Open Adoption and Diverse Families

Open Adoption and Diverse Families

Complex Relationships in the Digital Age

ABBIE E. GOLDBERG
Professor of Psychology at Clark University in Worcester
Massachusetts, USA

OXFORD
UNIVERSITY PRESS

OXFORD
UNIVERSITY PRESS

Oxford University Press is a department of the University of Oxford. It furthers the University's objective of excellence in research, scholarship, and education by publishing worldwide. Oxford is a registered trade mark of Oxford University Press in the UK and certain other countries.

Published in the United States of America by Oxford University Press
198 Madison Avenue, New York, NY 10016, United States of America.

© Oxford University Press 2019

All rights reserved. No part of this publication may be reproduced, stored in a retrieval system, or transmitted, in any form or by any means, without the prior permission in writing of Oxford University Press, or as expressly permitted by law, by license, or under terms agreed with the appropriate reproduction rights organization. Inquiries concerning reproduction outside the scope of the above should be sent to the Rights Department, Oxford University Press, at the address above.

You must not circulate this work in any other form
and you must impose this same condition on any acquirer.

Library of Congress Cataloging-in-Publication Data
Names: Goldberg, Abbie E., author.
Title: Open adoption and diverse families : complex relationships in the digital age / by Abbie E. Goldberg.
Description: New York : Oxford University Press, [2019] |
Includes bibliographical references and index.
Identifiers: LCCN 2019004982 (print) | LCCN 2019013511 (ebook) |
ISBN 9780190692049 (UPDF) | ISBN 9780190692056 (EPUB) |
ISBN 9780190692032 (hardcover : alk. paper)
Subjects: LCSH: Open adoption. | Adoption—Psychological aspects. |
Adoptees—Family relationships. | Social media.
Classification: LCC HV875 (ebook) | LCC HV875 .G593 2019 (print) |
DDC 306.874—dc23
LC record available at https://lccn.loc.gov/2019004982

1 3 5 7 9 8 6 4 2

Printed by Sheridan Books, Inc., United States of America

Contents

Acknowledgments   vii

Prologue—Setting the Stage: Open Adoption, Gay Parenthood, the Digital Age, and the Current Study   1

1. Getting to Adoption: The Path Before the Path   21

2. Orienting to Open Adoption, Considering Contact, and Reflecting on Race: Preadoption Perspectives and Preferences   47

3. "Meeting the Reality of Our Situation": Placement Experiences and Circumstances and Postplacement Openness and Contact   91

4. Imagining and Enacting Birth Family Contact Over Time: Trajectories of Openness Among Private Domestic Adopters   125

5. Navigating Openness and Contact in Child Welfare Adoptions   187

6. Adoption Talk: Communicative Openness Throughout Childhood   217

7. Weaving a Family Narrative: Genetics Talk   275

8. Facebook as Facilitator or Foe: Boundaries and Birth Family Relationships on Social Media and Beyond   313

9. Absence and Ambivalence: How Birth Fathers Fit Into Adoption Stories   341

10. Summing Up: Practical Strategies and Applications for Families   365

Appendix A: Demographic Information for Participants   395
Appendix B: Data Analysis Process   411
References   413
Index   425

Acknowledgments

This book has been a long time in the making. I started interviewing participants for this project in 2005—and have continued to follow them and talk to them up until the present day. First and foremost, this book is for these families. Thank you to all of you who have let me into your lives and parenting journeys—sharing your dreams, worries, fears, and struggles. I am honored by the level of trust and faith you have placed in me, and I hope that I have written a book in which you can see yourselves and your families' journeys—and one that captures the messiness and complexity, and the creative potential of adoptive families today.

I first began working on this book in 2016. I started by reading and poring over years of interviews I had done, developing pages and pages of notes and ideas. These notes and ideas gelled into something akin to a book prospectus, which I shared with and received feedback from my editor at Oxford, Sarah Harrington. It was with her guidance, experience, and wisdom—and the extremely insightful and helpful commentary from several anonymous reviewers—that I embarked on the actual writing of this book. A semester-long sabbatical and several summers provided me with some delicious blocks of uninterrupted writing time—something I treasured, even amid the inevitable frustrations and self-doubt that creep into book writing.

During my writing of this book, I had the fortune of sharing drafts with several colleagues and experts in the field who provided me with excellent feedback and insights—most notably, David Brodzinsky, Harold (Hal) Grotevant, and Sharon Roszia. David Brodzinsky has been an absolute rock during the process of writing this book. The author of several acclaimed and classic books on adoption, such as *Children's Adjustment to Adoption* (with Daniel W. Smith and Anne Braff Brodzinsky) and *Being Adopted: The Lifelong Search for Self* (with Robin Marantz Henig and Marshall D. Schecter), and an internationally recognized adoption scholar and clinician, he served as a sounding board for both the tone and content of the book. He read multiple drafts and provided extensive clinical insights and relevant research knowledge. He also provided a great deal of encouragement and support during the writing process. I'm very grateful to him for his generous contributions to this book, and for being a wonderful colleague and friend.

Hal Grotevant, a clinical psychologist and internationally recognized expert on open adoption, and the principal investigator on the Minnesota/Texas Adoption Research Project (MTARP), the longest running longitudinal study of open adoption, provided me with insightful, specific, and useful feedback on the book. I am extremely grateful to him for his kind, gracious, and always supportive stance in relation to my work.

Sharon Roszia, internationally recognized adoption expert and social worker, read and provided feedback from the perspective of a practitioner. Her input was incredibly valuable in helping me to sharpen my analysis and clarify the nature, needs, and expectations of my audience. Her feedback also helped me realize the necessity of a final chapter aimed at providing recommendations and suggestions to adoptive parents in particular.

I also spoke several times with experienced adoption practitioners, whose input significantly shaped and informed this book, and to whom I credit various insights throughout the book. I interviewed, and am extremely grateful to, the following individuals: Shari Levine, executive director of Open Adoption and Family Services, an adoption agency in Oregon; Dawn Smith-Pliner, founder and director of Friends in Adoption, an adoption agency in Vermont; and Roberta Evantash, a social worker who has worked for many years at Adoptions From the Heart, an adoption agency in Pennsylvania. I also interviewed Sharon Roszia and David Brodzinsky for the book.

During the writing of this book, I had many conversations with friends, colleagues, and students who have a personal and/or professional connection to adoption. Our conversations, their off-handed comments, and their personal stories often influenced my thinking in some way in relation to the material for this volume. Thank you to Marianna Litovich, Sarah Buttenwieser, April Moyer, and Rachel Farr, in particular, for your insights and conversation.

I am very grateful to my current and former doctoral students for all of their hard work interviewing participants. There is no way I could have singlehandedly interviewed all of these participants by myself over the past decade. Each of these students approached every interview participant with respect, curiosity, and appreciation. Thank you to Christine Sauck, Jordan Downing, Hannah Richardson, Lori Kinkler, April Moyer, Katie Black, Melissa Manley, and Reihonna Frost-Calhoun.

Always a lover of biography and memoir, I was drawn to reading and telling stories for as long as I can remember. I am especially grateful to my professor at Wesleyan University, Phyllis Rose, a prominent biographer and literary critic, who accepted me into her seminar on Writing Biography and supported me in writing my mother's story. I am also grateful to my mentors, colleagues, and friends, who share my passion for studying and understanding families—including Maureen Perry-Jenkins, Katherine Allen, and Kate Kuvalanka, who have always encouraged and supported me along my writing journeys.

I am also unbelievably grateful to the funders of my research. The research featured in this book was funded by the National Institutes of Health, the Spencer

Foundation, the Alfred P. Sloan Foundation, the American Psychological Foundation, the Williams Institute at the UCLA School of Law, the Society for the Psychological Study of Social Issues (SPSSI), the Gay and Lesbian Medical Association (GLMA), the Foundation for the Scientific Study of Sexuality (FSSS), and Clark University. This work would not have been possible without their support.

Families are complicated and intriguing. Thank you to my big, complicated extended family, including those who are joined to me by blood, marriage, remarriage, adoption, and kinship. Without you, life would be far less interesting. And thank you to my immediate family—human, canine, and feline—for joining me in this life. It certainly is an adventure.

Open Adoption and Diverse Families

Prologue—Setting the Stage

Open Adoption, Gay Parenthood, the Digital Age, and the Current Study

This book is about the experiences of a diverse set of families in open adoptions, from the perspective of the adoptive parents. It centers on the stories of lesbian, gay, and heterosexual parents who adopted their children, whom I had the privilege of interviewing over the course of a decade. In turn, this book has several goals. First, I seek to provide rich descriptive accounts of the diverse experiences of adoptive parents, particularly those who are navigating the possibility or reality of openness across their child's lifetime. In doing so, I seek to highlight the different trajectories that openness may take, the unique dynamics that emerge in contemporary U.S. adoptive families, and the ways in which the rise of technology and social media have transformed the experience of adoption for families, children, and practitioners.

Second, this book seeks to demystify the experience of open adoption—as well as the fears, concerns, and feelings of adoptive parents navigating openness. Open adoption is generally poorly understood by the general public—that is, people whose lives and professions do not involve adoption. In talking to people about my research, I am continually reminded that most people have very limited ideas about adoption. Even educated and worldly people have asked me the following questions/made the following statements: "Why would parents want to have contact with their child's birth family? Won't that be confusing for the children?" "Why would birth parents want to have contact with their child's adoptive family? Don't they want to move on and build a life for themselves?" "It seems like a clean break would be better for everyone." "I would be really jealous and upset if I had to see the birth parents of my child all the time." These quotes underscore the fact that families in open adoptions routinely contend with the reality that open adoption is generally invisible, overlooked, or misunderstood in mainstream society—at the same time that they actively navigate their own real-life, nonhypothetical open adoptions. Finally, this book seeks to offer guidance—in particular, in the final chapter—for adoptive parents and prospective adoptive parents, as well as, secondarily, the practitioners who seek to support them.

This book is aimed at multiple overlapping audiences. First, it is a book for adoptive parents and prospective adoptive parents. Second, it is for birth family members, adults who were adopted, and the family members and kinship networks of anyone touched by adoption. Third, it is for adoption practitioners and child welfare professionals, as well as social workers, psychologists, lawyers, child advocates, and other professionals (e.g., pediatricians, teachers) who work with adoptive families at different stages of the life course. It is also for scholars and students in the fields of adoption, family science, psychology, social work, law, human development, and related fields—or anyone seeking to learn more about the lived experiences of families in open adoptions.

Among the questions that this book aims to address are:

- How do adoptive parents feel about openness when they first learn about it, and how, when, and why do their feelings change over time?
- How do adoptive parents' initial feelings about birth parents inform the types of relationships that they form with the birth family?
- How do adoptive parents who strongly value openness cope with and handle the disappointment of matching with birth parents who do not desire and/or are unable to enact a similar level of openness—or who "fade away" over time?
- What types of complex, unexpected, and nuanced trajectories of contact unfold over time between adoptive families and birth families? What do these trajectories look like among child welfare adopters, specifically?
- What types of boundary challenges occur between adoptive and birth family members, offline and online?
- How do adoptive parents talk about adoption (i.e., communicative openness) with their children, and how does this vary depending on level and type of contact (structural openness)?
- How and to what extent do adoptive parents invoke environment versus genetics (i.e., birth family) in articulating children's strengths, challenges, and physical features (e.g., height, skin color)?
- How do the experiences of adoptive parents differ by parent gender and relational status/sexual orientation?

In this prologue to the book, I provide some historical context (e.g., how adoption has changed over time) and information about the parents whom I interviewed for this book. The remainder of the book is grounded in and centered on adoptive parents' stories, beginning with the preadoption process.

Over the past 30 years, marked changes have occurred in how adoptive families are formed and in how adoptive family–birth family relationships are negotiated and maintained over time.[1] Beginning in the 1980s, openness in domestic adoptions (i.e., contact before and/or after the adoption between birth and adoptive families, varying in type and frequency) increasingly became the norm (see *Dear Birthmother*, by Kathleen Silber and Phylis Speedlin, 1982; *The Open Adoption Experience: A Complete Guide for Adoptive and Birth Families*, by Lois Ruskai Melina and Sharon Kaplan Roszia, 1993). This was particularly the case for private domestic adoptions: namely, adoptions of newborns/infants via a private domestic adoption agency or lawyer. The late 1980s and early 1990s saw a marked shift in professional practices and attitudes, whereby the central question evolved from "whether to tell" children about their adoptive origins to "when and how to tell"—and many agencies moved away from facilitating predominantly confidential adoptions to offering a range of openness options. This shift occurred in response to both client demand and competition from other agencies that were increasingly facilitating open adoptions.[2]

Yet even into the mid-1990s, many adoption professionals did not question the notion that anonymity and secrecy could have detrimental effects on birth families, adoptive parents, and adopted children—although telling children of their adoption was almost always recommended by practitioners, in that secrecy is almost impossible to achieve, and discovery of adoption later in life is likely to be disturbing.[3] As adoption scholars Harold (Hal) Grotevant and Ruth McRoy) note, in their pioneering book on open adoption, some professionals accepted and upheld the notion that adoptive parents could have the child they longed for, birth parents could forget the child they did not plan for and "move on," and children could grow up in a traditional nuclear family.[4] In this way, adoption solved the "problems" of infertility, an unwanted child, and not having parents.[5] Openness—and specifically structural openness, or contact between adoptive and birth families—was viewed as having a variety of potential negative effects, such as interfering with closure on the part of birth parents, undermining parental identity development and parental entitlement in adoptive parents, and creating confusion for children.

The last 10 to 20 years has seen a continued movement toward consensus among adoption scholars and practitioners of the potential benefits of openness for all members of the adoption triad—birth parents, adoptive parents, and adopted children. Very few contemporary adoption agencies facilitate closed adoptions, where no information is exchanged between birth and adoptive families—about 5% of agencies, in one recent study.[6] In practice, openness arrangements vary considerably. They may be open/fully disclosed (where birth and adoptive families communicate directly with each other, typically exchanging identifying information), or they may be semiopen/mediated (where birth families and adoptive families exchange information and communicate via the adoption agency, to preserve identifying information). Contact arrangements vary in frequency, type, and length of contact. For example, contact may be time limited or ongoing.[7] Written contractual agreements between adoptive and birth families can clarify the type and frequency of contact or communication and may provide a way for the agreement to be legally enforced—although not all states have statutes that permit written and legally enforceable agreements.[8]

Both theory and research support the benefits of openness. From a family systems perspective, openness is ideal, insomuch as all family members are important to identity development and overall family functioning; even family members who are absent physically are psychologically present.[9] Further, a family systems framework recognizes that adoptive and birth families represent members of a "kinship network that forever links those families together through the child, who is shared by both," wherein the legal transfer of parenting responsibilities does not "sever the psychological tie to an earlier family [but] expands the family boundaries of all those who are involved."[10] In this way, family ties are additive, not substitutive.

Structural openness—contact and shared information between parties—benefits children by providing them with biological continuity and not denying the truth of their origins and background, thus aiding in identity development.[11] Encouragement of birth family involvement serves to honor a child's identity and origins in its complexity, as well as acknowledging the family's status as adopted.[12] Structural openness also benefits birth parents. For example, knowledge of the possibility of openness may support expectant parents to consider adoption as an option when parenting is not desired or possible; and, given that birth parents are unlikely to truly "forget" the children they place for adoption, openness may help to alleviate their pain and guilt. For adoptive parents, structural openness may ease their fears and questions, reassure them about the permanency of the adoption, and promote empathy toward the birth parents.[13] Research has taught us that structural openness is associated with greater satisfaction with the adoption and better postadoption adjustment for both adoptive and birth parents.[14] Birth mothers with contact, for example, report less grief, regret, and worry[15]—but also acknowledge that even ongoing-contact, open adoption is both "good and hard."[16] Even the option of simply playing a role in choosing the adoptive parents appears to benefit birth mothers.[17] Further, adopted youth who have more contact with birth family members are more satisfied with contact, and greater satisfaction with contact is in turn related to better adjustment.[18] Both communicative openness and structural openness have been linked to better outcomes for adopted youth (e.g., fewer behavior problems).[19] One study of adopted teenagers and their parents, for example, found that adoptive families who did have contact reported greater satisfaction with their openness arrangements, more positive feelings about the birth mother, and more factual and personal knowledge about the birth mother, compared to adoptive families that did not have contact with birth families. Furthermore, families with no contact tended to want more contact, and fewer than 1% of all participants wanted the intensity of contact to decrease.[20]

Another dimension of openness is communicative openness—parents' level of openness to thinking and talking about adoption within the family, which is also related to children's adjustment.[21] When parents choose to learn and talk about a child's background and birth family, this reflects and facilitates comfort with discussion of adoption and difference, thus facilitating child well-being and identity development. Research has shown us that the children of parents who engage in higher levels of communicative openness exhibit fewer psychological and behavioral difficulties, better self-esteem, and greater trust in their parents.[22] Communicative and structural openness tend to be correlated, such that parents who talk openly about adoption tend to engage in more contact with the birth family, and vice versa—but parents can indeed have communicative openness when contact is not possible (e.g., when birth parents are not responsive to adoptive parents' overtures for contact).[23]

Yet adoptive parents may struggle with structural and communicative openness. Structural openness may feel threatening and anxiety provoking, particularly early on as parents try to settle into their role as parents and bond to their children—often after a long period of wanting and waiting for children.[24] Communicative openness may also be difficult for some parents. Parents may worry that their child will not feel fully integrated into the family (e.g., one of the family; normal) if parents acknowledge, articulate, and discuss the meaning of adoption.[25] Notably, there is an important difference between insisting on difference (e.g., highlighting the child's adoptive status unnecessarily or in a way that seems to blame adoption for all of the child's, or family's, problems) and acknowledging difference (e.g., embracing the reality of the child's origins and birth family as part of the child's and family's story). Without an acknowledgment of difference, parents who underscore their family status as "just like any other family" may inadvertently communicate that they are in denial of or ashamed of their child's adoptive status.[26] Adoptive parents have a better chance of facilitating communicative and structural openness when they can cultivate certain personal qualities and skills: namely, empathy, respect, honesty, trust, adaptability, and tolerance of ambiguity and complexity; a commitment to maintaining the connection; and collaborative communication in planning for contact and in conveying needs and wishes. These same personal qualities and skills on the part of birth parents also facilitate the development of mutually satisfying open adoption arrangements.[27]

Most research on openness is with families who adopted via private domestic adoption. Yet there is increasing awareness of the potential benefits of openness in domestic *public* adoptions—child welfare adoptions, or situations where children are removed from birth families' homes, placed in foster care, and become eligible for adoption—amid recognition of the potential complexities of openness in these circumstances.[28] Of course, the appropriateness of openness will inevitably vary in foster care adoptions, depending on the situation. For example, it may be beneficial for a child to maintain contact with birth siblings or birth grandparents but not birth parents, if the birth parents were the perpetrators of ongoing abuse or neglect.[29] Likewise, it may not be advisable for a child to remain in contact with birth siblings, if they were the perpetrators of abuse. As Jeanne Howard, a child welfare expert, notes:

> Some degree of openness in adoptions from foster care is often positive for children . . . but there needs to be a formal assessment of the level of openness that is in the child's best interest—not only with birth parents but also with [other family members]. In some . . . adoptions, the courts or a supervising agency may recommend no child-birth parent contact when there is a history of severe abuse.[30]

There are many more children waiting to be adopted via foster care than newborns available for adoption via private agencies, and hence, the complexities and potential benefits of openness in this context are certainly worthy of attention. In 2016, 436,465 children were in foster care in the United States, and of these, 117,794 were waiting to be adopted.[31] The average age of children in foster care is 8.5 years old, and 52% of children are boys. The primary reasons for children being in care were neglect (61%) and parental drug abuse (34%), with many children in care for multiple reasons. A total of 57,208 children were adopted via foster care during 2016.[32]

A not insignificant number of adoptive families appear to maintain postadoption contact with the birth family in child welfare adoptions—39%, compared to 68% of private domestic adoptions, according to one national study.[33] Worth mentioning here are unique and creative collaborations between private adoption agencies that facilitate open adoptions and child welfare agencies, which are aimed at (a) identifying women at risk for state adoption and (b) empowering them by offering them alternatives—such as voluntarily placing their children via an open adoption. Open Adoption and Family Services (OAFS) has formed a collaborative relationship with the Oregon Department of Human Services (DHS), wherein high-risk mothers (e.g., women who have had other children removed by the state and are pregnant again; women who face chronic mental health or substance issues) learn about open adoption as a viable choice. DHS workers and service providers who work with high-risk mothers throughout the state can refer expectant parents to OAFS, which provides education and information about open adoption. Preliminary data collected by OAFS show that this is a successful alternative and meets the ongoing needs of birth parents and their children better than the foster care system (see *A Proposal for Change From OAFS*, by Shari Levine, 2017). Innovative programs like this one have the potential to reduce the number of children in state care and increase the number of voluntary adoptions that involve some level of ongoing postplacement contact between birth and adoptive families. Indeed, the voluntary and open nature of these placements has the potential to enhance outcomes for all members of the adoption triad (i.e., adoptive parents, adopted children, and birth parents)—but especially the birth mothers, by "introducing an element of respect for these women, by giving them all of their options in the beginning, allowing them to be in the driver's seat."[34] Additionally, this model has the capacity to reduce costs to taxpayers by avoiding involvement in the child welfare system.[35]

Beyond Openness: Other Societal Shifts With Implications for Adoption

Shifts in openness over the past few decades have been accompanied by other notable trends related to adoption. Significant changes in *who* is adopting in the United States have occurred over the past few decades. For example, it has become increasingly possible for single individuals and same-sex couples to adopt. According to the demographer Gary Gates, same-sex couples are between 4 and 10 times more likely to adopt their children than heterosexual couples.[36] The rise in adoptions by lesbian, gay, bisexual, and queer (LGBQ) parents has significant implications for our understanding of adoptive families, the types of issues that these families will encounter, and the types of relationships that LGBQ parents engage in and maintain with birth family members.

Same-sex adoptive parent families, for example, must navigate their children's identities related to their status in a two-mom or two-dad family, their adoptive status, and, often, their status as a child of color: Indeed, same-sex couples are more likely to be open to adopting, and to be placed with, children of color than heterosexual couples.[37] LGBQ parents are vulnerable to stigma surrounding their sexual orientation by birth family members specifically, at different stages in their adoption journey. Some expectant parents* will undoubtedly rule them out as parents, because of their sexual orientation; and those that do choose them to be the parents of their child may have homophobic family members who disapprove of their decision and do not want to establish a relationship with a

---

* I use the term *expectant parents* because these individuals are not birth parents until after they have placed the child for adoption. Likewise, prospective adoptive parents are not adoptive parents (or simply, parents) until after they have adopted the child.

two-mom or two-dad family.[38] However, LGBQ parents' sexual orientation and/or relational status may also uniquely and positively nuance the relationships that they form with the birth family. For example, male same-sex couples might find that some expectant mothers are drawn to them insomuch as there is no other "woman" or potential mother figure in the adoption triad, thus eradicating potential tension or jealousy in relation to a maternal or mother role. Likewise, gay fathers may be less likely to feel threatened by birth mothers, compared to lesbian or heterosexual parents—and may even feel especially excited about the prospect of birth mother contact and involvement. Such dynamics might foster easier or more fluid relationships between gay adoptive fathers and birth mothers.[39] It may also be that some female same-sex couples strongly desire or value strong relationships with birth fathers, as there is no "father" in the parental equation. And yet, they are potentially more vulnerable to disappointment in this arena, in that birth fathers are less likely than birth mothers to maintain contact with the adoptive family/child.[40] Overall, same-sex couples—male and female—may be more open to contact, and engage more easily, with birth family members because they possess more expansive ideas about kinship and family as compared to heterosexual couples, who have historically not been rejected from their biological families and thus forced to consider alternative constructions of family.[41] Studies of families who adopted privately[42] and publically[43] have documented higher levels of contact with the birth family among lesbian/gay parent families than heterosexual parent families—although significantly, rates of contact tend to be higher, and birth–adoptive family relationships more positive, among private domestic placements than foster care placements.

Another recent societal shift—beyond openness in adoption and family diversity—that has implications for how adoptive family relationships are enacted and unfold over time, especially as children grow older, is the increased accessibility and pervasiveness of the Internet and social media specifically in daily life. The Internet has facilitated easier matches and connections between expectant parents and prospective adoptive parents (e.g., many adoption agencies post "profiles" of hopeful/prospective adoptive parents online, and expectant parents can contact the agency if they are interested in a match with one or more prospective adoptive parents). The ease and accessibility of the Internet has also made it possible for adoptive and birth family members to find one another with limited information—even if the initial adoption arrangements were not initially "open" (i.e., identifying information was not exchanged) or if birth or adoptive family members have abruptly terminated contact or disappeared.[44] Both anecdotal data and limited empirical research suggest that Facebook and other social media sites are increasingly being used for such purposes.[45] That is, birth and adoptive family members may search for and directly contact each other online; or they may engage in "passive contact"—that is, gathering information about each other, including photos and demographic details. In turn, Facebook and other forms of social media have the potential to facilitate existing relationships between adoptive and birth family members and to create new opportunities for contact.

Yet the expansion of the Internet and the pervasiveness of social media also have the potential to create new challenges for families. Adoptive parents might find themselves navigating tricky issues related to boundaries, such as how they should interact with the birth family online, and how they should handle or confront what they perceive as violations of boundaries in the semipublic space of Facebook. They may find themselves learning information about the birth family that is troubling or unsettling to them, which may inform their feelings about the birth family and/or present challenges in terms of deciding whether to share such information with children. Alongside the ease, speed, and accessibility of the Internet is a lack of emotional preparation for how to approach and navigate adoptive family–birth family connections made online—for example, how should an adoptive parent respond when she receives a Facebook "friend request" from her child's birth aunt? How and when should an adoptive parent reach out to a birth parent who is unresponsive to offline contact but whom they find on social media? Alongside the increasing relevance and urgency of these types of questions, only a little bit of research has looked at the experiences of adoptive parents, children, or birth families with respect to navigating social media concerns and contact. Although several adoption professionals have authored articles containing guidelines on the topic,[46] very few articles draw from empirical data.[47]

Another relevant consideration is that, as they grow older, children themselves are increasingly likely to be navigating the Internet and social media independently, which may bring them into contact with their birth family—either through stumbling across a social media account, for example, or being contacted directly by members of the birth family. Inevitably, the level and type of offline contact they have with the birth family, and familial communication about the birth family (e.g., how their parents talk about their birth family—with respect or with disparagement, such as referring to the birth mother as a "crack whore"[48]), may shape how children approach and navigate these online interactions. As author Ellen Fursland[49] observes, children searching for a birth relative might find content on their Facebook page that could distress or confuse them—such as pictures of the person intoxicated, pregnant, or in provocative poses. Of course, in the context of ongoing direct but developmentally staged communication about birth family, such discoveries would not occur alone, via secretive searching; rather, they would occur with the support of and possibly in the presence of a parent. Open communication about adoption and education about Internet and social media risks and responsibilities are important tools for adopted youth, who may discover information about, or be contacted by, the birth family online.

Situating This Book in Contemporary Context

Despite ongoing shifts in adoption practice toward greater openness, and a proliferation of books about, by, and for parents in open adoptions (e.g., *Open Adoption, Open Heart: An Adoptive Father's Inspiring Journey*, by Russell Elkins, 2011; *The Open-Hearted Way to Open Adoption*, by Lori Holden, 2013), the social and cultural visibility and awareness of open adoption is fairly lacking. *Juno*, a feature film released in 2007, featured an open adoption, but there are relatively few other contemporary media examples featuring openness (e.g., the show *Sixteen and Pregnant*)—although adoption itself has been featured in a number of films (e.g., *Lion, The Blind Side*) and TV shows (e.g., *Modern Family, This Is Us, Parenthood*) in the past decade.[50] Alongside this type of (in)attention to openness in adoption—and the often problematic representations of openness when it is depicted in the media—many people continue to have outdated views of adoption, reflecting dominant cultural scripts that position openness, and birth families, as scary or threatening to the adoptive parents, child, and family stability. The fact that there are few cultural scripts surrounding adoption in general[51] adds to the problem of invisibility, wherein adoptive families face assumptions and insensitive or offensive questions regarding their family and their children's origins (e.g., Where did she come from?; What do you know about her background?; Where are her real parents?).

In sum, these societal changes in openness, technology, and gay parenting, amid the relative cultural (in)visibility of open adoption, have implications for adoptive family relationships as they unfold over time. Using data from my longitudinal study of lesbian,[†] gay, and heterosexual couples who all became parents through adoption, this book explores, in depth, and from the perspective of adoptive parents, the experience of anticipating, forming, and maintaining relationships—symbolic or actual—with the birth family over time. Of particular interest is how, among these adoptive families, communicative openness (openness about adoption within the family) and structural openness (contact with the birth family) are imagined and enacted amid recent changes in digital

---

[†] Not all participants identified as lesbian/gay. Thirty-four of 44 women in female same-sex couples identified as lesbian/gay, eight as bisexual, one as queer, and one as pansexual. Forty-two of 44 men in male same-sex couples identified as gay; one man identified as queer, and one as "mostly gay." We use the term *lesbian couples* and *gay couples* to signify female and male same-sex couples, respectively, while acknowledging that individual participants' sexual identities varied. All individuals in heterosexual couples identified as heterosexual.

communication and, in particular, social media. Of interest too is how parent (sexual orientation, gender, race) and child (age, gender, race) characteristics interplay with openness and adoptive family dynamics, issues, and challenges.

The People in This Book

This book draws upon interview data from a varied group of research participants who have been participating in a longitudinal study of adoptive parenthood for over 10 years (the Transition to Adoptive Parenthood Project [TAPP]). To participate, all participants had to be (a) in coupled relationships and (b) adopting for the first time. They were interviewed separately from their partners, typically over the phone (the couples live all across the United States) at various points across the transition to parenthood and beyond: preadoption (while they were waiting for a child), 3 months postadoption, 2 years postadoption, 5 years postadoption, and 8 years postadoption. They also completed questionnaires at each of these time points—as well as at 1 year postadoption and 3 years postadoption.

For this book, I chose a subsample of participants from this larger study to represent the diversity of the sample and to focus on those families with particularly rich, compelling, and interesting stories. Sixty-six families were chosen, consisting of data from 132 parents, at four time points. In writing this book, I used interview data from Time 1 (preadoption), Time 2 (3 months postadoption), Time 3 (5 years postadoption), and Time 4 (8 years postadoption).

The families in this book primarily adopted through private domestic adoption (n = 45 families; 90 parents: 15 lesbian parent families, 15 gay parent families, 15 heterosexual parent families). All of these families initially worked with adoption agencies that facilitated open adoptions—and in turn, all of them had to indicate openness to some level of contact with the birth family. Ultimately, not all of them had contact with the birth family—for a variety of reasons, including birth parent preferences, a lack of sustained effort to initiate or maintain contact, or some combination of factors. Yet even when parents did not have direct contact with the birth family (e.g., because it was not possible or reciprocated), they often maintained communicative openness, meaning they talked regularly and openly about adoption within the family.

Some families adopted via public adoption (the child welfare system; n = 21 families; 42 parents: seven lesbian parent families, seven gay parent families, seven heterosexual parent families). There is rarely direct, agency-encouraged or agency-directed contact with birth families in public domestic adoptions—in part because of the types of situations that caused the children to be removed from the birth family in the first place (e.g., drug abuse, neglect). However, at some point adoptive families may be contacted by, or may contact, the birth family (particularly family members besides the birth parents), in part due to the increasing ease of accessing personal information online. Further, even if adoptive parents do not have direct contact with their children's birth families, they may—regardless of whether they adopted privately or publicly—search online for their children's birth family members, and thus must negotiate what they will and will not share with their children, now or in the future. And indeed, as we will see, many of the child welfare adopters in this book ultimately had some type of contact with at least one birth family member—and all of them inevitably navigated issues related to communicative openness (i.e., talking about adoption within the family).

The families in this book are largely white and middle class. Of the 132 participants, almost all were white; only 13 (9.8%) were of color (four lesbians, seven gay men, two heterosexual men). In most couples, both parents were employed—typically in professional or managerial jobs, such as chiropractor, therapist, engineer, nonprofit manager, and communications manager (see Appendix A). The majority of children, on the other hand, were largely of color: Of the 66 "focus" children (i.e., parents' first adopted child), 44 (67%) were of color—16 by lesbian parents, 14 by gay male parents, and 14 by heterosexual parents.

Only parents' voices are featured in this book—although I did interview five adoption experts and practitioners as well, whose perspectives, voices, and direct quotes are woven throughout the book.‡ I cannot underscore enough how this inevitably shapes what we can know and take away from this book in terms of understanding the reality of open adoption. Adoptive parents inevitably have different perspectives and experiences than birth families or children. In fact, research on adoptive kinship networks tells us that adoptive parents, adopted individuals, and birth family members often have incongruent perspectives on the reasons for declines in contact between birth and adoptive family members— as well as who initiated the stop in contact.[52] Likewise, members of the adoption triad may have different feelings about (e.g., levels of satisfaction with) the nature and degree of contact.[53] Fortunately, there are a number of first-person narratives and edited volumes that center on birth family members' experiences (e.g., *Birth Fathers and Their Adoption Experiences*, by Gary Clapton, 2003; *Hole in My Heart*, by Lorraine Dusky, 2015; *God and Jetfire: Confessions of a Birth*

---

‡ I interviewed Dawn Smith-Pliner, founder and director of Friends in Adoption, an adoption agency located in Vermont; Roberta Evantash, a social worker who has worked for many years at Adoptions From the Heart, an adoption agency in Pennsylvania; Shari Levine, executive director of Open Adoption and Family Services, an adoption agency in Oregon and Washington; Sharon Roszia, a social worker and internationally known adoption expert; and David Brodzinsky, a clinical psychologist and internationally known adoption expert. Dr. Brodzinsky's interview is featured prominently in Chapter 10.

Mother, by Amy Seek, 2016) and adopted individuals' experiences (e.g., *In Their Own Voices,* edited by Rita J. Simon and Rhonda M. Roorda, 2000; *You Don't Look Adopted,* by Anne Heffron, 2016).

Also, although some families did adopt subsequent children (see Appendix A), I focus on parents' experiences with the "target child" or "focus child"—that is, their first adopted child, the child they adopted after the first interview. At times I do refer to other adopted children, but I am always clear when referring to these children that they are the focus child's siblings, all of whom were adopted after the focus child.

Names of participants, children, and birth parents have been changed—along with key identifying details. I tried very hard to preserve the integrity of each family's story while also eliminating or obscuring details that would identify them to people other than themselves. In certain chapters, such as Chapter 9, on birth fathers, I rarely use pseudonyms, because much of what many parents discuss is sensitive and may not be known to others in their families—and pseudonyms, in combination with other information reported about those families, could potentially lead to their identification. Appendix A contains the list of pseudonyms for each set of adoptive parents, their child(ren), and birth parents (if relevant), along with information about geographic location, adoptive parents' race and professions, and children's race and gender.

For details about data analysis—that is, the steps I took to make sense of, analyze, compile, and write up the interview data—please see Appendix B.

Theoretical Perspectives

Several theoretical frameworks and perspectives informed my analysis and interpretation of the interview data. I draw, in particular, from family systems theory.[54] According to psychologist and family therapist Carlfred Broderick, the family is "an example of an open, ongoing, goal-seeking, self-regulating, social system"—and yet its "unique structuring of gender and generation ... sets it apart from other social systems."[55] Further, each family system is shaped by "its own particular structural features (size, complexity, composition, life stage), the psychobiological characteristics of its individual members (age, gender, fertility, health, temperament), and its sociocultural and historic position in the larger environment."[56] A central concept in family systems theory—and this book—is social distance regulation, or the shifting balance of connection and separation, between and among family members, as well as between families and nonfamily members.[57] Too much connection (i.e., enmeshment) and too tight boundaries (e.g., not allowing others in) may be associated with dysfunction. Although strong ties and boundary maintenance are indeed adaptive characteristics of families, as a system a family needs to maintain a "selectively permeable boundary" between its interior elements and its broader environment.[58] Such boundaries allow systems to exchange resources (e.g., emotional and material support) while also keeping out perceived dangers (e.g., the media).

Family systems theory also emphasizes the creation and construction of shared (or separate) realities, or meanings, whereby family members develop shared (or discrepant) understandings of themselves, each other, and the family as a whole. For example, family members create family stories, in part by drawing on material objects and photographs, which serve to preserve knowledge and facilitate recollection of past experiences. Family rituals also aid in the creation and construction of family meanings and shared realties.[59] Celebrating adoption day, for example, is a way to acknowledge a child's adoption and to honor and uphold the child's integration into the family. It "recognizes socially an existing situation, thereby emphasizing that the participants in this family group now belong together."[60]

I also draw from life course theory.[61] From this perspective, understanding development requires awareness not only of the broader contexts in which it occurs but also of the particular life stage a person (e.g., a parent, a child) is in, how that stage is interpreted by the individual, and how the individual changes over time. Particularly distinctive of life course theory is an emphasis on the interplay of human lives—that is, the notion of "linked lives," or the idea that family/social networks' lives are interrelated and that relationships shift over time.

A life course perspective also emphasizes the transitions and trajectories that occur in a person's life. Transitions into and out of social roles across the life span involve changes in personal and social status, sense of self, and identity. Becoming a parent, for example, involves gaining an entirely new role as well as making adjustments to already-held roles (e.g., partner, daughter, employee). Normative family transitions may represent passage or change from one place or state to the next, or extended periods of change and disequilibrium between periods of stability and balance.[62] Nonnormative or unexpected transitions may also occur in the course of one's life (e.g., infertility, job loss, divorce). Both types of transitions may cause changes in roles, the quality of close relationships, and one's psychological sense of self. Individuals and couples who deviate in some way from normative transitions, such as the transition to parenthood (e.g., they do not become parents; they become parents at a later age; they become parents through adoption) may encounter isolation and lack of community. They may also be unprepared for what unfolds, due to a lack of cultural scripts.[63] For example, in his classic 1964 book, *Shared Fate: A Theory of Adoption and Mental Health*, David Kirk stated, about one of the many ways in which becoming an adoptive parent differs from becoming a biological parent, "Preparation for biological parenthood and parental roles is gradual; the period of pregnancy provides the couple with a known timetable that moves them imperceptibly toward progressive involvement in their coming parental tasks. In contrast, preparation for adoptive parenthood tends to be abrupt with no clear-cut timetable."[64]

Finally, I draw from developmental psychology frameworks, which recognize how children's chronological and emotional age informs their understanding of adoption, as well as aspects of openness, including conversations about adoption and the birth family.[65] Children's cognitive, social, and emotional development has implications for their understanding of adoption throughout the life course; indeed, children's understanding of adoption evolves over time, paralleling and mirroring their general cognitive development.[66] As children develop, they often ask more questions—or at least more complex and sophisticated questions, which warrant more complex and sophisticated answers.

David Brodzinsky is the most prolific and well-known writer on the developmental psychology of the adopted child.[67] He notes that what it means to be adopted changes at different stages of the life cycle, and he identified several key developmental tasks for the adopted child. During infancy, the primary tasks are adjusting to the transition to a new family and developing secure attachments to caregivers. During toddlerhood and the preschool years, children learn about birth and reproduction, adjust to the initial information they are given about adoption, and begin to recognize differences in physical appearance (e.g., skin color). Significantly, "being adopted" has little meaning to very young children. At the same time, preschoolers tend to feel very positively about being adopted.

With the growth of logical thought, by age 6 or 7, adopted children can now differentiate between adoption and birth and recognize that most children are born into the family in which they are raised.[68] During early school age, children also begin to recognize that being adopted means having two sets of parents: those who conceived/gave birth to them and those who are raising them—a distinction that sets the foundation for the more nuanced understanding that emerges later (e.g., the circumstances surrounding their birth). Whereas for young children, family membership is often understood primarily in terms of who lives with them, and biological connection is not seen as a key component of family membership, by age 7, the child recognizes that families are typically defined in terms of blood ties. In turn, children may voice confusion about their status as family members. Children also begin to grasp the loss associated with adoption. That is, they begin to "infer the flip side of [their] beloved 'adoption story'—that for [them] to have been chosen, [they] first have to have been given away."[69] In turn, adoption implies "not only family building, but also family loss," which accounts for many of the behavioral changes and challenges that are observed among school-age adopted children, including anger and self-image issues.[70] For children who do not have contact with their birth family, coming to terms with adoption loss can be additionally complex, as they lack "guideposts" for integrating key information about their identity, whereas open adoption may ease and mitigate this sense of loss by allowing children to have two families. In middle childhood onward, youth increasingly understand the meaning and implications of being adopted and may seek out more information about their origins. They are also increasingly aware of, and cope with, the multiple ways in which they differ from their parents (e.g., physical difference, learning disabilities).[71]

How parents respond to their children's growth in understanding has implications for the types of conversations that are likely to unfold across the life course—and, ultimately, for their children's identity development. As David Kirk notes, adoptive parents may be faced with the

> inchoate, inarticulate ways in which children are known to broach to adults their problems of understanding difficult concepts. If the parents feel that, for them, certain aspects of the subject of adoption are threatening, they obviously cannot readily deal with ideas and feelings that arise for the child as a result of his knowledge that he was adopted. In such circumstances the child is likely to feel that the door to communication with the parents is closed. Accordingly he will ask few questions and those he asks will be tame. If this happens, the parents may assume that there are no problems.[72]

Although parents who initially avoid communication about adoption may experience relief, David Kirk[73] David Brodzinsky,[74] and others argue that in the long run, such an approach carries liabilities. Acknowledging the realities involved in adoption helps parents to open channels of communication and ultimately to build relationships of strength and durability. As David Brodzinsky and his colleagues[75] note, adopted people handle adoption best when they are raised by parents who encourage exploration of adoption whenever opportunities to do so happen to arise. Parents are ultimately responsible for cultivating a family environment that either facilitates or minimizes opportunities for discovery and exploration.

Overview of Chapters

The chapters that follow take the reader through parents' journeys of navigating open adoption up through middle childhood. Most chapters open with an in-depth vignette of a specific family. Parents' quotes appear in every chapter to bring to life key themes and help readers to understand the diversity and commonality across families' experiences. Chapter 1 addresses the path before adoption—including navigating infertility and making the decision to adopt.

Chapter 2 addresses parents' process of orienting to openness—including their decision making and preferences surrounding contact with the birth family as well as key characteristics of their future children, such as race. Chapter 3 addresses parents' experiences with placement, including meeting (or not meeting) their children's birth parents and navigating contact with the birth family during the early postplacement period. Chapter 4 addresses trajectories of contact over time among private domestic adopters, with attention to boundary issues and challenges. Chapter 5 addresses these issues in the context of child welfare adopters. Chapter 6 addresses communicative openness, or adoption talk, exploring how parents with and without birth family contact navigate communication about adoption as well as race throughout childhood. Chapter 7 examines how parents invoke genetics and environment to make sense of their children's challenging and desirable characteristics, and their process of adjusting to having a child whose characteristics (e.g., intellectual, emotional) diverge sharply from what they envisioned or anticipated. Chapter 8 takes a closer look at parents' experiences with social media and the Internet—and how Facebook in particular is invoked as facilitating relationships with the birth family, magnifying existing relationship challenges, and/or raising new issues in their relationships. Chapter 9 explores parents' narratives surrounding birth fathers—both known and unknown—over the course of their children's childhoods. Finally, Chapter 10 provides guidance and advice to adoptive parents primarily, with practitioners representing a secondary audience, regarding the topics outlined throughout the book.

Notes

1. Herman, 2008.
2. Grotevant & McRoy, 1998; Henney, McRoy, Ayers-Lopez, & Grotevant, 2003; Pertman, 2012; Siegel & Smith, 2012.
3. Grotevant & McRoy, 1998; Kirk, 1964; Pertman, 2012.
4. Grotevant & McRoy, 1998.
5. Kirk, 1964.
6. Siegel & Smith, 2012.
7. Ibid.
8. Child Welfare Information Gateway, 2014.
9. Reitz & Watson, 1992.
10. Reitz & Watson, 1992, p. 11.
11. Brodzinsky, 2006, 2011; Von Korff & Grotevant, 2011.
12. Kirk, 1964.
13. Belbas, 1987; Grotevant, McRoy, Elde, & Fravel, 1994; Grotevant & McRoy, 1998; Sorich & Siebert, 1982.

14. Ge et al., 2008; Grotevant et al., 1994; Grotevant & McRoy, 1998.
15. Clutter, 2017; Henney, Ayers-Lopez, McRoy, & Grotevant, 2007.
16. Clutter, 2017, p. 3.
17. Cushman, Kalmuss, & Namerow, 1997.
18. Grotevant, McRoy, Wrobel, & Ayers-Lopez, 2013.
19. Brodzinsky, 2006; Von Korff, Grotevant, & McRoy, 2006.
20. Grotevant et al., 2007.
21. Brodzinsky, 2006, 2011.
22. Brodzinsky, 2006; Hawkins et al., 2007; Kohler, Grotevant, & McRoy, 2002.
23. Brodzinsky, 2006.
24. Turkington & Taylor, 2009.
25. Kirk, 1964; Turkington & Taylor, 2009.
26. Jones & Hackett, 2007; Kirk, 1964.
27. Neil, 2009; Siegel & Smith, 2012.
28. Child Welfare Information Gateway, 2013.
29. Crea & Barth, 2009; Faulkner & Madden, 2012.
30. Howard, 2012, p. 39.
31. U.S. Department of Health & Human Services, Administration for Children and Families, Children's Bureau, 2017.
32. Ibid.
33. Vandivere, Malm, & Radel, 2009.
34. Shari Levine, personal communication, August 21, 2017.
35. Ibid.
36. Gary Gates, personal communication, June 26, 2017.
37. Goldberg, 2009; Goldberg & Smith, 2009.
38. Goldberg, Moyer, Kinkler, & Richardson, 2012.
39. Goldberg, 2012.
40. Farr, Ravvina, & Grotevant, 2018; Goldberg, Kinkler, Richardson, & Downing, 2011.
41. Brodzinsky & Goldberg, 2016; Goldberg et al., 2011.
42. Goldberg et al., 2011.
43. Brodzinsky & Goldberg, 2016.
44. Child Welfare Information Gateway, 2013.
45. Black, Moyer, & Goldberg, 2016; Fursland, 2010a, 2010b; Howard, 2012.
46. Fursland, 2010a, 2010b; Howard, 2012; Krueger, 2014.
47. Black et al., 2016; Siegel, 2012a.
48. Holden, 2013, p. 67.
49. Fursland, 2010a, 2010b.
50. McNamara, 2014.
51. Goldberg, 2010; Kirk, 1964.
52. Dunbar et al., 2006; Grotevant et al., 2007; Neil, 2009.
53. Berge, Mendenhall, Wrobel, Grotevant, & McRoy, 2006; Dunbar et al., 2006; Neil, 2009, 2012.
54. Broderick, 1993; Reitz & Watson, 1992.
55. Broderick, 1993, p. 37.

56. Ibid.
57. Grotevant, 2009.
58. Broderick, 1993, p. 127.
59. Broderick, 1993.
60. Kirk, 1964, p. 69.
61. Elder, 1994, 1998.
62. Carter & McGoldrick, 2005; Cowan & Cowan, 2003.
63. Elder, 1998; Goldberg, 2010; Kirk, 1964.
64. Kirk, 1964, p. 7.
65. Brodzinsky, Schecter, & Henig, 1992.
66. Brodzinsky, 1987; Brodzinsky et al., 1992.
67. Brodzinsky, 1987, 2006, 2011; Brodzinsky et al., 1992.
68. Brodzinsky, 2011; Brodzinsky et al., 1992.
69. Brodzinsky et al., 1992, p. 18.
70. Ibid.
71. Ibid.
72. Kirk, 1964, p. 90.
73. Kirk, 1964.
74. Brodzinsky, 2011.
75. Brodzinsky et al., 1992.

1
Getting to Adoption
The Path Before the Path

As much as adoption is the *beginning* of a journey, for many parents in my research, it was also the culmination of a long process of considering or trying various methods of becoming a parent. No one arrived at the decision to adopt lightly. This chapter explores the factors that ultimately influenced couples' decision to pursue adoption, as well as their feelings, hopes, and fears surrounding adoption. Some couples—particularly heterosexual couples—recounted harrowing stories of struggling to conceive for years, often with the help of painful and invasive (not to mention expensive) fertility drugs and treatments. Others described genetic or medical barriers to conceiving. For gay male couples, biological options for parenthood were limited to the most expensive—surrogacy—which was simply *not* an option for most couples due to its costliness. This chapter also addresses the kinds of circumstances, beliefs, and experiences that fostered participants' openness to adoption as a path to parenthood. For example, having family members who were adopted enabled a basic familiarity with adoption as a family-building route, making it less "foreign" than it was to some people—and served as evidence that biogenetic ties were not prerequisites for family membership and love.

Family Vignette: Jackie and Bob

Jackie and Bob were a white heterosexual couple living in a Northeastern suburb. At the time that they began to pursue adoption, Jackie was employed as a pediatric nurse and Bob as a financial manager. The couple tried to conceive for several years. Jackie shared that she had always wanted a few children—but they had talked about having one or two biological children and then ultimately adopting, because Bob's cousin was adopted and it always felt to them like "a nice way to build or add to your family." At the same time, Jackie conceded that it took her a long time to abandon her efforts to have a biological child. Over the course of several years, Jackie had tried intrauterine insemination (IUI; 10 cycles) and in vitro fertilization (IVF; six cycles), as well as taking the medication Clomid for many months to stimulate ovulation. For several years, Jackie persisted with these treatments. It was very difficult for her to let go of the possibility of having a biogenetically related child, and, like some other participants, she referred to the process of abandoning fertility treatments and moving to adoption as a "grieving process":

> I've always wanted to have a child or children of my own, to be able to pass on what I know, and of course, my genetics and everything. And then that didn't work out, and that was a huge grieving process for me as far as having to go to, "OK, it's not going to be my genes or my husband's; they might not look like me, they might not act like me" or whatever. But, I want to have a child more than I need to go through the whole birthing process–type thing. I know that I want to be a mom, and I know I would be a great mom.

As in many couples, Jackie and Bob differed in when they arrived at the point where they were ready to stop efforts to conceive and move to considering adoption. According to Jackie, Bob was ready to move on from fertility treatments to consider adoption before she was. This was actually somewhat unusual among the heterosexual couples whom I interviewed, where it was typically the wife who brought up adoption first—and likely in part reflects Bob's familiarity with adoption within his own family:

> Bob was [ready] a little bit before me, because I wasn't willing to let go of the IVF thing as much as he was at first. I was like, ". . . absolutely I want to adopt, but after we have our own biological one" [*laugh*]. I was kind of stuck on that I think a little bit more so, and he was more like, "Oh my God I'm all set with the hormone injections and your changing moods" [*laugh*].

Likewise, when asked who was on board with adoption first or whether they were equally on board right away, Bob said: "I don't know; probably equally, but maybe myself, because I have a cousin who's adopted, and I've always [been] like, 'Hey honey, if it doesn't work out we can always adopt.' That was my stance. Jackie felt like, she wanted to carry her own child and wanted to keep going with the infertility route." Bob also elaborated on the varied factors that led him to conclude that it was time to move on—that is, emotional, health, and financial considerations:

> We had six [IVF] cycles that were covered by insurance, and after six of them were unsuccessful we decided that it's not worth—first of all health-wise for Jackie to attempt it any longer, but also financially we just could not have

afforded to do it on our own. Health insurance only covered up to six [cycles]. That was a 2-year process and at that point I was just both emotionally [and financially] spent with it.

Like many participants, Jackie and Bob both felt that enduring the pain, stress, and disappointment of infertility together served to both challenge and bond them as a couple. By the time they had arrived at adoption, they were exhausted yet hopeful. And, although both Jackie and Bob were initially hesitant about adoption, and about open adoption specifically, at the time that they were first interviewed they had fully committed to the process. While acknowledging that the paperwork, "Dear Birth Mother" letter, and cost were overwhelming, they also felt relieved to know that they were investing in something that "had a real shot at working out." By turning their attention and energy toward adoption and placing their financial and emotional trust in something that felt more like a sure thing, they had regained a sense of control and agency. Jackie shared:

As far as the application process and everything else . . . it's far less laborious than doing anything [related to] infertility. You fill out the paperwork, it's straightforward; you answer questions, you go on interviews, you pay the money. We've been to several workshops and stuff, which have actually been fun and very informative, and we've networked and met a lot of other people through that. So I would say on like a scale of 1 to 10, if I had to rate the infertility experience with 1 being miserable and 10 being positive I would say the infertility experience is about a 2. If I had to rate the adoption experience that we've been through to date, as far as home study, 1 being miserable, 10 being positive, I would rate it a 9 on the other end for adoption. Which is a good thing, because, you know, I really feel like we're in the right place here.

Jackie and Bob were among those couples that tried extensively to have a biological child but who ultimately felt positively about their decision to adopt. As we will see, not all families exerted the same level of effort to have a biological child; indeed, same-sex couples frequently expended far less time, money, and energy on biological parenthood before moving to adoption, and some never tried to have a biological child at all. Additionally, some couples who ultimately arrived at adoption were not as wholly on board as Jackie and Bob— even though, at the time that I first interviewed them, all couples were actively working with an adoption agency, demonstrating at least some level of commitment to adoption.

Trying to Conceive: The Path Before the Path

Most, but not all, of the heterosexual couples whom I interviewed had tried to conceive unsuccessfully and had used reproductive technologies, such as IUI and IVF, in their efforts to conceive. Most couples who tried IVF—the most invasive and expensive fertility treatment—tried for at least three cycles, and sometimes as many as 10. Several couples tried to conceive with egg donors. Their narratives regarding the physical and emotional process of trying to conceive using fertility treatments, as well as how and why they ended up considering and then pursuing adoption as a path to parenthood, were remarkably consistent across participants. Their narratives also echo prior research and memoirs that address infertility[1] and, more rarely, the path from infertility to adoption.[2] Several heterosexual women had long-standing medical issues or concerns (e.g., polycystic ovarian syndrome, endometriosis), which had prepared them, to some degree, for the possibility of difficulty conceiving—and thus adoption. Likewise, in a few cases, couples were in their late 30s or early 40s when they began the process of trying to conceive (e.g., because they had just recently married and/or decided they wished to become a parent) and thus had some sense that it might be difficult to conceive. In several cases, heterosexual couples never tried to conceive because of medical concerns on the part of the woman (wherein a pregnancy could be health threatening) and/or concerns about genetic risks (e.g., a heart condition that was likely to be passed down to biological offspring).

For lesbian couples, the process of trying to have a biological child was somewhat different. For them, becoming a parent was not as much a given as it often was for heterosexual couples. In turn, lesbian couples often described a more deliberate process of first deciding that they wanted to be parents before articulating what route(s) they would pursue. Mariette, for example, described how she and her partner, Jenny, first discussed "starting a family" but wondered "how are our families going to react? And . . . society, and is it fair?" After a few years, she and Jenny "just decided, 'We're both going to be miserable if we don't.'" Lesbian and gay couples sometimes had to first work out their worries about parenting a child as members of a stigmatized minority in society before they could fully commit themselves to pursuing parenthood.

Regarding parenthood route, some lesbian couples tried to conceive first, others tried at the same time as pursuing adoption, and others went straight to adoption. Notable was the fact that in only a few cases did both women actually try to conceive, and lesbian couples more rarely pursued the more invasive and expensive fertility treatments (e.g., IVF) as compared to heterosexual couples. Several lesbian couples did pursue IVF—and their physical and emotional experience of enduring IVF was highly similar to that of heterosexual women.

On average, however, lesbian couples demonstrated a less intense commitment to having a biological child. This was evidenced by the fact that often, only one partner tried to conceive, they typically tried to conceive for a shorter period of time than heterosexual couples, and they spent less money on fertility treatments than heterosexual couples.

Infertility and Loss: "It Was the Longest Road . . . and It Led Nowhere"

Among heterosexual couples in general, and among some lesbian couples, trying to conceive without success was described as an emotionally and physically draining process, filled with "anxiety, hope, and dashed hope." "It was really painful and really hard and really disappointing" (Charlene, lesbian). "We tried for a year and a half every single month and . . . I became depressed and it was not good for me" (Elora, heterosexual woman). Said Carly, a white heterosexual professor in the urban Northeast:

> It was devastating, the worst thing I could have gone through, ever. . . . It was a recurrent loss; it just kept hitting me again and again and again, every cycle. Getting our hopes up—just thinking maybe this is going to be it, and getting so excited and really trying to take good care of ourselves, and doing everything we could to make it work, and then to get so, so profoundly disappointed—it was devastating.

Participants often turned to reproductive technologies such as IUI and IVF, which were expensive, painful, and ultimately not successful. Ellen, a white heterosexual travel writer living in a large West Coast city, had done "several rounds of in vitro," which was

> pretty stressful, and I mean, it sounds so scientific, like they know so much, and you get in there and it's kind of like, "well, let's try this and see if this will work," and then, "well that didn't work; all right, let's try this . . . " and "maybe we should try this" . . . and it's all such a random guessing game, and there are these huge emotional ups and downs.

Eventually, Ellen and her husband, Matt, reached the point where they wondered, "'should we keep going with this when there are no guarantees? . . . What's our goal here?' and so we started considering adoption." Holly, a white lesbian civil engineer in a large Midwestern city, described how her partner, Tammy, had tried to conceive for several years, and had endured several miscarriages. After miscarrying a third time, Tammy was "done trying to get pregnant"—and Holly began to try to conceive:

> So then I started trying at home. And that wasn't working, and so then we went to the doctor, and he put me on the first round of fertility drugs and then the second round of fertility drugs and then the third round of fertility drugs. And after I became a screaming banshee—my body went all out of whack—I stopped that process. And that's when [we started to turn toward] adoption.

Damian, a white heterosexual software engineer living in a medium-sized city on the West Coast, recounted the "emotional roller coaster" of unsuccessful fertility treatments, and what it felt like to get off that roller coaster:

> Emotionally, it was very, very difficult. A lot of close calls, a couple of really sad moments, and there were times where there was physical pain for Monica. It put an extra burden on both of us. There's the emotional toll that it takes; you feel exhausted and frustrated. Luckily, we banded together, because it was very hard. There's a lot of emotional scars.

Michael, a white philosophy professor in a midsized East Coast city, shared the story of how he and his wife, Meg, got off of the roller coaster before it could "destroy" them:

> We started trying the old-fashioned way, it didn't work, and then we went through the IVF clinic, the diagnosis of infertility, and . . . the rather irritating, "Well, there's no good reason why you can't have children." And so we went through the IUIs and then the IVF. At that point we then decided that rather than keep doing that—we made the decision that look, this was not working, and we didn't want to become one of these couples who are—well, even just the couple of years we were doing it, it's incredibly stressful. Every time you go through a cycle, you have the whole buildup and come-down of it. And so I think we basically kind of said we're not going to have the next 3 years of our life going up and down that roller coaster. We've been through enough. . . . We'd done enough. We weren't going to keep putting ourselves through that.

Rachel, a white lesbian woman who worked as a computer systems training manager in a large Southern city, reflected on the multiple losses she and her partner, Nancy, had experienced prior to pursuing adoption:

> You want something to work so much. So it was hard. . . . You live your life in 2-week intervals. When you are trying to [have a child, you're always thinking],

"How is our life going to change in 2 weeks?" There is a whole ... myriad of emotion that is wrapped around it. There is frustration, you know—it didn't work. And ... disappointment. We [both] tried to get pregnant. I did become pregnant. We lost [that] baby. She became pregnant and lost [that baby]. So, [adoption] just seemed like the next alternative for us. I mean, we just kind of got to the point where, you know, I am 40 now and I think we just hit the age barrier where it was just, "Okay, now we're starting to risk health issues if we continue."

For Charlene, a white lesbian teacher in a midsized Northeastern city, feelings of loss, anxiety, and helplessness arose as she and her partner, Leila, faced disappointments on both the conception and adoption front. Charlene was trying to conceive via insemination (with the help of Clomid, IUI, and finally IVF) at the same time that she and Leila were trying to adopt internationally—hoping that "something would stick." Yet both routes led to frustration:

It's been a roller coaster, definitely. One of the hardest parts was when the international phase started to look not doable. We were pretty paralyzed for several months there. I felt kind of depressed, like, "What are we going to do and how's this ever going to happen?" And actually, that time paralleled sort of the end of my fertility treatment and attempts to get pregnant; we were kind of overlapping there for a little bit.

Leila, Charlene's partner, spoke to the relational aspect of managing the emotions associated with the roller coaster of unsuccessful conception attempts and fertility treatments. Leila recognized that the process of trying to conceive, unsuccessfully, was uniquely challenging for Charlene—but also spoke to how it affected her, and their relationship:

She was an incredible, incredible sport and doesn't do anything halfway, and the way that she tried was wholly, with her whole being, so the disappointment was with all of our whole being. So ... that was horrible. And it could have really messed us up, but it brought us a lot closer, and we had a lot of help during the time. So that was a really good thing. But, it was like ... eating ground glass or something—it was horrible all the way. It was really hard, because when she shows up for her life, [she shows up]. So she showed up for a devastating fertility experience.... It was very poignant and compelling at the same time. I'm happy to never go through that again. It was very hard.

It was fairly typical that both partners—heterosexual or lesbian—acknowledged that the partner who was actually experiencing the inseminations and fertility treatments had a different, often more intense, experience, than their partner. Molly, for example, shared that she was "grumpy and depressed," and noted that

> Taryn was too, but she wasn't going through it all like I was. I think I was in this pattern where, like, right before I was due to get my period we'd both get really grumpy. And I think it was right before we inseminated too. It was like, what if it didn't work? It was so stressful. Then I'd get my period, and I'd cry.

The nontrying partners generally did experience "big" emotions as well—but sometimes shielded or downplayed them as they sought to support their partners. Lucas, a Latino heterosexual lawyer in a suburb in the South, had been through a very difficult process of trying to conceive with his wife, Therese, who had endured a range of medical procedures, diagnoses, and treatments before they agreed to move to adoption. Now, as they waited to be placed with a child, Lucas said that he

> notice[d] that occasionally, I have this sudden rush of great sadness, but then it kind of subsides and I can tell that that's my own feelings that are—you know, they're not suppressed, but I postponed a lot of them. I've postponed a lot of feelings because Therese has really had to go through a lot. . . . I've been—my personality has been to be protective of her to make sure that she's okay, that she doesn't hurt excessively, and she knows that I'm here for her . . . so, yeah, [these emotions] have accumulated over the years.

Getting off the fertility train, moving forward with adoption. Getting off the fertility train was difficult. Even as participants came crashing down from the disappointment of another failed conception attempt, the promise of possibility ("next time could be the time!") kept them riding the train. Nauseous from uncertainty but buoyed by hope, they continued to pour their money and emotional energy into fertility treatments—until ultimately, their financial and emotional coffers began to run dry, often alongside or after devastating disappointments (e.g., miscarriages, stillbirths, and unexpected diagnoses such as endometriosis and polycystic ovarian syndrome). Seana, a white heterosexual sales associate at a jewelry store in a large city in the Midwest, shared how, after a change in insurance coverage, she learned that she and her husband, Ron, would now "have to pay for all of the cycles ourselves, which was a lot of money," prompting them to "move to adoption. At least we'd be putting money to something more or less a sure thing. It was starting to be very financially draining." Likewise, Lucas, the Latino heterosexual lawyer, said, "What we realized was that with adoption, at least in theory, if you go through the process, you will have a child at the end.

With these other procedures, we could spend a fortune and have nothing [but] a woman with ruined health." Angela, a white heterosexual environmental planner in a large West Coast city, had endured several miscarriages, several years of taking Clomid to stimulate ovulation, a diagnosis of fibroids, and several surgeries before she reached the point where "it was just really hard, and very devastating . . . and we started to say, 'Okay, how far do we want to go with this, with the reproductive technologies?' And we walked that path and then we were really able to say, 'Ok, let's go into adoption.'"

Partners within couples often differed in their willingness and readiness to "quit" the process of trying to conceive. For example, Seana noted that she was ready to move on before her husband, Ron. Whereas Seana espoused to be "okay with adoption all along," even when trying to conceive, Ron was, according to Seana, reluctant to adopt. Seana said: "He had always said he would never do it" because of "uncertainty that the baby was going to be taken away," but, even more so, because the baby " wouldn't look like him." In turn, Ron was initially less willing to abandon all efforts to conceive, preferring to continue past the point when Seana felt spent. At the same time he voiced an awareness that the physical and emotional process of trying to conceive "wasn't as hard on me as it was on Seana. . . . As a female, it has got to be so much harder on her—why she can't have kids, you know. And just that anxiety and the monthly waiting . . . it was tough on her." Thus, although he was reluctant to consider adoption ("just knowing that the bloodlines wouldn't be passed down; it wouldn't be ours, so to speak"), Ron was sensitive to the fact that their struggles to conceive were particularly "tough on her . . . they wore on her." Ron's sensitivity to Seana's distress echoes a fair amount of research showing that heterosexual couples tend to see infertility as more devastating for wives (e.g., a tragedy), whereas for men it is viewed as more of a profound disappointment.[3]

Other couples also described discrepancies between partners in their willingness and readiness to cease fertility treatments and move to adoption. Seana and Rob are fairly typical in that, among heterosexual couples, women were often "done" with the process of trying to conceive sooner than men, and were also more readily on board with the possibility of adoption. Thus, at the same time that they were often viewed—by themselves and their husbands—as more devastated by infertility, women were ultimately also more ready and willing to move on from it, expressing fewer hesitations regarding adoption and greater certainty that they could bond to an unrelated child. Cal, a white IT manager in a small city in the Northeast, shared:

> Having a biological child was our original plan and we had never sort of considered adoption until that didn't work out. I probably would have pursued more medical treatment longer than Shoshanna. But I was also in agreement

that I did not want to spend lots of money and time and risk and effort [for something that wasn't going to work].... It took a couple years before we moved forward with the adoption. It took me a while mentally to come to terms with the fact that that was what we were going to do.

Laura, a white heterosexual web designer in a medium-sized city in the Midwest, similarly described her husband, Lou, as less enthusiastic about adoption during their early conversations about it:

I was more open to the idea initially than Lou was. He was a little bit unsure about whether he wanted to pursue it. I think he was more—more focused on the idea of having a biological child; he didn't really know how he would feel about an adopted child, [whereas] I said all along that if we weren't able to have children I would want to adopt.

Lena, a white heterosexual operations manager in a Northeast suburb, who described the last 5 years of years of trying to conceive as "emotionally draining" and who "just want[ed] to have a child already," was in the early stages of working with an adoption agency when I first interviewed her. She noted that she was more on board with adoption than her husband, Thomas, although he was, in her words, "getting there." Lena provided this description of a recent conversation she had had with Thomas:

I'm like, "I want you to be on board with this. I don't want to feel like I'm pushing you," and he said, "No," he says, "I want a child more than anything in this world," and I said, "I know," and he said, "Obviously, I'm not going to lie to you. I never thought I'd be adopting." I said, "Well, I didn't either 5 years ago," but he said, "You know what, I'm okay with adoption because I really want a child." I said, "Okay." So, I'm more excited about adoption because I think it's great and he's more like accepting of it because he wants to be a parent really bad.... He wishes it happened ... naturally for us. He said he's just warming up to the idea [of adoption] a little more.

Getting off the train of fertility treatments did not mean that participants were ready to move on to adoption right away. Some participants recognized that it was important for them to fully process and grieve the loss of a biological child before seriously considering or taking steps toward adoption. Others, though, emphasized their desire to "dive right in" to adoption as a way to feel that they were moving forward, especially after feeling that they lost so much time and hope during the process of trying various fertility treatments. Sometimes, these different individuals were members of the same couple. Monica and Damian, for example, differed in their readiness to move to adoption. Monica, a white heterosexual graphic design artist living in a medium-sized city on the West Coast, shared, about her and her husband, Damian:

> We were in different places. . . . For me, after each [miscarriage] I lost hope a little bit where it's like, okay, you know, my expectations went lower, lower, and lower. And by the last cycle which was about a year later, I was like, "Okay, I just want to get this over with and just know whether it's working or whether I'm moving on to adoption." And so, of course, I was depressed after all, but . . . for my husband, he was positive the whole time and didn't want to think it through and then at the very end when it didn't work, it hit him like a ton of bricks that, "This is the reality, it's not working"—so he took it a lot harder than me at the very end. I felt like I was just ready to jump right in into the whole adoption thing, like: "Okay; *Plan B*," whereas he had a serious setback with it. . . . It just hit him harder. He didn't process it at each time like I did; he processed it all at once.

Taryn, a white lesbian radio personality living in a Northeastern suburb, shared that although she was disappointed each month when her partner, Molly, did not get pregnant, she did not feel that it was her right or role to tell Molly when to cease such efforts. Specifically, Taryn was aware that it was "even more disappointing for [Molly] because it's her body." In turn, Taryn felt that although it was a shared decision as to "when we would stop, I felt like as long as she wanted to keep trying—I mean, unless it was putting us in the poor house or something—I would just support however long she wanted to try. Like, she could be kind of the final call [as to] when she wanted to stop trying." Dominick, a multiracial heterosexual small business owner in a large West Coast city, said that he deferred to his wife, Elora, "when it came to the stopping of the fertility [treatments]; that was really, really her decision—but I think we both felt that it was the right thing to do because it's just really hard on the body and emotions and all that."

Sometimes moving away from a difficult process of trying to conceive and toward adoption did not happen in one grand and definitive gesture. At times, it happened in baby steps. In this way, participants took actions—including attending informational meetings at adoption agencies, talking to other couples who had adopted, and reading about adoption on the Internet—before they actually stopped trying to conceive. Dominick, for example, shared how he and Elora took a break from conceiving and then were

> considering in vitro, and then the idea of adopting came up. We researched it online, and finally just said, "ah, well, it wouldn't hurt to take the first steps. Let's just call an agency and just start the process, see what happens, and we can

always pull out if it doesn't seem like the right thing for us." And then it just kept moving forward.

Monica similarly noted that "most of the other people in [our] workshop, they went right from infertility—like, the next day, to adoption. Damian and I took like a year." Damian shared his process of slowly relinquishing his fantasies of biological parenthood and adjusting to the idea of adoption:

> [I had] those fantasies of being a parent and having a family and ... [it was challenging] to give up those fantasies. As much as I wanted to hang on to some of those fantasies, over time I started to transition into a more of an accepting concept of adoption and [accept that reality] doesn't always quite match up with your fantasy or your vision ... so we started slowly pursuing adoption, went to a workshop, and nothing felt wrong, so we just kept it going. Slowly I was able to [shift] my vision [of parenthood].... [I]t's not this perfect vision that I've had since I was 5 [but] it didn't work and I need to find something else. [Holding on] is not fair—it's not fair to myself; it's not fair to Monica.

A particularly emotionally detailed description of the process of learning about and slowly getting on board with adoption was described by Lou, a white heterosexual cartoonist in a midsized city in the Midwest. Lou, who had tried to conceive with his wife, Laura, for several years, shared:

> It was a big struggle, dealing with the medical aspect, and after a while it's just like ... I just want to have a baby. And so Laura was online looking around and she started reading about adoption, which I had never really considered. And I think that I got fairly—I got depressed fairly often during the whole medical thing.... [I]t was kind of a depressing [time] for me, on and off.... I'd be like, "Ok, we can do this, we'll figure out something else." But then I would get depressed. At a certain point I realized that I was going to have to let go of [having a biological child] if we wanted to go any further. And so, there was my wife saying, "OK well what about adoption?" and I was like, "Adoption! Oh, I don't want to do that." And then she convinced me to go to this weekend seminar and—I liked it. [Before that], I was just ignorant, I didn't know anything about it, and so I was reluctant because of that. But once I did know something about it, it seemed pretty attractive. It took a week or so to fully sink in, and then I thought, "Yeah, okay, we could do that, we could adopt." Because really what we want is a child. I definitely had thoughts about, you know, my biological legacy [is] coming to an end [*laugh*]. But you know, whatever. There's plenty of people in the world. Who's to say that my biology has to continue?

Adoption often seemed to promise more of a "sure thing" to couples. That is, after months or years of unsuccessful conception attempts, medical procedures and treatments, and what sometimes felt like "broken promises" by doctors and fertility specialists, they felt relieved to finally invest in something that seemed like it had "more of a guarantee." Donna, a white heterosexual nonprofit manager in a large city in the Northeast, said that once she and her husband, Max, had transitioned from pursuing fertility treatments to pursuing adoption, she felt "at peace with where we're at right now, and I'm excited, and—we know our outcome." Such sentiments were especially typical early in the waiting process. Yet some prospective parents had been waiting for a child for several years at the time that I first interviewed them—and they sometimes expressed feeling less certain about whether adoption was in fact the "sure thing" that they initially thought it was. A long fertility road that "led nowhere" was sometimes followed by a difficult decision to invest emotionally and financially in adoption—which in turn was often accompanied by its own set of uncertainties, false starts, and disappointments as couples wondered: "Will I ever be a parent?" As Seana, a white heterosexual sales associate who had been waiting for 2 years—and endured a few failed birth parent matches—when I first interviewed her, said:

> In the beginning we were so excited when we would get a call and we would want to run and tell everybody. Then now with things hav[ing] fallen through on us, I find it more that we're not telling anybody anything. . . . I didn't think it would be as difficult as it has been. . . . [I]t's been very emotional.

Disappointment in a "Process That Didn't Work Out"

Unsuccessful conception efforts were not always the source of deep pain and loss—particularly for lesbian couples. Couples who did not try for very long, and/or seriously entertain any of the more expensive reproductive technologies, typically described experiencing little to moderate levels of distress around their lack of success. Becki, a white lesbian group home supervisor in a midsized city on the West Coast, whose partner, Kathleen, tried to conceive, shared, "We tried about 6 months. And then . . . it was just too stressful and too expensive, and . . . [w]e just decided . . . to take a break and then just we never went back." Kathleen, a white nonprofit manager, agreed, stating that she came to realize that she did not "feel a need for a biological tie . . . to feel like that was my child" and decided that she did not have a strong desire to "get pregnant . . . or give birth . . . or go through labor, or any of that."

Mary, a TV production studio manager, and Andrea, a prison guard, were a white lesbian couple in a midsized city in the South who explained that they had ceased efforts to get pregnant after Mary did two rounds of insemination. Both women's age (late 30s), Andrea's lack of desire to be pregnant ("she was like, 'I'll try it if we need to but I really don't want to go there'"), and their experiences with a homophobic doctor during the insemination process led them to make the switch to adoption fairly early in their parenthood journey. As Mary explained:

> I did two [insemination attempts]. But . . . the doctor made me uncomfortable and made me feel like, "You know, I'm really doing you a favor by doing this for you." They basically told us that, that in any other city you'd have to go through a lengthy application process and, you know, "You can't keep coming off the street and expect someone to inseminate you," and so he didn't agree with our lifestyle. He made that clear without telling us that, and his bedside manner was atrocious.

Mariette, a physical therapist, and Jenny, a manager at a medical supply company, were a white lesbian couple living in the suburban Midwest who tried to conceive for about a year but also pursued adoption at the same time. Mariette shared that she and Jenny "were both completely interested [in] and open to adoption [but] Jenny has always had and expressed a desire to actually carry a child. I really want to be a parent, but I've never felt that need or desire to carry a child. We decided to give kind of both angles a try." After Jenny did five cycles of donor insemination, she became pregnant, but then had a miscarriage. After that, according to Mariette, they "waited about 6 months and tried about four or so more times, and it just never happened. But the whole time near that last year we'd already been in the process of doing the adoption, because our goal was to have a couple of children." Both Mariette and Jenny acknowledged feelings of sadness and disappointment associated with Jenny's lack of success in carrying a baby to term—but they also evidenced a flexibility and openness surrounding adoption that may have ultimately protected them from the deep feelings of loss that other parents described. The couple also had "close friends who adopted," which exposed them to adoption as a viable and positive family-building route, even before they eventually settled on it.

A similar feeling was expressed by Daniela, a white lesbian small business owner in a midsized city in the South. Daniela shared that although she had a desire to be pregnant, she did not have an intense desire to be biologically related to her child. Daniela shared, in turn, that when trying to conceive did not seem to be working out, turning toward adoption seemed like the "natural next step," as opposed to continuing to invest in the possibility of biological parenthood:

We did some treatments and then in vitro of course was going to be another $10,000 or whatever. And it was like, should we try this or should we just try for adoption and eventually we will have that baby? We've always wanted to adopt anyways. It wasn't a question about passing on genes or anything.

Daniela's partner, Heather, a white bookkeeper, was in complete agreement about moving on, in that she had always intended to adopt prior to meeting Daniela: "I always knew that I would probably adopt because I never technically had the biological clock ticking in my body. [I never] wanted to birth a child—but I definitely thought that I wanted to be a parent."

Indeed, several lesbian women who had attempted to conceive explicitly stated that they felt that they and their partners were approaching adoption from a different vantage point than heterosexual couples who had tried to conceive. They did not think of themselves as suffering from infertility; rather, they thought of themselves as trying "Option A" before moving on to "Option B." Stated Eliza, a white lesbian junior accounts manager in a large city in the Northeast:

We had always talked about adoption. Even before we tried to get pregnant, we had talked about adoption. Then one day Hannah decided, "I think I'm going to try to have a baby" ... but after about $2,000 we were like, how much more do we want to spend on this kind of stuff? Let's go back to option two.

Hannah, a white administrative assistant, echoed:

We, I had made up my mind the whole time that ... we were going to give it 6 months and so if it didn't work we were going to try [adoption]. I knew that I didn't want to have to go through all of that infertility garbage with the shots and all of that stuff.

Similarly, Meredith, a white office manager in a large West Coast city, explained that she and her partner, Erin, had "only tried three times for me to get pregnant" but stopped once they learned there were problems with the sperm quality of their known donor, a friend:

I was like, well this is silly to continue with a known donor, but that's what we kind of wanted to do. And then it was like, maybe we should revisit the idea of adoption. Because I was thinking of all the different ideas of what to do, and I was like, you know what? I guess I don't have to birth a child.

Meredith then described how she and Erin began to interview adoption agencies and realized that adoption was a good fit for them. Both women felt confident about their emotional readiness to move forward. Stated Meredith: "We don't have the infertility issues that some people go through and that's the reason why they're adopting. So we don't have a heavy—all the things that go with that. We're . . . ready [and] we want to do it."

In a few cases, heterosexual men and women also demonstrated disappointment, as opposed to a profound sense of loss, surrounding their inability to conceive. For example, Shoshanna, a white project manager in a small Northeastern city, said that she and her husband, Cal, had not always known they wanted to be parents and therefore had not started trying to conceive until they were in their mid-30s. After pursuing some additional avenues, including a minor surgery to address a potential source of their fertility issues (but saying "no" to IVF as a possibility), Shoshanna and Cal "took a break" before moving to adoption. About not being able to conceive, Shoshanna said: "I mean, I certainly would have liked to be pregnant so maybe there's a loss to that. But, not a loss that there won't be a child who is part Cal and part me. That doesn't feel important to me. It's just genes." Cal had a similar perspective. Regarding the significance of a biogenetic relationship to a child, he said:

> I don't know; I would say it's a little more than a "nice to have" . . . a genetic heritage and lineage. . . . [T]here's something about that—but to me, it's not a huge deal. It's more about pairing the child [and parent] and knowing that we're the people to raise that child.

Leigh and Billy, a white heterosexual couple in a small city on the East Coast, were similar to Shoshanna and Cal in that they had not started trying to conceive until they were in their late 30s. Like Shoshanna and Cal, they also demonstrated an unwillingness to pursue the more expensive and intensive fertility treatments, which led them to step off the fertility train and take steps toward adoption. Leigh, an assistant museum director, said that after a series of unsuccessful attempts to conceive, the doctor "basically said the next step is to do IVF . . . [and] I was just not interested in pumping myself with the hormones and the drugs. It seems to me to be very invasive and . . . nothing about that was appealing to me." According to Leigh, after a year of having conversations about "whether or not we wanted to have kids or didn't want to have kids, and if we do . . . were we willing to do IVF or [should we] move on to adoption," they went to an information session to learn about adoption. "Once we did that, it was like, 'Oh, OK, we can do this. It's not quite as scary.' Ultimately, we decided we wanted to be parents, and the biological thing wasn't as important as just being parents." Leigh's husband, Billy, an assistant principal, offered a similar perspective:

> We went to the fertility specialist, who came across as kind of sales oriented. We just didn't feel comfortable. We both felt like—this has been enough. We

crossed a threshold where we felt that that [IVF] wasn't needed. We don't have to spend more time with specialists to try and get a kid.

"We Didn't Have a Strong Desire or Need for a Biological Connection"

Some participants did not try to have a biological child. Lesbian couples, particularly those who adopted via foster care, were well represented in this group; additionally, one heterosexual couple who ended up adopting through foster care was among those couples who did not try to conceive. Even more so than the previously described group, these participants emphasized that they were approaching parenthood from a unique vantage point—distinctly different, they pointed out, than most heterosexual couples seeking to adopt. Greta, a white lesbian small business owner in a suburb of the Northeast, emphasized how different she and her partner, Robin, felt at their adoption orientation sessions, amidst mostly heterosexual couples:

> Adoption is not, like, our back-up choice, it's not sloppy seconds, so that made us completely outside the box. The majority of people who end up [pursuing] adoption are there because they couldn't get pregnant, and that's not where we are coming from. We can get pregnant, but we're choosing not to.

For Greta and Robin, their status as preferential adopters limited their ability to relate fully to the experiences of, and the type of programming geared at, the mostly heterosexual couples in their pre-adoption groups and trainings. Robin, a white freelance writer, said, with feeling: "Everything is about infertility, and so we get a little bit bummed out about that. We get it, and we understand why, we just wish it wasn't so much focus on that. A lot of people come to adoption because it's a great thing."

Adam, a biracial (African American and white) gay marketing director in a midsized West Coast city, shared how, in their adoption classes, "the counselors go through this thing where the parents-to-be mourn the loss of their fertility because a lot of them are adopting because they're infertile. For Will and I, it's kind of like, 'Wow, we're just happy to be here!' " Adam went on to say:

> We actually had to try not to look too happy, because a lot of the [heterosexual couples] had tried so many other things... and now they are at the end of their rope, where they are looking to adopt someone else's baby. We had to be sensitive to that in the beginning of the process when we were just getting to know the other couples.

A parallel narrative was provided by Darren, a white computer programmer in a large city on the West Coast, who described attending workshops offered by his adoption agency with his partner, Benji, where "the first class was really just about coming to terms with your sadness around the fact that you weren't able to have a child . . . [whereas] for me it was like, 'Wow, this is a great opportunity!' That wasn't the same place that other people were coming from." Indeed, having grown up and come of age in the 1970s and 1980s, lesbian and gay participants had not always assumed that they would become parents, given the lack of cultural scripts and numerous barriers surrounding same-sex parenthood. Recent shifts in the accessibility and acceptance of gay parenthood meant that they could indeed become parents—a reality that they embraced, sometimes with explicit gratitude.[4]

Often, these preferential adopters explained the fact that they had not tried to conceive prior to pursing adoption as deeply rooted in their desire to give a home to a child who needed it (i.e., via adoption). Shelby, a white lesbian postal clerk in a small Northeastern city, who stated that she had "no desire" to be pregnant, explained: "I believe there are so many unwanted kids around that it would be kind of selfish for me to want to have my own. And, we don't need any more human beings on this planet right now." Shelby went on to say, "And then we saw . . . adoption specials about how just in [our] county there are something like 12,000 kids that are waiting to be adopted so we thought that would be [the best] way to go." Mandy, a white heterosexual career services manager in a suburb of the East Coast, stated, "There's so many children out there that need good homes [and so], at this point, this is something that we really feel committed to; it feels like something that's right for us." Aisha, an African American lesbian woman employed as a human resources manager in a large Northeastern city, shared her and her partner Larissa's process of landing on adoption:

> We kept asking ourselves: "What is the inherent value of bringing yet another person into the world? Is it really just because we want someone who has a nose like ours? Is that really a good enough reason to go through all of the stuff we are going to have to go through in order to actually give birth?" And our answer, eventually, was no, it is not. There are so many children who are in desperate need of precisely what we have to offer, so many children in desperate need of someone to love them and believe in them and offer them a safe place. And so [having a biological child] just didn't seem right.

A lack of investment in biological parenthood, as well as a lack of desire to experience pregnancy and birth, was also emphasized by preferential adopters. Greta, a white lesbian small business owner in a Northeastern suburb, shared an early memory of seeing a pregnant woman and thinking, "'I don't want to ever do that.' So I never saw myself being a birth mother, but I always saw myself as being a mother." Stacy, a white lesbian school administrator in a medium-sized city in the Northeast, offered her perspective on having a biological child:

> I just never have [wanted to have a biological child]. And that was part of why I never wanted to have kids when I was a younger person. Even as a child, I never wanted to have a child—like, "there's a labor part and I'm not into that" [*laughs*]. I mean it might be something that I'm totally into but not enough to find out [*laughs*].... I'm the younger of the two of us... so if one of us were to try [insemination] it would probably have to be me because age-wise, it would be a better choice. There's so many... variables and I like the idea that our child will have the same relationship between the both of us because [having just one of us be related to the child] would just be too much. I like the idea of becoming a parent and not having my hormones and my body completely screwed up for a year and.... Both of us will be able to hit the ground running, at least theoretically—you know, in a way that we wouldn't be able to if one of us was carrying the child.

Indeed, among lesbian couples, women sometimes also spoke of a gravitational pull toward adoption as it offered the unique opportunity to be on an equal plane with their partner with regard to a (lack of) biological connection. By ensuring that neither parent had a "head start" on bonding, they would experience a more similar process of getting to know and developing a relationship with their future child. Larissa, a white bookstore manager in a large Northeastern city, stated, "[A benefit] of adoption is we are both experiencing the process equally." Peggy, a white lesbian occupational therapist in a large Northeastern city, recounted, "I felt like I'd rather adopt if a child wasn't going to be biologically both of ours anyway."

A few lesbian couples had considered or taken steps toward insemination before realizing that it was not the right choice for them. Kate, a white lesbian woman who worked as the director of a women's survival center in a large city on the West Coast, shared how initially, it was "really important to me to be pregnant," seeing it as a "really interesting unique thing to go through and potentially very rewarding," while also imagining that "we would adopt a second child." Then Kate and her partner, Cara, "got into the nitty-gritty about where we were going to get sperm from and we started looking at all these online sperm banks and I started reading all this stuff and doing the initial stuff like tracking your cycle and everything and it's a lot of work." According to Kate, she and Cara found the

> sperm bank process to be really weird. It is bizarrely objectifying and really odd.... [I]t just feels insane to make a decision based on the information you

have, like passing judgment on people's hobbies and favorite colors and their answers to these completely insane questions. That didn't feel good; it didn't feel like who we were.

To Kate, even having such choices seemed "so crazy too, because, you know, heterosexual couples [who want children] don't choose their partners this way!" Then, while spending time with some lesbian couple friends who had adopted, Kate had

> a sort of strange epiphany. We were all sitting there and I just thought, maybe it's not so important to be pregnant. None of these kids came from my friends' pregnancies. So I thought: "Wow, I'm going to sit with that for a while and see what I think about it." And Cara had always been interested in adopting.... So sometimes you realize you've been holding on to something for such a long time and you haven't fully re-evaluated it in light of who you are and where your life is right now. And that's what I did, and I realized that it was not so important to me.

Kate's movement toward adoption was facilitated not only by disillusionment with the insemination process and exposure to families formed through adoption but also by her realization of several "major benefits" to adopting:

> The truth of it is that there can be a lot more things that are equally shared. And there's always a little bit of this underlying homophobia thing in culture and maybe even within ourselves that sort of says that whoever gave birth to child is the "real" parent or "real" mom and it's hard to know the way that that might dig into your relationship and your parenting.

Kate recognized that

> if one parent is the one who is a little more physically bonded and doing all the breastfeeding, then that thing about who is the real parent just gets reinforced. It's kind of nice to avoid all of that. And plus there's just the practical benefits of just not putting your body through that.

It is worth noting too that according to Kate, her partner, Cara, "was always in support of adoption, and she always wanted to adopt; she didn't care about me having, giving birth to a child, but she knew it was really important to me."

Other participants shared Kate's experience of realizing, via exposure to other families who had adopted, that they could love a child who was not biogenetically connected to them. Miri, a white lesbian artist in a large Northeastern city, shared that she and her partner, Lindsey, had "talked about insemination, but that became really daunting and stressful and we didn't try it." Miri shared that she had cousins who were adopted and "always liked [the idea of] adoption," leading her to conclude that "love is love"—a sentiment that helped her to settle on the conclusion that adoption was the "right choice." Lindsey, a white physician assistant, similarly recalled that the process of "looking into fertility banks [was] very stressful, just the idea of tracking her periods and the monthly cost without the guarantee of actually getting pregnant." Then, a family member (who was not related to Lindsey by blood) had a biracial child, and Lindsey realized that

> here's this kid who doesn't look a thing like you, isn't blood related at all, and yet I have the same emotion of totally loving this child. Then I realized: Wow, this kid that we will have between us does not need to look like us at all for us to feel really connected to them.

Never tried because it was unlikely to be successful or it was dangerous. In a few couples, both lesbian and heterosexual, participants had come to the realization that they wanted to parent later in life—namely, in their 40s. They therefore landed fairly quickly on adoption once they realized that options for conception at their age were slim, were very expensive, and/or carried risks that they were unwilling to take (e.g., enhanced likelihood of birth defects due to their "advanced maternal age"). As Larissa, quoted earlier, shared: "I know a lot of women have babies when they are over 40, but I think a lot of my fears were coming into play [around that]." Similarly, a few women recounted significant medical or genetic issues that made it dangerous or impossible to conceive, carry, and/or birth a child; in turn, adoption was an option that they had considered and investigated since first deciding that they wanted to be a parent. Annie, a white heterosexual school administrator living in an East Coast suburb, explained that knowledge of a genetic condition within her family had led her to consider adoption long ago. This, combined with her sense that there is "no need to preserve our biological makeup, and I have no need to give birth," led her to pursue child welfare adoption with her husband, Chuck, who was also not highly invested in a biogenetic connection. "Those kids need a home," said Annie, "and we can provide one." Said Chuck, a white IT director: "There's kids [in foster care]. Why wouldn't you adopt them? They're here and they need a mother and a father."

Because of the fact that most of these participants had known about their medical issues for many years prior to actively pursuing parenthood, they had had a lot of time to think about and get used to the idea of adoption—which they had discussed with their partners early on in their relationship. Sandy, a white heterosexual health care advocate in a small city in the Northeast, stated: "I was honest with him from the beginning about my [illness] and you know, that

I probably wouldn't be able to have a biological child. We were pretty much on board about adopting right from the beginning."

Gay Men: When a Biological Connection Isn't Impossible... but "Out of Reach"

Lesbian couples can, at least theoretically, get pregnant with the use of donor sperm relatively inexpensively, barring any fertility challenges. Among gay male couples, the option of biological parenthood is simply a financial impossibility for most. In addition to being prohibitively expensive for many couples (i.e., upward of over $150,000), practical barriers abound. Surrogacy laws vary from state to state, such that surrogacy is prohibited in some states (e.g., New York), whereas others have no laws governing surrogacy. In states without surrogacy laws, courts may tend to lean relatively favorably toward surrogacy (e.g., Massachusetts), or they may have a reputation for unfavorable rulings surrounding surrogacy (e.g., Kansas). Notably, surrogacy law, whether by statute or case law, is constantly changing.[5] Another barrier that gay couples may encounter is homophobia, insomuch as clinics that arrange surrogacy may be unwilling or reluctant to work with gay male couples.

Half of the gay couples whom I interviewed had considered surrogacy, at least briefly—and in a few cases had taken steps toward pursuing it. Typically, they described the draw of surrogacy as enabling a biological connection between (one) parent and the child, and ensuring that couples would be able to parent their child from birth—that is, to have the "full" experience of parenthood. Several men also felt that surrogacy seemed to promise greater control over the child's prenatal environment, as a woman being paid to carry their child would likely be the host of a healthier womb than, say, a woman who found out she was pregnant after using drugs or alcohol. Yet upon learning more about the financial issues in surrogacy, these couples rejected it as a viable parenting route. Phil, a white graduate student in a midsized city in the South, shared that upon deciding to become parents together, he and his partner, Barry, had "assumed that we would do surrogacy." But upon looking into surrogacy and determining that it was prohibitively expensive, the couple began to explore adoption: "The expense turned us off.... If it were the same cost as the adoption... we probably would do a surrogate but being so vastly different, it was a no brainer; we just said 'no way.'" Dean, a white gay software developer in a large city in the South, shared, "There was a brief period where we kind of pursued going that route, to hire surrogates or surrogates' eggs, and it was just going to be extraordinarily expensive. We heard prices [up to] $150,000 to do the full surrogacy." Dean and his partner, Seth, quickly moved on, after just a few weeks, to consider "other options."

Sometimes, practical challenges associated with surrogacy were named as deterrents to pursuing it. Such challenges included access to donor eggs by a female relative or friend and access to a fertility clinic that would work with gay men. Seth, a white gay director of an after-school program in a large city in the South, said: "We thought about surrogacy [and did research] on the Internet. Logistically, it was going to be very difficult. [State] was the closest place that anyone would work with us. Certainly all fertility stuff is religious based around here, so that presented some obstacles." Ethical challenges were also identified, whereby surrogacy struck men as "artificial" and "weird" or it just did not "feel right." Terrence, a white anesthesiologist in a West Coast suburb, shared: "Surrogacy seemed too clinical and too medicalized."

Some men cited other concerns related to surrogacy. A few men, for example, spoke about how they had entertained the idea of having a sister or female friend be the surrogate. While attractive in that it would enable both men to be genetically related to the child, this possibility also introduced relational complexities. Joe, a white operations manager living in a large city on the West Coast, for example, noted that he and his partner, Jared, had considered asking Joe's sister to be the surrogate. But then they realized that they would have to deal with "all the emotional issues involved with all the physical people involved—and that's a whole lot of mess and a whole lot of money and . . . there are all these kids that need a home." Likewise, Will, a white accountant in a midsized city on the West Coast, shared:

> We did consider surrogacy; Adam was more in favor of it than I was. I had a lot of resistance to it just because of the various complications that I see in the process [such as] if the mother has a change of mind, a change of heart halfway through the pregnancy, or when the baby is born. That was a really huge concern for me, and just the complications of finding the right mother. We did have some girlfriends who volunteered, and I think they were quite serious about it. But my concern with that was that I wanted Adam and I to be the parents, more so than have a third fully functioning parent involved—and I thought that our friends would want to be fully functional parents as well.

Gay couples who considered surrogacy described minimal loss and grieving surrounding the process of "taking surrogacy off the table"—but several of them attributed this to the fact that they had already grieved the loss of biogenetically related offspring when they came out as gay. Related to this, they also asserted—as some lesbian participants did as well—that as members of the LGBTQ community, they were already oriented to and endorsed the idea of family as constructed through relational ties, not biogenetic ties. Doug, a white psychologist in a large West Coast city, shared:

> We have a really clear sense of family as created. Not family as born . . . I mean from the time we came out, we've each had 15 or more years to do whatever grieving around [not having biological offspring] that we would need to do, really. . . . I mean I always knew that it would be possible for me to be a parent but I always had it in the back of my head that it was fairly unlikely that it would be a baby that I created.

In some cases, gay men explicitly rejected surrogacy, emphasizing that their goal was to become parents, not biological parents. Nate, a white medical assistant living in a Southern suburb, had "no interest" in surrogacy. He shared that his own sister was adopted, which had shaped his ideas about the significance of biology to family and kin relationships. Specifically, Nate believed that "parenting is more about time and attention and actually being there than biological relationships." Some men viewed surrogacy as unjustifiable given the number of children already on the earth who were in need of families. Dave, a white gay radiologist in a large Midwestern city, said:

> We both talked about [surrogacy] but then came to the conclusion that it was too expensive. Also, just from a general principle of adopting a child that may need a home and is already going to be coming into the world anyway—I think we both kind of felt strongly about that too. We'd be helping someone.

In a few cases, men were quite familiar with surrogacy as a route to parenthood but felt it was not right for them. Eric, a white editor in a large Northeastern city, said:

> My brother did surrogacy, and he's got two great kids. I love them, but I feel like for Russell and I, it was very important to us to give a child a home. If it comes to, you know, if we have to do surrogacy, that's an option, and we're blessed with money and education and we can look into doing all those kinds of things. But for now, it's important to us that we create a family this way.

> One of the reasons we chose open adoption is that it is about community. It is about helping someone who is pregnant at a very inconvenient time for her. We've always created families in our personal lives, so this is just an extension of that.

Jamie, a white communications manager in a midsized city in the South, said: "We know about surrogacy. We just didn't feel like that was the way to go especially because there are so many other kids out there that need to be adopted . . . and trying to get a surrogate mother and all of that is just really expensive." Thus, for some gay men, surrogacy never really landed on the table as a viable option because of a whole constellation of reasons—including, most prominently, the desire to give a child who needed it a home and the expense. Deciding to become a parent, then, was often synonymous with or quickly followed by the decision to adopt.

* * *

For many couples, adoption was not the beginning of their parenthood journey. Heterosexual couples in particular are highly influenced by heteronormative scripts of "normal" parenthood, which have historically linked biology to kinship. The loss associated with the envisioned and often taken-for-granted template of "normal" parenthood was often greater for heterosexual couples than same-sex couples, whose deviation from heteronormative relationship and family scripts facilitated greater openness to nonbiological forms of kinship. Gay men in particular often embraced adoption—indeed, their parenthood scripts often fused "adoption" with "parenthood." In turn, gay men, and some but not all lesbians, often experienced less loss associated with not having a biological child, setting them up for an easier transition to adoption.

As discussed in more detail in Chapter 10, couples who encounter infertility or barriers to biological parenthood should consider seeking out a therapist who is knowledgeable about infertility, egg and sperm donation, and adoption, to ensure that issues of loss and communication are addressed meaningfully and sensitively. A competent therapist can help couples to address relational differences in perspective and preferences for biological parenthood and adoption, easing the couple through processes of grieving and/or decision making related to family building. An adoption-competent therapist or professional is also essential so that couples can accurately assess the reality and range of adoption options available to them, and determine what routes, if any, are an appropriate fit, given their own emotional and financial resources, and personal strengths and limitations.

Notes

1. Greil, Slauson-Blevins, & McQuillan, 2009; Orenstein, 2007.
2. Donovan, 2013; Goldberg, Downing & Richardson, 2009.
3. Greil, Leitko, & Porter, 1988; Kirk, 1964.
4. Goldberg, 2012.
5. The Surrogacy Experience, 2018.

2

Orienting to Open Adoption, Considering Contact, and Reflecting on Race

Preadoption Perspectives and Preferences

> Many open adoption relationships have a warmth that comes from having shared a common struggle—allowing yourself to be vulnerable to another human being, responding to that person's vulnerability, and being committed to a common goal that centers around the best interest of the child.
> —Friends in Adoption (www.friendsinadoption.org)

> It is one of our goals to help birth and adoptive parents get to know and respect one another. For some families, it takes longer to gain respect and trust for one another. Some birth parents and adoptive parents really hit it off and enjoy one another's company. They are likely to have more frequent and more face-to-face contact. Some birth parents and adoptive parents feel they need to take time to get to know one another and establish trust before they have any significant contact. These families may start off with less contact (letters, occasional phone calls, emails) and gradually move to more frequent and trusting contact (regular phone contact, visits).
> —Bright Futures Adoption Center (http://rfkchildren.businesshomepage.info/bright-futures)

These quotes are examples of what prospective adoptive parents—and prospective birth parents—might see when they first begin to investigate the possibility of open adoption, or adoption more generally. For many of the parents whom I interviewed, openness was initially a foreign concept. Familiar only with closed adoptions, they wondered about, and were sometimes wary or even leery of, the reality that openness now seemed to be more of the norm than the exception in adoption.

This chapter takes us through what happens during the preadoption stage: the kinds of patterns that parents exhibited with respect to openness. Some parents, as we will see, more easily boarded the open adoption train, whereas others lingered or held back, or immediately placed caveats on the level of openness they would consider. Adoption-related programming, conversations with social workers, exposure to other families in open adoption, and other experiences ultimately caused shifts in many participants' views and thinking about openness. In fact, some participants came to the conclusion that they would not actually be willing to pursue an adoption with expectant parents who were uninterested in some level of contact. In addition to considering participants' desired level of contact with the birth family, this chapter also considers their openness regarding children's race. Openness regarding contact and race are two of the most significant dimensions of prospective adopters' decision making and in part determine what placements are possibilities for them. I also briefly consider parents' openness with respect to prenatal drug and alcohol exposure, as this represents a final choice point that prospective adopters must grapple with, and set pen to paper on, during the preadoptive phase.

Family Vignette: Monica and Damian

Monica and Damian were a white heterosexual couple, both in their mid-40s and recently married, who lived in a midsized city on the West Coast. Monica worked as a graphic design artist and Damian was employed as a software engineer. Because of their older age and the unlikelihood of conceiving a child naturally, Monica and Damian began to consider adoption soon after they were married. At the time of the first interview, they were actively working with an adoption agency that primarily arranged domestic open adoptions. Yet as Monica explained, open domestic private adoption was not always their first choice—and in fact, she and Damian had vacillated between domestic adoption and international adoption for quite some time:

> We went to . . . a standard adoption workshop where they had guest speakers coming in and talking about different things and different roles, the facilitators, the lawyers. . . . They kind of go through [all this] stuff and we kind of gravitated in different ways in different times [to different adoption routes], depending on what they were presenting or talking about. With open adoption, the woman that was running the workshop had two children from open adoption. One had a birth parent that wasn't very involved, and the other had a birth parent that was very involved, and so it led to some equity issues amongst the children. Damian and I were like, "Oh my God, we don't really like that! . . . How sad." So then we're like, "Oh maybe international," and then we heard about . . . the attachment issues, and that pushed us back towards domestic. Then we saw a

show on open domestic [adoption] where they were showing, like, the birth families. And it was so traumatic and scary and just, it made us realize it wasn't just the birth parent you're dealing with, it's the whole birth family, there's all of these emotions, it's traumatic and it's kind of scary. And so then we were [thinking] international. [It was kind of] back and forth.

[Interviewer: And how did you finally land on open domestic—how did that play out?]

Well . . . we got a little less scared about the whole birth family relationship. We looked at the value to the child of having that connection, and that was probably foremost. Number two, there was really no perfect country. It wasn't like there was one country that was simple and wonderful that didn't have a million drug issues . . . [or other issues] . . . that just jumped out like, wow, that's the country! It's easy, everything's good, the kids are taken care of! . . . So, for us I think, we would both agree that . . . we would [rather] kind of suffer . . . going through the process of open adoption because it is really more traumatic for the *adoptive parents* and—that whole triad relationship is really challenging. But . . . the really bad part only lasts so long, and then the kid has a lifetime of connections. So for us, it's just like, "Okay, we can suffer a little because it's going to be worth it for the child."

Damian narrated a similar set of concerns related to openness, noting that international adoption had initially appealed to both of them. He had initially perceived it as a "sure thing . . . if you do the right paperwork, and you have the money . . . you can pick a child as opposed to domestic which forces a relationship with the birth mother, [who] can [also] change her mind about placing the child." In addition to highlighting the perceived lack of autonomy and control over the open adoption process as concerns that mitigated his enthusiasm for openness, Damian was also wary of "the fact that you're also related to not just the birth mother but to the birth father and . . . all of these other people," noting that such a scenario struck him as "difficult and potentially awkward and . . . unappealing." On the other hand, "with international, it was all of these health problems in all of these other more developing countries," which led Damian to more seriously consider and learn about domestic private adoption. Ultimately, he said, "it became obvious that [various] countries either were no longer doing adoption, or the reputation was such that we were no longer comfortable working with those countries, so we just decided that domestic made more sense."

Monica and Damian came to a place where, as Monica said, they expected "some contact with the birth family, for sure." They anticipated that the level of openness would depend in part on the characteristics of the birth family and the degree to which they shared "similar values," as well as how close the two families lived to each other. Monica asserted, "We're open to as much [contact] as . . . makes sense for all of us involved. . . . We don't think about it as in terms of some kind of intrusion or threat or any of that. It's more like what makes sense, what feels good for everybody, what's good for the kid . . . that kind of thing." Monica explained that their adoption agency had in fact corrected her assumption—and that of so many prospective adoptive parents[1]—that it was typically birth parents who desired more contact than adoptive parents wanted or felt comfortable with: "[We've learned] that it's often that adoptive parents are yearning for a bit more contact rather than vice versa . . . so I definitely feel open to . . . whatever happens." Damian's narrative echoed this sentiment:

> I'm sure everyone thinks that it's like a coparenting thing, [but then] you realize that's not the case. . . . We like the idea of developing a relationship [with the birth family], and that the child can fill in those gaps about where they came from. It would be great if we could have a relationship where they can actually *see* each other. . . . I think I would actually *prefer* that there be regular contact. Of course I say that now—that might change in the future, especially when you actually meet the birth family. . . . But I think right now, having the benefit of fantasy, I'd like to be able to have that for the child. They would feel like, "I wasn't abandoned by someone and I wasn't unwanted . . . and this is a good relationship and I know my place in the world."

Monica and Damian were placed with a girl, also white, whom they named Olivia. The placement was sudden; Olivia's birth mother, Tracy, had intended to try to parent but had decided to make an adoption plan after several weeks: "She is a teenager and realized that she was *not ready to be a parent*. It was super hard . . . she's so loving. . . . She couldn't give her the life she wanted her to have," explained Damian. Recalling their first meeting, Monica said about Tracy, "I loved her—her spunk, her attitude. We met her and her family. It went really well. At the same time, it was . . . awkward." Their current level of contact, both parents noted, was a bit less than they had expected. Over time, they anticipated that contact might fluctuate, but hoped that they could "maintain a good relationship with Tracy and her extended family" (Monica).

As Monica and Damian's vignette outlines, upon first hearing about open adoption, it can seem scary and unfamiliar. Given that the cultural narrative around adoption has historically involved secrecy,[2] the possibility of openness—which ultimately varies considerably across families and has many permutations—may strike families as threatening and impossibly complicated. Yet as Monica's and Damian's narratives detail, exposure to the potential benefits of openness, particularly for the child, and parents' growing awareness that there is no "perfect" adoption route may lead them to more seriously consider an open adoption—albeit with some hesitation and perhaps with some restrictions on the parameters of contact. Ultimately, though, parents may match with birth parents who cause them to further revise their feelings and preferences surrounding openness, possibly embracing a relationship that would have seemed unfathomable when open adoption was just an abstract concept. Indeed, Monica and Damian matched with a birth mother whom they liked and with whom they hoped for ongoing contact—a scenario that contrasted sharply with their initial imaginings.

"We Really and Truly Believe in Open Adoption": Choosing Openness

During the preadoptive stage, many participants vocalized a high level of enthusiasm for open adoption. They had not always been enthusiastic about the possibility of openness, as I discuss later—but at the time that they were first interviewed, while they were actively seeking to adopt with the help of an adoption agency, they had "drunk the Kool Aid." Many participants provided excited, detailed accounts of their reasons for valuing open adoption. Such reasons tended to center on the perceived benefits of openness for the child: that is, the anticipated effects of openness on children's adjustment, socioemotional health, and identity formation. In some cases, participants emphasized the perceived benefits of openness for all members of the adoption triad (i.e., the child, the birth parents, and the adoptive parents). Underlying this emphasis was a valuing of honesty and transparency in the adoption process, with the assumption that everyone in the adoption triad (i.e., adoptive parents, adopted child, birth parents) would benefit from communication, information, and truthfulness. Greg, a white gay software consultant living in a small Southern city, recognized that any child that he and his partner adopted would ultimately wonder about his or her birth family: "We wanted an open adoption because a child is going to have questions when they get older: 'Who's my mom?' To be able to say that your mom lives someplace else and she chose us to raise you, to be able to say 'here she is,' and have contact with her, is a good thing. It's very healthy."

Similarly, Lou, a white heterosexual cartoonist who lived in a medium-sized city in the Midwest, spoke to the benefits of openness for all members of the adoption triad. Lou was drawn to the idea of "being able to have all your questions answered from day 1" so that the child would "know whatever he needs to know." From Lou's perspective, openness also benefited "the birth mother. It's really unfair to have to go through life knowing nothing." In this way, openness was seen as allowing both adoptive parents and children access to birth family information, thus aiding the child's identity development, and enabling the birth mother to achieve a sense of peace and well-being that would not be possible in a closed adoption. Shoshanna, a white heterosexual project manager in a small Northeastern city, recognized all of these benefits of openness. She exclaimed:

> Everything that we read—I mean, it just seemed natural. If you're going to adopt . . . the person who can't parent for whatever reason shouldn't just have to send their baby off into the darkness and have no idea what happened to them. And [for the child], you know who your parents are and who raised you—but there's also that feeling of biology, like, "No wonder I can roll my tongue; it's because my mom could"; or, "I really love onions." I mean, that's biology more than nurturing that that comes from. Being an adopted person is already a challenge, and if you can know something about your birth family, or maybe have contact with them, I think that somehow helps you find your place in the world more easily. And to me, as a potential adoptive parent, I want to know who my baby's biological parent is and if I can have contact with them, all the better.

Here, Shoshanna demonstrates an awareness of the types of questions that adopted children might have at various stages of their life and the ways in which access to the birth family could help to answer those questions and in turn aid identity development. Shoshanna further acknowledges the birth parents' pain in placing a child for adoption—and recognizes the benefits of knowing where and with whom that child was placed. Finally, she acknowledges the possible benefits of birth family contact for herself, as an adoptive parent, whereby knowledge of her child's genetic background might enable her to have a fuller picture of her child and facilitate more sensitive parenting. Shoshanna also demonstrates a keen awareness of the birth mother's feelings and perspective and expresses a desire to "do right" by her. Indeed, Shoshanna and her husband, Cal, chose an adoption agency that allowed any birth mother who placed with them to

> go to them for counseling . . . from now until the end of her life. . . . They'll pay up to $2,000 on counseling for her. I love that. I love that they're conscious of that. That's something that you're going to need if you're going to make that choice. It's the whole adoptive family [that is being served by them], including the birth family.

Charlene, a white lesbian teacher in a midsized city in the Northeast, was one of several participants who became so firmly committed to open adoption that she was unsure of whether she would accept a placement by birth parents who did not want any contact:

> As we talked about it and read about it and learned more about it, open adoption just felt like a no-brainer to me—like, of course that's what we want to do.

I would love to have a relationship in some form with the child's ... biological parents. At this point, that's important to me—like, if we were presented with a situation where a birth parent wanted to place their child with us, but they wanted a closed adoption, I'd have to think about it. Because I feel like it's really a strong preference for me at this point—for our child to have some knowledge of and connection with their birth parents.

Angela, a white heterosexual environmental planner in a large West Coast city, similarly shared that her experience of attending an adoption conference, and also an adoption agency–sponsored panel of birth parents, children, and adoptive parents in open adoptions, had solidified her commitment to and comfort with open adoption. Now, Angela's only concern—what she was "really afraid of"—was that "someone will tell us that they want open adoption but then they don't do the work to make it happen. That's the one thing I fear—like, 'Okay, we come into this all hyped and ready, and then they don't ... it doesn't work out." After a pause, Angela mused that she did not think that she would accept a situation where "the woman, the family wasn't really committed to an open adoption, staying in touch."

Doug, a white gay psychologist living in a large city on the West Coast, was similarly opposed to pursuing a closed adoption. He shared his perspective that closed adoptions—and the secrets that were associated with them—were driven by fear:

I just really—I love the idea of putting a kid's experience at the center and then, whatever fears and anxieties the adults have, they need to work out. It's not appropriate to alleviate my own fear by adding to my child's anxiety or fear. That's completely inappropriate. I'm choosing to do this, so I have to choose to work through the stuff I have to work through. So ... I wouldn't do an adoption any other way. If it were that we would not be able to do a truly open adoption then I would opt out of parenting before I would choose to do a closed adoption. Secrecy ... cheapens the experience of a created family.

Like Doug, Lindsey, a white lesbian physician assistant in a large Northeastern city, felt strongly that concern for the child's well-being, development, and identity should dictate adoptive parents' decision making. Lindsey explained that she and her partner, Miri, had chosen an agency that only facilitated open adoptions. Similarly, Lindsey shared that when she and Miri were looking into donor insemination, they were "only going to choose a donor who was willing to be contacted." Lindsey believed strongly in the importance of children having contact with their birth parents, reflecting that she had close friends who grew up not knowing their fathers, and therefore had questions about "who am I in relation to this guy that I don't know?" Lindsey emphasized that she had

> every intention of trying to develop a relationship [with the birth parents] so that that kid knows that, you know, "Susie" is his birth mother, but we are his moms. So that's very important to us. I remember looking at my parents and thinking, "this is what I will look like when I'm older," and our kid needs to have that too.

Growing up gay, and feeling pressured to hide their sexual identity from their families and society as a whole, informed some participants' emphasis on and requirement for openness. They were intimately familiar with the shame and negative feelings that came with hiding a core aspect of who they were, and they were firmly opposed to choosing an adoption path that supported or encouraged secret keeping in any way. Roy, a white gay sales manager in an urban area of the West Coast, stated:

> I think for us, growing up gay, and just knowing what it's like to hide things and not be completely honest about things and how detrimental that can be—I would never want to start off a kid's life like that. And that's what open adoption is all about—is knowing everything really.

Roy acknowledged that when he started the adoption process, he had never heard of open adoption, but once he and his partner, Dante, began to learn about it, they thought, "'this is perfect.' We just thought it was the best way to go."

We can be out. Notably, about a third of lesbian and gay parents explicitly stated that open adoption felt more comfortable to them as sexual minority parents, in that "everything was out in the open" and there were no secrets (i.e., they were not hiding their sexual orientation). In many cases, they contrasted their decision to pursue private domestic open adoption against the alternative route of international adoption, which typically requires same-sex couples to choose one parent to act as a single parent, thereby erasing the identity of the other parent (and the sexual orientation and relationship status of both partners). Rick, a white gay nonprofit director in a large West Coast city, said: "We were adamant about not lying because of integrity [reasons]." Mariette, a white lesbian physical therapist in a Midwestern suburb, shared:

> I guess the biggest reason [for doing open adoption] is we both feel like it's healthier for the child, it's healthier for the birth mother, I think it's healthier for the adoptive parents. And ... especially, given our relationship, and being a gay couple, [we] just kind of feel we'd be more comfortable if the birth mother knew

that she was making that choice for herself. I think that's healthy too, to kind of know where your child is being placed.

For Mariette and others, the prospect of hiding their sexual orientation, or the birth mother not knowing that they were a same-sex couple, was uncomfortable. They did not want to introduce any secrecy or hiding into their child's adoption story—or somehow imply that being gay was something that should be kept secret. In turn, they felt that transparency and openness was "healthiest" for all members of the adoption triad. Will was a white gay male accountant in a midsized West Coast city who had considered international adoption but concluded that "it didn't really feel right because there would be deception involved, [and] we wouldn't have contact with the child's family, which we wanted." Similarly, Lindsey, the white lesbian physician assistant, noted that she and Miri had considered international adoption but discovered that

> there's no country in the world that will adopt to a gay couple, so . . . we'd have to do it [as] a single person. And [the social worker] would have to see our lives set up in such a way that it looked like we were roommates. . . . Neither of us want to start a family with that kind of façade, playing those games.

Lindsey later added, "And what if we were discovered? We're completely out and the last thing I want to do is go back in the closet for a child when it's not necessary."

Notably, several same-sex couples who had tried to adopt internationally or via the child welfare system had experienced pressure to hide their sexual orientation, or discrimination when they refused to hide their sexual orientation, thus prompting them to turn to private domestic adoption. Charlene, a white lesbian teacher in a midsized Northeastern city, shared that she and her partner Leila had terminated their efforts to adopt internationally in part because of political upheaval in the sending country, but also because "it was more taxing on us than we realized, to be not doing it as a couple." The couple's first visit to a private domestic open adoption agency was "a totally different experience; it was fabulous. [They] work with gay families, and were like, 'You need to be able to adopt a child, and we're going to help you do that.'" Similarly, Brent, a white gay brand manager for a small skin care company in a large West Coast city, initiated the process of adopting internationally but ultimately moved to domestic private adoption because "most countries were closed to gay men or single men" and "we really did want a newborn."

Experiencing discrimination in the child welfare context prompted Tiffany, a white accounts manager in a large Southern city, and her partner, Karen, to change course to pursue private domestic adoption. Tiffany recalled that although she and Karen had "consulted an attorney before we began the process, who said, 'It's no big deal; you'll fly right through—you're stable, you have a great relationship, etcetera,'" they ultimately had their application rejected and were told they could not adopt as an openly same-sex couple in their state: "We were expecting it to be easier than it was." After meeting with an adoption consultant and facilitator, who was now "guiding them through the process," Tiffany and Karen decided to meet with private domestic adoption agencies—which, they came to learn, were largely facilitating open adoptions. In turn, although the couple was disheartened by the fact that they were turned down by the welfare system, they felt buoyed by the possibility of pursuing an option that would allow them to be open and out, and ultimately found an agency they felt welcomed by.

Opportunity for female role models/"a mother figure." Notably, a number of gay men named the ability to access female role models as a unique and desirable benefit of pursuing open adoption. Dean, a white software developer in a large Southern city, said: "It is really preferential to have another female around. I think it's important to have the mother [involved]. I just don't see how it could be a negative thing." Terrence, a white anesthesiologist in a West Coast suburb, stated: "I have no concerns about open adoption. It will be nice to have female contact and the birth mother will provide access to a regular woman." Some men were specifically motivated to pursue open adoption in part because of the potential for a relationship with an engaged birth mother, so that when peers asked, "Where's your mommy?" their child could indeed point to or refer to his or her birth mother.

Openness to nonbiologically related people as kin. A final theme that was especially pronounced among same-sex couples was the perception that "open adoption means extending your family." That is, sexual minority participants described ways in which open adoption resonated with their own valuing of nonbiological kinship ties in creating family. They looked forward to the possibility of counting the birth family as part of their extended family—thus conceptualizing adoption as a unique form of kinship, or a "hybrid family form comprised of both biological and nonbiological ties."[3] Jenny, a white lesbian manager for a medical supply company in the suburban Midwest, shared:

> We really... loved the philosophy [of open adoption], and we just realized that this was the type of adoption we wanted to pursue, in that it is open, and just being able to have the biological mother, and/or father, the family, participate, and be a part of this family.

Sam, a biracial (Asian and white) gay man who worked as the director of human resources at a small company in a large West Coast city, exclaimed:

At first, I didn't know a lot about open adoption, so I was a little nervous and scared.... But the more I learned, and the more and more I thought about it, I'm now excited for it, because we talked about the fact that we would have [an] extended family network and kinship networks and that our children would have multiple safe adults in their lives and us. And that's wonderful! The more, the better!

Terrence, a white gay anesthesiologist in a West Coast suburb, mused that cultural norms may have also helped to foster his and his partner Rob's openness to open adoption, after an initial period of hesitation. Rob was Mexican American and, according to Terrence, "he's part of a large extended Mexican family, and in those kind of situations the lines between parents and children really blur. Rob's family . . . live close by and we're all kind of incorporated, the boundaries are a little bit more porous." In turn, the notion of open adoption as a means of extending one's family was not foreign—in fact, it seemed to "make sense" to Terrence and Rob. In this way, sexual minority parents were especially likely to endorse a concept of family that was inclusive and expansive, and which acknowledged as legitimate and significant both biological and nonbiological relationships.[4]

Evolution in beliefs. Even among the participants who described enthusiastic "buy-in" to open adoption, many acknowledged that, early on—either prior to or early in their process of working with an adoption agency—they were hesitant about or even scared of open adoption. They knew little about what openness entailed, and they were unaware of the spectrum and range of openness arrangements. Typically, these participants' fears centered on boundaries and roles: They did not like the idea of "sharing" parenthood with another person or people, and they worried about their parental rights in the process (e.g., they expressed concern that birth parents could reclaim a child even after the legal paperwork was signed). Lesbian and gay participants sometimes also harbored the fear that expectant parents would never choose them because of their sexual orientation and that they would wait "forever." In a few cases, prospective parents also shared worries about the effects of openness on the child—that it would be "confusing" and/or complicate their identity formation and adjustment in some way. In sum, they described initial hesitation and uneasiness about the prospect of open adoption.

But these individuals also spoke to an evolution in their ideas and attitudes about openness in adoption, from the time they first learned about open adoption up until the point when they were actively waiting for a child placement. Rob, a gay Latino administrative assistant in a West Coast suburb, acknowledged that initially, he was somewhat fearful and wary about open adoption: "We didn't want anyone intruding on our lives." Upon learning about open adoption from adoption professionals, trainings, and the like, Rob realized its benefits: "We don't want a child wondering for years where he or she came from ... [and we'll have] greater access to information about health issues." Dave, a white gay radiologist in a large Midwestern city, said: "The more I learned, I realized that my worst fears were unlikely scenarios ... and open adoption made sense, in that it helps the kid understand where they are from, and eliminates secrecy." Dean, a white gay software developer in a large city in the South, shared:

> When we started, I wasn't really even aware of open adoption. I did kind of have it in my mind that these poor, drug-addicted 15-year-olds were going to drop their kids off and never see them again. ... It seemed a little uncomfortable at first to think that the mother of the child would hang out all the time, or be stopping by, or whatever. But as with a lot of these things, all of our fears were unfounded, and the reality doesn't really support that.

Talking to adoption agency personnel, attending adoption-related programming, and reading articles and books about open adoption were all identified as influential in shifting participants' attitudes from that of scared, confused, or hesitant to hopeful, open, and excited. Nancy, a white lesbian pet store manager in a large Southern city, chronicled the evolution in her attitudes around openness:

> When we first started the adoption process ... open adoption was such a scary thing. We were like, "Oh my gosh. There is no way that we can do this." Then, the more books we started reading about, you know, how wonderful it was, and how healthy it was for the child, [how] it took away so many questions in their life and just—then we started thinking: Wow. And then the [agency personnel] would tell you the birth mother is just as scared as you are, and they don't want to be rejected any more than you do. So then when we started looking at it from both sides, [we realized] there is nothing to be afraid of.

Bob, a white heterosexual financial manager living in a Northeastern suburb, shared a similar shift in perspective. His initial hesitation and fearfulness surrounding openness was, he shared, influenced by his exposure to a closed adoption:

> I was very skeptical at first, just because we had no idea [about open adoption]. My experience with [cousin, who was adopted] was, everything was closed shut, you know, and you never have any information. But after learning about open adoption it was like, wow—I can see how this could really benefit all parties involved. ... Initially, you're kind of scared that, like, well, what if the

birth mother wants to steal our baby, that sort of thing. But upon learning more about it, it seems like it's the best thing to do.

In a few cases, it was not only talking to adoption agency personnel and social workers that helped shift their views but also seeing adoptive parents and birth parents speak on panels and/or talking to friends or other people they knew who had done open adoptions. Javier, a gay Latino gastroenterologist in an East Coast suburb, reflected: "One of the things we really like about the agency is that they're very focused on the well-being of the child. It really opened our eyes. They had a couple of birth mothers speak and [hearing them] really made us consider it."

Within couples, partners were not always on the same page with openness—particularly during the early stages of the process. Sometimes, one partner was on board earlier in the process and the other partner needed more convincing and assurance. For example, Therese, a white heterosexual teacher living in a suburb in the South, recalled:

> I was more into it than Lucas was. I had read a lot more about this. It's sort of a pattern in our marriage: When there's something going on, I tend to do more of the excessive reading. . . . So, I tend to forget that he may have a different opinion than me, just because he hasn't read everything I've read and doesn't know all the stuff I may know about it. But yeah—I was definitely ahead of him [early on]. And the more he learned about adoption, the more he was willing to consider it. Openness threw him more than it threw me.

Another example of a couple that initially differed in terms of their orientation to open adoption and their relative comfort with the notion of contact with the birth parents was Andrea and Mary, a white lesbian couple living in a medium-sized city in the South. Andrea, a prison guard, had some personal experience with adoption: Her mother had been adopted, and several of her cousins had adopted their children. All but one of these adoptions had been "traditional" closed adoptions; thus, although the idea of open adoption was appealing in some ways, it was also relatively unfamiliar. Nevertheless, Andrea was more open to openness than Mary, a manager at a TV production studio. Andrea explained:

> We talked a lot about it just because Mary wanted a totally closed adoption. She laughed that she didn't want to become the Lifetime movie of the week. For me, a totally closed adoption . . . I didn't want that. An open adoption would [make] a lot of things easier; it would . . . take care a lot of those questions. So . . . I talked to her a little bit, and I'm like, "Just because it's open doesn't mean we're going to be stopping by her house every week." And she went over and talked to my cousin about their adoption [who] impressed upon her, you know, they had

done an open adoption and this is how it had gone and . . . so then Mary finally came around and went "Okay, I can do this."

Mary herself voiced a preference for a "semiopen" adoption, where

you still have your privacy but the birth mother doesn't feel like they're giving up their baby to someone they don't know. So, it was a plus for our baby in the future if they want to know but it was a plus for us so that way we have a little bit of a separation.

Elaborating on what she meant by "separation," Mary explained:

My thing is, how am I going to go in and take this baby from its mother? . . . Me being an attachment person, I'm afraid I would get attached to the birth mother. . . . I would like a little bit of separation so I can keep my emotions in check.

Both Mary and Andrea preferred more indirect forms of ongoing contact with the birth parents; as Andrea said, "I think letters and phone calls would be good." About why she was less enthusiastic about in-person visits, Andrea said, "I'm just concerned our child would be confused as to why there's another parent in the picture."

Another example of a couple that differed in their feelings about openness was Brent and Travis, a white gay couple living in a large West Coast city. Brent, a brand manager, and Travis, a technical writer, took preliminary steps toward international adoption before moving to private domestic adoption. Attracted to the idea of a newborn and turned off by the bureaucratic hurdles that accompanied international adoption, they eventually turned to private domestic adoption. Brent said: "We both came to realize that was not what we wanted and that we definitely wanted open adoption." Travis, on the other hand, acknowledged more fear around open adoption, especially early on:

Originally, what appealed to me about international adoption was the idea of getting the baby and then getting thousands of miles away from the birth parents. . . . I think it was more of an issue for me than it was for Brent, but that was the main appeal to me. . . . With an open adoption—Brent had been more open to it than I was originally. Then, just kind of studying it and learning about it, I just came to understand it. . . . It's a very strong feeling for me to have a newborn, to adopt a newborn. The idea [that it may come with] some type of contact with the birth mother, or father, if he is involved, is kind of scary—but it may help to answer some questions.

When asked about desired level of contact with the birth parents, Travis and Brent differed. Brent was "open" to a variety of possibilities, whereas Travis preferred "limited to none. With limited being letters a couple times a year. Possibly one or two visits a year going all the way down to no contact." Thus, although the couple was officially working with an agency that primarily facilitated open adoptions, Brent and Travis differed in their feelings about the ideal level and type of contact with birth parents.

"We Are Doing It Because We Want to Be Parents": Open Adoption by Default

Some participants—and more often heterosexual couples than lesbian or gay couples—were forthcoming about the fact that they did not strongly value or desire an *open* adoption, but they were nevertheless *pursuing* private domestic adoptions, which had the potential for some degree of openness. In this way, these participants can best be described as reluctantly open, as opposed to enthusiastically open. Typically, they were doing open adoption for practical reasons. Between 2005 and 2009, when the couples in this study were initially interviewed, the majority of adoption agencies facilitating domestic private adoptions required some degree of openness. In turn, "we arrived at this by default" was a common sentiment. "We kind of sort of didn't choose it; we're learning about it," explained Matt, a white heterosexual realtor in a large West Coast city. Matt also noted that he was surprised to find that "there are 100 different flavors of open adoption." Seana, a white heterosexual jewelry associate in a large Midwestern city, shared that open adoption was "actually not . . . [our] preference. It just seems that everybody wants that now. When we started this process, I didn't even know that existed . . . but it's what [most agencies] are doing. So yeah." Laura, a white heterosexual web designer in a Midwest suburb, shared: "When I first started looking into it, it just kind of seemed that open adoption was, in terms of domestic adoption, the only option."

In some cases, participants specifically contrasted private domestic adoption—the route they were taking now—with private international adoption,* which they had considered or taken steps toward but eventually turned away from because it did not seem viable and/or they had too many concerns about it. Such concerns included bureaucratic issues, length of time to placement,

---

* Few couples who pursued private domestic adoption seriously considered child welfare (i.e., public domestic) adoption, largely because they wanted a newborn or infant and/or were concerned about the emotional and psychological "baggage" that a child adopted via foster care might bring. In essence, they worried about their ability to "shape" a child who had already had significant (and negative) life experiences.

the unlikelihood of being placed with a newborn, and the limited background information available for children. Notably, these concerns were more often named by heterosexual couples: Most same-sex couples did not view international adoption as a legitimate option because of the secrecy mandate associated with it and the increasingly narrow list of sending countries that were open to single parents.[†] Lena, a white heterosexual operations manager who lived in a medium-sized city in the Northeast, shared:

> I really wanted an infant. So that's really why we're doing a domestic adoption. . . . What we've read and heard and learned about international is that they [usually are] first in orphanages or foster care. I really didn't want to miss the first 12 or 18 months of the child's . . . life. We really wanted to bring an infant home from the hospital, so I think that's been our driving force doing domestic . . . and by default, most agencies do open.

Likewise, Carly, a white heterosexual history professor in a large city in the Northeast, shared that she and her husband, Brian, had started out looking at international adoption "pretty exclusively . . . that's just what we were drawn to right away," but found that

> with a lot of these programs, they sent you a picture or video, so you know who this child is, but you can't really travel to get them for another bunch of months, in many cases. And I had this big realization like, "Oh my god, there's no way I can survive." I think I would go out of my mind, knowing that my baby is out there, knowing who he is, and knowing that I don't know who's taking care of him and who's tucking him into bed at night and who's reading to him and making sure that he's okay. I realized that would be a really hard part about international. So we talked to [social worker] . . . and [got] more information about domestic, and it felt like there were really recent and ongoing shifts in this adoption world, that this [was] really a good way to go at this point, with a lot of things changing fairly unpredictably [in international adoption]. And it seemed that adopting domestically maybe would be a little more predictable.

Thus, practicality and expediency were foremost in Carly's mind, in terms of settling on private domestic open adoption. However, Carly had limits to the level of openness that she was willing to consider. She was open to contact, and possibly visits, but "I don't know how regular. I feel like once or twice a year [is enough]."

[†] Sending countries have historically not been open to same-sex couples, so same-sex couples have adopted internationally by having one parent present as a single parent during the adoption process.

Participants who were pursuing private domestic open adoption for practical reasons often emphasized that their goal was simply to adopt a healthy baby as soon as possible. They had chosen this route because it seemed to hold that promise—and not because it offered the possibility of contact with the birth family, which in turn might benefit their child. Eliza, a white lesbian woman employed as a junior accountant for a small county hospital in a large Northeastern city, shared how although she was pursuing a private domestic adoption and was now "okay" with the possibility of birth parent contact, she ultimately desired whatever route would bring her a child fastest. Thus, Eliza had moved from a place of fear regarding openness to greater comfort with—but not active preference for—birth parent contact:

> I think in the beginning, before I did a lot of reading on adoption . . . I was afraid about this whole birth mother thing. And I thought that [closed adoption] would be safer. Now, I don't think it would matter. I am just worried about the time frame. If I could get an international kid tomorrow I would go international. If I could get a domestic kid tomorrow I would go domestic. It doesn't really matter to me anymore. But I'm not really concerned about the birth mother anymore now that I've done research. . . . I don't think I have a fear of her snatching the baby away anymore. I have read a lot about open adoption and learned about different [scenarios] and stories and stuff.

In some cases, although participants' primary motivation for pursuing open adoption was practicality and ease, they also surmised that this method could end up benefiting their child as well. For Thomas, a white heterosexual financial planner in a midsized Northeast city, the primary reason that he and his wife, Lena, were pursuing open adoption was "the agency that we're working with [does open adoptions]. So open—I think number one, we think it may help us get a child faster." But Thomas went on to acknowledge the potential positive benefits of open adoption for a child, whereby "it probably isn't the worst thing. . . . If there is some contact, then maybe there'll be a lot less questions, a lot less anxiety for the child." Benji, a white gay dermatologist in a large city on the West Coast, expressed some reluctance surrounding openness, stating, "My reservation is that I want to adopt a child—not an adult and a child." At the same time, Benji shared his impression that "it's psychologically more healthy for the birth mother and the kid [for it to be open] . . . so we'll see how it goes." Roger, a white gay marketing director in an East Coast suburb, explained that he and his partner, Barry, discovered early in their adoption journey that "most [agencies] are pretty much open." Yet a recent potential match with an expectant mother had caused them to re-evaluate their decision to pursue an open adoption. As Roger recalled, it was a "crazy situation" that made them wonder, "Do we want this woman in our lives for the rest of our lives?" Yet Roger was reassured that

> you create a template of what the relationship is going to be like. You are not at the mercy of the birth parent. It [can] be very structured.... And there are some adopted people that I know that are adults and they were adopted when there wasn't open adoption and it is something that always will plague them: Who are my parents? So [open adoption] makes sense.

Thus, although Roger voiced some continued uncertainty and hesitation surrounding openness, he also recognized its potential to truly benefit the adopted children themselves.

Indeed, several prospective adopters continued to actively struggle with the concept of openness even as they pursued potential matches with expectant parents. Donna, a white heterosexual manager at a nonprofit organization in a large metropolitan area of the Northeast, shared that she was aware that she and her husband, Max, would "have to be flexible and change with the times, because of the trend [toward openness]." At the same time, she stated, "What I'm struggling with, and what I'm on the fence with, is if a child always knows their birth mother or birth father, you're never really giving them a choice in whether they want to know them." Similarly, Lucas, a Latino lawyer in a Southern suburb, said that he and his wife, Therese, were working with an agency that only facilitated open adoptions but that he continued to have reservations about it: "I don't like it. But, I don't think I like anything, if that makes any sense. Because, I mean, if we did it confidentially, on the one hand, we might have less of an opportunity for heartbreak, but then we would also know less of what's going on."

Phil, a white gay male graduate student living in a medium-sized city in the South, also shared some ongoing hesitation surrounding openness, voicing concerns about the potential lack of clarity in the adoptive parents' roles amid birth parent contact:

> Open adoption makes both of us nervous. But closed adoption... also doesn't sit completely right with me. So what seems to be growing on us is... the exchange of pictures through the agency, but no contact, and everything is mediated through the agency. And that to me sounds like the best of both worlds because it still allows the birth parent to have some updates about the child but doesn't... put the adoptive parents at risk or diminish the role of the adoptive parents in caring for the child.

Envisioning the Future, Considering Contact: How Much, and Who Decides?

Participants who expressed enthusiasm and excitement about openness were generally open to more frequent contact with the birth family, and more direct and intimate forms of contact (e.g., in-person visits as opposed to letters, direct contact as opposed to mediated through the agency) than those who voiced ongoing hesitation or reservations surrounding openness. But most participants, regardless of their overall level of enthusiasm about openness, generally felt that the exact nature and level of contact would depend on the particular birth parent situation that they found themselves in. Thus, although they tended to possess a general idea about the ideal level and type of contact, they did not necessarily feel comfortable specifying a set number or frequency of letters, photos, or visits in regard to the birth parents. Rather, they felt that these details would depend on the birth parents' emotional stability and personality, and the "fit" or connection between them and the birth parents ("I think it totally depends on the birth mother or parents or family and how we get along"). Thus, these parents demonstrated flexibility surrounding birth family contact—but also caution (e.g., they were comforted by the idea that they could restrict the level and type of contact if the fit was poor or the birth parents were perceived as unstable). Bob, a white heterosexual financial manager in a Northeast suburb, was optimistic about the possibility of a positive and close relationship with the birth parents—but also asserted that the relationship would depend on the birth parents and the fit between the two parties:

> It all will depend on the birth parent, how comfortable we, our relationship is with that person. We're hoping that we'll fall in love with the birth parent and we'll want to communicate regularly . . . through email, through visits, everything. One of the seminars we went on, we went to actually had a birth parent there with the adoptive parent and they're . . . friends . . . and it was just, it was amazing, the stories they were telling. And it's so good for the child as well to see that and to experience that. . . . It was amazing just to see that. Ideally that would be awesome, I would think. But it depends on the birth parent of course and how we relate to that person. [For example,] if it was an older birth parent or somebody was more mature and we got along great . . . we'd love to have them over for dinner regularly.

A similarly flexible and hopeful stance is also present in the narrative of Roy, a white gay sales manager in a large West Coast city. Roy and his partner, Dante, had put a great deal of thought into birth family contact, having attended programming offered by their adoption agency that included informational sessions and panels with birth parents, adoptive parents, and adopted individuals. In turn, even more so than Bob, who was just quoted, Roy had landed in a place where he hoped for a high level of contact—but he also centered the birth mother's desires and preferences as the ultimate determinant of contact:

> I think so much of it is going to depend on who the person ends up being—[and] we're really more open to deciding that based on the birth mother's desires more so than ours.... We know that the whole concept of open adoption is going to be important for the child—to know who she is and all that. But I wouldn't want to force anything.

Roy also discussed his awareness that contact might involve the birth parents' own parents—a prospect that "made sense" to him:

> A thing that's come up a lot in our classes is ... the extended relationships ... with her parents. I've heard lots of stories about adoptive families ending up being closer with the birth grandparents than theirs. Which I can understand, because maybe the grandparents ... want to kind of have more exposure in the child's life. And your age might be actually closer to them.... And we've heard of couples who were really close with the adoptive mother but it was much more of a parent–child kind of relationship—they helped them get through whatever it was that they needed to get through with the adoption, and they kind of formed more of a paternal and maternal bond with the birth mother.

Roy and Dante were among a handful of couples who indicated that they would take the lead from the birth parents in terms of the level and type of contact to pursue. These participants were generally hopeful and excited about openness and desired as much contact as the birth parents wished to pursue. They frequently spoke to the benefits of openness and contact and did not tend to endorse fears about birth parent behavior or boundaries in qualifying their response. Dominick, a multiracial heterosexual small business owner in a large West Coast city, stated:

> We're open to any—I think we would prefer if they wanted to ... kind of be treated as relatives. And to have some kind of role in the child's life. But we would respect whatever decisions they have, and whatever they feel comfortable with, especially the birth mom. We are sort of open to however they go.

Heather, a white lesbian bookkeeper in a midsized Southern city, shared similar feelings, noting that any restrictions or parameters surrounding contact would likely come from the birth family: "In our ideal world we would have ongoing contact with the birth mom and hopefully the birth father and even their extended family. We're never sure what type of an agreement they're going to want but in our ideal world, we would continue contact [past the placement]." Her partner, Daniela, a white bookstore owner, said that contact would

> depend on a few variables, of course. But ideally we would love to have ongoing contact throughout our lives with the birth family. We'd love to see them once or twice a year and maybe even more. It kind of depends on what they want. But we think it's so exciting for our child to be able to know them . . . and as a birth family it must be really nice to be able to know how their birth child is doing. . . . And then for [us], I think it's important because here's this birth mom and maybe a birth dad that we'll get to know too, [who] are giving up one of the biggest gifts of our life. . . . We [hope] we would know them and that we would continue to have a relationship. It just doesn't seem like it would make sense if we didn't know them.

These participants spoke with awareness of and gratitude regarding the "gift" that the birth parents—or more often just the birth mother—was giving them. In turn, they did not position or imagine her as a potentially intrusive figure, overstepping boundaries and demanding more contact than they preferred. Rather, they acknowledged that they did not know what the birth mother would be like or what she might desire regarding contact—and demonstrated an openness to allowing this unknown but important person to take the lead regarding contact.

Most parents who demonstrated flexibility surrounding contact indicated that they saw themselves, and not the birth parents, as the ultimate arbiter of frequency and type of contact. Notably, the frequency of in-person contact was typically the issue that they faltered at. Thomas, a white heterosexual financial planner in a midsized Northeastern city, stated, "It will be case by case. I'm certainly open to contact. I mean, if a woman wants to see her child, you know, five times a year, that might be a little bit too much, but if she wants to see it once a year, maybe that's OK." His wife, Lena, a white operations manager, expressed similar sentiments. Lena, who noted that she had significant respect for a birth mother who was "just trying to give a better life to her child," went on to say:

> We can meet the birth parents, send letters through the agency, send pictures. We have no problem with that. I'll just be so happy that the child's hopefully doing well—I don't know why I wouldn't want to share that with her! I don't know if we'll go as far as giving them our address and saying, "Come on over anytime," but . . . .

Lewis, a white heterosexual teacher in a small Northeast city, who was initially pursuing private and public domestic adoption simultaneously, was clear that he saw real benefits of open adoption—but also wished to "hold the line" on contact, although where that line fell would depend on the relationship that he and his wife, Sandy, formed with the birth parents:

> I like the idea of open, because it gives the birth mother a little more closure.... It's not [going to be] like a daily visit or anything. But I think it would make it easier for her to make the decision [to place the child] and it's easier as [the adoptive parent] to raise the child if they know where they're from, and who's who.... But we don't agree with interference—you know what I mean? There's that fine line when it becomes interference. So we're all for ... open[ness].... Letters and calls we agree with. But we wouldn't agree to, "Yeah, we'll bring the child over every week." We want the birth mom and the child to have contact. We are open to, potentially, birth mom seeing the child a couple times a month. But ... we may have an idea right now [about contact], but that could change. It could change—it could increase, depending on the relationship, the connection we have.... We are open to just seeing how things go, and not really setting the limits, "only two calls a month, only one visit" ... because it's very [hard to know] what will happen.

Shoshanna, a white heterosexual project manager in a small Northeast city, shared:

> We'd like a regular schedule with letters and pictures through the agency. And the agency has an event once a year [with adoptive and birth families] and we said we would be open to meeting at the picnic. Then I think, once we know who the birth family is, we can determine how much more openness we're open to. I think some of it will be based on who they are and who we are to them and all of that ... and where they are in their life. If it's not safe for the child to interact with them, then we'll want to limit the contact. That doesn't mean that we would say, "We're going to disappear." ... If it is safe and the birth parents are well and all that, then ... good.

Here, Shoshanna underscores a desire to ensure the child's safety as the central reason for potentially reinforcing certain boundaries and limiting contact. Thus, her child's well-being, as opposed to her own comfort, was emphasized as the determining factor in contact.

Prospective parents sometimes named the types of circumstances that might require them to restrict contact. Poor boundaries, emotional instability, and drug use were named as factors that might lead them to limit contact, out of concern for the well-being of their child and family. Leo, a gay Latino speech therapist in an East Coast suburb, said: "It really depends on the girl, the woman. My concern would only be the boundaries. It depends on the woman . . . where she is in her life, what's she's got going on at home, what she's bringing to this scenario." Taryn, a white lesbian radio personality in an East Coast suburb, surmised:

> If they have pictures of the kid all over, or they have a tattoo with the name they gave the kid, I think that could definitely freak us out a little. But I think if they have good boundaries, and are respectful of our role as the—I don't know if this is the right term to use, but as the real parents, the permanent parents . . . if they don't try to act like the parents, I think I'm fine with a lot of contact. But we kind of have to see what they are like. And if they don't live a lifestyle that we approve of . . . and wouldn't want our child to be exposed to . . . like if they had drug problems or something . . . we wouldn't shun them or anything, but we probably wouldn't want a lot of contact in that case. I think we kind of just have to wait and see.

Erin, a white lesbian librarian in a large West Coast city, imagined certain scenarios that would require her and her partner, Meredith, to limit contact with birth parents, out of concern for protecting their child. Regarding her desired level of involvement and contact with the birth family, Erin said:

> It totally depends on the birth parent. If the birth parent's totally got their stuff together, like, if the situation is the birth parent is a mom of three who just can't handle four, if it's that kind of situation, then maybe fairly active involvement in terms of visiting more often and spending time more often would be totally great. . . . If it's one of those situations where the birth mom is really not together or incarcerated or is still using drugs or has the potential to be abusive or is being abused or anything like that, then we're going to fight pretty hard to limit interaction, like keep it to maybe just letters. Because our job primarily is to protect our child. . . . So we'll just cross that bridge when we get there.

Will was a white accountant in a medium-sized West Coast city, who voiced great enthusiasm for open adoption and for contact with the birth mother—but at the same time acknowledged the (unlikely) possibility of poor boundaries:

> We're both very friendly, very open people. As long as the birth mom respects boundaries, [we're good]. . . . Healthy boundaries, we get together for an afternoon or a ball game . . . . that's great [*laugh*]! My only worry would be if the birth mother doesn't respect the boundaries and she becomes needy or clingy, but from what I understand that's kind of rare. They even said we might not hear

from the mother, the mother might drift away. That's kind of sad for the child, but we're okay with that too. I think the best of both worlds would be healthy boundaries, and the mother kind of being an auntie to the child, [with] phone calls occasionally, and letters and pictures, that kind of thing.

In a handful of cases, participants demonstrated little flexibility as they imagined the level and type of contact that they would be willing to consider. These individuals were among those who had the greatest concerns about, and ongoing reservations around, openness. They sometimes expressed reluctance, or at least caution, surrounding the idea of openness. They were okay with occasional letters and phone calls, for example, but were generally uneasy about in-person visits. Overall, they preferred little contact and voiced discomfort with the idea of a birth mother who wanted regular or frequent in-person visits. Of note here is that, according to authors and adoption advocates James Gritter and Lori Holden,[5] when parents use words like "willing to" or "consent," this usually means that they are missing the "spirit" of open adoption—that is, they are operating from a place of fear and anxiety (e.g., regarding parental roles) and may be setting themselves up for an adversarial relationship. Further, Lori Holden[6] suggests that when parents are thinking of what they will "give up" or "grant," this is a sign that they are viewing the birth family as an imposition rather than seeing the relationship as collaborative and mutually beneficial.

Anxiety surrounding boundaries and roles is evident in the following example. Donna, a white heterosexual manager at a nonprofit organization in a large Northeastern city, reflected: "In an ideal world, [I'd be open to] maybe emailing pictures a couple times a year, maybe a meeting once a year, but I want these children to know that there's only one mommy and one daddy." After pausing, Donna acknowledged that she was "still getting used to the idea of an open adoption," wherein ongoing contact with a set of birth parents was hard to imagine. Similarly, Ron, a white heterosexual manager for a retail chain in a large Midwestern city, stated, "I'm not totally into open adoption. You hear stories about people exchanging monthly letters or [having birth parents present] at their birthdays. I can't go that far. Yearly letters or photos, I don't mind that. But nothing extreme." Byron, a white gay graduate student in a large metropolitan area of the Midwest, preferred "very little" contact, which he acknowledged was "just selfishness on my part":

I would kind of get freaked out [if they were] calling three or four times a week. It's not like you can give them a schedule and say, "You can only call this many times or email." Realistically, when you agree to that up front . . . you just have to play by that rule. . . . We had one [potential birth mother] that pretty much wanted a postcard every 10 years. Then, there are some that say, "Oh, I might move to [your city]." Honestly, I would prefer less contact than more, is what I'm saying . . . and it would make me feel a little uneasy if I felt there was a [strong] interest . . . or desire to be close to the child from the get-go.

At the same time, Byron did voice a sense of obligation to both the child and the birth parents ("they are giving you a child . . ."). He noted that he did not want to "hurt the child" by limiting contact based on his own "selfishness." Yet Byron also did not want to expose a child to a high level of contact with "unstable" birth parents—simply "because such contact was promised, and you have to do what you agree to."

Considering Contact in the Context of Adopting From Foster Care

In some cases, couples who were seeking to adopt from foster care acknowledged the possibility of ongoing contact with the birth family postadoption and articulated their feelings and preferences regarding such contact. Many adoptions of older children are at least partially open, in that the children may already have knowledge of identifying information (e.g., contact information) for members of their birth families and/or may wish to stay in touch with siblings placed in other adoptive homes.[7] Even in newborn or infant adoptions through the child welfare system, there are situations in which continued contact with the birth family is a possibility following the termination of parental rights (TPR), and is often court mandated prior to the TPR. Openness and continued contact do have the potential to be beneficial in child welfare adoptions—and, in particular, when a history of maltreatment by the birth parents is absent and a collaborative relationship between the birth parents and adoptive parents is present.[8] Kate, a white lesbian director of a women's survival center in a large city on the West Coast, had given some thought to this matter:

I had no idea that there would be as much contact as it sounds like there [could] be. I mean, our social worker was saying that some judges with newborns are ordering [regular] visits with birth parents. . . . That's a big commitment, and it makes me a little concerned about our time. I don't know how often we'll have those visits or how old our kid will be. . . . I know about the studies and open adoption . . . and so, I think it's good if the birth family can stay involved. I can imagine all different degrees of involvements that might be just fine. I think in an ideal world, they would stay pretty strongly involved; they'd be like extended family. I do think involvement is important, even if they are really struggling, or even if they're just assholes, you know, because . . . like, as the kids get older, if they don't have a sense of who their parents are, it's really easy to idealize who their parents were. Like, if they're teenagers, hating you [*laughs*], and imagining how their whole life would be better [with their birth parents] . . . I can imagine that really being heightened for kids who never had much involvement with their biological parents, to really have to go through this process where they think everything could have been okay if you just hadn't come into the picture. I can imagine that would be really hurtful for us as parents and it also just seems really painful and difficult for the child. So for them to have a good sense of where they came from would help them put that together more clearly. That seems like a real benefit to me.

Kate's partner, Cara, a white landscape design artist, expressed similar feelings, noting that her willingness to engage in postplacement contact would depend in part on the birth parents' situation and stability, and the relationship they had formed. Cara said: "If the birth parent is able to do what they need to do . . . great. I'm not necessarily happy to hand a child over to a person that is drunk or on drugs—who knows what would happen. But I think it would definitely depend on the parents and how they are in the world. And even on how they are with me. . . . It will just depend on the situation."

Vincent, a white telecommunications director in a large Midwestern city, and his partner, Simon, were a rare couple adopting through foster care who said that they strongly preferred openness in the context of whatever adoption they pursued. At the same time, they were aware that openness, in the way that it is typically arranged and cultivated in the context of private adoptions, was not common among child welfare adoptions. Vincent shared that he would "love to do an open adoption . . . in the context of the foster care system," because

> we feel like that would be the best option for the child, and it would be the best option for the birth parents. It makes us feel a little queasy that there are problems with the system in the sense that it structured that make it difficult for some people to care for children. I mean, whether that's economic, social, whatever. And it feels a little creepy being—we have a lot of privilege in our lives and that's enabled us to get to a place where we can raise a child. And there are a lot of people who haven't had a lot, who've suffered a lot of oppression, and who have just had hard knocks, and made poor choices probably, but—and are unable to raise their children. So what we would like is—I guess the best solution for everybody in my estimation would be probably to give a birth mother the opportunity to know her child, and to give a child the opportunity to know her birth parent. It's something we've explained [to our social workers], that we would definitely be open to. . . . Going through the foster care system, we could make an agreement with a birth parent that we'll have kind of an open

relationship—but it's not something the court would write into the adoption agreement.

Vincent is unique in speaking to the systemic forces at play, emphasizing structural inequalities as opposed to personal deficiencies in characterizing a hypothetical set of birth parents. He recognizes the complexity of maintaining ongoing contact with birth family but also sees it as important and valuable—and far from just "talking the talk," he and Simon had in fact discussed their feelings and preferences surrounding openness with their social workers.

In a few cases, parents adopting through foster care expressed a desire to maintain contact with siblings specifically. They recognized the significance of sibling bonds, as well as the reality that siblings were often separated from each other in child welfare adoptions.[9]

In many cases, though, participants had never considered the possibility of contact in the context of child welfare adoptions. To them, child welfare adoption meant taking a child out of a bad situation and providing them with a better home. They did not see how continued contact with members of the child's birth family could be healthy or beneficial to the child. In addition, it is likely that no one (e.g., the Department of Social Services, social workers) ever raised the possibility of how, why, and when parents might maintain contact with birth family members.

Choices, Choices: "Checking a Box, Deciding Our Future"

Upon deciding to pursue open adoption and signing up with an agency, couples made the first of a long series of complicated choices that they would be asked to navigate—choices that would ultimately have implications for their birth family match and the child they would adopt. Prospective adopters are asked not only to decide their level of openness to contact with birth family but also to declare their openness with regard to child race, wherein they indicate the races and racial combinations they are open to and willing to consider. Prospective adopters must also decide upon the type and level of prenatal substance exposure they are open to (as well as what type of physical, emotional, and behavioral special needs they would consider—a dimension I will not be discussing in this chapter).

For now, I turn to race, which, like openness to contact, represented a domain that elicited complex and varied responses from participants. As with openness to contact, participants demonstrated a range of preferences surrounding race, from being very open to not at all open to adopting a child of a different race. And, as with openness to contact, participants varied in terms of the degree to which they possessed flexibility and willingness (an attitude of "yes") with respect to potentially altering aspects of their lives and communities to raise a child of a different race. Similarly, they varied in the depth of their reflection upon and analysis of their racialized preferences, whereby some simply emphasized their own (dis)comfort (e.g., "I don't feel comfortable raising a black child") and others engaged in a more probing inventory of their racialized attitudes and beliefs—a process that sometimes resulted in an acknowledgment of their own deficiencies but also an openness to acquiring the skills and resources that they would need to competently raise a child of a different race. In many cases, participants emphasized that the training and preparation they received from their agencies was instrumental in assisting them with clarifying their beliefs, limitations, and resources related to raising a child of a different race.

Racialized Preferences

In articulating their preferences and openness around race, participants often described considering the racial diversity of their family and friend networks, as well as their broader neighborhoods and communities. Heterosexual couples in which both partners identified as white generally preferred a same-race child or at least "mixed" with white/Caucasian—although there were exceptions.[‡] Lesbian couples in which both partners were white were the most likely to espouse an openness to a child of color. Gay male couples in which both partners were white tended to be more open than heterosexual couples but less open than lesbian couples. This pattern is documented in larger groups of adoptive parents.[10] Couples where one or both partners were of color were typically open to a child that matched the race of the parent(s) of color, or to a multiracial child.

Participants described varying levels of thought and consideration regarding their racial preferences. In some cases, they reported having spent a great deal of time and energy thinking about and exploring their personal, familial, and community resources for raising a child of a different race and/or of particular races. In turn, some had talked extensively to agency social workers, friends who were of color, and/or friends who had adopted children of color. In addition

---

[‡] Of note is that some adoption agencies no longer allow prospective adopters to indicate an openness to a biracial (mixed) child. For example, some agencies that formerly allowed prospective adopters to indicate an openness to very specific racial combinations (e.g., white/Hispanic, white/Hispanic/African American, white/African American, etc.) no longer do this. That is, prospective adopters can no longer indicate a willingness to adopt an African American/white child but not an African American child; they must be open to the possibility of both. This change is viewed as necessary, to prevent the adoption of children of color by people who are not prepared for the reality that a biracial child is indeed a child of color (personal communication, Roberta Evantash of Adoptions from the Heart, August 31, 2017).

to engaging in this kind of social inventory and crowdsourcing, these parents also examined their own racialized beliefs and ideas, comfort with becoming a multiracial family, and willingness to engage in the work that would be necessary to raise a child of color with integrity (e.g., making new social connections, moving). Other participants described minimal personal exploration, settling on their racial preferences and requirements relatively easily, and noting little movement from their original ideas and beliefs surrounding race.

Not open: "We prefer white; that is really our ideal." In some couples, especially those in which both partners were white, at least one partner was not open to any races other than white or Caucasian. These couples also tended to be among those who spent significant time and financial resources trying to conceive, perhaps underscoring the relative importance of having a biological child—and, likewise, the participants' preference to mirror as closely as possible the standard nuclear American family (SNAF).[11] In explaining her preference for a white infant, Laura, a white heterosexual web designer in a medium-sized metro area in the Midwest, said: "When we're just thinking about us and our family and making it as harmonious as possible, I guess we kind of wanted it to be as much like a biological child as it could be."

Even though they were building their family via adoption, these individuals wished to "look like" what is culturally accepted as the typical or dominant family form in the United States: a heterosexual couple with biological children.[12] Adopting a child of a different race would invite unwanted attention from outsiders—and possibly clues to the "atypical" way that they had built their families. Seana, a white heterosexual sales associate in a large Midwestern city, shared that she and her husband, Ron, "prefer Caucasian.... We have gotten calls from people that are like . . . half black, half white and I haven't pursued them. [Full Caucasian] is important because . . . I think that it does look more like us; there's not as many questions." Ron, a white retail chain supervisor, echoed these sentiments:

> We really want to adopt a Caucasian baby. If we can't have our own, I would at least like the baby to look somewhat like us. I know maybe that's not fair but that's what we want. . . . I don't consider myself prejudiced but . . . all of our families and friends are Caucasian. I don't know. I can't explain it. I don't want a black child of my own.

Participants like Seana and Ron noted the racial homogeneity of their friend and family networks as one reason they might not be suitable parents for a child of color. Yet ultimately, it seemed that their decision was less grounded in concern about their inadequate personal or social resources to raise a child of color and more directly a function of their personal desire to have a child that looked like them. They wanted to be seen and recognized as a "real" family—and, as Ron alludes to, they may have felt uneasy about their ability to bond fully to children of a different race and/or who did not look like they could have "come from" them.

Lena, a white heterosexual operations manager in a midsized Northeast city, similarly articulated that she and her husband, Thomas, felt "more comfortable with Caucasian" because of concerns about hypervisibility and a desire not to be "pegged" as an adoptive family:

> I don't want that the first thing that people say is "Oh, look there's Lena and Thomas and their adopted baby." You know, it's not our adopted baby. It's our baby, so we've always felt like—I don't know. I think it would be nice if it wasn't so obvious. . . . We've been so open—my whole family, all my colleagues at work, and everyone knows our 5-year struggle to have children. . . . With first appearances, it would be nice enough to be like—not automatically pegged as adopted parents.

Monica, whose story opened this chapter, expressed similar sentiments—although interestingly, she noted that her husband, Darren, was more open to adopting a child of color than she was. Monica's narrative differed somewhat from Lena's in that Monica focused more on the difficulties associated with hypervisibility for the child. Indeed, Monica described how she had discussed her racial preferences with her therapist, who had helped her to realize that "the decision is not just for you, like, what you can handle, you know? You're making a decision for your kid." In turn, Monica came to a place where she felt like

> with adoption, when you do choose somebody that doesn't necessarily look like you or is culturally different, there's yet another thing that divides you, that separates you. And then other people, of course—everybody else around you, you know, in the grocery store—it's a flag, and you're different. It's a really tricky issue, but it's one more thing that could be tough for a child. You might get a really resilient child [who says], "I don't care." But you might get one that's just very aware that they're the oddball and adopted—"I don't look like my parents." It just adds more to it. . . . So I'm kind of concerned about what I'm setting that child up for. That has me worried. Darren totally doesn't care. He was saying that . . . he kind of wants it . . . to be very apparent that we've adopted. I think he doesn't want to hide it or . . . make the child think that there's anything shameful or bad, so it's kind of like he almost wants, like, a very super [obvious] appearance [difference], whereas I'm kind of feeling, I don't want to hide this, it's nothing to hide, but it's just like, do I want every person in the grocery store commenting? And am I setting the child up [to make it] that much

harder for them to feel a part of a family, [a sense of] belonging? I know I'm just really afraid of making a really important decision that will affect somebody's entire life.

Limited openness: "We are open to a child of color (with restrictions)." Some white participants were open to a mixed-race child (i.e., white and some other race) and/or a limited number of racial categories and combinations. These parents often preferred a white child and acknowledged a desire to at least vaguely resemble their child—but they also emphasized child-centered concerns, such as awareness of the identity considerations that would necessarily be a part of raising a child of color. They frequently emphasized the racial homogeneity of not only their families but also their communities. A child of color, they implied, would not see racial/ethnic representation around them. Unmentioned was the possibility of moving somewhere else to ensure that representation. Cal, a heterosexual IT manager in a small Northeastern city, shared:

> We pretty much decided because of where we are and some concerns of identity concerns for adoptive kids [that] we're primarily looking at a Caucasian baby or mixed race. . . . Like half-Caucasian and half-Asian or Latin American . . . just based on where we live. This is one of the whitest states in the nation. And we live in a very rural [area]. I just think that a child being adopted raises some questions and identity issues that may come up for a child. You throw into the mix maybe an ethnicity where they have nobody around, peers to relate to [and] sort of say, "What's my history?" "What's my heritage?" and I think that just complicates things more.

Many of these parents had placed certain caveats on the type and amount of "color" they would consider. Most preferred that the child be at least part white. Many explicitly said they would not be open to a "full" African American child. Elora, a white homemaker in a large West Coast city, said, "We're open to Caucasian, biracial . . . not full African American. . . . I think I wouldn't be totally comfortable with that. . . . It's more of a society kind of thing. It would be harder on the baby." Lou, a white heterosexual cartoonist in a medium-sized Midwestern city, said:

> I lived [abroad] and feel an affinity for Latino, Hispanic people, and I speak Spanish, so I feel very comfortable with those. I'm not comfortable raising an African American child. I just don't really have the connection. I've never really had black friends. Everybody is basically the same as far as I'm concerned but— the cultural side, or the race issue in America; I'm unprepared to give a child the extra support they're going to need.

Sandy, a white heterosexual woman who worked as a health care advocate in a small Northeastern city, stated:

> We put our preference as Caucasian, but they have so many different mixed races. We probably wouldn't be willing to accept a full African American child, but a half African American child . . . it's a good chance that we would. That's just, I think, because of where we live. It's not an African American community. . . . I guess it's just our preference. We're in a farming community, a country area. I don't really know much about [African American] culture. But there are so many different mixed races. We couldn't believe it when we had to do the application, because it was like, a quarter Polynesian, a quarter African American, a quarter this, a quarter that. It was like, crazy, you know?

In some cases, participants described a fair amount of processing and consideration that went into determining "which boxes we were going to check." They spent time "thinking and talking" about what it would mean to raise children of various races. Attending mandatory programming by their adoption agency and talking to their agency social worker(s) were important in helping them to determine their comfort and capabilities raising children of color. Leo, a gay Latino speech therapist in an East Coast suburb, whose partner, Javier, was also Latino, noted that he had initially been open to adopting an African American child, "thinking that it wouldn't be a problem." But after doing a lot of "work with the agency on that, and watching videos of kids who were adopted interracially, we came out saying that we wouldn't do an African American adoption because it seemed like too many whammys." Rather, the couple "put down any kind of Latin, we put biracial, Asian American . . . thinking about it from the perspective of the child. It just kind of made us feel like we were putting the kid in more harm's way, if you will, if we [adopted an African American baby]." Leo acknowledged discomfort with the extensive and detailed paperwork regarding what they would be open to: "It's like Match.com for babies." Erin, a white lesbian librarian in a large West Coast city, shared:

> We spent a lot of time talking about that, as you can imagine. And our adoption agency was actually very helpful in helping me figure that out. We went to a 4-hour workshop on understanding the needs of adopted children who are from different races or cultures than you. So I think what we came down to is, we would love to adopt a child that's a mixed race, if that comes up. Of course, we're both white, so anything in that range would be fine too. But maybe we're not quite equipped to do a full race from a different, than us, child. . . . We would just . . . try to make sure they're exposed to their race, their family of origin culture. . . . There's a lot for us to learn there too.

Meredith, Erin's partner, a white office manager, was even more specific about their racial preferences, as well as the barriers she anticipated they might encounter if they, as two white women, were to raise a child of color:

> We said to the agency that we would be fine with half Caucasian and half anything else, or all Caucasian. Where we live, it's very... white, and we don't have many multicultural friends or—we have few friends who are from different countries. We went to a multirace education seminar, and after going to that—it really kind of explained to us that it's really important to incorporate the ethnicity of the child and to be part of that community. So, if we had an African American child or a 100% Latino child, we would have to find that community and then try to act like we're a part of that community. It's a little bit harder and, you know, you would want to be able to have access to that.

A lack of community resources—i.e., in the form of racial homogeneity, as well as, in some cases, community intolerance of racial diversity—was frequently emphasized as impacting participants' choices and preferences. Leigh, a white heterosexual assistant museum director in a small city on the East Coast, shared how she and her husband, Billy, recently had a "big, long talk" about whether they would be open to adopting a child of a different race:

> We kind of decided that that [would be] okay. But we live in a small town that is predominately white, so having a white kid makes things—you know—it's just one less thing that will set the child apart. One of the things we decided on is that if we do adopt a child from a different race, it would be really important for us to live in an area that is more diverse... but are we willing to do that? Are we willing to pack up and move to [nearby city] or some place that is more ethnically diverse? And we kind of decided that we like where we are, so probably not. The long answer is that we are happy with it and we will probably look for a white kid, as awful as it sounds. I really wouldn't want our kid to be the "token black kid" in our town. I wish it was more diverse, but it's not.

Ellen, a white heterosexual travel writer in a large West Coast city, was open to "white or Hispanic, because, living in [city], it's not a very diverse place, and we're kind of worried about having a baby in our family who doesn't look like anybody around them; I just think that would be really difficult growing up like that." Donna, a white heterosexual manager of a nonprofit in a large Northeastern city, said, "I'm a little worried about my husband's side of the family to be quite honest, and their religious community in general in terms of acceptance of a baby that's a different race." Jerry, a white heterosexual appliance installer in an East Coast suburb, shared, "My dad and brother on occasion use racial slurs. And while I'm not really seeking their approval, I do think stuff could come up." Byron, a white gay graduate student in a large city in the Midwest, noted that he and his partner, Dave, were currently living in an area that was not

> the capital of acceptance and liberalism. It's . . . challenging enough, maybe, to have two same-sex parents; do we really want to add on race components? I believe what we put officially was that we were open to biracial, including like full Hispanic and Caucasian. I think we did pretty much rule out like full African American, maybe even full Chinese or Asian. Mainly, we just had issues with that about what it could potentially put upon the child in this environment, unfortunately.

In explaining his specific racial preferences, Byron articulated considerations that many prospective parents hinted at but did not state directly. Namely, in explaining why they were open to "biracial or Hispanic" but not open to a "full African American," Byron pointed to both community and societal intolerance as well as internal biases and a lack of preparation for the type of discrimination that an African American child—with gay parents—might face:

> I kind of said to Dave, "I don't want to be politically correct in the sense of saying we'll just take any child in all of the world, [to make] myself look good." Like, "Oh, I'm so accepting of everything in the world." The reality of it is, maybe I am, but how am I going to handle this? Am I going to be the greatest defender of my child? How am I going to deal with those issues that would come up? We had pretty long conversations about it and—we did end up in agreement as to what we would accept and what we didn't think we would accept.
> *[Interviewer: How did you decide you were open to biracial or Hispanic?]*
> I think it's a matter of degrees. . . . It just seemed like there would be maybe a little more tolerance of that than a full—you know, where it's obvious that you have people from different races.

Participants sometimes emphasized racialized attitudes within their own families of origin contributing to their racial preferences. Nate, a white gay medical assistant in a large Southern city, explained that they preferred a white child because "Dwight's parents, who live in the area, and who would be a definite part of the kid's life, definitely have a preference towards Caucasian, which we both are." Nate went on to say that they had discussed this with their social worker, who "said that she would not recommend anything outside of that, just because—the issue of racism—you don't want to inflict that on a child within a family." Other participants—even those who were of color—pointed to their parents' unwillingness to accept a child of particular races. Javier, a gay Latino gastroenterologist in an East Coast suburb, said that he and his Latino partner, Leo, had entered the adoption process "thinking we'd take any race." Then, "an agency workshop on black children raised by white parents opened our eyes to the limitations and deficiencies within our extended families [in terms of] accepting us as a couple, accepting a child of ours, and accepting a child of a completely different race." A similar scenario was described by Will, a white accountant, and his partner, Adam, a biracial (African American and white) director of marketing, who lived in a midsized West Coast city. Both men agreed that Will's family would not accept a "full African American child." Will explained:

> We put down [that we were open to] white–black mix, white, white–Latin mix, but not Asian or black. Only because—it's not so much a problem for us, but for the acceptance of our families. My family, I'm ashamed to say it: My mom said [about the rest of my family], "they'll accept you, they'll accept the baby," but [*whispers*] "*if it's a black baby they might not.*" So I'm like, okay; that's my family. They're already taking a big leap to accept a baby adopted by two gay men. So that's kind of that, and Adam is mixed race, black–white, so that's a good thing; the child could look like him, and that's great. . . . We just had to be realistic about what would fit in this situation.

Adam stated that he personally would have been open to any race,

> the reason being, I'm mixed race myself, so I flow well in different cultures. . . . And I also have a family that—even though I may be half black, half white—I have family members that are from everywhere. I have aunts that are Latino, I have aunts who are completely black, aunts who are completely white; so to me, it doesn't make a difference.

However, Adam acknowledged that they had not indicated an openness to "full" "African American. . . . The logic behind that was Will's parents were from the South and [*laugh*] it would just present more complications for that." Thus, despite his own racial background and comfort with an African American child, Adam took seriously the potential problems this might raise for his partner's family of origin and, in turn, agreed on a more restricted range of potential racial categories that would theoretically cause fewer concerns.

Some lesbians and gay men also highlighted identity concerns, with the added emphasis on their child's status as a child of two men or two women. That is, they shared their worry that as a child who was adopted, who had two moms or dads, they would inevitably feel different from many of their peers, especially at certain stages of the life cycle. They explained that "adding the race piece"—that is, adopting a child of color into a white family—would represent a third form of difference that their child would have to navigate. Reed, a white alumni relations director in a large West Coast city, said: "I have in my mind that it would be much more difficult for an African American child to grow up with two gay, white parents." Lauren, a white therapist in a large Northeastern city, said:

> The only hesitancy we have is, we feel like . . . the child's going to have some obstacles and barriers with their peers and with their friends' parents and with society, having two moms. To add on some race issues—we're afraid might make it harder for them. But we haven't ruled it out, because we think that's something that with support, we could all get through together as a family.

Russell, a white gay policy analyst in a large East Coast city, explained, "Our reasoning [for preferring a white child] was that we were already going to be a same-sex couple raising a child, and that would create its own set of issues, and we just didn't feel like we wanted to also deal with transracial or transcultural adoption issues." Al, a gay white insurance sales manager in a midsized Northeastern city, shared that the adoption classes that he and his partner, Geoff, had taken were very helpful in that social workers were "so honest and up front" saying, "Don't be a hero; don't do this because you're trying to make a statement or a hero. It's not bad to say, 'I prefer a child my own race.'" With the support and guidance of their social workers, Al and Geoff had reached the point where

> we are very open to Latino, Hispanic, or mixed. We're not open to African American right now only because we think that in our town—probably less than 3% of the school district is, you know, African American. We're thinking that we [are] already presenting a child with a few challenges. One adoption, two gay parents—really, when you start throwing more on, how much can one little family maybe handle? So, we don't want to come across as biased, but we're trying to be very honest—looking at the big picture when we think about what's best.

Very open: "Bring it on. We see no need to limit ourselves. We'll figure it out." A minority of couples—typically lesbian and gay—shared that they had placed few caveats or constraints on the race of their future child. Sometimes they did acknowledge a mild *preference* for a white child, but they did not restrict themselves to white children, or any race for that matter. Dean, a white gay software developer in a large Southern city, reflected:

> I think originally I just imagined a little white boy. And I don't anymore. I've kind of worked through whatever thought processes [shaped] that. . . . It's just

kind of a picture I had in my head, before I thought about it.... I don't have a strong preference anymore.

Dean further noted:

> Our information that we sent out about what we would accept had the option to choose race as far as—even to the level of half Hispanic and half African American, or half Asian and half Caucasian. You could get *that detailed* with it. We just checked everything, like, this is silly [*laugh*]. Like ordering sushi off a menu. [That's] what some people do, and we chose not to.

These prospective parents tended to acknowledge the potential challenges that might come with raising a child of color but did not see their whiteness as an insurmountable barrier. They often emphasized that they would have work to do in order to raise a child of color with integrity, and they were up for the challenge. Simon, a white gay social worker in a large Midwestern city, had spent a lot of time thinking about and working on "issues of social identity and social justice and cultural competence" and was aware of "all of the dilemmas related to white people raising children of color, and all of the dynamics that come into play when you have a multiracial family." In turn, Simon knew that "it's not going to be easy—but because I recognize the issues and I'm willing to deal with them, and I can adequately do that in a critical way, I am [open] in terms of race." Simon's partner, Vincent, a white telecommunications director, said:

> If the child we do adopt is from a different race, the child will also have two dads. One thing we would want to be really sensitive to is, like, openly talking about that and giving the child role models of his or her own ethnicity, like choosing stories or kids book[s] or toys or whatever that reflect the child's race or ethnicity. Trying to find as many opportunities for the child to interact with the kids that not only look like him or her, but kids who are different [in other ways] too.

Kate, a white lesbian woman who worked as the director of a women's survival center in a large city on the West Coast, said:

> We don't have a strong racial preference. If we were going to take a baby of color—I mean, we told the agency [that] probably a Latino baby would be the best match for us just because of our neighborhood and my language skills and our background. If we get a child of color from a community that we're less connected to, it will just be additional work for us; it's not that we can't do it.... I mean, it'll [be] hard; we're both white. And as parents of children of color, a

big part of what you have to teach them is how to deal with racism in the world. I don't know as much about that; I mean, I know a little about it but I have never had the daily lived experience with coping with racism. So, I'm not going to be as good at that. It's also tricky for kids of color to look at their parents and [not see their own race]; it just means we would have to work really hard to make sure that that child is connected to a community of color that represents them. So, it would be more work in terms of providing for them and their cultural needs. I think we can do a lot of it but we'll have to make sure we do it. . . . [T]here are certain things that your kid is going to need that you can't fully give them and you have to make sure you get them from somewhere else.

Like Kate, Carly, a white heterosexual history professor in a large city in the Northeast, also acknowledged gaps in her racialized awareness and knowledge and an openness and desire to learn more. Carly also demonstrated sensitivity to the controversies surrounding transracial adoption:

We've explored [adopting a child of color] a lot, and we're feeling good about it. I think because we said that we are open to that, it's probably a very real possibility, because I'm realizing there are a lot more couples saying that they're not open to it, and so that [is] making it more likely that we will end up adopting a child that is not Caucasian. It's funny . . . I've thought a lot about identity development and racial identity, ethnic identity.

I know we barely even know the half of it—what we're getting into—but it makes me worried because I really want to do right by this child and I know it's a controversial area. I feel like we're in a good place with it because we recognize that it's huge and it's complicated and it's not going to be everything about our raising this child, but it's going to be there and we're going to be mindful of it and we're ready to embrace and become a transracial family, whatever that means. . . . I don't totally believe "what's meant to happen is going to happen," but there's something about this—the more that we get into this, that I'm feeling like I think we're really supposed to be doing it this way.

Here, Carly also highlights practical reasons for their openness to adopting a child of color: That is, she alludes to the reality that because there are more children of color available for adoption, indicating less restrictive racial preferences may result in a quicker placement. Eliza, a white lesbian accountant in a large Northeastern city, also recognized that she and her partner, Hannah, could improve the likelihood and speed of a child placement if they were open to African American children. In addition to saving them time, this choice might also save them money:

We are in the African American book,[§] so we will [get a child] who has at least a portion of African American descent. It doesn't really matter to us. Race doesn't matter; it is a kid. But . . . it was cheaper [to be open] and the time frame was faster. The time frame was more of an issue than the money. It is not that they are putting values on the kid, but there are technically more of them out there and less people who want them. So we're not saying that they are worth less. You shouldn't think about kids that way, but they said if you really want a white baby then you are going to wait 2, 2½, 3 years . . . and if you are willing to take any variation of race it will be a lot faster for you.

Several lesbian and gay prospective parents suggested that, as same-sex couples, they might already be less likely to be considered or chosen by birth mothers in general—and therefore it did not make sense to further limit their options based on race. Stated Eddie, a white physical therapist in a midsized Southern city, "For us, [race] is still pretty open; it just depends on what baby comes up that we're eligible for and that the birth mother is willing to let us have."

In a few cases, participants emphasized their families, friendship networks, religious communities, and broader communities as racially and/or ethnically diverse and framed these contexts as informing their openness and offering potential resources. Seth, a white gay afterschool program director in a large Southern city, said, with regard to racial preference:

[Race] doesn't seem like that big of [a] deal to us. Dean's sister's husband is African American, and their children of course [are] biracial, and it just has not ever been an issue; it just seems that's normal for our family. . . . The people that we interact with who are of different races—they have the same values as us, the same attitudes as us. Obviously it's important to be around people who look like you, and to be aware of positive role models, people of the same race. [A child of color in our family] would get that.

A few participants acknowledged that their "total and complete openness" had been effectively modulated and in some cases dialed back by the agency programming and dialogue to which they had been exposed. In other words, they came to adopt a more informed approach to adopting a child of a different race, whereby they possessed a more nuanced idea of their own limitations in regard to providing fully for a child of color, and the kinds of challenges they might encounter. Roger, a white gay marketing director in an East Coast suburb, shared:

[§] Here, Eliza is referring to the compilation of profiles of prospective adopters who are open to adopting an African American child, which are then shown to expectant parents considering adoption.

We went into this [thinking] that the race and ethnicity didn't matter. When we told people about that, the reactions were pretty unanimous. They said: "Are you sure? You should really think about that." People have talked to us at length, including social workers, about what it really means to bring a kid of another race into your home and if that affects the kid.... I think... that, in the case of raising a black child or something, you are going to know they are different and they are going to know they are different. They are also going to know that they are loved and part of the family. But, from what everyone said, it just makes me wonder if it just makes more sense to adopt a child that is white or Hispanic white. [They say] African American ... would be such a challenge versus like an Asian American child—but I don't really know what the thinking is there.

In just a few cases did prospective parents' "total and complete openness" seem to reflect a color-blind philosophy, whereby they asserted that "race doesn't matter" and often focused on themselves rather than their child in their response—in contrast to many of the aforementioned examples of openness, where parents acknowledged that race did matter and that parenting a child of color would require a mindful approach that involved hard work and a lot of integrity. Chuck, a white heterosexual IT director in a suburb on the East Coast, was adopting through foster care with his wife, Annie. Regarding race, he said:

Nah, [it doesn't matter]. I grew up in an ethnic neighborhood and race really doesn't matter to me. I think it's just more socially acceptable [now] to raise a child of color. I mean, maybe like 50 years ago people would be like, "Why are they doing that?" But now, I'd say a large percentage of the population is either accepting to that or they would just be indifferent, and every now and then maybe narrow-minded.

Drug/Alcohol Exposure: Pressure to "Check That Box"

Along with indicating preferences around openness and race, prospective adoptive parents must also indicate the type and level of drug and alcohol exposure they are willing to consider—assuming that this information is available, known, and disclosed. Navigating these decisions was challenging, given that most participants had little prior knowledge of the impact of drug and alcohol exposure on a developing fetus and found it difficult to "tick a box" as to what type and level of exposure they were willing to entertain in the context of a potential birth parent match. As Adam, a biracial (African American/white) gay marketing director in a medium-sized West Coast city, said, about the paperwork they completed for their agency:

> Where it became more difficult is when I didn't have the information and I had to ... research it ... like, we had to choose which, what types of drugs we would be willing to tolerate that the birth mother had used. So for example, we had to say we would be willing to tolerate low, medium, or high heroin use, cocaine use, or alcohol during the first trimester or the second trimester. We had all these things that we had to research, to see what's the impact on the child and development. That took a long time and that was kind of challenging. And the thing is, you could say, for example—"no alcohol use" because alcohol can have [a] significant detrimental effect on a developing fetus. However, if you say "no," a birth mother who may have had a social drink before she knew she was pregnant is eliminated from your pool. So you have to be careful how you answer the questions. And if we [say yes], we [have to be] willing to tolerate a low amount or a moderate amount just so that we don't eliminate people who may have just had a glass of wine in their second month.

Many participants articulated feeling pressured to indicate a greater level of openness to potential drug and alcohol exposure than they were comfortable with to increase the likelihood of a potential match. Lesbian and gay participants were particularly likely to grapple with this: Amid an awareness that their sexual orientation rendered them less likely to be chosen by certain expectant mothers, they sometimes felt compelled to offset this reality by indicating greater openness and flexibility surrounding drug/alcohol exposure so as to effectively broaden the pool of prospective matches. Taryn, a white lesbian radio personality in a Northeastern suburb, shared that she and her partner, Molly, were aware that the wait time for a child placement was longer for lesbian couples than for heterosexual couples. In turn:

> we kind of felt like we should be pretty liberal in terms of what we were open to ... in terms of the level of the birth mother's drug use and what level of prenatal care. . . . I guess you say what you're willing to do, and then when they call you with a referral you can say yes or no ... but I can see that's going be really hard when there's a baby and it's like, "Oh, you know, it might be okay."

Jamie was a white gay communications manager in a midsized city in the South. He observed that he and his partner, Evan—and same-sex couples in general—tended to be more open than heterosexual couples in general, not only with respect to drug/alcohol exposure but also with regard to other child characteristics (e.g., race, gender) and birth parent characteristics (e.g., history of mental illness). Jamie described what he saw as the root of this difference:

> In [our adoption classes], a lot of the straight couples ... are there not because they want to be; it is because they sort of have to be. They come into it [with] this expectation that they are going to get this perfect little while baby. That is what I see over and over, and so their profiles are very limited and very narrow. Whereas, like, with our profile, we are willing to take more risks with interracial children and with past drug abuse, and the stage the drug happened, and what the drugs are—because they give you a big sheet of drugs that you are willing to accept and not accept and at what time in the pregnancy, etc. [The heterosexual couples], they are just not willing to do [much].

Sometimes the pressure to be open to drug/alcohol exposure was not internal—it was external, coming from their adoption agencies. Mary, a white lesbian TV production manager in a midsized Southern city, shared how her adoption agency, which "prided themselves on being, you know, the gay and lesbian agency," had made some significant missteps in how they handled Mary and her partner, Andrea, and their preferences surrounding drug/alcohol exposure:

> We felt like, you know, babies would come up and we would say no, and we would feel like they were like, "Well, you should just take this, given your situation." So we're like, "No, we don't want a baby whose mother's been on crack cocaine for 6 months." You know? We don't want that. But we had several offers of those kind of babies, but, you know, our money is green just like everybody else's. We didn't feel like we should have [to choose] that.

Indeed, when prospective parents maintained limited openness to drug/alcohol exposure, they were sometimes cautioned by social workers that these restrictions might mean a longer wait time. Hannah, a white administrative assistant in a large Northeastern city, said:

> We are being very stringent on alcohol and drug use so that is kind of holding us up [from being placed]. We are trying to work out what we are comfortable with and if we would take more usage ... but we're not sure. The social worker said because we are a lesbian couple it is going to be longer and since we are so strict on drugs and alcohol use that is going to be longer.

Notably, some prospective parents ultimately ended up relaxing their criteria regarding the range and severity of substance abuse exposure they would consider. Donna, a white heterosexual manager at a nonprofit organization in a large Northeastern city, shared that initially, she and her husband, Max, had indicated that they were not open to any alcohol use during the pregnancy—but were now revisiting that decision: "We haven't been contacted by anybody. We haven't had any even potential matches so we may need to discuss things further and expand our horizons. I'm open." Donna added: "We don't want to corner ourselves and . . . never be matched." Notably, Donna and Max had already relaxed their criteria for what they would consider in terms of drug use—and still weren't seeing any matches. Thus, the process of opening up to a different reality than they had initially envisioned (i.e., an expectant mother who did not smoke cigarettes and who took prenatal vitamins) was a gradual one, with many points of adjustment as prospective parents reconsidered their options and modified their expectations.

* * *

Orienting to open adoption is a process. As we saw, participants arrived at open adoption for a variety of reasons, and varied in the degree to which they embraced versus tolerated the concept of openness. Likewise, racial preferences and openness to drug/alcohol exposure varied considerably—but, as with openness, prospective adopters balanced their preferences and ideals with structural realities (e.g., the likelihood that the more restrictive and stringent they are in their preferences, the longer they will wait for a child placement). Members of same-sex couples are at least theoretically released from the pressures of conforming to the heteronormative biologically related family ideal,[13] thus facilitating greater openness in terms of what a family might look like (e.g., in terms of contact with the birth family and racial diversity within the adoptive family). But they are also aware that their positionality as "less than ideal" parents may make the adoption process more difficult for them, thus exerting pressure to declare openness to child characteristics and attributes that they may not fully embrace.

As discussed in Chapter 10, an essential part of the preadoption preparation process is exploring feelings about openness with an adoption-competent professional who is able to provide authentic emotional support alongside fact-based guidance and education surrounding openness. Further, guidance surrounding openness should be provided not only preadoption but postadoption, when navigating open adoption is no longer hypothetical but a reality. Regarding race, prospective adopters similarly need support and guidance in a nonjudgmental space where they can examine their beliefs, attitudes, and resources regarding the adoption of children of various racial/ethnic backgrounds. Prospective adopters should avoid capitulating to internal or external pressure about what they "should" do regarding race or prenatal drug/alcohol exposure, yet they should ensure that they are armed with the facts needed to make informed, educated decisions.

Notes

1. Siegel & Smith, 2012.
2. Ibid.
3. Baxter, Norwood, Asbury, & Scharp, 2014, p. 253.
4. Baxter et al., 2014.
5. Gritter, 2000; Holden, 2013.
6. Holden, 2013.
7. Child Welfare Information Gateway, 2013.
8. Boyle, 2017.
9. Child Welfare Information Gateway, 2012.
10. Goldberg, 2009; Goldberg & Smith, 2009.
11. Smith, 1993.
12. Kirk, 1964; Smith, 1993.
13. Smith, 1993.

3
"Meeting the Reality of Our Situation"
Placement Experiences and Circumstances and Postplacement Openness and Contact

After completing the paperwork, programming, and other requirements to adopt, couples wait—until an expectant mother or agency chooses them and they are placed with a child, an event itself that is often preceded by many false starts and stops, including matches that fall through (e.g., because the birth mother changes her mind and decides to parent). When birth parents and adoptive parents meet, a relationship is born that, whether negotiated symbolically or relationally, will forever change the lives of everyone involved: birth parents, adoptive parents, and the child at the center of it all. This chapter first explores some of the reasons adoptive parents are typically selected by expectant parents (or agencies, when birth parents do not wish to make the decision). I then address parents' accounts of their initial meetings with the birth parents. I also address the varied circumstances that surrounded the placement of children (e.g., financial difficulties, emotional instability). Finally, I explore initial patterns of openness and contact, alongside a discussion of how adoptive parents' expectations surrounding openness may be unmet in ways that are potentially difficult or possibly rewarding.

Family Vignette: Rob and Terrence

Rob, a Latino administrative assistant, and Terrence, a white anesthesiologist, were a gay couple living in a suburb of a large city on the West Coast. They were chosen by a birth mother, Alena, who was attracted to the idea of helping a couple that otherwise might not have the opportunity to become parents fulfill their dream of parenthood. According to both men, Alena's own personal history of same-sex sexual experiences also impacted her decision to place her son with them. Unable to parent in part because of poverty and difficult life circumstances, Alena was also seemingly drawn to their self-described personal, emotional, and financial stability.

Rob and Terrence were typical of many gay male couples who described a parental orientation toward their children's birth mothers, who were often young and facing emotional and financial challenges. When I talked to Rob a few months after the adoptive placement, he shared how he gave Alena a 1-800 number that forwarded calls to his cell phone, so that "she can always reach me.... Because if she's got, like, a pain in her chest, I want her to always feel cared for—just call." Rob further described how he sent Alena pictures each month. When we talked a few months after the adoptive placement, Rob felt that the current level of contact between his family and Alena was "just about right.... We had agreed to a couple of visits a year.... She just wants to know that David's okay, and to see how he's growing up." Terrence shared:

> Since David's been born, we had a lot of contact with her. She hasn't decided yet whether she wants to actually see him or not. We showed her the pictures and—she took a long time to pick the pictures up, so I know that she was trying to debate whether or not she wanted the pictures. But she did get the pictures. And she talks to Rob pretty frequently, and I spoke to her, speak with her. She's doing well.... She's been trying to find a job.

Reflecting on whether the current level of contact matched his expectations or hopes, Terrence said thoughtfully:

> I don't know that I necessarily had an expectation going in.... My thought was that we'd hear from the birth mother occasionally and send her pictures and letters and whatever. But I hadn't really had any expectations about how it would look after the adoption, to be honest with you. You know, the thing is—it's very different for us, because I think if we were a heterosexual couple there might be some threat, like the birth mother coming in.... There's no adoptive mother here—there's two adoptive fathers, and so there's no threat or feeling like she's coming in on our territory or something like that.... It's just kind of—it feels like another aspect of our child's life. So it feels very different than I imagine it is for a heterosexual couple.

Terrence also shared how, at the same time that they wanted Alena to be involved, he and Rob were sensitive to the emotionally challenging circumstances surrounding the placement of a child. In turn, they were trying to respond appropriately to Alena's needs and boundaries:

> We really want her to be involved on some level in his life, but also we don't want to push her or make her do that. She had a really hard time in the first few weeks after the adoption. She was really sad, crying a lot, and then she called our attorney and she was really upset. I think she's kind of processed

a little bit now, but [in terms of] inviting her [to visit], we're trying to let her have the lead on that. I think at, we will at some point visit her.... When she ... was talking to our attorney, she was saying things like, "I just wish I had my child with me, and I wish we were together, and I was nursing him and stuff like that." But I think ... she was just saying this is what she wished she had been able to do, but her life situation wasn't [in a place] so that she could [do that]. I don't think she was actually saying that I want my baby back. It was just the sense of loss around it. She didn't get any counseling around it or anything like that. So I think that that's probably created a lot of sadness for her. But she's better now. Every time we talk with her, she seems much happier and I think she's resigned to what's going on.... She's really, I think, grieving the loss [of this child and the other children that she placed].

Rob and Terrence were typical of many couples in open adoptions who, amid the chaos of adjusting to life with a new baby, were also navigating the uncharted emotional terrain of birth family relationships and contact. They acknowledged the loss that Alena must be feeling—yet resisted the possibility that she could really be regretting her decision to place the child for adoption. They wanted her to be involved—yet they also did not want to overstep boundaries or interfere with her grieving process. They defaulted to letting Alena "take the lead" on letting them know when she was ready to make her first visit to see them—yet it is possible that Alena herself was waiting to be invited. Indeed, it is not surprising that many couples talked about the unfolding of their relationship with the birth family as a "dance," with both parties managing the space around them and between them, trying to anticipate their partner's movements, and occasionally stepping on toes. This process of social distance regulation[1] was especially complex during the postplacement period, a time of heightened emotions and relational intensity.

"Why She Chose Us": Making a Match

How do expectant parents decide who will be the adoptive parents of the child they are awaiting the birth of or have recently given birth to? The chain of events typically starts with a phone call: Expectant (or new) parents call an adoption agency, lawyer, or mediator, who introduces them to the idea of adoption and provides them with potential adoptive parent matches. Most adoption agencies, for example, present expectant parents with the profiles of hopeful adoptive parents (which include photos, background information, and often a "Dear

Birth Mother" letter*) to determine which individuals or couples they might consider for placement. (Now that these profiles are typically online, expectant parents may view them on the Internet directly and then call the agency with ideas about which adoptive parents they are interested in learning more about.) Often, expectant parents will meet with one or more hopeful adoptive parents during their pregnancy and then decide who is the best "match." In other cases, expectant parents wait to make an adoption plan until after their child has been born—in which case they typically have less time to consider various families and thus may select just one family with whom to "match."

Many parents discussed the reasons their children's birth parents—and typically birth mothers—chose them. Parents typically obtained this information from their children's birth parents themselves or, in some cases, from their adoption agencies and lawyers. In a minority of families, the birth parents did not choose the adoptive parents but elected to have the agency make the decision. In some cases this was because they contacted the agency very late in their pregnancy or when they were at the hospital giving birth. Charlene, a white lesbian teacher living in a medium-size Northeastern city, shared, "The birth mom had no issue with the fact that we are gay. But the agency officially chose us because we were waiting the longest at the agency."

Parents often described birth parents as choosing them because of general impressions of them as happy and emotionally and financially stable. In essence, according to the participants, birth parents chose them because they seemed to have a warm and joyful home that offered a child many opportunities that they themselves could not provide. As Mariette, a white lesbian physical therapist in a Midwestern suburb, shared: "She said, 'I saw your website . . . and you looked really happy, and you talked about the importance of family, being close to family.'" Carly, a white history professor in a large Northeast city, reflected:

> I loved . . . that she really liked that we [place] a lot of value on our friends and family and that we really have a large circle of people in our lives that are really important to us and she just really got the impression that this child would grow up surrounded by people that love her; she really liked that about our profile.

---

* The "Dear Birth Mother" letter (or "Dear Expectant Parent" letter) is written by the hopeful or prospective adoptive parents as a means of introducing themselves to potential birth parents. It is typically encouraged by adoption agencies and is included as part of, or constitutes, the adoptive parents' portfolio or "profile," where they describe themselves and, often, why they are pursuing adoption and the kind of life they hope to create with a child. In addition to only addressing the birth mother (as opposed to both birth parents), one problem with the term *Dear Birth Mother* is that the person who is reading the letter is an expectant parent who is considering placing her child for adoption—but may never be a birth mother, in that she also may very well be considering parenting the child.

Noting that these were values also shared by their daughter's birth mother, Carly asserted her sense that "we really share some fundamental qualities with her, [which in a sense] approximates the nature that we don't share with this child.... [There is something] shared between us and the birth mother who saw us and resonated with these kind of qualities."

Sometimes, birth parents were described as having been drawn to specific personality traits or personal qualities. As Marcus, a white gay graduate student living in a large West Coast city, said:

> She thought that we would be a good balance—that Rick was kind of the humorous one, and I was kind of the serious one. So, Rick would be good at making sure he got the play time, and I would ... make sure that he got places on time and got his homework done.

Shared hobbies or interests were also emphasized as a gravitational pull for some birth mothers ("she is also a bookworm, so she liked that about us": Carly). Some couples asserted that they were selected because of a shared background trait or characteristic, such as religion (e.g., Catholicism), race (e.g., African American), or language (e.g., Spanish).

Occasionally, birth parents reportedly named a relatively idiosyncratic detail of the couple's life, background, or living situation as especially compelling in their decision-making process (e.g., the presence of a dog, the couple's penchant for travel). As Marcus recalled with a laugh, "She looked through the birth parent letters and saw ... the picture of our cats, and she said she saw the cats and was like, 'This is them.'" Likewise, Lewis, a white heterosexual teacher in a small Northeast city, recalled, "She liked the fact that we had a lot of family, and the spot that we lived in—near the woods."

In some cases, birth parents supposedly just "knew" or "had a sense" that they were the right parents for their child. Shannon, a white lesbian school psychologist in a large city on the West Coast, recalled, "She said she was just looking for a couple that felt like the right people. We were the right people." Dante, a gay African American vice president of operations in a large metropolitan area on the West Coast, stated:

> I was just astounded that this single African American woman in [the Midwest] would pick a mixed race gay couple.... And I asked her, I said, "I'm, you know, I'm flattered of course that you chose us but if you can answer this, I'm really curious to know, not even, why us, but why a gay couple?" And she said: "To be honest with you ... that didn't even cross my mind. You just seemed like the right people." I almost fainted; I mean, I felt guilty, because I prejudged her already and, I mean, that was like the most enlightened statement I've heard in my whole life.

In a few cases, parents described a spiritual element of the birth parents' decision, whereby the birth parents felt "moved" by their profile or felt an "immediate, mystical connection" upon first meeting them. Donna, a white heterosexual director of a nonprofit in a large Northeastern city, shared: "They were presented [with] four profiles, and when they got to [husband's] picture, the birth father said, 'That's the guy I dreamt about.'" Brent, a white gay brand manager living in a large West Coast city, shared:

> It was just a very moving story. . . . [The birth mother] said [that when she looked at our profile], the baby was kicking the whole time and it had chosen us. So that is what she believed. She believes that the baby chose us and she wanted someone that had been waiting and she liked that we had been waiting a long time.

Same-sex couples were highly aware that some expectant parents would be unwilling to place their child with a same-sex couple because of certain religious and/or political beliefs. They also knew that many expectant parents, even if not explicitly "against" the idea of gay parenting, would prefer that their child be raised by a mother and a father and/or might worry that a child of two mothers or two fathers would be teased. As Eric, a white gay editor in a large East Coast city, said:

> We were so concerned about being a gay couple, with all the prejudice, and that we would be getting a very small sliver of people from which to be selected from or whatever. . . . Not everyone is going to want to place their child with a gay couple living in [city].

In turn, it is notable that same-sex couples narrated a unique set of reasons as to why they specifically were chosen by expectant parents. Gay men in particular tended to state that they were chosen because expectant mothers liked the idea of retaining their role as the only "mother" (symbolic or otherwise) in the child's life.[2] That is, expectant mothers did not want to place their child with a lesbian couple or a heterosexual couple because of the potential for tension surrounding parental roles and for maternal entitlement on the part of the adoptive parent(s). In some cases gay men were told this particular narrative by expectant mothers themselves; in other cases their agencies or lawyers reportedly provided this account; and in some cases they came to this conclusion themselves. Regardless, men's shared male gender was regarded as a facilitative factor in some women's decision to choose them as the parents. Greg, a white gay software consultant living in a small city in the South, shared: "She pushed aside the lesbian couples because she didn't want to be mom number three. She gave most of her interest and attention to the male couples. Ultimately, she picked us because we were close, we were willing to have an open adoption, and she liked what she saw." Roger, a white gay director of marketing for a small company in a Northeast suburb, shared that his adoption agency had "said, well actually in a lot of cases birth moms gravitate to gay male couples because [they] seem to feel like they're not being replaced as the mother." Doug, a white gay psychologist in a large West Coast city, surmised, "Some portion of her decision was probably about her desire to be the baby's only mom. There's something there for her that's very tangible and real about choosing two dads so that her role remains untouchable in some way."

According to gay fathers, some birth parents had also chosen them because they wanted to give a child to a couple who could not easily have one themselves. Thus, they were motivated by altruism—a desire to do good—and in some cases social justice, in that they wanted to benefit the most vulnerable or disadvantaged group. Leo, a gay Latino speech therapist in a Northeastern suburb, said that his daughter's birth mother had "looked for a gay male couple.... She felt it was best with two guys because obviously there's no shot for a biological child." Terrence, the white gay anesthesiologist whose story opened the chapter, said: "When she called the attorney, I don't think she said, 'I want a same-sex couple.' But when they sent her five families to look at, she was very clear that she wanted to choose the gay male couple because we couldn't have kids ourselves."

Several lesbian couples, in contrast, emphasized the birth mother's negative history with men as a reason they were chosen as parents. These birth mothers liked the idea that there would be "two moms and no dads." Andrea, a white lesbian prison guard who lived in a midsized city in the South, stated: "She thought it was great that we were both women, because she was like, 'She'll always have two mommies.' And I'm like, 'Yes! That's the point we've been trying to sell everyone!'" In one case, the agency, not the birth mother, chose the couple for a similar reason. Eliza, a white lesbian junior accountant in a large Northeast city, stated:

> When she came in [to the agency] to place her [child for] adoption ... she said that she had no particulars. She let the agency pick and the agency picked us because they didn't want to have a man involved at that time, because the mother was dealing with so many man issues. It's interesting that that's how we got picked—[because] there wasn't a man involved. She didn't have an issue with [us being a same-sex couple], but she didn't have a preference at all. She was like, "Whatever. Just find me somebody to take this baby."

The lesbian and gay parents whom I interviewed also articulated other, more generalized reasons that expectant parents chose same-sex couples—regardless of gender. A few parents commented, sometimes with humor, on the fact that their child's birth mother or birth parents were young, liberal, and "counterculture" and wanted to do something "different"—such as placing a child with a same-sex couple. They observed that they benefited from birth parents' youthful desire to go against the grain of what society would expect or prefer from them (i.e., placement of their child in a mother–father household). Jamie, a white gay communications manager in a medium-sized Southern city, said: "She wanted a nontraditional family and she saw something in us and chose us."

Some lesbian and gay parents also noted that the birth parents had gay siblings, relatives, or close friends, and therefore expressed a comfort with and even a preference for a same-sex couple. In some cases too, birth parents wanted their children to be raised with an appreciation for and tolerance of diversity—and believed that same-sex couples would be especially likely to cultivate such qualities. Adam, a gay biracial (African American/white) director of marketing in a midsized West Coast city, recounted: "She was looking for couples that she thought would allow her child to be raised in a loving, stable family, that were both open-minded. And that was one reason why she thought that maybe a same-sex couple would be appropriate."

In a few cases, same-sex couples were reportedly chosen because the birth parents related to them as marginalized individuals. Rachel, a white lesbian computer applications training manager in a large Southern city, said:

> Her main reason for picking a gay couple is that they were biracial, living in, like [predominantly white city in the South]. So they felt like they really wanted somebody who kind of understood the importance of diversity—who kind of knew what it felt like to take a knock on the chin every once in a while, and still pick yourself up.

Among some same-sex couples, the match did not arise as a function of the birth parents' preference for, or even openness to, placing their child with a same-sex couple. Rather, the placement came about because of a match between the characteristics of the child being placed (e.g., of color, drug exposed) and the characteristics that the prospective adoptive parents were open to considering. This was particularly the case among same-sex couples who lived in the South and Midwest, who frequently alluded to racialized tensions in their communities and a dearth of heterosexual couples who were open to adopting a child of color. Mariette, a white lesbian physical therapist in a Midwestern suburb, for example, noted that her son's birth mother was limited to only "two couples who would accept multiracial children, [including us]. If we had not had that box checked, we would not have been considered." Jamie, a white gay communications manager in a midsized Southern city, said that his son's birth mother had reportedly chosen him and his partner in part because "with her being African American and the father being Caucasian, she needed potential adoptive parents that were open to a child that is a different ethnicity. That slimmed the choices down in the South as to people that would be open to that." Tiffany, an accounts manager in a large city in the South, said, about the birth mother: "She was given a stack of profile books of people that were willing to accept a biracial child and [chose us] from there. She really liked our profile." Mary, a white lesbian TV production studio manager in a midsized metro area of the South, recounted how their openness to a child of color ultimately led to them matching with a birth mother who was not actually looking to place her child with a same-sex couple:

> She called the agency when she gave birth: "I'm ready to sign the paperwork." Well, they had no families available. The agency mainly places white, you know, Caucasian babies, and they only deal with 10 or 12 families at a time, so that they didn't have a place for her. So the agency called our social worker and said, "Do you know anybody who would want this baby?" And she was like, "Oh my God, yes I do." So the agency social worker went over there to talk to her about us. And in the beginning, she was a little hesitant about us being a same-sex couple, but the more that she thought about it and even at the end of the conversation she said, "You know what? That's kind of neat. My baby is going to have two mothers. You know, what more could I ever give her than two mothers?" Then after she met us . . . you could tell that she totally bought into it.

Likewise, Russell, a white gay policy analyst in a large city on the East Coast, noted that his son's birth mother was not initially looking for same-sex couples. He reflected that perhaps their agency's strategy of simply putting their profile in the pile of those to peruse served them better than first asking the birth mother if she wished to consider a same-sex couple:

> I think she was actually—not thinking of a gay couple. . . . She looked at us and liked us and then decided to pick us. But I kind of get the sense that she wasn't specifically looking at gay couples, and maybe if the agency had asked her, "Do you want to look at gay couples?" she might have said no. We're not quite sure.

The Nature and Timing of the "Match"

The timing of the "match" between birth parents and adoptive parents varied considerably across families. Some families were chosen by birth parents or birth mothers during the second or third trimester, enabling the families to get to know each other prior to the birth.

In other cases, birth parents made an adoption plan late in their pregnancy, and there was only one or two meetings between the birth parents and adoptive parents prior to the actual birth and placement. Finally, in some cases, birth parents waited until they had given birth to connect with an adoption agency, and thus, in some cases, parents had limited time—for example, 24 to 48 hours—to make a decision about whether they would accept a particular placement.

An example of a family that had an extensive "getting to know you" period was Roy and Dante, a white sales manager and African American vice president of operations, respectively. The couple lived in a large West Coast city and matched with their son's birth mother, Liza—who lived in another state—during the second trimester. When Liza began to have contractions, they took a red-eye flight out to be at her side, along with a friend of hers. Recalled Dante, "We were sitting there together for 10 hours before Liza had her baby so—it was a very natural response for me to just get up and be the person that held her hand while she pushed." After the birth, they stayed at a hotel in a room with their baby, whom they named Ethan, with Liza and her friend, Marisol, right down the hall. They then flew back to their home state—all of them: the two men, Ethan, Liza, and Marisol, so that they could "do all the relinquishment and counseling" in their home state—as opposed to the state where Ethan was born, which did not allow two men to jointly adopt a child.

The trust and rapport that Roy and Dante had built with Liza during the pregnancy was beneficial to their relationship. It allowed them to relax into the unknown—but also remain cautiously optimistic that Liza would indeed place her baby with them. It also enabled them to offer the option of Liza spending time with them in their home state with minimal anxiety. Indeed, the couple was hopeful that spending some additional days with Liza after the birth would allow them to further develop their relationship; they did not believe that it would not lead to "unhealthy interactions or expectations," as some family members had hypothesized. Ultimately, Liza and her friend, Marisol—who didn't stay with them "but in a hotel across town for 4 or 5 days"—had a "wonderful time" visiting their city; indeed, Dante "took them shopping and was the consummate host" whereas Roy spent more time at home with baby Ethan. Ultimately,

> on the last day that they were here we asked them—I mean we felt a little weird; we didn't know whether it was appropriate or not, but we asked them if they wanted to come to the house, and they did. And so they came over and I was very nervous about it, but it ended up being a really really phenomenal, wonderful evening. By the time they left, it was like family had been there.

About Liza, Dante said thoughtfully:

She is just a ... really sweet genuine person ... very easy to talk to, more of one-on-one person than she is a group person. She's very shy and—she just kind of reminds me of a family member that I have, like a cousin, that I haven't seen in a long time and I went to visit and got to spend some time with—but, so, we really liked her.

A number of other couples also described being contacted by birth mothers early on in the pregnancy. Lena, an operations manager, and Thomas, a financial planner, were a white heterosexual couple living in a midsized Northeastern city who matched with their son's birth mother, Mandy, during the second trimester. This allowed a certain intimacy to develop over the months preceding the birth. Lena recalled: "Mandy said, 'I was actually thinking of this more as a surrogacy. That's why I wanted to find parents early on.'" In turn, Lena, Thomas, and Mandy all attended prenatal visits together, and Lena and Thomas came to the hospital soon after the birth and stayed overnight in a separate room. Although matching early on in the pregnancy meant that there was a longer period of uncertainty about whether or not the expectant mother would actually place the child with them, some adoptive parents, like Lena, said that they resisted allowing this possibility to interfere with their process of bonding with the expectant mother and/or their hopefulness about the possibility of parenthood. According to Lena, Thomas "was more cautious and like, 'honey, don't get ...' and I'm like, 'I know!' Like, the night when Mandy chose us, my mother started buying little clothes, and Thomas is like, 'She could change her mind,' and I'm like, 'I know, but just let me be happy.' I have to do this either 100% or not at all. I can't just be so cautious about it."

Adam, a biracial (African American/white) marketing director, and Will, a white accountant, were a gay couple in a midsized West Coast city who matched with their son Isaac's birth mother, Julie,

when she was just 8 weeks along. So it was very soon. For her, it was just an accidental pregnancy and her boyfriend had wanted her to have an abortion, and she didn't want to do that but she couldn't afford to raise her child herself, so she chose open adoption for that reason.

Even though the agency "wanted us to be very careful because it was so early in the process; it's very risk[y] to [match] so early because they can change their minds," Adam and Will did begin to talk to Julie regularly on the phone, "and then maybe a month a two after talking to her we ... had lunch with her and things went well from there." It was not until Julie was "in her sixth or fifth month that we did the official match [meeting], but we considered ourselves matched long before that, so we knew her very, very well before we actually did the paperwork. We pretty much spoke, text[ed], or email[ed] every day."

Even when birth parents and adoptive parents matched just a few weeks before the birth, this was often enough time to communicate regularly and feel that a solid relationship foundation had been built. Daniela, a white store owner, and Heather, a white bookkeeper, lived in a midsized city in the South and met their daughter Stella's birth mother, Joy, only a few weeks before the birth. However, they had spent a great deal of time during that period "getting to know each other more intimately," said Daniela, "to the point where Heather remarked how wonderful it was and how much she felt like Joy was a friend to us."

Sometimes, as with couples who had a more extensive rapport-building period, those who matched during the tail end of the third trimester had to overcome their initial cautiousness—which had been conditioned after several failed matches and/or suspected scams—before they could fully warm up to an expectant mother. Darren, a white gay computer programmer in a large West Coast city, recalled how he and his partner, Benji, were contacted by their daughter's teenage birth mother, Emmy, a week before she gave birth: "[When we first spoke to her], we were, I think, a little detached. I mean, there was a certain sort of healthy distance that we had created in this whole process, because of some experience with scammers—you know, when someone would pretend to be pregnant, for the attention." After talking briefly to her, the couple found Emmy to be "just amazingly trusting and open" and they relaxed into the process of learning more about the woman who would become their child's birth mother. Rob, the Latino administrative assistant whose story opened the chapter, shared that he had approached the initial meeting with his son's birth mother, Alena, with mild caution, in that "we had had a couple of meeting[s] before with moms-to-be, and they hadn't all gone so great." However, Rob found Alena to be "nice, and forthcoming, and very friendly—very open about why she was making this decision and why she picked us. We just felt very comfortable once we met her."

In several cases, matches occurred very suddenly. In such cases, birth parents typically did not make an official adoption plan until they got to the hospital and couples therefore had little time to make a decision about the potential placement. They typically received a phone call from their agency (after the birth mother selected them or after the agency selected the couple on the birth mother's behalf) and had a matter of hours to decide whether they would accept the placement. Holly, a white lesbian civil engineer in a large Midwestern city, recalled that their social worker "called . . . and said the birth mom had picked us when the baby was a day old, and as soon as we could get all the paperwork ready, we could go and pick him up." Stated Christy, a white lesbian nonprofit director in a midsized Northeastern city:

We found out [we were picked] an hour after she was born. The birth mom didn't tell anyone in her family she was pregnant. She walked in, delivered a week overdue, and then said, 'I don't—I don't want to pick. . . . I just want to put the baby up for adoption.' We had 24 hours to get there.

Cal, a white heterosexual IT director in a small city in the Northeast, recalled his experience of one of these "hospital calls":

It was very short notice. We were assuming that we would . . . match and meet the birth mother and have . . . even a month to be prepared. But that's not how it happened. We got the call and had to decide within a few hours if we wanted to move forward with it and then the next day drove out to meet the birth parents and basically had Morgan [our daughter] the day after that. It went by really quick! I guess in some ways it was probably better that way because we didn't have time to think about it; it just all of a sudden happened and then we had her. [Meeting them] was awkward, but not as awkward as I thought it would be. The fact that we hit it off with them, and they're very nice people, and we got along, made it much easier.

Shoshanna, Cal's wife, gave a more elaborate description of their first meeting and what made it special—but also awkward:

We met them and—actually it was definitely really awkward at first, but . . . we met at a casual restaurant and once we got talking it was really good. I felt like we connected and they asked us a lot of questions and we asked them questions and it seemed apparent to me that they wanted the best home possible for Morgan. And what the best home meant for *them* was people who shared some of their beliefs and had the kind of outlook that would be good for raising a child. So at the end it was great, but at first it was so—it feels so strange because I mean, really, we are there because we want to grow our family. We want a baby to raise and they are there because they are hoping to find a home for their baby. But you feel so—we felt anxious, they felt anxious, and you somehow feel greedy because, it is like, we want that baby. You know, you look at these people and we think, "God, what could we do to help you keep your baby?" in a way. It's like . . . adoption is very complicated.

Indeed, parents experienced a whole gamut of emotions during these initial, and sudden, meetings with birth parents. Brian, a white heterosexual dentist in a large Northeast city, recalled meeting his daughter's birth mother the day she gave birth. Comparing it to jitters before a first date that ultimately went well, he said: "At first I thought it was going to be a little bit frightening, but—it was sort of equally scary on both sides. We were 10 seconds into this relationship and I think everybody was relieved; she was very calm, and she seems great."

"The First 24 Hours": The Birth and the Immediate Aftermath

Before adoption, there is birth—an intensely emotional and uniquely personal event. In many cases, adoptive parents were present for the actual birth—often in the company of the birth mother's extended family, particularly when she was a teenager and still living at home. Paul, a white gay principal in a small Southern city, recalled how both sets of extended family members—their own and their daughter Louisa's birth mother, Nina—had congregated at the hospital during Louisa's birth:

> The day that Louisa was born, Greg and I were actually in the delivery room.... We were right there watching the whole thing. Our parents were all in the very next room with a bunch of Nina's friends and her parents' friends and everything. Everybody was just hanging out the whole time.... The nurses treated all of us wonderfully.... No questions asked. I'm sure that's not a scene they see every day... a teenage girl [placing her baby with] two dads.

In a few cases, sharing the birthing space with birth mothers' parents and extended family was awkward. Insomuch as they were therefore not yet legally the parents (i.e., birth parents do not sign paperwork relinquishing their parental rights until after the birth occurs—and sometimes not for several days afterward, possibly longer[†]), figuring out their roles and boundaries—as well as how to relate to the birth mother's family—was sometimes tricky. Mariette, a white lesbian physical therapist in the suburban Midwest, shared how she had initially felt somewhat uncomfortable in the presence of the mother of her son's birth mother. Didi, the birth mother, had a contentious relationship with her mother, who was present for the birth. Three months postadoption, Mariette shared:

> The only time her mother was close to her was when Jacob [child] was there and they gave him to her, and ... her mom was standing there saying, you know,

---

[†] Relinquishment of parental rights typically refers to voluntarily giving up parental rights. Sometimes, parental rights are terminated involuntarily (e.g., as in the case of severe and/or chronic abuse or neglect). The exact grounds for parental rights termination vary from state to state. Termination of parental rights ends the legal parent–child relationship. The time period within which the biological parent can revoke their consent after signing the relinquishment paperwork is generally fairly short, usually 48 to 72 hours after birth, although in some states it is longer (e.g., 30 days).

"This is your time, they'll have a chance." ... I said to Jenny [partner], "It makes me so sad. I felt like I'm as much Didi's mom as I am Jacob's mom. ..." And there was a period of time then when I stopped feeling uncomfortable; I got the feeling that Didi was more supported by us being there. And so I stopped feeling like kind of the second fiddle.

The incredibly intimate and emotional event of childbirth, coupled with the impression of birth mothers' own parents or families as emotionally absent or neglectful, created the perfect storm for protective feelings toward birth mothers. Lucas, a Latino heterosexual lawyer living in a Southern suburb, stated: "I wanted to adopt her, practically [*sigh*]. ... I really wanted to hug her. ... She's been ... emotionally neglected a lot of her life."

In several cases, adoptive parents were the recipients of hostility from birth mothers' parents and extended family, in part because these family members believed that the birth mother was making a mistake by considering adoption and that she should "keep the child." In turn, they saw the adoptive parents as unwelcome intruders and direct threats. These clashing perspectives had the potential to force a confrontation. Leo, a gay Latino speech therapist in a Northeast suburb, shared that his daughter's birth mother, Leandra, had invited him and his partner, Javier, to be in the room during the birth, but then they encountered pushback from Leandra's mother. Leo recalled that when Leandra's mother "started acting out," he

> said to her then and there, "Listen, we made this ... emotional contract with your daughter, and we're going to take our lead from her. If she doesn't want us in the room, we won't be in the room. If she wants us to be here, we're going to be here." Her mom kicked Leandra out of the house ... because she finally gave the baby up.

In contrast, several parents noted that members of the birth mother's family were explicitly supportive and appreciative. This was particularly the case in situations where the birth mother was a teenager and extended family members felt that she was too young to parent. In such cases, the adoptive family members were viewed as welcome agents of support as opposed to disruptive forces to the family system. Roger, a white gay marketing director in an East Coast suburb, recalled how he met his son's birth mother's mother at the hospital soon after the birth, and she told them, " 'I fully support [my daughter's] decision ... and I think it is the right decision.' Then she came over and gave us both a hug. That was great—it was really nice." This type of validation from birth parents' own parents was experienced as a "blessing" by adoptive parents—and one that carried added impact when the adoptive parents were lesbian or gay, and thus alert to the potential for homophobic bias from extended family members.

The immediate aftermath of the birth was sometimes stressful, as adoptive parents waited for birth parents to sign the legal paperwork relinquishing their rights as parents and/or for the designated time period within which birth parents can change their mind to be over.[‡] In most cases, birth parents signed the relinquishment papers at the hospital, often in the presence of the adoptive parents. This experience was often emotional and bittersweet: a mix of sadness (especially for the birth parents), joy, and relief. Many of these adoptive parents had already had one potential placement fall through: They had matched with expectant parents who ultimately changed their mind and decided not to place the child. In turn, participants were sometimes vigilant and "on edge" during the hours and/or days following the birth. Phil, a white gay graduate student in a midsized Southern city, who, with his partner, Eddie, had matched with the birth parents during the pregnancy, shared:

> [During the pregnancy], we probably had a phone call once a week—we were staying in really good contact with them and developing a really wonderful relationship. That was great, and at the same time, we would always catch ourselves thinking, "Gosh, this is going to make it even harder if it falls through!" First time around, we didn't really get to know them at all. This time, we were really becoming friends with them. So, if they decided in the end either legitimately or for reasons I didn't understand to not follow through with it, it was going to be even harder.... By the time that we got to the delivery—at that point we were so nervous, but she did fine, and we were there, and to watch the birth happen was just completely incredible and overwhelming and emotional. But then again, knowing that she still had 48 hours to change her mind—and we couldn't begrudge them, really, if they did change their mind at that point, you know? And now that we had told everyone about it, it was going to be so hard to go back and tell everyone that it wasn't happening.... We were very nervous, excited—every single emotion. But the birth mother never wavered; the birth father never wavered. There was nothing that was a red flag at all, but still the possibility was really nerve-racking for both of us.

Phil's description of the emotional aftermath of the birth was typical of the parents I interviewed. They wanted to trust the process, the relationship, and the expectant parents—and at the same time, they were anxious amid prior experiences of coming to the hospital for the birth and leaving without a baby.

[‡] The specific amount of time that birth parents have to change their mind (i.e., revoke consent to have their parental rights terminated) varies from state to state.

Rob, the Latino administrative assistant whose story opened this chapter, recalled similar "uneasy feelings" up until the point when his son's birth mother signed the paperwork:

> We had been matched with one other birth mom before, and she changed her mind. It was a pretty nasty, prickly experience. So having gone through that . . . we were apprehensive about whether or not it was going to happen, whether or not she would change her mind too. I didn't want to get attached.

Somewhat like parents who experience pregnancy loss, these parents found themselves reeling from failed matches, not wanting to be caught off guard by an expectant mother's decision to parent. In turn, these failed matches cast a shadow of anxiety over their current potential placement.

Despite this sense of anxiety, and the ongoing reality—up until the actual placement—that an expectant mother could change her mind, some adoptive parents were able to maintain a sense of empathy toward the birth mother and continued to interact with her even amid evidence that she might be wavering in her decision to place her child. Monica, a white heterosexual graphic designer in a midsized West Coast city, said:

> Meeting her and her family went really well. There were a few little teeny roadblocks or bumps with religion. But that was really it—I mean, it was awkward in that situation because everybody feels like they're on display, and it's awkward, but I think everybody handled it really well. . . . When we got back and texted her and didn't get a response I think I immediately felt a little bit concerned. So the next day I texted her, like, "I understand if you're having second thoughts—and just let me know where you're at" and she texted back that yeah, that was the case. . . . So we just felt horrible—it was devastating. . . . We thought it was all over but [we continued to] stay in touch. And then . . . we got a call from her, and she was like, "Are you still interested?" and we were like, "Yes!" . . . and then we had a great talk and I think she felt a lot better about the situation.

Circumstances of Placement: "She Was in a Really Bad Place in Her Life"

Most couples knew something about the circumstances surrounding their child's placement—that is, why, in the case of private domestic adoptions, birth parents had chosen to place their child for adoption. Drug abuse, mental health issues, financial challenges, unemployment, housing problems, young age, lack of a committed relationship between the birth parents, and lack of emotional preparation for parenthood were frequently cited reasons for the decision to place a child for adoption. Sometimes, domestic violence (allegedly perpetrated by the birth father against the birth mother), incest, rape, and homelessness were named as reasons for placement. A desire to reach higher educational goals was also cited by several parents. Carly, a white heterosexual professor in a large Northeastern city, said: "She came up with an adoption plan because she wanted to go back to school. . . . She'd like to be a physician but she hasn't even been able to get through college yet because she's been a single mom."

Indeed, in some cases, birth mothers were already parenting one or more children, and their emotional and financial resources were stretched very thin, such that they "just couldn't afford another mouth to feed." Max, a white heterosexual communications manager living in a large Northeastern city, explained, about his son's birth parents, "They're having a tough time financially. When we met them she was living in the shelter, and they both have other children. . . . They didn't think it was fair to raise this child, and they didn't want to raise this child in poverty." Similarly, Mary, a white lesbian production manager in a medium-sized city in the South, explained:

> They had [several children] already. She says, "Both my husband and I have a ninth-grade education. He does manual labor; I'm a stay-at-home mom." She says, "I'm an only child, but he comes from a [large family]. And they just continually have more and more children, more and more children. And those children . . . they all wear second-hand clothes. They're never going to have any sort of education. . . . I want more for my kids."

In some cases, participants described their children's birth mothers as dealing with a variety of other family obligation, beyond childrearing—for example, caring for ailing or infirm parents or other relatives. Barry, a white gay teacher in an East Coast suburb, stated, about his son's birth mother: "She is 23 . . . and she was trying to take care of her elderly relative . . . and financially she couldn't take care of the child. And she just wanted to make a decision to actually do something good. . . . It's what she needed to do." Byron, a white gay graduate student in a large Midwestern city, similarly said: "She's really young, and . . . she lives with her mom and her grandmother and her mom is disabled. She also has [one child]. I think she just thought it would be too much. So, she had to do what was best for him."

This sentiment—that the birth parents did what they needed to do and that placing the child was the right decision for everybody involved—was threaded throughout the narratives of these new adoptive parents. Eddie, a white gay physical therapist in a medium-sized Southern city, asserted: "They said that they weren't economically or emotionally stable enough to take care of the child. They realize that, and it's wise on their part that they were able to realize that." Rob, the Latino administrative assistant, said, "She didn't feel capable of raising him at this point. And this just wasn't a good situation for her or the baby. So she decided to place him for adoption; having done it before, she knew it was a good choice." This assessment—that birth parents realized they could not raise the child and subsequently decided to place the child—was in some cases accompanied by the assertion that the birth parents made not only the right choice but also a very brave and courageous choice. Women in particular tended to convey this sentiment regarding the birth parents' decision. Stated Jenny, a white lesbian manager at a medical supply company in a Midwestern suburb, about her son's birth mother:

> Oh gosh, [I have] just admiration [for her]. She's courageous; she's a bright young woman. You know, she took the initiative [to acknowledge] her mistakes [with me]. She has done some things that are not, um, for the best, but she—it's kind of ironic, but we think she's a great mom [to her other children].

Shoshanna, a white heterosexual project manager in a small city in the Northeast, shared:

> I really respect them. They are young, early 20s. And when they had Morgan, they were like, "Oh my god, we are not in a place where we can raise a child together." Financially, maturity wise. When they said, "We just don't think we are mature enough to raise her," I'm like, "Oh my God; that is such a mature thing!"—to recognize that and to look and go, "Oh my God, we are not fit to be parents right now; we are still growing ourselves." So yeah, I completely respect them.

It is notable that the sometimes vast socioeconomic differences between adoptive parents and birth parents were typically acknowledged only in passing as a reason for the placement, and as a matter of fact (as in "They couldn't afford to raise a child"). In some cases, such accounts were followed by statements indicating recognition of the birth parents' reliance on the money that they were receiving through the adoption agency. A typical response was provided by this gay father:

> Neither of them had jobs at the time. . . . He had a felony conviction that has made it very difficult for him to find a job. They're young—early 20s . . . and

emotionally young and immature too. They just don't have it together, and they somehow know that it's going to take them a long time to get it together—longer than they have to pull it together to have to raise a child, you know? . . . They would have been homeless if it wasn't for the adoption agency giving them money. So even if they decided to keep the child, the adoption agency would have had to cut them off financially, which would have made them homeless. They couldn't afford to. . . . They always talked about that they had bigger goals and dreams for their life that having a baby would have prevented, and they also knew that they had bigger better dreams for their child than they would have been able to provide for. They wanted opportunities that they wouldn't have been able to afford her. . . . This was their act of responsibility and selflessness. During the [entire process], I don't think they ever wavered [in] their decision that this was the right thing for the baby.

Thus, some parents acknowledged the birth parents' dependence on the financial support they were receiving from the adoption agency (and, indirectly, from them) and in some cases explicitly identified these funds as the singular barrier to homelessness ("she would be on the street if it were not for the added help from the agency"). Yet it was rare that these parents articulated any further thoughts or feelings about the socioeconomic divide or discrepancy between themselves and the birth parents. Only a few parents described ambivalence or discomfort surrounding the difference in their financial circumstances—and the uncomfortable but indisputable reality that this difference privileged them. Bob, a white heterosexual financial manager in a Northeast suburb, said:

Financially she did not have any way of raising another baby. She already has one baby. At the time, she did not have a job, she was on welfare, she was not with the birth father anymore, and she was struggling just to get by. It's sad; and that's why it was very awkward initially to see her, because—not that we're wealthy or rich or anything, but we are definitely better off than her, and it almost felt like we were buying her baby type of thing, you know? So it was pretty awkward initially. But she seems to be doing better now—she does have a job.

"Like an after-school special"; "It's a dream situation": The (almost) mythical college student (or young adult emotionally unprepared for parenthood). In a few cases, participants described the placements as occurring simply because of the birth mother's lack of emotional preparation for parenting—or lack of interest in parenthood. That is, these parents emphasized that the birth mother did not have any mental health, substance use, or housing issues, and ultimately "was fine . . . except for not wanting to parent." Holly, a white lesbian civil engineer in a large Midwestern city, stated:

I mean, it was truly like an after-school special how this whole thing worked out. I mean, she didn't do any drugs, she didn't drink during her pregnancy, she didn't smoke.... She said that she just wasn't in a place in her life where she could care for a child the way she wanted to.

Travis, a white gay technical writer in a large West Coast city, exclaimed: "It was really an amazing situation. She had good prenatal care. She doesn't drink and doesn't smoke; [there's] no drug use."

Heather, a white lesbian bookkeeper in a midsized city in the South, asserted that her daughter Stella's birth mother was "totally uncharacteristic" of what her agency and her own research had prepared her to expect of a pregnant woman considering adoption. Heather recounted that both the birth mother, Joy, and the birth father, Danny, were "very educated. For Joy, growing up, knowing a gay person was not a threat. She was introduced to a lot of diversity, so she thought that having two moms would be wonderful, and that Stella would be exposed to a lot of diversity, and that was very exciting for her." Heather also added that Joy was

> a professional; she has got a really good job, has really good insurance, and she's such a self-aware person so she immediately started taking care of herself physically.... It's scary how much this is a dream situation.... We were prepared to have a 16-year-old birth mom.... She didn't smoke, didn't drink, didn't do any drugs, and in turn, took really good care of herself. She thought, "This is a person I have inside of me." She's a very self-aware person.

Byron, a white gay graduate student in a large Midwestern city, also described a "dream situation" that he didn't believe at first: That is, the birth mother's profile had said "no drugs and no alcohol," which gave him and his partner pause: "that's not typical." But then,

> after meeting her, I would say that I totally believe that. She just seemed incredibly responsible in terms of like . . . taking care of one child already, going to school. She didn't seem like someone who would do drugs on a regular basis. She just seemed pretty straight-laced, I guess.

Thus, when birth parents seemed to deviate from the script that parents had been taught to prepare for, participants were surprised—and pleased. Significantly, their narratives underscore the reality that they viewed as optimal and preferred, a placement situation that was low risk from their perspective—and, in turn, not necessarily one in which the birth mother was in the middle of a major crisis that had the potential to harm her own and thus her child's health.

In this way, in private adoption, becoming parents to the healthiest child possible is often a central priority—rather than a desire to alleviate an expectant parent's crisis or to become parents to a child who is highly vulnerable and/or may need special care or services.

Foster-to-adopt placements. Among the 21 families whom I interviewed who adopted via the foster care system, the circumstances surrounding placement were inevitably narrated somewhat differently. Parents outlined not why birth parents chose to make an adoption plan but why the children ended up in the foster care system, available for adoption. Despite this marked difference in choicefulness, circumstances surrounding placement in the foster care system were similar in some ways to the reasons birth parents chose to place their children: Drug use, mental health issues, and financial instability all featured prominently. These data echo broader trends in the United States in regard to why children end up in state care,[3] wherein children were typically removed from their birth parents' care due to the neglect or abuse that unfolded as a result of substance abuse, mental illness, or financial issues and homelessness.

Eva, a Latina lesbian communications professor who resided in a Northeastern suburb, shared, about her son, "He was removed partly for the neglect issue.... [Initially] the birth mom was supposed to get treatment and get certain things in order that never happened and so her rights were terminated." Joe, a white gay operations manager in a large West Coast city, shared that his son was "pulled out of the home [because of] chronic neglect. She just didn't know how or couldn't take care of them. There were drugs [and] they were on the borderline of homelessness, living in disgusting filth." Michael, a white heterosexual philosophy professor in a midsized city in the Northeast, explained that his daughter was removed from her birth mother's care because the Department of Social Services (DSS)[§] was "monitoring the household, because birth mom had had a previous child taken from her, and she just wasn't—there were drugs in the house, there was abuse in the house, and in the middle of winter she wasn't dressed appropriately and also wasn't being fed appropriately."

Most parents who adopted via foster care noted that their child's birth family already had prior involvement with their state's Department of Social Services at the time that the child was removed. In some cases, other children—their child's siblings—had already been removed from the home. Greta, a white lesbian small business owner living in a Northeast suburb, said: "The parents were ... homeless, and [staying] with a relative.... The family was on DSS's radar, [in part because] the mother had several previous children who were taken from the home.

[§] Every state has some version of DSS; for example, Child Protective Services (CPS), Department of Children and Families (DCF), Department of Child and Youth Services (DCYS), or simply Social Services.

So [neglect] was ultimately the reason [child was removed]." Annie, a white heterosexual school administrator in the suburban Northeast, who was placed with a young boy named Grayson, said, about the birth mother:

> She had a first child; she kept the first child. They had two more children, put those up for adoption, had Grayson and sometime [during her pregnancy] she started having real big issues. The issues started before Grayson's birth but [the Department of Social Services] didn't seem to do too much. And then his sister would go begging around for food . . . and then they found that [the family's house] didn't even have electricity or running water . . . and [DSS] spent [years] trying to remove these kids. If the world was perfect, Grayson would have never lived with them, but it doesn't work that way.

In a few cases, children were removed at birth because the birth mother tested positive for drugs and the children were born addicted to drugs. Leigh, a white heterosexual woman who was the assistant director of a museum in a small Northeastern city, explained, "His mom was a heroin addict. He was born testing positive for heroin. So he spent like a month in the hospital detoxing and then went to his foster home."

"It's Like a Dance": Navigating Postplacement Contact and Boundaries

The metaphor of a dance was often invoked by parents to describe the often uncertain and sometimes awkward "getting to know you" period following the birth and subsequent adoptive placement. This "dance" varied in terms of its ease, reciprocity, predictability, and stability. Indeed, adoptive parents described a complex process of anticipating, responding to, and in some cases actively regulating the level of closeness versus distance between themselves and the birth parents.[4]

Parents' descriptions of initial contact tended to follow several general patterns. Specifically, when they were interviewed 3 to 4 months after adoptive placement, many adoptive parents described a pattern of fairly regular communication immediately after the birth that had tapered off in the past month or so. Barry, a white gay teacher in an East Coast suburb, stated that the contract** that they had with Beth, his son's birth mother, was for "letters and pictures four times

---

** A written contractual agreement between birth and adoptive families can specify the type and frequency of the contact or communication and can provide a means for the agreement to be legally enforced. About 28 states and the District of Columbia currently have statutes that allow written and enforceable agreements (Child Welfare Information Gateway, 2014).

a year," via the agency, and one in-person meeting per year at their adoption agency's annual event for adoptive and birth families. So far, according to Barry:

> we've exchanged emails a few times. . . . It's sort of tapered off a bit. In the last two emails she would take a little bit longer to respond and when she did she was very nice, but [they were] brief responses and then she'd say "Well, I've got to run."

Parents often described the current level of contact as mutually agreed upon and as evolving naturally. Adam, a biracial marketing director in a midsized metro area on the West Coast, shared:

> We text, we email. . . . When I take pictures I send it to Julie [birth mother] along with everyone else we care about. . . . We talked to her earlier this week. But at this point we only talk about every 2 or 3 weeks, and that's really her because once the baby was born, she actually moved to [state]. And she's kind of starting her life over. I don't know if she's pulling back deliberately and guarding her own emotions or if she's just starting her own life, but she's busy. . . . So, we certainly don't communicate every day, but she said from the beginning that she wouldn't be contacting us every day like before Isaac was born. We told her she's welcome to visit, because we really honestly do care about her and we actually feel kind of parental towards her as well. Financially, she's just not in a place where she can just do that [yet]. . . . But because she can Skype with us and she gets pictures from us all the time just informally, I think she is very happy.

Here, Adam wonders whether the tapering of contact is a reflection of "deliberate" efforts on the part of the birth mother to "guard her . . . emotions" or whether the reduced communication is a reflection of the fact that she is just "busy." Regardless of the reason, Adam voices a desire for the birth mother to know that she is cared for and "welcome to visit."

Many parents who described a recent reduction in contact were on alert to any indication that the birth mother felt left out or abandoned. Gay men in particular shared their sensitivity to such dynamics, wishing to respect the birth mother's boundaries but also wanting to ensure that they were meeting their obligations. As Will, a white gay accountant in a midsized West Coast city—and Adam's partner—stated:

> [We are sensitive to the possibility of] something to be misunderstood, for feelings to get hurt. I mean, the more we know each other the more chances there are of that happening. So we are very careful. . . . If we say we are going to

do something, or if we say we were going to call at a certain time, we keep our word. And [we] keep our outputs and advice to a bare minimum and just let her talk and let her listen and let her get to learn who we are, get to know each other, and it's worked pretty well! . . . We Skype [and] she asks us relationship advice, questions, and she kind of sees us as her big brothers. We were Skyping with her yesterday and she started crying because she realized that Isaac was in such a good place and she could see Isaac from Skype. . . . When we say goodbye, she says "I love you" and we'll say "I love you" back and she's really like a sister to us, or a niece or something like that. We feel very close to Julie.

Daniela, a white lesbian store owner in a small city in the South, shared the challenge of the "dance" between trying to communicate respect for the birth mother's space and not staying so distant that she felt rejected or uncared for. Daniela had wondered, during the months after the birth, whether their daughter's birth mother, Joy, might perhaps be willing to consider more contact than they had initially discussed—but Daniela did not want to intrude on Joy's space:

At our match meeting . . . she said she only really wanted to hear from us once a year or twice a year on the baby's birthday. Those were the two times she really wanted to hear from us. . . . But [I wonder] if things have changed in terms of how much contact she wants with us? And so I felt bad asking her some of that because it's only been 3 months since the child was born and we're trying to give her space . . . but at the same time I don't want to make her feel left out. So it's all fine but it's definitely still something that takes away conscious thinking, you know, because I want it to be a relationship that works.

In several cases, parents felt relatively certain that their initial level of contact had grown less frequent and intimate because of the birth mother's difficulty adjusting to the loss and her tendency to "pull back" amid a normative grief reaction. These parents expressed sorrow regarding the depth of their children's birth mothers' grieving but were uncertain of whether and how to reach out or offer support. They struggled to balance their joy at being new parents with the sobering awareness that their child's birth mother—and in some cases, birth father—was experiencing a profound loss. Phil, a white graduate student in a midsized metropolitan area of the South, shared:

Even now, talking about it, I try not to get emotional about it. [Early on], it was exciting but [at the same time], I think that we felt their loss, you know? It was hard to be ecstatic over the circumstances that led to this child having an adoptive family as opposed to being able to be with her birth family.

Often their sensitivity to the birth mother's feelings led parents to adopt a stance of extreme carefulness with respect to reaching out to her. They wanted her to feel appreciated and cared for—not abandoned—but also did not want to interrupt her grieving or intrude on her privacy. Damian, a white heterosexual software engineer who resided in a medium West Coast city, reflected that Facebook currently seemed like the ideal means of maintaining connection with his son's birth mother, Tracy, in that it enabled her to control the timing and nature of contact (e.g., passive viewing of pictures vs. active communication):

> I thought we would have a really close relationship with Tracy and it turns out to be a little less so. And I don't know if she's just going through some things—because I'm sure it's a very emotional time for her and she may need a little emotional removal from us.... I don't really know. But maybe it'll be off and on. We're connected through social media like Facebook so she can be a part of his life without actually being here or talking to us, at her own discretion. And we can be a part of her life; we can see what she's got going on by checking out her Facebook status and stuff like that.... It's like, "We're there to reach out to if you want to connect."

In a few cases, parents had reason to believe that their children's birth mothers had pulled back out of fear of overstepping the adoptive family's boundaries. Max, a white heterosexual communications manager in a large Northeast city, shared that he had initially been a bit perplexed by the drop-off in contact by his son's birth mother, Gloria—but ultimately determined that this was a function of her sensitivity to boundaries and her fear of alienating their family. Max said,

> We had great contact up until about a month ago. Gloria was calling Donna [wife], she was talking to her, and really wasn't invasive or anything like that. We really liked her phone calls; she was always calling, and then she sort of dropped off—she wasn't calling as much. We weren't sure if we should just pick up the phone and call her.

Max decided to call their adoption coordinator for advice and insight. The coordinator let him know that " 'Gloria's feeling that maybe she's calling us too much.' But we really didn't have that feeling at all, so hopefully we'll get that cleared up.... [I don't want her] to feel [like] she can't call." This situation highlights how, amid the emotional vulnerability and complexity of the "dance," and in the absence of direct and clear communication, actions or words—or lack thereof—may be (mis)interpreted in ways that have important consequences for the birth family–adoptive family relationship.

More rarely, contact had not dwindled but had remained relatively constant over the first few months. Bob, a white heterosexual financial manager in a Northeast suburb, shared that he had been told by his adoption agency that there is often a sharp reduction or total loss of contact with birth mothers fairly soon after the placement. In turn, Bob was prepared for this possibility—but expressed pleasure at the fact that it had not come to pass: "We've been emailing back and forth, corresponding and sending pictures and she seems very eager to get information about Serena [child], so you know, we have been in touch regularly as far as email goes." At the same time, Bob was aware that contact, and their relationship with Serena's birth mother, Thea, would

> naturally evolve or change . . . but I would hope that we continue to—we're still going to send pictures regularly and updates regularly. I think it's very important for Serena that she has contact with her birth mother as she gets older, so we hope that it does continue [even if] not at the level it is now.

In some cases, participants were enthusiastic about contact but, like Bob, acknowledged a sense of uncertainty regarding the future. Often, they shared an awareness of the financial, familial, or emotional challenges that might impede the birth mother's ability to remain in contact. In turn, parents were appropriately wary of assuming consistent and reliable contact and communication over the long term. Mariette, a white lesbian physical therapist in a Midwestern suburb, for example, noted that she and her partner, Jenny, were optimistic about their future contact with their son Jacob's birth mother, Didi: "She's been so positive about wanting to be involved, wanting this to be an open adoption, being glad it was us. We have every commitment to, you know, stay in touch with her if she's going to do that too." At the same time, Mariette was aware that "she's very fragile. I feel like she very well could fall off the radar."

In several cases, parents and birth parents had agreed to have a fair amount of contact after placement—but this contact had not materialized. Doug and Sam were a white psychologist and biracial (Asian/white) human resources director, respectively, who lived in a large West Coast city. Both men felt strongly about the benefits of open adoption, with Doug being among those participants who expressed, preadoption, that they were unlikely to agree to a match that did not hold the probability of true openness. Yet the couple had matched with a birth mother, Lara, whose living situation was unstable, and who was also struggling emotionally, both of which had prevented her, it initially seemed, from being able to make contact. Doug shared that, as of 4 months postplacement, they had not seen Lara, which he felt terribly about:

> We still haven't been able to see her since we all left the hospital together, which is horrible. But yeah. It's tough. It's definitely what I had feared would happen with our relationship and what I had hoped there was enough in place to

prevent.... She's right now having a lot of life transition. She's not at all stable right now and really kind of having a difficult time of her young adult, or newfound adulthood.... She definitely... wants to have contact and wants to see the baby but—the difficulty is she doesn't really have a way to get to [city] or even to get halfway. We don't certainly have any interest in throwing a 4-month-old in the car and driving for 10 hours.

Doug spoke with great compassion about the difficult circumstances that had brought Lara to her current place in life, noting that she had never had stable housing, that she grew up with various family members and on the streets, and that this type of upbringing "does not make good, caring, and safe adults." Doug also added that Lara currently had very few life skills and was working to put her life together but had the cards stacked against her: "She doesn't have much going for her. She's currently living somewhere in the state . . . and sometimes she has power and electricity, and sometimes she doesn't." Yet significantly, Doug also reflected upon Lara's personal strengths. For example, in his eyes, Lara currently had

a lot going on for her, but being able to see . . . her motherhood as a strength . . . her ability to carry a baby, her ability to deliver a healthy beautiful baby, her ability to find a family for that baby, her willingness to do all that—I think is a real source of strength for her. I think that's one of the places where she feels a great deal of confidence. I don't think it's this lingering sense of, "Oh my gosh, I really screwed up." I think it's really like, "Yeah, look at what I can do. I did this and I did it right."

Boundary Challenges

In some cases, parents narrated ways in which their children's birth parents—and typically birth mothers—had toed the line of what they viewed as comfortable or desirable boundaries. These parents often described a tension they experienced during these early months between expressing appreciation and communicating a welcoming stance while also drawing boundaries around their newly formed family. This process of responding sensitively while also establishing boundaries was complex and did not always unfold seamlessly.[5] Rick, a white gay nonprofit director in a large West Coast city, shared how, a few days after returning from the hospital, he received a call from their adoption social worker, Jane. Jane indicated that their son Jack's birth mother, Sara, was "was crying and depressed and upset and worried that she's never going to see Jack again." She was also reportedly worried that Rick and his partner, Marcus, were not "really committed to an open relationship." Jane suggested that it might be helpful if the couple could go visit Sara, to provide her with some reassurance and allow her to see Jack. Rick shared his initial reaction, and what came next:

> So we're like, "Oh, well, this wasn't exactly on the plan, but. . . ." We wanted to reassure Sara that we were committed to this openness. . . . [Jane felt] it would really be helpful to Sara . . . in her grieving process. Because Jane had said that . . . Sara was kind of in denial during the whole pregnancy that she would have any sort of emotional attachment to the baby, and Jane was trying to counsel her during the pregnancy, saying, "These are the feelings that you may feel, and . . . you can't pretend not to feel them." . . . So we were like, "Okay, we'll be happy to drive down and visit" . . . so we arrive and Sara is there to greet us and gives us big hugs and is happy to see us and is smiling and is all excited about Jack and we go inside and we play with Jack and . . . then he got fussy and she gave him back to us, and then he got happy so she took him again and he wet a diaper so she gave him back to us to change the diaper and then she held him again.

Later, Rick noted too that Sara had been "refer[ring] to herself as the mom. I think we'll refer to her as the birth mother to Jack, but I don't feel the need to correct her at this point . . . and Jack will figure that out too." Indeed, gay fathers were fairly consistent in their "cool" approach to boundary challenges or concerns. They tended to acknowledge some discomfort with a request or action by the birth mother—but in the same breath suggested that they did not feel the need to confront or contest the behavior. In this way, the unique gender dynamics that characterize two-dad, one-birth-mom relationships may have led to greater ease and less tension surrounding roles and boundaries, in that there was no real or perceived competition for the title of "mom."

Leo, a Latino gay speech therapist in a Northeastern suburb, shared how his daughter Elizabeth's birth mother, Leandra, had asked to see Elizabeth several weeks after they brought her home. "And we were both like, 'Oh my God, that's so fast!' And then I was like, 'You know what, [the termination of parental rights] is irrevocable; what's the freak=out about at this point?' So Leandra came to the house [and] we took pictures of the three of us." In this way, Leo ultimately concluded that it was not a big deal to give his daughter's birth mother what she seemed to want and need; it did not threaten his sense of entitlement or authenticity as a parent. It is also notable that Leo and his partner, Javier, had encountered several other situations during the initial weeks and months that they ultimately rolled with but that other families might have "freaked out" about. Specifically, the two men had discussed possible baby names with Leandra and accepted her influence when she voiced a dislike for several of them. Accepting influence is widely recognized as a characteristic of healthy relationships and coparenting specifically;[6] by listening to and accepting Leandra's feedback, they communicated to her that her perspective mattered, and that they were not interested in a power struggle around whose opinion mattered "most." In this same vein, Benji, a white gay dermatologist in a large West Coast city, described how his daughter Ryanne's birth mother, Emmy, had wanted to weigh in on her middle name—and, specifically, had wanted a traditional Spanish middle name for Ryanne. Benji shared how he and his partner, Darren, handled this—at first reluctant, but then accommodating:

> Emmy, at the hospital, asked us if we would give her the middle name that she had and we said we already had a middle name in mind . . . but it was the least we could do, and the name that she wanted was Isabella; she liked the name and so now Ryanne will be Ryanne Isabella.

This decision can be seen as a valuable means of explicitly honoring the birth mother and also recognizing that a child comes from two different places or has roots in two different families.[7]

In just a few cases did parents express feelings of frustration or irritation with the birth parents' level of desired contact early on and/or their method of asking for more contact than was happening. Lena, a white heterosexual operations manager in a midsized Northeast city, described how her son Joey's birth mother, Mandy, had made a request for more visits than initially planned, which elicited unexpected feelings of being put upon and pressured:

> We tried to let her initiate contact in the beginning because I didn't know how upset she was going to be . . . [and a week later] I emailed Mandy a bunch of pictures from then and then I think she waited a couple weeks and called me and said, "Hey, how's he doing?" and so I gave her an update of Joey and then she waited another month and called me. . . . And then she kind of hit a brick on me and said, "How about we have four visits instead of two visits a year?" This state is one of the only places that you can have a contract [and] we had in our contract twice a year visits . . . and she's like, "Well you know, he's going to change so much, so I'm thinking, how about four times a year. Would you be okay with that?" And I can't just say, "Yes, I'm going to be okay with four times a year" because how am I going to feel? I haven't even had one visit with her yet. So I said, "Mandy, let me talk to Thomas," and I kind of just skirted around the issue, and she said, "Okay, okay, I don't want to make you uncomfortable." She ended up talking to her social worker, I talked to my social worker, and they ended up talking, and what we decided was, we're willing to give Mandy a visit [soon] and then I said "Let's play it by ear. We'll keep our schedule to two a year,"

but I said I'm not committing to four a year; that's every 4 months. By the time I'm thinking of one and it goes by, we're thinking of another one. I said, "Maybe after I have one it'll be fine," but this first 3 months have been like—I mean, I'm kind of upset. I'm like, here I am, I just brought Joey home, I'm really enjoying my [time] off with him, and I get a call from the birth mother saying, "Hey, can I see him four times a year instead of two times a year?" He's just so fresh and new and fun for us and we're loving it and now I'm getting hit over the head with like more requests and it's like enough already.

Carly, a white heterosexual history professor in a large Northeastern city, shared similar feelings of wishing for more space and time to nest as a new family and for fewer immediate "obligations" to fulfill with regard to contact:

I really am glad that we can be in touch if we really need to, but I feel like if we were too in touch right now, it might make me feel like less of a parent in some way.... I don't know, maybe that's just a worry that wouldn't actually be the case. I feel like we're really, really Eve's parents—there's so no question about it—and we'll see what evolves over time in our relationship with her, but it is sort of nice to not have major obligations right now.

That the parents who described the greatest sensitivity and protectiveness around their familial boundaries were heterosexual women suggests that they may be the most likely to experience tension surrounding their maternal "role" in relation to the birth mother. Lesbian mothers must by definition navigate and negotiate the reality that they will be sharing the maternal role with their partners. In turn, the fact that another woman bears the child whom they will parent may not prompt the same level of anxiety and boundary maintenance as it did for some heterosexual women. Likewise, heterosexual men and gay men did not tend to experience or perceive the birth mother as threatening to their parental role insomuch as she did not occupy a parallel status (i.e., by virtue of gender). Birth fathers were rarely prominent figures in open adoptive family arrangements (see Chapter 9)—and so it was rare that heterosexual and gay fathers were faced with a similar situation: that is, a highly involved, same-gender birth parent.

Notably, a few parents—all heterosexual women—had initially been very concerned about potential boundary challenges but ultimately matched with birth mothers whose behavior allayed their fears. In turn, they came to a place of expressing greater openness to ongoing contact than they had preadoption. Donna, a white heterosexual nonprofit manager in a large Northeastern city, initially expressed significant concerns about openness, worrying that contact might interfere with their ability to bond with their child and/or cause confusion about who were the "real" parents. Postplacement, however, Donna expressed an openness to and appreciation for contact with the birth mother with whom they matched—although Donna was clear that (a) she would not have felt similarly about all birth parents, and (b) it was still very important for the birth mother to "respect" boundaries. Donna shared:

> We've talked a couple of times, and nothing's been established, it's just whatever we feel comfortable with.... She doesn't want to disturb us, and you know, I'm the Mommy and he's the Daddy, and she doesn't want to intrude on us and our family, and that kind of thing, [but] I would like him to grow up knowing her. I mean, we're pretty flexible. If it had been the first birth mother, we would say uh, absolutely not, I don't feel comfortable with it, because she... was stalking the birth father.... But with [birth mother] and [birth father], because they're such wonderful, wonderful people, and we both felt such a connection with them, we feel comfortable being flexible. I mean, they gave us a gift, and we consider them part of our extended family.

* * *

This chapter articulated the matching process and addressed the varied reasons that couples were reportedly chosen by birth parents, highlighting the specific and often unique reasons cited by sexual minority parents in particular. Inevitably, two-father and two-mother households were deprioritized by some birth parents—but in other cases, their shared gender and/or sexual minority status seemed to be regarded positively. Significantly, in narrating the reasons that birth parents were placing their children for adoption (or that children were removed from their birth parents), adoptive parents rarely acknowledged the economic privilege that separated them from the birth parents—despite its unavoidable reality and its potential to shape postplacement dynamics and relationships. The initial postplacement period was sometimes marked by awkwardness and, more rarely, tension—with gay fathers highlighting the greatest ease and heterosexual women the least.

As detailed in Chapter 10, it is important for individuals and couples embarking on open adoption to be prepared (e.g., by their agencies, therapists, and other professionals) that the postplacement phase represents a period of huge adjustment for everyone, as they seek to articulate their roles in relation to one another amid feelings of loss (for birth parents) and the establishment of parental entitlement (for adoptive parents). Emotions run high, feelings are easily hurt, and relationship patterns and expectations have not yet been firmly established. In turn, taking a deep breath, "checking" one's own insecurity and fears, and assuming the best possible intentions can go far in creating more space for ease, growth, and closeness in the relationship between adoptive families and birth families.

Notes

1. Broderick, 1993; Grotevant, 2009.
2. Goldberg, 2012.
3. U.S. Department of Health & Human Services, Administration for Children and Families, Children's Bureau, 2017.
4. Broderick, 1993; Grotevant, 2009.
5. Grotevant, 2009.
6. Walsh, 2015.
7. Personal communication, Sharon Roszia, adoption consultant, November 21, 2017.

4
Imagining and Enacting Birth Family Contact Over Time

Trajectories of Openness Among Private Domestic Adopters

Openness and contact are related—but not the same. Some parents who embraced openness preadoption and who, in turn, often desired a moderate to high level of contact with birth parents ultimately had less contact than they envisioned or desired. These parents tended to describe feelings of disappointment with the level of contact that unfolded (structural openness) yet were able to enact openness in other ways, such as through how and how often they talked about adoption and the birth family (e.g., communicative openness). Further, some parents who had little contact with birth parents nevertheless regarded these relationships as quite meaningful and important. Other parents possessed a more reserved and conditional approach to contact preadoption, emphasizing the importance of communicative openness but noting that the "match" between birth and adoptive parents would ultimately inform structural openness. Some of these parents matched with birth parents whom they respected and cared for and ended up having more contact than they initially expected or hoped for. Others matched with birth parents who possessed characteristics (e.g., drug use, perceived emotional instability) that they viewed as concerning or dangerous and perceived these as reasons to dramatically limit the type and level of birth family contact. Still other parents were uncomfortable with openness preadoption and typically desired limited (and usually no in-person) contact with the birth family. These families usually ended up having very limited contact, if any, with the birth family.

This chapter draws from interview data at multiple phases of the family life cycle (i.e., preadoption, 3 months postadoption, 5 years postadoption, and 8 years postadoption) to describe the diverse patterns and trajectories in adoptive–birth family relationships that unfolded—from the perspective of parents who pursued private domestic adoptions. (Chapter 5 discusses structural openness among child welfare adopters.) This chapter's primary focus is parents' attitudes about and practices related to birth family contact, or structural openness—and how such contact unfolds over time. A secondary focus is communicativeness openness: that is, how their approach to adoption communication intersects with contact. (For a more focused and in-depth exploration of communicative openness, see Chapter 6.) These stories are messy and complicated, and obviously do not represent every perspective in the adoption triad. Yet they offer insight into the dynamics of adoption and openness and the types of contact trajectories that may unfold.

Particularly relevant to this chapter is family systems theory[1] and, specifically, tenets related to emotional distance regulation,[2] or the process by which adoptive and birth families negotiate, navigate, and (re)calibrate relational dynamics, especially the level of closeness versus distance in the relationship. Individual differences in comfort with closeness may shift over time, thus informing changes in contact.[3] Families negotiate contact dynamics from the beginning of their relationship. Indeed, initial contact agreements, which may be formal and written or informal and verbal, often involve discussions about the level and form that contact will take and who will initiate it—and these agreements often inform the contact that unfolds. However, through processes of emotional distance regulation (e.g., bridging or distancing behaviors), families may end up with contact arrangements that are different from what was initially discussed or preferred. The amount of contact that unfolds is impacted by a range of factors (e.g., negative vs. positive interactions between families; life events, such as the birth mother remarrying or having another child) but often reflects the contact comfort zone of the "lowest common denominator"—the person(s) with the preference for the least amount of contact.[4] The chance of positive adoptive–birth family relationships is optimized when the comfort zones of adoptive and birth families are similar, or well matched, and when both parties can tolerate the ambiguity and complexity of the relationship they are forming and allow it to grow gradually.[5]

Contact both reflects and intersects with the broader dynamics of the adoptive family–birth family relationship. In turn, structural openness (i.e., contact, in its various forms) and communicative openness (i.e., openness about adoption, in its various forms) are interrelated—and both appear to benefit children. Access to information about one's origins, including one's birth family and the circumstances surrounding placement, and contact with the birth family are generally recognized as facilitating positive adoptive identity development.[6] And when parents' communications about adoption are open, supportive, and empathic, children are better equipped to integrate their adoptive status into a positive sense of self.[7] Hence, this chapter addresses the intersecting dimensions of both structural and communicative openness, with attention to how they change over time. It outlines a typology of contact dynamics over time, such that couples were classified as embodying one of the following patterns: (a) low enthusiasm for openness maintained, little contact; (b) increasing enthusiasm for openness, some contact; (c) increasing enthusiasm for openness, little contact; (d) high enthusiasm for openness maintained, some contact; (e) high enthusiasm for openness maintained, no contact; (f) decreasing enthusiasm for openness amid boundary challenges, contact terminated or reduced; and (g) enthusiasm for openness maintained amid boundary challenges, contact maintained. This chapter and Chapter 5 do not open with a family vignette, because a key goal of these chapters is to provide in-depth discussions of a limited number of families to illustrate the complexity and nuance of their stories over time.

Low Enthusiasm for Openness Maintained; Little Contact Maintained

Some parents did not embrace the concept of openness preadoption and ultimately found themselves in adoptive arrangements where they maintained little contact with the birth family. In most cases, these adoptions were described as semiopen[*] and mediated through an agency; thus, birth parents were presumably aware of the adoptive parents' wishes and preferences surrounding openness from the very beginning. Formal contracts specifying the number and nature of contacts per year were executed and signed by all parties, adoptive parents sent pictures and letters through the agency to be delivered to the birth parents, and birth parents initiated all contact with the adoptive family via the agency.

One exemplar of this pattern was Tammy, a graphic designer, and Holly, a civil engineer, a white lesbian couple living in a large Midwestern city. Tammy and Holly had both tried to get pregnant. Tammy suffered several miscarriages, and both women tried fertility treatments. The painful experience of enduring infertility and the desire to move on to a more promising family-building route led the couple to adoption. Preadoption, Holly noted that she and Tammy had initially been interested in pursuing international adoption, because they were, in her words, "freaked out" about open adoption: "There is ... a period of months until the adoption becomes final. The [birth parents] can change their minds." Part of Holly's anxiety stemmed from a prior potential placement that had not worked out, where an expectant mother had chosen them but changed her mind after delivery and decided to parent. Frustrated, sad, and profoundly disappointed, Holly found herself wary and mistrustful of the motivations and commitment of potential birth parents. Holly and Tammy were eventually matched in a "semiopen adoption," where the birth mother chose them based on a review of their profile and also a phone conversation. Although the couple never met

---

[*] Typically semiopen adoptions are arrangements where both parties exchange nonidentifying information. Often, contact is mediated by a third party (e.g., adoption agency).

her, they planned to "send her pictures, and someday we'll encourage Madden and his birth mother to meet."

Five years postplacement, Tammy shared that talking about adoption was not a regular or ongoing occurrence in their home. Rather, she and Holly talked about adoption primarily in the context of telling their son Madden, who was also white, the story of how they brought him home. Tammy affirmed that she was somewhat more comfortable than Holly in talking about adoption: "She tends to be a little bit more cautious. She may be worried that she might say the wrong thing. . . . I'm probably more likely to talk about it or bring it up. I'm the one who asks thoughtful questions all the time and provide[s] opportunities to talk about it." Tammy described adoption-related conversations as relatively rare and parent initiated, and minimized Madden's level of interest in the topic of adoption. "I've asked him questions on occasion. I'm like, 'Oh do you wish that you were with your birth mom?' or 'Do you wish you had a "real mom"?' And he sometimes says yes to that."[†]

By the 8-year follow-up, Tammy had lost contact with Madden's birth mother. For several years, Tammy had been sending her updates through their adoption facilitator, but "then her address changed . . . and so we're trying to find out where she went." Yet so far, their efforts were minimal. Holly stated: "We haven't hired a private investigator to find his birth mom. I bet if we did, it would be relatively simple." Likewise, Holly noted that they "hadn't looked on social media"—although she recognized that in the future, this could be an avenue to pursue, particularly given that Madden had recently begun to ask more questions about his birth mother and to "say he wants to meet her"—a possibility that, Tammy said, they were not "ready for yet."

Tammy and Holly represent an example of a couple who was minimally invested in fostering a current or future relationship between their son and his birth mother or extended birth family. They appeared to struggle with complicated discussions in relation to adoption, despite the fact that Madden was vocalizing both curiosity and loss in relation to his birth mother.

Seana and Ron were another couple who demonstrated reluctance surrounding openness early on, and who ultimately established a semiopen adoption. Seana, a sales associate at a jewelry store, and Ron, a retail chain store manager, were a white heterosexual couple living in a large Midwestern city. Like Holly and Tammy, Seana and Ron had dealt with infertility for several years

---

[†] Tammy's use of the term *real mom* is notable, as it reflects societal stereotypes of adoptive parents as not "real" parents and contradicts researchers' efforts to disentangle biology from parenthood (Miall, 1987; Robbins, 2016; Wegar, 2000). It is also a sentiment rarely explicitly expressed by the adoptive parents in this book; indeed, many adoptive parents express a great deal of pain and hurt associated with this type of statement—usually said to them by an unassuming outsider, as in "where is her 'real' mother?" (Robbins, 2016).

prior to pursuing adoption—a switch that was particularly hard for Ron, who, preadoption, continued to struggle with the idea of not having a biogenetically related child. Seana and Rob arrived at adoption because of their inability to conceive—and soon learned that open adoption was now the norm, whereby "most birth mothers seem to want to have some say [in choosing the adoptive parents]" (Ron). Seana emphasized that open adoption was "actually not [our first choice]. It just seems that everyone wants [that] now." Having adjusted to the notion that they would be adopting—a major shift in how they envisioned their journey to parenthood—they were now further (re)adjusting their expectations to accommodate the prospect of openness in adoption.[8] The couple decided that they were open to "letters and photos" but voiced anxiety about the prospect of in-person visits. Ron explained: "You hear stories about people having monthly letters or at their birthdays—I can't go that far. Yearly letters or photos, I don't mind that." Ron and Seana ultimately matched with a set of birth parents, Dana and Brad, who were a couple at the time of placement (although they broke up shortly after) who agreed to a semiopen arrangement involving annual photos and letters.

Five years after Ron and Seana had adopted their son Joseph, who was also white, they recounted a pattern of dwindling contact over the past several years. Specifically, they described themselves as responsive to the contact that Dana and Brad initiated but did not appear to initiate contact themselves. Over time, they had maintained more contact with Brad. Seana explained:

> I'm Facebook friends with Brad . . . so he sees pictures. . . . I used to keep in contact with both of them [but] then Dana kind of like dropped off. I didn't really know what happened and then Brad one time called me—he has our phone number—and told me the situation with her, something criminal, and advised that I drop her off of Facebook based on what was going on in her life. . . . So I did.

Elaborating on the contact she maintained with Brad, Seana said: "I do talk to him occasionally. Joseph has two biological siblings that Brad had gained custody of . . . but [recently] lost custody of. He calls occasionally . . . once or twice a year, and occasionally he'll drop a message or something or he'll comment on a picture [on Facebook]." Notably, however, a recent exchange with Brad had given Seana pause—and also reaffirmed her reluctance to open the relationship further to include Joseph:

> One time last year Brad made a comment—I guess I wouldn't say it's concerning, but—saying something about he can't wait till Joseph [is] 18 so he can . . . contact him. I guess I had never really thought about it. . . . I guess we

wouldn't be opposed to it. It's just not something we've really given that much thought to yet. I guess it would depend at the time if I felt comfortable with where they are in their life.

[Interviewer: So part of your reason for being hesitant is just given the instability of their lives?]

Yeah. I mean, I see now, just with the other children that are involved—they've been bounced around.... I don't know that I want to expose Joseph to [the chaos]. I guess Brad's thought when he said "18" is that Joseph will be an adult and can make his own decisions. And I guess in some ways that was good that he picked 18, that he doesn't have expectations before then.

Unlike other families who considered the benefits of contact, Seana only considered the potential risks. And, unlike some other families who were excited to hear about the existence of half or full siblings, Seana did not appear to consider seriously the possibility of Joseph making contact with his biological siblings. She seemed surprised by Brad's statement regarding the possibility of meeting Joseph when he turns 18—and although she found this statement "concerning," she was also reassured that Brad "doesn't have expectations before then." Thus, although Seana was willing to have some contact with Brad, she was clearly uncomfortable with the possibility of involving Joseph in this arrangement.

Ron also shared his anxiety about the prospect of contact between Joseph and his birth family. Ron said that he personally was not in contact with Brad or Dana—"Seana kind of keeps them up to date"—and disclosed that

it's tough for me, because I always think that I might lose Joseph to his parents someday. It's, like, one of my biggest fears. I don't know why.... That's just how I feel sometimes.... We'll just see what happens. I just don't know. I don't want to—I'm not going to tell him not to do something [like contact them]. He has the right to know.

Noting that a friend who placed a child for adoption had recently met that child as an adult, Ron shared his perspective that

it's nice that they reconnected, but at the same time I think, 'God, do I want Joseph hanging out with his birth mom someday and calling her Mom or whatever?' I guess I won't mind if he wants to know them or find out who they are. It's an important part of his life. It's just going to be hard on us.

Ron's and Seana's apprehensive stance regarding contact with Joseph's birth parents was reflected in how they interacted with Joseph about the facts of his adoption. Five years postplacement, Seana and Ron described limited communicative openness in relation to adoption: "It's always just been, 'You grew in someone else's tummy.' . . . On his birthday, we told him the whole story of how he was adopted and how we drove to [state] and all the details and asked if he had any questions and he didn't" (Seana). Seana asserted that Joseph did not ask many questions about his adoption or birth parents. "I say, 'If you have any questions, let me know.' I would tell him the story and see if that would generate anything, and it didn't." Seana added: "Visually, nobody would ever know [that he's adopted]. People think he looks just like me." Thus, here and in other families, racial similarity between parents and children was invoked as an explanation for why outsiders did not "recognize" their child as adopted. In turn, in the absence of unsolicited prompts for adoption-related conversation, some parents, like Ron and Seana, were unlikely to initiate adoption talk on their own.

Eight years postplacement, Seana stated that she no longer had any contact with Dana, although Dana's parents did send them occasional letters. Seana continued to "talk to the birth father maybe once a year" and to maintain him as a friend on Facebook, "so he sees updates of Joseph. We don't really comment back and forth on each other's stuff [but] I know he's seen . . . how Joseph is doing, and that makes him happy." When asked about Joseph's understanding of adoption and what types of conversations they had about adoption or the birth family, Seana continued to maintain that there wasn't much discussion, noting that Joseph had "never asked anything." However, Seana did share that she had recently told Joseph that she had pictures of his birth parents—and his response was one of interest and curiosity. He said:

"Oh! Do you have them?" and I said yes, and I asked if he wanted to see them and he said, "Sure," but never brought it up again.

[Interviewer: And how do you feel about talking about it more, showing him the pictures?]

I don't think I'll bring it up. If he does—we'll have to address that when that happens. I suppose we would show him a picture. I guess Ron and I will have to discuss that. Joseph never really asks much, yet. The birth father has made comments in the past like that he can't wait till Joseph is 18, so he can meet him. So, I don't know. . . . I guess that time is so far away.

Ron's narrative also suggested that conversations about adoption within the family were rare, and most likely to occur between Seana and Joseph. Ron also maintained his earlier perspective: Namely, he was not enthusiastic about the possibility of Joseph making contact with his birth family in the future. Noting that he personally had "no desire . . . to reconnect with the birth parents," Ron shared that Joseph says he does want to meet them, I guess, when he's older.... That's what he told Seana. He's never said it to me. I've never discouraged it, but—I mean, I don't want to, that's how I feel about it—but I never told him he can't.... But if that's the choice he wants to make, then he can do that. That's his choice.

Both Seana and Ron, then, maintained a minimal level of contact with their son's birth parents. Far from valuing the possibility of future contact, they expressed a fairly consistent level of anxiety and concern regarding contact, seemingly plagued by worries about role-related boundaries—and for Ron in particular, the possibility that Joseph might see Dana or Brad as his "real" parents. They also framed their wariness as in part reflecting concerns about Joseph, wherein they did not want him to get "caught up" in the chaos of his birth family's life. In turn, when faced with Joseph's curiosity about his birth family, as evidenced by his inquiries about his birth parents' photos, Seana avoided further discussion of the topic.

It is notable that Seana and Ron were one of a subset of heterosexual couples who had experienced infertility (and often underwent fertility treatments), and who also preferred and ultimately enacted a low level of contact—typically in the context of semiopen agreements. A parallel narrative was provided by Therese, a white heterosexual teacher in a Southern suburb, who, with her husband, Lucas, a Latino lawyer, adopted their son Josh, who was also Latino. The couple experienced a painful journey with regard to infertility and various fertility treatments—and Lucas in particular was forthcoming about his disappointment about pursuing parenthood via open adoption, noting that it did not appeal to him, but also acknowledging that adoption in general was difficult. "It's been somewhat hard, but I think adoption is hard, no matter what. So I think that people who say, 'There must be a way to do this so that it won't hurt' are deluding themselves." The couple matched with a very young birth mother and maintained some agency-mediated contact with her—and her parents, even more so—early on. But Therese, by her own acknowledgment, was not as good at "keeping up" with that contact as she could be. By the time Josh was 8, Therese said:

> We've never tried to hide [his adoption] from him. I guess the only thing about it that would make me uncomfortable is if he said, you know, "Well why haven't I met her yet?" And I don't have a problem with that, but probably I'd feel a little bit guilty because I was supposed to be sending pictures to the agency and we haven't done that. And I don't really have a good excuse, other than, just, life gets busy and—maybe I'm just such a perfectionist; I want to put together a nice album and everything, and I just don't get around to it because that's not the kind of thing I do. I'm a very lousy correspondent. So, I feel really guilty about

that—that I didn't live up—we didn't live up to . . . [*sigh*] everything we said we would do. Other than that I would be particularly happy for him to meet his birth mother. I think it would be a little awkward just because, as I said, we have not followed through—but other than that, I would [be] fine with it.

Despite acknowledging her minimal efforts to maintain a line of communication with Josh's birth mother, Therese had recently considered reaching out to the agency to try to get her address so that perhaps she could attend Josh's upcoming first music recital ("I think that she was [very musical]"). At the same time, though, Therese wondered: "Do I want to add that pressure of him meeting her at that time? Maybe not. But I do think that it would be good for him to meet her." Thus, whereas some families' ongoing avoidance of contact appeared to be related to anxiety about birth family "chaos" and/or jealousy about the potential relationship that could unfold between their child and the birth parents, Therese's ambivalence about contact seems more directly tied to her own guilt about not being a better communicator—and possibly anxiety about what would happen if and when she did initiate more direct contact.

Dave, a white radiologist, and Byron, a white graduate student in linguistics, who resided in a large city in the Midwest, represent a final example of a couple who had little interest in and expressed fears surrounding birth parent contact. Preadoption, both men articulated some anxiety surrounding open adoption. In that they were primarily working with a lawyer, they had not been exposed to the same level and type of education that many couples pursuing open adoption had received via their agencies. With regard to direct contact, Dave initially voiced that he would be uncomfortable with regular visits, and Byron said that he would prefer very little, adding that his desire for minimal contact partially stemmed from "selfishness on my part." At the same time, both Dave and Byron imagined that they could be somewhat flexible about contact: That is, it was something that they were "willing to negotiate with the birth mom," if she met a certain threshold of emotional stability.

Dave and Byron matched with their son Aidan's birth mother, Keira, a few weeks before she gave birth. Their agency notified them that they had been chosen by a prospective birth mother, but one who, according to Dave, did not want to meet them at first, "which was fine with us; we understood that." Then, several days later, Keira changed her mind:

She said that she was really kind of—not torn about—she wasn't conflicted about giving him up . . . but just really would feel better if she got to meet us. So we met her . . . for about an hour or so. It was nice. . . . I think it just reassured her that she had made the right decision.

Then, after the birth, Keira wanted to hold Aidan, a request that initially made Dave and Byron slightly uneasy. Ultimately, however, Dave said that he came to regard this event as a "positive thing. Now that is part of the story when he gets older and we discuss it with him."

Three months postplacement, Dave described contact as initiated predominantly by Keira. Dave also described a recent change in the level and frequency of contact, stating: "I think she is more at ease with the decision she made, just by the fact that she's eased off on the contact a little bit. It was a little bit more just the beginning." Further, although Dave on the one hand said that he felt comfortable allowing Keira to drive the level of contact, he also acknowledged that in-person contact was limited by the fact that "we're so far away that it's not like we can get out there often, if at all." Dave noted that "emails, maybe even a phone call when he gets old enough is fine; I don't really have any concerns about it."

For several years, Byron maintained email contact with Keira—until, when Aidan was about 3, she stopped responding. In trying to make sense of this, Byron said:

> We don't know why or what happened. We've made several attempts to reconnect and she hasn't responded.... She's a very sweet person and I think it was very difficult and I think at some point she just had to make a break and move on with her life. Or I don't know if she just found a new relationship, or I thought maybe she even has another kid. I don't know.

When Aidan was 5, neither email nor phone contact with Keira had resumed. Both men had looked her up on Facebook but had not initiated any contact. Dave acknowledged that one reason for his not reaching out was a desire to avoid discomfort: "Part of it may be self-serving for me, just not wanting to feel weird. I just took her nonresponse as her way of telling us, you know—she kind of let go." He also wondered if connecting via Facebook could be harmful for Keira, in that "seeing pictures of Aidan [could be] hurtful, not intentionally—but it would open up wounds.... I don't think it would be a positive thing."

Alongside their fairly passive approach to contact, Dave and Byron voiced a reluctance to make "too much of Aidan's adoption." Dave in particular expressed his opinion that many adoptive parents "overdid it" in terms of talking about adoption, particularly when children were young and did not possess the capacity to understand the meaning and nuances of adoption. Yet Dave also indicated that his own discomfort may have also informed his cautious approach to adoption talk. Indeed, when Aidan was 5, Dave shared that he and Byron possessed pictures of Keira but had not yet shown them to Aidan, feeling that it would be more appropriate "later when he sort of understands it better and it's more—I don't want to say comfortable, but less weird [*laughs*] and less sort of stressful." Byron expressed anxiety about the questions that Aidan would eventually ask about his birth mother and worried about how knowledge of his adoption "is going to affect him. He's a very sensitive kid and I worry he's going to take it personally."

When Aidan was 8, he had begun to ask more questions—reflecting the more active role that children often take as they develop a deeper and more nuanced understanding of the concept of adoption and begin to integrate their status as an adopted person into their identity.[9] Both Dave and Byron noted that their lack of contact with Aidan's birth mother made answering these questions more difficult. Dave said that when Aidan asked questions, they explained that they used to have contact with his birth mother but it stopped:

> We just tell him we don't know [why] for sure. . . .He's been asking more about contacting her. So we said, "First, we'd have to find her and see if she's ready," and then he's like, "Well, why would she have to be ready?" and we say, "It may be something she's nervous about," and he's just like, "Why would she be nervous?"

Aidan's questions prompted Dave and Byron to consult with their home study social worker, with whom they had kept in touch, to ask: "How do we handle this? What do we say? What do we do?" The social worker, Byron said, had helped them come up with a "game plan" that involved reaching out to Keira via Facebook to let her know that they were thinking about her and that if she wanted to contact them, "that's great, and if you're not comfortable, we understand."

Thus, among those parents who initially expressed little enthusiasm for openness and who came to enact arrangements with limited to no contact, some couples, like Seana and Ron, continued to deflect and avoid their children's questions, seeming to believe that the risks of contact outweighed the potential benefits. Others, like Therese and Lucas, described their children as minimally interested in their adoption and/or birth parents—but also did not actively seek out opportunities to discuss what continued to be a somewhat uncomfortable and unwelcome topic. Still others, like Dave and Byron, responded to their children's growing curiosity by making contact—or at least taking steps toward doing so amid their own ongoing anxiety and discomfort. Indeed, when children's curiosity became more prominent, some parents re-evaluated their current level of (and preferences surrounding) distance versus closeness, recognizing that exposure to an imperfect birth family situation was better than nothing at all.

Increasing Enthusiasm for Openness With Some Birth Parent Contact

Not all families who started out suspicious or dismissive of open adoption maintained these attitudes. Parents' feelings about and comfort with closeness to birth parents sometimes changed over time, thus informing changes in contact.[10] For example, some parents who were initially hesitant or even fearful about open adoption became increasingly open to contact over time amid a growing awareness of the benefits of openness or a shift in perspective wherein birth family members were no longer seen as threatening, but as resources—and complex human beings.

Travis and Brent are an example of a couple that was initially reluctant about the idea of open adoption—but dramatically shifted their orientation to openness when they matched with a birth mother whom they liked, and with whom they established a connected and trusting relationship. Travis and Brent—both of whom were white and lived in a large West Coast city—had initially hoped to do international adoption. But, because they wanted a newborn and because so few countries were open to single male applicants, they were guided by adoption professionals to consider domestic adoption.

Regarding contact, Travis, a technical writer, initially preferred "limited to none, with limited being letters a couple times a year." Brent, a brand manager, described somewhat greater openness to contact, asserting that occasional visits would be fine with him. Recent disappointments with failed matches had fueled the men's hesitation regarding contact. Travis explained that a number of matches "just didn't pan out. There was one woman who contacted us that turned out not even to be pregnant. We've been sad and . . . we're tired of the process." After a series of unpleasant experiences, Travis and Brent were frustrated and fatigued with the adoption process and could not easily imagine a birth parent situation where they would want ongoing contact.

Then, Travis and Brent matched with a birth mother, Adalia, who did not speak much English but who shared that she felt spiritually connected to them the moment she saw their profile. The couple felt warmly toward her and trusted her. Adalia had not shared her pregnancy with her family—a not uncommon scenario. Presumably in part because of the secrecy associated with the pregnancy, Adalia was hesitant to commit to a specific schedule or plan for contact. Initially, the two parties discussed monthly visits, yet Travis and Brent ultimately found that it was difficult to keep track of Adalia once she had been discharged from the hospital and they returned home with their son, Samuel, who was Latino. Three months postplacement, Travis—who initially had more restrictive ideas surrounding, contact—said:

We have seen her twice and talked to her on the phone two or three times but she has not returned the last two messages we left for her. So at this point, we are not really sure [what's going to happen]. At this point, it's up to her to reach out.... Originally we talked about seeing each other once a month just so she could see him and how he is doing. At this point, we don't really know what is going to happen.

Brent shared his desire for contact alongside his uncertainty about how to proceed, and his efforts to be respectful of Adalia's privacy and boundaries:

I would like contact with her.... I am just trying to balance respecting her space with just letting her know that we are still around and we still would like contact. It has been about 3 or 4 weeks since I called her last. She did call me 2 months ago to tell me that her phone number had changed. So obviously, there is some sort of wanting to stay in touch, somehow.

Five years postadoption, the couple continued to have intermittent contact with Adalia, which they typically initiated. As Travis said: "We see her at least once a year, sometimes every 9 months. Oftentimes it will take a few phone calls or texts from us to get her to respond." Aware of the many constraints on Adalia's time and ability to be in contact (e.g., her family did not know about the pregnancy; she lived over an hour away) but also attuned to the benefits of maintaining such contact, especially as Samuel grew older, the couple did not always know what to do when Adalia was unresponsive. Brent shared: "I want to stay in touch with her, but ... I'm afraid—like when she doesn't respond, I don't know if it's because she can't literally, or doesn't want to—and how often do I try to initiate contact? It's hard to figure out." When the family did see Adalia—often in a neutral in-between spot like a park or restaurant, she was "always—I can't imagine her being more appropriate. She gives the right level of loving, care, affection [toward Samuel], but not too much. She really likes us. So, I don't really know.... It's really complicated" (Brent).

Amid the sometimes unpredictable nature of their contact with Adalia ("what typically happens is I'll start texting her to ask if she wants to get together and she'll say yes, but it takes a lot of coordinating before it actually happens": Brent), the two men cultivated and maintained communicative openness. For example, in talking to Samuel about family, Brent noted, "We're always conscious about birth parents and birth siblings. They're part of the family. In fact, Samuel had something they did at school and he drew one diagram for his birth family and one for us; that was unprompted." Both Brent and Travis also specifically sought to encourage open communication and conversation about birth family and adoption. Said Brent: "We try to open the door [to conversation]." For example, recently, he asked Samuel whether he thought of his birth mom on his birthday, "and he said, 'Yeah, I do.' I said, 'Well, do you want to tell that to Adalia?' and he said, 'I want to tell her myself.' I was like, 'OK.'"

Eight years postplacement, the couple continued to describe a good relationship with Adalia, although they also described ongoing difficulties related to the predictability of contact. Brent, for example, noted that the "language barrier . . . she doesn't speak great English" made texting and talking on the phone challenging at times: "It is particularly hard to understand her on the phone." Adalia had also still not told her extended family about Samuel, so "there are times where we can't really call her or communicate with her because there are people around her that can't know about him." Adalia had recently become a parent and had expressed a desire to introduce her daughter to Samuel. Yet, as Brent noted, this had not yet occurred. Indeed, although Bent described their relationship as "positive . . . she is always open to hearing from us, always open to getting together," her ability to "deliver on that is not always consistent, either because of her work schedule or because of other commitments." And yet: "the baseline [relationship] is one of affection and one of respect and positivity."

When Samuel was 8, both Brent and Travis described efforts at continuing to foster communicative openness amid the ongoing barriers to contact. Said Brent:

We try to bring it up and we do bring it up. It can often be like pulling teeth. [A close friend] just adopted a child, who we met recently. We brought that up and he seemed really interested in that. That was a surprise. We talk about it; we have books about it; we talk about his birth mom; we try to see her when we can. We talk about the fact that we don't know anything about his birth dad and what that's like and maybe he has certain qualities that Samuel has.

Travis shared this example:

There are times when Samuel will ask us questions and I'll say, "You know, I don't really know that. You can ask Adalia when we see her." Then we'll see her and it will be like, "Do you want to talk to her or tell her anything?" and he'll just be very quiet. He'll want to see her and touch her and be there for a while, and then he'll go off play and do something else. . . . We try to follow up [after visits]. See how he's feeling.

Another development that had occurred by the time Samuel was 8 was that Brent and Travis had recently become Facebook friends with Adalia. Since Adalia had moved out of the home she shared with extended family members, she had become, according to Brent, a lot more open to contact, including Facebook. So now we're Facebook friends with her. Whenever she posts pictures or stuff that involves her or her daughter that are appropriate to show Samuel, we always share it. And she always "likes" our posts, and we'll let him know, "Oh, your mom liked our post." It makes a sense of connection even when we aren't able to see her.

At age 8, Samuel was having some direct, albeit parent-facilitated, contact with his birth mom: According to Travis, Samuel "will call her sometimes, text her, or we will text a message for him."

Travis and Brent represent an example of a couple that faced multiple barriers to contact: a birth mother who spoke little English, kept her pregnancy a secret, and was not easy to get a hold of. All of these barriers were present alone or in combination among other couples whom I interviewed. And yet, unlike some of these couples—and amid their own (and particularly Travis's) initial hesitancy surrounding contact—Travis and Brent ultimately maintained a fairly high level of contact with their son's birth mother. Mutual respect for one another, an appreciation of the complexity of the relationship they were forming, and an acknowledgment of circumstances out of their control (e.g., Travis and Brent did not blame or get upset with Adalia when she was unable to consistently communicate with them) facilitated their growing comfort with closeness and ongoing contact.[11]

Eliza and Hannah, a white lesbian couple living in a large city in the Northeast, experienced a similar shift in openness and ultimately demonstrated a high level of commitment to ongoing contact. Preadoption, both women asserted that they were open to pursuing an open adoption but provided a variety of caveats surrounding the level and type of contact they were willing to engage in. Hannah, an administrative assistant, said: "As long as the birth mother or family is willing to respect the boundaries, I have no problems with letters and cards and emails . . . and stuff that is appropriate." Eliza, a junior accountant, shared that after "reading a lot . . . about open adoption" and participating in adoption agency programming related to open adoption, "I don't think I have a fear of her snatching the baby away anymore. . . . I've gotten a lot better. I think I could do once a year or something like that, or sending letters and taking pictures. . . . It depends on the birth mother." For Eliza, key factors in determining the nature and extent of contact were the birth mother's access to technology and location:

> If she has access to a computer then I can send her pictures every day. . . . Now, if she lives like 8 hours away, I'm not going to go visit once every 2 months; it will be like once a year. We can do visits here and there and sending letters and pictures and stuff like that. . . . Rather than dealing with calls and writing letters, I would rather do emails and photo attachments and stuff.

Eliza and Hannah were eventually placed with a biracial (African American/white) boy named Luke. Luke's birth mother, Amy, was already raising one child, a daughter—and was in a relationship with an abusive boyfriend, Luke's birth father. Prior involvement with the state's Department of Social Services meant that Amy was on their radar when she gave birth. In turn, according to Hannah, Amy was told that

> if she didn't sever ties, if she refused to leave him, then they were both going to foster care. If she chose to leave him, then she had the chance of keeping the kids—but then she realized that she couldn't keep both of them; she couldn't do it 100% on her own.

Eventually, Amy did leave her boyfriend—but awareness of the emotional and financial burdens of raising two children on her own, with little outside help, led her to make an adoption plan—a decision that was "very difficult for her," according to Eliza. According to Hannah, Amy had placed a child for adoption essentially because she felt she "did not have many choices."

Three months postplacement, Eliza and Hannah were sending pictures and letters once a month to the agency but had not heard from Amy directly. Amy was "not in a place ... where she can [have contact] or know anything about him or see him or anything. She's still struggling with her—not with her decision, but with the follow-up. I guess she's still struggling with the loss" (Eliza). Eliza noted that she hoped for a future relationship with Amy, as well as her daughter, Reese ("I really want Luke to know his sister"), but was unsure whether this would realistically unfold. Eliza stated:

> I think either we're going to be in contact on a regular schedule or we're never going to hear from her again.... There's not going to be an in-between ground... so we kind of left it open. She knows that we're willing and she knows that we'll send monthly updates, but right now she just can't deal with it.

The prospect of not having contact was upsetting to Eliza. Despite her initial hesitations surrounding birth family contact, 3 months after adopting Luke, Eliza was grieving the possibility of not having an open adoption. She said: "I mean, I really, really, really want—really want an open adoption with the mother. I really want contact. This will be good for all parties.... But it just—it's not—this is not working out the way I wanted." Eliza's disappointment regarding a possible lack of contact was likely facilitated by the fact that she had developed a strong empathy and respect for Amy: "She's incredibly strong." Further, far from signaling to Eliza that there might be reason for boundary or role concerns ("she said, 'Here. Here's your son,' and we both kind of relaxed a little and were like,

'There's not going to be much of a problem here'"), Amy indicated her need for a fair amount of distance between herself and Luke—at least early on, as she managed her own feelings of loss. Hannah believed that Amy wanted him to "have a good home, but was also having a hard time with how she wanted to know him and his life." Both women maintained hope that Amy would eventually seek out contact with them. Three months postplacement, Hannah sighed: "Hopefully she'll realize that she actually does need to read the letters [we sent] and does need Luke to know his sister."

So what happened? The relationship ultimately opened up to involve a fairly high level of contact. After about 6 months, the two families connected directly after mutually communicating their desire to do so to the agency. According to Eliza, Amy's interest in contact was motivated in part by a desire to "make sure the siblings have a relationship." The families, in turn, maintained visits every 3 or 4 months until Luke was about 5. He saw his birth sister, Reese, regularly during that time and strongly identified her as his "sister." Both Eliza and Hannah also regularly text messaged with Amy during Luke's first 5 years.

When Luke was about 5, Amy and Reese moved several states away to be closer to extended family. This presented new challenges for Hannah's and Eliza's relationship with them. No longer were they separated by a long car ride; now, it would take the family a plane ride to reach Amy and Reese. In turn, Eliza and Hannah were considering buying Amy something "like an iPod touch, something with video conference [to facilitate contact].... She doesn't have the money to buy something like that... and Luke keeps talking about how he wants to see them." The family did maintain regular Facebook contact as well as texting after the move, and talked by phone about once a month—although, as Eliza noted, "I think she's a little afraid to call us, because she doesn't want to butt in, but she has no problem when I call her." Hannah shared:

> We are in contact with her all the time. She gets regular updates, pictures, that kind of stuff. She talks to him on the phone. Luke's birth sister, Reese—they talk on the phone and act like you would think they were living next to each other. That's how much they talk to each other.

Indeed, Luke's relationship with his birth sister, who was a year older than he was, was very special. Reese had even visited Eliza, Hannah, and Luke independently of Amy, which Eliza and Hannah viewed as emblematic of the trusting relationship they had developed: "Amy seems to be happy with us, and we're happy with her."

Lena and Thomas, a white heterosexual couple in a midsized city in the Northeast, represent an example of a couple who dramatically shifted their approach to openness across the transition to parenthood, successfully navigated some communication and boundary challenges during the early postplacement period, and came to enact a structurally and communicatively open adoption. Lena, an operations manager, and Thomas, a financial planner, experienced a long and painful road to adoption. They tried to conceive for many years, underwent numerous cycles of in vitro fertilization, and suffered several miscarriages. When they arrived at adoption, however, they were in a place where they acknowledged their loss and pain, yet were also remarkably excited about adoption. At the same time, the couple voiced a sense of uncertainty and caution surrounding openness. Preadoption, Lena stated:

> We'll probably have a semiopen—you know, they'll have nonidentifying information about us. We can meet the birth parents, send letters through the agency, send pictures. We have no problem with that. I don't know if we'll go as far as giving them our address and saying, "Come on over anytime," but we haven't really talked about when the child is a teenager—after 18. . . . We really haven't discussed postplacement. That might be [where] some of my concerns [lie].

Despite her uncertainty regarding the level of contact, Lena expressed a sense of respect for and gratitude toward the birth mother of her future child. She said:

> If the birth mother didn't give us her children, Thomas and I wouldn't be able to have a family, so I really think of her—I have a lot of respect for her. . . . [I think I'd be] open to her getting pictures and letters, 'cause I'll just be so happy that the child's hopefully is doing well.

Thomas was interested in domestic open adoption "because number one, we think it may help us get a child faster. And number two, it probably isn't the worst thing. . . . What is best for the child is probably to have some contact." Yet at the same time that he recognized certain potential benefits of openness, he acknowledged worrying that when his future child was a teenager, and "I yell at him or her to go to their room, I don't want them running to their *'real parents.'* That's something that concerns me, [but] from what I understand, it doesn't happen much, [except] on after-school specials."

Lena and Thomas matched to a "bright" and personable birth mother whom they liked a lot. Lena exclaimed how impressed she was that Mandy, her son's birth mother, "just followed the doctor's orders to a T." Lena shared:

> It's awful, but I had in my head a woman on drugs who wants to give up her baby and doesn't give a crap about it. And Thomas and I were like, we could have not gotten a better birth mother. She took such good care of him. Any time she felt a

twinge or a ping she was at the hospital.... She took *such* good care of him. And that's why I'm like "Why would I not want her to see him twice a year?"

But Lena also found herself navigating some tricky dynamics wherein Mandy made requests that Lena struggled to respond to, as they were outside of her comfort zone with regard to boundaries, including more visits per year than they initially agreed to. According to Lena, Mandy also, at one point,

asked, "Can I be called Mama Manda?" And I'm like, "Eeeh, nah." I talked to my social worker and said, "I don't really want her to be called Mama." She said, "I agree, that's kind of hard."... So I [said to Mandy], "I think that's a little too confusing and he has one mother...."

Significantly, Mandy responded positively: "Oh, I think it's fine just for Joey to call me Mandy. Don't worry about it." Both parties in this situation had the potential to feel as though their roles were not adequately acknowledged and respected. Yet potential tension was seemingly resolved through the cautious "dance" of establishing comfortable emotional boundaries for all parties, and relational equilibrium was restored.

Lena and Mandy navigated other challenges as well. According to Lena, "she would always email a lot, like the first year she'd say, 'Oh, can I have another visit?'" In responding to such requests, Lena juggled her own complex emotions—which encompassed gratitude and admiration as well as mild irritation. Notably, when Lena responded in a way that conveyed a sense of being relaxed and "okay" with whatever Mandy was requesting—even if that is not how she felt—Mandy responded in a way that was respectful and reassuring. Indeed, Mandy often did not ultimately have time for an extra visit—but seemed comforted to know it was a possibility. Likewise, early on, when Mandy asked for their address, Lena initially bristled at the request—but then relaxed when she found out that Mandy only wished to send them a card.

Despite the initial bumps in the road, the families established a strong connection. When Joey was 5 years old, Lena and Thomas spoke with excitement and pride about Mandy's professional advancements and how the nature, content, and tone of their conversations (e.g., via phone and email) had changed over the past few years. Recalling the last conversation that she had with Mandy, Lena said:

She ended up talking about her career most of the time. It was because I kept asking her questions. She was interested in Joey, and talking to him, but a lot of it is what's going on with her is her career. She was so excited and is so... career focused right now.

The families enjoyed visits together several times a year, sometimes along with Mandy's own parents and siblings. Joey was sometimes shy at the beginning of visits, but by the end he was comfortable and carefree, and he always gave Mandy a big hug goodbye. When Mandy visited, Lena tried to give her alone time with Joey, so that Mandy would not feel monitored, crowded, or inhibited—and so she could develop her own independent relationship with Joey ("I go into the kitchen and do something, and I'll let them do something together.... She reads stories to Joey, and they made cookies together"). Their growing comfort with one another, and the fact that Mandy was doing so well personally and professionally, had shifted the relationship dynamics. Lena felt increasingly relaxed and at ease, which manifested in terms of how she spoke to Joey about Mandy and how she related to Mandy:

> In the beginning it was like, we had to watch what we said. Now, we talk about how wonderful she is. And with visits, in the beginning, I was like, "Oh my God, the house should be perfect." Now I'm like, "Yeah, whenever." It's a home, and you know, she's happy, he's happy. The visits are not stressful at all anymore.

Increasing Enthusiasm for Openness Amid Little to No Birth Parent Contact

In some cases, prospective adoptive parents came to a place where they embraced openness—only to match with birth parents whose own preferences and/or efforts surrounding contact did not match their own. Ellen, a travel writer, and Matt, a realtor, were one such couple. A white heterosexual couple living in a large city on the West Coast, both shared some initial reluctance surrounding open adoption during the preadoption period. Matt had experienced some evolution in his views about openness over the course of the adoption process and had reached a point where he was not exactly excited about but was willing to pursue open adoption: "Initially I wasn't so hot about open adoption. Now I'm pretty okay with it." Matt shared that in terms of preferred level of contact, "We're pretty okay with every year or two [with] less and less contact as time goes on." Ellen, on the other hand, seemed somewhat more sold on the potential benefits of open adoption, noting that children should have the option of knowing as much as possible about their birth families. Further, Ellen demonstrated greater flexibility surrounding contact, stating that the amount of contact would depend on the situation and that although she was definitely open to letters and pictures, "meeting face to face on a regular basis—I'm not sure how we feel about that."

Ellen and Matt matched with a birth mother who agreed to a semiopen adoption, mediated by the agency, such that all communications (e.g., photos, letters) occurred through the agency. Further, although the birth mother knew their first and last names, Ellen and Matt only had access to the birth mother's first name—Dania. Initially, both Ellen and Matt—as new parents preoccupied with the excitement of becoming parents—did not express strong feelings about their arrangement. In the early months postplacement, engrossed in caring for their son, Anthony, they simply stated that they "hoped that eventually" Dania might respond to the quarterly photos and letters they had agreed to send via the agency. They did not express positive or negative feelings (e.g., relief or disappointment) about the one-sided, fairly limited nature of their contact arrangement.

By the time that Anthony was 5, however, a great deal had changed. Anthony was an inquisitive and questioning child and asked many questions about and expressed great interest in his adoption—possibly in part because, as a Latino boy with a noticeably darker skin tone than both of his parents, his adoption was a topic that sometimes came up at school and with peers. Ellen and Matt both described how their regular reading of the adoption book (or "life book") they had put together for him prompted "random questions about his birth mom":

> We've always talked to him about it from the very beginning—as much as we thought he would understand. We had those books we made for him with his adoption story in it, so we'll bring it out. . . . It's got a picture of his birth mom [in it] and stuff. . . . So it's just explaining, just making sure he starts to understand, and that he's exposed to this. . . . There are questions that are harder in terms of, like, birth mother questions, like "Why can't I see her?" or "Why doesn't she want me?" that we have to deal with. . . . I worry about that, but I think it's important that we talk to him and it won't be better if we ignore it.

When Anthony was 5, Ellen and Matt had recently been contacted by the agency about a half-brother of Anthony's—a little boy, Finn, who shared the same birth mother as Anthony, who had been placed with a family several hours away. They began to spend time with Finn and his parents and observed its significance for Anthony—who spontaneously referred to Finn as his "little brother." This contact, in turn, had raised more questions about adoption and the birth family. As Matt explained, "We'll explain why his little brother doesn't live with us, and why he lives with his parents, his adoptive parents. We explain, like, 'Your birth mom and his birth mom are both Dania, so you have the same birth mom.'" Amid Anthony's increased curiosity and the growing salience of the birth family context in their lives, Ellen had recently intensified her efforts to make direct contact with Dania; for example, she had offered up their email address as a means of getting in touch with them. Ellen had also considered other ways of trying to find Dania—but with limited personal information, she was unable to find anything:

We send pictures and letters to his birth mom. We used to send them once every 3 months but now it's not as often—maybe once every 6 months or so. But we haven't gotten anything back from her. . . . I had actually sent her our email address on a couple of letters and said if she decided, we would be very welcoming of contact. But she never does. . . . I tried searching for her on the Internet a while ago. . . . I don't think I found anything. I've thought about looking for her since she's probably at that age where she has Facebook. But we don't know her last name. . . . She has our name so all you would have to do is search us and it takes 30 seconds. Again, we would welcome contact. For adoption, I think it's better for the kids to have contact if they can have that. But I'm not sure what she's kind of open to. . . . We've been sending the pictures and encouraging her to contact us if she wants to.

By the time that Anthony was 8, his questions had increased in specificity, intensity, and frequency, reflecting a growing understanding of adoption and an increased curiosity about birth origins,[12] likely prompted in part by the fact that he was seeing his younger half-brother Finn more frequently. Ellen and Matt had also recently adopted a second son, Benny. In turn, adoption and birth family had become even more prominent topics in family conversations—especially since Benny's adoption arrangement was much more open than Anthony's, and Benny's birth mother had in fact visited their home a number of times over the past few years. These visits sometimes "brought up questions. . . . [After a visit] we just make sure Anthony's okay, and we talk about his story again, and we [emphasize] that he can always ask questions, whenever he wants" (Matt). Thus, Matt and Ellen maintained a high level of communicative openness in the absence of much structural openness. Ellen stated:

He sees his half-brother every month or so. . . . He's been asking a lot more. He's always asked questions. I mean, we always talk about it or we'll bring it up occasionally and then he'll ask questions about it. We've tried to just emphasize with him that you can just ask us questions any time, and it doesn't make us feel bad, and we tried really hard to kind of pound that in a little bit. And he's brought up a lot more. . . . With Benny's birth mom, it's a very open adoption. She's in the picture, she comes over . . . so it's been hard for Anthony to understand, well, "Why does Benny get to see his birth mom and I don't?" It's been really upsetting to him on a couple of occasions. We say, "We understand that . . . it might make you a little bit sad," and he has been, a little bit. We kind of talk about, "Well, he gets to see [birth mother] but you get to see your brother. Finn is your, you know, other family member that we have as part of our family" kind of a thing. Which helps, I think—but there's been a lot of questions about "Why didn't she want me?"

Matt elaborated on how they sought to address such questions:

That realization of "Why doesn't she want to have contact with me?" I think is—we're getting those questions now, particularly since we have pretty regular contact with Benny's birth mom. We tell him, "We wish we had contact with her too" and that we send letters, and we've talked all about the letters and pictures we've sent to Dania over the years. Recently we've been involving him in the letters that we send. So he reads it and we ask, "Is there anything you want to add?"

Ellen remarked on her own shift in how she thought about openness. She put into words what so many parents eventually experienced: that openness was less scary than she had initially envisioned, and now—seeing the difference between a more open adoption arrangement and a more closed arrangement, up close—she truly understood the benefits of openness and, in some ways, how it made parenting as an adoptive parent easier. Openness was still challenging and emotional at times, but Ellen could see how it would ultimately benefit her younger son Benny, Benny's birth mother, and herself:

It seems like the longer we've done the adoption thing, the more okay we are with open adoption. I remember when we first started the process and it was like, "Oh my God, birth parents—I don't—that's too scary, we don't want anything to do with them. We want, you know, whatever!" We were scared. But I've been really sad that Anthony hasn't had that access with his birth family. I mean, he has [had access] with his brother, which has been awesome. But I just think . . . I don't know. I mean, it was scary, we were in the hospital when Benny was born and . . . you're sitting there with her and trying to figure out if she's really going to go through with this or not, and you're invested immediately of course. There were parts like that that have been really hard and—she's sad when she comes over, and it's hard to see that. But I think it's good—I don't know; I *hope* it's good for her to come over and see him if she wants to; we let her initiate that. [And] I mean, I feel like it's really good for Benny, or will be. To know this person and to know a little bit more about where she came from and to sort of have this relationship. And we're all just kind of figuring it out, I guess.

In direct contrast to his initial reluctance about openness and especially the possibility of in-person visits, Matt emphasized the positive nature of their relationship with their second son Benny's birth mother, stating:

She's really great. . . . I worry about her sometimes—how she's doing with it. I just hope it's not too hard for her. But . . . we have each other's phone numbers and she knows where we live and we have her over and we keep just repeating that—whenever, just give us a call. We've said, "We don't want to push seeing Benny on you. It's whenever you want to—give us a call or contact us and we will make it happen."

Matt's remarkable shift—from general uneasiness with openness and a reluctant willingness to entertain the possibility of limited (i.e., not in-person) forms of communication with the birth family to a stance that was empathic toward the birth mother and welcoming of contact that included visits to his home—is a powerful reminder of the potential for change in how parents approach openness. Matt and Ellen were ultimately presented with a series of factors that had the potential to facilitate greater openness: a child who asked questions, a birth sibling, and a second child whose birth mother seemed emotionally stable and was open to contact. Matt and Ellen could have shut each of these potential doors to openness. But they opened each one—and although the conversations they engaged in with Anthony were not easy, their willingness to continue to engage in such discussions, and to facilitate contact with his birth brother, will likely enable a deeper level of honesty and openness in the relationship that they enjoy with Anthony as time marches forward.

Another example of a couple who ultimately came to a place of greater appreciation for and interest in contact were Andrea and Mary. Both white, and living in a conservative area of the South in a midsized city, they were employed as a prison guard (Andrea) and a manager at a TV production studio (Mary). Preadoption, Mary wanted a totally closed adoption, whereas Andrea was more willing to consider some openness. Andrea recounted how she had spoken to family and friends about their experiences in both closed and open adoptions and had reached the conclusion that indirect contact—namely, letters and phone calls—could be good for a child. In turn, Andrea "talked to [Mary] a little bit.... I'm like, 'Just because it's open doesn't mean we're going to be stopping by her house every week.'" In fact, both Andrea and Mary expressed concern about in-person visits, viewing them as intrusive, and feeling that they could lead a child to feel "confused as to why there is another parent in the picture." Ultimately, both women decided that they would be okay with some openness—but they placed various caveats on the type and level of contact that they would be comfortable with.

By the time that Andrea and Mary were placed with their daughter, Jessie, who was Latina, the couple had endured several failed matches, whereby one expectant mother had decided to parent, and another woman was determined (by their agency) to be "scamming" them. These experiences left both women, but especially Mary, feeling anxious in relation to birth parent relationships. Mary explained that, after their most recent "horrible" experience, "I was really questioning if I could do an open adoption." To the couple's relief, Jessie's birth mother, Luciana, was not interested in visits and did not want to receive letters or pictures directly; rather, because of the circumstances of placement (i.e., the birth father was not her current partner), she preferred all communications to be sent to the agency. Luciana was, however, open to having her children meet Jessie "eventually... she said it would be good for the siblings to all connect'" (Andrea). The plan for ongoing contact was "pictures four times in the first year, and then every 2 years after that.... That's the minimum the agency likes" (Mary).

About Luciana, Andrea expressed that she was

> happy we got to meet her, and got to know the story and she gave us pictures, which we have in Jessie's nursery, and she wrote out a letter to Jessie. She put a lot of thought into it, and she explained everything in the letter: "Why I did this, and I don't want you to feel like you weren't loved, but these are the circumstances and this is what I want to give you."

Indeed, according to Mary, Luciana's perspective was, "I'm not going to have to go on welfare. We shouldn't have kids we can't provide for." Luciana invoked her limited resources and inability to provide for Jessie in the letter as part of her explanation for why she made an adoption plan. The photos and letter, in addition to the "15-page document that she filled out [for the agency] about... her favorite foods, movies, music, all of that stuff," would, the two women felt, assist in answering Jessie's questions down the road.

When Jessie was 5, Mary and Andrea shared that they had, over the past few years, sent Luciana "pictures and letters [through the agency] probably three times a year"—far more than the minimum of once every 2 years that they had agreed to at the outset. Both women noted that Jessie had a lot of questions about her birth family: "We keep a picture of her birth family in her room. She's started asking [for] almost a year now about, 'Well I want to meet my birth mom, and I want to meet my birth brother and sister'" (Andrea). Andrea acknowledged that they found it hard to "explain why we can't just pop up and see her birth family any day of the week. I feel really bad when she's like, 'But I want to meet them,' and I don't have a good answer." Jessie's intensified interest and curiosity, combined with a letter that they received from Luciana, prompted Mary and Andrea to intensify their efforts at making contact—and to indicate their willingness to meet in person. Andrea said:

> Her birth mom had sent a letter that said, "Hey I'm [separated] now, I'd like to get to talk to you guys, here's my number." We kind of sat on it for [a few weeks] going, "Hmm, what do we do with this." And then we decided we were going to make a trip to the city where she's located so we started calling... but nobody picked up. So we sent a letter going, "Hey, Jessie is really asking; if you're ready,

here's how you find us." . . . So I don't know if Luciana's back with [the boyfriend] or what's going on. So . . . with Jessie, I definitely don't want her to have negative perceptions of her birth mom but at the same time I don't want her to think we're not trying. So it's been trying to balance her desire for or need for contact with our inability to make it happen, because it's really . . . it's outside of our realm of control. If I could make it happen I'd drive her up to [city] tomorrow. I've told her if they make the call we'll make the trip.

Mary noted that she hoped that they could make contact, because Jessie was increasingly looking to them to fill in the holes of her story, and although they had some information about her birth family, it was relatively superficial and incomplete and did not address the increasingly detailed questions that Jessie was asking about her birth family. Mary further noted that she wasn't sure how "tech savvy" Luciana was, given her relatively low level of education, but emphasized that she was more than willing to be friends with Luciana on Facebook if she asked: "It hasn't been something she asked for . . . but I think in this day and age it would be wonderful because you could share information . . . in an instant. But at this point we haven't asked."

Thus, Mary and Andrea came to pursue far more in the way of contact than they had initially envisioned. Jessie's persistent questioning had certainly impacted this shift—but, notably, they were already sending more pictures and letters than they had agreed to by the time Jessie had requested to make contact. They appear to have realized that they could not answer Jessie's questions on their own; they needed Luciana. And yet, at the same time that the couple opened the door to potentially meeting Luciana, they remained somewhat cautious, given their uncertainty as to whether she would eventually respond, agree to meet, and follow through—and how they would manage Jessie's feelings should her hopes of meeting Luciana go unmet.

High Enthusiasm for Openness Maintained Amid Some Contact

In contrast to parents who initially had tentative or restrictive preferences surrounding openness and contact, some parents strongly desired openness from the "get-go" and ultimately matched with birth families wherein they were able to maintain some level of contact, although it was not always predictable and was sometimes easier to maintain with extended birth family than with birth parents. Mariette, a white lesbian physical therapist in a suburb in the Midwest, and her partner, Jenny, a white manager of a medical supply company, were one such couple. Mariette and Jenny were among those couples that seemed to embrace openness from the outset. They specifically chose to work with an agency that only did open adoptions because "we both feel like it's healthier for the child, it's healthier for the birth mother, I think it's healthier for the adoptive parents" (Mariette). Preadoption, Jenny exclaimed that they "loved the philosophy" of open adoption, and that they would "love to be able to have the biological mother, and/or father, the family, participate and be a part of this family." Both women desired ongoing contact with the birth family, although they were also sensitive to the need to consider the birth parents' preferences in determining the exact nuances and nature of contact. Jenny said:

> We definitely want [the] birth mom and the child to have contact—as long as they want that. As far as what amount, we go back and forth with that. Visitations—we're open to, potentially, [the] birth mom seeing the child a couple times a month, depending on . . . where she is traveling from. Phone calls are fine. But you know, we may have an idea right now, but that could change. It could change, it could increase, depending on the relationship, depending on the connection we have. . . . We are open to just seeing how things go, and not really setting the limits—like, only two calls a month, only one visit.

Mariette and Jenny matched with a birth mother, Didi, who was fairly young, was already a parent, and still lived with her family of origin. Didi gave birth to a boy, Jacob, who was biracial (African American/white). Mariette and Jenny both felt very "parental" toward Didi and "truly hoped" for ongoing contact with her. Yet they worried that her extended family might interfere with contact, because they disagreed with Didi's decision to make an adoption plan, wishing that she had chosen to parent. Postadoption, Mariette said that she and Jenny continued to be optimistic about maintaining contact with Didi: "I don't doubt [that we will]—she's been so positive about wanting to be involved, wanting this to be an open adoption, being glad it was us. We have every commitment to stay in touch with her if she's going to do that too." Said Jenny: "We are planning to fly out in the spring for a visit with her. We told her . . . this is what we'd like to do . . . at least once a year, given the distance, and . . . perhaps most of the [traveling] would be done on our side." Yet at the same time that they remained hopeful about the possibility of ongoing contact ("all I can say is that she's receptive to it now" [Jenny]), both women also worried about the possibility of Didi disappearing. Mariette shared:

> I feel like she's very fragile. I feel like she very well could fall off the radar if her family just kind of pushes her to the edge. . . . So, I have a really good feeling about her, but I also realize that—I emailed her about a week and a half ago, I sent pictures from Christmas to both her and . . . his birth father, Jim, and

Jim emailed right back and said, "Thanks so much, they're really cute"—and I haven't heard from Didi. When we were emailing her when she first contacted us, she'd email nightly—but then there would be periods of time where she'd go a week and [a] half without emailing. One of the reasons was that she didn't have a computer. . . . So that may be one of the issues. I don't worry about it, I just—it builds on our worries if we don't hear, don't hear, don't hear.

Five years later, Mariette and Jenny had maintained contact with the birth family, although, as before, contact primarily flowed from them to the birth parents. Interestingly, they now described the birth father, Jim—whom they had initially expected to drop off in terms of contact—as more responsive to communications than Didi. Mariette and Jenny had recently begun to employ Facebook as a way of maintaining contact with Didi and Jim, and this served to be an important tool in sharing photos. They were initially hesitant to accept Jim's and Didi's requests to connect on Facebook (i.e., friend requests) out of concern that their respective families might see their interactions on social media and that these would not "sit well" with them. But Mariette and Jenny came to realize that Facebook could be a valuable way of maintaining the tenuous connection they had with the birth parents, especially Didi. Mariette explained their current contact:

> They are both [connected to us] on Facebook. It's very sporadic and it's very us-driven. His birth parents are not together. If I write them, Jim will write back very quickly. Didi might write back quickly or it might be 3, 4, 5 days before she writes back. If I post a picture or make a comment, every once in a while, and more frequently than not, Jim will write something real quick. I don't think until like last month that Didi had ever made a "like" or a comment. But not too long ago, I posted something that Jacob said, something hysterical, and she wrote, "That's really cute. I can't wait to see you guys." But that's really it. Every once in a while—you know how you can instant message at the bottom? Every once in a while Jim will send a "hi" and asks how we're doing and says he really misses us or something, so we chat for a few minutes. But with Didi it's not like that . . . although I did ask her if she had a few more pictures of her that she could post so I could show Jacob. She wrote back and [put] a couple on there.

Regarding direct contact, Mariette said that their last visit with Didi and Jim occurred when Jacob was a toddler. Despite the fact that "the birth parent agreement that we put together was that it would be alternating years; so a visit once a year and it would be we go there one time, they come here," they had ultimately not had these yearly visits, which Mariette attributed to difficulty scheduling on both of their ends. They were, however, planning a trip to visit both Didi and

Jim during the upcoming year. Mariette and Jenny were looking forward to the trip, as they hoped that it would enable Jacob and his birth parents to "connect." Mariette reiterated her commitment to, and hope for, a truly open adoption:

> It's been disappointing for me because we did an open adoption and we really wanted there to be more of a connection. When we were out there and going through the whole adoption thing, I really did get a sense that there would be more of a connection than there is.... I guess I was just hoping there would be more of an emotional connection. Maybe there will be when we go out again and they actually see him again.

When Jacob was 8, he had visited his birth family three times and was aware that his mothers were friends with his birth parents on Facebook. Jim, his birth father, continued to be the more active one on Facebook. As Mariette said:

> He is a little bit more quick to write a kind, quick hi, or like, "Oh my gosh, I can't believe how big he is getting!" Didi is a little bit less; and now for the last year I've really heard very little from either of them—although I [posted] something not too long ago, and she wrote ... to us and said, "I just can't thank you enough; you guys have given him what I would have wanted for him and so much more."

At the same time that communication with the birth parents was not as extensive or intimate as they had imagined, Mariette and Jenny had established an unexpected and positive relationship with Jacob's paternal birth grandmother, whom they called "Gamma." Gamma had visited them several times, "because she has the means" and was in fact "the biological family member we have the most contact with" (Jenny). During her most recent visit, Gamma had stayed with them—a new development that they felt very positively about, as it had allowed Jacob to spend more time, and deepen his relationship, with Gamma. It is notable that Gamma was African American—and Jacob was biracial: half African American, half white. Mariette and Jenny viewed this relationship as significant and noted that as Jacob became more aware of his racial identity, he would increasingly benefit from connections with birth family members who looked like him.

Thus, Mariette and Jenny, who maintained a solid commitment to birth family contact, had maintained ongoing, if somewhat sporadic, contact with Jacob's birth family. They had also, rather unexpectedly, developed a relationship with a birth grandparent, who came to play a key role in their own and their son's lives. Further, Mariette and Jenny represent a couple who, although initially hesitant about some of the privacy issues inherent to using Facebook, came to view it as a valuable and reliable tool for maintaining contact and connection to the birth family.

Like Mariette and Jenny, Paul, a white school principal, and Greg, a white software consultant, embraced the philosophy of open adoption, and came to establish an open adoption arrangement characterized by a high level of ongoing contact that was fairly close to what they had initially envisioned. Residents of a small city in the South, both Paul and Greg strongly believed in openness, in part because they valued a "mother figure": In fact, explained Paul, "that is a big reason why we chose open adoption." In contrast to "other adoptive parents who might feel threatened by the birth parents," Greg saw regular contact with and involvement by a birth mother as "beneficial to and healthy for the child."

Paul and Greg were matched with a teenage birth mother, Nina, who claimed not to know the birth father. They had their first meeting when Nina was 7 months pregnant, giving the two parties some time to get to know each other. By the time Nina delivered a girl, Louisa (who was biracial: African American and white), both men felt "very comfortable" with Nina, as well as Nina's parents. At 3 months postplacement, the two men had had "quite a bit of contact with Nina.... I think that's really what she needed. One of her fears was that we would just take the baby and disappear and she would never get to see her," said Paul. The couple sought to reassure Nina by "sending a lot of pictures. Plus she's been [to see us] twice and we've met in between. I think it's been good" (Paul). Yet like most adoptions characterized by fairly high levels of contact overall, there were periods of less contact. Greg explained:

> There was a stretch there where all three of us got busy and there wasn't a whole lot of contact.... We had sent Nina several emails.... She was busy with work and... didn't reply. We were kind of worried that she was fading off into the distance, which we really don't want to happen. But now she's back.

Five years postadoption, there were new challenges to deal with—but Paul and Greg had continued to maintain contact with Nina and felt that things had recently been going well. Reflecting on the past few years, Paul said:

> The only time it really got kind of frustrating was when Nina [had a baby] a few years ago. Louisa was so used to getting all of her mom's attention whenever we went to visit her—and then she had to share the attention, so there was tension with that. After visiting her mom, we'd have to drive home 2 hours with this kid that was just crushed, because her mom didn't acknowledge her hair, or her mom didn't acknowledge her dress. But like I said, that's kind of subsided now that her brother, Sebastian, is old enough to play with her.

Both men used Facebook to maintain contact with Nina—as well as Nina's mother. The whole family also Skyped with Nina "once in a while": "Louisa will say, 'Can we Skype?' and we'll talk with Nina, Louisa will talk with Sebastian" (Greg). Both men also texted regularly with both Nina and her mother, particularly in advance of making plans for a visit, but also to exchange photos and to keep each other updated on their lives. Greg noted that having technology-based options for maintaining contact "does make a difference, that's for sure." Thus, Facebook and Skype served as important means of maintaining contact amid the changes in Nina's life (e.g., parenthood) that sometimes made meeting in person difficult. Indeed, adoptive parents' and birth parents' life circumstances may not always be in sync in such a way that facilitates contact. For example, birth parents may be starting new romantic relationships or becoming parents during the adopted child's school-aged years, causing a decline in contact as birth parents adjust to new roles and responsibilities.[13]

Both Paul and Greg nonchalantly referred to Nina as Louisa's mother. Louisa too seemed to conceptualize her role in this way. As Paul noted, 5 years postplacement, "In assignments Louisa brings home where they ask her to draw her family, she will typically draw both our family: Greg, me, and her, but she'll also draw her mom and her brother." The tendency to describe and refer to their children's birth mothers as their mothers, without any caveats or additional descriptors, was specific to gay fathers. Several gay fathers did this, whereas no lesbian mothers or heterosexual mothers did so. Notably, gay fathers did not refer to their children's birth fathers as their fathers. This pattern speaks to (a) the primacy of mothers in society, whereby gay fathers may feel especially compelled to maintain a relationship with birth mothers, and (b) the reality that, in the absence of a woman within the parental unit, gay men are less likely to experience tension or jealousy surrounding the "claiming" of maternal labels and roles.[14] Thus, gay fathers are simultaneously released from the pressures of having to compete with another "mom" while also being compelled to prioritize "moms" in their children's lives.

Another couple who was very enthusiastic about openness from the start and who entered an adoption arrangement characterized by a fair degree of contact was Elora and Dominick, a white heterosexual couple in a large metropolitan area on the West Coast. Like Doug and Paul, Elora and Dominick also experienced periods of lower contact, especially early on, and seemed to maintain a high level of communicativeness about adoption within the family regardless of the current level of contact. Preadoption, Elora, a homemaker, and Dominick, a small business owner, both expressed a view of open adoption that included birth parents as extended family. As Dominick said:

When you get married, you extend your family. When you adopt, you extend your family. It's just another way to increase your family size. And my suspicion is that if the birth parents still want a role in their life, they turn out to be more like an uncle or an aunt in terms of role. That makes perfect sense, and it's not shameful and not filled with regret.

Elora and Dominick matched with a birth mother, Shari, who was young, had some mental health challenges, and had hidden her pregnancy from most of her family. Given that her pregnancy was a secret, Shari expressed some caution regarding the possibility and frequency of future contact with Elora, Dominick, and baby Maeve. Like other parents who matched with birth mothers in their teens or early 20s, both Elora and Dominick acknowledged that Shari brought out "protective" feelings in them. As excited as they were to be placed with Maeve, the couple worried about Shari. Elora conveyed her empathy and concern for Shari, stating:

> What's most important to me is that this situation is a positive situation not only for us, but for Shari. I am really kind of concerned about her. . . . I feel really sad for her, but really happy for us as the same time. I've been always kind of thinking about [this] even before we even meet her. How hard [it is] to, you know, see somebody else's pain like that. I'm worried about her. I'm not worried about the birth father because he's got other children that he doesn't have any contact with.

Elora and Dominick formed a positive relationship with Shari during the weeks leading up to the birth and postplacement. They were clear with her that they would really like to have contact but would respect whatever she preferred. They were delighted when Shari seemed to shift from her initially cautious stance, wherein she was open to fairly limited contact, to expressing greater openness about the possibility of future communication. Stated Dominick: "At the beginning, she really had said that she didn't want any. But [then] I think she was bonding more with Elora and I—and I didn't want to push her, but I suspect she [came to a place where she was glad] that we are open to other possibilities." Thus, the trusting relationship that evolved between the two parties may have served to shift Shari's ideas about the type of relationship she could imagine and would want with an adoptive family.

Five years postplacement, Elora described how their relationship had transpired over time. She noted that they had "kind of lost track of Shari for a little while, but now she's back in the picture with us, and on my Facebook page, and she emails me [about] what's going on in her life a lot." Like many birth parents, Shari had experienced numerous changes in her life over the years following the adoption. She had formed and ended several new romantic relationships and moved multiple times. In turn, contact was sometimes sporadic. Yet during the period when Elora and Dominick "didn't hear back as much" from Shari, the couple had formed a relationship with Maeve's birth grandmother—the birth father's mother—who "sends cards and notes and letters to me, and . . . gifts to Maeve, [and] I send her photos and things" and who also visited occasionally. This contact was welcome yet unexpected, given that the couple had limited contact with Maeve's birth father, other than him occasionally sending small gifts.

Five years postplacement, Shari had been to visit several times ("it's like extended family that we don't see every often": Elora), although not recently. As Dominick said, "It's grown a little more distant. . . . I guess it's kind of nice to know that she's okay, and moving on, and that she continues to feel very good about her decision, and that she is well and things like that." Most of their contact at this point was facilitated via Facebook, which was viewed as a helpful tool in sharing information and photos, although, like some other parents, Elora expressed concerns about some of the information Shari posted—but did not comment on it, feeling that doing so would be inappropriate and would overstep a boundary: "I make sure I don't reply on some of the stuff that she has there because it's just not appropriate, I think. . . . I'm a little bit concerned about . . . the boyfriends that she chooses sometimes."

Eight years postplacement, Elora and Shari continued to be in contact via Facebook, and Elora described a deeper sense of connection to Shari: "She and I . . . talk on Facebook, and on the phone, and keep in touch on a regular basis." Elora also noted that she and Dominick had sent money to Shari when she was in a difficult situation and needed to leave the place where she was living: "She kind of got stuck, so . . . we paid for her plane tickets to get her home." Elora regarded their relationship as very close, adding that "she probably would be, more so like a daughter to me, more than kind of a peer kind of friendship." Elora and Dominick had also formed connections with other birth relatives, including several aunts, via Facebook. Elora and Dominick felt very positively about these connections, especially as they imagined a future in which their daughter Maeve might want to make direct contact with these individuals.

Elora and Dominick were one of a number of couples where contact was primarily maintained among adults, with the intention of eventually facilitating contact between birth parents and children (e.g., when they became teenagers or, more specifically, when they turned 18). For the first 8 years following placement, most communication occurred between them and Shari; Shari had only met Maeve a few times. Yet amid the fairly limited direct contact between Shari and Maeve, Elora and Dominick remained committed to a fairly high level of communicative openness that was evident in the frequency and nature of the adoption-related conversations they initiated and engaged in with Maeve. Five years postplacement, Dominick shared:

> We talk openly about it. . . . Elora's made these really nice books of photos—they're little bound books, and the first one basically tells Maeve's birth story. . . . There are pictures of her birth mom and birth dad and she knows what their names are, and some of her extended family. Her birth grandmother stays in contact regularly, and sends her presents. We include her as one of Maeve's grandmas. . . . We stay in contact with her birth mom. There is no secret to Maeve that she's adopted. The way we think of it, and I think she probably thinks of it too, is that there are many ways that families are formed, and one of them is through adoption. Some children are adopted and some aren't, and both are perfectly normal. . . . That was our approach from the beginning and it seemed like a good one to take. . . . She hasn't asked a lot of questions about her birth mom, or birth dad yet. I suspect it's partially because . . . people aren't bringing it up at school, you know. She's not being pressured.

Eight years postplacement, both Elora and Dominick said that they were still typically the ones to initiate conversations about adoption; Maeve, in general, "didn't seem too interested." But both parents observed something that many parents alluded to: the reality that although "adoption talk" was regular, normalized, and casual within the household, there were apparent gaps in Maeve's comprehension of adoption. That is, as Maeve matured, she asked questions that revealed a lack of understanding of certain aspects of adoption. For example, Elora and Dominick had recently begun proceedings to adopt a second child via foster care, a little girl named Opal, when Elora realized that Maeve did not understand some aspects of adoption:

> When we were setting all this stuff up, all of a sudden she didn't know what it meant. It was like, what? In talking about it all these years, I was really kind of surprised! I think she was talking about more, like, the legal aspects of it [that she didn't get]. But . . . I was surprised that she didn't get it, because she knows she has a birth mother and a birth father and a whole other family. We kind of have always treated them just as, like, extended family. Like, there are people you just don't see as much. So, it's just been so normal that, it's kind of not been. . . . It would be like saying to somebody, you know, "What's it like to have a birth parent?" or something. You know, I don't know. You don't know any different than what you've kind of lived, or whatever.

As psychologist and adoption expert David Brodzinsky[15] has noted, an ongoing task, and sometimes challenge, that adoptive parents face is the sharing of adoption information with children in such a way that they come to understand the meaning and implications of being adopted. Young (i.e., preschool-aged) children may understand the language of adoption (e.g., they learn to talk about "being adopted") without grasping what this actually means.[16] Parents of young children frequently overestimate the depth of their children's understanding of adoption—possibly leading them to minimize the significance of, or their efforts to address, adoption with their children[17]—although that did not appear to be the case for Elora and Dominick. As Maeve grew, both parents asserted that she did appear to grasp much more about what it meant to be adopted, reflecting the changes in cognitive and emotional development that occur in middle childhood,[18] which ultimately led to more "tough discussions" about what it meant to "have a birth mother, but not to live with her" (Elora).

High Enthusiasm for Openness Maintained Amid No Contact

Some couples were highly enthusiastic about openness prior to adopting but matched with birth parents who were described as wanting no contact. (Many of these were emergency placements, where a birth mother made an adoption plan from the hospital, soon after giving birth, and in some cases did not actually choose the couple themselves—the agency or social worker chose them.) In such circumstances, parents were challenged to maintain communicative openness amid a regrettable absence of birth family contact. Indeed, these couples found the absence of birth parent contact difficult to reconcile with the fact that they had pursued domestic private adoption with a wish, and often expectation, for ongoing contact.

Jamie and Evan, a white gay couple living in a midsized Southern city, represent one such couple. Preadoption, both Jamie, a communications manager, and Evan, a hospital office manager, were very enthusiastic about openness: "It just [makes] perfect sense," said Evan. Both men were especially excited about the possibility of birth mother involvement, imagining how she might function as a key female figure in their child's life. Jamie and Evan waited several years to be placed with a child. During this period, they made contact with multiple expectant mothers, some of whom ended up choosing other couples, and others whom their agency determined were "scammers . . . not really pregnant at all." Then, one hot summer day, the couple received an emergency placement phone call from the hospital. Although an expectant mother had indeed chosen them—in part because of their openness to a biracial or multiracial child (she was black and the birth father was white)—she did not want to meet them. Furthermore, she claimed not to know who the birth father was, and thus, there was no possibility of meeting him either.

She was open to the possibility of being contacted through the agency in the future, having "signed papers that when Timothy is 18 he can find her" (Jamie). Not wishing to give up on his dream of an open adoption, Jamie stated: "I hope that she changes her mind and goes to the agency. We would welcome her to be able to see Timothy and see how wonderful he is." The reality of the situation certainly clashed with both men's hopeful vision of a truly open adoption. Having been sold on the idea of openness, they were unprepared for the possibility of no contact at all. As Evan said, 3 months postadoption:

> I was . . . disappointed. We opened ourselves up to have this relationship with the birth mom because . . . all the classes that we took and all the books that we've read, you know, it's supposed to be so good, emotional development-wise, for the child to know their roots. And, from what we understand, it somewhat helps the birth mother with this whole process as well. We would have liked to meet her [at least] but I have to respect her wishes. . . . But we have totally left the door open for her, if she changes her mind. I think the biggest disappointment for me is for Timothy.

Thus, Evan's principal reason for desiring openness was for the benefit of his child. In turn, his disappointment centered around the loss of these anticipated benefits for Timothy.

Five years postplacement, Evan and Jamie had adopted a second child, Daria. Daria had a relationship with her birth mother—and this, as in other families, had raised a lot of questions for Timothy surrounding why he did not see his birth mother. Jamie shared:

> Timothy continues to ask questions. I think some of his questions in the last year have been more because of the difference between himself and Daria—that his birth mom is not involved, and we don't have conversations with her. She placed, and she moved on. So in that situation of just placing and moving on versus with Daria where we were there for the birth and for [subsequent] visits . . . those kinds of questions come up just because he's wondering why there's a difference between . . . having a birth mom or not having a birth mom. So he's trying to understand that, and we've had those kinds of discussions with him about the differences. . . . He hasn't talked about his birth father yet; that's the topic that hasn't come up. [Fortunately] the agency is there to help us, you know—counsel us to say the right things. I just want to make sure I say the right thing to him.

Jamie noted that he had looked for Timothy's birth mother on the Internet but was unable to find any information about her. He also acknowledged that if they were able to find her on social media or elsewhere, he was not sure what they would do with the information, because, as Evan said, "from what I understand we're supposed to honor her wishes, so I have a feeling that [contact] would have to come from her." This was frustrating and disappointing for Evan in particular, who felt that contact would "benefit us all. It would be so healthy for Timothy. So if she wanted to [contact us through social media], it would be great. But like I said, I don't want to—I guess we could pursue it. What would stop us? I don't know." Evan's uncertainty about how to proceed stemmed from a fundamental conflict between his strong desire to make contact with Timothy's birth mother and his wish to avoid overstepping boundaries, as well as concern about violating the "rules" of their contract.

When Timothy was 8, both Evan and Jamie emphasized that he had become more sensitive about the fact that he did not have contact with his birth mother, whereas his sister Daria did. Jamie said:

> In Daria's situation, she knows . . . her birth mom and birth siblings. And Timothy doesn't understand why that's—it's not fair to him. And kids are about fairness, right? So now we just don't really talk about that so much with him just because we know that it bothers him and makes him upset. . . . When Daria's birth mom reaches out and texts us or wants pictures we send them and we text back and forth. She's wanted to Skype a few times. So we've done that every now and then. . . . We typically take Timothy out of the house during this time. But we also understand that as Daria gets older, that conversation's going to start happening again. My hope is that in a couple years Timothy will have a few more years of maturity on him; it'll be a different kind of conversation.

Evan shared how he had sought to explain the current situation to Timothy:

> I said, "You know, Daddy really wants your birth mom to possibly want to reach out to us and she can. And we told the lawyer, if she reaches out to me to contact us we will make that happen." I want her to see how wonderful he is. And . . . we do have her information, and if she moves or anything she's supposed to let the agency know . . . so if we ever needed her for some kind of family background history information . . . she can be found.

Thus, Jamie and Evan struggled with communicative openness in relation to Timothy. In possession of very limited information about his birth mother, and uncertain about whether and how to reach out to her amid her desire for privacy, they were sometimes unsure of how to respond accurately and sensitively to Timothy's questions—which had intensified as he grew older and as he also began to contrast his situation with that of his sister, Daria. The couple acknowledged leaning on their adoption agency for support as they navigated Timothy's current questions and anticipated future ones, such as those related to his birth father. They were frank with Timothy about their own ongoing desire to make contact with his birth mother—yet also acknowledged the reality that, as of yet, she had not responded to their letters and photos. Evan and Jamie were highly engaged in the ongoing process of helping Timothy to make sense of his adoption amid a sometimes frustrating set of circumstances. As parents, they could not give Timothy all of the answers that he wanted—which was no doubt incredibly painful at times.

Peggy and Elana were another couple who desired an open adoption but did not get one, yet who maintained communicative openness nonetheless. Both white, and living in a large Northeastern city, Peggy was an occupational therapist and Elana was a website editor. Neither woman had a strong desire to be a biological parent or to experience pregnancy or childbirth, and thus landed on adoption—and specifically open adoption—fairly soon after solidifying their shared goal of becoming parents. They were excited and enthusiastic about the idea of openness. Preadoption, Elana spoke passionately about the various benefits of openness that she imagined, for both the child and the child's birth family:

> Open adoption is, I think, a way to recognize what kind of effects adoption has on a child. There probably will be some sort of grieving process for our child—when that child begins to realize that they were born into a family and then they're no longer with that family, for whatever reason. As they get older, having more information about that family and what they were like, and who they're related to—I think that's an important thing for getting through that grieving process, and realizing what kind of person you are—kind of figuring out your identity. That's really important for everybody, and it's especially important for people who are adopted. And on the other side of it, with the birth parents—being able to provide them with information about their child, even if they don't really want it right away, or they're nervous about it, may help them with their kind of process too. So I really hope we do end up with some sort of open adoption situation.

Although similarly excited about the benefits associated with openness, Peggy also acknowledged, and seemed prepared for, a range of circumstances that might impede openness, including those that set the birth parents up to place a child in the first place:

> Obviously, people place their children for adoption because there's something going on in their life. So, that could potentially be an issue. But I don't see it as

a huge issue, and I think the benefits of it outweigh [the challenges]. Even if is difficult for the kid, I think it's more difficult not to have contact.

While describing her desire for, at a minimum, "yearly visits, and sending letters and pictures and that sort of thing," Peggy also acknowledged that "sometimes what happens is ... [you] end up with a child where the birth mother just places them and they don't want contact."

Almost a year after waiting to adopt, Peggy and Elana received an emergency placement call. A woman who had had several children removed from her care by social services, and who was "actively trying to get those children back," had just given birth. This woman was aware that "having a fourth child would kind of make it hard for her to get her other children back" and she was struggling financially. Because her children were not currently in her care, she had been advised to make an adoption plan to avoid her baby being placed in foster care. This is how Peggy and Elana came to become the parents of their daughter Kacie, who was biracial (African American and white).

Kacie's birth mother did not want to meet them. "She left the hospital the same day that our daughter was born. So it's an open adoption in the sense that we're open to being contacted, but she hasn't really made any contact" (Peggy). Although they were disappointed, Peggy and Elana regularly "sent pictures" through the agency and remained hopeful about the possibility of some future contact, while also recognizing that it might not happen. "We wanted more. The [lack of contact] was the only thing about the situation that wasn't exactly what we wanted. But that's the way it was, so . . . and she might always change her mind" (Peggy). Echoed Elana:

> I hope . . . the situation will change [but] right now the birth mom is not interested in contact. We hope that eventually it will be an open adoption. [We'll] send letters and pictures to the agency that will just be held by them, and if the birth mom ever wants to find out about Kacie, she can contact the agency and pick up that information. So there's a door open that way.

By the time that Kacie was 5, nothing had changed with respect to contact. Peggy and Elana continued to send yearly updates, including a letter and photos, to the agency, but they were uncertain as to whether Kacie's birth mother was receiving them. Stated Peggy, "We are not even sure whether the agency has a good address for her anymore." They also had very limited information about Kacie's birth family, which made it challenging to talk in depth with her about some aspects of her adoption. Yet they did the best they could to foster open communication with Kacie amid their limited knowledge of her birth family. Peggy explained:

Kacie knows where she was born and her birth mom's name and the fact that we don't know her birth dad's name. We [made] a story book about her adoption process [with pictures] and the story of how we went to go pick her up and pictures of her the first day we met her and all the people she met.... Sometimes we drive by the hospital where she was born and casually say, "Oh that's where you were born." So if we drive by some place that looks like it, she will say, "Oh that's where I was born" [*laugh*]. She knows the story.

In the absence of ongoing information about or contact with the birth family, but in the presence of strong ideals surrounding openness, some parents—like Peggy and Elana—sought to cultivate an environment where adoption talk was "no big deal" and their children in turn would feel comfortable asking questions and sharing feelings about adoption. So far, Peggy and Elana thought they were "doing okay with that"—but continued to long for birth family contact.

A final couple who embodies this pattern of "high openness, no contact" was Charlene and Leila, a white lesbian couple living in a large Northeastern city, who waited several years for a child placement. A teacher and physical therapist, respectively, Charlene and Leila maintained communicative openness with their Latina daughter Sofia despite a lack of structural openness. Although both women were strongly invested in the benefits of open adoption, Sofia's birth mother, Jasmine—whom they had met once, soon after Sofia's birth, an opportunity that Charlene was "so grateful" for—had not maintained contact. Jasmine had expressed a wish for a semiopen adoption: She wanted to receive letters and pictures twice a year via the adoption agency but did not want direct contact with Sofia. Jasmine was also open to receiving emails from Charlene and Leila, which they did initiate, but which went unreturned after several brief replies from Jasmine during the early weeks postplacement. Charlene and Leila remained hopeful about the potential for future contact but also expressed an awareness that it simply might not happen, given Jasmine's stated wishes.

Five years later, the couple shared that they had heard from Jasmine only once—however, her words meant the world to them. Leila explained how over the past few years, the contact had been overwhelmingly initiated by them—punctured by one meaningful response from Jasmine:

We send letters and pictures twice a year to our adoption agency where they're in cold storage forever—they've never been read, she's never requested them. And we have faithfully, every single month, written her a breezy email, "Hey," you know, whatever ... "it's spring here." We never mentioned Sofia's name—we didn't even mention Sofia all that much. We just said, "This is what our family is up to. We continue to think of you, we continue to cherish the day that we met you. You continue to be about one of the most important people we've ever met.

We hope you're well." And then she actually informed us of a change in email address, but she would never write back. We just desperately—this is like our only connection, her email, but she would never write back. Then one time she did write back and just said, "It's clear I made the right choice." Everybody burst into tears.

In the absence of ongoing reciprocal contact, Charlene and Leila cultivated communicative openness through activities (e.g., the collaborative construction of Sofia's life book) and daily conversation (e.g., about her adoption day, about other children they knew who were adopted). Three months postplacement, Leila emphasized that they "told her she was adopted from the beginning.... We have Jasmine's photograph on the piano along with lots of other baby photographs. We use books to talk about it." When Sofia was 5, Charlene said:

> She doesn't bring it up much. We bring it up more than she does. But when we bring it up she'll talk about it, you know? We'll find ways to kind of just tell her stories about when we adopted her. We'll look at pictures. We always celebrate her finalization. And this past year we finally decided, "Okay, we've got to do the life book." We had just not gotten our act together so we involved her in it and it was remarkable how into it she was.... We had photographs and we wanted to do it in somewhat chronological order so we would say, "Let's start at the beginning. So you grew in Jasmine's tummy..." and then we would kind of tell her, "Well maybe we should write your mood down in words," and she said, "Yeah, that sounds good." So we would write words and then she would draw pictures... and [we'll bring it out regularly now] and say,... "Do you want to do another page?"... We said, "You know, this is something you can keep adding to... as you grow and you think about parts of your life that you want to put in your book."

It was around this time that the couple had begun seeing an adoption therapist, as Sofia had begun asking more questions about her birth parents. For example, Leila note that Sofia had recently

> asked about her birth father, and I kind of put it back on her birth mother and said she didn't tell us much about him. We know his name and we know he was really good at math. That's about all we've got. So we respond to questions she asks us if we're able.

Charlene and Leila also maintained contact with their adoption agency and sometimes reached out for ongoing support from them, particularly amid Sofia's growing curiosity about her birth parents.

For the next few years, contact continued in the same way, such that "every 4 to 6 weeks, we make sure we get an email out to Jasmine. . . . We're pretty general; we don't want to give her too much information and scare her away; we want to maintain this fragile connection that we have so we're careful," explained Charlene. The absence of more reciprocal contact was difficult for both women. Charlene said wistfully: "I mean, I would much prefer to have her in our life and in Sofia's life in some fashion. So I definitely feel that loss. I still feel oddly very connected with her even though we don't really have any contact."

Around the time that Sofia turned 8, a rather major change in indirect, or passive, contact occurred: Namely, Jasmine friended Charlene and Leila on Facebook—which led to some complex back and forth until, with the support and guidance of their agency, they gently requested some boundaries related to "liking" and commenting on posts and photos. Charlene explained how, when they received the Facebook request,

> we were so excited—we started liking photos that each other posted and making some comments, and then we realized—what can other people see of what we're saying about each other's photos or comments or whatever? So we talked with our adoption agency about it and the director really helped us kind of frame a conversation over email about Sofia's story being her own story and wanting to kind of protect that and have her know her story before other people know her story. And so if people that we know see that we're having contact with Jasmine and Sofia doesn't know that, it didn't feel right, and could we just be private, couldn't we just sort of enjoy each other's photos but you know, message each other privately or communicate about things over email and not over Facebook? And she wrote back a really nice letter saying, "Absolutely, I respect your privacy and . . . thank you for respecting mine and I totally understand." That was the last written contact we had with her. Since then she has totally respected that. . . . Mostly, frankly, I put pictures up on Facebook of Sofia for Jasmine. I mean I'm happy to share them with our family and friends but the main motivation is so that she can still see Sofia.

Charlene and Leila's story is a version of a scenario that occurred in other families as well (see Chapter 7): A birth parent who has been relatively unresponsive to communication via "traditional" means (e.g., letters) reaches out via social media to make contact. As Charlene and Leila articulate, the excitement of finally having some contact—even if indirect—was so great that they made some impulsive decisions regarding sharing that they came to regret. In turn, the couple had to renegotiate boundaries with someone who was extremely important to them but with whom they had not had direct contact in 8 years. The stressfulness of this situation was mitigated by the fact that they consulted their agency, received solid guidance, and deployed good judgment amid a variety of competing concerns and pressures. Yes, they strongly desired openness—but they were also aware of the potentially problematic nature of their Facebook communication and the ways that it might jeopardize their daughter's privacy. Ever fearful of the possibility of losing all contact with her birth mother, they took a chance by requesting certain boundaries on their communication—and it was, thankfully, respectfully and appreciatively received.

Birth Parents, Boundaries, and Difficult Circumstances: When Contact Is Threatened

Some parents encountered difficult circumstances with the birth family, which often involved birth parents' mental health challenges, as well as, in some cases, drug abuse/activity or criminal behavior. Navigating such situations was especially difficult when parents highly valued birth contact. In some cases, the birth parents' difficulties were seen as a threat to the stability and functioning of the adoptive family, and the child specifically, and efforts to maintain contact were muted. In other cases, parents sought to (re)negotiate boundaries and mutual expectations in an effort to maintain contact.

Enthusiasm for Openness Diminished in the Context of Difficult Circumstances and Boundary Challenges; Contact Markedly Reduced, Limited, or Terminated

Some parents demonstrated enthusiasm for (or at least interest in) open adoption preadoption and expressed a desire for some level of contact, but ultimately matched with birth parents who had emotional or substance use difficulties that prompted adoptive parents to place certain restrictions on contact. This type of situation highlights the power of the adoptive parents in managing the relationship and the level and type of contact that unfolds—that is, they are the ultimate arbiter of contact.[19]

Rachel, a computer applications training manager, and Nancy, a pet store manager, were a white lesbian couple living in a large metropolitan area of the South. Preadoption, Rachel shared her perspective that

> for us, open adoption was an interesting prospect because we got to continue a relationship with the mother, which we felt was important, but ... we didn't feel that we wanted to coparent, but we wanted to be able to be honest with the baby

almost from the beginning—about their adoption, how they came to be, how we all ended up together.

Nancy, in turn, acknowledged that although initially "open adoption was such a scary thing ... we were like 'Oh my gosh, there is no way we can do this,'" through reading books and attending adoption programming, she realized "how healthy it was for the child, in that it took away so many questions in their life." Thus, both women seemed to be on board with openness preadoption—although in noting that the birth mother would not be another coparent, Rachel suggests that she felt strongly about establishing mutual expectations related to boundaries and roles.[20]

The couple was matched with a birth mother, Jade, who had "significant emotional problems" including a long history of depression, and a birth father, Donny, who had a history of physical and emotional abuse against Jade. In turn, the couple vocalized a sense of caution in their early interactions with the birth parents while also trying to fulfill their side of the agreement, especially in relation to Jade. After they were placed with their daughter, Moriah, who was biracial (African American and white), they "emailed Jade with [pictures] every week just to let her know that we are still here and we are not going anywhere. . . . She is working through some abandonment issues [in counseling]. We are trying to back off . . . without having her feel . . . isolated" (Rachel). To Rachel, it was "important that she doesn't feel like we just kind of [up] and left." Rachel added that when they spoke on the phone—which happened every few weeks—she purposely "[did] not initiate the hanging up. I let Jade kind of guide that." Given Donny's history of violence toward Jade, both Rachel and Nancy were tentative about future visits with Donny specifically—but also maintained an openness to seeing how things unfolded over time. Said Rachel: "He will probably at some point come out to see Moriah. . . . We had some reservations because of some of his actions, but . . . we'll make those decisions as they come."

Five years postplacement, Nancy and Rachel shared that they had seen Jade only once, when their daughter Moriah was about a year old—and they had not seen Donny at all. The couple continued to speak with Jade on the phone occasionally; such calls were typically initiated by Jade. Rachel, who was the primary communicator within the couple, "sent pictures, emails . . . probably just about every 3 months. It's been like this the last few years." Despite the fact that Jade had requested more contact, the couple had denied this ("She . . . wanted to be able to Skype with Moriah on a daily basis. I just don't think that's healthy. . . . She wants more than we're willing to do, and more than we ever agreed to do" [Nancy]). Both women described feeling forced to redraw their boundaries surrounding contact and communication based on what they perceived as inappropriate behavior on Jade's part—for their daughter's sake. Nancy shared examples of what she saw as Jade's manipulative behavior and how it led them to "double down" on their efforts to protect Moriah, although she also acknowledged that Jade's emotionality was a personal trigger for her, activating her own fears surrounding losing Moriah:

> Jade is in a really bad place. She never went and got help from it. She was just calling and crying and saying that her kids are staring at Moriah's picture and crying.... Jade was crying, like, "There's a hole in my family and... her brothers and sisters need to speak with her on the phone. We want to get one of those webcam things so I can see her every night." That became really hard for us. We're not going to subject Moriah to that.... It's like this whole big gamut of emotion because I know she can't take Moriah from me, but it's always something that hangs over your head anyways.

Indeed, although she maintained that she "admired and respected" Jade for placing Moriah, Nancy emphasized that she felt that it was important to place clear and firm limits on Jade's behavior, in order to protect Moriah. She stated:

> When Jade called this last time and was finished crying... we finally told her, "You know what, Jade, you gave up Moriah, entrusting us that we would do the right thing for her, and that is not the right thing for her. It is not fair to Moriah [to] get on the phone with her and tell her that you're her mother; that's not your place. You need to get some counseling because you're not in a good place at all."

Nancy asserted that they had offered to pay for Jade's counseling but that Jade had said, "Oh no, I don't need it."

Rachel shared how she struggled to continue to be responsive to Jade's overtures amid her frustration and irritation:

> Usually when she calls, she's obviously upset and she's crying—and it's really the truth that I haven't changed the cell phone... so that's how I try to reassure her, like, look, if this was about bait and cut, you wouldn't be talking to me on the same phone number that you've been talking to me on for... years. But time is the one thing that you don't get to push and manipulate. I'd say that her life is pretty filled with pushing and manipulating.

Rachel described a variety of ways in which she had responded to what she perceived as problematic expectations for their relationship on the part of Jade: "If she calls and leaves a message and asks me to send pictures, when I send pictures I'll say, 'Okay, now I've sent you pictures. You send me pictures.' I want her to understand that there's, like, an equal [relationship] here. This isn't all about her asking. Like, one-sided." Rachel had also recently altered the type of pictures she sent to Jade as a way of clarifying the boundaries as well as trying to encourage Jade to see their family as a separate and complete entity:

> I used to send her pictures of just Moriah. More to protect her . . . I thought if she had the pictures out or whatever she wouldn't have to explain anything, if it were the three of us or . . . like, if somebody came over, it wasn't like, "Well what's going on here . . . [with two moms]? But then honestly, I believe that she almost thought that Moriah was still her child . . . almost like we were just raising Moriah for her. And I don't think she necessarily respected or saw us as like a true family unit. I got that feeling. The only pictures I send now are of the three of us.

In considering the reality that her daughter Moriah currently had little contact with her birth mother—which Rachel viewed as necessary and protective, given Jade's emotional difficulties and boundary challenges—Rachel also acknowledged the importance of being open and honest with Moriah about her origins and adoption story. Thus, amid relatively low structural openness, communicative openness was viewed as doubly important:

> I think that the more honest and the more forthcoming we are from the very beginning, the easier it will be long down the road. No matter how we ever slice this, until the day we die, we will never be Moriah's biological mothers. It's an impossibility. So it's our responsibility to make sure that she knows what she needs to know.

Nancy elaborated on the challenge of maintaining these boundaries with Jade amid Moriah's growing interest in adoption and meeting her birth mother:

> Moriah is just now kind of understanding what adoption is, and asking, "What is a birth mother?" We read adoption books, and Moriah asks, "Mommy, do I have a birth mother?" "Yes you do." "What's her name?" "Jade." "Can I meet her?" "Of course you can, if that's what you want to do. Later on."

Nancy struggled to balance her awareness that "openness is important" with the difficult challenges that they were currently facing with Jade and the "huge stress" that contact had placed on them:

I wish that we had no contact with them. I mean, I know it's the best thing for Moriah [so that she doesn't] wonder where she came from and struggle with that and have to search to find Jade and Donny. So that's one reason why we're sending pictures and answering the phone and doing those things. It's not for them but for Moriah. . . . We committed morally to keep in touch, to have an open adoption. So we're trying as best we can.

Rachel and Nancy, then, were a couple who had not always been highly enthusiastic about open adoption but whose exposure to education and information via their adoption agency had impressed upon them its potential benefits—although they continued to believe in the importance of clearly delineated roles and boundaries. They matched with a set of birth parents who were struggling with a fair amount of internal and situational chaos. As time progressed, Jade's emotional spillover and requests for contact, which seemingly exceeded what the two parties had agreed to, were viewed as increasingly disruptive and frustrating. In turn, Rachel and Nancy sought to maintain forms of contact that allowed greater distance between their family and Jade—while resisting more direct forms of contact, such as Skype.

Adam, a biracial (African American and white) marketing director, and his partner, Will, a white accountant, were another couple that had been enthusiastic about openness but ultimately—after a very positive initial relationship—faced an abrupt cessation of contact with their child's birth mother. The couple, who lived in a midsized city on the West Coast, were contacted by their son Isaac's birth mother, Julie, very early in her pregnancy: namely, during her first trimester. In her early 20s, Julie was not in a relationship with Isaac's birth father and was emotionally and financially unprepared to become a parent. Adam and Will formed what both men described as an excellent relationship with Julie during her pregnancy. Three months after adopting Isaac, Will described their relationship like this:

We still talk; we Skype. She asks us relationship advice, questions, and she kind of sees us as her big brothers. We were Skyping with her yesterday and she started crying because she realized that Isaac was in such a good place; she could see Isaac from Skype. . . . When we say goodbye she says "I love you" and we'll say "I love you" back, and she's really like a sister to us, or a niece, or something like that. We feel very close to Julie.

Julie maintained regular contact with them for the first few months, and then contact dwindled somewhat as she got a job and moved farther away. Adam and Will described Julie as emotionally fragile, and, aware that she had been disappointed by many people in her life, both men strove to always follow through on any promises they made to her—for example, by calling her exactly when they said they would call. Yet after about 2 years, Julie stopped returning their calls and emails: "Suddenly [it was like] we went from being her best friends to her enemies." The two men pulled back, continuing to send pictures but halting their efforts at phone and email contact.

When Isaac was a toddler, they saw Julie for the first time since Isaac was born. Adam, Will, and Isaac were planning a vacation to the state in which Julie was now living and contacted her ahead of time to ask if she wanted to get together. Julie did respond this time and seemed excited about the possibility of a visit. But the visit was a "disaster," because, as Adam said,

> Isaac did not really care who she was, and she was very hurt by that ... so she got very angry and upset, and thought he was disrespectful. But ... he was a 3-year-old bouncing around, he could care less who she was ... and so ... this is kind of part of Julie's mental health issues; she immediately lashes out when she feels rejected. So she got very angry, and really quite vicious. And it hurt a lot. Especially Will. For me, it didn't really hurt me [as] much, because I had always sort of kept, I guess greater ... emotional boundaries with her than Will had. So it was very rocky after that for a year or so. Our agreement said we would send pictures at least once a year ... so we sent pictures to her without much of a comment, because at this time she was just still really, really angry and venomous. But I was sticking to the agreement we had with the open adoption.

During the year that followed the visit, Adam and Will became guardians to a little girl, Clementine. Clementine—whom they eventually adopted—became part of their family quickly and unexpectedly when a close friend became ill and passed away. Julie, upon seeing the pictures that the couple sent her, which included a new and unfamiliar child, was reportedly very upset, having not been notified of this addition to their family. Adam shared:

> It threw her over the edge. She just got very, very ugly.... "I never want to hear from you again!" So I wrote her back, and I said, "I understand this is how you feel now. But we have a contract we have to honor from the open adoption. So if you really want us never to contact you, I would ask you to go to our agency, and just tell them that so that it's documented." And so she did ... and when we next contacted them, they said, "We have it on file that she doesn't want any communication." And so that's where we have left it.

Will elaborated:

> She actually told the agency that she wants to release us from our obligation to send her pictures once a year. And so we said we won't do that unless she sends

a letter to the agency. The agency . . . can have that on file if it ever comes up again. So we haven't had any contact with her at all. It is hard, because I kind of wanted to stay in touch. But now, no way. Because I don't want Isaac . . . having a relationship with her [only to have her] flip against him. We can take it, but he couldn't.

With Isaac, in the meantime, Adam and Will continued to share the "same story—that Julie loved him so much that she wanted him to have a better life than she could provide." They also had "lots and lots of pictures of Julie . . . alone, with Isaac [when he was born], and so on." When Isaac was 5, Adam and Will had not had contact with Julie in over a year. Adam had tried searching for her on the Internet but "she doesn't show up." The couple remained hopeful that they might re-establish contact with Julie in the future, yet they felt strongly about protecting their son from the type of emotional reactivity that they had experienced from Julie.

A final couple who started out very open to contact but ultimately had to curtail their efforts at maintaining contact with their child's birth mother was Kelly and Gil, a white heterosexual couple employed as an environmental planner and property manager, respectively, in a large West Coast city. Kelly and Gil were strongly in favor of an open adoption, even noting that they were not sure they would accept a placement situation with birth parents who didn't want at least some openness: "We were very wary of closed adoption." And in fact, Zoe, their daughter Rosa's birth mother, was drawn to them in part because "she liked our take on open adoption; she had placed other children before and was not in as much contact with her birth kids as she wanted and we were really very, very pro-open adoption. That made a difference to her." Despite the fact that Zoe initially struggled with her decision to place Rosa for adoption, she ultimately did—reassured, according to Kelly, by the couple's commitment to openness.

The two families maintained regular contact over the first few years, particularly via text messaging ("she's a big texter") but also via email ("we email her photographs and keep in touch by email"). When Rosa was 6, Kelly described how they had recently navigated some boundary challenges with Zoe. Although Kelly had accepted a friend request from Zoe via Facebook, she was dismayed to find that Zoe—who struggled with "emotional instability"—frequently posted about Rosa, including pictures of her, in a way that felt "intrusive." In addition, Zoe had given out the family's address and phone number to other birth relatives without asking them—including one birth relative who declared their intention to "take custody" of Rosa (a legal impossibility but a highly upsetting statement to the couple nonetheless). Kelly asserted that Zoe's behavior prompted her to make "two nonnegotiable demands." One was that Zoe "not post anything on the

Internet about Rosa again and two ... she not give out our contact information ever again to anybody. We are in charge of who's in touch with our family, not her. We email her." Gil shared his frustration and their efforts to stay calm amid their sense that their privacy had been threatened and their relationship with Zoe seriously compromised:

> It's just like, "What?!" You are screwing with our family to the point of—like, I may never talk to you again. These weren't things that.... But everything I said to her I said in a calm tone.... We were very calm with her, but explained that this is not okay. This is not acceptable. You cannot give our information out, all that. She got really ... pissed off and hung up on us basically.

In consultation with their adoption agency, several therapists, and an adoption expert, Kelly and Gil developed an understanding of Zoe as having mental health issues wherein she "loses all rational thought [sometimes] and does these things." Their therapist pushed them to "think about if this is somebody you want in your life or not." After some deliberation, Kelly noted that they

> wrote her a really long email that kind of said, "You can't do this. [We may need to] go back to court, and change [our contract] to make this explicit." Basically Zoe kind of came around. I think she settled down ... and I think things got a little more stable emotionally for her, but she minimizes [the breach in trust] ... [like it was] a bump in the road.

Recently, they had had a visit with Zoe, who was, in their eyes, entirely appropriate with them and with Rosa. But Gil continued to feel wary, concerned about future potential breaches in trust and the long-term viability of their relationship with Zoe. He said: "We're willing to continue a relationship—but if anything even remotely along those lines comes up again, I think it might be done." He added:

> It's like being in a relationship with a deadbeat dad, or something; [there are things] like her insensitivity [that] you have to deal with because we share this child—we have something in common. The incident with [our information] has made it difficult, to the point of saying, "Are we going to sever this relationship?" We've got to do what's best for our family.

Thus, these parents often voiced a tension between their original intentions surrounding openness and their current feelings about birth parents. On the one hand, parents voiced a desire to honor their agreements with their children's birth parents, aware that as their children grew older, they would want and need contact with their birth parents—regardless of how emotionally dysregulated and chaotic they were. But on the other hand, these parents felt manipulated or mistreated by birth parents and/or expressed concern about how the birth parents' behavior could negatively impact their child or family, currently and in the long term. They struggled to reconcile their often conflicting feelings toward the birth parents—but in the meantime, their default was often to place new or additional limits on contact or set boundaries for appropriate behavior. One gay father's narrative illustrates the back-and-forth internal debates that parents often engaged in:

> The birth mother has . . . issues and PTSD [posttraumatic stress disorder] and trauma [but] I think about the fact that she's basically—her actions and what she did [substance abuse–wise and crime-wise] basically has really affected all of her children, our child to the least extent. . . . At the same time, she's responsible for making us parents, right; she birthed our child. I don't really know how I will react to her on an ongoing regular basis. . . . I really like her as a person; it's just hard for me to [deal with her].

Enthusiasm for Openness Maintained Amid Difficult Birth Parent Circumstances and Boundary Challenges; Contact Maintained

Not all couples curtailed contact in response to difficult birth parent interactions or circumstances. Some found ways to maintain it, even amid challenging ongoing dynamics with birth parents. One such couple was Stacy, a white school administrator, and Deb, a white chiropractor, who lived in a midsized city in the Northeast. Stacy and Deb were placed with Marlo, a biracial (Latina/white) girl, via a private domestic adoption that "could have been" a public domestic adoption situation. Namely, their social worker called them about a baby who had been born drug exposed and would require temporary hospitalization in the neonatal intensive care unit (NICU). They were told that Marlo's birth mother, Krista, had made an adoption plan "very last minute" after realizing that Marlo would likely be removed from her care. To alleviate the stress of going through the courts to have her parental rights terminated involuntarily, Krista chose to voluntarily terminate her parental rights with the hope of maintaining a relationship with the individuals who would become her child's parents. Stacy and Deb were thrilled when presented with this situation; in fact, they been pursuing both public and private adoption options and were more open than many couples pursuing only private adoption with regard to drug exposure. (They had come to terms with the reality that some drug exposure was likely in most child welfare adoptions where a child was removed from parental care at infancy.) Further, they were pleased that this situation meant that the birth mother—and birth father, as it turned out—had some say in choosing the adoptive parents and would not have their rights terminated involuntarily.

Deb and Stacy soon learned that the birth parents, Krista and Jay, struggled with drug and mental health issues, as well as housing challenges (i.e., they did not have a permanent residence and had experienced periods of homelessness throughout their adult lives). Krista and Jay had also had other children removed by the state—which is one reason they voluntarily terminated their rights to Marlo. Yet the couple did not place Marlo immediately, and the days following her birth were difficult. As Stacy recalled, Krista and Jay were "turning to us for counseling, and . . . I'm glad we were there and I'm glad that we shared that time, but it was an intense few days, and they needed . . . professional support." Both women tried to support the birth parents as they made their decision but found this to be quite difficult. Deb recounted:

> They said, "We need more time, but she's definitely yours. We just need more time to finally sign the papers," and we were like, "She's yours until you sign those papers, and you don't have to promise her to us. This is your decision and we want you to make it without thinking about us, unless you want to. We're honored to even be here right now."

Deb went on to say:

> Open adoption is the hardest on adopting parents . . . but the best for the adopted child. . . . We were right in the thick of it, and seeing their tears . . . but those are memories that we hold for Marlo, and no matter what her birth family is able to do in terms of contact with her, she will always know that they loved her. They *love* her, and this decision was not made out of anything but out of love. And she'll know that. We can always let her know that.

After placement, Deb and Stacy sent photos, letters, and emails to Krista and Jay "very regularly." The two parties had not agreed to a specific number of photos, letters, and emails—although they did talk about visiting once a year. Their agreement was therefore flexible and informal; neither party had felt compelled to delineate the details of contact. When Marlo was 5, Stacy said that they currently had contact with Krista and Jay by phone and text messages ("about 10 times a year"), in addition to exchanging letters and pictures about every 3 to 4 months. Stacy explained that contact had changed. We had more phone contact in earlier years. This year we [received] more gifts for Marlo from them but had less phone contact. We haven't really had many text messages this year. The quality of the contact is still pretty steady. They think Marlo is wonderful and that we are doing a good job; they feel like they have made a good decision. They do their best to call us on the phone.

Krista and Jay faced multiple barriers to maintaining contact—including their chronically unstable living situation and a lack of a computer, "which we have offered to them . . . but is not something we have all been able to follow through with" (Stacy). In addition to these practical challenges, Krista and Jay continued to struggle with mental health problems and drug abuse, which impeded their ability to remain reliably and consistently engaged. Notably, Stacy and Deb were among only a few parents to explicitly name the fact that the problems that had impeded Marlo's birth parents' ability to raise her also made ongoing, stable, and predictable contact difficult. These problems also inevitably influenced the nature and quality of the relationships that Krista and Jay were able to form with Stacy, Deb, and Marlo. Said Deb:

It's something I have thought about since meeting her birth family and when she was placed with us . . . the fact that they have certain issues that might impact their ability for a healthy relationship with Marlo and the potential for her being hurt by that. . . . That's part of why they chose us to raise her. I think there will be some sad lessons ahead, but I think one thing that makes it easier is their decision to place her with us was a decision made out of love. They loved her . . . and they made one of [the] toughest decisions of their lives. We feel that every time we talk with them in person or on the phone; you can feel that pain still. It's awful to witness and it must be horrible to feel, but that pain comes from the fact they do love her. If we can help her know that they love her, that she wasn't abandoned, that would be one of the greatest gifts I think we could give her.

Both Deb and Stacy described how, in telling Marlo her story from early on ("she has always, always been told she was adopted, since day 1": Stacy), they always emphasized the great love that Krista and Jay had for her. It was this love, Deb and Stacy emphasized, that prompted Krista and Jay to make an adoption plan, as they recognized that they could not effectively parent amid their own personal challenges.

By the time that Marlo was 8, contact had continued to shift and change. Both Deb and Stacy reported that they had more regular contact with Marlo's extended birth family, including both sets of birth grandparents; previously, contact with these individuals had been infrequent and somewhat erratic. Over time, their relationships with the grandparents had evolved to the point where these were now described as valuable and positive connections. Both women talked to the grandparents on the phone semiregularly, and Marlo had met them a few times. Stacy described them as "friendly, fantastic people.... It's a nice relationship."

Contact with Krista and Jay, in contrast, had grown less frequent by this point—although Facebook had proved to be a useful tool for maintaining at least some connection to them. As Deb said:

> We used to talk to them on the phone, and via email, and send them things. But that has been harder to do. They don't answer, or phone numbers change, or packages get returned to us. But [recently] they found us on Facebook and that seems to be helpful; Facebook is a connection to all people. So we are having some connection with them through that.

The two women did still make an effort to maintain phone contact with Krista and Jay, because, as Stacy saw it, "our jobs as parents is to facilitate Marlo's relationship with them and maintain that until she is in a place to make whatever decision she wants." Indeed, even as they spent a significant amount of time cultivating an ongoing connection with Krista and Jay, both Stacy and Deb recognized that their personal difficulties would likely continue to present challenges for Marlo and the relationship that she developed with them in the future.

Rick, a white nonprofit director, and Marcus, a white graduate student, were another couple that had maintained contact with their son Jack's birth family amid some moderately challenging dynamics with Jack's birth mom, Sara, who struggled with addiction and mental health issues. Rick and Marcus, who lived in a large metropolitan area on the West Coast, originally considered both public and private domestic adoption—but chose private after attending seminars on both and deciding that they were committed to adopting an infant and realizing that the philosophy of open adoption, which was enacted much more routinely in private adoptions, "just made sense." The couple found an agency that they liked and trusted, and were eventually matched with Sara, a young woman who lived about a day's drive away, toward the end of her second trimester of pregnancy. Despite her upbringing in a conservative rural working-class area, Sara's worldview and values were progressive, according to Rick and Marcus, and she "specifically sought out a gay male couple." Though noting that she was "kind of immature for her age," the two men also remarked favorably on Sara's self-awareness, such that she recognized that she was not in a position, emotionally or financially, to care for a baby. Rick and Marcus enjoyed getting to know Sara during her pregnancy, describing her as friendly and warm, and noting that she "treated us like Jack's dads from the very beginning."

Despite some initial ambivalence about whether she would want them in the delivery room, which both men said they understood, Sara ended up inviting them in to be present during the birth and to cut the umbilical cord, alongside her mother and sister. Rick and Marcus shared that Sara became very emotional while signing the papers for relinquishment—and then again a few days later, wondering aloud to her case worker whether the couple was "really committed" to an open adoption—which the couple promptly responded to by driving many hours with Jack to visit her. The couple ultimately agreed to an arrangement with a fairly high level of contact: Said Rick:

We were certainly hoping for . . . a lot of contact, and she said that she'd probably want a lot of contact in the first several years and then it would probably kind of back off—after that, I think that she figured 4 or 5 years from now, that she might kind of have her life a little more together and she'd be either going to school or moving on into a relationship and maybe a little further away in distance, so . . . [we settled on] frequent visits for the first year, then maybe taper off to three or four visits a year, after all of the big changes in development had happened. We'll see if that's what she continues to want.

Marcus shared how he had, in a simple yet explicitly welcoming overture, communicated to Sara that she was invited to holidays at their home. He said:

We're definitely encouraging her to have as much contact as she wants . . . and she knows that our family tends not to do too much for the holidays, and just like for Thanksgiving and Christmas, just kind of whoever shows up is family and so she knows she's more than welcome to be here at Thanksgiving and Christmas.

During the early months following the adoption, Sara made "comments about her being the mom." Although noting that "one of the things we learned from the agency was that it is important from the child's perspective to differentiate between mothers and birth mothers, because it's . . . confusing for kids," Rick did not currently feel the need to discourage or correct Sara. "Right now she refers to herself as the mom; I think we'll refer to her as the birth mother to Jack." Indeed, both men demonstrated a high level of responsiveness to and compassion toward Sara, highlighting her young age and the fact that she had just placed a child for adoption as inevitable factors in her current emotional needs and overall mental state.

During the first few years, Marcus and Rick saw Sara regularly—as well as her parents and her two children. However, by the time that Jack was 5, Sara had been in and out of rehab for 2 years. This meant that they "hadn't really communicated directly with her much." However, the two men had maintained regular contact with her parents and saw them more regularly. Despite Sara's ongoing drug and alcohol issues ("she's had a lot of instability and addiction issues") and the removal of her two children from her custody (they were placed with relatives, whom Rick, Marcus, and Jack now saw regularly), Rick and Marcus continued to talk with Jack about Sara regularly and with positive regard. Said Rick:

> Jack is very fascinated with his story about when he was born. And so probably once a week, he asks me to tell him the story about—we talk about how "when we met Sara when she was pregnant, and she had picked us to be [your] parents because she wasn't able to take care of you. And we went to the hospital, and you came out of her tummy, and I got to take you down the hall." So he knows that he grew inside Sara's tummy, and he knows she's his birth mom.... It's certainly something that we discuss regularly. And it's just kind of part of the background noise, so it's not going to be any big surprise. I think that his thinking around it is just going to evolve.

Marcus said, "We always . . . keep the talk about the birth family as positive as possible. So certain things we don't talk about sometimes so that he always has a positive relationship with his birth mom and with his birth family."

Like many families, Rick and Marcus came from a different background than Sara's family. Political, regional, and social class differences lay between them and Sara's parents—a white working-class couple living in a very rural area—and yet, particularly in Sara's absence, the couple was committed to finding common ground between them. And they did; as Marcus asserted, "We're a similar age as them, so we have a lot of cultural commonalities." In turn, they developed a "very friendly, really good" relationship with Sara's parents, and, during the years when Sara was not physically or emotionally available, they regularly made the long drive to visit her parents as well as the relatives who had assumed custody of her other children, Caitlin and Jayden, whom Jack now knew as his siblings. Marcus said: "[Her parents] are very supportive of us and very encouraging, and really like us." Although Sara's father was "a little slower coming around," in part because of initial discomfort with their sexuality, "he is now like, 'I couldn't be happier with where Jack's at, and how you guys are raising him'" (Marcus).

By the time that Jack was 9, Sara had continued to struggle with addiction issues. Both men voiced concerns about the choices that Sara was making in her life, from what she put on Facebook ("there's a lack of filter for what she puts out there . . . so sometimes I'm fearful for her because, like, it is out there and it doesn't go away": Marcus), to her relationships with "questionable" men, to her lack of birth control (she went on to have several more children). Amid their discomfort with Sara's choices, they spent several years continuing to spend time with her parents, children, and other relatives, but not her, "because we didn't want to expose him to [the] bad choices ... she was making." They did maintain a relationship with Sara via email and Facebook during this hiatus from in-person visits. When asked if they had explained this break in visits to Jack, Marcus said:

> He was pretty young at that time, so not really. I think we would say we're going to go see his birth grandparents and Caitlin and Jayden [birth siblings], so we're not going to be able to see your mom this time. We didn't really say why. She actually moved for a little while in there too so it wasn't even really an opportunity to just see her and so that.... And then she was in rehab for some of it as well, but we never really talked about any of that. We don't even really talk about that in front of other people because we don't want other people to have a negative impression of Jack's birth family inadvertently passed onto him ... and [we didn't want him to] think negatively of her. We want that relationship to stay as healthy as possible.

At the time that Jack was 9, they had resumed some contact with Sara—although they continued to see her less often than Jack's other family members. Rick and Marcus typically tried to meet her on neutral ground and to do an activity together "so it takes a little bit of the pressure off." In their eyes, Sara "want[ed] to see Jack" but also struggled to "relate to him." Still, both men felt that these interactions were important, and they were committed to maintaining them. Rick and Marcus, then, valued and strove to maintain a relationship with their son's birth mother even amid her ongoing personal struggles. They chose not to explain periods of distance from her to Jack, as they saw this as developmentally inappropriate and possibly unnecessary given their ongoing communication with other birth family members. Their flexibility with the format of contact—and, it seems, Sara's as well—also enabled them to maintain communication when in-person visits were impossible or undesirable.

A final couple who managed difficult and unexpected dynamics with their child's birth parents was Doug and Sam, a gay couple living in a large metropolitan area on the West Coast. Doug, a white psychologist, and Sam, a biracial (Asian/white) human resources director, strongly desired openness, even noting that they would not enter into a closed adoption. They matched with their daughter Catie's birth mother, Lara, when she was in her third trimester. Lara was young and had an unstable living situation. Although both men acknowledged that Lara's nomadic lifestyle might be a barrier to reliable ongoing communication, they nevertheless "really enjoyed getting to know her, and definitely feel like she is part of our network and family" (Sam), and "hope[d] that we're in each other's lives for the long haul" (Doug). The two parties agreed to a very open adoption, with plans for "visits, letters, phone calls, etc." (Doug). Yet both Doug and Sam found that it was quite difficult to maintain contact with Lara, whose whereabouts were often unknown and whose behavior was unpredictable. Sam said, 3 months after they adopted their daughter, Catie, who was white:

> We have not seen each other since we tried to do one visit [and] she didn't tell us where to meet her or where she was going to be or how to get a hold of her. . . . But we do talk to her, and we email. . . . Now she doesn't have regular access so it's kind of hit or miss. She does call once in a while [but she's always on the move]. That really throws a wrench in terms of visiting. She's stuck in [state] because she doesn't have any money to get back.

When Catie was 5, the couple asserted that their one-sided efforts to maintain contact with Lara had become increasingly difficult: "It's a strain" (Doug). In turn, the couple had modified their expectations, and management, of the relationship. Doug said that they currently saw Lara

> at least once a year. We go visit. Lara doesn't do very well at sort of calling Catie, or remembering birthdays, or those kinds of things. So, over the last few years, we've just sort of stopped forcing [those aspects of the] relationship, and just sort of taken Catie's lead; when she says she wants to call Lara, we do. And we make sure that we go and see her at least once a year.

Sam felt that this arrangement was less than ideal. He explained that because Lara lived in another state, it was at least $1,000 for the three of them to travel to see her for a day; in turn, they did not see her as often as they initially planned. Further, the ongoing one-sidedness of their communication felt increasingly burdensome. Sam desired more mutuality and "back and forth" in their communications, and worried about how Lara's more passive approach to contact might affect Catie in the future:

> Contact between visits is all driven by us, which I find is getting more and more challenging for me as a parent. I find myself getting annoyed and a little bit resentful. And I'm getting really protective of Catie, being like, "Look, if you want a relationship, you need to invest in her"; like, she's . . . gonna ask us, "Why doesn't Lara call me ever? Why doesn't she call on my birthday, or send any holiday cards?" So it's like, we have to do all the work to maintain that relationship. And we're fine because we want that for Catie. But at some point we can't be responsible for that. And her birth mom will have to decide whether to step in or not.

In addition to struggling with Lara's passive communication style, Doug and Sam also described interpersonal challenges in relation to Lara. Both men struggled with some of the ways that Lara seemed to be seeking or asserting connection to Catie, noting: "Lara claims a ton of ownership over Catie and anything that she does. Lara maintains sort of a narrative in her head that she is an active parent to Catie" (Doug). Doug elaborated:

> She's like, "I loved swimming too when I was little; I bet she gets that from me"—not because we [signed her up for swim lessons] a few years ago. And . . . I'm not like 100% convinced that love of swimming is a hereditary trait. But maybe it is, I don't know. So, it's extremely important for Lara to be able to—I think how she sort of is okay with her decision to not parent, and to have chosen us, is, is totally wrapped up with still being able to claim some sort of ownership. So that's fine. I mean, it's annoying. And—well, Sam and I both get reactive in terms of how we read that as Lara's undervaluing our role as Catie's parents. But again, that is not about Catie; that's about our reaction to Lara's reaction. And Catie started sort of calling Lara out gently on some of that kind of stuff too. So I'm pretty sure that as their relationship ages, they'll have to work that out, and part of our job is to just hold the space for them to have that set of conversations once it's time for them to have it.

Sam offered his perspective on these same dynamics, stating:

> When we do go down to visit Lara, I don't know how to describe it other than she seems to want to take credit for everything about Catie. She doesn't want Catie to have anything to herself, so anything Catie can do it's because Lara did it. It's like she gets it all from Lara. It's like, "Catie is an individual, a separate person in and of herself, like, give her that." I'm starting to question whether she really gets that she's not parenting, like—"Do you really understand that we're not just long-term babysitters?"

Thus, both men felt somewhat slighted by their perception that Lara did not respect or appreciate their parental role or status. Indeed, among the families I interviewed, members of same-sex couples were especially likely to be sensitive to this dynamic, perhaps reflecting the invalidation and lack of recognition that lesbian and gay parents face in the broader society.[21]

By the time that Catie was 8, the couple had continued to maintain contact with Lara via email and Facebook but, according to Doug, had modified their in-person contact agreements. Specifically, after a recent visit to see Lara, they had made a plan ... that we were not going to subject Catie to going back in the near future. Because what happens when we go there is that Lara is really invested in showing Catie off and claiming a lot of ownership over Catie, which all makes sense—I mean, I think the birth parent experience is in a lot of ways harder than the adoptive parent experience, especially in an open relationship, but I don't think that she really grasps what openness could mean—anyway, so she shows Catie off and she doesn't take any interest in getting to know Catie at all, beyond just as a trophy extension of herself ... and she competes in some ways with Catie; it's like two kids each trying to tell a story and neither one actually listening to the other. ... And so Catie really mourns what could be. And so part of what we've done for the first several years was try super hard to push Lara to be in the relationship. And we recognized that at some point we weren't going to be able to keep doing that and they were going to have to have their own relationship and Catie was going to have to go through a really painful experience, probably, of [realizing] what that relationship was going to be. And it was our job not to try to make it happen but try to support her and make meaning out of what does happen. ... So we told Lara that we're not willing to go back down there. We will certainly pay to fly her and her family up here. ... But it's more important for them to come be in Catie's space than Catie to go be subjected to being in her space again. And although Lara says that's great, we've been saying this for months and we have yet to find a date. ... One of the things that we've been hearing from Catie for a very long time is that she wishes that Lara paid more attention to her life ... and I've never said, "You're right, Catie, I think your birth mother doesn't care about you." We always say, "Lara cares a lot about you, honey, and it's probably super painful for her and probably super hard for her to work out her life. Her life isn't super stable and she has lots of transition and lots of other things going on that make her not able to pay attention in the ways that I think she wants to pay attention."

Thus, Doug and Sam renegotiated their contact arrangement in a way that they hoped would promote more relational equilibrium,[22] such that Catie and Lara would still see each other, but in a setting that would hopefully enable Catie to feel more empowered and supported. The couple also maintained communicative openness, not shying away from the difficult emotions that Catie was experiencing, but offering potential insights into Lara's behavior in a way that would hopefully support Catie's growing understanding of her birth mom and their relationship.

Adoptive families form complex relationships with birth families. Structural and communicative openness are deeply intertwined and inform one another, but communicative openness is possible in the absence of contact (see also Chapter 6). The nature of birth family connections may be unpredictable and may change over time. However, certain types of personal and structural factors may facilitate continued contact over time. Tolerance of ambiguity and complexity, and relational skillfulness were assets for adoptive parents—and maximized relational harmony even amid unpredictable dynamics and uncontrollable life events.

As Chapter 10 addresses in more detail, parents who desire an open adoption but who match with birth families who do not want contact, pull back from contact, or prefer very little contact can experience profound disappointment—for themselves and for their children. Parents in this scenario are encouraged to consider the complex and diverse range of emotions that birth parents may be going through that may explain their disappearance (e.g., shame, relief, loss) as well as the varied circumstances that may make contact difficult (housing challenges, poverty, mental health challenges, or drug and alcohol dependence). Parents can maintain contact—albeit one-sided—in ways that honor the birth family (e.g., writing letters or emails on special days, such as the child's birthday) and possibly increasingly include the child in such communications (e.g., drawing a picture, picking out a photo to send), if this type of involvement appears to benefit their child's sense of agency as opposed to causing stress.

Parents who encounter boundary-related challenges with the birth family should ideally initiate a respectful and direct conversation about feelings and wishes for future interactions while also maintaining an openness to what the birth family members are thinking, feeling, and experiencing. Inevitably, there will be situations where parents need to limit contact out of concern for their child's or family's safety; however, some situations that initially present as difficult may not warrant cutting off contact. Parents who are experiencing ongoing difficulties with communication and boundaries in relation to the birth family should consult with an adoption-competent practitioner and consider seeking support from other adoptive parents who have dealt with similar issues—either in person, if available (e.g., via support groups or community connections), or online.

Notes

1. Broderick, 1993.
2. Grotevant, 2009.
3. Ibid.
4. Ibid.
5. Ibid.
6. Brodzinsky, 2011, 2014.
7. Ibid.

8. Daly, 1992; Grotevant, 2009.
9. Brodzinsky, Singer, & Braff, 1984; Brodzinsky, 2011.
10. Grotevant, 2009.
11. Ibid.
12. Brodzinsky, 2011.
13. Grotevant, 2009.
14. Goldberg, 2012.
15. Brodzinsky, 2011, 2014.
16. Brodzinsky et al., 1984.
17. Brodzinsky, 2014.
18. Brodzinsky, 2011, 2014.
19. Grotevant, 2009.
20. Ibid.
21. Goldberg, 2012.
22. Grotevant, 2009.

5
Navigating Openness and Contact in Child Welfare Adoptions

As Chapter 1 details, openness has, for a long time, been conceptualized as applying only to private domestic adoptions. Because of the nature of child welfare adoptions—wherein children are being removed from their birth family because of abuse, neglect, substance abuse, and/or criminal activity—there has not, historically, been much attention to or confidence in the possibility that retaining some contact with birth family members could be beneficial to all members of the adoption triad. Understandably, adoption professionals, advocates, and researchers have tended to prioritize child well-being and safety, which are typically assumed to be under threat—hence children's removal from the birth family. Yet at the same time, children adopted via foster care, especially older children, are the most likely to have an established relationship with birth family members. There is currently increasing but cautious acknowledgment of the potential benefits of openness in domestic public adoptions, amid recognition of the significant complexities that are often associated with openness in these circumstances.[1] Whether and with whom openness might be appropriate will inevitably vary in foster care adoptions, depending on the situation. It might, for example, be beneficial for a child to maintain contact with birth siblings or birth grandparents but not birth parents, if the birth parents perpetrated ongoing abuse or neglect.

A little bit of research—particularly in the past 15 years—has examined openness in families whose children were adopted via foster care. This work indicates that (a) some contact between children and the birth family (parents, grandparents, siblings) involved in child welfare adoptions is common but less likely to occur than in private domestic adoption, (b) adoptive parents with more positive views of the birth family are more likely to have contact, and (c) adoptive parents who feel a sense of control over the arrangement tended to be more satisfied with it.[2] Furthermore, older youth are more likely to accept an adoption plan if they understand why their birth family cannot take care of them and are assured that adoption will not preclude contact with their birth family.[3] For adoptive parents, assisting their children in remaining in contact with the birth family can be time-consuming and emotionally exhausting,[4] particularly when parents have a low tolerance for the complexity of such relationships[5] and do not like or trust the birth family.[6] However, it may also be valuable, in terms of helping youth to accept, and more easily transition to, adoption; communicating respect for children; easing worries and promoting the ongoing exchange of information; facilitating youth identity integration and development; and helping birth family members to accept and support the adoption.[7] Ultimately, even when relationships with the birth family are maintained, the meaning of such relationships may change over time, such that, for example, children come to attribute more or less significance to these relationships over time.[8]

Some agencies and adoption professionals are encouraging a revisioning of openness as it relates to child welfare adoptions. For example, since 2010, Open Adoption and Family Services (OAFS), an adoption agency on the West Coast, has been involved in a unique collaborative relationship with Oregon's Department of Human Services (DHS). The empowering model that OAFS offers allows DHS workers and service providers who work with high-risk mothers throughout the state to refer expectant parents to OAFS. Specifically, pregnant women (or new mothers) who are at high risk of having their children removed by the state (e.g., based on having had prior children removed) are informed preemptively of an alternative to state adoption: namely, entering into an open adoption agreement. Women—especially those who struggle with chronic mental health and substance abuse challenges—may view this option as more viable and desirable than state involvement. According to Shari Levine, the executive director of OAFS, preliminary data show that it is a successful alternative and meets the ongoing needs of birth parents and children better than the foster care system.[9]

As this chapter details, many families involved in child welfare adoptions had complex feelings about openness. Some families had significant concerns that mitigated their willingness to pursue contact. Other families were opposed to birth parent contact but, to varying degrees, were willing to pursue birth sibling contact. In some cases, contact was initiated but then halted temporarily or permanently because of the perceived risks and drawbacks associated with such contact. Yet amid a lack of contact, families often remained communicatively open with their children, and some did not rule out contact in the future.

It is notable that some families simply did not discuss the possibility of contact with their children's birth family. I do not discuss these families in depth, because they barely mentioned contact as something they were opposed to or in favor of. It just was not on their radar. An example of this particular type of family narrative comes from Sandy, a white health care advocate, and Lewis, a white teacher, a heterosexual couple living in a small Northeastern city, who adopted their son Todd, who was also white, via foster care. Todd was placed in foster care as a toddler due to parental neglect. Noting that the child welfare system "pits birth families and adoptive families against each other," Sandy said that she had "never even considered" the possibility of ongoing contact with Todd's birth family postadoption, viewing it as "interference. I don't want a birth mother or grandmother calling us twice a week—you know what I mean?" Yet at the same time that she had not considered the possibility of contact, Sandy was aware that the sudden absence of contact with his birth family might indeed have some effect on Todd. Regarding the fact that Todd would no longer have contact with his biological family, Sandy conceded that this "concerns me too. . . . I just have to hope and pray that everything works out for everybody's benefit."

"We Have Too Many Concerns at This Point": Caution Regarding Contact

Some families voiced serious concerns about contact amid the circumstances of their children's removal from their birth families. Kerry and Shelby were one couple that expressed a high level of caution surrounding potential contact with the birth family. Kerry, a housepainter, and Shelby, a postal clerk, were a white lesbian couple living in a small city in the Northeast when they adopted two school-aged brothers, Cameron and Cole. Parental drug abuse, neglect, and domestic violence were the primary reasons for the boys' removal; indeed, at the time that Cameron and Cole were removed from their parents' care, they were living in what Kerry and Shelby described as a communal "crack den." The boys' birth parents voluntarily terminated their parental rights when it became clear that they were unlikely to regain custody of the children, and they learned that upon relinquishing their parental rights, they could have ongoing letter and photo updates from the adoptive family via a post office (PO) box. Kerry and Shelby were relieved that there was no protracted trial and gladly agreed to this level of contact. They also agreed to maintain phone contact with the boys' grandmother. However, upon learning, fairly soon after placement, that the grandmother often handed the phone off to other relatives—possibly including the birth parents—Kerry and Shelby temporarily terminated phone contact with the boys' grandmother. The two women wanted to give the boys a chance to develop a "new normal" in their home. They viewed continued contact with the birth family, and particularly the birth parents—who continued to use heavy drugs and were intermittently homeless—as counterproductive to that goal. Kerry explained the circumstances of their decision to restrict contact with the boys' grandmother:

> I just had to set a boundary with her because every time she called, we let them speak to her and you can't tell—we don't know who's on the other line and she's handing the phone off to relatives, and we don't know if the parents are around, because we don't have them on speakerphone. So we had to have a

conversation about that and a conversation about how often she calls. Finally the therapist said, no more grandma for 3 months. And then I had to tell her that, and just yesterday she phoned and we talked last week and she phoned and said, "Oh I haven't talked to you in a while." I'm like, "I talked to you last week—boundaries."

Five years postplacement, the couple had continued to send occasional letters and pictures through the PO box, although they never received anything from the birth parents after the first year. "I never hear anything. None of their family ever tries to contact them," said Shelby. However, the two women were very aware that their older son, Cameron, was at the age (i.e., a teenager) where he might begin to search for the parents online—and they were not ready for that. Even though Cameron was limited in terms of what he could do online,

he does have some freedom and he does have a Facebook [account]. And he was contacted by his cousin. And it was interesting because his cousin said to him, "I can't wait until you come back and things can be like they used to be." And Cameron's response to that was, "Why would I want to come and sit on the couch all day doing nothing?" Like, "I'm not coming back, like for that." But I do worry about that . . . that cycle . . . continuing.
[Interviewer: And you worry that you might, if they gain contact, that that would be a bad influence?]
Yes, yes.

Shelby expressed concerns about how things would continue to unfold in the future:

Right now, he doesn't want to have anything to do with them, but I think he does plan to [get back in touch] eventually. Right now, he just doesn't have the means to go wherever he needs to go. I think if they said, "Come live with us, we've got this place and a bedroom for you," I think he'd be on the bus there.

This sense—that children who were adopted at an older age via foster care might return to their birth family after age 18—is not uncommon. Some youth do ultimately reconnect with and in some cases return to their birth families once they are legally adults, as online parenting blogs—and the much-discussed story of Rosie O'Donnell's daughter Chelsea—serve to highlight.[10]

Another couple that was ambivalent about contact with the birth family was Jake, a white hotel manager, and Carl, an African American day care supervisor, who resided in a small city on the West Coast and adopted their African American daughter Sharice via foster care when she was 3 years old. Sharice's mother was a drug user, living on the street and in homeless shelters, when Sharice was finally removed from her care ("She just couldn't take care of her anymore, and left her at the shelter": Jake). Several years later, Jake and Carl adopted Sharice's half-sister, Sheree, after a social worker in the child welfare system alerted them to the fact that Sharice's birth mother had given birth again. Feeling strongly that they should "keep the siblings together," Jake and Carl decided to adopt Sheree. One year later, they were contacted about a third sibling—a little boy, Amos, who shared the same birth mother as Sharice and Sheree. Again, despite financial concerns about the implications of doing so, the couple agreed to adopt Amos, feeling that it was the "right thing to do." Despite their strong commitment to ensuring that Sharice grow up with children who shared the same birth mother and who resembled her in race and appearance, Jake and Carl were deeply ambivalent about the possibility of making contact with the children's birth mother, or other biological relatives. Indeed, when Sharice was placed with them, neither Jake nor Carl seemed to even consider contact as a viable, much less desirable, possibility. Jake asserted that contact was out of the question, in that "they don't know who the father is and the mother is apparently long gone and they've lost track of her." As Sharice grew, they gradually began to introduce facts about her family in what they felt was a developmentally appropriate way. When Sharice was about 8 years old, Jake said:

> At first, I think we just said that her birth mother was just too sick to take care of her. And then I think we introduced the idea that she was mentally ill; she knows what mental illness is. Then finally we talked about the issue of drug abuse. So I think Sharice has known for about a year now that her mother had problems with drug abuse. I think she definitely went through a period, probably 2 years ago, where she missed having a mother; she said she felt different because she didn't have a mother. That was tough; we just had to listen to her, validate her feelings, explain to her that well, "This is your situation; you don't have a mother...." I think since she has two fathers, she doesn't ask about their birth father at all; it doesn't occur to her.

Also around the time that Sharice was 8 years old, Jake and Carl had heard from a source that Sharice's birth mother had "reappeared" on the streets of a nearby city, "in a terrible physical state and mental state." Upon learning from this source that Sharice and her siblings were living nearby, the birth mother had apparently said: "'No, no, no; I don't want to see them.... I don't want to see them or hear about them. I'm just too sick.'" Although these details saddened Jake and Carl, they also served to reinforce the two men's decision to delay any efforts to make contact.

By the time that Sharice was 11 years old, both men seemed to be thinking more about the potential for future contact—with either the birth mother or several birth relatives who supposedly lived nearby—but also had not made any movement toward initiating contact, although, as Jake noted, "we've definitely kept records, so that if there comes some point where the kids want to find out more, we want to help them." Indeed, Jake had recently determined Sharice's birth mother's current location, in a nearby city, via an Internet search, but had not used this information to initiate contact. Likewise, Carl shared that when they had adopted Amos, the social worker had not "blacked out" the birth mother's name or her siblings' names on the paperwork, affording them key identifying information about the children's aunts and uncles. "If we wanted to get a hold of them ... we could do that; we have names. That'd be easy." And yet, the couple had not made contact—despite the fact that, as Carl noted, Sharice was "all about family," and he expected that she would "probably want to make contact in the future."

A couple that firmly rejected the possibility of making contact with any member of their child's birth family—at least until he was 18—was Nate and Dwight. Nate, a white medical assistant, and Dwight, a white health program administrator, were living in a large Southern city when they adopted their 5-year-old son Parker, who was biracial (Latino and white). According to Nate, Parker's parents were drug addicts and very young when he was born. In turn, his grandmother assumed custody when he was an infant but she "did not care for him. He was neglected ... and severely malnourished ... and taken out of the household. He said many times that she was really bad. So he is glad to not be with her." Nate, reflecting that Parker's grandmother had left him "scavenging [for food] in garbage cans," and noting that Parker himself had quite negative memories of his grandmother, saw no potential for future contact with her. Nate stated: "We absolutely do not know who she is and we certainly would not—that is not something I would ever support, having contact."

According to both men, by the time he was 10—5 years postplacement—Parker had expressed some interest in his birth mother but more ongoing and intense curiosity about his birth father, whom he did not remember: "It's been the birth dad that he's expressed the most interest in lately. We know absolutely nothing about him, but once Parker gets older, he will be able to request information about his birth circumstances that we cannot legally request" (Dwight). Nate recalled:

> I told him that [many] kids have a very strong curiosity about their biological parents ... and he said that he really wants to, like, at some point, get to meet his biological dad. And we've told him, when he gets older he'll have access to more

information that will allow him hopefully to find out more about his bio dad, and perhaps locate him. And if that's the case we will certainly support him and help him try to find this person. It's perfectly natural to wonder about things like that.

Neither Dwight nor Nate mentioned the possibility of trying to assist Parker in finding out more about his birth family, either currently or in the near future. In fact, Dwight appeared to believe that searching was not appropriate or possible prior to Parker turning 18, stating:

Parker mentioned that he would like to see—to find his family. . . . I said, "Not a problem; when you are older, 18, we will gladly help you. Not at this point." . . . As an adopted child, once he becomes of legal age he can find out more information about the circumstances of his birth.

This couple's resistance to make contact appeared to stem from a constellation of beliefs related to what Parker needed to be a healthy and happy human being. Although they validated Parker's curiosity—namely, the fact that it was normal and natural—they did not appear to believe that meeting this curiosity with additional information would be helpful or healthy. Their approach to openness, wherein they downplayed the significance of knowledge about or contact with biogenetic kin, can be further contextualized by their attitudes about and approach to racial identity development. Parker was biracial—yet this couple also, by their own admission, did not do anything to facilitate his racial or ethnic identity exploration, because it was "not important" to them. Thus, this couple's approach to such topics—that is, birth family, racial identity—was passive and marked by little communication, which may have discouraged Parker from asking questions or asserting interest in his origins over time.[11] About his son's racial/ethnic identity, Nate said:

That's something that we talked about it initially and we were wondering what we should do to be more culturally aware and it just—we didn't take any specific steps because it felt inauthentic. Anything we talked about seemed really artificial; and, also, his own self-identity hasn't really seemed to have gone in that direction. I guess he's been very sort of mainstream and that's not been something that he has been interested in exploring . . . so we haven't done anything with that. It hasn't been important to us.

Thus, underlying this passive approach was a belief that racial identity exploration was not "important," as well as, perhaps, a sense that such exploration would be uncomfortable for them to try to facilitate as two white men. Similar to the subject of birth family contact, Nate did not perceive racial identity development as significant enough to actively address—and he may have imagined negative consequences associated with even talking about it. In turn, both Nate and Dwight tended to avoid such discussions.

A final example of a couple that voiced significant concerns about making contact was Kathleen, a manager of a nonprofit organization, and Becki, a group home supervisor. Both white, the two women adopted their infant daughter Ana, who was Latina and white, from foster care in a midsized city on the West Coast. Throughout Ana's childhood, they maintained a high level of communicative openness about adoption (see Chapter 6). Although they did not think that contact with Ana's birth mother would be beneficial, they did regularly search the Internet for her in order to "keep tabs" on her whereabouts, as well as any notable developments in her life (e.g., arrests). Ultimately, they were able to determine that she was in jail. The couple also regularly looked into the whereabouts of Ana's birth siblings, as they knew that several other children had been removed from the birth mother's care and were subsequently adopted. As Ana grew, both Kathleen and Becki considered a variety of potential benefits of making contact with birth siblings specifically. Such contact might allow them to gain valuable medical history information. It could also provide Ana with valuable connections to family members who shared her mixed-race background, and who therefore mirrored her in ways her adoptive parents and extended family did not. Yet when Ana was 8 years old, neither Kathleen nor Becki were ready to make contact. Both women expressed their desire to find out more about the children and their circumstances before facilitating introductions, in part because Ana was having some emotional and behavioral difficulties, and they worried that introducing new relationships into her life at the current time might lead to an escalation in such difficulties. Kathleen said:

> A caseworker at DHS wanted to know if Becki and I would be interested in meeting with them. [I would like to know first] whether they are healthy or not and then maybe set up a meeting. Ana knows she has siblings . . . I do have an interest in it, in medical stuff, if anybody else is kind of dealing with the things we are. . . . I just want to make sure that we know all is there is to know . . . but I haven't done anything yet. I'm just curious. Ana's probably going to want to [meet them] when she's older; now she doesn't. She doesn't express an interest at all. But . . . I'm also just curious about what, what are they like? . . . What do they look like? And wouldn't it be great if . . . she looked like these other kids? That's such a big part of our culture—that you look like your family and Ana doesn't have that. I think it would really be cool for her to look like somebody out there in the world.

Kathleen, then, in considering whether and when to potentially establish contact with Ana's siblings, imagined the potential benefits to Ana's identity development—but also took into account Ana's current functioning as well as her current (lack of) curiosity about birth sibling contact. Although Kathleen remained open to the possibility of future contact, the risks seemed to outweigh the benefits of current contact.

Contact with siblings amid concern about birth family. Several families felt strongly that contact with birth parents and other adult relatives would not be healthy or helpful for their children—but they were interested in and committed to pursuing contact with siblings. Yet these relationships themselves were sometimes fraught with challenges. Noah, a white school psychologist, and Reed, a white alumni relations director at a college, were one couple that described such challenges. The couple, who lived in a large West Coast city, adopted Shayne, who was biracial (Latino and Native American), via foster care when he was 5 years old. Shayne's birth mother had reportedly been a drug addict and had neglected him, his two brothers, and his sister. By the time that Shayne was placed with Noah and Reed, his birth mother's parental rights had been terminated, his birth father was reportedly "long gone" and his whereabouts unknown, and his three siblings (Robert, Mason, and Bonnie) had already been adopted into two other families—Robert alone, Mason and Bonnie together.

By 3 months postplacement, the couple had already formed a relationship with these two families, with whom they had agreed "to try to keep the siblings connected." Noah shared that he appreciated the opportunity to get together with these families. In particular, he valued the chance to talk to the adoptive parents about everyday parenting issues and challenges as well as issues specific to the children's shared history and upbringing. Five years later, Noah, Reed, and Shayne continued to get together with these families, several times a year— including on birthdays and some holidays. According to Noah, Shayne seemed to enjoy these visits, expressing excitement as they approached—although notably, according to Reed, the actual visits sometimes seemed to overwhelm Shayne.

By 8 years postplacement, when Shayne was a teenager, things had changed. One of Shayne's brothers, Robert, was "having some really difficult—he has got a lot of emotional issues, and his parents did not think that he, at that time, could deal with seeing Shayne" (Noah). Significantly, Robert's challenges appeared to be related to early childhood trauma: older than Shayne, Robert had been exposed to severe neglect for a longer period of time, and had more intense memories of his birth mother's drug abuse and the unpleasant conditions in which they were raised. Reed explained that Robert's parents

> asked if we could just not have contact for a while, because they [felt] it would just agitate an already bad situation. So we're in contact with [the] parents

through Facebook and holiday cards, and there is no negativity, but they're having a hell of a time ... so we've sort of sidelined ourselves.

Contact had not resumed, however, a year later. In part this was because of Robert's ongoing difficulties—but it was also related to what Noah described as a lack of interest on Shayne's part, wherein he "just wasn't that into it," referring to the last time they had gotten together with Robert's family. "We even asked him, 'Would you like to see Robert? Or what about Mason and Bonnie?' And he said, 'No, not really.'" To Noah, it did not make sense to

> try to force it.... Those relationships are there for him when he is an adult, if he wants to try to develop them.... Things change. It's kind of sad, but they're all adopted into different families. If nothing but the blood type is there, it's not on us to try to make them be there.

Although Noah did not feel that contact with Shayne's birth parents would be appropriate or healthy, he, like others, acknowledged that Shayne might be "curious" about his birth mother. Noah in turn communicated to Shayne that he would be open to helping him search for his birth mother—in the future:

> I said, "When you're older, if you want to reconnect with her, I can give you all the stuff [I have from your mom] and we can talk about it ... and [we can] help facilitate that."... So far, he has no interest in it, which I think is good.

Another example of a couple who sought out birth sibling contact amid a lack of birth parent contact, but with less positive results, was Lauren, a social worker, and Victoria, a medical assistant, a white lesbian couple living in a midsized city on the East Coast who adopted their 6-year-old Latina daughter Kiley via foster care. Initially the women were open to sending annual letters and pictures to Kiley's birth parents postadoption. But upon learning the birth father was in jail for a crime that made them concerned for Kiley's well-being, their interest in and commitment to providing such pictures waned. Kiley's birth mother "bounced around" so much that, as Lauren said with exasperation, "the county couldn't even keep up with her.... They have no clue where she is." Thus, contact, at least during Kiley's early childhood, was not a possibility.

Yet Lauren and Victoria voiced a desire and commitment to uphold birth family relationships and actively tried to establish a connection to Kiley's birth sister, Abigail. However, Abigail's adoptive parents had, according to Victoria, said that Abigail would "probably be better off not knowing Kiley—like, talking to her. [It was better] for Abigail to kind of forget about her. I felt so bad! Why would you want to forget about this child?" They were uncertain about how to talk to Kiley about the multiple unmet bids for contact that they had initiated—but nevertheless strove "not to use pejorative language about her family. We just emphasize that people who experience a lot of trauma have a really hard time sometimes being loving and . . . treating other people well."

"We See Them as Part of the Kids' History and Identity": Openness Regarding Contact

Some families were attuned to the potential benefits of ongoing contact of some kind, with at least some birth family members, for their children—and for other members of the adoption constellation as well. Even amid challenging circumstances, these families made efforts to maintain at least some level of birth family contact. One such family was Kate and Cara, a white lesbian couple who were employed as the director of a woman's survival center and a landscape artist, respectively. At the time that they adopted via foster care, they were living in a large city on the West Coast. Preadoption, Kate and Cara were fairly unique among child welfare adopters in their shared openness to and preparation for possible ongoing contact with the birth family. They recognized that there was a good chance that whatever child would be placed with them would probably have been removed from their parents' care due to neglect or abuse. Yet both women emphasized that they would not rule out ongoing contact with birth parents, birth siblings, or other relatives. They recognized that parental neglect could be due to drug abuse, intellectual disabilities, or mental health issues and, in turn, contact would not necessarily be harmful to children—and could arguably be positive in terms of honoring the children's past and promoting a more integrated identity. Preadoption, Cara reflected:

> I want my child—or not my child, *the* child, regardless of whether or not we get to adopt or if [they are] reunited with their birth parents—to have a connection with the birth parents, who brought them into this world. I think that I would want to deal with the birth family as much as I can. I plan on taking a lot of pictures and trying to create a story, like a life book, for that child even as they grow older. . . . I think it's really important for the child to have this sense of where they came from, who their parents were, what did they look like. . . . I think that's important. I'm more than willing to do my best to provide that to them.

Cara's approach to contact was flexible and responsive: She was open to contact but also recognized that the amount and type of contact that unfolded would depend on birth family circumstances, life events, and the nature and quality of birth–adoptive family interactions.[12] For example, Cara acknowledged that certain circumstances might make ongoing contact unwise or untenable:

> I mean, I'm not necessarily happy to hand a child over to a person that is drunk or on drugs—who knows what would happen. So it would definitely depend on the parents and how they are in the world. And even on how they are with me. It will just depend on the situation.

Her partner, Kate, had a similar perspective preadoption—but was even more insistent about the benefits of maintaining contact amid less-than-ideal circumstances (e.g., because it helped to mitigate children's tendency to fantasize about their birth family[13]):

> I think it's good [for the children] if the birth family can stay involved. I can imagine all different degrees of involvements that might be just fine. I think in an ideal world they would stay pretty strongly involved; they'd be like extended family. . . . I do think involvement is important even if they are really struggling, whatever their issue is, or even if they're just assholes, because—as the kids get older they don't have a sense of who their parents are, and it's really easy to idealize who their parents were, especially when they're teenagers, and hating you, and imagining how their whole life would be better if you weren't there [laugh]. . . . I can imagine that really being heightened for kids who never really had much involvement with their biological parents, to really have to go through this process where they think everything could have been okay if you just hadn't come in to the picture. I can imagine that being really hurtful for us as parents and it also just seems really painful and difficult for the child. So, for them to have a good sense of where they came from would help them put that together more clearly. That seems like a real benefit to me.

Kate and Clara were placed with a Latino baby boy, Daniel, who was removed from his birth parents' care at birth due to documented neglect in relation to other children in the birth mother's care. Kate described her own, and the agency's, rather unique approach to the situation; indeed, Kate was unusual in that she worked with a private agency—much like OAFS, discussed earlier—to facilitate this child welfare adoption:

> It is very much the philosophy with this agency that it's good to be in touch with the birth parents, and I tend to think that that's true. But I think that it's true even more because they are who they are. I do think it's good for Daniel to continue to have relationships with his birth parents and his siblings as much

as possible and that's going to be facilitated by my having a relationship with them. Also, it's always really nice when it [is] clear what's going to happen if parents can *relinquish* their rights instead of the state having to *terminate* them, you know? In the same way that it's always a little nicer than it is to quit your job than it is to get fired. And [if they relinquish], it means that they have the possibility for an open adoption and all that stuff. And if they know that, then I think they're more likely to [relinquish parental rights], because they have a much better sense of where their child is and who's taking care of him and whatnot.

For several months, Daniel's birth parents engaged in social worker–supervised visits with Daniel. Early on, these visits were more common; then, the birth parents began to miss visits and "fade away" a bit, before they finally relinquished their parental rights. Kate and Cara did meet Daniel's parents prior to the relinquishment—and both women noted that despite a language barrier, such that both of the birth parents only spoke Spanish, the four adults were able to "talk a little bit" and communicate in a way that felt "not completely awkward." Daniel's birth father, Rafael, was, they sensed, a bit resentful "because, you know, your baby gets taken away from you . . . and gets given to of all people, white lesbians [laugh]. . . . I get the sense he doesn't like us as much and is not super appreciative" (Kate). Daniel's birth mother, Camila, on the other hand, struck them as "really nice—thanking us for taking care of him and bringing him . . . and she seems like she likes us, which was a concern of us since we're obviously a lesbian couple" (Kate).

Upon relinquishment, Kate and Cara had to wait 6 months before Daniel was legally free for adoption, at which point they completed the legal adoption. In the months that followed, contact with Daniel's birth parents was infrequent and unpredictable: "I'm not sure what they want. . . . I mean, Kate and I would love to have them be a part of our life but I don't know [if that will happen]" (Cara). It was around this time that Kate and Cara learned that the state was in the process of removing two other children in Camila's care—and that they could be considered as potential parents to these children. They did eventually adopt these two children, Gabriela and Adriana, several years later.

When Daniel was 5, Kate and Cara recounted that they had maintained intermittent contact with Camila. Early on, during the first few years, Camila had drifted in and out of their lives—she will "just sort of pop up . . . and then you can't find her for a few months" (Cara). When Camila re-emerged, she was usually staying at a friend's apartment in a neighboring city—so, Kate conceded, "I kind of always thought that if I really super super needed to find her, I could probably, like, hit the pavement, and . . . find her."

But she didn't have to. Camila had recently resurfaced and reached out to them, expressing a desire to see them. This marked a turning point in their relationship. Kate shared how Camila had

> come over for dinner one night. Then, like a week later, she couldn't stay with her friend anymore and didn't have a lot of options, [just] places where people were doing a lot of drugs and she didn't feel very comfortable. So she wanted to know if she could stay with us. So we said, "OK, good [*laugh*]." And there you go.

Now, Kate said, "we see her all the time. She's over at the house at least once a month. We see her constantly." The current level of contact was perceived positively—although it had not unfolded without some boundary negotiation. Cara explained:

> We've always tried to be pretty close but we didn't have her start coming to our house until recently. . . . There was a steady movement towards more involvement and at some point we did have to say like, "No, Camila actually can't stay the night at our house," you know? Like, we did have to draw the line. So that's been a little—that part right there has been a little tricky.

Kate shared that these boundary negotiations extended to the relationship between Camila and Daniel as well: "We have this dynamic that we've struggled with where she, like, swoops in and wants to, like, take him and kiss him and he's like, 'back the hell off of me' . . . and then she has her feelings hurt."

When Daniel was 8, they had maintained a high level of contact with Camila, and had also formed relationships with several extended family members. In turn, Daniel seemed to possess a good understanding of adoption, according to his mothers. As Kate explained:

> She's his Mama Camila; we're Mama Kate and Mama Cara, and we've talked about it, and he knows that Mama Camila is the mama who gave birth to him. He grew in her uterus and she gave birth to him and now he lives with us and we're his moms who take care of him . . . and isn't he so lucky that he has three moms who love him? And he rolls with that.

Kate noted that the circumstances of Daniel's placement

> used to come up a lot more; it doesn't come up as much now, but he knows that [he] doesn't live with her because, even though she loves him a lot, she wasn't able to take care of him, and we can take care of him. And we just kind

of divided up all the tasks so that all of our skill sets can be used equally—that's how we kind of talk about it and that's how he understand[s] it.

Kate and Cara, then, were successful in maintaining a high level of structural and communicative openness amid some structural (e.g., language) and dynamic (e.g., boundary) challenges, thus facilitating the creation of a dynamic web of extended birth family that was inclusive of biogenetic and adoptive kin.[14]

Kate and Cara's situation is notable in that boundary negotiations were minor and easily resolved—something that was facilitated by their own, and Camila's, ability to tolerate ambiguity while growing their relationship, and their shared commitment to contact.[15] A different situation was that of Greta and Robin, a white lesbian couple living in a racially diverse suburb of a major city in the Northeast, who adopted Shawn, a 3-year-old Latino boy, from foster care. Like Kate and Cara, Greta and Robin were also very open to contact with the birth family, and did establish regular contact with the birth family—but ultimately had to terminate this contact after a series of difficult birth family interactions.

Greta and Robin were a unique couple. Both women expressed "zero desire" to have a biological child. Rather, they shared a mutual, passionate commitment to adopting children through foster care, such that adoption was not, as Robin said, "a back-up plan. . . . We are choosing it." They were placed with their son Shawn, who, at 3 years old, had had a difficult early life history. Shawn had experienced severe neglect by his birth parents, who were addicted to drugs and did not have stable housing, and he had lived with relatives off and on before being placed into a foster home for several months. Further, Shawn was born addicted to cocaine and methamphetamines and, in turn, displayed difficulties with attention and impulsivity.

Despite these difficult circumstances, both Greta and Robin demonstrated empathy for the birth parents. Greta said: "People get wrapped up in a lot of things that are really bad, and I feel for these parents, the birth parents, I do. And I think about Shawn, on the other end; when he entered into the system he didn't have any services, [which is] baffling." Robin described how the complexity of the situation meant having some difficult conversations with Shawn:

> It's tough because his family violated all the family covenants. And then we're saying, "Family takes care of each other . . . and family doesn't hurt each other, they have your back." But it's like, [my birth mom] yanked my arm out of my socket—so what's up with that? So we try and address those honestly and directly without throwing the parents completely under the bus. . . . I mean, the only way to get around adoption is to completely support birth families, with high-impact interventions, but I don't see society doing that. I would prefer that—but I do think adoption is a necessary evil. So . . . any adopted family is [there]

because... something fundamental went wrong and [resulted in the] severing of birth bonds. I mean, I can't think of a worse thing. And so that's tricky.

Robin and Greta appeared to believe in and value, and not be threatened by, birth family involvement. In fact, they spoke to the birth father, Esteban, prior to his termination of parental rights hearing and assured him that if he terminated, they would be willing to maintain contact with him. Robin said: "At the termination we said to him, 'If you don't contest this, we will do an open adoption agreement with you. We'll shake on it, but if you contest this I can't promise anything.' And he didn't contest it, so we started visiting him."

Five years postplacement, both Robin and Greta had maintained some contact with Esteban and had also established contact with other birth relatives. The couple had encountered a few challenges ("this particular family . . . just wants you to show up, and that was hard for us to take seriously, because we are planners") but were ultimately settling in to a more comfortable groove in their relationship ("everyone was playing really nice and polite . . . and now we're more relaxed"). Shawn's extended family was, to Greta's surprise, totally "embracing" of them as a lesbian couple:

> We're totally accepted.... We couldn't have gotten luckier. I can't imagine trying to establish contact with a birth family who didn't approve of us. I don't know that I would—I don't know how we would handle that. We didn't have to think about it. We have so much to think about, I'm so *glad* we didn't have to think about it.

Robin explained:

> They've all lost children [to drugs]. They're thrilled that we want to maintain contact—they're very welcoming. And our friend said that in Latino culture particularly, family is everything—that they will do anything to keep in contact. So it made me feel very glad that we're keeping Shawn in their lives.

Such efforts to keep Shawn in their lives were not always easy. Some family members lived hours away, and many of them spoke little English. In addition to logistical and language barriers, Greta and Robin contended with the reality that the visits were not always easy or fun for Shawn. They noted that although Shawn always seemed enthusiastic and excited about visits beforehand, the actual visits appeared to overwhelm him—a dynamic also described by other families. For example, Shawn often had meltdowns, particularly early on, after visits. This led the couple to keep the visits relatively short—no more than a few hours. As Robin noted, contact with the birth family brought up painful memories, and the process of "purging" those memories was difficult: "He's processing a lot." Robin acknowledged that she wasn't sure "exactly what he gets out of these visits. . . . I guess we won't know for a long time. But we're trying to make it work." In addition to visits every few months, the couple also established a relationship with one of Shawn's birth siblings, Mateo, a boy who had been adopted by a couple in the next state over.

Alongside this structural openness, the family also maintained notable communicative openness with Shawn. Robin said:

> We're probably brutally honest. We're kind of unconventional but it works for us at least. And we think it works for Shawn. We just, we've said since day 1, your birth parents made you, but they couldn't take care of you. Because they couldn't take care of you, you got really hurt in terms of, you're separated from your siblings, you don't live with them. You were thrown into a house with these two crazy girls [*laugh*], but we're gonna make the best of it.

Eight years postplacement, things had changed somewhat. Robin and Greta had pulled back on the level of contact they were having with Shawn's extended family, due to concerns about continued drug abuse within the family, as well as possible criminal activity—and some explosive family dynamics (e.g., arguments among family members) that occurred in front of them and Shawn. In explaining to Shawn why they had put the brakes on contact, they said, " 'It was all about them, and that's not family. It can't be all about you.' They were really quite disruptive and quite volatile and . . . we just can't [expose him to that]." Yet their relationship with Shawn's biological brother Mateo was stable—in fact, they had deepened this connection over the past few years, and the two boys now spent long weekends and some vacations with each other. They were aware that Shawn would likely want to reconnect with his birth family in the future. In turn, according to Robin,

> What we tell Shawn is that when you're that magical age of 18 and . . . you want to visit your birth father[*] or any of your other birth family relationships, knock your socks off. You can do that, but right now we're not doing that and we have our hands full with managing your relationship with your brother, which is a positive relationship and we've worked very hard at that . . . and I want to pour my energy into that working. And I don't really [want] to feel encumbered by having to make something work that's clearly at odds with our family values and our family time. We don't have that kind of time. I want to spend that time on you and your brother.

---

[*] The birth mother was at this point deceased.

The couple had not ruled out reconnecting with Shawn's birth father in the future—but worried that in doing so, they would also be reconnecting with the extended family members who were of the greatest concern. Greta and Robin were not yet sure how to "make it work." Said Robin: "We don't have a good solution yet but we want to try to keep that connection, if we can; we'd like to try. We just have to figure out how."

Another couple that strongly valued the possibility of birth family contact from the very beginning of their adoption journey was Simon, a white social worker, and Vincent, a white telecommunications director. Simon and Vincent, who lived in a large Midwestern city, were one of just a few couples that adopted via foster care that, preadoption, explicitly emphasized their desire for birth family contact. The couple had always been drawn to openness but did not pursue a private domestic adoption—where openness was more normative—because of financial considerations and a desire to provide a home to a child who was unlikely to be adopted (i.e., they were open to older children and children of color). Simon explained:

> We originally wanted to do, and we still would like to do, an open adoption. And we'd love to do that in the context of the foster care system, because we feel like that would be the best option for the child, it would be the best option for the birth parents.

The couple was placed with Ayo, an African American boy, when he was a little over a year old. The placement was initially a foster care placement; the couple hoped to adopt Ayo upon termination of his mother's parental rights. According to Simon and Vincent, Ayo's birth mother was drug addicted and had severe mental health issues. She also had a history of violence (but not toward Ayo) and had had several other children removed from her care due to drug abuse and neglect. Thus, the couple felt relatively confident about the long-term viability of the placement and the likelihood that they would be able to adopt Ayo. Sure enough, after 6 months, Ayo's birth mother had not initiated any type of visit, and the court moved ahead to file for abandonment and terminate her parental rights. Neither Simon nor Vincent seemed to know a way forward that involved maintaining contact with the birth mother; she "never made it to any of the court appointments and wouldn't communicate with the social workers. We never met her in person." To Simon and Vincent's relief, the birth mother resurfaced to voluntarily terminate her parental rights, which they viewed as far more ideal than having them involuntarily terminated. She also wrote them "a letter which basically thanked us and said, 'I couldn't take care of a child,' and 'thank you for raising him.'" And, she wrote Ayo a letter that said, "I am not giving you up because I don't love you. Right now mommy is sick and

I can't give you the best in life as I want to. Therefore the people who have you [who I] trust with you."

Upon adopting Ayo, the couple reaffirmed their intention to do what they could to maintain contact with his birth family. Although contact with Ayo's birth mother did not seem possible as she had disappeared soon after voluntarily relinquishing him, the couple had been able to locate an older birth brother of his named Gamba. The couple made immediate contact with Gamba and the white heterosexual couple who had adopted him, and established a strong relationship with this family. In fact, 5 years after Ayo had been placed with them, they were seeing Gamba and his family—who lived a little over an hour away—at least once a month. The two boys, they said, had formed a "strong bond."

Five years postadoption, Simon and Vincent had also located and met several cousins of Ayo's. One of these cousins was much older, and she maintained intermittent contact with Ayo's birth mother. When Ayo was about 6, this cousin "recommend[ed] at this point not having any [contact]. . . . She doesn't want to hear from her children [because of her instability]; so, she wouldn't recommend us having contact with her for the same reason." Simon and Vincent continued to feel ambivalent about the lack of contact and found themselves wanting to "offer pictures to her . . . to figure out how to do that." Upon mentioning this possibility to Ayo's cousin, she stressed that she "wouldn't do that, just with what she [has going on] at the moment. Because you don't want to stir things up.' So we're kind of following her lead on that" (Simon).

Furthermore, at the age of 6, Ayo was not "really even asking" about his birth mother—who, they had explained to him, had "adult problems" and had "asked us to take care of you"—and they felt that it made sense to hold off. Furthermore, Ayo had "a very large extended and loving family that includes connection to her through his brother and his cousins. . . . I think that's enough for now" (Simon). Indeed, Ayo's older cousin was open to "answering Ayo's questions, if anything ever comes up; she said she'd be happy to." Both Simon and Vincent maintained Facebook contact with this cousin, several other birth family members, and the parents of Ayo's brother—and they both made a point of showing Ayo photos of these family members as a means of bridging the gap in communication between visits.

When Ayo was 9, the two men continued to revisit the possibility of contact—but were repeatedly told not to initiate it. Vincent said:

We were advised by both the social worker and Ayo's cousin that safety was an issue. She just had a really unstable life and was very angry for a period. . . . We were told was that she was unpredictable when she—she has some mental health issues that have caused her not to be in her right mind sometimes . . . [and she] self-medicates [with drugs]. So both his cousin and the social worker said that it was probably best for Ayo not to have contact, and for her not to be able to find him. I have kind of deferred to [cousin] about this. And we maintain a relationship with this cousin so if he ever does want to get in contact with his birth mom he can do so though his cousin.

Yet Vincent continued to "feel guilty about not contacting her. I have asked [cousin] three times [about reaching out] and she is afraid that making contact will open a wound for her and bring no good to Ayo. This is a really tough one for us to navigate." He went on to say:

> We could find her. We could send her pictures. I feel guilty for not doing so. It was just a tough call. We were intending to do open adoption before we [decided to pursue foster care]. We were never opposed to open adoption and really liked the idea of it. We tried to create the next best thing by connecting with the cousin and Ayo's brother, but I still have mixed feelings about not having contact with her.

Another couple that was decisively on board with open adoption from the very beginning of their adoption journey was Joe, an operations manager, and Jared, a sales associate, a white gay couple living in a large city on the West Coast. Joe and Jared worked with an agency that facilitated both public and private domestic adoptions and encouraged some level of openness "when possible." Jared explained: "In our case, with foster adoption, there will still be some level of openness, most likely, depending on the situation—but it may be more with grandparents, or uncles or something." Jared was hopeful about the possibility of

> ongoing meetings with the parents or other relatives. . . . It would be nice to maintain contact through actual meetings and letters. I think it's really important for the child and it just seems to make the most sense. To keep the child aware of where he really came from—I think that's important.

Interestingly, Joe attributed their ease surrounding openness and contact with the birth family in part to their sexual orientation, observing that he and Jared seemed to find the prospect of open adoption less startling and more appealing than the heterosexual couples at their agency. "By time we came to adoption, we had already restructured [our] idea of family . . . so open adoption to us is like 'Oh, OK, maybe I hadn't thought about that before, but sure.'"

The couple was ultimately placed with their son Chase, a toddler, who was also white. Initially, it was a foster care placement. Chase's birth parents continued to have visitation during the early months of their life together. These visitations created stress, because the birth parents were unaware of "the fact that we're a gay couple—we have to try to be secretive. It sucks that we can't be more open" (Jared). Of particular concern was that the birth father, who was "sort of" in the picture, and who was rumored to have expressed homophobic sentiments, might use their sexual orientation against them as a weapon (i.e., as a reason for rejecting them as potential adoptive parents). Given this, and the fact that he had a criminal background, their social worker had advised them to keep a safe distance. Despite these circumstances, Jared nevertheless expressed regret about not meeting the birth parents, offering his estimation that "as much as they have problems taking care of him, they both love him." Joe also described a complex set of feelings about the predicament they were in, prior to legally adopting Chase: "For the birth mom to succeed means we lose out, and we think Chase loses out. For us to succeed in our desire to adopt Chase, and to provide Chase with a really good nurturing home with two parents, you know, she loses out. And it's sad, and complicated."

Ultimately, Joe and Jared were able to legally adopt Chase. Notably, what eased the process was the couple's agreement to ongoing meetings between Chase and his birth mother, Allison, postadoption. (The birth father eventually disappeared and was not involved in postadoption visits.) Initially, the visits were between Chase and Allison at his day care center. Gradually, the visits became less structured, and more frequent, than initially agreed upon—and Joe and Jared began to participate in the visits (e.g., they met Allison at a park, playground, or casual restaurant). This ease was facilitated by their assessment that Allison was "in a better place, mentally," in part because of some changes in her medication regimen, which had improved her emotional stability. Sometimes Allison brought her sister to their visits, and sometimes she brought her children, Chase's older half-siblings. Notably, these changes did not happen overnight. Rather, they were slow, and facilitated by both men's increasing comfort with Allison, as well as, it seemed, her gradual recognition and acknowledgment of her limitations (e.g., her inability to parent several young children in the context of her current mental health struggles). Over time, Jared said, Allison seemed to

> really recognize that she was always not capable of parenting him. She was always cooperative, but now, she's kind of taken that to the next level and she's glad that Chase is with us. She knows that he's happy and doing well with us. She doesn't seem to have any problem with us being gay. She's happy that he's in good hands. And she respects the limits that we set for him and doesn't do anything to undermine them. And she really cares about his well-being.

Their relationship was not without its challenges. As Joe noted, with mild frustration:

because of her limitations, we have to kind of do all the management of the logistics and the visits, so, that's one more thing that we have to do. On the other hand, the reason we're doing this is for Chase, so he doesn't really get hurt. That's part of our job as parents.

While acknowledging that for "convenience sake, I would like a little less [contact]," Joe and Jared nevertheless acknowledged that they were committed to upholding contact between Chase and Allison for the long term. In fact, although they had only agreed to four visits a year, they were currently seeing Allison every month, which reassured them that "we will have no problem meeting the minimum—and if we ever feel like we need to back off, we have a lot of room." Chase, in turn, seemed to be doing "okay" with the arrangement. Five years postplacement, Jared said:

> He asks about her occasionally and we talk about going to see her. He'll often draw her a picture to bring. . . . I'll happen to be making cookies and he'll say, "Oh, let's save some for my mom." So I clearly appreciate that role that she has in his life, and I think it would be a mistake to make it more frequent, because it would send the wrong message to him about the extent of her role in his life. She's not a parent—or really part of the family in any way. We don't leave him alone with her; I don't know that we will as he gets older. . . . I think he realized that she's not—not only is she not here, but—he likes to see her, but I think he also sort of understands that she doesn't give him the kind of support he needs. So I think this is good, and we'll just continue with this as long as it feels right.

The couple also maintained contact with several of Chase's birth siblings—two boys, Perry and Jax—who had been adopted by other families, and, in turn, acknowledged that at times they felt "exhausted" by these multipronged efforts at contact. For example, Joe noted that when Chase "first came to live with us it was at least every couple months we would [drive] to celebrate their birthdays." As Chase grew older, Joe and Jared tried to allow him to dictate the timing and frequency of visits. Although they felt that it was good for him to see Perry and Jax, both men observed that Chase was not asking about them as much, which was "okay, because it's hard to schedule time. . . . We follow his lead now." Joe and Jared, like other parents, were highly attuned to how Chase was responding to visits with the birth family. Indeed, parents were typically aware that children's preferences, needs, and feelings about contact might shift over time and were ready to respond accordingly.

"Sometimes things like this happen—we can't pretend his birth family does not exist": A return to the birth family amid ongoing contact. Several of the families who adopted older children via foster care expressed concerns that their

children would be confused by ongoing contact, worrying that it would interfere with children's adjustment and ability to develop a healthy attachment to their new parents. In turn, they expressed concerns that continued contact with the birth family might increase the likelihood that their children might ultimately choose to return to their birth parents once they turned 18. In one family where there was ongoing contact with their child's birth family, this situation did indeed come to pass—but was short-lived, and well managed by all parties amid the fairly high levels of structural and communicative openness that the adoptive parents had established.

Al, a white insurance sales manager, and Geoff, a white waiter, lived in a midsized city on the East Coast. They originally adopted a 10-year-old boy, Nick, followed by two additional school-aged boys several years later—Mitchell and Brad, who were siblings. The couple maintained contact with Nick's birth family, but not with Mitchell and Brad's birth family—largely because of the very different circumstances that surrounded their early life and removal from the home. Nick was removed from his parents' home primarily because of neglect, which was attributed to his parents' low intellectual functioning and severe mental illness, whereas Mitchell and Brad were removed because of their birth parents' severe physical and emotional abuse.

Al shared how, 5 years postadoption, he and Geoff had continued to facilitate and maintain contact with Nick's birth parents, Nina and Steve, who were "very low-functioning. I mean *really* low-functioning. And they're kind of sweet and nice. And we've always maintained contact. They don't drive or anything, so we always make sure Nick gets to see them at least once a year. We get together with them at a restaurant." Geoff added: "Everything has always been supervised. [Early on], they would send us emails; we would review them before we would give them to him. And gradually they all earned that trust and everything, so that you know, over time we grew comfortable, to make sure everything was safe." Furthermore, Al and Nick ultimately became "Facebook friends with both Nina and Steve, so if they have any issues or things they want to talk about they can contact us that way." In addition to maintaining contact with Nina and Steve, Al and Geoff had maintained relationships with Nick's siblings, who had been adopted by other families, "for the kids' sake" (Geoff).

When my research team interviewed Al and Geoff 8 years after Nick was placed with them, Nick had recently turned 18. According to the two men, Nick's transition to legal adulthood had prompted him to consider moving back in with his birth mother, Nina. Al and Geoff supported him during this short-lived exploration, which culminated in Nick's realization that he could maintain a relationship with his mother without living with her—and also that she was not capable of parenting him in the way that he had fantasized about. This realization, and the relatively low level of turmoil that seemed to surround it, was likely facilitated by the fact that Al and Geoff had ongoing contact with Nick's birth family over the years—as well as their calm and sympathetic response to Nick's proclamation that he was returning to live with Nina. Al explained what happened after Nick made his announcement:

> Nina told him: "I can't take care of myself, I can't take care of you." And he realizes that now. We've had good relationships with his birth family. We felt that at first they were kind of freaked out that he was going to, you know, two guys, but once they met us and they saw what a great job we were doing... they were like, kind of, "If we can't have him, we're glad they're with you" type of thing. We've enjoyed good relationships there. And we think that's important. We don't want any of the kids to feel like their loyalty's being pulled upon. And you have to be secure as adoptive parents. You can't let your insecurity get in the way of that relationship that's always going to be there between a birth parent and their child. Yet they're all very realistic and understand that they were separated for reasons, and you can't go back to that.

Al and Steve encountered what some parents imagined as the "worst-case scenario"—a child returning to their birth family. However, they—and Nick—successfully navigated what was an undoubtedly painful experience with a remarkable level of honesty, warmth, and acceptance.

Managing Children's Feelings Amid Declining or Unreciprocated Contact

Some families acknowledged a desire to stay in contact with their children's birth families—at least specific birth family members, such as siblings—but ultimately, contact declined over time. Parents tended to describe this decline in contact as resulting from birth family members' difficulties staying in touch due to their chaotic or unpredictable personal lives (e.g., a recent relapse into drug use, a sudden departure into rehab, a stint in prison). In some cases, however, parents were unsure of the reasons for inconsistent or unreliable contact. Parents often tried, with difficulty, to manage their children's expectations and/or desires surrounding contact amid its general unpredictability. One such couple was Tina, a multiracial engineer, and Eva, a Latina professor, who lived in a Northeastern suburb with their son Devon, who was Latino. Adopted at age 4, Devon had several biological siblings with whom Tina and Eva had strived to maintain contact. Initially Devon had contact with his older brother, Rick, at least once a month—which Tina regarded as very important in that Rick was Devon's "primary family attachment," having taken care of Devon when he was a baby and their birth mother was actively using drugs and unable to parent effectively. But by the time Devon was 10, he had not had contact with Rick in almost 2 years. Tina voiced frustration about this drop-off in contact, stating:

> [After the initial period] we had some get-togethers with Devon and Rick, but it wasn't so often. We invited Rick to his birthday party a couple times. We would invite Rick over. But it was harder to get the families together. I mean, we would invite and they would invite us, and then it became a little bit harder and harder to get together and then it became, maybe we'd see them once a year and Devon would really miss them. And we would actually contact Rick's father and mother and then sometimes the phone numbers would change—so it wasn't regular contact. Then it got to the point where we'd maybe see them [once a year].... We tried really hard. Rick's phone number kept changing. We would keep calling, send texts, say, "Can we get together?" ... Devon always said, "I really want to see my brother." And I'd say, "Devon, I'm really trying, I'm calling."

Tina described frustration with the fact that Rick was not consistent in responding to their overtures to get together—as well as the reality that Devon blamed them when Rick did not respond. "It was like we were keeping him away from Rick," she said with exasperation, "when I was really reaching out and not getting any response." At this point, Tina said, she pulled back: "He knows how to get in touch with us; I've left him messages if he wants to see us." Finally, Rick did respond—and they had a visit with Devon. Immediately, Rick promised another visit—to which he did not show up. Again, Tina found herself pulling back in order to manage Devon's expectations. While she cautiously maintained contact with Rick, she did not tell Devon about any upcoming visits until she was fairly certain that he would come (i.e., he had confirmed with her an hour before the intended visit).

In some cases, unpredictable or intermittent contact was described as a complex product of inconsistent communication and adoptive parents' own worries about how contact might impact their child, especially at certain developmental phases (e.g., when their child was struggling more intensely with loss and/or anger). Mindy was a white career services manager in an East Coast suburb, who, with her husband Earl, a white therapist, had adopted her biracial (African American/white) son, Brett, at the age of 4. Mindy maintained email contact with Brett's birth mother, Barbie, early on, after her parental rights had been terminated—and the two women had discussed the potential of a future visit: "We talked about potentially meeting up. And then suddenly she fell from the face of the earth," recalled Mindy. About a year later, Mindy received an email from Barbie, in which she explained that she had been in rehab for drug abuse.

Again, Barbie requested a visit. Mindy was cautious, and asked that she finish her rehab treatment program before discussing a visit. Barbie agreed, and "then we never heard from her again . . . until about 6 months later . . . and she emailed a couple times, but then we lost communication again." This type of intermittent contact went on for years. Mindy explained why she continued to hesitate to facilitate a visit:

> We heard from her right before the holidays—and then not for a while . . . so we've left it in her court, to kind of keep in touch. And then if we feel like it's [an] appropriate time, we'll consider it. But a lot of times that she's come back, it's just not been an appropriate time for Brett. He might be going through a huge phase of concerns or issues. And part of it feels like this is more for her than it is for him . . . at this point. And yeah, I mean he has questions about her. He has torn [feelings] about missing her, yet being angry with her. . . . So our communication with her has been limited. . . . And you know, she clearly is trying very, very, very hard. . . . And she's never been, for lack of a better word, bitchy about it. When we push back, she's . . . always, "I understand a lot is going on and a lot has gone on."

Two years later, this pattern had continued—with Barbie increasingly asking for visits. Mindy explained:

> Brett . . . says things like, "Well, why won't you let me have a visit with her?" . . . But she doesn't contact us. When she does, she . . . demands a visit right then. And then . . . when she realizes that she has to follow through on something, she disappears again for 9, 12 months. And then pops up and says, "I'm going to visit."

Adding to Mindy's—and Earl's—hesitation about actively pursuing these visits was Brett's trauma associated with his early childhood, which was marked by neglect, substance abuse, and witnessing intense domestic violence. And yet, at the same time, both Mindy and Earl recognized the benefits of having a continued line of communication—particularly "because we may need to know family history later down the road. . . . So it's best to keep an eye on both of the parents, just so that we know their health history, so that we can have an idea of what's coming around the bend for him" (Earl).

Of note is that Mindy and Earl had initially agreed to a contract wherein Barbie would have visits twice per year at their family's home. Yet the contract also stated that if the birth mother did not contact them or missed consecutive visits, then the contract was officially terminated. Despite the official termination of the contract, both Mindy and Earl continued to emphasize their desire to "keep in touch" and to maintain an open line of communication with Barbie—especially for medical reasons.

Meg, a graduate student, and Michael, a philosophy professor, were a white heterosexual couple living in a midsized Northeastern city who adopted their biracial (African American/white) daughter Shaylene as a toddler. Like Mindy and Earl, they also had a contract with Shaylene's birth mother, Penny, in which they agreed to twice-a-year visits—and they expressed concerns throughout Shaylene's life about the impact of these visits. For example, early on—when Shaylene was not yet legally adopted and continuing to have visits with her birth mother prior to her termination of parental rights—Meg observed that postvisit, "Shaylene didn't eat or sleep or poop or pee and she stopped talking and everything. Everything shut down." Despite their alarm at this situation, both Meg and Michael, and especially Michael, saw a variety of benefits to maintaining contact with Penny. Three months after Shaylene was placed with them, Michael noted that one advantage of ongoing contact was that

> if an adopted child says, "I want to know who my biological parents are," you can actually say, "This is them," or you've already had contact with them and they know who they are. You can actually give them that. You don't have this kind of psychological disruption around, "Who the hell am I? Where do I come from?" . . . I wouldn't say that [contact] is something that makes me comfortable and cheerful, but at the same level, it's a good thing. It is something that hopefully—it's something that will help down the line, even if it's not an easy thing, even if it's difficult to do, watching someone deal with the idea of identifying who is their "real" parent, which probably would not be—which will not be easy when it happens—if and when it happens.

Ultimately, the contract that they signed was officially terminated. Penny had a few posttermination visits with Shaylene, during which Shaylene reportedly "hid" from her under a table, appearing unhappy and unsettled, and after which Shaylene "cried all the way home," eventually withdrawing into herself for several days. These visits fizzled after about a year. Five years after Shaylene was adopted, Meg shared:

> The visits were going to be twice a year and Penny was going to come to [our city]. And she just never managed it. [Our contract was] that if she didn't contact us or have visits within a year, like, if she missed two or three consecutive visits, the contract would be terminated. So we had the contract officially terminated. But we've kept open our post office box and once a year I send her a few photos of Shaylene. . . . We have to be able to tell Shaylene we tried—so that's the reason we kept open the post office box. But Penny had trouble

making visits when we were actually going through the process, so the fact that she hasn't made visits after the termination has made it easier for us.

Marianna, a homemaker, and Jerry, an appliance installer, were a white heterosexual couple living in an East Coast suburb who tried to establish contact with their daughter Lola's birth mother several years postadoption but were unsuccessful. When they adopted Lola, who was white, at the age of 10, Lola had not had contact with her birth mother in several years, having "lived out the past few years of her life in various foster homes" (Marianna). Lola had a lot of anger at her birth mother, who had an extensive history of drug abuse and who had "neglected all her kids pretty bad" and "never showed up to any of the court hearings or scheduled dates for supervised visits" while Lola was in foster care (Jerry). When Lola was about 13, she indicated that she wanted to reach out to her birth mother. According to Marianna, Lola said, "I just want to be friends." Marianna responded by saying to her:

"You know what, your mom might want to do that, knowing that we have legal custody now that you're legally ours." But I told Lola, I said, "It's up to her and she might say no." So the lady from the adoption agency, I sent an email to her, and she said would see about getting her mom's information. And I asked Lola, I was like, "Do you want me to call your mom?" ... And she said, "I'd like you to call her," and I'm like "All right, I will." Because it doesn't bother Jerry or I if she gets to know her mother. I think it would help her to not hate her mom and to see her mom has different struggles and different limitations.

Marianna did reach out to Lola's birth mother—but her calls went unanswered. Lola, in turn, seemed to experience the loss of her birth mother all over again, as well as the pain and disappointment of having been "left." "She is really pissed off about it. She tries to make sense of it. 'Why would my mom want to get rid of me?'" (Jerry). Although Lola did express an interest in "getting in contact with her mom at some point down the road—maybe [to] forgive her then, if not [to] have a relationship," for now, Jerry asserted, it seemed as though there would be no reunion. In turn, Marianna and Jerry were currently struggling with the fact that Lola was dealing with a great deal of anger—initially at her birth mother, but now "at, like, everything" (Jerry). Marianna said:

Not only is she dealing with this anger, but also she is feeling all these emotions from when she was a kid and trying to understand them, and then she's having to deal with all of her teen emotions on top of it! So she's getting swamped by all of this stuff she doesn't understand. And it's frustrating. For her and for us. We're trying to support her. We have an appointment with a psychiatrist next week.

Contact with the birth family is complicated—and even more so in the context of child welfare adoptions. Some parents—particularly heterosexual couples—never considered it; others did and rejected the notion that the benefits could outweigh the risks; and still others engaged it, sometimes cautiously—and sometimes creating relationships that all members of the triad appeared to benefit from. As children grow older, they appear to be increasingly likely to express their own preferences in terms of the who, what, when, and how often of birth family contact—a reality that some families accepted and responded to and others resisted.

As discussed in Chapter 10, contact in child welfare adoptions must be on a case-by-case basis—yet it also behooves adoptive parents to take a broad perspective when considering birth family contact, whereby the possibility of contact with a range of birth relatives—not just birth parents—is evaluated. Indeed, parents should seek out information about the range, type, and depth of birth family relationships that the child has (e.g., Does the child have cousins, aunts, and uncles? If the child has birth siblings, were they in the home at the same time as the child, and what are those relationships like?). Even if contact does not seem advisable early on, postplacement, parents should remain open to the possibility that they may be called upon to shift their approach to contact throughout their child's life. In that children's interest in and need for birth family contact may change as they develop, parents should request and/or seek out birth family contact information as early as possible, so that it is available if and when it becomes appropriate to reach out and establish contact. Having a long-range view of these relationships is ideal. Likewise, in some circumstances, parents may need to establish boundaries around contact with birth relatives—such as when these birth relatives are perpetrators of physical, emotional, or sexual abuse against the child.

Notes

1. Boyle, 2017; Child Welfare Information Gateway, 2013.
2. Barth & Berry, 1988; Crea & Barth, 2009; Faulkner & Madden, 2012.
3. Leathers, 2003; Wright, Flynn, & Welch, 2007.
4. Riggs, 2007.
5. Grotevant, 2009.
6. Neil, 2009.
7. Neil, 2006; Riggs, 2007.

8. Jones & Hackett, 2011.
9. Shari Levine & OAFS, 2017.
10. Gregorian, 2015.
11. Skinner-Drawz, Wrobel, Grotevant, & Von Korff, 2011; Wrobel, Kohler, Grotevant, & McRoy, 2003.
12. Boyle, 2017; Grotevant, 2009.
13. Riggs, 2007.
14. Grotevant, 2009.
15. Grotevant, 2009; Neil, 2009.

6
Adoption Talk

Communicative Openness Throughout Childhood

In contrast to advice given in the early 20th century, when adoption was taboo and secrecy was the norm, telling children about their adoption has been the directive given by adoption agencies to adoptive parents at least since the 1940s.[1] Scholars and practitioners now recognize that (a) secrecy surrounding adoption is almost impossible to achieve, (b) discovery of one's adoption later in life is likely to be distressing, and (c) disclosure of adoption is consonant with dominant societal values such as the importance of honesty and communication between parents and children.[2] Thus, the vast majority of parents tell their children about their adoptions, although when, how, and how much they say varies considerably.

Children's understanding of adoption changes throughout childhood, particularly during early to midchildhood. Adoption expert and psychologist David Brodzinsky and his colleagues[3]), in their seminal work on children's understanding of adoption, note that what it means to be adopted shifts according to children's stage in the life cycle alongside their growth and maturation in both cognitive and socioemotional domains. During infancy, a child is transitioning to a new family and developing secure attachment. During toddlerhood and the preschool years, children are learning about birth and reproduction and adjusting to initial information about adoption; they can also recognize differences in physical appearance, such as skin color and tone. By age 6 or 7, with the growth of logical thought, adopted children can usually differentiate between adoption and birth, recognize that most children are born into the family they are raised in, and are aware that being adopted means having two sets of parents: those who conceived/gave birth to them and those who are parenting them. These distinctions set the foundation for the more nuanced and complex understanding of adoption that emerges later.[4]

David Brodzinsky and his colleagues[5]) observed that parents' telling of the adoption story typically emphasizes joy and happiness—and, in turn, young children tend to feel very positively about being adopted, although "being adopted" also has very little meaning to them. As children's cognitive abilities develop, children begin to understand, in a more nuanced way, that adoption is an atypical way of coming into a family, and that there is another family out there that is related to them; an, by middle childhood, they begin to "infer the flip side of [their] beloved 'adoption story'—that for [them] to have been chosen, [they] first have to have been given away."[6] In turn, adoption begins to mean not just family building, but also family loss—thus accounting for many of the challenges that some adopted children begin to manifest during their school years, including anger, difficulties with communication, and poor self-image.[7]

How parents talk to their children about adoption can profoundly impact their growing understanding of adoption and how they integrate their identity as "adopted" into their overall sense of self.[8] David Brodzinsky has argued that even more important than structural openness (i.e., contact arrangements) is communicative openness: that is, adoptive parents' ability to create a flexible, open, nondefensive, and emotionally attuned family dialogue.[9] Communicative openness can be cultivated regardless of the level of contact—as it is independently related to positive child and family outcomes[10]—but the two types often overlap, with parents who are communicatively open also establishing and maintaining more structurally open arrangements.[11] When parents are open, flexible, and responsive in their general, and adoption-related, communication, this is believed to promote positive adoptee identity development, including greater ease and comfort asking questions and seeking out information regarding birth family and background.[12] Communicative openness may ultimately have the effect of encouraging more open and honest family communication about other important family topics; as one young adult participant in a longitudinal study of open adoptions said, "The openness makes it easier for us to talk about other situations, like drugs, alcohol, boys. It's made our relationship more open."[13] Likewise, a lack of flexible adoption-related communication within the family (e.g., because parents feel threatened by or wish to avoid the topic of adoption) may discourage children from expressing curiosity and asking questions, thus undermining adoptee development.[14] According to adoption scholar Gretchen Wrobel and her colleagues, there are three phases of communication about adoption that families may engage in across the family life cycle. First, adoptive parents may provide children with unsolicited information about their adoption and birth family. They may then address children's growing curiosity by answering their questions related to adoption and the birth family. Finally, adopted teens and young adults may begin to seek out information independently of their parents.[15]

This chapter traces how parents communicate about adoption with their children over time, with attention to how children's developmental stage reflects and impacts parents' approach to talking about adoption—as well as the topic of families more generally and the topic of race specifically. What parents say about adoption (adoption narratives) and how they talk about adoption (the emotional undertones) communicate important messages to the child about the nature and meaning of family and identity and have implications for children's personal self-concept and identity formation.[16] Many parents describe an awareness of and commitment to communicative openness. However, not all parents believe that it is necessary to talk about adoption—possibly reflecting a desire to avoid talking about difference[17] and their own concerns about the consequences of doing so (e.g., provoking feelings of loss in their child, causing their child to view their adoption as the most central feature of their identity). A key task for parents is to balance the importance of acknowledging difference (e.g., between adoptive and birth families) while not overemphasizing difference, thus enabling children to feel fully integrated into their adoptive families while also accepting their adoption as a part of themselves—and something that can be discussed openly, without fear.

The opening vignette in the chapter illustrates many of the themes that are discussed: namely, adoption talk at various stages, the role of the child in shaping the nature of adoption talk, and the possibility for difficult but honest questions and conversations to unfold over time.

Family Vignette: Kathleen and Becki

Kathleen and Becki, a white lesbian couple living in a midsized West Coast city, were employed as a nonprofit manager and group home supervisor, respectively. The couple adopted a newborn baby, Ana, through the foster care system. Despite having no contact with Ana's birth family (i.e., they lacked structural openness), they maintained a high level of communicative openness. Namely, they engaged a flexible and engaged approach to talking about adoption with Ana—and one that was responsive to the changing developmental and emotional needs of their daughter, whose feelings and questions about adoption shifted considerably over time.

Kathleen and Becki were placed with Ana when she was just a few weeks old by the Department of Social Services—an emergency placement that came about when Ana was removed from her birth mother's care in the hospital after it was determined that she was drug exposed. Her birth mother disappeared shortly after—which led to a slightly more expedient process of legally adopting Ana, insomuch as efforts at reunification halted after multiple unsuccessful attempts to locate the birth mother. Both Kathleen and Becki acknowledged relief but also discomfort with the reality that Ana's birth mother's disappearance made their lives, and the process of adopting Ana, "easier." They were aware that the birth mother's disappearance represented a loss, and one that would have anticipated and unanticipated echoes throughout Ana's life.

Both Kathleen and Becki talked to Ana about her adoption throughout her childhood ("it's our reality as a family"). They never sat her down to tell her "the whole story"; rather, "we would share little bits when she would ask questions—age appropriately." Three months postplacement, they had already begun practicing telling Ana her adoption story, with the intention to "just talk about it as openly as possible. Then we'll just let her ask the questions, with how much information she wants to know. But always give her space to talk about it." As Ana matured, both Kathleen and Becki described engaging Ana in more complex, nuanced, and detailed conversations. Both women's explanations of how they responded to their daughter's questions and fears revealed a deep attunement to her developmental and emotional needs as well as their own comfort and ability to sit with some of the more difficult relational dynamics that surfaced. They demonstrated a high level of tolerance with ambiguous, complex, and painful feelings, an important and adaptive characteristic for adoptive parents in particular.[18] When Ana was 5, Kathleen shared:

> Sometimes she'll just be kind of looking a little pensive or whatever, and I'll say, "What are you thinking about?" and she'll say, "I'm just thinking about my birth mom, and where she is and I miss her." So we'll kind of talk through, like, "Well what would she do if she was here?" and try to get to some of the fears she has and the sadness that she has. Lately she has started doing this whole "You're not my real mom, and I wish I could live with my real mom." . . . Usually [she says this] when she's in her rages, so we wait for her to calm down, and then we say, "I am your real mom. A mom is somebody who loves you and cares for you and wipes your tears and stays up with you when you're sick; that's your real mom. Whereas the woman who carried you in her body for 9 months, it's different. She created your body, and we're developing your heart." So that's kind of how we've been doing it . . . and we're looking for a therapist who is skilled in adoption and has families with two moms so that Ana has a place to work through some of this stuff.

Both Kathleen and Becki were unique in their ability to "hold" the complex reality of adoption—its joy and its loss—for both themselves and their daughter. They also recognized and embraced Ana's challenges as well as her strengths. Kathleen said:

> Ana has some attachment stuff, and there's some anxiety going on with her. . . . She [also has] some rage issues where she'll just fly off the handle at nothing . . . so trying to get a handle on that is our focus. . . . We're connecting with a therapist and she's being assessed for medication. But Ana is a bright,

beautiful child, with a huge heart—and I just think that because of the drugs that she was exposed to in utero, and because of her grief and loss that she feels so deeply, she just needs extra help.

Becki shared:

I think that Ana's experience in utero and also what she inherited from her birth family—that does have a significant impact on her. And the adoption itself... I think it impacts Ana that she... is being raised by two people that are not biologically related to her, that she has grandparents that are not biologically related to her—but not in the negative. It just is part of the impact. It's part of who she is and it creates her. At their core everyone has something that's not their parent, but you don't really talk about that with bio kids. I think it definitely matters, and we're very open about it. We talk about it. We've talked about it forever. I think she worries and wonders about her birth parents. Both are heavily tragic stories, and that's for sure had an impact on her.

Kathleen's and Becki's approach to sharing Ana's story with her, and Ana's own understanding of adoption, continued to evolve as Ana grew older. When Ana was 8, Kathleen shared how Ana had repeatedly, over the past few years, asked to see a picture of her birth mother—which they were reluctant to show her, because she "looked terrible... it's one of the most depressing pictures in the world." But Kathleen finally relented, revealing how different pieces of information might be shared at different points in the adoption life cycle, depending on the developmental needs and requests of the child.[19] Sharing this picture with Ana had a number of important consequences—including solidifying the reality of her birth mother's substance dependence, and in one instant eliminating any perfect fantasies that Ana might have had of her. "She really examined [the picture], and we talked about ways that she looks like her... and then she immediately stopped talking about her altogether and it hasn't come up much since." Kathleen explained that they had already talked to Ana about the reality of her birth mother's addiction—but Kathleen suspected that seeing the picture made it real:

I guess she wanted it to be something different than what it was and then seeing the picture of her birth mom made her understand what it was. I think to actually see that... was hard for her. I don't know. She really never wanted to talk about it. And I mean I've always been, you know, "When you want to talk about it, anything you want, we'll talk about." So sometimes late at night she'll bring things up, but it hasn't come up for [a while]. I think she's cut off the brakes on that piece of her story and that's okay. And I'm sure it'll come back.

Kathleen and Becki did not try to minimize their daughter's loss or trauma. They took her cues in terms of how and when to talk about her story, in developmentally appropriate terms. They were generous in their view of her, highlighting her strengths as well as describing her challenges. They remained flexible in terms of how and when to talk about adoption and remained optimistic that their own comfort and willingness to talk about the tough issues would in turn encourage Ana to continue talking to them, even when it was challenging.

Talking About Adoption Early On, "When They Don't Understand, So We Can Practice"

Soon after bringing their children home, and often in the midst of navigating early relationships with birth parents, parents were also figuring out how to talk to their children about adoption. Although their children were typically infants—just a few months old—when I first talked to them after they had adopted, parents had often already begun to "practice" what they would say when their child was older and would understand. Many parents voiced an awareness that in order to get comfortable with talking about adoption, and to ensure that talking about adoption was always "normal and natural ... an ongoing conversation," they needed to start right away. Thus, they—sometimes awkwardly—tried on what to say, and how to say it, with their infant children, as a way of establishing a solid foundation for future conversations about adoption. Indeed, some parents felt strongly about honoring their commitment to openness, and thus took such personal discomfort in stride. Rob, a gay Latino administrative assistant living in a suburb of a large city on the West Coast, who, with his partner, Terrence, ultimately adopted two Latino sons, David and Nolan, acknowledged that such conversations would likely not always be easy, but

> I'm very open because I don't want them to have an issue later—because we didn't talk about it or because it was taboo, or whatever. When we decided to have kids, we knew that we needed to be very open about this because obviously they didn't come out of either one of us. So we made that agreement that we would always be open, we would always talk about it, and whatever questions they had, we would furnish to the best of our ability and to the best of their understanding and mental capacity at that age.

Here, Rob reveals how his approach to communicative openness incorporates a consideration of family structure as promoting such openness (i.e., via his children's eventual realization that two men can't make a baby), as well as a consideration of developmental stage (i.e., his children's cognitive capacity would inform the timing, amount, and type of information shared).

Photos (e.g., of birth parents) and books about adoption were used as tangible prompts for these (initially one-sided) conversations. As Shelby, a white lesbian postal clerk in a small Northeastern city, who adopted two biracial (Latino/white) sons, said, "I think using books to bring out discussions is a great way to introduce subjects. . . . We already have some same-sex adoption books, and just regular adoption books." Rosie, a white heterosexual magazine editor living in a suburb of the Northeast, shared how she had begun writing a book about how her daughter Lila, who was white and adopted as a toddler via foster care, "came to live with us," which Rosie intended to read to her, "just so that it is so matter of fact, so it's never like, you're thirteen, and it's like, 'by the way, you were adopted.'" Engaging with a book, photo, or other artifacts (e.g., a gift from birth family) enabled parents to initiate conversations about adoption with more ease and comfort. Further, treating their child's adoption as basic factual information, "like the sky is blue, birds fly, that's your birth mom," was seen as key to ensuring that it "always just seems natural" and there was never any "big reveal." Cara, a white lesbian landscape design architect in a large city on the West Coast, who adopted her young Latino son Daniel from foster care, said, "I have a bunch of pictures of his parents and of him as a baby and of us with him . . . and I'm going to sort of build a storybook that he can look at . . . over and over as long as he wants to . . . even before he can talk." Shoshanna, a white heterosexual project manager living in a small city in the Northeast, shared, regarding her daughter Morgan, who was also white:

> I tell her all the time [*laugh*]. I tell her her story. I tell her about how we got the phone call and . . . met her birth mom and birth dad. I'm always telling her about it. She will know the whole story. It will be one of those things where it is her story, and she probably won't even know when I first told it to her, and she will be meeting them once a year every year, too.

Shoshanna's husband, Cal, a white IT manager, provided a very similar account, stating: "We just kind of figure that we talk about it with her now, so as long as we are talking about it with her all of the time, she will always know. . . . It will always be that [this] is just the way it is." Leo, a Latino gay father employed as a speech therapist in an East Coast suburb, gave this account of how he practiced talking about adoption in the presence of his daughter Elizabeth, who was biracial (African American/white):

> I kind of do already [talk about adoption] with Elizabeth, which I think is a little practice for myself. Like when she's looking in the mirror and I'm holding her

up to the mirror and saying stuff about her, how she looks. Because, you can't really notice it when her hair is cut—but Elizabeth has curly hair and Leandra, the birth mother, is biracial and that curly hair doesn't obviously come from me or Javier—not obviously, but it doesn't come from me or Javier. So I talk about that. I feel very comfortable with the idea of saying, "These are the things that come from your birth mom" and stuff like that.

Here, Leo seems to recognize the importance of getting comfortable with talking about visible physical differences between himself and his daughter—differences that were racialized (e.g., hair) and which might become more noticeable in the future (e.g., when Elizabeth's hair was longer). Likewise, Daniela, a white lesbian small business owner in a medium-sized city in the South, shared her experience of beginning what would be an "ongoing conversation" about adoption with her infant daughter, Stella, who was also white:

We have this multisided photo frame in her nursery that has a picture of me and Stella, a picture of Stella and her other mommy, a picture of my sister and Stella, a picture of her birth grandma, and a picture of Joy, the birth mom, and Stella. In the last couple of weeks, when I changed her she started looking at herself more and see what's on them so we get to talk about that ... you know, show her Joy's face. You know, start the dialogue now. As she gets bigger it will just be a natural part of her nursery to have pictures around and for us to identify who that is and who this is and as questions arise from that then we'll talk about it. And of course we'll also have storybooks that also talk about alternative families and that will just be something that she will always be exposed to, stories with other family types, so it's just natural for her to realize that not all families have a mommy and a daddy.... I think it will be a natural conversation that we will always have, and the fact that we will have some contact with Joy and most likely fairly heavy contact with the birth grandmother—it will be a very natural progression for us to talk about them as if they are a part of our extended family. And in Stella's mind, the word *birth mom* will mean very much to her like what the word *aunt* means to me.

Here, in Daniela's narrative, she also not only articulates a desire to make adoption a natural and comfortable conversation topic but also identifies a number of other messages she hopes to convey. First, Daniela wishes to normalize the notion of birth family as extended family—for example, the idea that the birth mother occupies a role that is similar to that of "aunt." Indeed, birth parents are featured prominently in Daniela's description of family, and she appears confident that contact with the birth mother and grandmother, for example, will facilitate conversation about adoption and birth family, rendering these topics (as inextricably linked as they are) less abstract and mysterious. Second, Daniela wishes to normalize her daughter's membership in a two-mom family. Conveniently, talking about adoption will also mean talking about their status as a two-mom family, and vice versa. As both Daniela and Rob, quoted earlier, imply, the reality that their families look different from the dominant heterosexual nuclear family model in multiple ways might make adoption talk easier in two-mom and two-dad families. In other words, their family structure and visible differences make avoidance of adoption talk harder.

Many participants' narratives suggested that talking about adoption during these early months of parenting was facilitated by their two-mom or two-dad status. The dual fact that most families had a mom and a dad and that two moms (or two dads) can't make a baby (alone) made the topic unavoidable—and thus somewhat easier to engage with their children. Terrence, a white gay anesthesiologist in a West Coast suburb—and the partner of Rob, quoted earlier—said, about his son David:

> He's going to know immediately that we didn't just spawn him from our ankles. It's not like with a heterosexual couple where the child can still maintain a fantasy that he or she is a biological child until you actually tell them that they're adopted. We have to really deal with that, I think, up front and immediately. So even now we talk to him about, "Oh, we just got off the phone with your mother." We're really trying to make sure that we're talking with him about who she is.

Lesbian couples pursue biological parenthood at rates higher than gay couples (in part because donor insemination is less expensive and involved as compared to surrogacy[20]), and thus, lesbian couples who share the same race as their children may not necessarily be seen as an adoptive family. But in that gay male couples' primary route to parenthood is through adoption, concealment or avoidance of their adoptive status is unlikely—particularly in cases where children are of a different race than both parents. Terrence's son David was biracial (Latino and white), and his partner Rob was Latino. Thus, though it was possible that an observer might see Rob and David as biogenetically connected (based on David's "darker skin tone") and Terrence as an outsider to the family, it was as or more likely that they would be seen collectively as an adoptive family. In turn, Terrence and others recognized that in general, gay parenthood and adoption seemed to "go hand in hand," as one gay father put it, making it almost impossible to talk about one without talking about the other.

Heterosexual adoptive parents, in contrast, were pursuing a family-building route that was distinctly different from the heterosexual nuclear family standard—and the majority of their children's current and future peers. This might help to explain why some heterosexual parents explicitly wove in their inability to have a child with the adoption story they shared with their child as part of the "background" for how their child came to be with them. Perhaps—unlike same-sex couples—they felt compelled to address the "why" behind their choice to adopt. Lena, a white heterosexual operations manager in a medium-sized city in the Northeast, said:

> I envision telling him when he gets old enough. You know, "Mommy couldn't have a baby and Mandy was your mommy and you were in her tummy and she was just too young to take care of you and she wanted you to come to Mommy and Daddy." I think it's just going to be so—it's a fact. Everyone in my family knows, all of our friends know, it's just "Joey was adopted." It's not going to be this whole, like, thing.

Similarly, Seana, a white heterosexual sales associate in a large Midwestern city, said: "I've explained that 'The doctors said that I couldn't grow a baby in my tummy, but we really wanted to be parents.' So I've explained that part of it. And then, 'This other couple was having a baby and they chose to let mommy and daddy raise you.'"

Lesbian parents did not describe discussing or planning to discuss their inability to get pregnant as part of the adoption narrative, even when they had tried to conceive for a considerable length of time prior to pursuing adoption. They likely did not feel the need to explain why they did not have a biological child or how they arrived at adoption. Again, whereas heterosexual couples were pursuing a family-building route that deviated from societal norms about "ideal" or "typical" families (i.e., heterosexual married couples with biologically related children), same-sex couples already deviated from such norms in multiple ways (e.g., via their same-sex, and often unmarried, relational status). In addition, media and societal images of same-sex parenthood encompass a range of family-building routes, including donor insemination, surrogacy, adoption via foster care, and domestic private adoption. In turn, same-sex couples likely felt much less pressure to justify, explain, or provide context for their particular family-building route.

When It's (Extra) Complicated: Addressing Loss and Sensitive Circumstances in Adoption Talk, Early On

In practicing adoption talk during these early months, parents typically emphasized "the basics": namely, (a) the general circumstances that led to the adoption and (b) how much the child was loved by both adoptive parents and birth parents. In crafting the adoption narrative, parents also often acknowledged, directly or indirectly, the loss inherent to adoption. In telling their children's adoption story, they recognized that alongside the albeit important messages of joy and celebration they wished to communicate, it was also necessary to articulate aspects of adoption that were harder to talk about—most significantly, the fact that their child had a set of birth parents that were not parenting them due to a variety of complex circumstances, as illustrated in this chapter's opening vignette.

In private domestic adoptions, where children were not removed from their birth parents' care, it was possible to position the birth parents' inability to parent within the context of these individuals' bravery and love, whereby they actively made an adoption plan out of a desire to give their child the best life possible. Although clearly simplifying a very complicated set of circumstances and decisions, this framing served to, in parents' eyes, place the birth parents' love (as opposed to their limitations) front and center, and also to underscore the collaborative nature of the birth parents' and adoptive parents' relationship, whereby they worked together out of shared love for the child. Jackie, a white heterosexual pediatric nurse living in a Northeastern suburb, said, about her daughter Serena, who was also white: "I tell her, you know, that Thea loves you. She loves you so much that she chose us to be your parents, because she couldn't do it alone, and she had [other kids], and not the means or support system that she needed in place." Here, Jackie acknowledges the circumstances that prevented her daughter's birth mother from parenting, but also clearly frames the decision to make an adoption plan as loving and child centered. Hannah, a white lesbian administrative assistant in a large Northeastern city, shared, "We explain it to Luke, like, Amy couldn't take care of you, and she thought it would be the best for you—so you'd have the best possible [life]. She . . . decided it would be the best for [you] to be with our family."

Notably, parents sometimes highlighted the fact that their pursuit of an open adoption enabled them much greater insight and detailed knowledge into their child's story than they would have possessed if the adoption had been closed. Jackie, for example, had met and maintained contact with her daughter Serena's birth mother, Thea, and thus had knowledge of the challenging circumstances surrounding the placement ("she didn't have a job, she was on welfare and food stamps") but also the birth mother's personal qualities ("she seemed honest and up front, and healthy"). This knowledge informed Jackie's ability and confidence to construct an adoption narrative that felt authentic and sufficiently nuanced. Shoshanna, a white heterosexual project manager in a small Northeast city, stated:

One of the things we started telling Morgan about her adoption was that her birth parents felt that they were not responsible enough to parent her when she was born and they felt like the most loving choice they could make for her would be to find parents who would parent her.... That was really what Leanne and Tucker offered to us as to why they were making that choice, so it is honest; it is not anything we made up. It is not—if you had a closed adoption, you know, "Your birth mother loved you very much," but really you don't know, right? You have no idea what the circumstances are. [For us], it's right there.

Sometimes the reasons and circumstances surrounding the adoptive placement were complex and difficult to explain to a child (e.g., their birth parents were drug involved, suffered from mental illness, or were engaged in criminal activity and/or in prison)—especially as parents balanced the desire to be honest with the desire to be positive in how they talked about the birth family.[21] For parents who adopted via foster care, whose children were typically removed from the home at least in part because of these issues—and whose birth parents often did not voluntarily relinquish their parental rights—acknowledging the circumstances surrounding placement was especially challenging. Three months postplacement, Kathleen, one of the lesbian mothers whose story opened this chapter, was keenly aware that she and her partner, Becki, would need to explain the "why" behind Ana's adoption in the future—and they had already started to practice these conversations:

We've started talking about it now, just to kind of practice. So we say things like, "Your birth mom had a really tough life." I think the phrase that we use is that she was not able to parent you, she wasn't able to love and care for you, provide for you in a way that was healthy and safe. And I tell her a lot that her birth mom really, really loved her and that's why she let her go. I don't know; we'll figure it out as we go. But the thing I want Ana to know is that her birth mom loved her, but she just wasn't able to provide a safe, loving home. And eventually we'll talk about the addiction because we want Ana to know [about] the possibility that she could get into trouble with drugs and alcohol too, because it runs in her family.... We're going to be totally open, as open as we can be. I just think that's important for her sanity really.

Vincent, a white gay telecommunications director in a large Midwestern city, who had adopted his African American son Ayo from foster care when he was a toddler, shared that Ayo's birth mother had substance abuse and mental health issues, and had several children removed from her care when Ayo was placed with them. However, Ayo's birth mother had eventually voluntarily relinquished her parental rights—which Vincent was very happy about, because it enabled him to say, "She had adult problems and couldn't take care of a child, so she asked us to be [your] forever family, and we adopted [you]."

Parents whose children's adoptions involved difficult or sensitive circumstances were sometimes uncertain about how to talk about these issues and sought guidance and advice from their adoption agencies as well as therapists and other helping professionals. Sandy was a white heterosexual health care advocate in a small city in the Northeast, who, upon adopting her toddler-aged son Todd, who was also white, via foster care, said that she was "not sure" how to talk about adoption with him—particularly given the circumstances of the placement, such that his birth parents had cognitive and mental health issues that rendered them unable to parent. In turn, Sandy had gone to

> a presentation on how to talk to your child about adoption at different stages. And, you know, jeez; they're talking about how you should start really from birth. And, like, wow—now we're at the 2½ [mark], and he's going to be 3. And we kind of don't know. Okay, what do we say?

In some cases, parents were aware of highly sensitive details about the adoptive placement that simply could not be easily woven into the adoption narrative—and which were difficult to imagine telling their children about, at least not directly, for a long time. For example, in several cases, parents worried about whether, when, and how to acknowledge the role of rape or incest in their child's conception and eventual placement. "The one thing we haven't figured out yet is [what to do] when she asks who her dad is. You know, with the sexual assault—at what age can you tell a kid that situation?" wondered one gay father. This father went on to say that he was coordinating with the birth mother—with whom he had contact—to determine that they were on the same page in terms of what to share. He said:

> I think the whole story of her early life and the adoption—if we keep the current contact that we have with the mom, the story is just going to evolve. I don't think it's going to be a "We need to sit down and tell you something." It's going to be the story she knows.

Likewise, a heterosexual father shared the fact that his daughter was the product of incest. Given the sensitive and "high risk" nature of the adoption, he expected to be "fairly circumspect" about certain aspects of her story, at least during early childhood. "It is not a happy thing," he said soberly. Regarding the future, he said:

She doesn't need to know the myriad of ways in which human beings can be horrible to each other. The family in question has issues. . . . One of the things that we realize now is that we have to—there may be things that we're going to have to explain at some point. But . . . I don't know. I can't—I cannot . . . I just can't fathom explaining this to a child; I don't even know how I would. So—I think as time goes on, I think it's going to be one of those things where, you know, since all of it is not a big secret, only parts of it are a big secret, it'll be more a matter of, you know—what portion of the secret does she not know, as opposed to, she didn't know any of it and now it's like a ton of bricks. . . . It breaks my heart a little bit in anticipation, but I can't suffer what's not happened yet.

Not Talking About Adoption Early On: "It Seems Unnecessary"

At this early stage—several months after adopting—a minority of parents, mostly heterosexual fathers, voiced concern about finding a balance between acknowledging and addressing adoption as part of their children's story and not making it a "big deal." These parents wanted to keep things "simple" and did not view ongoing conversations about adoption at this early stage to be necessary or meaningful. Some of these parents did note, however, that they expected such conversations to be more important as their children grew, and thus they effectively saw themselves as "tabling" adoption talk for the future. Lewis, a white heterosexual teacher in a small Northeastern city, considered the possibility of introducing his son Todd—who was white and adopted as a toddler—to a "family tree" at some future date, believing that this visual exercise

> would start explaining it and getting it into his mind, and discussion. We don't want to overburden him with it, you know? But we will tell him, we want to tell him, we feel it's important to tell him—we're just waiting for the moment. Not right now, but the right time.

These narratives of these men's wives reinforced the possibility that these men struggled in talking openly about adoption with their children—and that women in turn tended to take on this role early on. For example, Lewis's wife, Sandy, was quoted earlier as describing her attendance at an adoption event aimed at helping parents to talk to children about adoption. Carly, a white heterosexual history professor in a large Northeastern city, contrasted her husband's and her own approach to adoption talk with their African American daughter Eve, stating, "I'm definitely more of the talker and 'emoter' parent. He talks about things but . . . in a little bit more of a matter-of-fact kind of way. It may even be a little more academic, I would say." Carly acknowledged that talking about adoption felt "hard . . . but practice had helped." Carly described how she would practice reading adoption books, with the knowledge that her daughter had "no idea what I'm saying," in an effort to "get [the crying] out of my system."

In some cases, the desire to keep things simple and to put off adoption conversations until some future date also appeared to be related to the fact that parents had had minimal contact with birth parents and were unsure of the role they would be playing in the child's life. Uncertain about what exactly to say at this early stage, they held off on practicing their stories until they felt they had a better grasp on the birth parents' role and involvement and therefore a better sense of how to talk about them.

Talking About Adoption to School-Aged Children: Emphasizing Love, Acknowledging Loss

At every interview, most parents emphasized that the primary messages they wanted their children to internalize about adoption were that families are diverse/different; families are not defined by blood but by love; and adoption is normal, positive, and nothing to be ashamed of. Thus, they sought to normalize the idea of adoption while also ensuring that it was internalized as a "positive thing"—thus recognizing the critical importance of their child developing a positive and integrated sense of self as an adopted person.[22] These parents aimed to establish that although a statistical minority, adoptive families were real and valid, and there was "nothing to be ashamed about" in regard to being adopted or a member of an adoptive family ("we're a minority but that doesn't mean we're any less than or better than": Christy, a white lesbian mother). Aisha, an African American lesbian human resources manager in a large city in the Northeast, shared how in parenting her 8-year-old biracial (African American and white) daughter Elise, she had tried to cultivate an awareness of the ways in which Elise's family and background might differ from those of other children. However, Aisha sought to frame these differences as positive—and to underscore that there really was no family "norm":

> [We try to convey] the message that there's difference all around you. Like, it can be easy to feel like you're the only one that's different but it's rarely true. There are other people who have differences embedded in the way that their families operate and that's okay. The difference is what makes you extraordinary, right? It's the ways in which you are different from other people that make you special.

Erin, a white lesbian librarian living in a large West Coast city, explained her approach with her 5-year-old son Jeremy, who was also white:

> He's got a variety of books with two dads and two moms—things like that. But it's in his life. Some of his friends just have one parent, some of them live with two parents.... Just, every family is different. He's been raised always being told, "Yeah, it's not a big deal." That's always how we've kind of put it: "This is how our family is, other families are different." And the same thing [with race]—he has a very diverse friend group. And some of them have really dark skin, some of them have light skin, some have curly hair, some have straight hair—it's just, "It's different, that's just how it is. Isn't that great?"

Many families emphasized the notion of "love makes a family." Donna, a white heterosexual nonprofit manager in a large city in the Northeast, said, about her 5-year-old biracial (African American/white) son Ace, "We sometimes talk about [how] family members are not necessarily blood related. And family is made up with love, and family is probably the most important thing to us." Lewis, a white heterosexual teacher in a small Northeast city, mused, regarding conversations with his 7-year-old son Todd, who was also white: "I guess the main message we throw out to him is, family is made up of love. It's generally made up of love and caring over any kind of other tie. I mean, it's whoever is loving and caring for you, from this day to forever."

As their children grew older, parents increasingly considered how, alongside this emphasis on love and connection as the foundation of their families, it was also necessary to acknowledge the often difficult circumstances surrounding the placement: that is, the fact that, as much as adoption is about love, it also involves loss. In turn, as children entered school age, parents' narratives surrounding the adoption often grew more specific and elaborate, shifting to accommodate their children's growing understanding of and questions about adoption. Research on the adoption family life cycle shows that as children develop, they gain a more sophisticated understanding of family formation (e.g., facts about reproduction) and become more attuned to differences between people, within and across families.[23] Aware of their children's developmental gains—in some cases because of the changing nature of their children's questions—parents often began to modify their telling of the adoption story and the circumstances of the placement. When they were interviewed 5 and 8 years postadoption, most parents explained that conversations about adoption had gotten more specific, nuanced, and interactive.

Parents' conversations with school-aged children often involved details surrounding past and present birth parent circumstances, and sometimes addressed the particulars of family formation and reproduction. Such conversations in part echoed parents' narratives of the stories they told their children soon after placement, whereby adoption was emphasized as overwhelmingly positive, with messages of being "chosen" as their children's parents (by the birth parents or in some cases by God) woven in. Yet by school age, parents' stories were typically more elaborate and detailed, in part because their children were now able to ask direct and often very specific questions about aspects of the placement and birth family. Rick, a white gay nonprofit director in a large city on the West Coast, shared, about his 5-year-old son Jack, who was also white:

> He's very fascinated with his story, about when he was born. And so we talk, probably once a week, he asks me to tell him the story about how when we met Sara when she was pregnant, and she picked us to be his parents because she wasn't able to take care of you.

Roy, a white gay sales manager in a large West Coast city, shared that adoption-related conversations with his 8-year-old African American son Ethan had increasingly focused on his birth mother, Liza. Roy said:

> It's definitely less about actually adoption than it is about—I'd say that 80% to 90% of the conversations, when they do come up, are about his birth mom and his birth origins. He's just interested in a lot of origin-related things or little facts about his birth mother—just wanting to know more about his birth mom.

As their children grew older, parents were also increasingly likely to acknowledge the difficult circumstances that led to their child's placement. Stacy, a white lesbian school administrator in a midsized Northeast city, described how their discussion of the difficult circumstances surrounding her biracial (Latina and white) daughter Marlo's adoption had grown more detailed over time. Around the time that Marlo was 8, Stacy shared:

> She has always, always been told she was adopted since day 1. So it was never a surprise to her. She has always grown up knowing. What has changed is the [level of] details [we provide]. When she was younger, the narrative was much more about, "Because of what was going on in your birth parents' lives they couldn't care for any child at that time." Now we fill in what those things were that were going on in their lives. So, Marlo knows that Krista and Jay, her birth parents, were having a hard time staying housed—that they were living with friends, that they didn't have a stable house where they could stay, or a stable apartment where they could stay. She knows that her birth brother has been

taken into foster care because of the challenges around drugs and alcohol that her birth parents were having.... She knows that they put her up for adoption[*] because they couldn't be parents to anyone.

Robin, a white lesbian small business owner in a Northeast suburb, had adopted her son Shawn, who was Latino, with her partner, Greta, via foster care. A toddler when they adopted him, Shawn was asking more complicated—and heartbreaking—questions about his birth family by the time he was 6 and 7. Robin described how she and Greta sought to emphasize to Shawn that "our big thing about family is [that] we take care of each other. We talk about how families are made in a million different ways, about the different ways families work . . . but reiterate that family is the place where you belong. They're never going to quit on you." For Shawn, such conversations

> bring up, "Well, why did my birth family quit on me?" And . . . we're pretty honest and say, you know, they didn't take care of you and they couldn't do their job. When you bring kids into the world, your job is to take care of them . . . to have a roof over their head . . . to teach them . . . to be a role model.

For Robin, naming the reality that Shawn's birth parents had "messed up" was challenging but necessary, she believed, in order for him to have a true sense of how and why he was removed from his birth parents' care, placed in foster care, and adopted by his two moms. In turn, Shawn had to confront the painful losses and injustices that he had suffered as a consequence of his birth parents' mistakes, recognizing that what was supposed to happen "didn't happen in [the early] years of [his] life. And we say, 'You're absolutely right. That's not the way it was supposed to be . . . [but] the three of us have got to fix it, because that's not a way to move forward'" (Robin).

Similarly, Mindy, a white heterosexual career services manager in an East Coast suburb, had adopted her son Brett at the age of 4 via foster care. Mindy made a point of emphasizing that Brett, who was biracial (African American and white), was in fact chosen—while also acknowledging the painful circumstances that led up to his placement with them (i.e., parental substance abuse, physical abuse, and neglect) as well as Brett's feelings of anger and abandonment. When Brett was 9, she mused: "I think the overarching theme that we've always tried to emphasize with him is that we chose you. We were told about some children who needed a family and needed a safe home, and we chose you. You're a part of this family forever and ever." Alongside this emphasis on the fact that Brett was

---

[*] Of note is that "put up for adoption" is not ideal language. "Placed for adoption" is considered more adoption-positive language (Henry & Pollack, 2009).

chosen, she conceded: "We talk about how yes, he has a past. Yes, he has a history. There are certainly things that he has a right and reason to be upset and angry about . . . and we can talk about it . . . we can deal with it." Noting the complexity of Brett's feelings surrounding his birth family, she said:

> We also talk about, it's also okay to love and miss your past as well. We realize that there's some bad things about your past . . . and you might be angry with them. But we realize you also miss some [of them] and that you do wonder and have questions about that. . . . That's okay. We get that. We can try to help fill in any issues or questions you might have. But you are here to stay—and it's also okay to love them and miss them.

Parents ultimately faced the task of acknowledging the birth parents' inability to parent while also remaining respectful and compassionate. Some parents, like Jessica, a white heterosexual homemaker in a midsized Midwestern city who adopted an African American boy named Jerome via private domestic adoption, carefully navigated this dialectic—in part drawing on religion (i.e., the presence of God) to help her 6-year-old son make sense of his adoption:

> We just say that . . . every person who has ever been born has a birth mother and a birth father. God uses a birth mother and birth father to create a child, and sometimes children live with their birth parents or birth mothers or birth fathers and sometimes they don't . . . and so Jerome said, "Well so are you my real mom?" And so I say, "Well, yes and no. Carolyn is your real mom and I am your real mom." "Well why don't I live with my birth mom?" And that's kind of tough because I don't want him to think of his birth mother as a lesser person because she couldn't take care of him. And so it's a hard question because—it's so hard to say to him at such a young age. "She . . . loved you *so* much that she sacrificed raising you to give you what she wanted you to have. She knew she couldn't give you what she wanted you to have." And that's a big thing to kind of give to a kid that age—so at this point it's just, "You know what, she prayed and God asked her to let mommy and daddy raise you, but she still loves you." . . . I want to portray—and, you know, it's difficult as an adoptive parent who is supportive of all members of the adoption triad, because a lot of people don't—they just think that these birth families throw these kids away, that they don't love them, that they don't want this kid to bring them down or whatever. And maybe in some cases it's like that but I can't imagine that every birth family, at some point, every birth mother doesn't at some point feel that ache. And I know that Jerome's birth mother, regardless of how everything turned out, she cares and cared about him. And I would always want him to know that.

In addition to becoming more detailed, adoption talk also sometimes shifted to reflect and accommodate children's own growing awareness of the loss inherent to adoption. Some families described ways in which their children had communicated their own understanding, and personal experience, of loss ("he finally sort of made the connection between him being adopted means that somebody gave him up": Leigh, a white heterosexual mother). These families were often those in which (a) children had been removed from their parents' care, at a very young age (birth to toddler age), or (b) children had been adopted privately, as newborns, but had little to no contact with birth families. Both the involuntary removal from birth family and a lack of birth family contact raised difficult questions and feelings for children regarding why they could not see their birth parents. Sandy, a white heterosexual health care advocate in a small Northeastern city, who adopted her son Todd, also white, via public adoption, shared:

> He actually says, "Why don't they want to see me?" I told him that "It's not that they didn't want to, that they just feel that it might make them sad or hurt them to see you." . . . He doesn't understand why he doesn't see his birth family. He's asked if I have pictures; I don't.

Sandy added that she tried to counteract the loss and sadness she could see in Todd by emphasizing her own happiness and gratitude: "I say, 'We're so happy we adopted you.'"

Lucas, a heterosexual Latino lawyer in a Southern suburb, had adopted his son Josh, also Latino, via private domestic adoption, and although he and his wife, Therese, sent letters and photos to Josh's birth mother via the agency, they had never had direct contact with her. Both Lucas and Therese conceded that although Josh's adoption was "no secret," they did not talk about it much ("we don't shy away from it but we don't necessarily bring it up unless it's relevant, and most of the time it just doesn't fit into conversation": Therese). Then, when Josh was around 7, it became clear to Lucas that Josh did indeed have a sense of loss surrounding his birth mother:

> There was one particular point when we were talking about, you know, things that you might lose; you might lose this, you might lose this. . . . And suddenly he kind of looked sad and was like, "I lost my birth mom." And that broke our heart. But—this is how I see it—the sadness is going to be there no matter, [but] by never making it a great secret, whatever sadness is there is always allowed to express, heal, and flow away. It never gets pent up . . . so, he's expressed a little bit of sadness a couple times, and we've never made a secret of it, and it doesn't seem to be a great part of his thought process. I may be wrong though.

Kathleen, one of the women whose story opened the chapter, shared how her 8-year-old daughter Ana was making sense of the loss inherent to her situation:

> She knows that her birth parents couldn't parent and that we were dreaming of a baby and that she was meant to be with us as her parents. She has a very deep awareness—not conscious, she's too young for it to be conscious—but that thing really terrible and tragic is also . . . good. That's something that we learn over the course of life, how things can be horrible but also can lead to good. [I think] she is trying to puzzle out, what does it mean that there's this loss in her birth mom and the tragedy in her birth mom's story, but also, that [loss] means that she's our kid? She wouldn't want to be anybody but our kid. Like, those two things are really hard to reconcile and it's a really grown-up concept. She can't really, doesn't completely understand it, but it's—like, the story of her life.

Here, Kathleen acknowledges the "tragic" and "good" components of adoption, and in so doing highlights the deep complexities of adoption that few parents acknowledged so directly.

Charlene, a white teacher, and Leila, a white physical therapist, who lived in a midsized metro area of the Northeast, similarly described how, when their biracial (Latina/white) daughter Sofia was 8, she began to have increasingly complex feelings and questions about adoption. Furthermore, Sofia appeared to be experiencing loss in a more intense way—particularly around birthdays as well as temporary separations from her parents, such as when one parent traveled. Such events seemed to activate feelings of loss, fear, and sadness. Charlene and Leila, in turn, tried to create space for a mixture of positive and negative emotions surrounding adoption. Charlene described how Sofia had asked to put their picture of her birth mother—whom Sofia had never met—in her room. Her mothers responded, "Absolutely." At some point, Charlene asked her:

> "Do you want to have the picture in your room because you'd like to have your birth mother kind of closer by to where you are, or because . . . ," I can't remember, something more benign. I gave her some other reason. And she said, "Oh yeah, I want her nearby." . . . And she talks about her birth family sometimes, and every time we talk about it, I find a way to leave in something like, you know, "Kids can feel really happy to have the family that they have, but you might also miss your birth family and that [is] really normal." You know, because she's had both of those feelings and she has kind of acknowledged it.

Vincent, a white gay telecommunications director in a large Midwestern city, described his African American son Ayo's sense of loss related to his birth mother. Adopted via foster care as a toddler, Ayo would occasionally, when very upset, say he wants his mom . . . he'd threaten to leave and go find his mom. We have a few pictures of her, so I think he has an image of what she looks like. I think he really wants to connect with her. . . . With female teachers and aunts, he's always exceptionally snuggly. I think that there is a void there for him.

When Ayo made these exclamations, Vincent and his partner, Simon, tried to respond empathically and with care. The couple also noted that Ayo also talked about memories "from when he was little," which, based on their level of detail and the young age at which he was adopted, seemed to be "invented." Yet they "didn't correct him or anything" but simply tried to understand and appreciate their function for Ayo.

Rob, a Latino administrative assistant in a West Coast suburb, observed that by the time his biracial (Latino/white) son David had turned 5, he had begun to express more complex feelings about his adoption. Both Rob and his partner, Terrence, maintained contact with David's birth mother, Alena. However, given the circumstances of Alena's living situation—she was intermittently homeless or in intensive drug rehab programs—David had not seen his birth mom since he was an infant. David struggled with why Alena did not parent him, why he was adopted, and why he could not see her:

> He's aware that he's adopted, he knows where his mother is, he knows that we're his adopted parents. And there are some things he's not very clear on, like why things worked out the way they did. And so I think sometimes that comes out in his behaviors. I think there's an underlying resentment there. I don't know if its resentment or pain or what, but I see a glimmer of it when he's upset, when he's angry with me or with us both, where he'll say things like, "Well you're not my real dad." And I just say, "I'm as real as it's going to get. I am your real dad, whether we are blood relatives or not, it doesn't matter. I am your real dad and it's okay to be angry at me." So, there's stuff going on in his mind that he doesn't discuss with me.

Rob went on to explain that David was,

> at some point, very interested in meeting his mother. We talked to his therapist and she said it wasn't a good idea at the time because he . . . didn't have a clear distinction between reality and fantasy, and he fantasized about his mom and who she was and how she would be if they were together.

In turn, the therapist recommended that it might be appropriate for David to meet Alena when he was older and he had a better handle on his birth mother's difficulties and why she could not be a parent to him—and, in turn, when he was emotionally and cognitively prepared to "ask Alena [the] questions he has for her."

Finally, Aisha, an African American lesbian human resources manager in a large Northeastern city, shared how she and her partner, Larissa, had sought to respond to their 8-year-old biracial (African American/white) daughter Elise's increased vocalizations of loss and longing, and fantasies of searching for her birth parents:

> We've had times when she's cried about what it feels like to know that her birth mother is out there and that she doesn't know who she is . . . and I guess we've just tried more just to let her know that all of that is okay. It's all part of who she is and that we accept that and we see it. We recognize that this is part of her and we embrace that too. We've talked multiple times about what it will look like when she goes on this search [for her birth parents] and we just always tell her, "We will help you in any way that you need us." Like, "Maybe you'll go by yourself. Maybe we'll go with you if you want us to. Maybe we'll just—whatever you need is what will happen at that time. We don't know what it will look like but—all you need to know is that we'll be there for you." With all the reading I've done, it's one of the most common things said by adopted children—that that sense of that whole, that piece of yourself that's missing. I mean, that's practically universal, that experience, and so the reality is that this is likely how she feels as well and that she is going to go looking for that and need that. And so for us to pretend that it's not there or doesn't matter, that we don't want to listen or talk about it—there's no winning in a situation like that. That's just bad for everybody.

Even when children did have contact with birth parents, issues around loss sometimes came up frequently. Residents of a large West Coast city, Doug, a white psychologist, and Sam, a biracial (Asian/white) human resources director, had intermittent contact with the birth mother of their daughter Catie, who was white. Several years after placing Catie for adoption, her birth mother, Lara, had had another child who she ended up parenting. The loss associated with not having a mother and not being raised in the prototypical heteronormative family structure, alongside the reality that Lara was now parenting a child with her boyfriend, sometimes prompted Catie to make "comments like, 'Why can't I have a mom and a dad?' . . . and to ask, 'Why didn't she try to parent me? Was I bad?'" When Sam was interviewed around the time that Catie was 9, he recalled:

> After her birth mom had another child, about a year ago—when that first happened, Catie had a lot of abandonment issues come up and . . . jealousy . . . and she went through a period of time where she was like ". . . throw me

away like Lara did"—you know, really big stuff for an 8-year-old to be dealing with, but she's been dealing with it.... And now it comes up ... I'd say once a month. But I think she thinks about it all the time.

Sam explained how he and Doug had sought to help and support Catie as she processed the loss, grief, and abandonment that sometimes overcame her:

> Initially, her reactions were huge. I remember the first big fit that she had over it and I had never seen her in so much pain physically and emotionally. And you know our job was just to be there and hold her and say no matter what's going on, we're here for you, we're not going away, we're always in your life, and just let her feel and deal with those and just keep telling her, our job is to make sure she knows she's loved, wanted ... and I think as time has evolved we've had conversations about her birth mom being in a different place when Catie was born than she is now as she's trying to parent this other child. And so we would talk about why and how Lara chose us to parent her and that we're her family and we're always going to be her family and nothing she can ever do or say will ever change that. So we try to solidify in her this idea that she does belong and she's not—her relationships with people are not disposable.

Jackie, a white heterosexual pediatric nurse in a Northeastern suburb, also described how, despite having regular contact with her birth mother, Thea, and her half-siblings, her 5-year-old daughter Serena, who was also white, struggled to understand why Thea "gave her up." This was a question that was undoubtedly magnified by the reality that Thea had in fact chosen to parent her other children, who were born before and after Serena:

> She knows Thea is her birth mom, Debbie is her half-sister, and John and Jake are also Thea's children. They have a different father. And so, as she gets older, it's "Why did my birth mom keep Debbie?" And John and Jake—Serena is in between them in birth order.... So I explain it as, "She was living out of her car when she was pregnant with you; she was trying to take care of Debbie at the time. She really didn't have a place to live and made a plan because she loved you."

Amid these circumstances, Jackie was aware that Serena would continue to have "a lot more to process than the typical kid" as she got older and would probably feel, at some points, "like she's missing out" on the family life that Thea, Debbie, Jake, and John shared.

Kelly, a white heterosexual environmental planner in a large West Coast city, shared that her 5-year-old multiracial daughter Rosa had always brought up adoption regularly—amid Kelly and her husband Gil's efforts to "always be open," an approach that seemed to have encouraged ongoing conversation and questions. According to Kelly, Rosa's interest in the specifics of her adoption had intensified over the past year, when she began to "really want to talk about when we first met her—just really granular descriptions of the crib that she was in, the place we first met her birth mother, when she was first put in our arms, what outfit, what her birth mother said." During the past 6 months, Kelly said that she and Rosa had these types of conversations

> over and over again. She tends to seize on a piece of it and then need to process it, like, ferociously. . . . We went through a period where she was, and I mean, *howling* with grief over being adopted, and she would just sit and sit and need me to rock her.

Despite having been with Kelly and Gil since birth, and having met her birth mother, Zoe, several times, Rosa's grief was, as Kelly described it, "intense":

> She would just cry for, I mean there was a couple-week period where it was just like an hour or two a night, she would just sob and say, "I don't want you. I want my tummy mommy." It was just . . . extraordinary. I don't know—we, I tend to go with the . . . the idea that she needs me not to be fragile when she's going through that. My job is to just kind of hold the space. . . . She's just, she's got a very profound process around being adopted and there's always a little something going on. [Even when] she was 3, [there was a period], almost daily, [of her] pretending to be a baby in my tummy—under blankets and being born. . . . She's clearly got some, at every developmental stage, has got some extra developmental task. . . . [Even today], she talks almost daily about her "tummy mommy." She has expressed . . . extreme grief.

Significantly, both Kelly and Gil spoke to the fact that although they talked regularly about Rosa's birth mother, Zoe, as well as the context of her placement, they did not use the word *adoption* itself on a regular basis. Thus, their narrative highlights the many forms that talking—or not talking—about adoption might take. Although both parents described themselves as attuned to adoption-related dynamics, they nevertheless drew distinctions among talking about birth family, adoption, and race/physical differences. For example, Gil mused:

I mean, we talk about race; we talk about the color of our skin a lot and, well, she brings it up a fair amount and then we always—we don't try to change the subject. And . . . she asks questions about Zoe, her birth mother. Zoe moved to [state] so Rosa was like, "Why don't I see her as much?"

When their therapist asked them, "Do you guys use the word *adopted* much?" Gil had the realization that

> we don't, that much. . . . I think at times she doesn't want to talk about it, like she doesn't like the word at some times. . . . I think there may be a little bit . . . denial—you know, she doesn't want to be different. She doesn't really like being adopted, so it's like she has to grapple with that.

Communicative Openness About Adoption

As highlighted earlier, the parents whom I interviewed did not hide their children's adoption stories. The fact that most were in open adoptions—and many had ongoing contact with the birth family—inevitably facilitated such conversations. Adoption was a reality that was, at the very least, acknowledged superficially and/or rarely. Yet the degree to which parents engaged in adoption talk, as well as the nature and nuances of those conversations, varied quite a lot. A key question then, is: What are the characteristics and nuances of engaged, developmentally responsive adoption talk—communicating openly about adoption, the birth family, and the circumstances surrounding placement—and what type of factors seem to facilitate it? On the flipside, what type of factors seem to inhibit open communication? In addressing this, it is worth revisiting the meaning of communicative openness about adoption.

As detailed earlier in this chapter, psychologist and adoption expert David Brodzinsky[24] and other adoption scholars, such as Elsbeth Neil,[25] have distinguished between *structural openness* (contact with birth family) and *communicative openness* (adoptive parents' openness to thinking and talking about adoption). Communicative openness in adoptive families is focused on the parents' willingness to discuss adoption and share whatever adoption-related information they may possess, regardless of the amount of information or level of contact they have in regard to birth parents. Although structural openness may facilitate communicative openness (e.g., in the sense that regular contact can facilitate the ease or "naturalness" of conversations about adoption),[26] communicative openness can exist regardless of the level of contact. This is important, insomuch as a lack of contact with the birth family does not preclude, and should not be regarded as a rational reason for, an absence of conversation about adoption.

Communicative Openness: "It's a Natural Part of What We Talk About"

Parents who espoused a strong engagement in communicative openness often grounded this in beliefs about the importance of honesty and openness to healthy family communication and, in turn, to optimal child development and well-being. Open, fluid, and interactive dialogue about adoption was viewed as necessary to ensuring that their children did not experience shame surrounding their adoption origins. When his son David, who was biracial (Latino/white), was about 5 years old, Terrence, a white gay anesthesiologist in a West Coast suburb, shared: "I think it's been essential that we're open about all of it from the very beginning. [One of] the reasons we're up front and honest about that from the very beginning is because we don't want to teach David that it's anything to be ashamed of." Will, a white gay accountant in a midsized West Coast city, asserted that his philosophy was to make adoption "matter of fact" so that for his 5-year-old son Isaac, who was biracial (white/Latino), "there's no 'what's behind the curtain' sort of moment. This is just the way it is." Will emphasized that he had "always been puzzled at people who say [adoption] is too complicated for the kid to figure out.... A child only asks you what they are prepared to know. It's not too complicated. They get it a lot easier than adults do."

Responsive Communicative Openness: Open, and Taking the Child's Lead

It is important to underscore the nuances of communicative openness, whereby some parents, even preadoption, voiced a strong philosophical commitment to open dialogue and discussion about adoption—and then assumed an approach that was grounded in a philosophy of openness and honesty but was also contextually and developmentally responsive.[27] The reality was that, in some cases, parents were faced with painful birth family circumstances—sometimes punctured by emotionally difficult visits or other contacts—that were quite "activating," stirring up difficult emotions and challenging conversations for their children. These parents therefore took their children's lead in regard to conversations about adoption, the birth family, and related topics. Sensing anxiety or distress, parents sometimes "backed off," taking a more cautious approach to adoption-related communication. Kathleen, one of the lesbian moms whose story opened the chapter, said, when her biracial daughter Ana was 8 years old:

We talk a lot about how families come in all different ways and some people have families through birth, and some people have families that [are formed through adoption], and that every family is beautiful and unique the way that they are. And we started by always telling her her birth story. It's helped teach her, and we've just always talked about it. But in the past year or so, since her anxiety has increased, we pulled back on being the ones who bring up the story and let her ask questions now, and then we'll talk through it. . . . It's been a long time since she's wanted to talk about her birth mom, but every once in a while . . . I'll just ask Ana, "How do you think your birth mom's doing right now?" and she'll say, "I don't know," and "I don't want to talk about it."

In other cases, parents reigned in "adoption talk" due to a perceived lack of interest. Elora, a white heterosexual stay-at-home mom in a large city on the West Coast, said, when her biracial (Latino/white) daughter Maeve was 5 years old:

We've talked about it since birth; it's just so kind of organic that it's hard to even . . . I mean, we'd look through [adoption and photo] books, and I'd talk to her about it. But it really is me [initiating], so I've kind of backed off on initiating any conversation about that unless she asks. But she doesn't really ask; she's just playing with her fairies and things like that.

Elora later added, as means of illustration:

Yesterday, I guess I was looking at Shari's [the birth mom's] Facebook page, and she had a picture . . . [that] I showed Maeve and I said, "Oh, look, there's Shari, you have her chin, and her nose." You know, that kind of thing, but she's really not all that—if I bring it up she's not that interested. She'll say "Oh" and then go off and do something else. . . . I mean, because we've talked about it constantly, it's kind of like, "All right, mom." She's aware of everything, so it's not like anything really new to her.

Here, Elora provides descriptive evidence that she has continually sought opportunities to make adoption a normal, natural part of everyday life and conversation—but also highlights how her daughter's lack of interest had informed her decision to "back off" on such overtures. Having established adoption as an acceptable and welcome topic of conversation, Elora can presumably quiet—but not silence—her conversational efforts while remaining attentive to possible changes in Maeve's intellectual or emotional engagement with the subject of adoption. Especially when considered alongside parents' narratives at earlier time points, this type of responsive communicative openness seems distinctly child centered, and quite different from allowing a child to "take the lead" because of a parent's own discomfort with or avoidance of adoption.

Larissa, a white bookstore manager in a large city in the Northeast, stated that her biracial (African American/white) daughter Elise, who was adopted via foster care, had a complex set of early living circumstances, involving living with her birth mother, then relatives, and then finally a foster family. In turn, when Elise was about 5, although she seemed to "understand that she's our daughter, and knows she's adopted," she was "still confused about her biological mother . . . about, like, coming out of the tummy . . . she's just fixated on that" . . . and "didn't understand why . . . she was then raised by these relatives." Sensing that Elise was becoming increasingly confused, in part because of her developmental stage, Larissa and her partner, Aisha, decided to

> focus on, you know, we're your moms, we're your parents. You're our daughter, whose been adopted, and you're here with us forever. Everything else will just come into place, we're just trying to focus on making her understand that this is home. . . . [Right now] she's just too young for us to sit down with her and really just go over all of the details; it's just too much.

Jessica, a white heterosexual homemaker in a midsized city in the Midwest—which she described as predominantly white—shared that she had pulled back on adoption- and race-related conversations with her 8-year-old son Jerome, who was African American, because it was clearly a difficult topic for him. When asked about adoption-related communication, Jessica said, with a sigh:

> You know, yes and no. I think it's kind of hard. I think it depends on the kid. I think that as he gets older I think that he kind of maybe—and this is just guessing, I mean he hasn't verbalized this—that maybe adoption is kind of a private thing for him. He doesn't want to be any more different than he already is. He notices that his hair color—he has curly hair, I have straight hair, he's darker-skinned than I am, so I think he probably already always feels like he's different. So my guess would be that he wouldn't want to be any more different than anybody else. It's hard because I would like adoption to be talked about more, but at the same time I think that in our culture today, even still, there's a lot of shame involved in adoption—maybe like, "Why don't I live with my birth parents?" You know, "I wasn't wanted." . . . So it's a tough—it's a tough issue I think. I mean, I'm proud of it—but I'm not the one that doesn't . . . live with my birth parents.

In other cases, parents had adapted their approach to adoption-related conversation not because their child had expressed distress or disinterest, but simply in response to their children's developmental stage, corresponding intellectual and emotional capacities, and type and frequency of questions. Thus, these parents enacted a developmentally informed approach to adoption communication. Dante, an African American vice president of operations, stated, when his African American son Ethan was 5 years old:

> One of the best pieces of advice I think I've ever got from someone was that . . . when the questions come, the best approach is to just answer; it's very simple, just answer them [*laughs*]. But also not feel like when that first question comes from your 3-year-old, or 4-year-old . . . or whatever, that suddenly the entire flood gates are open and you have to sit the kid down and tell them everything from the beginning. It's just answer that question, and after that question gets asked, that may be all the kid cares about—or they might ask another one, or they might not have another question for a year. That's kind of the approach we've taken. We're not hiding anything from him, but I'm also not pushing anything on him about it. And so I feel like . . . I'm not nervous about anything.

An example of how parents engaged in responsive communication over time is contained in the following passage. When her daughter Stella, who was white, was 8 years old, Daniela, a white lesbian small business owner in a midsized Southern city, articulated how she and her partner, Heather, had enacted adoption talk since Stella was born:

> Like, when she was little, I made photo albums with all the major people in her life, and I put their names on the pictures and we'd leaf through that every once and a while, and as she grew, there'd be a question here and there on "who's that?" And I'd just prompt conversation sometimes—for example, when we were about to take a trip to visit with her birth family—and as she grew, that conversation would get more in depth. And it was always based on Stella's interest level—or, on occasion I would facilitate conversation . . . because I anticipated a visit and I didn't want to run into a situation that would make Stella . . . uncomfortable. So I tried to prep her a little bit. So, that's just always been an open dialogue. And Stella is the type of child who keeps things in her head sometimes. So every once in a while Heather and I will manage to figure that out and bring her to talk about stuff. When we can see that something's going on in her head, I will wonder if it's an adoption question and I will prompt her a little bit. But I won't prompt it directly, because I really want to let *her* be the one who runs that conversation. I don't want to *force* it on her, is what I'm saying.

Here, Daniela describes her effort to balance open discussion about adoption with sensitivity to not overdoing it. Aware of the importance of allowing Stella increasing control over the timing and nature of adoption-related conversations, but also conscious not to assign complete responsibility to Stella for initiating these conversations, Daniela looked for natural opportunities to talk about adoption and also remained sensitive to any indication that Stella had "adoption questions" on her mind.

Daniela, Heather, and Stella's story illustrates why it is so important for parents to keep talking while also allowing space for children to increasingly direct the conversation. Indeed, Daniela went on to say that

> mostly, Stella hasn't been super interested in talking about the adoption—until recently. She's been pretty interested in genealogy, and she's continued to put together pieces about different family types and, you know, "this child in class has a mom and a dad at home, this one doesn't." And so it's come up, over the past 6 months, "I don't have a daddy; I miss that," kind of thing.

Then, Daniela said:

> a few weeks ago, we mentioned *again* that she has a birth dad. And for some reason, this time, she heard it—differently. It really was something she clung to. She was like, "Wow, I—I have a birth dad." Like, it didn't dawn on her before, even though we'd talked about him, even though she's met him a couple times—but it hasn't been since she was small. And there's a picture of him in the photo album. So she has known he existed but she hasn't really let that sink in until recently. So we talked about that some more. It brought up some strong feelings from her, mostly because she felt like she didn't know him at all.

Daniela, Heather, and Stella were a family that had ongoing contact with Stella's birth family. Yet responsive communicative openness can occur even in the absence of contact. Leila, a physical therapist, and Charlene, a teacher, were a white lesbian couple living a midsized city in the Northeast who did not have contact with their biracial (Latina/white) daughter Sofia's birth mother—other than Facebook contact that was initiated when Sofia was about 8 years old. The couple possessed minimal information about Sofia's birth family, other than the fact that she did have a half-sibling who lived with her birth mother. About 8-year-old Sofia, Leila shared:

> She asks questions sometimes: "Do I have a birth sister?" "Do I have any birth siblings?" We've told her about her birth sister. All of the conversations are led by her, pretty much. . . . Our policy is, we answer the question that she asks; we don't answer any more than that. And we share information as she seems to ask for it—we answer the truth, but just sometimes we don't know.

Charlene provided a more elaborate description of their approach to Sofia's questions, which was clearly embedded in a general family communication style that was responsive, direct, and child centered:

> She brought it up, something about her birth sister and she said something about, "Well my birth sister . . .," something like, "my birth sister was adopted, right?" And I said, "No, actually." And she said, "Really?" I said, "Yeah, no, Jasmine didn't put her up for adoption." And she said, "You never told me that!" And I said, "Well, you know, that's not a question you've ever asked, I'm happy to tell you." And then the next day, Sofia and I talked about it and I said, "Kids at different ages have different questions about their adoption and their adoption story and how it all came about and all of that, and I want you to know that Mama and I take your lead, and any question you ever ask us, we will answer and we will always be honest with you. But we are only going to answer the questions you ask, and we assume you will ask us questions when you are interested or ready to know or want to know more." She said, "Okay."

Allowing children's adoption story to become their own. A specific way in which parents enacted developmentally responsive communicativeness was through allowing children's adoption story to become their own—that is, via the gradual "handing over" of their children's adoption story to their child. That is, as their child grew, parents became increasingly sensitive and careful about what they shared with people beyond the immediate family, recognizing—and sometimes outwardly modeling or stating explicitly—that their child's adoption story was their child's to tell. In turn, they acknowledged and supported their child's autonomy in determining if, what, when, and how to talk about their adoption. Kate, a white lesbian mother in a large West Coast city who had adopted several Latino children via foster care, said, "I don't want them to hear me explaining their story over and over again, because I don't want them to feel like objectified or exotified in some way. . . . It's their story. . . . Less is more [and they] can decide what to share." Charlene, the lesbian mother quoted earlier, shared how her practice of addressing Sofia's adoption had changed over time:

> She's old enough now that I think if we were in line at the grocery store and someone said to me, "Oh, is she adopted?" I would probably look at Sofia and say, "Sofia, what should we say?" I would probably either engage her or say, "Do you think we should talk about that?" Or, "Sofia, she wants to know if you're adopted, do you want to answer that?" or something, I don't know, something to kind of engage her in it so it's not like we're talking about her. There was one time, I do remember someone saying, "Where is she from?" and I remember

turning to Sofia and saying, "What should we say to that?" and Sofia said, "Delaware!" and I said, "Delaware ... that's where Sofia was born" or something like that. And that was it.

Kathleen, one of the white lesbian mothers whose story opened this chapter, shared a similar approach, clearly illustrating the fact that families can maintain communicative openness within the family while also establishing firm boundaries with outsiders with regard to the sharing of adoption-related information:

That Ana was adopted is just part of our conversation always, whenever it comes up. But we don't share it without outside people, because we feel like that is her story to tell. So like I'll tell doctors and things like that, because they need to know, but for the most part we try to just keep it to ourselves. So the thing's like, you share it [and] then people will make their own assumptions, like, "Oh, this is something terrible." But yeah, Ana really takes the charge on that.

Miranda, a white lesbian director of career services at a university in a large West Coast city, shared how she had gently began discussing with her 5-year-old daughter Eloise, also white, how the details of her adoption, though not secret, were not necessarily appropriate to share with a "total stranger." To Miranda, sharing information about Eloise's birth family seemed most relevant and appropriate in the context of an "ongoing relationship." In turn, Miranda struggled with how to respond to a stranger's innocent questions (e.g., about whether Eloise had siblings, about who Eloise "looked like") in front of Eloise: "Especially when she's there with us, [it's hard to figure out] how to demonstrate being open and honest about it—but not wanting to share too much either—because it is a very personal thing, and it's her [story] to tell."

Stacy and Deb were a white lesbian couple employed as a school administrator and a chiropractor, respectively, who lived in a midsized city in the Northeast. They shared how it was their 5-year-old biracial (Latina/white) daughter Marlo who prompted them to realize that Marlo needed to increasingly "own" her own story. At five, Marlo had recently become more sensitive to the multiple ways in which she was different from many of her peers. "Instead of being like, 'Yeah I'm adopted' like she had been all her life, she started feeling different about it," explained Deb. Marlo was, according to Stacy,

concerned that other people would think she was different because she was adopted, has two moms, and has braces. . . . It was just a little wake-up call [for us]. She was like, "You can tell [my teachers] that I'm adopted, but tell them [that information] is just for adults, not for children to know."

Stacy acknowledged that she was a bit "floored" ("I was like, 'wow' . . . '') and yet, she did share with Marlo's teachers "that it's her story [and] she can share that or choose to keep quiet on that. . . . She knows all the pieces of her story. She can choose what to share or what not to share."

One gay father shared an example of how he gently encouraged his 5-year-old son to consider the idea that he did not need to share all of the details of his story, some of which were sensitive, with others. Delivering such a message requires a careful balance between teaching children they have a right to privacy without making them feel ashamed of the details they have shared:

> He has talked about [his adoption and having two dads] at school, and the kids, for the most part, have been receptive. They're just like, "Oh, okay cool, your family is different." Last year he was sharing [that his birth mother was in prison] and I had to talk about it with him. I said, "You know I don't really care that these people know, but there are some aspects, some chapters in your life story that belong to you, only you. Some things we only discuss at home with our family because they're family matters. And this is one of them. Your friends don't need to know who your mom is, where she is, why she's there; that's something that belongs to us, just you and me, and that conversation belongs at home." And he got it. He was like, "Okay I get it." . . . I know he's said a lot of things about himself at school and he's had no real consequences from it other than we had the conversation with him and hopefully he knows the difference between private and public matters.

What Facilitates Communicative Openness?

Of interest is what types of factors seemed to facilitate or increase the likelihood of communicative openness. Regular contact with birth parents (i.e., structural openness) was invoked as contributing to or at least deeply intertwined with communicative openness, in that seeing birth family regularly meant that conversations about adoption were initiated and maintained more easily and naturally (see Chapters 4 and 5). Parents did not necessarily have to "bring it up"; rather, an upcoming or recent visit with birth family members, an email from the birth family, or sharing or receiving a photo on Facebook all served as potential jumping-off points for conversations about adoption. Mariette, a white lesbian physical therapist in a Midwestern suburb and mother of a 5-year-old biracial (African American/white) boy named Jacob, described how she used tools such as photos and Jacob's "birth book" to talk about adoption:

> We have a . . . birth book in the family room that we pull out every once in a while so he can look at it. We've always talked about it. It's never been something

that we would have to sit down and have "that talk" about. He knows he's been adopted forever. He knows his birth mother and father and knows he has half-siblings.

Benji, a white gay dermatologist in a West Coast suburb, shared that he and his partner had fairly regular contact with their Latina daughter Ryanne's birth parents, Emmy and Luis—for example, yearly visits and phone calls every month or two. In turn, adoption was

> not a taboo topic for us. We talk about her birth parents all the time. She'll put something on and I'll be like, "Is that the dress that your birth father gave you?" It's so open and not taboo. We just treat it all so matter of fact, and I think that's how she internalizes it.

A high level of contact served to normalize, and to some extent invalidate the need for "explanations" of, adoption. Kate, a white lesbian director of a women's survival center in a large West Coast city, explained that her 5-year-old son Daniel, who was Latino and adopted via foster care as an infant, saw his birth mom, Camila, "very regularly":

> I don't know how much we talk about adoption exactly, but the family is here all of the time. I think people who adopt their kids who don't see their birth families probably need to talk about it in a really specific way, but for us, Camila is here several times a month, and [other relatives] are always around. He knows he came out of her uterus and that she loved him very much and wanted to see him as much as possible. He's really clear about who she is.

Shoshanna, a white heterosexual project manager in a small Northeastern city, stated, in regard to conversations about adoption with her 8-year-old daughter Morgan, who was also white:

> They wax and wane. We usually go see her birth family in the summer and so sort of leading up and a couple weeks after that we talk about it a lot. That's when all the questions will stir up from the bottom about, you know, just how it was. She likes to hear stories about herself.... She likes to know, well, "Remember when we...?" and then you have to tell her the stories.

Shoshanna elaborated on the types of questions that Morgan had asked, the nature of which seemed to be shaped by the fact that Morgan had regular contact with her birth family, as well as Shoshanna's ongoing willingness to respond to Morgan's questions:

Mostly it is [questions about] the stories of her adoption; it's less of like, "Why did Leanne and Tucker choose adoption over parenting?" Or, she is more likely to say, "So how old are Leanne and Tucker now?" and "How old were they when they had me?" and that kind of a question as opposed to why—I don't know. . . . I mean, she still feels that she has them [in her life]. There isn't the probing questions like, "Whose eyes do I have?", "Who do I look like?" Like, those sorts of things haven't come up because it is apparent; you can see it.

Taryn, a white lesbian radio personality in a Northeast suburb, had regular contact with the birth mother of her daughter Quinn, who was white. In fact, Quinn's birth mother, Sharla—and Sharla's mother—sometimes stayed with them during overnight visits. This regular contact helped to normalize adoption and validate the idea that these individuals were members of Quinn's extended family. Taryn explained:

We have some books—quite a few books about adoption. And we have an open adoption with both [birth parents], so we just saw Sharla and her birth grandma for her birthday party. . . . We see them frequently. We have pictures of them on the wall and stuff like that. So they're like a constant presence. Quinn knows she grew in Sharla's belly—but it's funny; she hasn't really asked too many deeper questions [than] about how babies were born. . . . We have friends who have an adopted child [who] asks a million questions. They don't have an open adoption. They have one picture and some really small sketchy info about that birth mother. Nothing about the birth father. So sadly they don't know a lot to tell her, but the girl is constantly asking questions. It's interesting. I mean, is it the way they talk about stuff? Is it her personality? Like, why does this child ask a million questions? And Quinn doesn't . . . is it because she sees them so she doesn't really—so she's somewhat satisfied already?

Finally, Lena, a white heterosexual operations manager in a midsized Northeastern city, described how she had maintained regular contact with the birth mother of her son Joey, who was white, since his birth. The family saw Joey's birth mom, Mandy, at least twice a year. Arranging these meet-ups far in advance, and in a location that Joey would look forward to (e.g., near a beach or amusement park), served to build excitement for the visit and also functioned as regular, and natural, lead-ins to conversations about adoption (e.g., via discussions of who Mandy was in relation to Joey and their family). Lena elaborated on the types of conversations she typically engaged in with Joey and the types of questions he asked:

He's pretty matter of fact. It's usually before visits. "Oh remember we're going to see Mandy." "Oh yeah, yeah." And then we'll talk about what she's doing.

If she's in Minneapolis, or what we're going to do. You know, it's more like, "Oh we're going to go visit Mandy; what are we going to do?" Every once in a while, he'll surprise me. He'll say something like, "Did my birth father know my birth mother?" And I'm like, "Yeah, a little bit." You know, he's really not at that age where he knows what a birth father really entails; I don't think it's really clicked—like, the birds and the bees and the birth father and what role he's played. But, it'll come up . . . and like, "You were in Mandy's belly." So . . . they're quick conversations . . . and he's comfortable. Like, his friends will be over and he'll be like, "Oh my birth mother, Mandy, got that for me." . . . So he'll definitely throw the word *birth mother* out like it's just "aunt." . . . So it's not like—I don't think he thinks it's something to be ashamed of or he's not supposed to talk about it 'cause he definitely says that word and he's open about it.

Thus, contact with birth family had the effect of reducing the need for parents to initiate certain types of conversations, such as those related to physical resemblance. At the same time, contact opened the door for other types of conversations to occur.

In addition to structural openness, being a two-mom or two-dad family also facilitated communicative openness. Indeed, some lesbian and gay parents specifically noted that their status as a two-dad or two-mom family encouraged ongoing and regular acknowledgment and discussion about adoption, in that their children's adoptive origins were potentially recognizable or surmised "wherever we are: grocery stores, day cares, or whatever." As Terrence, a white gay anesthesiologist in a West Coast suburb, stated: "Being a two-dad family, it's easier to talk about adoption because . . . some woman delivered him, right?" Likewise, Doug, a white psychologist in a large city on the West Coast, reflected that "there was never any . . . being in the closet about being an adoptive two-dad household; I mean, I guess there are other ways to become dads, but. . . ." Several parents also noted that their status as sexual minorities led them to embrace a general philosophy of openness, whereby either their own experiences being closeted during their younger years or simply their awareness that being "out" had benefited their own well-being facilitated an emphasis on the importance of open communications about family diversity and origins. As Cara, a white landscape design artist in a small Northeastern city, stated: "My feeling is, you know, that secrets just kill you. Secrets are just poison. So I definitely make a point of being very open about our family in every situation that comes up. I just think it's healthier for kids."

Racial differences between parent and child also served as a "tip off" regarding adoption origins in both same- and different-sex adoptive families, thus prompting acknowledgment or discussion of adoption as part of their family story. "People always want to know about her heritage . . . which leads to the fact that she's adopted" (Charlene, a white lesbian mother, whose daughter was Latina and white). Simon, a white gay social worker in a large Midwestern city, whose partner, Vincent, was white and whose son, Ayo, was African American, alluded to how both the multiracial and two-dad nature of their family appeared to invite questions from outsiders—which in turn facilitated regular acknowledgment of their adoptive family status, something Simon welcomed:

> With a two-dad family, clearly there's something to explain [*laugh*]. And then it's interracial on top of that, and, like, there's something very different about us that anybody can tell just by looking at the three of us walking together. So yeah, what's nice is that they ask about it routinely . . . because with us, [the adoption is] obvious; with others it might not be.

Finally, adopting additional children also appeared to facilitate family communication about adoption. Children who ultimately acquired younger siblings—who were typically adopted from another set of birth parents—often asked questions related to the similarities and differences across adoptive placements ("He asks, 'Why did [brother's] mom give him up?' And I say, 'Same reason as you. His birth mom decided it would be the best for him'"). Insomuch as children were increasingly sensitive to differences as they grew older, children with siblings often voiced growing curiosity about the reasons for differing levels of contact with birth family. Jamie, a white gay communications manager in a midsized Southern city, had adopted his son Timothy—who was biracial (African American and white) 5 years earlier, and another child, Daria, a few years later:

> We read through books, and we have conversations about birth parents and different types of families. The books we read talk about two dads, two moms, people that are . . . biracial or multiracial, and mixed families. . . . With age, it continues to change and Timothy continues to ask questions, but I think some of his questions in the last year have been more because of the difference between his birth mom [and Daria's birth mom]. His birth mom is not involved, or hasn't been, and we don't really have conversations with her. . . . She placed, and she moved on. But with Daria—we did a visit [recently], and so those kinds of questions come up . . . wondering why there's a difference between . . . having a birth mom or not having a birth mom. So Timothy's trying to understand that, and we've had those kinds of discussions with him about the differences.

A similar narrative was provided by Dan, a white gay software developer who lived with his partner, Seth, in a large metro area in the South. When their son Bobby, who was white, was 5, the couple had adopted a second child, a girl named Samantha. The couple maintained some contact with Samantha's birth mother—but not with Bobby's birth mother. Their divergent situations had prompted an increase in questions and discussion around adoption and birth parents, and "mommies and daddies," which Dean expected to continue to increase in the future:

> The concept of him not having a mommy in his life—we've kind of tried to explain to him as to why that is. That's going to be difficult because Samantha does have a mom who's much more active and visible. So that's going to be a little difficult to kind of work through.

Muted Approach to Communicative Openness: "I Haven't Really Pushed That"

Some parents took a cautious, muted approach to communicative openness. Rather than emphasizing adoption talk as a regular, ongoing, natural phenomenon in their household, these parents were more restricted in their efforts to engage in conversation about adoption. Underlying this more cautious approach was typically a set of beliefs and concerns surrounding the relevance and necessity of adoption talk. Such beliefs were invoked by parents as they explained why they took a more "hands off" approach to conversations about adoption—although notably, they often stated that although they themselves did not initiate conversations about adoption, they were "willing" to engage in adoption-related discussions if their children initiated them.

Men—gay and heterosexual—were especially likely to assert that they preferred to keep things simple, believing that their children were too young to grasp the details or meaning of adoption or the circumstances surrounding placement, or that sharing "too much" information about their placement or birth family would confuse or overwhelm their child. Lou, a white heterosexual cartoonist in a midsized Midwestern city, grounded his more "minimalistic" approach to adoption talk in his desire for his Latino son Dennis to feel "normal" and his belief that too much of a focus on adoption could be harmful. When Dennis was 5, Lou said:

> It hasn't really come up. We don't really put the fact that he's adopted forward. Just so that he's considered like any other kid. I mean, he and Tate [his adopted brother] are very well aware that they're adopted and that they have birth parents. It'll just come up in conversation every once in a while. Especially— you know; they're starting to talk about, like, the birth process and "Well, is she

a pregnant woman?" It'll come up then, and we'll be like, "Yeah, you used to be inside your birth mom's tummy like the baby is for that lady." Things like that. So it's just normal. Laura and I both, we've made it like not a stressful thing to discuss. It's just normal. It's just *one* more fact about [their] lives.

Further, Lou added that Dennis was also "not very interested" in talking about adoption, which further muted Lou's efforts to engage him on the topic—although Lou also noted that he would be "fine with answering questions" as Dennis grew older. Men like Lou, therefore, saw themselves as following their children's lead. Similarly, Barry, a white gay teacher in an East Coast suburb, acknowledged that he rarely spoke about adoption with his son Xavier, who was biracial (African American/white), but also offered, "If he ever came up with these topics, I would be totally fine with it."

Developmental considerations were explicitly or implicitly raised by many parents who took a more muted, minimalistic approach to adoption talk. That is, they viewed conversations about adoption as developmentally inappropriate or unnecessary at the current time but voiced an openness and willingness to address adoption more deeply with their children in the future. Dave, a white gay father employed as a radiologist in a large Midwestern city, said, about his and his partner Byron's orientation to adoption discussions with their 5-year-old Latino son Aidan:

> We've kind of let it develop naturally, rather than kind of forced conversations. We've kind of waited until he brings things up and then have a discussion. . . . He went through a phase where he was asking where his mother was and we just explained that she's in Fresno and that's all he needed to know. There are times when he's gotten emotional about it. We've just reassured him that we know it's really hard for him or it's really sad. But his mom did a really great thing and we kind of left it at that. Our plan is, as he gets older, we'll kind of tell him the details of the story. It hasn't been a major thing that we've talked about. Like on a regular basis.

Dave later added that their cautious approach was in part informed by their consultation with a therapist, who had advised them to "just answer truthfully and answer honestly and don't overanswer or make it complicated because that will just confuse him." Armed with this advice, Dave stated that he and Byron

> basically just explain that your mom lives somewhere else and she has a lot going on and she really couldn't take care of you and she was really brave and she made a decision to let us take care of you and everything. . . . We never used

the word *adoption*. I don't know that I've consciously avoided [it] but I'm trying to keep it super, super simple.

Likewise, Byron, a white graduate student, stated that 5-year-old Aidan sometimes did ask

where his mother was, and we just explain that she's in Fresno.... There are times when he's gotten emotional about it, and we've just reassured him that we know it's really hard for him, or it's really sad, but his mom did a great thing and we've kind of left it at that. Our plan has been that as he gets older we'll tell him the details of his story.

Despite some parents' assertions that they wished to "keep things simple" because of their children's young age and they planned to talk more about adoption at some unspecified future time point, some continued to describe the same approach when their children were school-aged. That is, they expressed ongoing hesitation about talking "unnecessarily" about adoption and preferred to downplay it as a central aspect of their child's, or family's, story or identity. Indeed, when Aidan was 8, Dave continued to describe a sense of caution surrounding discussion of adoption. He and Byron tended to wait until Aidan brought it up—which typically occurred "in the context of [asking about] his birth mom.... He'll ask questions like, 'Why did this happen?' or 'Why did she do this?' or 'Where is she?'" Dave, in turn, believed that not initiating such discussions but simply engaging in them when Aidan initiated them was a more natural approach than "forcing these conversations, [which feels like] overdoing it.... My personal feeling is that there are some families that overdo it. They make so much about the adoption that it becomes almost a stress. So I try not to do that."

In addition to believing that talking about adoption could create feelings of difference in their children and/or that their children were too young to handle adoption-related information, difficult circumstances or relationships with the birth family sometimes seemed to underlie parents' reluctance to engage in adoption-related conversations. Rachel, a white lesbian computer applications training manager in a large Southern city, had encountered some challenging early dynamics in her relationship with her 5-year-old biracial (African American/white) daughter Moriah's birth parents. For example, Moriah's birth mother, Jade, had requested daily or weekly phone or Skype contact with Moriah, leading Rachel to assume a more detached and avoidant stance in relation to contact—which in turn seemed to spill over to adoption-related communication with Moriah. Rachel said:

I'm expecting that all of these conversations are going to come, but I can't say that we decided that now is the time for them. I think little by little Moriah's going to come to us, and it may not be the best move to wait for her to come to us, but I'm not sure that it's good news to tear down that path yet either.

Thus, at the same time that she planned to wait for her daughter to come to her with questions about her adoption, Rachel acknowledged some uncertainty about whether this was the best approach.

In one case, a lesbian mother shared that her daughter "knows that she came from somebody else's tummy; they were not able to take care of her. That's pretty much what she knows. She knows nothing about their history." This mother was quite concerned that disclosing the details of the drug abuse and criminal behavior that caused her daughter to be removed from her parents' care at birth might lead to some "pretty intense emotions"—a consideration that was especially important insomuch as her daughter already suffered from anxiety. In addition, her daughter "wasn't asking questions, like, 'Why didn't they want me?'" which to this mother seemed to justify the withholding of adoption-related information. (Notably, this mother was somewhat uncertain about her current strategy and had recently sought out an adoption therapist for "good guidance" about how to navigate disclosure of "the painful and unknown parts of adoption.")

Indeed, some parents asserted that their children did not bring up adoption or their birth family. In some cases this seemed to reinforce parents' belief that adoption was "not on their minds" and thus not important to talk about, thereby justifying a continued de-emphasis on such conversations. In essence, these parents' feeling was this: If adoption was important to talk about, their children would bring it up—but their children were not bringing it up, and it therefore must not be important to talk about, at least not yet ("I don't know if adoption should be more of an issue or not, but it almost seems to be not an issue. It hasn't come up much"). Chuck, a white heterosexual IT director living in a Northeastern suburb, said, about his 8-year-old son Grayson, who was white and adopted as a toddler via foster care:

> I think he understands that his biological parents were neglectful and that's why he's not with them. I don't really ask him too many details about that. He doesn't really ask me either, so I think that's all good. . . . I don't know; I haven't really pushed that and he hasn't pushed it either, but it could be a guy thing. Maybe he talks to my wife more about that. . . . He may still get upset about adoption every now and then; it's not clear to me.

Thus, the absence of questions seems to reinforce these parents' decision not to focus or dwell on adoption. Of course, if parents who believe their children are uninterested at a particular developmental stage use this as a reason not to talk about adoption, their children may sense that this topic is off-limits, and thus may continue to avoid asking questions about it as they grow older. In turn, parents may read their silence as lack of interest and may not broach the subject. The longer they go without making it a part of normal family discourse, the more difficult (i.e., forced, uncomfortable, awkward) raising the topic will become. The children, in turn, may sense that certain aspects of their adoption are "threatening" to their parents—and, as adoption scholar David Kirk observed more than 50 years ago, will feel that the "door to communication with the parents [around] adoption is closed. Accordingly, he will ask few questions and those he asks will be tame. If this happens, the parents may assume there is no problem."[28]

When children were of color but looked like their parent(s)—either because one parent was of color or because that child was biracial or multiracial but "looked white"—this sometimes served as a rationale for not addressing adoption. When his son Josh, who was Latino, was 8, Lucas, a heterosexual Latino lawyer in a suburb in the South, said:

> The fact that he is adopted is not immediately apparent to anyone. So that's the first thing. It's not something that comes up in conversation on a regular basis. People don't go around asking, "Are you adopted?" Nobody asks that. I've never seen that asked.... So he's just a kid, and these are his parents. So it's not an issue.

Noah, a white gay school psychologist in a large West Coast city, noted that his 12-year-old Latino and Native American son Shayne, who was adopted at age 6 from foster care, did not

> bring up ... adoption or race—and I think maybe part of that is because he looks white. I don't think that people see him as anything *but* white. He's frequently, you know, mistaken to be my biological son, so he looks like me. I don't, you know ... I just don't think that it ever comes up.

Navigating Challenging Child Questions and Difficult Dialogues

Many parents noted that as their children grew, their questions became more specific—and sometimes raised complex issues. Parents struggled to sensitively navigate their children's questions—and, sometimes, difficult emotions—especially when they were "caught off guard" by their inquiries. Andrea, a white lesbian prison guard living in a medium-sized city in the South, reflected, about her 5-year-old daughter Jessie, who was Latina:

> She does ask questions out of the blue sometimes. I have to tell her, "You know, I need to think about it and, you know, we'll talk about it." ... Her questions are getting more specific instead of more general, so I have a feeling that the next year is going to be interesting!

Several key themes in children's questions recurred throughout parents' narratives. Specifically, "Did my birth mother/birth parents have other children? Did she/they parent them?" and "Why didn't my birth mother/birth parents keep me?" were the most common. Eddie, a white gay physical therapist in a midsized Southern city, shared, very matter-of-factly, how his daughter, Anastasia, who was multiracial, frequently asked questions about her birth mother and the circumstances surrounding her placement—which Eddie expected to increase in the future:

> [She talks about it] all the time. Sometimes she asks to see her birth mother, or if we can call her birth mother. She'll tell us that when she was a baby she was in Elle's belly. Elle now has another child that she's seen ... and Anastasia asks about her baby, and she talks about her birth mother not being able to take care of her so Phil and I have to take care of her and that we love her a lot. It'll come and go and it'll just be out of the blue when she'll say something like that, and we'll talk about it for a minute and then it moves on to a different subject. ... You can tell it does go through her mind. I'm sure the older she gets, the more she'll think about it and have more questions.

For children with two dads, the question of "why don't I have a mommy?" became increasingly salient during middle childhood, whereas for children with two moms, the question of "why don't I have a daddy?" took greater hold. These questions took on more urgency and were generally harder for parents to navigate when families did not have contact with the birth family member in question. As Heather, a white lesbian small business owner in a midsized Southern city said, about her 8-year-old daughter Stella, who was also white:

> We have enough [of a] relationship with her birth mom, Joy, and her birth grandparents that I think she's doing very well with it. I think the only thing that she would have an issue with is, we don't have really any communication with her birth dad, Danny. And I think if anything, if she has any issues with adoption it would be this unknown person out there that's her birth father. That

could be the sticky wicket in all of this. . . . I think that as she gets older that could be significant.

Indeed, birth fathers were more often "unknowns" than birth mothers, and thus, questions about birth fathers were especially hard to navigate (see Chapter 9).

Parents of only children also noted that questions surrounding birth siblings were increasingly likely to come up as their children grew older—and parents often struggled to provide answers to their children's questions, especially when they had little to no contact with birth parents. Miranda, a white lesbian mother employed as the director of career services at a university in a large metropolitan area of the West Coast, shared that although they had an open adoption, her daughter Eloise's "birth mom, Emily, has chosen not to see her since she was about 4 months old. . . . We exchange pictures and letters, but [that's it]." When Eloise, who was white, was 5 years old, she was "talking a lot recently about wanting to see her sister." Not wanting to upset Emily, Miranda had struggled with knowing exactly how and how much to probe her for personal information, including facts about her other children. Significantly, although Miranda was surprised at Eloise's insistence on using the term *sister*, she did not question or resist it. (Miranda recalled that when a child had asked her whether Eloise had any siblings, Miranda had said no, causing Eloise to became upset and say, "No! I have a sister!" Miranda recognized the significance of this moment and subsequently followed Eloise's lead in how she described that relationship, which was clearly important to her.)

Sometimes, children were not asking difficult questions per se—but parents themselves found it challenging to discuss certain aspects of the adoption with their child. For example, Sonja, a biracial (Native American/white) data analyst in a midsized Northeastern city, shared how she had hesitated to disclose to her daughter Arielle, who was white, that her birth mother had actually given her a different name when she was born:

> She knows, like, there's this little gift bag on the top of my cabinet with a stuffed animal from her birth mom. . . . And she was born in a town next door, which is really nice. We often drive by and that gives me an opportunity to say, "Oh, look we're going by [town]! This is where you were born! This is, this is where Ann gave birth to you" . . . just because I've been to some of those adoption workshops, [where] they say, "Just bring it up, just so the kids know it's safe to talk about or ask about or something." Recently, we had a conversation— it was the first time I've told her that her birth mom actually gave her a different name—'cause we did not like the name her birth mom gave her. I was like, "Gosh, I don't want to keep that a secret. She needs to know that." And even

if she's not going to remember it now she can still just have it somewhere in the back of her mind that she's heard it before—"Yes, I was given a different name by the birth mom and then Mommy and Mama changed it." So I had that conversation with her, and I shared with her about the name. And I shared with her why we changed it—not that we didn't like it, but we didn't think it suited her.

Race Talk: Communicating About Race and Racial Differences

Intertwined with discussions of adoption were discussions of race. As children grew older and began to notice, and sometimes point out, difference across families (e.g., most families have a mom and a dad; I have two dads), they also demonstrated increasing awareness of differences *within* their families. For children who were of a different race than their parents—and, more specifically, who differed noticeably in skin tone or shade—these observations were more likely to occur. Indeed, children were not themselves the only ones who were noticing such differences; outsiders (e.g., peers, teachers, neighbors, and people at the supermarket) were often the first to point out and bring children's attention to such differences. Thus, alongside consideration of how parents talk about adoption with their children, it is worth exploring the interrelated issue of how they talk about race, skin tone, and ethnicity, and what factors appear to shape the regularity and nuances of such conversations, as well as the strategies parents employ to help children make meaning out of race and racial differences.

Many parents, especially when their children were kindergarten age, acknowledged racial differences between themselves and their children but limited their acknowledgment to physical differences, thus neutralizing the topic of race. They explicitly recognized the existence of skin tones but did not address the social construction of race (e.g., racialized attitudes/attributions), the consequences of such constructions (e.g., discrimination), or strategies for dealing with racial bias or discrimination. Nor did they acknowledge ethnicity or culture in any way.

For example, when his multiracial daughter Anastasia was 5 years old, Phil, a white gay graduate student in a midsized West Coast city, said that he and his partner, Eddie, had talked

> a little bit . . . about her skin color being different from ours, how everybody's skin color is a little different and where it comes from. . . . We've talked about skin and eye color and where that comes from biologically. The biological explanation of skin color and eye color and stuff like that."

Phil, then, used the language of biology and genetics to explain and make sense of skin tone for his daughter. He also grounded this discussion in the larger idea that "everyone is different"—a common way that parents sought to help their children develop an understanding of and comfort with the idea of adoption.

Significantly, some parents—especially those who were in contact with children's birth family—invoked birth family members to help their child make sense of race, as well as, to some degree, genetics. That is, they pointed to or referenced birth parents as sharing a particular characteristic with their children (e.g., race, skin tone, hair). Such overtures served to communicate a larger lesson: namely, that part of what makes you unique is what you get from your birth parents (genetics, biological origins), whereas you get other important things from your adoptive parents (environment, family) (see Chapter 7). As Greg, a white gay software consultant in a small city in the South, stated, about his daughter Louisa, who was 5 years old and biracial (African American/white): "We get into genetics—like, 'Your mommy is one color, you're another color, your sister Magdalen is this color.' And she knows people are different colors and I don't think she cares. I mean she's aware of it, but it's like, 'Okay, yeah, next subject.'" A similar narrative was provided by Leo, a Latino gay speech therapist in an East Coast suburb, whose daughter Elizabeth was African American and white:

> We still talk to her birth mother, Leandra. We have pictures of them together, and we always keep that as something in the book, or like on the coffee table, so it's just like a very "Oh, yeah, that's just who she is." And sometimes we'll talk about her hair and Leandra's hair, and her hair is curly. You get some things because of me—you like some place because I take you to it—but you get your genes from her. We try to just separate the difference between what she gets from each person.

In some cases, children initiated these conversations. Eliza, a white lesbian accountant in a large Northeastern city, shared that her 5-year-old biracial (African American/white) son Luke

> just started asking about why his brother Stewart is really dark and he's light, and this kid's white, and this kid's dark. I explained to him about how his mother's white, and his birth father's black, and Stewart's birth parents are both black.... I know he's going to ask about it again.

Stacy, a white lesbian school administrator in a midsized Northeastern city, who maintained ongoing contact with her daughter Marlo's birth parents, Krista and Jay, shared that Marlo, who was Latina and white, often commented on the fact that

> she and I have similar colored hair but hers is really curly, mine is straight. We [talk about that]. We have different eye colors. We track that directly to her birth parents and to her heritage. "Oh, you have dark eyes like your birth dad. Jay has eyes like you do.". . . She knows she has Puerto Rican heritage too.

Some parents incorporated additional complexity into their discussions of race, whereby they acknowledged ethnicity, language, and cultural traditions—even though they were not always clear about how these differed from or were related to race—in their conversations with children. Cara, a white lesbian mother who was employed as a landscape design artist in a large West Coast city, had adopted her Latino son Daniel 5 years earlier via foster care—and subsequently, two other birth sisters of Daniel's, Gabriela and Adriana. She and her partner, Kate, were unique among families who had adopted through the child welfare system in that they maintained strong ties to their children's birth mother, Camila. Cara appeared to recognize the ways in which family relationships and racial/cultural history and identity were deeply intertwined and intermingled:

> It's important to know what your roots are and where you come from . . . so we try to meet those needs as much as possible. I think keeping them in contact with their birth mom is a big step, right? I mean that's their history right there, you know? And where they come from and the traditions they have, the type of food they eat. . . . We have made food with Camila so we can make the same kind of food that is pretty traditional and talk about [where] in Puerto Rico they came from. And we've even thought about actually taking a vacation there and seeing relatives. . . . We also read Spanish language books and we listen to Spanish lullabies.

Adam, a gay father employed as a director of marketing in a midsized West Coast city, was himself biracial and had a biracial 5-year-old son, Isaac. Adam voiced a view that was rare among parents whose children were biracial: Namely, it was important for his son to understand that even though other people might see him as white, he was not white:

> We want him to understand that yes, the world might view you as white. And in fact, I think that's what they even put on his birth certificate, but your birth father was half Latino, and Daddy—I am half black and half white. So he's kind of growing up knowing that even though he hasn't processed it as any different. I mean, he has cousins that are black and he has cousins that are white. He just

hasn't processed that that's different—unique. It's just going to be, "Yeah, you're half Latino. Your dad—your birth dad was . . . half Latino. And your godmother is Latina too. And she speaks Spanish."

Adam was sensitive to the importance of articulating and discussing with his son the different components of his "unique" background and family constellation—possibly in part because as a biracial person himself, he was acutely aware of the need to counter a monoracial identity narrative. Significantly, Adam's own positionality as a biracial person also aided his ability to talk about difference in a way that incorporated his own identity, as opposed to seeming to suggest that Isaac was the (only) one who was "different."

The desire and ability to address racial and ethnic complexities was enhanced among parents who articulated an explicit awareness of their own racial privilege—and, indeed, far from avoiding it, were actively wrestling with it. Simon, a white social worker, lived in a large city in the Midwest with his partner, Vincent, also white, and their African American son, Ayo. Reflecting on both his own white privilege and the reactions of other African Americans to their family, and Ayo specifically—which, as Ayo grew, prompted more conversations about his own racial identity in relation to how the world saw him (i.e., black with two white parents, who were presumed potentially inept at racial socialization)—Simon said:

> There are a lot of white gay men who aren't prepared, in [terms of] racial consciousness, to be able to raise African American children or children of color period. So I think about that . . . and when I see an African American woman react negatively, it sort of reminds me of the fact that, yeah, you're a white man, and you're raising a black child in a white supremacist culture. It just brings to mind the kind of political ramifications of [this] very personal choice. And that's a really complex and difficult issue; it's overwhelming.

The tendency to introduce greater complexity into conversations about race was particularly evident as children entered middle childhood (e.g., 8 and 9 years old). Jenny, a white lesbian medical supply company manager in a Midwestern suburb, spoke to the role of her biracial son Jacob's birth grandmother in communicating to him his "heritage." Specifically, when asked how important it was to her for 8-year-old Jacob, who was African American and white, to learn about or have information about his racial/ethnic background or heritage, Jenny said:

> It is important to us—especially as he gets older. As much as he wants to have, we want him to have it, and that was a big part of what prompted us to do an

open adoption.... His birth grandmother that comes and visits, she is African American ... so he absolutely knows that this woman who comes and visits him is his birth grandmother and she's African American. And we want him to know as much about her heritage ... as we can get for him.

Similarly, Charlene, a white teacher, and Leila, a white physical therapist, who lived in a medium-sized metro area in the Northeast, sent their 8-year-old daughter Sofia, who was Latina and white, to an after-school Spanish language immersion program. They had initiated this about a year earlier alongside the growing recognition that "Sofia's identity as a Latina, as an adopted person, her identity as a child in a two-mom family ... are just coming more to the fore. These pieces are starting to come together in different ways.... They are live issues for her" (Charlene). This couple purposefully sought out a setting that promised to facilitate their daughter's cultural identity and language development but that might not necessarily be immediately comfortable for them as a white same-sex couple ("we're way in the minority there"). Of note is that they were ultimately "really warmly welcomed" by the program's teachers as well as most of the other parents.

Some parents noted that as their children grew older they had become more racially aware, and were in turn increasingly likely to confront and in some cases internalize racialized assumptions related to their skin and hair. Some children had expressed confusion, sadness, or distress related to the negative attention they had received related to their skin or hair. Parents responded to and managed these concerns in a variety of ways. Sometimes, they focused on emphasizing the positive aspects of their child's race—that is, building racial pride by countering dominant societal messages. Max, a white heterosexual communications manager in a large city in the Northeast, was the father of a biracial (white/African American) son named Ace. When Ace was 5 years old, Max noted that race

> comes up a little bit. More his hair than his color. He's said a few times that he, he wants to have [hair like] one of his friends ... a little white blond boy; "I don't like my curly hair." And it's just ... of course we tell him that he's got the most beautiful hair in the world. Daddy wishes he had hair like you.

Here, Max acknowledges a difference that exists between them and tries to challenge the racialized attractiveness norms that have already impacted Ace by voicing a desire to be "more like" him, as opposed to trying to figure out ways to help Ace be or look more like him (e.g., by cutting his hair).

Larissa, a white bookstore manager living in a large Northeastern city—whose partner, Aisha, was African American—also responded to her biracial (African American/white) daughter Elise's expressed desire to look more like her with concerted efforts to foster racial pride ("you're beautiful . . . you're special"). At the same time, Larissa recognized that this longing expressed something deeper than just wanting to resemble her mother physically—and Larissa also felt that longing:

> I know Elise has said a number of times, "I wish I had the same skin color as you, Mama." It's just one of those things that, you know, in our situation, we don't look the same, but we're a family and it's a struggle she's going to have and I think that I'm going to have too. But I wish we did; I wish we looked exactly the same, I wish—because she is my daughter and it's one of those wishes that's like—it's not a real wish, but it's like, it just speaks that kind of honest yearning that people have when they are really close; they wish that they could look the same, right?

Miri, a white lesbian artist in a large Northeastern city, described her 5-year-old daughter Ava, who was African American, as highly attuned to skin color. Miri tried to instill positive messages about race alongside providing factual information about skin tone:

> We talk about it *all* the time. She will literally ask us when she hears a song come on the radio, "Is the singer of the song pink or brown?" and she'll ask to see a picture, and she started asking questions about what makes skin different colors. And we're just like, "Well, skin has melatonin," and she has said something about . . . painting one's skin a different color. And we say, "Well you can paint your skin, you can put makeup on, but the color of your skin doesn't change. What you're born with is what you are." Mostly we've really emphasized and spent a lot of time on things like pride and love and how wonderful it is to have the beautiful skin that she has, the beautiful hair that she has.

By the time that Ava was 8 years old, she had become even more racially conscious. As Miri noted, "She hears stereotypes, and she observes. In her old school, she was like, 'All the black kids are always getting in trouble.' So she observes patterns and she hears about stereotypes, but I think that those are the sort of, the implicit biases in the environment." Miri and her wife, Lindsay, in turn, tried to challenge these stereotypes—not the fact that they existed, "but the idea that they are true."

Max, Larissa, and Miri, notably, all lived in urban areas that were quite racially diverse. Other parents were trying to instill racial pride in communities that were primarily white, presenting challenges in terms of racial representation and role models. Rachel, a white lesbian computer applications training manager in what she described as a "very white" city in the South, described how her 5-year-old daughter Moriah, who was African American and white, had also recently become more aware of skin color differences and had noticed that there were not many people in her family, school, neighborhood, and community who shared her skin color:

> She was very bothered by the fact that she does not see many people that have the same color skin as she does. She didn't understand that. And so what we tried to do is, we try to like, [point out people of color] in a few positions that play an important role in our lives, like policeman, fireman, teacher. Because we don't want her to feel like because her skin is darker that she's not important. And [celebrities] . . . all of those people that have darker skin, we're pointing those out. We always tell her . . . be proud of who you are. So it bothered her in the beginning but now she's really looking and seeing that, you know, there are lots of people that have different colored skin.

Here, in the absence of regular contact with Moriah's birth parents—who shared her race—and in the absence of people of color within their family, Rachel sought to highlight potential role models of color in their community, as well as in the broader society (e.g., President Barack Obama).

When children expressed unhappiness about their race or skin tone or had racially charged experiences, these (predominantly white) parents were challenged to respond in a manner that was attuned and supportive, and aimed at promoting their children's racial pride and resilience. Roy, a white sales manager in a large urban, progressive area on the West Coast, whose partner, Dante, and son Ethan were both African American, shared how Ethan had, at various points, expressed unhappiness about his skin shade and hair texture. When Ethan was 9, Roy recalled:

> [I remember] when he didn't like his skin color and wished it was more like mine, and it was just, it wasn't like a constant thing, but it came up frequently. It was just like the most heartbreaking thing for me to deal with, because at the age he was, it just seemed crazy. But it was less about him not recognizing what it meant to be black and the hardships that that might bring with as it is, just wanting to be more like Daddy [me]. It wasn't as much of a race thing as it was identification with me . . . and same with hair, and that's actually a little bit more ongoing still. He does not like having tight curly hair; he really wishes he had straight hair.

Roy also shared that although he had conversations with Ethan about skin shade and race, ultimately, "Dante, being African American, that's kind of a special bond that they have with each other. It's something that while I certainly feel like I can talk to him about, and do, that's kind of the territory that Dante is very equipped to talk about." In particular, Roy was not "comfortable" talking to Ethan "about the intense hatred that some people have for people just because of their skin color" and preferred to center his racial socialization efforts on emphasizing that

> everyone is a unique individual, and that all colors are beautiful and amazing. We stay away from categories of people, and say ... there's brownish people, and there's darker brown people, and there's white people—it's not sort of this category of, well there's white people and there's nonwhite people. It's more about a spectrum.

Another example of a white parent seeking to respond empathically to the racialized experience of his child of color is Simon, a white gay social worker in a large city in the Midwest. Simon shared that his 9-year-old African American son Ayo was—and had been for several years—acutely aware of how his hair set him apart from many of his classmates. Ayo, who had braids (which he loved), received a great deal of largely positive attention about his hair, but this attention made him uncomfortable. Simon described how he responded to Ayo's discomfort by validating how frustrating it was to be singled out in this way and offering support—and also noting indirectly that it was not just Ayo, but their whole family, who was different in some ways:

> I remember he asked in kindergarten, "Why is everyone always talking about my hair?" Always positive, like, "Oh my God, I love your hair; dude, those [braids] are awesome!" It is just all this unwanted attention on what frankly is *hair*. I have hair. So he is acutely aware of when he is singled out. Because even though he is in a school where he is not a token black student by any means, a lot of African American boys [don't have braids] in the third grade. So it is still something that is seen as interesting and unique. He gets a lot of attention and praise for it. So he hates when that happens but he handles it well.... I would think it was a problem if he couldn't talk about it, or if he lashed out when these sorts of things happened. But he is always very patient and matter of fact, and he talks to us about the frustration and we reinforce or reflect back that [it] is naturally frustrating to be singled out. "We are different and we do stick out in a number of ways. If you ever need help handling it, let us know."

Parents who shared their adopted children's minority race tended to describe their racial socialization efforts with a frankness and directness that parents who were parenting across racial lines did not possess. Carl, an African

American day care supervisor who lived in a small city on the West Coast, and whose partner, Jake, was white, shared emphatically that he felt strongly about introducing his 8-year-old African American daughter Sharice to literature and poetry written by or featuring women of color and also talking directly to her about what it means to be black and female in America: "It definitely needs to be direct, and there's nothing wrong with being direct." Yet Carl was also uniquely attuned to the fact that as a black man, he did not share the same positionality as his daughter:

> We don't have a female perspective, and until we have a female perspective, we'll read things like bell hooks and Paula Giddings and . . . poems by Maya Angelou. We'll read things about other woman of color's struggle. . . . We definitely need to incorporate women's issues of struggle because Sharice needs to identify that she's part of a sisterhood too.

Carl was mindful of his male privilege in parenting his daughter, recognizing the potential negative consequences of having two men take an overly authoritative approach with a daughter: "I can't bully her. She has to be able to see and understand when she's being bullied." Further, Carl was also sensitive to the fact that his partner, Jake, was not only male but also white; in turn, he asserted that Jake had to be cognizant of his "privilege[s] of being male and white" in parenting their daughter.

"Not a Big Deal": Minimizing—or Not Emphasizing—Race

As with adoption, however, some parents were hesitant to make race a "big deal." They voiced concerns that regularly discussing race and racial differences could have a negative effect on their children, possibly making them more sensitive to race and racial differences "than is necessary at this stage." Furthermore, they sometimes worried that routinely noting racial differences between themselves and their children would have the unintended effect of diminishing their children's sense of connectedness to the family, introducing questions about whether they really "belonged."

One variation on this perspective was voiced by Matt, a white heterosexual realtor in a large city on the West Coast, who voiced reluctance about "overemphasizing" race, preferring to allow his son Anthony, who was Latino and white, to "take the lead" in talking about race and exploring his racial and ethnic identity. Matt was distinctly uncomfortable with the idea that he should define the significance or meaning of race or racial identity for his son. When Anthony was 5, Matt said:

I don't want to impose the importance [of race and ethnicity] upon him. I want him to find out how important it is for himself. I think that what's most important to me is that he has access and opportunity and whether or not he finds that identification with Hispanic culture as super meaningful in his life or a big part of who he is, down the line I want that to be his decision. . . . I want to empower him, I don't want to necessarily force it down his throat.

When Anthony was 8 years old, Matt said: "Anthony is definitely darker than Benny [adoptive brother] too. We talk about it—about why his skin is different and, you know, what that means—it means you're Latino, and all that stuff."

Matt's wife, Ellen, a white travel writer, provided the following description of their approach when Anthony was 8. Like Matt, she notes that they talk about racial categories and labels—but, as with Matt's description, it is unclear whether and how they have articulated the meaning behind these labels:

We were talking about MLK and segregation [after a Martin Luther King event at school] and [we said], well, you know, "MLK is black," and well, "Who else is black?" And you know, "What color am I?" And you know, "You're Latino" and so the other day he kind of brought it up again and he was like, "Well okay I'm Latino; are you Latino?" "No, we're not Latino." . . . So yeah . . . this year [he's] trying to figure out the labels a little bit.

It is useful to contextualize these comments with Ellen's description of their general approach to adoption talk: "We talk about it a decent amount, yeah. I mean . . . we try not to force it or anything. We try to keep it kind of organic if it comes up and then we talk about it [and ask], does he have any questions."

Laura, a white heterosexual web designer in a medium-sized Midwestern city, whose 8-year-old son Dennis was Latino, also described a minimalist approach to talking about race, stating:

We mostly are at the point where we talk about everyone's different. He's brown and we're white. It's okay to be whatever you are; that's kind of where we're at with that. We acknowledge it. We haven't really gotten any deeper; we're kind of waiting for him to bring up the issues he wants to talk about."

Laura's overall approach to communication about adoption was similarly characterized by cautious acknowledgment of difference and little emphasis on parent-initiated conversations (i.e., she and her husband, Lou, both said that they tended to "wait for Dennis to bring it up"). Thus, in relation to both adoption and race, Laura emphasized commonalities across individuals and assumed a more tentative, muted stance in relation to differences. Significantly, parents who do not proactively initiate discussion and information sharing related to adoption may find that their children are less likely to voice curiosity and ask questions about adoption—a dynamic that may also extend to discussions about race.[29]

In some cases, parents described a more open stance in relation to adoption-related communication than race. Indeed, parents may have felt more equipped to talk about the former than the latter, especially if they were white.[30] Eliza, a white lesbian accountant in a large city in the Northeast, voiced a reluctance to talk about race. When her son Luke, who was biracial (African American/white), was 5, Eliza noted that he surprised her by commenting on the fact that "he's brown, and we're whiter . . . and so we had this discussion about how he is biracial," adding, "I didn't think that kids recognize race yet." But despite indications that Luke was curious about race, Eliza did not think it was a good idea to "dwell" on it, noting that Luke tended to "worry about things a lot," and thus felt that "if we talk about it before there's a need to talk about it, then he would worry about it . . . so, like, if I start focusing on racism and all that stuff, he'll internalize it and start to worry." Meanwhile, Eliza contextualized her approach to adoption as "very open; we talk about his adoption and anything else with him. And we talk about our family with him. But [race] rarely comes up as important to talk about."

* * *

Communicative openness, which is known to be beneficial to child and family functioning, is "absolutely possible even in the absence of contact."[31] Yet communicative openness is neither static nor inevitable. Namely, the likelihood and amount of communicative openness that parents engage in is informed by a range of personal and family characteristics, including parents' own tolerance of ambiguity and complexity (e.g., of the loss inherent to adoption), the level and type of birth family contact, and children's own curiosity and questioning. Children's race and family structure represent physical features that may also invite more opportunities for openness—which, of course, parents can choose to engage or shut down. Furthermore, parents' openness regarding adoption is sometimes intertwined with their approach to racial socialization, whereby openness and tolerance of complexity in one domain are associated with openness and tolerance of complexity in the other.

As Chapter 10 details, parents should seek to cultivate an environment of openness that encourages questions and conversation about adoption. This will help to ensure that children who may seem disinterested in adoption talk now will ask questions later. Indeed, some parents noted that their child did not talk or ask questions about his or her adoption, but parents also recognized that this did not mean that adoption lacked salience or meaning for the child. In turn, parents simultaneously affirmed their child's sense of belonging to the adoptive family while also acknowledging the child's origins. Sometimes, the topic of adoption was not avoided, but difficult and painful emotions associated with adoption were—for example, some parents expressed dismay when their child expressed grief or loss associated with their birth family, and in turn chose to focus on the positive aspects of adoption (e.g., parents' own joy). Parents should be aware of how their own discomfort, anxiety, or fear may underlie such avoidance tactics. They should aim to show their child that they as parents can handle these painful emotions, are not scared by them, and will be there to listen in the future.

Notes

1. Kirk, 1964.
2. Herman, 2008; Kirk, 1964.
3. Brodzinsky, Schecter, & Henig, 1992.
4. Brodzinsky et al., 1992; Brodzinsky, 2011.
5. Brodzinsky et al., 1992.
6. Brodzinsky et al., 1992, p. 18.
7. Brodzinsky et al., 1992; Brodzinsky, 2011.
8. Neil, 2012.
9. Brodzinsky, 2006, 2011.
10. Farr, Grant-Marsney, & Grotevant, 2014.
11. Ibid.
12. Brodzinsky, 2006; Campbell, Silverman, & Patti, 1991; Wrobel, Kohler, Grotevant, & McRoy, 2003.
13. Siegel, 2012b, p. 137.
14. Wrobel et al., 2003.
15. Ibid.
16. Hays, Horstman, Colaner, & Nelson, 2016; Kranstuber & Koenig Kellas, 2011.
17. Kirk, 1964.
18. Neil, 2009.
19. Ibid.
20. Goldberg, 2010.
21. Jones & Hackett, 2007.
22. Brodzinsky et al., 1992; Neil, 2012.
23. Brodzinsky et al., 1992.
24. Brodzinsky, 2006.

25. Neil, 2009, 2012.
26. Neil, 2009; von Korff & Grotevant, 2011.
27. Grotevant, 2009.
28. Kirk 1964, p. 90.
29. Wrobel et al., 2003.
30. Goldberg & Smith, 2016.
31. Shari Levine, Open Adoption and Family Services, personal communication, November 30, 2017.

7

Weaving a Family Narrative

Genetics Talk

Science tells us that genes and the environment shape human development. For example, research indicates that intelligence (which encompasses a range of cognitive and interactional abilities and skills) is one of the most heritable behavioral traits,[1] whereas almost all personality traits appear to have both biological and environmental bases.[2] Yet it is gene–environment interaction that, though less frequently invoked in common parlance, is perhaps most significant in impacting human development—and represents a particularly meaningful context when we consider the development of adopted individuals.[3] Despite the common misconception that genes represent a "blueprint" for development— that is, that who one ultimately becomes is "set in stone"—research indicates that early life experiences profoundly impact whether and how genes are expressed (i.e., turned on or off). Early life experiences, then, play a major role in the development of "brain architecture."[4] Exposure to growth-promoting environmental experiences early in life, such as rich learning opportunities, can promote children's ability to develop into healthy and productive adults, whereas exposure to negative environmental experiences, such as malnutrition and abuse, impede positive development. Indeed, adverse early experiences, including nutritional deficiencies and chronic stress, can have long-term and even lifelong consequences by impacting the foundations of brain architecture. Yet by the same token, children with biological and environmental risks who are adopted into resource-rich environments characterized by committed and skilled parents and access to therapeutic resources can show gains in functioning (e.g., in their cognitive and physical development).[5]

When considering the development of adopted children, it is absolutely necessary to consider the significance of bidirectional influence: namely, how what children bring to the table affects adoptive parents, and vice versa. Depending on the adoptive parents with whom they are placed and by whom they are raised, a temperamentally difficult child with sensory integration issues may "pull" for different types of parenting, which in turn will shape the child's development in the long term. A parent who is impatient, easily frustrated, and has few economic resources might interact with that child differently than a parent with an abundance of emotional and financial resources, who may, for example, be better able to meet the child's needs.[6] Whether and how parents understand this interplay—namely, the reality that what they bring to the table (e.g., their own temperament) interacts with what their children brings, and that these interactions build on one another and unfold over the life span to affect child and family development—likely will influence how they approach and parent their child.

Of interest in this chapter is: How do parents think about, and talk about, the sticky and complex issue of similarities and differences between themselves and their adopted children—both those that may be immediately visible (e.g., skin color, hair), even early on in parenting, and those that are not as apparent until later on (e.g., abilities and interests)? How do parents invoke birth parents to help children to understand, make sense of, accept, and/or experience pride in aspects of themselves that may not be mirrored in their adoptive parents—including physical features, abilities, and talents? And, insomuch as mental health and physical health are both, to some extent, genetically and environmentally mediated, how do parents anticipate, make sense of, interpret, and address challenges in these domains—and how does the presence or absence of contact with or information about birth family affect this process? To what extent, and how, does information function as a source of *power* (e.g., in terms of anticipating certain issues or challenges, such as substance abuse or mental health problems) or a source of *anxiety* (e.g., in terms of prompting parents to be highly sensitive to certain features in their children or to anticipate issues in the future)? Finally, how do parents' ideas about the relative influence of nature versus nurture change across their children's life course?

Family Vignette: Therese and Lucas

Therese, a white teacher, and her husband, Lucas, a Latino lawyer, were living in a Southern suburb when they adopted their son Josh, who was also Latino, after dealing with infertility for several years. Prior to adopting Josh, the couple struggled to reconcile the loss of the biological child they would never have—particularly Lucas, who wrestled with the fact that he was the "end of the family line," in that he had only one sister, who had decided not to have children. Both Therese and Lucas also acknowledged a sense of loss associated with the fact that their future child might be dissimilar from them in terms of personality, intelligence, and interests. During the preadoptive stage, Therese noted that they could not predict or anticipate any aspect of their child, and surmised that this might be difficult for them as parents:

> It would challenge us is if the child we adopt is radically different in some way than we are. We're both readers, we're both bookworms, we're both not athletic,

we both love school, we both were good students. I think if our child turns out to be totally different, if they are very much an athlete, and turns out to be disinterested in everything we like, that would be a challenge—to appreciate him or her for who they are and not . . . we don't want to expect them to be just like us, but it's hard not to have that underlying expectation. And, that's kind of hard thinking—"This is my daughter, she just finished her course in cosmetology and she's a hairdresser at such-and-such salon." . . . I mean, every parent, I think, has to come to grips with the fact that their child is *not them*. Even though you share half their genes, the child is not you. But adoptive parents—we have to come to grips with that before the child is even there. The child is not genetically ours, so we don't have that illusion that somehow they're going to turn out just like us. And who knows? Our child may wind up being very similar to us in terms of interests or in who knows what, but we . . . have to be prepared that that might not happen.

The couple ultimately matched with Josh's birth mother, Coco, a teenager. Because of Coco's young age, Therese and Lucas developed the adoption plan in coordination with Coco's parents. The two parties agreed to a semiopen adoption, whereby Therese and Lucas would send letters and photos to Coco and her parents several times a year through the agency. According to Therese, Coco's parents "would actually prefer she has no contact with us," in that they "want her to kind of try to put this behind her, and not identify as the teenager who gave up a child for adoption." This sentiment, expressed to Therese and Lucas early on, somewhat undermined Therese's motivation to be vigilant about regularly sending the photos and letters they had promised, "when I know she [might not] see them for years." Similarly, Lucas noted, 3 months postplacement, that Coco's parents "want her to get over it, and in their view getting over it meant doing something else with your life, and not having things that remind you on a daily basis of what you went through."

By the time Josh was school age, Therese and Lucas acknowledged that they had been sending photos and updates less frequently over the past few years. Their efforts to maintain regular contact were undermined by general "busyness" as well as their continued awareness that Coco might not even be accessing or reading the materials they sent. When Josh began to show symptoms of attention-deficit/hyperactivity disorder (ADHD), as well as a learning disability, the couple had little to go on; the only medical and background information they had access to was what they had obtained from his birth family at the time of the adoption, 8 years earlier. In turn, the couple relied heavily on this limited data, in combination with their own personal observations and hypotheses, as well as testing and input by school professionals. Lucas, for example, relied on his knowledge of the birth father's criminal involvement to make sense of his son's behavioral issues: "His birth father had impulse control issues, I'll just say that. And our son is impulsive." Also contributing to Lucas's diagnostic impressions was familiarity with the symptoms of ADHD:

> We were kind of suspecting he would have [ADHD] because his cousin does too. Not that they're biologically related—they aren't—but, some of the early signs that Therese's sister had seen with her son we were seeing with Josh. So we're [relying on that], and we're just kind of following him along, and [listening to] school personnel.

The couple also did their own research and determined that "adopted kids tend to have a higher incidence of ADHD," which further informed their understanding of Josh's current challenges and potential diagnoses.

Adjusting to his son's diagnosis of ADHD and several learning disabilities was challenging for Lucas, who had done quite well in school and never encountered any academic difficulties. Both he and Therese were, by his own description,

> very precocious and bookish kids.... We didn't have all that much trouble with impulse control. So, this is new for us. And, for us, [we have been faced with] the complete realization that the child is very much—is another entity that you're taking care of. Not an extension of you, not a reflection of you, not "you version 2.0."

Lucas shared that he tried to assume the mindset that "my kid is an individual; he's not supposed to be a clone or just like me or anything. And sometimes it's hard, sometimes it's easy.... Even if a kid is your biological child, that doesn't mean it's going to be easy." Thus, Lucas chose to approach Josh's individuality as something that was not unique to adoption but was simply a lesson of parenthood—a cognitive reframe that seemed to facilitate a greater sense of acceptance and ease with regard to Josh's difficulties.

Upon receiving what appeared to be accurate diagnoses, 8-year-old Josh was finally receiving services that allowed him to manage his difficulties while also revealing his strengths—thus illustrating the powerful role of context and resources in shaping children's ability to reach their highest potential.[7] Lucas was delighted to find that "apparently, Josh is very bright"; this news came as somewhat of a surprise to him and Therese, who had become accustomed to thinking of Josh as average based on teachers' assessments of Josh's academic progress and performance. Learning that their son was above average in intelligence was especially powerful for Therese, who had modified her initial hopes for an academically inclined child and seemed to accept the idea that Josh might not be especially bright or bookish:

It surprised me—to learn more about Josh's intelligence. We went into this thinking, we have no idea what our child would be like, and we joked about, "Hey, here we are, two nerd brainy types; maybe we'll get somebody who really is not terribly scholastically minded." So we were, you know, trying to set our expectations to that we could get someone who's totally different from us in every way.... And we had his IQ tested as part of some educational screening, and he came out as average. I was like, "Okay, so we have an average kid." But then, once we got the learning disability treated, and once we got the ADHD worked on, then all of a sudden we're like, "Wow! We have a really smart kid!" And then his tutor told us that in 30 years of teaching, he's never seen a kid advance as quickly as Josh has through the material—that was a very pleasant surprise.

Lucas wondered whether the speed and ease of obtaining an accurate assessment of Josh's abilities and challenges was undermined by the school's assumption that Josh was their biological child—and, in turn, that a learning disability was unlikely given Therese and Lucas's professional successes. Stated Lucas:

I mean, [the school forms] ask us questions about ourselves: We both have advanced degrees. So there may be some bull-headed assumption that because we're brainy, then the kid should have no issues, so why does he have issues?... I mean, we've never shared [his adoption] arbitrarily, and it's not particularly obvious. And they never asked.

Lucas and Therese explained that they had not shared Josh's adoptive status with the school in part out of concern about how this information might be used to label him and/or become overly salient in teachers' understanding of him. For example, they worried that teachers or school officials might inappropriately attribute certain behaviors or issues to Josh's adoptive status. In turn, Lucas and Therese surmised that not sharing that Josh was adopted may have had anticipated and unanticipated consequences.

Reflecting on Origins, Preadoption: Nature Versus Nurture

As Therese's and Lucas's narratives reveal, some adoptive parents have ideas about what it means to parent a child who is not their own biogenetic kin, even before they are placed with their child. Although not all parents discussed this—perhaps in part because it is a sensitive topic that some parents may rather not deeply interrogate, especially amid a history of failed conception attempts—some did. Some parents, particularly those who adopted from the child welfare system, recognized the power of both genes and early environment, and noted the possibility that a child's postadoptive environment may not fully heal or erase their early difficulties or trauma. Others acknowledged the unknowns of a genetically unrelated child—but followed this with assertions about the unpredictable nature of a biological child's personality, needs, and behaviors. Thus, they normalized, neutralized, and potentially challenged the supposed differences between having a biological versus an adopted child.

Nature Matters, and "We Will Do Everything We Can to Maximize Nurture"

The most common type of narrative was a straightforward acknowledgment of the power of nature, while not dismissing the power of nurture: "With adoption, there's only so much that you can influence." That is, parents recognized that they could not control a child's prenatal or early postnatal environment, their genetic predispositions, and so on—but they could control the type of childrearing environment that they cultivated. These parents' narratives were realistic but hopeful. Mariette, a white lesbian physical therapist in the suburban Midwest, stated her intention to raise her child in "a positive environment," while acknowledging that one can't "erase and backtrack" what came before that. Carly, a white heterosexual history professor in a large Northeastern city, mused that, especially in the academic context, she had internalized a sense of the "[significance] of nature.... The contributions of genetics are really huge, and make people who they are in a lot of ways." At the same time, Carly emphasized that she felt confident about her parenting abilities and asserted her belief that parenting and environment "matter too."

This type of narrative—acknowledgment of nature, but hopeful enthusiasm regarding the role of nurture—was especially salient among parents adopting via foster care. These parents knew that any child who was "in the system" was there for a reason. At the same time, they were willing to adopt from foster care, suggesting that they felt hopeful about their ability to make a difference in a child's life, wherein offering a good home could help to facilitate a meaningful life and future. Preadoption, Randy, a white gay operations manager for a retail chain in a large city on the West Coast, recognized that

> there is a reason that most of the kids are in the system.... Drug exposure, alcohol exposure, abuse—I have concerns about that. But I mean I could have a [biological] kid who has issues too.... So, it is more about their environment and rehabbing them from their previous caregiver.

Al, a white gay sales manager in a midsized city on the East Coast, recognized that any child that he and his partner adopted via foster care would also come with "scars"—but Al also emphasized the skills, compassion, and preparedness that he hoped would make a difference in parenting a child through foster care:

> The children come with a lot of issues. We obviously don't have experience parenting... but we know there's a potential for sexual or physical abuse, or a child that may have chemical dependency problems or fetal alcohol syndrome, stuff like that. So, are we prepared?... This isn't like *Annie* where you get a cute little red-haired girl singing and dancing.... I guess, any way you have a child, you just—you know something's coming; you don't know what's it going to be and you don't know what the challenges are. You hope that you've prepared as best you can and that you'll be open-minded and you hope that love will conquer all. We realize that these children already have had tough breaks in life.... But, we really believe we're good guys, we really believe we can provide a good loving home. So we're just hoping that, you know, that love will conquer all.

Several parents noted how their professional backgrounds (e.g., as therapists or teachers) might be an especially important asset in supporting a child adopted through the child welfare system. Noah, a white gay school psychologist in a large West Coast city, was hopeful that his professional experience would be a resource in parenting a child through foster care. Yet at the same time, Noah was realistic, stating:

> I know the adoption literature fairly well, and you're talking about a population that has a lot of—certainly a lot of environmental baggage, but a lot of genetic crap as well.... You have think about, "Well, how much of this is stuff he's inherited? How much do we have to worry about any predispositions to substance abuse later on, given his family's biology?"

Parents like Noah were committed to adopting children from foster care—but also spoke candidly about the fact that such children would likely come with a set of complex prenatal and early childhood environmental experiences that were neither ideal nor under their control. They were fairly savvy about the types of challenges that these children might have, and the reality that although their parenting would "matter," it could not erase a child's experiences prior to arriving in their home. Lauren, a white lesbian therapist in a midsized Northeast city, acknowledged that adopting a child from foster care held many unknowns but also affirmed her commitment to building her family in this way:

When you have your own biological child, during the pregnancy, you know that you do the prenatal care, you take care of yourself a certain way. You can never know, unless she disclosed it, if mom did drink or do any drugs during pregnancy that could affect the child. A lot of these parents have mental health issues, which can be genetic. I worry about that. You don't always have a complete medical history to know what all of the medical concerns might be. So yeah, we definitely have those kinds of concerns. Also because when you have your own baby, you build that attachment from birth, and with adoption, you don't have that same level of attachment in the beginning ... even kids who have been adopted at a young age. So that kind of scares me. But I [do know of] some really successful adoptions, and I've heard of some really great things that have happened through adoption, so that's why I think we continue to want to do this, but it is very scary because it's much different than having your own biological child.

The notion that the older a child was at the time of adoption, the more challenging it would be to positively impact the child's development, was frequently invoked by private domestic adopters as a primary reason they were not pursuing child welfare adoption. These parents wished to adopt a newborn, in order to have the "biggest influence possible." Byron, a white gay graduate student in a large metropolitan area of the Midwest, described how his partner, Dave, had asserted strong feelings about not adopting via foster care, because his opinion was that

> when a kid reaches such and such an age, the dye is set.... His concern is, and it is mine too—but maybe not to that degree—is that worst-case scenario, we would end up with a child that we would have limited effect on what we could do for them, depending on the circumstances they are coming from.

Adam, a biracial (African American/white) gay marketing director living in a midsized West Coast city, explained that he and his partner, Will, were seeking to adopt a newborn because "there is so much hardwiring that occurs in the infant stages of development. We wanted to be the ones to sort of shape that hardwiring, as opposed to having to try to fix something that may have been damaged by negligent parents."

All Kids Are Different: "You Don't Know What You're Going to Get, Bio or Adopted"

Another type of narrative—which was particularly common among men—was one in which parents minimized the differences between having a biological or adopted child, emphasizing that children are all "unknown packages," parenting was a "crap shoot," and, just like an adopted child, biological children could have unknown or unforeseen "liabilities." Dwight, a white gay health program administrator in a large city in the South, said:

> [Parenthood is] unpredictable, no more so than being a biological parent; who knows what you're getting yourself into. You're about to have a kid, and whether it's biologically or not, this is a separate individual with separate distinct personalities. As an adoptive parent, your child is coming to you with a host of issues from a background that you don't necessarily know about. However, when you have a child by birth it's also a crap shoot, in that you don't know what kind of mental or physical or emotional liabilities or disabilities the child is going to be born with. You're getting an unknown package.

Lucas, the heterosexual Latino lawyer whose narrative opened the chapter, endorsed a similar perspective, stating: "Even when it's your biological child, it does not come with a guarantee and it's not going to be a copy of you anyway.... All those things are things that you can fool yourself into thinking, that you're immortal through your children, when your children are related to you." Michael, a white heterosexual philosophy professor in a midsized Northeastern city, asserted, "I've never been a great believer in the biological connection.... I think people kid themselves about what they think is going on. Also I'm a born cynic in terms of, kids don't come with guarantees."

A variation on this type of narrative was to note concerns about the unknown challenges that an adopted child might bring, followed by an assertion that a biological child might also present with unanticipated issues—but these could simply be more easily addressed amid readily available background (e.g., medical) information. Taryn, a white lesbian radio personality in a Northeastern suburb, mused that she sometimes had "the concern, like, what if the child has like some disease that they inherited from their parents or what if the child.... But that's stuff that could happen with a child that we had too ... although [we'd have more] background on that." Erin, a white lesbian librarian in a large West Coast city, said:

> I think that probably my biggest concern is that you really don't know what you're going to get. With biological kids you don't know that too, but you have a little bit more genetic influence and so you can look at your family history and say, "Well you know, all my family has turned out good." [With an adopted child], you're never sure what's going to kind of come up; you don't really know the history of the child as well as ... you would know your own family history.

We might get some surprises, medical or mental health surprises, [but] I try to be optimistic.

A few preadoptive parents, all women, actually framed the "unknowns" of an adopted child as a positive. They chose to view the fact that they could not anticipate their future child's physical or psychological characteristics as an opportunity; that is, their child would be revealed to them, in a series of "exciting surprises." Leigh, a white heterosexual assistant museum director in a small city on the East Coast, asserted that she was

> totally okay [with not knowing] what we're going to get. I've given it a lot of thought. I know it's going to be different, but I also think that there's something neat about the idea of getting to know a kid that's biologically different. There's a whole bunch of stuff you won't know about the kid.

Likewise, a few preadoptive parents spoke to the notion that becoming a parent to a child that was not related to them guarded against the tendency to have certain "expectations" of what their child would be like or accomplish, rendering them more open to their child's unique strengths, abilities, limitations, and challenges. In this way, adoptive parenthood was framed as an opportunity for discovery. Stacy, a white lesbian school administrator in a midsized Northeastern city, said thoughtfully:

> I think that it is a strength [in adopting], just knowing ... that a child is going to be his or her own person ... whereas if you had your own biological child you'd be like, "Ohhh little Susie's got grandpa's eyes, or is going to be a piano player like her brother."

Benji, a white gay dermatologist in a large West Coast city, shared his sense that

> it probably helps in that you don't have a genetic predisposition about what this child should be able to do, so the child can really be their own person ... [and not put expectations] on the child based on DNA. Like if it's my biological child and they're not an academic achiever, I would be disappointed; but if it's my adopted child and they weren't, it's more okay. That's kind of bad, but in the sense that—some people are above average, some people are average, some people are below average. I can't demand or have an expectation that the child that we'll adopt is going to be above average in academic talent. So, we're going to push this child and encourage this child and make this child maximize their potential but ... if it was my biological child, I would have certain expectations

about academics or whatever. And I have lower expectations because I'm going to the grab bag.

Thus, Benji underscored what research has suggested: that a child with difficult early beginnings (e.g., prenatal drug exposure, genetic vulnerability to mental illness or intellectual deficits) could ultimately achieve more in an environmentally rich setting (i.e., one marked by educational resources and parental encouragement) than an environmentally poor one.[8]

Weaving a Family: We Get Different Things From Different People

Once parents actually adopted, they had to make sense of, and help their children make sense of, the different components of their child's identity, and thus acknowledge the contributions of both adoptive and birth families. In weaving a family narrative, some parents underscored the notion that "we get different things from different people," whereby both birth and adoptive families contributed to children's unique selves in meaningful ways. Some parents also emphasized that both adoptive and birth family members were included within their larger definition of family. Much like a series of concentric circles, adoptive family members were typically situated at the center or "heart" of the family tapestry, and birth family members occupied outer rings of that tapestry (e.g., "we stress to her that, you have this whole other family that loves and thinks about you. They are not parenting you and they are not your parents, but you really have a big family, including [an] extended birth family that she gets to see").

By acknowledging birth family as family and directly or indirectly pointing to ways in which they were connected to children, parents validated the importance of birth family in their children's identity. Making these connections was relatively easy in the context of shared resemblances or talents, especially when parents maintained contact with their child's birth family. This process was more complex, however, when birth parents' contributions were viewed less positively—such as a genetic predisposition to mental illness, or prenatal drug use that may have contributed to children's medical, emotional, or behavioral difficulties. Parents typically drew these types of connections privately, sometimes in consultation with mental health professionals or doctors—but did not share them with children. Thus, when and how the birth family was invoked as part of their child's "makeup" varied, depending on whether the characteristic in question was physical, medical, or psychological, and whether it was regarded in a negative, positive, or neutral manner.

Making Sense of Medical and Mental Health Issues

Among the families I interviewed, parents' descriptions of their children's health—emotional, behavioral, and physical—varied considerably. However, parents of children adopted via foster care tended to describe more medical and mental health difficulties than parents of children adopted as newborns via private domestic adoption. This is consistent with research showing elevated rates of physical, psychological, behavioral, and cognitive difficulties among children adopted via foster care, particularly noninfant children, compared to children adopted as newborns via private domestic adoption.[9] Such difficulties are related in part to impairments in brain development that are more likely amid circumstances of neglect and trauma. As the American Academy of Pediatrics notes:

> More children are entering foster care in the early years of life when brain growth and development are most active. During the first 3 to 4 years of life, the anatomic brain structures that govern personality traits, learning processes, and coping with stress and emotions are established, strengthened, and made permanent. If unused, these structures atrophy. The nerve connections and neurotransmitter networks that are forming during these critical years are influenced by negative environmental conditions, including lack of stimulation, child abuse, or violence within the family. It is known that emotional and cognitive disruptions in the early lives of children have the potential to impair brain development.[10]

Parents who had limited knowledge of their children's health and medical history, and who also had little to no contact with their children's birth family, were especially likely to speak to the multiple ways and settings in which this lack of information introduced frustrations, by virtue of the "unknowns." These parents felt somewhat unprepared for what issues might arise in the future (e.g., Will my child have allergies? Will they need glasses?). When his Latina daughter Ryanne was just a few months old, Darren, a white gay computer programmer in a large West Coast city, shared his frustration that because the birth father was unknown, "we don't have the benefit of knowing her [full] medical history.... There's some mystery, some unknown, about her health." Lauren, a white lesbian therapist in a midsized Northeastern city, adopted her Latina daughter Kiley via foster care. Kiley, who had multiple developmental and medical issues, came with "no medical records prior to age 4; we don't know her early medical stuff [or] her family's medical stuff, [which] makes everything more challenging." Jake, a white gay hotel manager in a small West Coast city, noted that his daughter Sharice, who was African American, had considerable "challenges with reading.... I mean, it seems like it's a full-on reading disability; we obviously weren't expecting that." Jake found himself "wondering sometimes... I wish I knew more about her birth family, [to have a] better medical history and better idea of... what potentially may arise in the future." Further, when faced with behavioral issues, Jake found himself wondering, "Well, is that genetic? Or, is that something that happened because of what she was exposed to when she was in the womb? But we don't— we'll never really know." Indeed, genetic determinism, or the societal belief that human behavior is controlled by an individual's genes or physiology, has a "particular effect on adoptive families.... [T]he adopted child whose genetic origins cannot be clearly defined becomes a carrier of the unknown,"[11] which can promote an ongoing sense of uncertainty and helplessness.

When his son Isaac, who was Latino and white, was 5 years old, Will, a white gay accountant in a midsized metro area on the West Coast, put it like this:

When you're genetically related, you kind of know what runs in the family— illnesses and what have you. And we're kind of a blank slate. And although we have a thumbnail sketch, we don't have it all. For example, Isaac has really severe asthma. We weren't prepared for that, because we don't know if it runs in his family. We weren't looking for that. [It's hard], just the unknowns about medical history.

Such unknowns meant that parents often felt helpless when asked to provide basic medical information for their children—for example, at school and at the doctor. Indeed, Will's partner, Adam, a biracial (African American/white) director of marketing, observed that such unknowns were particularly evident in the medical context:

We always have to kind of remember—in all of that paperwork, did [birth mother]... have high blood pressure? Did they have this... or that? There is always this sort of academic exercise we have to go through when we're in the doctor's office. We try and connect Isaac's biological history with whatever the doctors are asking us.

Amid uncertainty about the origins of their children's difficulties and an absence of birth family contact, some parents felt compelled to draw their own conclusions about the role of genetics or prenatal drug exposure or environmental stress in their children's disposition. Lindsey, a white lesbian physician assistant in a large Northeastern city, shared that her 8-year-old African American daughter Ava struggled with anxiety. Based on the limited information she had about Ava's birth mother, and the input of a therapist, Lindsey drew her own conclusions about the potential contributors to Ava's anxiety:

> Her therapist said, "Oh, she probably had some sort of intrauterine trauma." And her birth parents were [splitting up] at the time and God knows what other sorts of stressors were happening in their lives. I'm like, yeah, this little fetus probably had this huge infusion of cortisol and it made her all jumpy, so now she's an anxious kid. So, I guess I can imagine where it came from.

Among the families who lacked medical information about and did not have contact with their children's birth families, several parents of girls described how their children had shown signs of entering puberty early. This "threw [them] for a loop" and (re)alerted them to the reality that "we don't know a lot of the genetics here!" The absence of medical information, they realized, was becoming more salient as puberty unfolded and "there are all these milestones and we have no roadmap of what to expect or what will happen when."

By contrast, parents who did have access to their children's birth family shared ways in which contact had enhanced their ability to address and answer medical questions. Elora, a heterosexual stay-at-home mother in a large West Coast city, had recently encountered a situation where her biracial (Latina/white) daughter Maeve, at 8 years old, was experiencing some confusing medical issues. As part of her quest to determine the nature and origin of these "mystery symptoms," Elora sought out input from multiple birth family members. "We just had some genetic testing done for Maeve, because she had been experiencing some pain. . . . [We were able to do it] because we have an open adoption with her birth family." When his biracial (Latino/white) son David was 5, Rob, a gay Latino administrative assistant in a West Coast suburb, described how he had maintained ongoing contact with David's birth mother, Alena, which enabled him to reach out with medical and mental health questions on an "as needed" basis:

> I have a relatively close relationship with her, because I cultivated it, so that if David ever wanted to talk to her I wanted to be able to tell him, "Well let's call her up" or "This is where she is, you can find her here." That was important to me. . . . So I've kept track of her . . . and I've had questions myself like, "Did any of this happen with your other kids?" And questions of the family history health line . . . [like,] "Did any of the other kids have ADHD? How did you manage? How did you deal with this situation compared with the other?" And sure enough, Alena has kids who do have ADHD. She thinks she may have had it, or has it. She says his temper comes from her, that she is very much like that,

very reactive, that her parents didn't do a good job of giving her direction and helping her with her temper ... so she's also made me very afraid [*laughs*]. But I'm grateful that I have that communication with her.

Access to birth family information was also a source of power in that it allowed parents a sense of agency and control in anticipating their children's future needs and challenges. Leigh, a white heterosexual assistant museum director living in a small city on the East Coast, adopted her son Kevin, who was white, from foster care, and ultimately established regular contact with his birth siblings and their adoptive parents. Five years postadoption, Leigh described how comprehensive information about Kevin's birth parents' history, combined with ongoing contact with Kevin's birth siblings, allowed her to anticipate the types of supports and services he might need in the future:

His birth family has a history of ADHD and learning disabilities, and he was prenatally exposed to drugs, so I anticipate that he will be needing some services and special ed services as he gets older. ... Both of his birth parents had various diagnoses from ADHD to ... whatever, and his birth siblings also have those diagnoses. And so I fully anticipate that he will have ADHD or a learning disability or whatever, and so I'm just making sure that he is in environment with teachers who [are] supportive [and] who can provide the resources that he needs in order to succeed, and making sure that I am able to advocate effectively.

Indeed, in a number of cases, parents did not have contact with birth parents—but they did have contact with birth siblings, which facilitated parents' ability to draw conclusions about the origins of their children's difficulties, and thus more easily and quickly seek out appropriate assessment and intervention. Eva, a Latina lesbian communications professor in a Northeastern suburb, had adopted her Latino son Devon via foster care, 8 years earlier. Eva described how although she did not have contact with 12-year-old Devon's birth parents, she did have contact with his birth siblings and their adoptive parents. Knowledge of those children's behavioral profile had supported her "suspicion" of prenatal substance exposure:

What's to say she didn't drink with Devon? He has a lot of symptoms around the way he processes things and his understanding of ... consequences that kind of go with a fetal alcohol spectrum disorder. The neuropsych testing suggested ... that that might be the case. We don't have clear documentation or evidence of alcohol intake by his bio mom. It's just my suspicion because of what we know about his younger brother.

Eva's partner, Tina, a multiracial engineer, also commented on the challenges that they had encountered in the absence of solid evidence of prenatal substance use—and the benefit of having contact with the adoptive families of his siblings. Tina noted that Devon "meets all the criteria, has all the symptoms" of fetal alcohol syndrome, so "we really need to test for that." However, to achieve diagnostic certainty, "technically, you have to have someone who observed the mother drinking while pregnant. We don't have contact with the birth mother, but we feel pretty certain that that's what had happened because she had several children and they were all taken away because of drug and alcohol use."

Georgia, a white heterosexual realtor living in a large West Coast city, also relied on knowledge and contact with birth siblings in the absence of regular contact with birth parents. Georgia described how her 8-year-old son Henry, who was biracial (Latino and white) and adopted privately as a newborn, had recently been showing signs of a learning disability—and how she had relied on her ongoing communications with and knowledge of his birth siblings to make sense of the situation:

> I think about all the genetics, [in terms of] Henry having a hard time writing, and I just wonder, like.... This morning I said to Stan, "Do you think he's dyslexic?" My husband was saying no, because he can read; he's just having a hard time writing [and] his spelling is not very good.... So, I think, does he have a learning disability? Because I know that—sometimes we'll receive letters from his half-sister, and her writing is horrible... meaning like... instead of "w-r-i-t-e" she might just say "r-i-t-e." So, things like that. Henry does have a temper, and then being diagnosed with ADHD—I wonder, you know, about that genetic aspect of his life.

Annie, a white heterosexual school administrator in a Northeastern suburb, had adopted her son Grayson, also white, via foster care when he was 3 years old. Grayson was placed in their care with very little medical information in his file, and no formal medical records at all. This led to frustration and concern on Annie's part when Grayson began to exhibit some physical difficulties, including gross motor delays. "As an adoptive parent, dealing with a child that has these [problems], we ask... is this normal? We don't have a family history of [physical delays]." Then, several years postadoption, Annie and her husband, Chuck, successfully made contact with Grayson's birth brother, Christian, who, Annie discovered from talking to Christian's adoptive parents, was exhibiting some of the same challenges as Grayson—and who had undergone some testing, which had informed a preliminary diagnosis. Knowledge of Christian's struggles and diagnoses ultimately helped Annie and Chuck to speed up the process of seeking help for Grayson, including services to support him at school.

Extensive knowledge about birth family members—obtained either during the preadoptive stage or via ongoing contact with the birth family—was not always experienced as an unequivocal blessing. When parents had knowledge of mental health problems, addiction, and criminality on the part of birth family members, this information was sometimes described as a source of anxiety and concern. For example, Elora, a white heterosexual homemaker in a large city in the Northeast said, 5 years postadoption: "Both of Maeve's birth parents have had some mental health issues . . . so I keep that in the back of my mind [although] I don't see anything like that. She's such a well-adjusted, happy little child [who's] just very . . . shy." Parents sometimes worried that their knowledge of mental health or addiction issues caused them to "overreact. . . . I always have the family history in the back of my mind" (Elora). Terrence, a white gay anesthesiologist in a West Coast suburb, noted that his biracial (Latino/white) son David's birth parents had struggled with drug addiction. In turn:

There's been a challenge in kind of knowing the family history, trying not to overreact. . . . I have to really take a step back [sometimes] and say, okay I really don't need to overreact in this circumstance. Genes are only a small part of this. I mean, it's difficult. And I think that's probably worse being an adoptive parent than it would be as a natural parent. At least I would know how, what genetic issues we're [dealing with].

Knowledge of possible genetic predisposition to substance abuse or mental health issues led some parents to have frank discussions with their children about possible future vulnerabilities (e.g., a greater than average likelihood of developing a difficult relationship to alcohol or drugs). One gay father discussed how knowledge of his daughter's birth mother's drug abuse history—which was intertwined with a history of homelessness and mental health issues—affected how he talked with his daughter about alcohol, and influenced his own decision to stop drinking:

My daughter and I had a conversation yesterday [spurred on by a school assignment] on the effects of heredity and environment on fetus development. She didn't know what that meant, so we talked about that, and I said, "I am concerned about some of the hereditary things because we don't know. . . ." I do have a concern that—how far does the mental health piece in their family go back? And . . . the birth mother was taken away from her own mother because the mother had a drug habit. And then my daughter was [also taken away] because of that. So these are things I wonder about—what kind of addictive behaviors [she] might have . . . and I do talk to her about it—"Just be careful, as you start to grow and develop." The conversation is basically, "Just because your friends do it and they enjoy doing it, think about that—that may not always be the right thing for you to do, because, there's a lot of stuff that we're still discovering about ourselves as we grow." She says things like, "Well, I don't want to drink. I definitely don't want to [do] drugs, but I hear kids talk about it." And nobody in our house does drugs; we drink wine, but what I've done is, I've stopped drinking wine, because—I'm trying to model things for her. I also know I shouldn't drink, because—I always tell her, "People on Grandpa James's side of the family: they drank, they died." And then she's like, "Well, why do you drink?" and I'm like, "That's a good question." And so instead of trying to justify hard liquor from wine, I just stopped drinking.

Similarly, Deb, a white lesbian chiropractor in a midsized Northeastern city, noted that she and her partner, Stacy, both saw openness about adoption and birth family circumstances as encompassing direct communication about substance use and other biogenetic predispositions and vulnerabilities. About their conversations with their daughter Marlo, who was biracial (Latina and white), Deb said:

> We do talk about genetic issues and familial patterns ... in a developmentally appropriate way to help her understand where she is coming from and the hurdles she might have. ... Krista and Jay [birth parents] struggle with substance abuse and we want her to be aware of that. It's like your teeth, and stuff like that. We say, "Your birth mom talks about that she always had teeth issues, so make sure you brush your teeth."

Making Sense of Intellectual Ability

Only a few parents raised intelligence in relation to genetics. As with mental and physical health, parents appeared to have private theories and opinions about their children's intelligence, which they did not communicate to them (e.g., in terms of how a child's intelligence might relate to their birth parents' intelligence). Many parents spoke about trying to prepare themselves for the fact that their children would not necessarily "take after them" with regard to physical characteristics, intellectual curiosity, talents, and interests—yet ultimately, a few parents noted that they were pleasantly surprised by their children's intelligence. Heather, a white lesbian small business owner in a midsized Southern city, said, about her 8-year-old daughter Stella, who was also white: "She's a very, very smart kid and her birth parents were, are brilliant people, so ... I mean, her birth parents are *really* ... brilliant people." Jenny, a white lesbian mother employed as a manager at a medical supply company in the suburban Midwest, was taken aback by what she described as above-average intelligence on the part of her 8-year-old son Jacob, who was biracial (African American and white):

> You just never know how your child's going to be and how your child's going to take to learning and growing and . . . Jacob has just, you know, there's never been an expectation, but if there ever was one he's, well, exceeded it. He just, he keeps us—I'm amazed. I'm just truly amazed. . . . I would have never thought this, but it can be challenging at times because he's such an avid reader and we have to constantly . . . really think about [appropriate reading] material for him.

A few parents, on the other hand, acknowledged that they were surprised, and somewhat sad, to learn that their child appeared to be less traditionally intelligent than they had hoped for or expected. Tony, a white heterosexual small business owner in a Northeastern suburb, said, about his 9-year-old daughter Lila, who was also white, whom he had adopted via foster care:

> A couple years ago . . . she had to repeat first grade, and after that we had her tested and her IQ came back extremely low. And so, we certainly knew there would be issues because of her mother doing drugs and stuff but the whole IQ thing kind of—and really her abilities—wasn't something we expected.

Tony was currently struggling to adapt to the reality of his daughter's challenges. In particular, navigating school services and Lila's newly developed Individualized Education Plan (IEP) was stressful: "I feel like they're just pushing her along at school. It's very frustrating." Significantly, Tony's wife, Rosie, a white magazine editor, expressed more optimism than Tony about Lila's capabilities, emphasizing that the IQ test "did not capture . . . aspects of her abilities" that Rosie believed might become more apparent in the future.

Another couple who had to drastically adjust their expectations for their child's intellectual functioning was Seth, a white gay after-school program director, and Dean, a white software developer, who lived in a large city in the South. The couple adopted a son, Bobby, also white, who was eventually diagnosed with severe cognitive deficits. This diagnosis was difficult to adjust to, but both men ultimately found that the healthiest thing they could do for their own well-being was to accept their situation, and their son, and parent the child they had—not the child they imagined. The couple was in fact aware that the placement was high risk (Bobby's birth mother had developmental and mental health challenges) but believed, early on, that "if he does [end up] having any kind of problems, we have so many resources and we're educated people, so we think we can deal with whatever comes up" (Seth). Yet the reality of adjusting to Bobby's diagnosis was challenging. When Bobby was 8, Dean said:

We knew his mother has disabilities, so we knew there certainly was a genetic component there. She also [took] medication that has [side effects], so we knew there were going to be issues, and it's just a matter of finding out how severe and what can be done about it along the way. There was a point where we were just doing all this testing we could find and talking to all the therapists ... [about] his delayed walking, delayed talking, delayed everything. And doing occupational therapy and speech therapy. You know, on and on and on. But at a point you have to learn to accept things as they are. He's going to have a difficult life, and we're just going to have to give him whatever tools we can to do it. But it's certainly [been] challenging along the way.

Making Sense of Talents, Personality, and Physical Features

Parents, in general, did not tend to talk directly to children about the ways in which their medical background, mental health, or intellectual abilities may have been linked to birth parents—for example, via genetics or prenatal stress or substance abuse. That is, they did not try to help their children make sense of these challenges by highlighting their possible origins. Parents were likely aware that such attributions would not be particularly useful—and in fact could be quite damaging: For example, they could suggest that parents blamed birth parents for their "inferior" or problematic genetics, or for the lifestyle choices they had made; or such attributions might imply that children were or came from "bad seeds." In my interview with Dawn Smith-Pliner, founder and director of Friends in Adoption, an adoption agency in Vermont, she stated:

> Despite the fact that parents often have strong preferences about drug/alcohol exposure, a number of children whom they adopt will ultimately be diagnosed with ADHD, learning problems, and so on. It's hard for them to make sense of this. Is it genetics? Drug exposure? I see them struggling about how to make attributions without blaming the birth parents directly or indirectly—especially in front of the children. However, I've seen that they do invoke birth parent characteristics when their child displays a positive quality (e.g., a gift for music).

Consistent with this on-the-ground observation, the parents I interviewed did not tend to invoke the birth family when attempting to explain children's challenges—but they did sometimes invoke the birth family when noting a special talent, personality attribute, or ability in their children—thus highlighting birth parents when they believed that it might help their children to internalize a sense of positive regard for their birth parents and themselves. Physical features, such as skin color and hair (as discussed in Chapter 6), as well as other physical attributes such as height, were also sometimes linked directly or indirectly to birth parents.

These linkages were made more easily and naturally when parents had contact with their children's birth family. In the context of ongoing contact and communication, parents possessed a more comprehensive knowledge of and familiarity with birth parents' strengths, abilities, and talents, possibly rendering their observations (e.g., to children) more credible and less abstract. Heather, a white lesbian small business owner in a midsized Southern city, said, about her 8-year-old daughter Stella, also white: "I definitely see things in her that, knowing her birth mom, Joy, that I say, 'Wow, that's so like Joy.' Stella is very musical, Joy is extremely musical . . . so there are things where I think, 'Wow, she definitely took after Joy on that!'" Mariette, a white lesbian physical therapist in a suburb in the Midwest, described how she had often observed to her 8-year-old son Jacob, who was African American and white, that he must have gotten his strong spelling and reading abilities from his birth father, Jim. Inturn, Jacob began to make statements like this as well, suggesting that he had positively internalized this association. Mariette said:

> Jacob is very bright . . . and kind of on the far end on the chart, verbally. And we do know both his birth parents, and so we're like, "Hmm, wow, he probably wouldn't have gotten that from us!" . . . And one day recently, Jacob said to us, "I think Jim is a good speller." And those kinds of comments start a long conversation.

Jacob's comment reveals that he had been listening closely to the associations that his parents were making—and that he had internalized the notion that he got his spelling abilities from his birth father. In turn, parents who supported and responded to their children's efforts at meaning making and identity integration—for example, by affirming and building on the associative linkages their children were making—likely contributed to their children's positive identity development.[12]

Molly, a white lesbian environmental engineer living in a Northeast suburb, whose daughter Quinn, who was also white, was 8 years old, shared that their younger adopted son, Dillon, had demonstrated some behavioral issues, which they wondered about in relation to genetics—but did not articulate to Dillon. In contrast, "with Quinn it's more like, 'Oh my gosh, you look so much like your granny or your birth mom, or, your birth mom really likes art, and she's creative, and so are you.' So with her, it's just looking at the similarities." Her partner, Taryn, a white radio personality, also remarked on Quinn's physical resemblance to her birth mother, Sharla, and birth grandmother—an observation that was facilitated by the fact that they had regular contact with Quinn's birth family:

> We see her birth grandma... more than we see her birth mom. She comes and stays with us. She looks like her birth mom and her birth grandma *a lot*. So sometimes, I'll just randomly say—she'll make a face, and I'll be like, "Oh my God, that was a Granny face. You look just like Granny when you make that face," and we'll laugh about it or something. So it just comes up in random ways like that.

Robin, a white lesbian freelance writer in a suburb in the Northeast, had adopted her Latino son Shawn from foster care 8 years earlier. She and her wife, Greta, actively sought to maintain contact with Shawn's birth family members. This facilitated their ability to comment on the positive qualities that Shawn shared with them—which seemed especially important in light of the various challenges his birth parents had, and thus the tendency for their strengths to be missed or rendered invisible:

> We try really hard to point out—we know, for example, that their birth father, Esteban, is really good with, like, fixing cars and being good with his hands and computers. So we definitely see those in Shawn and so we try really hard to point those out and say, "Gosh you remind me a lot of Esteban, the way that you're trying to build that" or "You know, Maria [birth aunt] is really fashionable and you have a great sense of fashion and I think you probably get that from Maria."... So we try to... point out where maybe some of those strengths have come from.

Even when parents did not have ongoing contact with the birth family, the emergence of certain abilities or strengths were often used to make "reverse attributions" about the potential or likely role of birth family members and in turn genetics. Thomas, a white heterosexual financial planner in a midsized city in the Northeast, said, about his 5-year-old son Joey, who was also white, "He seems like he's very artistic and also... analytical, things like that.... He probably gets that from his birth parents." Lindsey, a white lesbian physician assistant in a large Northeast city, who, in addition to describing her African American daughter Ava's struggles with anxiety, which she surmised might be linked to prenatal stress, also commented on Ava's physical abilities and talents, which she guessed might reflect a "genetic contribution":

Her physical health is really good. She's a really strong and able kid. And I don't mean "oh I'm so glad she's not handicapped." I mean just her physicality; she's got a lot of talent there. She's really good at gymnastics, Zumba, and dancing and running. It's like, that's cool. It's not so much surprising, but just sort of like "Oh!"

Carly, a white heterosexual history professor in a large Northeast city, did not have ongoing reciprocal contact with her 6-year-old African American daughter Eve's birth mother. However, Carly held her in high regard and looked for opportunities to highlight special connections between her and Eve, such as a shared love of reading: "Sometimes I'll just say something about her birth mother—like, her birth mother had loved to read, she told us, so . . . I'll say, 'Oh yeah, your birth mom really loved to read; I wonder if you get that from her a little bit too!'"

When parents invoked birth parents in relation to children's physical features, it was sometimes in the service of providing context for and understanding of characteristics that were noticeably dissimilar between adoptive parents and children and in turn often identified as "clues" to their children's adoptive status. Race (discussed in Chapter 6) was one such physical feature—and along with race came skin color and hair. Jenny, a white lesbian manager of a medical supply company in a Midwestern suburb, noted that her son Jacob, who was biracial (African American and white), "knows his birth father, Jim, and he's African American." Although Jenny did not think that Jacob currently bore a strong resemblance to Jim, she routinely showed Jacob pictures of him and made a point of noting shared physical characteristics between them, out of an awareness that Jacob might increasingly identify with his birth father as he developed, both in general and with respect to skin tone and hair specifically.

Another physical feature that parents sometimes directly linked to birth parents was height. In a handful of families, children were much shorter or taller than would be expected if they were biogenetically related to their adoptive parents. Parents directly or indirectly invoked genetics in explaining this dissimilarity. Lena, a white heterosexual operations manager in a midsized Northeastern city, said, about her 8-year-old son Joey, who was also white:

It sounds silly, but Joey is very short [*laugh*] and we are tall. We are sensitive to it and I don't want him to be made fun of, so we're trying to, you know, "Joey, it doesn't matter if you're tall!" Sometimes, every once in a while, he'll walk around on his tiptoes and I'll be like, "What are you doing, buddy?" and he's like, "I want to be taller." Then he'll say, "If I was in your belly, I would have been taller." I mean, we try to have a good attitude about it. I said, "Yeah, but you're . . . green eyed and gorgeous." So we try to make sure he doesn't feel inadequate because he's in a family with tall people. His biological parents are . . . short. So I think we just want to make sure he doesn't feel . . . slighted.

Sometimes, parents had contact with one birth parent, typically the birth mother, but not the other, typically the birth father. In turn, they used the information they had to make sense of their children's abilities, personality, and physical features—while also acknowledging the "missing piece" in the puzzle. Gordon was a white heterosexual property manager in a large West Coast city, who maintained contact with his biracial (African American and white) daughter Violet's birth mother, Nessa. When Violet was 8, he reflected:

> Violet is full of energy, has lots of passions about things, and her birth mother and grandmother are not necessarily so strongly opinionated, maybe don't have the same passion, so we see similarities and we see differences, but this is only one side of her birth family we know about. We feel unfortunate that we don't really have contact with the birth father, so I think it would be—I'm really curious about a number of physical attributes, but also just other things that perhaps would help better explain who she is.

Acknowledging Nature but Emphasizing Nurture: "What We Do Makes a Difference"

Even as they acknowledged the role of their children's genetics and sometimes early life experiences in their behavior, health, physical attributes, and intelligence, parents inevitably maximized nurture to the extent that they could. That is, they understood that they had control over how they parented and, in turn, the types of settings, experiences, and opportunities that their children were exposed to. In this regard, it is interesting to note that research shows that families with both adoptive and biological children may in fact invest more heavily (e.g., through financial, social, and educational resources) in their adopted children.[13] This greater investment may in part reflect a "compensatory strategy" on the part of adoptive parents, such that they aim to mitigate disadvantages that adoptive children are suspected or known to have experienced preplacement, including prenatal experiences.[14] Indeed, although a definitive explanation for these patterns in parental investment is difficult to come by, it is reasonable to suggest that many adoptive parents recognize that although they do not have control over their children's genetics (or prenatal and/or preadoptive environment), they do have some control over their children's postadoptive environment. In turn, they seek to use their existing resources to support and optimize their children's development and well-being.

Preadoption, most parents acknowledged the power of nature, to varying degrees, but they also hoped that their nurturing would make a difference—and now, as parents, they had the opportunity to see, and believe in, the ways in which parenting, school, and other key contexts impacted their children. When her son Joey was 5 years old, Lena, the white heterosexual operations manager quoted earlier regarding Joey's height, reflected: "You always wonder, as a parent, about [intelligence]. But I don't see any concerns. A lot of that is also nurturing. We're in an environment where he sees us reading, so I don't have any concerns about him starting school." When Joey was 8, Lena said: "We thought Mandy [birth mother] was bright and well educated—but I think we [also] try to compensate; like, I read to Joey all the time, but that's just because I love reading too. But it's nice to know that . . . he seems on track, and he's not behind." Thus, even amid impressions or beliefs of Joey's birth mother as "bright," Lena conceded that she and her husband also aimed to foster intellectual curiosity and academic progress through their own parenting practices, such as reading aloud to their son.

Jamie, a white gay communications manager in a midsized Southern city, also reflected on the roles of both nature and nurture in his children's intellectual and academic functioning, emphasizing the role of education specifically in fostering their abilities. A parent of two adopted children—8-year-old Timothy and 4-year-old Daria, both of whom were biracial (African American and white)—Jamie said:

> We're really fortunate because—I know Timothy's birth mom smoked but other than that—they're really sharp kids. So genetics does play a part in that. At the same time, investing in early education, I think, is just as big a part as genetics, to be able to foster and develop [their abilities]. Because we see Daria's birth siblings and they're smart children but they're also falling down a path that's probably not such a great path . . . a lifestyle [that happens] more likely than not because you get caught up in the system and all you know is what's around you in your environment. But we do talk about genetics and both of the kids are really sharp and we're fortunate with that, because we've seen other adoptions where that is not the case. We've been lucky.

Jake, a white gay hotel manager in a small West Coast city, acknowledged that his African American daughter Sharice's birth mother's history of mental illness and substance abuse was "always hanging in the background" of his consciousness. In this way, he worried about Sharice's elevated risk for mental health and substance use issues "simply because of nature." At the same time, Jake chose to emphasize what he could control—namely, "making sure she gets all of the support she needs, that she feels safe, that she gets all of the mental stimulation that she needs, mechanisms for dealing with challenges in life . . . and that [we foster] open and honest communication." Dave, a white gay radiologist in a large Midwestern city, said, about his son Aidan, who was Latino, "As far as his physical health, genetics plays a role. He's in the 98th percentile for height and weight. [He] struggles with eating healthy, and . . . I think he's genetically predisposed to struggling with it." Yet like Jake, Dave emphasized what he and his husband, Byron, were doing to offset their child's risk profile, noting that they were committed to "monitoring eating and exercise and all that." Likewise, his partner Byron, a white graduate student, asserted: "We don't dine on fast food a lot. We don't really let Aidan eat junk very often."

Finally, Jenny, the white lesbian mother who was described earlier as being "pleasantly surprised" by her biracial son Jacob's above-average intellect and strong reading ability, shared that she believed that genetics were "mostly responsible" for these qualities. Yet Jenny also felt that she and her partner, Mariette, played a role in allowing Jacob to optimize his potential (i.e., amplifying his heritable traits[15]):

> I kid all the time with my friends . . . that we can't take any credit for [how bright] Jacob is. So they're very quick to say, "Well, actually yes that's a part of it, but . . . ," meaning his genetics, but they remind me, "You're his parents, you're his mother, and certainly you guys are doing something that is contributing to that." I absolutely think that genetics is a part of that. But I also do think it's what you do as a parent, or caretaker . . . that [matters] too. You can know your child can do something, but if you're not supporting that and you're not helping to nourish that, then whether or not that child will grow to full potential, I think, depends on that.

It is notable that some parents, while acknowledging their role in possibly shaping their children's abilities or interests, ultimately came down on the idea that their child "just is who he is." Larissa, a white lesbian bookstore manager in a large Northeastern city who had adopted her biracial (African American/white) daughter Elise from foster care 8 years earlier, shared her sense that by virtue of having adopted, she approached parenthood with far fewer expectations of who and what her child would become. This, Larissa believed, had enabled Elise to develop into her own "unique" self:

> She has a love of reading and a love of music and she's a very unique human being. It's just so enjoyable to watch her be like, "I'm interested in this, and I'm

interested in this...." It's awesome. I think certainly a lot of it is just who she is.... We never made her do anything. We wouldn't say, "Okay now you got to practice your flute. Okay now you've got to read." We just kind of let her grow, let her develop. I think a big thing that has been such a strength in our parenting approach is, because she started so far behind, she's never had those really heavy expectations. We had high expectations within what we thought she was capable of at the time, but we wouldn't be pushing for "excellence." We weren't like, "If you don't come home with anything less than an A . . . if you don't play this flute perfectly. . . . So all of that pressure, I think, we were able to let go of, so she was just able to develop in her time. And we knew that our relationships were the most important thing and everything else would just come. I know that a lot of people, when they have their own biological children, have expectations about what their life will be like and what their kids should do, as like a reflection of themselves. We were relieved from all that because we just couldn't have any of those expectations. We had to grow with her and couldn't force anything, and we always had so many other things to focus on in terms of our bonding and emotional stuff. So I think that's one thing—that we just let her be herself.

Rick, a white gay nonprofit director in a large West Coast city, voiced a similar narrative. Like some other parents, Rick shared that he "could not have predicted" his 8-year-old son Jack's personality, strengths, and challenges. According to Rick, Jack, who was also white, had historically struggled with behavioral problems at school, which had culminated in a recent diagnosis of ADHD. Rick was frank about these challenges but also highlighted the opportunities associated with parenting a child that was "not from [him]." Rick marveled about the differences between himself and Jack: "My entire family is introverts, and now Jack—he is clearly an extravert. It's like, 'Wow, you are not from this family' [*laugh*]. It's like, 'You are a different person than me.'" Rick reflected:

> You read about it, and you intellectually understand that this is going to happen—but your child is going to be their own individual and they're not going to be whatever you imagined them to be. You have to come to terms with that. It's a source of delight, frustration, and amazement every day when I'm like, "Wow, Jack is really, absolutely nothing like me. He's just his own person and that's all he can be [*laugh*]." You go into parenting wishing and hoping for things and you have to recognize that you get what you get and they're their own person. You don't get to choose who they're going to be.

Growing Appreciation for Nature: "God Grant Me the Serenity to Accept the Things I Cannot Change"

Some parents described how, over the course of their children's development, they had become increasingly dubious of the power of context (i.e., parents, school, resources, tutoring) to shift or alter aspects of their child's makeup (e.g., academic abilities, personality). In essence, they increasingly felt that certain aspects of their child were less mutable than they had once hoped or believed. These parents were typically among those who adopted via foster care. Leigh, a white heterosexual assistant museum director in a small East Coast city, had adopted her son Kevin, also white, 5 years ago from foster care, when he was a toddler. Noting Kevin's birth parents' low levels of formal schooling, Leigh emphasized that a crucial concern for her was ensuring that 7-year-old Kevin was exposed to opportunities that would hopefully help him to enjoy learning and thrive academically:

> Both of his birth parents dropped out of high school and he has an older birth sibling who ... is definitely not [going to college], and so I would love, you know, not college necessarily—whatever the kid needs to do!—but I definitely want Kevin to be able to finish high school and be a successful productive member of society. I don't want him to be in an environment where he gets turned off from learning. So just making sure that he can succeed in school, making sure, you know, that he has a love for learning—that's my biggest, biggest, biggest concern.

At this point, Leigh felt relatively optimistic about the role of environmental supports to enhance Kevin's functioning and set him up for success, personally and academically. But by the time Kevin was 10 years old, Leigh expressed less confidence in this regard. Kevin had continued to struggle with attentional, behavioral, and attachment difficulties, and Leigh had begun to wonder if there was an "upper limit" on what she—and schools and therapists—could do:

> I think that even though in our foster parent training they sort of gave the whole "love doesn't overcome everything," I really truly believed that despite that, if you just throw enough interventions [at them] ... like, we did play therapy there for a while and Kevin had a full neuropsych evaluation—I totally thought that if you just throw enough stuff at them, that by the time they hit school age, they'll be just like every other kid. And yeah—I think I just didn't really have a good concept that some of these issues, whatever they are, whether or not you can put a label on them, that they might not ever go away.... So, I feel like I had expected these issues to have resolved themselves by now. I had expected

doctors and therapists to be able to understand them, and they don't.... At this point, I am slowly being able to put together a picture that—clearly, Kevin had some organic brain damage before he was born, and there's some attachment issues.... He was prenatally exposed to heroin, possibly alcohol, and who knows what else.

Leigh reflected directly on how her attitudes and beliefs surrounding nature–nurture had shifted as a function of parenting an adopted child:

Prior to embarking on this whole journey, I would have totally been in the nurture category—that parents and the community and who you surround your kids with will determine who they are, what they become and such. And I have been sort of leaning more and more towards . . . I suspect that there is a large nature component to some of what we're running into, right? Whether that be addiction-related things or mental illness–related things or just sort of, it sounds awful to say this, but just how academic, smart, they'll end up being.

Leigh further reflected on her sense that the child welfare system had set her up to view any evidence that her son was likely to "turn out" like his birth parents as inherently negative—a true tragedy:

They only tell you the negative stuff about the birth parents and the birth family. And the only way you can accept the whole process is to also really believe that they're bad people, right? Someone took their kids away from them and said they're never getting them back so clearly, they're bad people. And even though intellectually that's not the case, that still is totally the message that you get all the way along. And so—when I think about my son turning out like his birth parents, that's a negative thing, even though I know it shouldn't be. I just don't have any information for it to be otherwise.

Tina, a multiracial lesbian engineer in a Northeastern suburb, was similar to Leigh in that she had adopted her Latino son Devon through foster care at the age of 4. Like Leigh, Tina increasingly wondered about the ultimate impact of nature on her son. When Devon was about 12, Tina mused:

Maybe he is at his capacity to understand and connect.... It's really difficult for him to look beyond his own feelings, which are incredibly deep. I don't think I would ever be able to do anything to satisfy his sense of loss or disappointment, so.... [Agencies should] definitely give people more information about the cognitive problems that may show up later. Because I think that those are very significant for him.... On the surface [it's like], "Oh, he's a cute kid" and he looks like he's okay—just like other kids. But he just really struggles, especially [with] school and learning. I think there's an expectation that he can figure things out and be organized—and he just really can't.

In several cases, parents described how their children had begun to show neurological challenges during childhood—challenges that were "pretty clearly . . . classic signs of the consequences of prenatal drug abuse." Earl, a white heterosexual therapist in a suburb on the East Coast, explained that his son Brett, who was biracial (African American and white) and adopted via foster care at age 4, was, at the age of 9,

> experiencing some really significant school issues. It's really neurological issues, related to [exposure] to drugs. But you know, it just shocked me how much it has affected him. He was pretty delayed socially. And, due to the prenatal exposure, he cannot walk in bare feet without socks on. He feels that his feet are on fire. And so the running belief is that he might have sensory processing disorder. . . . And I have had so many people tell me that kids born addicted to cocaine have no issues. I'm like, "No, that's where we have our main issue." So now it's popping up and we have these people like, "Well you know maybe it's, you're feeding them red dye number 5 or whatever it is." Like, NO! . . . Like, no, I'm sure that it's what we're feeding them, not the fact that she was overindulging on heroin, cocaine, crack, and meth [*sarcastically*]. No, nothing to do with it.

Here, Earl highlights how a key source of frustration for him was the fact that "so many people" he encountered invalidated the reality that Brett's challenges stemmed from prenatal drug exposure—choosing to emphasize, instead, the possibility of a more easily modifiable contributor, such as a food additive. Earl recognized that the less attractive but far more likely reality was that his son's physical, social, and neurological difficulties were the result of drug exposure—and in turn, they were far harder to address than simply eliminating artificial food coloring from his son's diet. Earl had accepted this fact and wished that others would stop resisting the difficult truth.

Indeed, a number of parents noted that a key parental task for them had been to modify their expectations for their children. That is, upon realizing the "fundamental nature of who this kid is," they had tried to make mental and behavioral adjustments that reflected their growing reality of who their child was and would likely become, and who they were not. This type of cognitive shift is arguably adaptive, in that it allowed parents to shed false and unrealistic hopes about their child's future and more clearly see—and meet the needs of—the child in front of them. Reed, a white alumni relations director in a large metropolitan area on the West Coast, adopted a school-aged Latino and Native American boy named Shayne. Soon after the adoptive placement, Reed described both himself and his partner, Noah, a white school psychologist, as very education oriented. Although Reed felt that both he and Noah saw the reality of what Shayne brought to the table, he also observed that Noah had somewhat elevated expectations as to what Shayne was likely to achieve under their roof. Reed said:

Noah operates on a pretty idealized, "Shayne's going to be brilliant, Shayne's going to be very successful, Shayne did something better than all the other kids." So, I think Noah's operating based on what he wants versus what he—I think that's caused him a little conflict sometimes, because you know—Shayne will tantrum and . . . I really think that Noah wants him to settle down and be brilliant [*laugh*].

Eight years later, both Noah and Reed shared their sense that although Shayne was not "the best student . . . he likes school well enough but is not super academically oriented" (Reed) and was "average . . . in terms of all the testing" (Noah), he was "probably performing . . . higher than he would if he wasn't with us . . . with a steady household, and no real drama, and security, and food, and all those things that make a kid be able to function" (Reed). Thus, Reed came to understand that "there's an upper limit to what we can expect from Shayne":

We just sort of realized that he was always going to be the average performer. I think I thought that if we put him in private school, he would blossom academically. He would be, I don't know—he would show some academic prowess. And he didn't. He didn't, like, all of a sudden love school and want to learn. It was kind of like, "It's a nice place. I like the kids."

Some parents, especially those who were highly educated and/or self-described "intellectuals" or "nerds," found it difficult to adjust to the fact that their children might not share the same educational or academic interests or aspirations. Doug, a white gay psychologist in a large metropolitan area on the West Coast, said, about parenting his 8year-old daughter Catie, who was also white:

Something about parenting that I just didn't expect was—I think our whole household, except for Catie, is pretty intellectual—like we're both, "Oh I would rather sit and read a book quietly"—you know, be a little chill. Catie is . . . just very physical and has a lot of energy and is constantly making noise and . . . we're not that kind of household. And so a challenge for us is figuring out how to parent someone who fundamentally mismatches us in so many ways and trying to make sure that she gets the kind of needs and outlets to meet those needs. So it has been a bit of a surprise, or an awakening, of like, "Oh okay, this is my job to push myself a little bit." At the same time, we've pushed her and said, "Now it's quiet time, we're all going to be quiet, we're all going to read, or we're all going to take a break. You can go sit in your room and these are the things you can do..." so that she learns that she also [has] to adjust to people.

Nature Versus Nurture: It's Not Always That Cut and Dried

Parents who adopted via foster care had to consider not only their children's genetic makeup and prenatal environment but also the postnatal, preadoptive environment—all of which may have impacted their mental health, physical health, and intellectual abilities. Negative early life experiences (i.e., adverse childhood experiences, or ACEs) include psychological abuse, physical abuse, sexual abuse, exposure to substance abuse, mental illness of a household member, criminal behavior in the household, and violent treatment of a parent.[16] The number of ACEs that children are exposed to represents a measure of household dysfunction and is associated with an elevated risk of negative outcomes, including depression, suicide attempts, drug abuse, and health challenges.[17] In turn, parents who adopted via foster care were sometimes uncertain about the exact origin of their children's challenges. Aware that in many cases, their children were exposed to unfavorable early life circumstances, in addition to possessing prenatal and genetic risks, they did not know whether to situate their children's difficulties in the context of their prenatal environment, postnatal environment, and/or general genetic risks.

For example, Rosie, a white heterosexual magazine editor in a Northeastern suburb, adopted her daughter Lila, who was white, as a toddler. When Lila was 6, Rosie said:

> It's a little challenging in the sense that there are a lot of nuances with Lila because of, like, how she came to us. So... I don't like to label people in general, but... there are certain... behaviors that are exhibited, like [low IQ and learning difficulties], that are just kind of—it's hard [to know where they]... came from.

Annie, a white heterosexual school administrator in a Northeastern suburb, adopted her son Grayson, who was white, when he was 3 years old. Five years later, Annie similarly expressed confusion about the "what" and "why" of her son's behaviors:

> There are some things going on where—my husband and I, we don't know. Is it autism? Is it that he was adopted late that he has such this crass behavior output? I don't know what it is from. They're calling it autism; I'm calling it—I

don't know. It's Grayson's personality, period. Life experience, period. I don't know if it's because he's adopted late ... or what.

Lewis, a white heterosexual teacher in a small Northeastern city, who had adopted his son Todd, also white, 5 years earlier via foster care, stated:

The main issue for Todd is that ... he was adopted at 2 rather than as a baby. Maybe ... the ADHD has to do with that. And he's got kind of a reactive—they're kind of intermingled things—reactive attachment disorder. So, that was the main challenge, getting through that. And in the 5 years now since he came with us, it's gotten better. It's gotten a lot better, but it's been very slow progress for Todd and for us to deal with. That's probably the main challenge; he had those disorders that he could not help having.

Lewis's wife, Sandy, a white health care advocate, articulated a complementary perspective, stating: "I guess you don't know, if you're a biological parent, how your child will be, but it's kind of hard when ... I don't know. All these diagnoses; sometimes it just feels a lot harder than if you had biological children. It's an added stressor, I guess."

Lauren, a white lesbian therapist in a midsized city in the Northeast, had adopted a school-aged Latina girl, Kiley, who had a variety of medical problems. In the context of parental neglect, many of Kiley's health difficulties had been ignored, and thus, she had not received needed treatments and interventions. It was therefore difficult for Lauren and her wife, Victoria, to parse out whether the severity of Kiley's problems reflected an organic origin, and were thus fairly intractable, or whether they were treatable but had simply worsened in the absence of appropriate care:

A lot ... didn't get done because they just neglected to take her for follow-ups. ... She has issues with weight, which we think is partially, if not solely, because of the neglect that she had when she was with her parents. ... Her parents weren't very good at encouraging her or getting her to eat, and they also weren't giving her the right amount of food. ... So she really was malnourished, and they diagnosed her with failure to thrive. ... It's sad, because she was so neglected. ... So we're just doing everything we can to fix what we can for her. Sometimes it's hard, because we wish we could do more for her. But when you have years of neglect—it's going to take time for everything to resolve.

Jessica, a white heterosexual homemaker living in a medium-sized metro area in the Midwest, did not adopt her African American son Jerome via foster care but, rather, via a private domestic adoption. Still, amid the conditions of this placement, whereby Jerome was born several months premature and spent his first 6 months of life in a hospital, Jessica found herself wondering about the origins of his behavioral profile in ways that were very similar to parents who adopted via foster care. When Jerome was 5, Jessica reflected:

> I think about him sometimes, and his personality, and how he acts, and I think, "Is this biological? Is this environmental? Is this . . . ?" Like with Jerome—is it because he born at 25 weeks? Is it because he's a boy? Is it because he was poked and prodded in an incubator for 5 months like a little alien? Why is he doing this or why does he act like this? Is it those very beginning feelings of—is it abandonment? You know, he literally was abandoned by his birth mom and when I got to the hospital, I said, "What do I do?" and [the nurse] said, "You need to hold him; if someone doesn't hold him he's going to die. He has not been held yet; he has to be held."

Growing Appreciation for Nurture: "She's Just Like Us"

Whereas some participants' parenting experiences led them to develop greater confidence in the power of nature in shaping development, in a few cases, parents' experiences led them to believe more decisively in the power of nurture. These parents emphasized the influence of the family and social environment such that ultimately, emphasis was placed on "the mimicking process," which was "considered more influential than genetic or biological components in identity building."[18] Shoshanna, a white heterosexual project manager in a small Northeastern city, was one of several parents who said that they had come to believe, in essence, that nurture was more important than nature. Both 5 and 8 years postadoption, Shoshanna marveled at the ways in which her daughter Morgan, who was also white, resembled and reflected her and her husband in terms of habits, sense of humor, and interests. When Morgan was 5 years old, Shoshanna said:

> There's definitely the question of nature versus nurture [when considering] all these things that are fabulous about her. . . . She's so much like us. I look at her and I'm like, "Holy cow!" I mean nurture is big. People say, "Oh she was just born that way." And I'm like, no way, because . . . she hasn't got any genes from us, but she knows so much from our raising her. . . . I feel like nurturing means a lot. . . . I think she'd be a totally different person if she had been raised by her birth family.

When Morgan was 8, Shoshanna said:

The funniest thing for me has been—and this has evolved over the last 8½ years—that I think nurture plays a bigger part in growing a child than nature. And I don't know if I would have thought that if we hadn't adopted Morgan, or if we didn't have children, or if we had a biological child. I'm not sure I would have understood that as well as I do. Because she is a lot like we are. It's crazy when you hear you know your child say something and you are like, "Oh, that's me! That's what I look like from the outside!"

At the same time, Shoshanna did acknowledge the ways in which genetic and prenatal influences may have affected Morgan. For example:

Her biological mom didn't know she was pregnant, or at least did not admit to herself that she was pregnant. So she got no prenatal care . . . and Morgan was delivered by caesarian section and [it was a difficult delivery]. I mean we wondered about how that would play out when Morgan was growing up because she wasn't quick for a lot of physical stuff. Like she didn't walk until late. She was a terrible sleeper. I wondered how much those kind of things had to do with her . . . early birth life.

Some scholars have argued that "trying to separate out nature and nurture as explanations for behavior . . . is . . . both impossible and unproductive" but also acknowledge that "in practice the nature-nurture model persists as a way of framing discussion on the causes of behavior in genetic research [and] in the media and lay debate."[19] These ideas are echoed in the narratives of the parents I interviewed: Indeed, their struggle to understand and make sense of their children's characteristics suggests that the nature–nurture distinction is overly simplistic but reveals the power of dominant narrative (i.e., the idea that they *should* be able to pinpoint said characteristics as genetically or environmentally mediated). Their narratives also lay bare the ways in which the nature–nurture distinction has been erroneously mapped onto, or treated as synonymous with, intractability versus changeability—or, in other words, "just the way things are" versus "amenable to intervention."

Significantly, even as they attempted to make attributions about the origins of their children's characteristics, many parents acknowledged that they were incapable of distilling their children's unique personality, strengths, and challenges into a neat set of "nature" and "nurture" categories. One gay dad summed up this perspective by saying:

I'm definitely not putting a lot of stock in what we think we know right now about genes.... I think we [tend to] view the data in terms of what supports our existing biases. So I try to interrupt my impulse when I find myself going to "Oh this is genetics." At the same time, she does have a lot of behaviors—even just facial gestures and things like that—that are quite reminiscent of her birth mom.

Ultimately, what may be most important is that (a) parents are open to and prepared for a diverse range of possibilities with regard to their children's needs, strengths, challenges, and characteristics and (b) parents are thoughtful about how they invoke the birth family with respect to attributing origin or contribution to said characteristics. As some of them recognized, their children were attentive to the nature and tone of such attributions, and were therefore internalizing what was being said about them—and their birth family.[20] And, just as parents wonder about and try to make sense of where their children's characteristics came from, so will children. As they grow, they are likely to have questions about their medical history, racial/ethnic heritage, and personal characteristics—prompting feelings of loss and uncertainty that may fluctuate over time according to developmental shifts in the salience of their adoption or changes in their lives and/or contact with birth family.[21] Parents in turn should be prepared for shifts in their children's questions about, meaning making surrounding, and uncertainty regarding their origins.

As Chapter 10 notes, parents who face intellectual, behavioral, or medical challenges in their children that are far more severe than parents anticipated may benefit from consultation with adoption-competent medical professionals and therapists who are knowledgeable about how early trauma (including prenatal and postnatal experiences) can affect brain development and psychosocial functioning. Indeed, adoptive parents may struggle with formulating realistic expectations for their children, especially when faced with well-meaning friends, family, and helping professionals who minimize the role of prenatal drug exposure and early trauma in their children's difficulties. Parents do not need platitudes or false assurances; they need support from knowledgeable and compassionate providers who can help them to develop an informed understanding of their children and a plan for supporting them.

Notes

1. Plomin & Deary, 2015.
2. Bouchard, 1994.
3. Reiss, Leve, & Whitesel, 2009.
4. National Scientific Council on the Developing Child, 2010.

5. Reiss et al., 2009; Lavner, Waterman, & Peplau, 2012; van IJzendoorn, Juffer, & Poelhuis, 2005.
6. Reiss et al., 2009.
7. Ibid.
8. Ibid.
9. Goldberg & Smith, 2013; Howard, Smith, & Ryan, 2004.
10. American Academy of Pediatrics, Committee on Early Childhood, Adoption, & Dependent Care, 2000, p. 1145.
11. Chateaneuf & Ouellette, 2017, p. 193.
12. Neil, 2009; Wrobel, Kohler, Grotevant, & McRoy, 2003.
13. Hamilton, Cheng, & Powell, 2007.
14. Hamilton et al., 2007; Werum, Davis, Cheng, & Browne, 2016.
15. Reiss et al., 2009.
16. Felitti et al., 1998.
17. Simmel, Barth, & Brooks, 2007; Simms, Dubowitz, & Szilagyi, 2000.
18. Chateaneuf & Ouellette, 2017, p. 193.
19. Levitt, 2013, p. 13.
20. Shari Levine, personal communication, November 30, 2017.
21. Powell & Afifi, 2005.

8
Facebook as Facilitator or Foe
Boundaries and Birth Family Relationships on Social Media and Beyond

In contemporary U.S. society, many people regard social media as an integral part of online life—as well as a key medium by which individuals develop, maintain, and deepen social ties, and also access support and information.[1] Yet the pervasiveness of social media is relatively new. When the Pew Research Center began tracking social media adoption in 2005—the year that I first began to interview the participants in this study—just 5% of American adults used a social media platform, such as Friendster, MySpace, and Facebook.[2] By 2011—just 6 years later—that number had risen to half of all Americans.[3] As of 2018, 69% of the public (and 80% of Internet users) reported using some type of social media.[4] Facebook[*] is the most widely used of the major social media platforms—which enable users to interact and exchange pictures and messages—although Twitter and Instagram are also increasingly popular.[5]

These relatively recent advances in technology and social media have made it easier to connect to people across time and place, and have implications for the nature and frequency of communication between adoptive and birth families.[6] For example, the ease and convenience of texting and emailing, and messaging via Facebook, have the capacity to shift interpersonal communication in adoption away from more "traditional" means of communication (e.g., phone calls, mailed letters), potentially raising questions related to boundaries, control, and contact. (Indeed, in a recent study of lesbian, gay, and heterosexual parents with school-aged children, 42% reported using social media to connect with birth family; social media use was as common as email [41%] and phone contact

---

[*] Facebook is a social networking site aimed at connecting people with friends and family online. Users can post comments, share photos and links to news or other creative online content, play games, chat live, and stream videos. Within each member's personal profile, there are several networking components, including the "wall," a virtual bulletin board. Messages left on the wall (by one's "friends"—namely, those whom one has accepted into one's network) can be text, video, or photos. Facebook offers a range of privacy options. Members can choose whether to make all of their communications visible to everyone, they can block specific connections, or they can keep all of their communication private. Members can also choose whether to be searchable, decide what parts of their profile are public, and determine who can see their posts. Facebook also contains a message feature that allows people to communicate privately.

[41%][†] and more common than letters [38%][7]). In addition to facilitating direct contact between people who know each other, advances in technology and the Internet specifically has also made it easier to access information about, and reach out to, people with whom one has had no prior contact.[8] Further, even limited personal information (e.g., surname, city of residence, photos) can be used to find detailed personal information on the Internet and social networking sites, including phone numbers, email addresses, and home addresses.[9]

This raises the possibility that both birth family and adoptive family members might be the recipients of contact that they do not expect, and may not want. Social media sites such as Facebook, and the Internet in general, have the potential to introduce complexity into adoptive family–birth family relationships—for whom online contact might be a welcome extension of offline contact, a temporary or ongoing substitute for offline contact, or, in some cases, an unwelcome and unreciprocated medium of communication. Particularly in the early days of Facebook, adoption professionals often expressed caution and concern about the implications of social media for adoptive families,[10] but many contemporary adoption professionals situate Facebook in the context of larger discussions about open adoption. They see Facebook as one possible means of maintaining contact that warrants mutually agreed-upon guidelines and may work better for some families than others.[11] Indeed, amid the changing realities of the digital age, the majority of families—regardless of adoptive or biological status—are constantly revisiting and sometimes redefining the boundaries among family members and between families and the outside world.[12]

In this chapter, I describe the different patterns and functions of Facebook and social media in general, whereby some parents engaged it as a means of establishing or maintaining reciprocal contact, others engaged it "passively" (e.g., as a means of finding out details about the birth family), and still others did not desire or pursue such contact. I also briefly address parents' ideas about their children's future relationships with their birth family—relationships possibly facilitated by social media, and maintained without parental oversight or monitoring.

Family Vignette: Rick and Marcus

Rick and Marcus were a white gay couple in their early 40s living in a large city on the West Coast with their son Jack, who was also white. Rick worked as the director of a nonprofit, and Marcus was a graduate student. The couple had

---

[†] The study did not differentiate between phone calls and texts.

ongoing contact with Jack's mother, Sara, who was a teenager when she gave birth to Jack. Both men maintained Facebook contact with Sara, and they described how this had been beneficial to their relationship, enabling them to stay in contact in between visits (they lived in different states, hundreds of miles away from one another). Yet Facebook contact had also provided Rick and Marcus with a window into personal details about Sara's life that they otherwise would not have known (e.g., boyfriends, substance use). Both men interpreted Sara's willingness to share such details as reflective of her younger age, noting that she had grown up with a generation of youth who were used to, and comfortable with, their online lives mirroring their offline lives ("I think there is a bit of a generational gap, or certainly a maturity gap, between us": Marcus). When Jack was 5 years old, Rick shared:

> I'm glad to have that connection, but we do learn a lot of things that I guess it's better to know than not know. Because she's so much younger, there's kind of a generational difference in what 20-somethings feel comfortable sharing on Facebook. And so, she'll talk about going out drinking or going to her boyfriend's house or whatever. We don't ever comment on those things, or pass judgment on anything, or monitor [her behavior].

Both Rick and Marcus expressed their feeling that in order to preserve their relationship with Sara, it was necessary to respect her boundaries—which meant not responding in any way to behaviors that they felt were questionable or concerning. They maintained a strict policy of not commenting on her posts, choosing to limit their public comments on Facebook to their own page—such as when Sara commented on the photos of Jack that they posted. Rick said, "Any time she does respond to anything we post, I always reply back. [She'll be] like, 'Oh, he's getting so big! I miss you guys; hope to see you guys soon!' And we'll always say, 'I hope we can touch base next time we're in [city]!'"

Thus, Rick and Marcus appeared to follow a set of spoken and unspoken guidelines for social media use in relation to Sara. They did not comment on her page, but they commented quickly and freely—with positive affect—on any posts she made on their page. Both men were therefore quite purposeful in the way that they utilized Facebook and expressed feeling that it was helpful to their relationship by enabling a connection that was "convenient" and easy to maintain.

The Multiple Functions (and Faces) of Facebook

The families that I interviewed often invoked social media, and Facebook specifically, as a key medium of communication with the birth family. Among parents who had regular direct contact with the birth family, Facebook often provided an easy, inexpensive, and reliable means to maintain contact and share updates. For families who did not have regular direct contact, it presented opportunities for searching out and finding information about birth family members. In some cases, parents acknowledged passively "stalking" (monitoring)[‡] birth family on social media sites or elsewhere on the Internet, making note of information they felt might eventually be useful in helping to fill in details of their child's story. In fact, one of the appeals of Facebook is that the platform allows for "individual surveillance and mediated lurking . . . including creeping on others' sites (which involves scrutinizing a person's Facebook profile, photos, posts, and friends); stalking individual pages (through repeatedly accessing and viewing them in a short period of time); and watching what others post and interact online about . . . from a distance."[13] In this way, Facebook is a unique online context wherein both known and unknown audiences can gain access to posted content.[14]

Indeed, some families found information or images online that they downloaded to their computers or printed for future sharing with their child ("I did some Googling, and I printed out a picture I found, and an article about [birth family member] from the paper, so she could have it when she got older"). Some parents searched for birth family simply as a means of "keeping tabs" on them: That is, they monitored the Internet and social media sites for evidence that their children's birth family had moved, been arrested, or were still alive. Other parents acknowledged the temptation of social media as a means of accessing information about the birth family but claimed not to have used it for such purposes. Still others had such limited personal information to go on (e.g., no last names) that online searching for birth fathers was regarded as futile.

Parents who did not have direct contact with their children's birth family at the time that their children were school aged often acknowledged that their children would eventually be able to search for and possibly make contact with their birth family. These parents, as well as those who did have contact with the birth family, recognized that social media sites might eventually play a central role in facilitating their children's access to their birth family—and vice versa. This possibility sometimes created a sense of unease for parents, as they realized that their children would likely become more Internet savvy in the future—possibly alongside increased curiosity about and interest in establishing independent contact with birth family members.

[‡] As Chaulk and Jones (2011) note, Facebook, in particular, has spawned its own jargon pertaining to the profile browsing people engage in while using the social media site (e.g., "profile stalking," Facebook cyber-stalking," "Facestalking," "Stalkbook," "status-creeping," and just plain "stalking"; see p. 245).

Understanding and interpretation of parents' feelings about and use of Facebook and new technologies are enhanced through the lens of an emotional distance regulation framework,[15] discussed in Chapter 4. Emotional distance regulation refers to the process of negotiating, navigating, and (re)calibrating the closeness–distance dimension in adoptive family–birth family relationships, wherein adoptive and birth parents work to establish a mutually agreeable level of closeness—which may change or evolve over time (e.g., as comfort and role security increase). According to this perspective, the relational processes of connection and bridging, and separation and distancing, which are driven by individual differences in comfort level over time, underlie the contact dynamics between adoptive and birth families.[16] Contact can be viewed as "a dynamic process that ebbs and flows over time, characterized by establishing boundaries and managing intimacy across relationships in the adoptive kinship network."[17]

An emotional distance regulation framework, then, offers a number of useful tenets for understanding contact dynamics in adoptive–birth families. A complementary perspective is communication privacy management (CPM) theory, which defines private information as any information that causes people to feel some level of vulnerability, resulting in the desire to control dissemination of that information.[18] CPM theory proposes that individuals need to disclose private information to others but at the same time protect information from others in order to manage their relationships effectively. The theory, when extended to information shared via social media, distinguishes between individual and collective privacy boundaries. In the case of Facebook, personal information that an individual refuses to share with others on Facebook remains in his or her individual privacy boundary. However, once an individual posts status updates or photos, allows others to comment on their own Facebook page, or comments on others' posts or photos, this information is converted into a co-owned, collective boundary.[19] When individuals establish mutually acceptable parameters surrounding privacy (e.g., commenting on posts, sharing information online), this decreases the likelihood that there will be "breakdowns" in privacy (e.g., one person releases information in a way that is not acceptable to another). A lack of established privacy rules thus creates the possibility for miscommunication, hurt feelings (e.g., over the revelation of too much sensitive information), and relationship breakdown.

Adoptive–Birth Family Contact: Using Facebook to Bridge and Sustain Relationships

For parents who maintained contact with the birth family, Facebook was a unique mechanism for sharing photos and information about themselves—albeit often curated—with birth family members. Facebook also provided a means for some parents to engage with birth family members who lived far away, and with whom regular in-person contact was not possible. And it was often regarded as a far more convenient way to share photos and general updates as opposed to mailing photos and/or letters: Indeed, over time, many families who had regular contact with birth family gradually transitioned from sending snail mail to using email and social media as a way of exchanging photos and updates—a trend that other adoption researchers have also documented.[20] In this way, Facebook was a convenient, casual, and cost-free means of contact, thereby helping families to maintain, or sometimes initiate, relationships with birth family members.[21] Yet Facebook also presented certain challenges, as parents navigated the murky waters of appropriate online etiquette amid an often complex set of birth family relationships, which were sometimes tenuous and/or fluid in closeness and contact.

One example of a family that found Facebook to be an important means of staying in touch with the birth family were Stacy and Deb, a white lesbian couple employed as a school administrator and chiropractor, respectively, who lived in a midsized Northeastern city with their biracial (Latina/white) daughter Marlo. The couple initially had some contact with Marlo's birth parents, Krista and Jay, involving, for example,

> us send[ing] a card or something on Mother's Day and Father's Day. . . . On birthdays she will pick out presents for them. We really feel that . . . our jobs as parents is to facilitate Marlo's relationship with them and maintain that until she is in a place to make whatever decision she wants. (Deb)

Maintaining contact grew increasingly difficult, however, throughout Marlo's childhood, insomuch as Krista and Jay were not consistently responsive or even reachable. Their ever-changing housing situation resulted in returned packages, letters, and photo bundles, and frequently disconnected phone numbers, which translated to months of "not knowing where they were or how to contact them." Both Krista and Jay also battled ongoing issues with substance use and mental illness; in turn, a lack of contact was anxiety provoking for Deb and Stacy, who worried about their safety and well-being, wondering at times "if and when we'll hear from them again" (Deb).

This pattern of intermittent contact continued for years. Then, when Marlo was 8, the couple recounted how, about a year earlier, they had established a relationship with Krista and Jay on Facebook. Facebook served as positive source of connection for the two families, proving to be a more reliable, convenient, and accessible means of communication amid the constant changes in Krista and Jay's housing situation and phone numbers. Facebook also enabled Deb and Stacy to "quickly and easily ask questions" of Jay and Krista—questions that were frequently being posed by Marlo, as she grew more curious about details of her birth family. Stacy recalled, "I asked them, 'How many other birth siblings does she have?—because she has been interested.' And we found out from Krista . . . that she has eight siblings." The use of Facebook, then, provided Deb and Stacy with the opportunity to experience a more sustained connection to Jay and Krista, which helped to minimize their anxiety and concern about the couple's well-being as well as frustration surrounding unreciprocated contacts. In turn, they arrived at a level of contact that, though less than what Deb and Stacy would have preferred, was mutually agreeable and unmarked by tension.[22]

Both Deb and Stacy described their relationship with Krista and Jay in measured terms, framing it as positive and mutually respectful. Yet they were sensitive to the fact that as Marlo grew older, and became more cognitively and emotionally mature, she would inevitably become more attuned to the ways in which Krista's and Jay's personal lives were marked by instability and chaos, and to the challenges that they faced on a day-to-day basis. Deb stated:

> Her birth mom and dad suffer from substance abuse and mental illness. So that—they have always been great with us. But, those things may be very challenging for Marlo, especially as a young adult, as she initiates and expects to take on more of a relationship with them. It can be very hard and heartbreaking. I just have my eye on it, not in a bad way, but as a protective mom—and wanting to help her navigate those relationships in a healthy way, because they are going to be complex.

Deb and Stacy did, however, feel that contact via social media would be a positive and fairly "safe" way for Marlo to begin to connect with her birth parents, in that both women could maintain a watchful eye on their online social interactions and stay abreast of—and guide Marlo through—any potentially challenging conversations or dynamics that unfolded. Deb and Stacy were therefore optimistic about the positive potential of Facebook for facilitating independent contact between Marlo and her birth parents, while also recognizing that they would need to continue to operate as guides or "brokers" of this contact,[23] at least until Marlo felt confident to assume independent reins of this relationship herself.

Leila, a physical therapist, and Charlene, a teacher, were a white lesbian couple living in a midsized city in the Northeast who established contact with their biracial (Latina/white) daughter Sofia's birth mother, Jasmine, through Facebook. But unlike Deb and Stacy, they had had no contact with the birth mother until Sofia was school aged. One day, not long after Sofia had turned 6, Leila received an "out of the blue" Facebook friend request from Jasmine. Leila and Charlene were delighted, as they had longed for contact with Jasmine and had sent her many unanswered letters and photos since the initial placement. Yet upon recovering from the initial shock of Jasmine's friend request—which Leila immediately accepted—they realized that they needed to set some boundaries around their online social interactions. They were concerned about Jasmine's frequent "liking" of photos and posts, recognizing that people in their respective networks could see the two families interacting on social media and might ask questions about their connection. Leila and Charlene consulted with their adoption agency, who agreed that their caution was warranted and guided them to request less public interaction with Jasmine. Wishing to preserve Sofia's privacy (i.e., regarding her "story"), Leila and Charlene requested less engagement with their posts from Jasmine, who agreed. At least on the surface, these negotiations seemed to represent a successful and mutually acceptable "recalibration" of the boundaries of information sharing (i.e., rules surrounding disclosure and privacy), which restored some degree of equilibrium in their relationship.[24] Regarding the future, Leila recognized that eventually, "Sofia will be able to find these people in seconds, probably, when she has the technology." She further noted:

> Yes, Sofia can reach out once she's asking more [questions about Jasmine], but I think when she's asking more is when *we* reach out. To the extent possible, it's our job as parents to have a plan for that, and help her deal with the disappointment if [Jasmine and other birth family members don't want contact].

Both Leila and Charlene struggled to balance their desire for contact with Jasmine—something they had hoped for over a period of years—with a desire to protect their daughter, while also worrying that by requesting certain boundaries around online contact (i.e., privacy rules[25]) they would upset Jasmine and "scare her off" for good. They also recognized that even though Jasmine was seeking contact now—and specifically with them, and not with Sofia—Jasmine might not always be open to contact in the future, especially considering the many years during which she did not respond to their letters, photos, and emails. Thus, the couple juggled a complex set of feelings and concerns as they sought to establish shared expectations and mutually comfortable agreements surrounding contact.

In addition to being an easy (i.e., quick, convenient, and accessible) means for birth families and adoptive families to connect, Facebook sometimes appeared to offer other benefits over other forms of contact, such as being a more "neutral" and emotionally safe forum for connection. Eliza was a white lesbian accountant in a large city in the Northeast who had maintained regular contact with her biracial (African American and white) son Luke's birth mom, Amy. Over time, Eliza found that Amy seemed to favor Facebook over phone contact, inasmuch as Amy seemed concerned about calling them at inopportune or unwanted times. Facebook offered a way of connecting that seemed less intrusive than the telephone in that there was no immediate pressure on either party to respond to a post, photo, or message—and it seemed to be an acceptable, if not preferred, mode of contact for both parties. When Luke was 5, Eliza said:

> I think Facebook made it a lot easier [to connect]. I think Amy is a little afraid to call us, because she doesn't want to butt in, but she has no problem—like, when I call her, she always answers, and talks to Luke, and Luke talks to Reese [biological sister]. So I keep telling her, if you want to call, call. And if I don't want to answer the phone because I'm doing something, I won't answer the phone. Amy doesn't usually take the initiative to call. She waits for me to call her. But, like, now when I post things on Facebook, she'll respond to it, and like it, and vice versa: If she posts something, I'll like it or whatever.

Eliza's wife, Hannah, a white administrative assistant, observed that Facebook and texting had made contact with Amy easier, and had replaced photos and letters as a means of communication. And yet, echoing other families—like Rick and Marcus, whose story opened the chapter, as well as Leila and Charlene, described previously—Hannah highlighted the unique considerations that accompanied social media contact, wherein they were navigating their relationship in a semipublic forum. Hannah, for example, noted the need to remain careful about boundaries and language: "I think sometimes you have to watch what you say. Like, you have to do that anyhow, but especially on [social media]." But Hannah also pointed to the many benefits that she saw for Amy in particular—such as being able to witness Luke's development as it unfolded—sometimes in (almost) real time:

> I think it's good, because Amy can see how he's doing, and she doesn't necessarily have to . . . be worried about him as much, because she can see it pretty much as it happens. Last week we went on vacation, and we posted pictures as we were going, so if she really wanted to sit down and see how our week was, she could have. Some people think that's a little weird, but at this point, it . . . makes it a little bit easier.

Some families' primary concerns centered not on their own online behavior and how it might be interpreted or construed by the birth family, but on birth family members' online behavior. Some families—like Rick and Marcus—encountered mild discomfort in response to birth family members' Facebook activity. In their case, the birth mother's questionable disclosures (e.g., about drinking or boyfriends) were contained to her own Facebook "wall," or profile; she never wrote anything they viewed as potentially problematic in response to their own posts or photos. But in other cases, families had encountered mild challenges in this regard. Miranda, a white lesbian career services director in a large West Coast city, expressed that she liked being Facebook friends with the birth mom of her daughter Eloise, who was white, and saw numerous benefits of this mode of communication: "It just made contact easier; it seems to be a format that we can both deal with.... [For several years], Emily didn't have Internet access, didn't have email, and didn't necessarily have a stable address." At the same time, Miranda acknowledged that Facebook was "not my favorite format" and

> struggled with, like, when Emily has posted her personal stuff on my timeline: Do I leave it there? Do I not? And I've come to the conclusion that she's the one that put it there, not me: It's not a reflection of me, it's her process, so I've always left it there.

Thus, although Emily's self-disclosures—for example, sharing her mental health challenges or her feelings of missing Eloise—on Miranda's Facebook wall (i.e., her "timeline") were a bit unsettling, Miranda nevertheless did not feel compelled to ask for changes in her online behavior. For Miranda, who was "simply delighted" to be in regular contact with her daughter's birth mother, such a request carried the unwanted risk of offending Emily or losing contact with her—and Miranda's empathy for Emily ultimately outweighed and mitigated any irritation with Emily's emotional displays on her wall. Whereas another parent might have been frustrated and asked for or set certain boundaries on Facebook, Miranda was aware that such a request could lead to greater distance between herself and Emily, and she did not want to take this risk. Miranda therefore relaxed her own preferences surrounding privacy to accommodate Emily's apparent need for disclosure and sharing.[26]

Parents' concerns about privacy were magnified in the context of situations where their children's conception was a secret. Several parents described how their children's birth mothers had never revealed to anyone—or at least not their immediate families—that they were pregnant and/or had placed a child for adoption. The secrecy surrounding their children's conception, birth, and adoption made adoptive–birth parent connections via Facebook especially complicated and sensitive, whereby there was a need for a certain degree of caution by all parties ("she actually told her family that the baby had died, so I can understand her reluctance"; "our daughter's birth mother didn't tell her parents"). One couple who encountered this scenario was Roy and Dante, a white sales manager and African American vice president of operations at a small company, respectively, who lived in a large city on the West Coast with their African American son Ethan. Roy and Dante developed a very positive relationship with Ethan's birth mother, Liza, during the pregnancy, but she wanted minimal contact—through email only, and none with Ethan—postplacement. Liza's preference for this level and type of contact appeared to be driven by the fact that she had kept her pregnancy and the subsequent adoption a secret from most of her family. Email was preferred over phone contact, because "with email, there's a sense of privacy involved. She can express as much emotion as she wants, but it's [private]—whereas on the phone, there's more of a potential for interruption. She can't show her emotions because [her family members are] going to say, 'Well what was that about?'" (Dante).

The two families maintained "sporadic" email contact throughout Ethan's first 5 years of life, interspersed by periods of relative radio silence on the part of Liza. Then Dante joined Facebook, and soon after, he received a friend request from Liza. When Ethan was 9, Roy recounted the initial negotiation surrounding, and ongoing use of, Facebook as a means of communication:

> She friend requested me, and before I said yes—because we hadn't had very much contact with her—I told her, "Look I'm totally happy to be friends with you but you have to understand that 70% of what I post on Facebook is related to the family, and Ethan. So if you want to see him growing up and all that, I'm more than happy to be friends with you, but if you don't, you might not want my stuff to start appearing in your feed." She did, and I think that's very much in her nature; she is kind of shy, a little ... passive, and ... I think she cares about us and about Ethan but doesn't want to be a super active part of his life. But I think that sort of voyeuristic nature of Facebook has been a nice thing for her and, likewise, it's the same for us: We see what's going on in her life and with her kids, primarily through Facebook, with the occasional phone calls.

Thus, contact through Facebook had allowed Liza to watch Ethan grow up from a distance ("She knows what he looks like, she knows what things he does, she knows ... what his life is like": Dante) but also to retain a sense of privacy surrounding her pregnancy and decision to place Ethan for adoption. In this way, Facebook enabled Liza to maintain some degree of (digitally mediated) connectedness, without violating her sense of control over the parameters of contact.

Roy and Dante occasionally showed Ethan photos of Liza on Facebook. Although Ethan had never spoken to her, there was a "loose plan" for him to meet Liza when he was a teenager: "We'll think about going to [state] or flying her out and we can all meet up" (Roy). When Ethan was about 9 years old, Dante shared that Ethan had recently begun to express more excitement and interest about the possibility of meeting Liza, as well as her son—his half-brother. Reflecting his increased interest, Ethan had recently made Liza a holiday craft project. "That was the first time we actually made a really tangible connection [between] him and her. He never talked to her, but he made something specifically for her. And she was completely beside herself when she got it" (Dante). Thus, as children grew older, even among families in which birth parents did not want to have direct contact with children, adoptive parents found ways to "close the gap" and enable some type of communication between children and birth parents that would be acceptable to all involved.

Some parents reached out to birth family members via Facebook—often after an extensive period of deliberation and "working up the nerve"—but with disappointing results. Leigh, a white heterosexual woman employed as an assistant museum director in a small city on the East Coast, who had adopted her son Kevin, also white, as a toddler via foster care, had not had contact with his birth parents—who both had "significant substance abuse issues"—since his birth. The adoption was closed, with no contact—yet when Kevin was about 7, Leigh found herself growing increasingly curious about his birth family and wondering whether healthy relationships could ever be established with at least some extended family members. Leigh saw the potential benefits of maintaining some connection to Kevin's birth relatives—although not his birth parents, whom she described as "people who really struggled in life" who had made a series of poor life decisions that landed Kevin in foster care. Leigh joined Facebook in part out of a desire to search for Kevin's birth family, and soon after found several birth relatives. Leigh did not reach out right away, stating, "I wanted to wait . . . until I was absolutely certain that they were actually the people I thought they were." For several years, Leigh "snooped on Facebook, just out of curiosity, every couple of months, just checking in, to see if anything is going on that I might be interested in," but did not make direct contact. Then, Leigh determined that Kevin's uncle worked at a nearby business, and so she went to meet him, and gave him her family's contact information. Leigh began corresponding with Kevin's uncle and his wife, emailing with them every month or so. But contact was ultimately not as regular, reciprocal, or satisfying as she had hoped:

> She emailed me some photos, I emailed her some photos. I put them on our Christmas card list this year, so sent them a Christmas card with some photos. So, technically—I mean they have my information—my address, my phone number, my email address, and I have theirs, but they haven't really shown a lot of interest, which is sort of surprising. . . . I mean, from sort of watching them on Facebook, [it seems like aunt and uncle] have got loads of issues, so I am not terribly surprised not to hear from them, but . . . disappointed. I was actually hoping to hear a little more from them. And so far it's been me. Kevin does not have any sort of direct communication; it's just all been me emailing and sending photos.

Even though reaching out had opened herself up to be disappointed by the level of contact that ensued, Leigh nevertheless valued the contact she did have with Kevin's relatives, as well as the opportunity to "keep tabs" on the family on Facebook—although the constant monitoring did cause her some distress. She acknowledged that her husband, Billy,

> would probably say that I spend too much time thinking and worrying about his birth family ... [being in] poverty ... [and so on]. He thinks that I know too much and I spend too much time worrying about something that I have no control over. There is nothing I can do to help ... so it would be better not to even know.... But I also want to be able to answer Kevin's questions [down the road].
> [*Interviewer: So it is a source of information as much as it's a source of concern?*]
> Yeah, yeah. Exactly, yeah.

As Leigh's narrative reveals, one potentially difficult and disruptive side effect of such Facebook "stalking" was parents' knowledge of details about the birth family that were hard to bear, and about which they could do very little. Other families also described how they witnessed posts and photos on Facebook that led them to worry about birth parents' mental health, relationship functioning, and life choices—but did not feel that it was appropriate, helpful, or warranted for them to comment or in any way "step in."

Facebook contact, then, offered the possibility for (re)connection as well as disappointment. It was so "easy" to connect on social media—but these initial connections did not always lead to the sustained, in-person contact that parents desired, insomuch as birth family members' zone of comfortable contact was lower than that of adoptive parents.[27] Miranda, for example, was described earlier as reaching out to her daughter Eloise's birth mother, Emily, via Facebook after years of intermittent contact, wherein she and her partner, Shannon, sent letters and emails but Emily was frequently nonresponsive. Reconnecting via Facebook was significant to Miranda—but it did not lead, as she had hoped, to face-to-face contact with Emily. After reconnecting, she and Shannon had tried to arrange a visit with Emily, but, despite Emily's initially saying that she would "love to see [them]," the visit did not materialize. In fact, Emily "dropped off the face of the earth" during the period of time when Miranda was trying to finalize trip details: "She couldn't quite manage it." Then, Emily re-emerged on Facebook several months later. The Facebook contact the two parties did maintain was important in solidifying for Miranda that Emily was "very clearly connected to Eloise," even if Emily was not able or ready to meet her. On Eloise's birthday, Emily changed her Facebook profile picture to a silhouette of an infant, which, to Miranda, wordlessly communicated that Eloise was in her heart and thoughts— "but for whatever reason, [she] doesn't want to see her."

Like Miranda, Jessica, a white heterosexual homemaker in a midsized Midwestern city, had reached out to her African American son Jerome's birth mother, Carolyn, on Facebook, with the hope that it would lead to connection and contact. Specifically, when Jerome was about 5 years old, Jessica sent Carolyn a message with a picture of him but received no reply. Prior to this, their contact had been one-sided, with Jessica sending photos and letters. In turn, the lack of a response from Carolyn was consistent with prior interactions, but "very disappointing":

> His adoption was, I guess, technically open, or semiopen; I had her identifying information. She didn't have any of ours, but it was because she—kind of walked away. So I just contacted her—I tried to be as polite and respectful as possible; I don't want to invade her life, but if there's any chance—I mean, we believe in open adoption if it can be done in a safe way that is healthy. And so that's kind of how we approach it.

Over the next few years, Jessica tracked Carolyn on Facebook (i.e., her settings were such that Jessica could "watch" her, or view her activity even without being "friends" with her, despite not hearing back from her). Then, to Jessica's dismay, she "got off Facebook." Then, all of a sudden

> she came back on. And so I just happened to search for her and she was on, like she had her profile up again and so I just messaged her and I said, "Hey, can I talk to you?" and she said, "Yeah, what's your number?" and she called me! She's very, very pleasant and kind, and I said, "I apologize, I don't want to interrupt your life, but I just want to talk to you and give you an opportunity to talk to Jerome."

Paralleling Miranda's experience, Jessica also mentioned to Jerome's birth mother that their family would be "passing through" her state of residence in a few months, stating: "If you wanted to meet we'd love to," but also quickly adding, "I know I'm throwing this at you and I know this is a lot." In response, Carolyn said, "Yeah, let me think about it." Jessica recalled: "Her hesitancy made me think that she probably won't want to, but I felt like at least I threw it out there." Jessica's husband, Ned, a white engineer, provided a similar perspective, surmising that insomuch as Carolyn had other children, she was likely considering the implications of making contact in terms of "not just what her parents or sisters or brothers might think, but what her kids might think." In fact, the two families did not end up meeting—but Jerome did ultimately speak to his birth mother on the phone, which elated Jessica: "It was great; it was really cool. I think he has no idea what's going on, but for me and for us that was pretty cool." Ned shared:

Carolyn didn't take Jessica up on the offer [to meet], but we're hoping that maybe she might change her mind at some point. [We'd love to] actually see her and visit her, and hang out at [our house] together. I don't know what she told her family—so I could see that it might be quite some time before she might be comfortable with saying, "Okay, now I want to build a relationship."

For some families, then, Facebook did not facilitate the level and frequency of contact that they had hoped for but offered a more consistent and reliable medium of communication than mail or phone contact had achieved. It was also seen as better than nothing. Indeed, Mariette, a white lesbian physical therapist in the suburban Midwest, had hoped for more contact with her biracial (African American/white) son Jacob's birth parents than had come to pass, but nevertheless felt that Facebook served as a useful form of communication:

I recognize that his birth parents, Didi and Jim, do not really have the means to travel and to come to visit. They absolutely have the means to write on Facebook or something . . . and [our hope] is that when Jacob gets a little bit older, he can get on Facebook, read, message, type, just to feel a little bit of a connection. So, that's where we're at. We are currently planning another visit [especially] with Didi and his birth sister, who we saw at the last visit. So yeah. Still, the communication now isn't really what we pictured, what we would like.

Jenny, Mariette's partner, echoed her sentiments, asserting that the level of contact with Jacob's birth parents was less than they had envisioned, having "really wanted more from an open adoption, but we'll take what we can get."

Maintaining connections with birth siblings. In several cases, parents who adopted via foster care had relied on Facebook and social media as a means of sustaining relationships between their children and their children's birth siblings, who had been adopted via other families. Maintaining contact with the parents of these siblings on Facebook enabled them to show their children pictures of their siblings and to keep track of what these children and their families were "up to . . . what they're doing." Vincent, a white gay director of telecommunications in a large city in the Midwest, shared how he maintained contact with his 6-year-old African American son Ayo's birth family—including siblings and cousins—via Facebook and texting: "We share and put up pictures on Facebook. Ayo doesn't have a Facebook account, so I sometimes will show him pictures of his cousins or siblings when they are posted." This family also maintained ongoing contact offline with these family members too, arranging in-person trips with one of Ayo's siblings, a boy named Gamba, at least twice a year.

These parents often spoke to their appreciation of the convenience and ease of Facebook for maintaining connections, in that their children's siblings typically lived far away. Facebook therefore served as a valuable tool for relationship maintenance.[28] Chuck was a white heterosexual IT director in a Northeast suburb, who had adopted his son Grayson, also white, via foster care. Five years postplacement, Chuck shared that he and his wife, Annie, maintained contact with the adoptive parents of one of his son's birth siblings, Christian, almost exclusively via Facebook:

> It's just so much easier than trying to make a phone call at the right time or trying to drive, because of the distance involved.... You can find out [information] relatively quickly without having to call everybody or send postcards to everybody; it's just so much easier to stay in touch.

Annie agreed, saying: "I do have the cell phone numbers for the parents, but we really do just use Facebook. It's just easier; everyone just uploads photos and we can see everyone's photos." Notably, Facebook was perceived as even more essential 3 years later, when Chuck wanted to stay in touch but also felt that it was appropriate to keep some distance from this family, as Grayson's brother Christian was having a "hard time":

> He was older when he was adopted, and he may remember more of some bad, neglectful experiences from when he was younger. So maybe as he gets older, we will have more contact with him. But I think it's probably best, just the way things are now—[keeping in touch] through Facebook and email.

Amid challenging life circumstances wherein in-person contact might be difficult or unwise, Facebook provided an ideal way to maintain "connection at a distance."

Passive Facebook Contact: "It's a Way In"

In some of the stories described earlier, adoptive parents monitored or "tracked" their children's birth family on Facebook prior to eventually reaching out to them. In other cases, parents tracked (or, in their own words, "stalked") birth family members but never reached out to them. Their decision not to friend or directly message birth family members on Facebook was grounded in a variety of reasons, including not wanting to intrude on their privacy, not feeling "ready," or concern about making contact after seeing "disturbing details" about birth family members online. Yet in some cases, parents stored or saved the information they obtained—sometimes printing out hard copies as well—to give to their child at some point and/or facilitate future searching. This type of activity—that is, the saving of data—represents one perhaps unanticipated consequence of releasing one's personal information into the collective privacy boundary of Facebook.[29]

Travis, a white gay father employed as a technical writer in a large West Coast city, expressed concerns about respecting the privacy of his 5-year-old Latino son Samuel's birth mother, Adalia, as the principal reason he had not friended her on Facebook—although he noted that his partner, Brent, "look[ed] up her page on Facebook from time to time." Travis felt that this type of behavior was "a little bit of a slippery slope.... I just feel like—it feels a little bit like peeking into her window." After a pause, Travis stated:

> Also, I don't necessarily want to by chance find out some information that I don't want to share with Samuel. I don't want to feel like I have to keep a secret from him. So that's the other side of it. I just feel like that I'm somewhat invading her privacy by doing it.

(Notably, several years later, it was Adalia who "friended" the couple on Facebook—and Travis found that this type of contact "actually made things a whole lot easier" in terms of communicating with and maintaining a relationship with Adalia. Further, Travis said, "Now, I can let Samuel know that she is aware of what he is doing—the successes and the joys in his life, and that she is seeing what he looks like.")

A number of parents in semiopen adoptions (i.e., those mediated through their agencies) described hesitation surrounding using the information that they had discovered online to contact birth family members directly. For example, Christy, a white lesbian director of a nonprofit in a midsized city in the Northeast, had stumbled upon information about the birth mother of her daughter Arielle, who was white, online. Noting that Arielle's birth mom, Ann, had not historically reciprocated contact to the degree that Christy had hoped, Christy had not used this information to reach out to her directly, noting that she wanted to "respect her privacy." Rather, Christy hid this information away for the future: namely, for when Arielle was older and wanted to "track her down on Facebook, things like that." Christy noted that her first obligation was to her daughter, and so she felt strongly about storing away the information she had acquired: "I know her full name. She lives in [city]. So, I suspect if Arielle has an interest when she's a teenager, then ... she could probably find her on the Internet." Likewise, Carly, a white heterosexual history professor in a large Northeastern city, who had a "semiopen" adoption, had searched for her African American daughter Eve's birth mother online but was not yet ready to make contact. Similar to Christy, Carla framed her decision to "hold off" as rooted in respect for her daughter's birth mother's decisions and preferences surrounding privacy. Noting that she did mail Eve's birth mother letters and photos every 6 months but had never heard from her, Carly not wish to "disturb" her with a more direct method of contact, such as an email or Facebook message:

> We had such a nice initial encounter with her birth mother, so when things do happen, I think, "She would be so proud! Wouldn't it be so cool to tell her this?" But I need to recognize that ... maybe she doesn't want to be found right now. I want to be respectful of that too.

At times parents possessed or discovered information about birth family members that mitigated their enthusiasm about reaching out to them online. One heterosexual father, for example, had found evidence that members of his son's birth family were involved in illegal activities and "had a lot going on" and, in turn, felt strongly that he and his wife needed to hold off on making direct contact: "Not everybody out there is a good guy, and if we randomly went out there trying to seek potential family members, without any understanding of what their backstory was, we could be inviting the wrong type of people into our family's life." In a similar situation, a heterosexual mother had discovered via online searches and Facebook "stalking" that her son's birth mother "is kind of trouble . . . she's in prison." This information, coupled with her knowledge that the birth mother had placed her son for adoption amid ongoing criminal involvement—gave this mother pause in reaching out. This mother also contemplated if, when, and how she would share and process this information with her son: "He doesn't know. I am kind of waiting for the right time to break that all down for him."

One gay father shared how, because of the sensitive circumstances surrounding his son's placement, he did not want to reach out directly to his son's birth father, whom he had found online, via the Internet or Facebook. Specifically, this father noted that "part of the reason the birth mom gave him up was because when she got pregnant, the birth father wanted her to abort him, and so they broke up over it." This father had, up until recently, possessed very limited information about the birth father ("the only things we know about him are from the birth mom"). In turn, he "downloaded everything [he] could" from the birth father's Facebook page, "every picture, all of his interests, where he was born, where he went to school . . . pictures of him," so that his son "could have it one day. He will want to know where he came from." A few years later, when his son was 8, this father expressed how glad he had done this when he had the chance, because the birth father's Facebook privacy settings had changed, and now he could no longer view the information that had previously been easily accessible. Armed with the information he had obtained and downloaded previously, this father said confidently, "We kind of know how to find him if we ever did want to."

In a few instances, parents had indeed been curious enough to "stalk" their children's birth parents online yet expressed no interest in reaching out. Their curiosity was satisfied by what they found, and they did not discuss any potential benefits of making contact—for themselves, their children, or the birth parents. One heterosexual mother said, "I mean I know she has a Facebook because I've stalked it, and she may have done the same although most of mine's private. But she's never tried to contact me through any social media or anything." When asked if she would ever reach out to her son's birth mother directly, she said: "No. She has problems. I don't know what good could come of [direct contact]." This mother, then, had a strong desire for distance from her son's birth mother—in the sense that she did not want reciprocal contact, imagining only negative consequences of such contact—but at the same time, she did crave information about her. Facebook provided this mother with an opportunity to access such information anonymously, and seemingly without direct contact or relational consequences.

"I'm Not Comfortable With That": Avoiding or Resisting Facebook Contact as a Means of "Preserving Boundaries"

In a few cases, families had ongoing contact with the birth family—letters, phone, email, and/or even in-person visits—but resisted the idea of Facebook as a means of communication. Phil, a graduate student, and Eddie, a physical therapist, were a white gay couple in a midsized city in the South who had maintained a lot of contact with their multiracial daughter Anastasia's birth mother, Elle, during the first 2 years postplacement, including weekly emails and monthly visits. By the time Anastasia had turned 2—and Elle had another baby, whom she chose to parent—their contact had gradually diminished to monthly emails and yearly visits. A year later, when Anastasia was 3, their email contact had further diminished in frequency, to about every 2 to 3 months, with yearly visits. Both men felt positively about their current level of contact and did not want to introduce Facebook into the equation, feeling that it might introduce new "stress." When Anastasia was 5, Phil surmised:

> In hindsight it was actually a smart move to constrain it to only email. We've got each other's phone numbers, but I think it helps take out stress that I've heard from other people, about birth families popping up and wanting to be parts of their life on Facebook or on Twitter. [So I think] just always having been highly controlled about that [avoids] just another source of stress. I think not friending the birth mother on Facebook was an early and probably important thought about how I wanted to manage the relationship. And I will say, whenever she

emails me, I email right back. Like, priority; I email her right back. I think if you asked her, I try really hard to be accessible. Accessible on kind of these terms.

Thus, Phil was committed to maintaining contact—within the parameters the families had initially set about acceptable modes of contact. Unlike families who adjusted their primary methods of contact to accommodate texting and social media, Phil was not interested in this, feeling that doing so could lead to situations that might be difficult to control—such as lots of extended birth family members "friending" them on Facebook. Significantly, Phil described himself as highly accessible to his daughter's birth mother, noting that he quickly responded to any emails that he received from her—but at the same time clarified that his accessibility was on "[his] terms," meaning he was reachable via the modes of contact that he had established as acceptable. Phil viewed Facebook as a potentially disruptive mechanism of contact, with the potential to open the floodgates on role confusion and boundary crossings. Phil therefore took a "preventive" approach to the privacy and boundary challenges that could accompany interactions on social media, as opposed to a "corrective" approach: By avoiding online interconnectedness, he sidestepped potential challenges in this arena.[30]

Donna, a white nonprofit manager, and Max, a white communications manager, were another couple who resisted the idea of establishing Facebook contact with their biracial (African American/white) son Ace's birth mother or birth grandmother, despite maintaining fairly regular contact via email and text messaging with both women over Ace's first 5 years. Like Phil, Donna was not open to Facebook contact, seeing it as a boundary violation (or potentially leading to boundary violations), as opposed to an extension of their existing relationship. When Ace was about 5, Donna explained that she and Max had, up until a few months ago, exchanged at least monthly emails and text messages with both women, with about one visit per year. Currently, though, Ace's birth mother, Gloria, was "dealing with some mental health issues," resulting in some concerns on Donna's part about future in-person visits. Donna asserted:

> It's great that . . . this relationship has stayed intact this whole time, and it feels like it is, for the most part, kind of a sure thing . . . and we'll continue to [do visits] if she's comfortable and we're comfortable. But, like, now she's not very stable, so we are a little reluctant.

Donna also noted that both Gloria and Gloria's sister (i.e., Ace's birth aunt) had recently "tried to add Max and I on Facebook," which Donna was not comfortable with:

It kind of crossed the boundary, and we didn't accept [the request]. We don't want them to know every detail of our lives. So . . . so we didn't accept that. I mean, in terms of communication, we email and, and we text, and I've been in contact with her . . . and that's about it.

Max was aware that not accepting their friend requests could be experienced as a rejection by Gloria and Gloria's sister, and he had tried to couch their decision to decline such requests in the context of his and Donna's Facebook habits: "We just told them in an email that . . . email is more private . . . and also, we don't go on [Facebook] much. I tried to put it like that."

When her daughter Morgan, who was white, was 8, Shoshanna, a white heterosexual project manager in a small city in the Northeast, shared that she had maintained continuous contact with Morgan's birth family, including her birth parents, Leanne and Tucker, throughout Morgan's childhood. This contact included yearly visits, and pictures and letters every 3 months. Over the years, Shoshanna had increasingly relied upon email to send the pictures and letters—but also continued to create bound photobooks for Morgan's birth family every holiday season. Both families had each other's addresses and phone numbers—"there's nothing top secret about that"—although they did not typically talk on the phone. Yet at the same time that contact was fairly regular and Shoshanna had not made an effort to conceal identifying information, she nevertheless maintained a separate email for communications for the birth family, preferring to "keep aspects of our lives separate." And when Morgan was 5, Shoshanna emphasized that she was not open to being "Facebook friends [with them] or something like that." In explaining why this was an important boundary for her, Shoshanna said: "I think they're living their life, right? So [this way] it's not like they're—it doesn't feel intrusive." When Morgan was 8, Shoshanna continued to draw these boundaries between the two families, stating:

We do use email. We have a separate email account that we email to them with. But we don't use anything else. I think . . . Facebook is problematic. We haven't integrated Morgan's birth family with our day-to-day family events. I don't know if we will. . . . When Morgan is an adult she can then decide if she wants to integrate them more fully, but for us the open adoption and the way that we all communicate for us is 100% for Morgan. Her birth father's [relatives] wanted to be able to Skype with Morgan, and wanted more contact, and wanted us to leave Morgan with them for a weekend, and we were like, "No, no that's for you. We are not here for you. . . . Morgan is our daughter. And we are fine with her knowing you . . . but that does not mean we are going to leave her with you for a weekend. Boundaries."

To Shoshanna, then, communicating and interacting via Facebook had the potential to muddy the boundaries that she had delineated between their family and Morgan's birth family. Such a prospect was unwelcome and undesired; indeed, Shoshanna, unlike some other families, was satisfied with the current type and level of contact and did not have an interest in expanding their agreement to include new forms of technology or a greater intensity of contact.

In a few cases, parents were not on Facebook and did not want to join. Hence, this was cited as the primary reason for not establishing social media contact with their children's birth family. For example, Lena, a white heterosexual operations manager in a Northeastern suburb, had ongoing contact with the birth mom of her son Joey, who was white. However, Lena emphasized that she was not on Facebook and did not intend to join the social media platform because she regarded it as a

> huge time sink.... I email to keep in touch with people I need to, but I don't go on Facebook. So, his birth mom, Mandy, doesn't see me there, and I don't see her there. I know it's old school, but I do [online photo albums] and send them out to her and her parents. And obviously I text them and send pictures and stuff like that, but Facebook—no.

Thinking About the Future

Families who had contact with the birth family, especially on social media like Facebook, sometimes discussed what they saw as a natural or inevitable evolution of contact: That is, their child would eventually take more of the initiative in managing birth family relationships. Parents expected to guide and facilitate the evolution of that contact—both offline and online. For those with positive relationships with the birth family, the prospect of this contact was typically viewed neutrally or positively. When her daughter Eloise, who was white, was 8, Miranda, a white lesbian career services director in a large metro area on the West Coast, said that she supposed that Eloise would eventually connect with her birth mother and birth siblings via social media:

> Yeah, I think she probably will. It seems like it's such a big part of so many kids' lives. I could imagine, when she has the tools to do that on her own, that she might do that. And she's definitely an independent creature, so what she wants, she will try to do.

Yet even parents who felt relatively positively about the prospect of their children developing independent relationships with their birth family sometimes expressed discomfort about the unsupervised nature of online contacts in general, noting that the idea of their children engaging in unmonitored online conversations and relationships was "disturbing; I'm not ready for that yet!" As Leigh, a white heterosexual assistant museum director in a small city on the East Coast, reflected:

> There will come a point in time where Kevin will have his own Facebook account or email account or whatever the technology will be, and then there will be the issue of him having unmoderated communications with his birth family. But right now I still have control over it. . . . I'm not ready to let that go yet.

Research suggests that negative interactions between birth and adoptive families typically result in less contact over time.[31] Similarly, research has highlighted that negative (e.g., intrusive or violating) interactions on social media may cause individuals to recalibrate their disclosure norms (i.e., what they typically share online), as well as their online privacy settings (i.e., who gets to see what).[32] In turn, some parents described how, in response to difficulties with boundaries or communication (which they often attributed to birth family members' mental health issues), they had taken steps to decrease contact or place greater restrictions on contact. These parents expressed concerns about their children's "taking the reins" of that relationship in the future, both online and offline. One heterosexual mother, who had approached open adoption with a high level of enthusiasm and commitment, shared that by the time her daughter was 5, she had developed significant concerns about the birth mother's increasingly erratic behavior and evident emotional instability. After this birth mother displayed some explosive and unpredictable behaviors, which included showing "blatant disregard for our privacy" online and offline, this heterosexual mother sought to establish some new guidelines related to their relationship and ongoing contact. In turn, when thinking about her daughter's future relationship with her birth mother, she said:

> We just don't know about—just the two of them. . . . We don't want to prevent her from having a relationship with her birth mother. We just want—you just don't always know which version of her you're getting. To the extent that we're able, we want to help negotiate the relationship for our daughter until those times we're not able to do that anymore.

Speaking specifically about her daughter connecting with her birth mother on social media, she said:

It concerns me a lot. The reality is, she is going to have conversations with her birth mother that are unsupervised at some point. That scares the hell out of me, because [birth mother] has some very strange notions at times that her children are going to come back to her. And I think [about] an impressionable teenager—obviously years down the line—but when she gets there, I think that could happen with technology, with Facebook . . . cell phones, texting . . . and who knows what's around the corner. [Daughter] is going to have contact with her and all we can do is just prepare her as much as possible. Instead of protecting her all the time, I think we're trying to give her a little bit more reality in pieces that she can actually digest.

Donna, a white heterosexual nonprofit manager in a large city in the Northeast, maintained ongoing communication with her biracial (African American/white) son Ace's birth mother and birth grandmother—but no Facebook contact. In thinking about the future, Donna—like the previous mother—was concerned about how Ace's birth mother's mental health issues would impact the type of relationship that unfolded between them. Donna shared her sense of unease ("it concerns me") while also acknowledging its inevitability: "Once he knows how to search on the Internet, he can pretty much find out any information that he wanted to. And because it's an open adoption he can easily find out their last names." Similarly, Adam, a gay biracial (African American/white) marketing director in a West Coast suburb, was aware that his son Isaac, who was also biracial (Latino/white), would inevitably be able to find his birth family members ("I'm sure he will search. . . . When you've got a name and Google, you can pretty much find anything you want"). Yet at the same time, Adam hoped to prepare Isaac for the reality of what he might find—family members who might not match his fantasy, and people who "don't really want anything to do with him."

Parents balanced their desire to shield their children from disappointment or worse with their awareness that their children would eventually come face to face with the reality of their birth families' difficulties and challenges—challenges that were often the reason they were placed for adoption in the first place. Still, amid awareness of birth family members' emotional challenges, substance abuse history, and criminal activity, the prospect of their children making contact with birth family members was a source of concern for some parents: "She's got a lot of psychological issues and substance abuse issues and it makes her kind of unpredictable and dangerous," said one gay father. Another gay father said:

I think he will use the technology to try and find more about them when the time comes. [The big] concern I would have is if she is unstable with him, in terms of her relationship with him. You know, I am going to be very protective of him. Part of what her illness does is, she will love you until she hates you. And then once she—she has borderline personality, so once she flips, she will hate you like nobody's business. And I am very afraid that he will experience that personally... and we will have to deal with it.

For families that did not have contact, the idea of their children finding their birth family on Facebook—or the birth family finding them—was especially likely to be described as unsettling. Miri, a white lesbian artist in a large Northeastern city, did not have contact with her African American daughter Ava's birth mother—she didn't even "know her last name"—but also mentioned wondering if it might be "in some paperwork somewhere." Reflecting on the likelihood that Ava would probably search for her birth mother or other birth family members in the future, and that such searching would probably start online, Miri said:

> I'm positive that she'll be curious. And I just want to do all I can to help her answer the questions that she has. And my feeling is whatever she needs is fine with me as long as she's safe. The idea of her going out online and meeting somebody is like super scary—not because of it being her biological family, but because of her meeting a stranger on the Internet. So my biggest concern is her safety. Anything she wants me to find or whatever—I would just try to facilitate that in a safe way using the agency.

Parents who had either previous reciprocal contact with the birth family that had become one-sided (i.e., the birth family had stopped responding) or consistently one-sided contact with the birth family (i.e., they had never gotten a response) often described the possibility of future online searching and contact in positive, hopeful terms. These were families who had typically desired more openness than ultimately unfolded and remained hopeful for a future increase in contact, especially between their child and the birth family. Carly, a white heterosexual history professor in a large Northeastern city, had voiced interest in pursuing an open adoption but matched with a birth mother who was working with an agency that predominantly facilitated semiopen (i.e., agency-mediated) adoptions. When her daughter Eve, who was African American, was 5, Carly expressed frustration with the agency, which "had not kept in touch with her; [despite] imposing on us that this is a semiopen adoption, they [haven't lived up to] their responsibility to keep track of both parties." Carly had looked for birth family information online and was hopeful that she had uncovered enough details to aid Eve in searching later on:

> I've gotten to the point where I have her birth mother identified in a person search, which is just preliminary information, and I could take it further if

I wanted to. I just check that every now and then to make sure that there's some preliminary lead that I could go off of on the Internet.... Should my daughter want to pursue that further at some point, it hopefully won't be that difficult to take the next step and [pay] to get the current address or something. I'm not on Facebook, so I haven't tried that—it would be a reason to join if Eve was pushing us to get in touch with her birth mother and the agency couldn't help us.

At the same time that these parents were hopeful about the possibility of future contact, they were typically aware of and sensitive to the possibility of nonresponse or rejection. Dave, a white gay radiologist in a large city in the Midwest, had emailed with his 8-year-old Latino son Aidan's birth mother, Keira, for several years, until she abruptly stopped responding to their emails. They had no other contact information for Keira. Aidan was upset by this and expressed a persistent desire to be in touch with her. Like other families, Dave and his partner, Byron, were cautious about reaching out, not wishing to intrude or overstep boundaries, yet they remained interested in the possibility of making contact—and were in fact aware that Keira was on Facebook. Dave explained:

A lot of it came up after Mother's Day. That was the trigger. Aidan just got really emotional and just got really upset and started crying, and was wondering why he couldn't see her. So we started thinking about it. And then he's asked a couple times, "When will I see her?" So [after consulting with our old adoption agency social worker], we just decided we'd try to make contact. Keira is on Facebook—we're not friends or anything; we just know she's out there. So there's possibly a way we can get in touch with her. The plan is that we would just send a general Facebook message and say, "Hey we're thinking about you; hope you're okay; if you wanted to contact us, that's great, and if you're not comfortable, we understand" and go from there. The reality is that she may not want to, and Aidan may not get the opportunity, and that may just be how it is. So it's just more of putting out some feelers and just seeing if she responds.... It's going to take me some time to process if she says she doesn't want to have any contact. That would be upsetting for me, and I know it's going to be hard for Aidan.... So we're thinking of doing that pretty soon, just because he's been asking more. And I think at some point when he's older, he'll be able to do it on his own, and he may just track her down. But for now, we'll just get an idea of whether or not she's remotely interested.

* * *

Adoptive families used Facebook in many ways: to sustain relationships, to establish connections, and to find out information. For some, it was a valuable means of communicating and maintaining contact, especially when relationships were positive and physical distance prevented regular visits.[33] For others, Facebook was a convenient and emotionally safe means to (re)establish communication with birth family members—such as those who had previously been inaccessible. For still others, it provided a window into birth family members' lives, allowing them to lurk without being seen, and enabling them time to figure out their "next move" with regard to contact. Notably, parents were on Facebook; their children, in contrast, were typically not yet teenagers and did not yet have access to social media. Thus, parents typically spoke about their children's social media access (and use of the Internet and social media to connect with birth family online) in the future tense.

As Chapter 10 discusses, these children will inevitably have access to the Internet and will be able to use the information that they possess about birth family to search for additional information about them. Furthermore, amid the recent rise in genetic ancestry testing via websites such as ancestry.com and 23andme.com, there is the growing possibility that these youth will employ these services to find out more information about their background—particularly if they sense that their parents are not telling them everything.[34] Thus, in an ideal world, parents will increasingly (a) communicate with their children about the reasons they have, or have not, sought out contact with birth family via social media; (b) help their children to develop responsible and safe social media etiquette; and (c) remain open to the possibility or probability that their children will probably search for their birth family online and be available to support them through that process. This searching can be scary for both parents and children—yet online information seeking can be a potentially powerful means of assuming agency and managing uncertainty for adopted children.[35]

Notes

1. Hampton, Goulet, Rainie, & Purcell, 2011; Webb, Ledbetter, & Norwood, 2015.
2. Pew Research Center, 2018.
3. Pew Research Center, 2016.
4. Pew Research Center, 2018.
5. Ibid.
6. Black, Moyer, & Goldberg, 2016; Farr, Ravvina, & Grotevant, 2018.
7. Farr et al., 2018.
8. Hertlein, 2012.
9. Kearney & Millstein, 2013.
10. Fursland, 2010a, 2010b, 2013.
11. Black et al., 2016; Greenhow, Hackett, Jones, & Meins, 2016; Siegel, 2012a.
12. Sharajevska & Stodolska, 2015.

13. Child & Starcher, 2016, p. 2.
14. Child & Petronio, 2011.
15. Grotevant, 2009.
16. Ibid.
17. Farr et al., p. 11.
18. Child & Petronio, 2011.
19. Child & Starcher, 2016.
20. Farr et al., 2018; Siegel, 2012a.
21. Greenhow et al., 2016.
22. Grotevant, 2009.
23. Dunbar et al., 2006.
24. Grotevant, 2009; Petronio, 2002.
25. Child & Starcher, 2016.
26. Child & Petronio, 2011.
27. Grotevant, 2009.
28. Hertlein, 2012.
29. Child & Starcher, 2016.
30. De Wolf, Willaert, & Pierson, 2014.
31. Dunbar et al., 2006; Grotevant, 2009.
32. De Wolf et al., 2014; Hertlein, 2012.
33. Fursland, 2010a.
34. Dawn Smith-Pliner, Friends in Adoption, personal communication, August 21, 2017.
35. Powell & Afifi, 2005.

9

Absence and Ambivalence

How Birth Fathers Fit Into Adoption Stories

Few adoption researchers have focused, in depth, on the gendered nature of adoptive family dynamics.[1] Yet there are numerous ways in which gender interplays with adoptive family processes—including the marginalization of both adoptive fathers and birth fathers in the adoption process, leaving "women to address emotion, connection, and communication."[2] This chapter deals with birth fathers—and the ways in which they were often implicitly or explicitly marginalized in the adoption process, as evidenced from the narratives of the adoptive parents I interviewed.

As a number of authors have observed,[3] birth fathers have been largely invisible in adoption discourse for a long time, and for a number of reasons. During what has been termed the *forced adoption* (or "baby scoop") era, which occurred between the mid-1940s and the early 1970s, unmarried women who became pregnant had few options and were often pressured to "give up" their "illegitimate" children. Adoption was often presented as the only option, and little to no effort was made to assist women in parenting their own children. Further, it was generally assumed that the fathers in these situations did not care about the women or the children—if they were even informed about the pregnancies.[4] Among those fathers who did know about the pregnancies, some fought to keep their children, even amid the shame and secrecy associated with "out of wedlock" pregnancy. Indeed, unmarried couples were severely scrutinized during this period and regarded as an inappropriate context for raising children.[5]

In fact, until the 1970s, unmarried birth fathers were not necessarily even parents in the legal sense, insomuch as birth mothers often listed the birth fathers as "unknown" on birth certificates. Then, several Supreme Court decisions during the 1970s recognized birth fathers as legal parents—and some states' laws have elevated their status further.[6] Today, birth fathers can contest adoptions where they were not informed of the placement. Yet at the same time, in many contemporary adoptions, the birth father is treated as either an afterthought or a legal problem.[7] Birth mothers may have personal reasons for not wanting to involve the birth father in the decision making surrounding the adoption or the adoptive placement itself, as well as, in some cases, not even naming the birth father as the known father.[8] No social worker or lawyer can force a birth mother to name the birth father if she is determined to keep his identity a secret—and she very well may be, if she believes he will want paternity rights or visitation. In turn, a birth mother who wishes to avoid birth father requests, demands, or involvement might state that the pregnancy resulted from rape or that she did not know the birth father's name when she engaged in sexual activity with him.[9] Importantly, adoptive parents can choose to decline to work with birth mothers who declare the identity of the birth father unknown or a secret.

Birth fathers who are aware of an unintended pregnancy vary in their response to the situation. Some men—perhaps in part because of larger societal pressures (e.g., to provide) or ideologies (e.g., of birth fathers as peripheral)—do avoid involvement or responsibility. Others care about the pregnancy and the baby but are not encouraged to participate in the adoption process, in part due to societal stereotypes of birth fathers as "unsuitable" to be parents,[10] which may further inhibit them from imagining and/or asserting a role in the child's life. Indeed, birth mothers are typically front and center when the possibility of openness is being considered, whereas the role of and contact with birth fathers may not even be part of the conversation.

In turn, some birth fathers do disappear, for their own reasons, or because they feel there is not a place for them postplacement—due to the birth mother's or the adoption professionals' unflattering characterizations of them (e.g., as uncaring, callous, and/or sexually promiscuous, or as uninvolved and hard to reach, and therefore problematic[11]). Notably, among children who lack information about their biological parents, it is often especially difficult for them to find their birth fathers. Children tend to first search for their birth mothers, who may be the only ones who know the birth father's identity—but are not necessarily open to providing it (e.g., they may possess ongoing anger or resentment toward birth fathers), leaving children with little information to go on in their search.[12]

Research on birth fathers' involvement in open adoptions is scarce. Most research that addresses birth parents focuses almost exclusively on birth mothers (even when terms like *birth family* or *birth parents* are used[13]), in part because of the reality that birth fathers are simply less likely to be involved in the initial adoption arrangement or ongoing contact.[14] But the use of neutral terms like birth parents obscures the reality that birth mothers, not birth fathers, are most often the focus of adoption research, policy, and practice.[15] In addressing birth fathers' lack of inclusion in studies, researchers typically cite their "unavailability or unknown whereabouts."[16] There are exceptions to this trend, however—one being a recent study that explored 323 matched parties of adoptive parents and birth mothers and a sample of 112 birth fathers.[17] Notable findings from this study included that (a) birth fathers' perceived choice or control in determining the degree of openness was positively associated with their satisfaction with the adoption experience and (b) birth fathers' reports of level of openness were positively associated with their satisfaction with the adoption experience and postadoption adjustment. In other words, birth fathers who felt a sense of control in determining openness parameters were more satisfied with the adoption, and birth fathers in more open adoptions were also more satisfied with the adoption and showed better psychological adjustment after the adoption. Another study found that the presence of birth father contact was associated with satisfaction with birth father contact among 167 adopted young adults—thus showing how birth father contact has the potential to benefit not only birth fathers but also the children themselves.[18]

Another relevant study examined 107 adoptive families in open adoption arrangements—including lesbian, gay, and heterosexual parent–headed households—and reported on families' contact with specific birth family relatives of their school-aged children.[19] The researchers found that 88% of families reported contact with birth mothers, 48% with birth grandparents, 33% with birth fathers, and 30% with birth siblings. No differences by family type were found except with regard to birth fathers: Intriguingly, gay fathers were more likely to have had contact (52%) than heterosexual parents (29%) and lesbian mothers (22%)—perhaps in part reflecting gay fathers' shared gender with birth fathers as a facilitative factor in contact. Lesbian mothers were more likely than other family types to say that they desired more birth family contact than they currently had. Other studies that ask about contact with specific birth family members have also found that adoptive families are much more likely to have ongoing contact with birth mothers than with birth fathers.[20]

This chapter addresses birth fathers—but often in the context of their absence. Terms like *negative space* and *in the shadows* (a term that Mary Martin Mason used in her 1995 book, *Out of the Shadows: Birthfathers' Stories*)—come to mind when I think about how parents talked about the birth fathers of their children. Despite the fact that our interview questions probed experiences, impressions, and beliefs related to the birth family or birth parents, many participants responded to these queries by speaking about birth mothers only. There were, however, exceptions. Some parents—particularly as time unfolded—became increasingly interested in their children's birth fathers. And some families did have ongoing contact with birth fathers, as we will see.

Of note is that in this chapter, as in other chapters, no names are used when the specific family circumstances being referenced are particularly sensitive (e.g., they involve emotionally charged information that some family members are unaware of). This chapter in particular contains a number of these sensitive circumstances.

Family Vignette

"He waived his parental rights.... He already has three other children who he doesn't see." This is the single statement that one lesbian prospective parent made in reference to the birth father during the entire postadoption interview. Such a paucity of explicit discussion of birth fathers was typical of the interviews in general. Again, even though the interview questions were constructed in such a way that they probed first for general birth parent experiences and beliefs, many interviewees responded to these general queries by referencing birth mothers only.

Typically, contact with birth fathers was not established initially—which made it quite difficult to track down or establish contact with birth fathers later on. Often, parents not only did not have contact with birth fathers but also possessed very little information about them—a lack that sometimes became more unsettling over time, as children grew curious and asked basic questions that parents could not answer. More often than not, parents who lacked birth father information tended to adopt a strategy of avoidance. As the lesbian mother referenced previously stated, when her daughter was 5:

> I don't want to deny that she has a sister—and she actually has a half-brother too, on her birth father's side, but her birth father—we've never met him, we've never had conversation with him, he's never really acknowledged her, so we have not been open with her about talking about that. And it doesn't come up.

By age 8, her daughter had been "talking more about her sister," who was being parented by her birth mother, with whom the family had intermittent contact. Yet this mother had still, at this point, not told her daughter about her half-sister—in part because this revelation would introduce the topic of her birth father, with whom they had no contact, and about whom they knew "almost nothing." Regarding the birth father, this mother stated that she would probably

> Talk to [daughter] about him at some point but at this point it's not really something we ever discuss.... So far she hasn't asked, and since the birth father is not really part of the picture, she's never really asked about it. When she does we will say everything that we know about him but at this point, we haven't [brought it up].

Difficult or Uncertain Circumstances Surrounding Placement: How Birth Fathers Become "Invisible"

Many families matched with birth mothers who declined to name the birth father or claimed to know very little about him. For example, one heterosexual mother who had matched with a birth mother in another state said, about the birth father:

> We have no information about his health or his family history.... He is "unidentified," is what they say. In [state], this is as a category that you can designate— so she was only able to say—she didn't have any information about the birth father; it was a one-night stand, basically a guy she met at a party. In [state], it's a little weird.... If a man has any sense that he may have fathered a child, the responsibility is on him to go ahead and register with the birth father registry with the state and then they can get potential information. So, the birth mother was probably advised by this agency that it's going to make things a lot easier if this is a one-night stand. He has no reason to believe that he was a father, and if she wanted things to go more smoothly and easily, then it's just easier to not identify him. I don't know ... I guess ... it sounds a little bit tricky—yeah, like maybe she was told not to identify him specifically.

This mother was a bit rattled by the information that she gleaned from the adoption agency. She and her husband talked extensively about the potential match and the "tricky" story that the birth mother was telling, and "whether this was something we could live with ... in a situation where everything else sounded really good." She noted too that the birth mother was working with an agency that was

> very different than the agency we worked with.... The people we worked with [are] so all about openness and transparency and how that's important for the mental health of all parties involved, including the adoptive child. The folks there ... the way they were doing adoptions is how they were done in the 1960s—much more closed off [and] private and protective of information.

This mother struggled to reconcile the guidance and education that she had received from her agency about the benefits of openness and honesty for all members of the adoption triad with the reality that the birth mother's agency was operating in a manner that seemed secretive and "old school." This woman's husband described the situation similarly:

Birth mothers can basically just say that they don't know who the birth father is [in state]. It's a little odd. . . . It's probably really an easy thing to do to just say, "Oh, I don't know who that is," so they don't have to get permission or whatever. [I think] they have to publish something in [the] paper, some kind of notice that a person is making an adoption plan. But [saying you don't know who the birth father is] is an easy way for the agency to get out of doing any follow-up on birth fathers.

When birth mothers declined to identify the birth fathers or asserted that they did not know their names, this presented a challenge for prospective adoptive parents, wherein they desired more information—but did not want to upset or alienate prospective birth mothers by insinuating that they doubted the veracity of their claims. In turn, many parents were left to "take the birth mother at her word," in one mother's language—that is, to accept that the birth father was unknown or that the birth mother did not have sufficient information to contact him, even if they doubted her claims or suspected otherwise. The difficulties of not knowing the identity of the birth father persisted over time. When his son was 5, one gay father shared that his "lack of knowledge of the birth father" was an ongoing challenge—for example, in regard to the "question marks" regarding his son's racial/ethnic and medical background. Specifically, this father shared that his son's

birth mother says she met the birth father the night she got pregnant at a party, and that there has been no contact since; she does not know how to get in contact with him. So there is kind of a big blank mark there in terms of what his history is.

In another case, a lesbian couple had been told by their agency not to question the birth mother about her story that her child had been conceived through rape. Yet this couple continued to have questions about the story 5 years later, as they struggled to navigate the lack of information they possessed about their daughter's birth father, and wondered whether and how they might address this issue with the birth mother. One of the women put it like this:

We don't [know] anything about the birth father so it's an issue because we need to know a little bit more. The agency told us that she was conceived from rape, and we—I never want to disbelieve a woman who says she was raped, you know? But there was something, something I was like . . . I don't know. There's something missing here, even though we knew so little about it. . . . But the agency had said to us don't mention it, and if she brings it up and wants to talk about it, that's fine, so we were like OK. So we didn't mention it, she didn't bring it up, and then she's never brought it up since. But all this time, I've [thought] that we probably should try to bring it up. Not that I want to make her relive any bad memories, but we need to know a little bit of information. I would like to know a little bit of information and so . . . we're having an open adoption. We're seeing her. It's going great. Let's just let it come up naturally, which I'm always a fan of letting it come up naturally, but now, it's been 5 years and it's never come up, and—you know how when you wait to bring something up, then it's weird to bring something up? So we have that issue now . . . and she has some mental health issues [so I don't want her to go into] some tailspin of whatever, depression, but . . . [daughter] is 5 now. We need to give her a little bit of information. She's going to start asking at some point, and we need a little bit of foundation to [know how to proceed] . . . just a little bit of information. [Birth mother] knows more . . . and I feel for her; whatever it was it must have been sucky and we care about her and don't want to make her feel bad—but it's just a weird situation.

This mother felt caught between her desire to respect the birth mother's clear desire for privacy and her wish to provide her daughter with even "a little bit of information." She was conscious of the risks of asking for information—for example, to the relationship they had established, and the birth mother's well-being—but she was also aware that her daughter was "going to start asking" about the birth father and wanted to be prepared when she did.

A similar situation was described by a gay father, who, when his daughter was 5, had continued to wonder about the birth mother's account of her pregnancy (i.e., that it was the result of a rape) but was told by the agency social worker not to press her about it. This father did not want to jeopardize the relationship with the birth mother—who was a teenager at the time of the pregnancy and, he suspected, possibly dating someone older than 18—but also did not want to tell his daughter that she was conceived by rape if it was not true:

She said that [daughter] was conceived during a rape, which is a huge deal, and it's something that we're going to have to talk to [daughter] about, and it's something that I'm open to talking to [daughter] about. However—no, trust me, I'm a feminist, you know, if someone says this happened to them, I am with you 100%. But given everything else that she talks about, I wonder: Is there someone after that was not a rapist but a boyfriend that did not work out? Who could have had the opportunity to meet [daughter]? Not now, but maybe eventually? I don't want to tell [daughter] that the fairytale of her life is that she was conceived in rape. If that didn't happen, that's going to be a lot for her, so it's tough. I'm worried to ask the birth mother questions; I don't want her to freak. But I'm going to have to talk to her about this because I don't want to have to tell [daughter] that story if it's not true.

A lesbian mother also described this scenario, noting that the birth mother "said that it was an unreported rape" and that the caseworker they worked with "said that we really do need to disclose that to [son] at some point—in age-appropriate language. I am really not looking forward to that." What gave this mother particular pause was the fact that the caseworker "told us that she saw a case where somebody said that but then as it turned out, actually it was her boyfriend, and—you know? There is a lot—there's a lot of them that say that, and it might mean something really different than what we're thinking." In turn, this mother concluded that "when we do say that to [son], we'll share with him the full story—but we'll also say we don't really know what that means. But maybe by that point we'll have contact with the birth mother, and she can explain it to [son] herself."

In some cases, birth mothers did identify or name the birth fathers—but ultimately these men were not part of the adoption plan. For example, one gay father described how his daughter's birth father wanted "nothing to do with the situation. . . . He wanted her [birth mother] to have an abortion from the beginning." In turn, "we've never met him, we've never emailed with him, and we've had no contact whatsoever." Another gay father shared that his son's birth father was aware of the adoption plan ("He had to be served with papers, so he knows about it. . . . He knows the baby was born, that he's been adopted . . . his parental rights have been terminated"), but he and his partner were unsure of how to engage the birth father, because the birth mother did not want anything to do with him ("she finally did give us his email, but requested to keep her out of it"). Since their priority was maintaining contact with the birth mother and they did not wish to alienate her, the couple did not reach out to the birth father—although they kept it in mind for the future, as they had "heard he has a daughter and we would like [child] to know her sister someday."

In some cases, the possibility of establishing a positive relationship with the birth father was thwarted or undermined by the tense legal interactions that preceded the adoption. One gay father shared that his son's birth mother was a teenager who became pregnant by an "undocumented worker . . . in his 20s." In turn, the dual issues of both statutory rape and immigration status meant that "lawyers were involved." Because the birth father in this situation did not want to relinquish his rights initially, this couple "hired a lawyer . . . to kind of convince him why he would lose if he challenged." Notably, at no point did this man or his partner discuss the possibility of engaging the birth father in discussions about openness or postplacement contact. In turn, it is perhaps no surprise that the birth father disappeared after the birth and subsequent adoption. In another case, a heterosexual mother described how the birth mother of her son denied knowing who the birth father was—and then the agency "found the birth father; he had just been released from jail after 4 years from the state prison. And he petitioned for custody. But then on the day of the trial he didn't show up." Noting her relief at this outcome, this mother noted that they never heard from him again after that.

In a few cases, birth fathers were described as angry about the birth mother's decision to place the child for adoption, and therefore cut off contact with the birth mother and adoptive parents during the pregnancy or soon after the birth. One lesbian mother stated:

> He was furious that the birth mom placed our daughter for adoption, though he couldn't step up and do anything—he chose not to do anything—so he's rageful and he's got some pretty severe problems of his own, and has wanted nothing to do with her or us, so we've never had contact.

Significantly, in several cases, adoptive parents found themselves surprised when birth fathers were actually involved in the adoption process, reflecting the reality that whereas birth mothers' connection to their children is often taken for granted, birth fathers' investment is questioned and must be "proven."[21] In turn, birth fathers who pushed for involvement were viewed with suspicion. One heterosexual woman described her anxiety when, preadoption, the birth father of her daughter was more engaged and interested in the adoption process and the prospect of openness than she had expected. This woman had been prepared for openness with a birth mother, but her agency had "never really talked about birth fathers being involved." She mused:

> I never thought I'd have to deal with the birth father. I really thought—I was really shocked [that he was involved], because you never read anything about it online. You never hear anything but how they relinquish their rights and then most of the time they don't really even really care. But he's like totally actively taking this role. It just seems odd to me.

Despite her apparent hesitation regarding her daughter's birth father's unexpected involvement, this woman ultimately formed a positive relationship with him. Yet as she notes, she was unprepared for "hav[ing] to deal" with the birth father, suggesting that her adoption agency—which did promote openness—may not have sufficiently described the range of openness arrangements that could unfold, or the potential benefits of birth father involvement. Had this birth father not been so persistent about being involved, he might have been "counted out" by the birth mother and the adoptive family. It is easy to see how a birth father in this situation, where he is expected to disappear, could easily disengage.

Had this woman's adoption agency effectively prepared this mother for birth father involvement (e.g., via preadoption discussions about him or by recommending educational resources that promote a balanced, constructive perspective on birth fathers), she might have been less surprised about and more open to such involvement. Indeed, adoptive parents who feel sufficiently prepared by their agency for contact tend to experience more empowerment and satisfaction surrounding open adoption.[22] Adoption professionals, then, play a powerful role in shaping adoptive parents' views of the birth father.[23]

When Birth Fathers Are Absent: Families With No Contact

To understand how birth fathers were viewed and described by adoptive parents and the role, or lack thereof, that they were presumed to have in children's consciousness, it is necessary to explore adoptive parents' narratives about birth mothers. Parents often only invoked birth fathers in relation to or in contrast to birth mothers—who were regarded as more psychologically significant, whether or not they were physically present. Shortly after the adoptive placement, one heterosexual mother, who had an open adoption agreement with her son's birth mother, mused: "His birth father—maybe he'll want to know about him eventually, but . . . he'll know his birth mother. So I don't know if he'll ever say, 'Well who's my father, or birth father?'" Likewise, even when the birth mother and birth father remained a couple—which was the single most important predictor of whether birth fathers had some level of contact and involvement with adoptive families postplacement—birth mothers were sometimes regarded with more reverence than birth fathers, especially by gay fathers, who lacked a female presence within the parental unit. Said one gay father, shortly after placement:

> With [daughter] having two dads, it's very important to us that she knows that she has a mother and father—but mostly that she has a mother. If [birth mother] wants to be part of that, great. I hope [that our contact with both parents] does last, but they're young, and who knows where they're going to be in the future.

By the time that their daughter was 5, the birth parents in this scenario were no longer a couple—and although the gay couple had ongoing contact with the birth mother and her extended family, they had "no contact" with the birth father. The birth father reportedly "never at any time wanted to see her" and thus "we've never had any correspondence with him at all."

Parents' presumption that birth fathers would occupy a less central position in their children's consciousness, or identity, influenced whether and how they solicited their involvement—not only during the process of establishing contracts surrounding postplacement contact but also throughout their children's early childhood. One gay father acknowledged that he had expended significant effort to "keep tabs" on his son's birth mother during the first 5 years of his life. Regarding his son's birth father, however, he stated:

> I have no contact with his biological father. I never have. I had one phone conversation with him when he was first born and he was just—he said he wanted me to know that he had agreed fully with the adoption plan and that he felt that the baby was better off with us than with his mother. That was the extent of the conversation. After that he sort of disappeared. I think he's in prison too, somewhere. But I've lost track of him.

As children grew, they sometimes began to ask about their birth fathers. Some parents seemed genuinely surprised by this, having anticipated their children's questions about birth mothers but not having expected a similar level of curiosity about birth fathers. This was particularly the case among gay fathers and heterosexual parents (i.e., couples where a man was present). Gay fathers tended to be attuned to the fact that a woman was not represented in the parental unit— and were especially interested in cultivating birth mother involvement (e.g., see Chapters 3 and 4). By extension, a few fathers seemed to assume that because their child had two dads, they would not be especially interested in the existence and meaning of a "birth father." One gay father, for example, shared that his 5-year-old daughter had asked him questions about her birth father in the context of trying to grasp how "a man and a woman make a baby." In turn, this father was "thrown off guard" inasmuch as he, by his own admission, had not given his daughter's biological father, who was unknown, much thought:

> The "where do babies come from" conversation got extraordinarily in depth because, you know, she just keeps asking, "Why?", leading me down this road. So she started asking about her biological father. It never even occurred to us that she actually has a biological father too. She kept asking about it, and we didn't know, and she wanted to know exactly how a man and a woman made a baby and I told her, "Sweetie, it's just human nature," and kind of changed the subject [*laugh*]. Talking about her biological father, that was harder—just because I don't know him and I wasn't—I never think about him, so it wasn't something I was prepared for.

Even when children had not yet begun to ask, some parents worried about future birth father–related conversations with their children. They often had little information about birth fathers, and were unsure of when and how to share the sketchy and incomplete details that they did possess. One gay father who had contact with his 8-year-old son's birth mother shared that his son "understands that she's part of his family, part of our family." This father noted that he did not know much about his son's birth father; in fact, he was unsure about whether the birth mother was even certain of his identity. For this reason, this father had not discussed the birth father with his son. Considering the future likelihood of more in-depth, engaged conversations with his son about his birth father, he said:

> I think that's going to be a little hard. I mean, I'm anticipating the question will come up at some point. He's on the cusp of becoming old enough to . . . understand what a birth father means and understand what it means to not know who the birth father is. I think that could become a potentially painful topic for him. I'm not sure what we're going to do when that question arises, but I think I would encourage him to ask his birth mom, and reach out to her and see if she can say anything about it.

Often, the incomplete details that parents did possess about birth fathers were less than flattering or favorable, creating additional concerns regarding how to talk about these men in such a way that was honest but not overly negative. One heterosexual mother explained how her 5-year-old daughter was now asking questions that indirectly referenced her birth father—namely, asking why her birth mother placed her for adoption but was parenting her half-sister, who had a different father. This mother worried about having to share what she did know with her daughter: "I just hope she doesn't ask too much about it but that's probably because I don't know much about him. I don't know if he's incarcerated or what the deal is there."

Likewise, when his son was 5, one gay father noted that he had begun to think more about whether and how he would eventually share certain sobering details of his son's birth father with him. Such details included criminal activity and history of violence, and were a key reason he was not interested in maintaining contact with the birth father in the first place:

> Because we see his birth mother [regularly], [son] and I talk about stuff [pertaining to adoption]. The only thing that we haven't talked a lot about with him is his birth father. That's because he hasn't asked a lot of questions about his birth father. He doesn't see him. We don't want them to have contact, but he does have a picture of his birth father. . . . He doesn't have a great story, so—so it's going to be hard. It's going to be hard explaining to him that he comes from a dad that doesn't have a good story.

Parents struggled to determine the best way to talk about the challenging circumstances that sometimes surrounded birth fathers. In regard to drugs, criminal involvement, and prison, parents often articulated that they had or would discuss such issues in terms of "poor decisions" that birth fathers had made.

A few parents invoked broader dynamics such as poverty and racism, which served to contextualize these "poor decisions," and also softened the "finger wagging" implications of their commentary about these men. In other cases, such as when abuse, sexual assault, or rape was implicated, parents struggled a bit more. One lesbian mother, who had been told that the birth father was abusive to the birth mother, said simply, about her son: "He does know he doesn't have a dad. But he did ask me about his birth father, which we don't talk about—ever—and he's never met, never will meet, because he's a jerk." Another lesbian mother talked through how she might talk to her 5-year-old daughter about the issue of rape that was implicated in her story:

> She hasn't asked about her birth father. And that's a little sensitive. Her mother said that it was an unreported rape. So we don't really what to—you know, I mean, we're going to have to share that with her at some point. But at this point she doesn't know what rape is anyway. I wouldn't want to put that word in the head and have her blab it to a hundred people, you know? Like, it wouldn't be appropriate. So I might have said something like, "You know, I don't think your mother was in love with your birth father." Or, "I don't think your mother was very close to your birth father." Something like that.

Sometimes, though, parents were less avoidant of these difficult topics, planning for how they might talk about these issues in ways that would be developmentally appropriate and also not explicitly denigrating to birth fathers. A heterosexual father of an 8-year-old boy shared his "vague concern" about how he would talk to his son about his birth father's extensive criminal rap sheet as well as the fact that he was currently in prison for charges related to sexual assault and rape. However, he did plan to talk to his son about these issues, stating: "As time goes on, I think it's going to be one of those things where [he learns] portions of what's going on [gradually], as opposed to, he didn't know any of it and now it's like a ton of bricks."

In a few cases, parents described an even more direct approach to sharing difficult or complicated details about the birth father. One gay father, for example, stated that he had never "shied away" from talking to his son about his story—which included details that were unpleasant as well as some that were uncertain or unknown. When his son was 6, this father said:

> Since he's been a baby we've talked about adoption. We have not hesitated to tell him his life story.... He knows that we're not sure—that there are two men that could have been his father, we think one of them is his father, but we're not 100% sure. One of them is in prison for assault. We've talked with him about how to live with that uncertainty.

When Birth Fathers Are Present: Families With Contact

Significantly, some parents did describe their children's birth fathers as involved in the placement process. Such involvement was most common when the birth mother and birth father were in a committed relationship. In these cases, birth mother resentment or negativity toward the birth father was typically not an issue, and adoptive parents often reported positive initial interactions with both birth parents. One lesbian mother, Jenny, a white medical supply company manager in a Midwestern suburb, shared that her biracial (African American/white) son Jacob's birth father, Jim—who was in a relationship with the birth mother, Didi—was quite involved in the placement. Three months postplacement, Jim responded to their emails with positivity and support, saying on one occasion, " 'We're so glad you met us.' You know, just complimented us." Eddie, a white gay physical therapist in a midsized Southern city, shared a positive impression of his 3-month-old multiracial daughter Anastasia's birth mother and birth father. Speaking about them as a collective, he described them as

> good kids. I feel sorry for them, and I feel so fortunate that we have Anastasia, and to have taken them out of a situation [like this].... It's good that we can talk with them and they can see Anastasia and see that she's doing well.... Every couple of weeks we call and every month we let them see her.

Stacy and Deb, a white lesbian couple in a midsized Northeastern city, employed as a school administrator and chiropractor respectively, described themselves as very engaged with both the birth mother and birth father during the placement process. Immediately postplacement, the couple created a photo album for the birth parents "that was addressed, like, 'Dear Jay and Krista,' instead of like, 'Dear Birth Parents,' or whatever. And we tailor[ed] it a lot to the few things we knew about them by that point" (Stacy). Both adoptive parents were in the room when their biracial (Latina/white) daughter Marlo was born. Deb recalled "how excited they were that it was a little girl, and how excited the birth dad was to get to cut the umbilical cord." Both Stacy and Deb valued open adoption, and desired ongoing contact with Jay: "I hope he'll have an influence, her birth father.... We just don't have a lot of male friends."

Ongoing contact with birth fathers was, again, most likely to occur when the birth parents were a couple—at least initially. These families were the most likely to have established an open adoption agreement with both parents, as a unit. Shoshanna, a white heterosexual project manager in a small city in the Northeast, explained that, as of 3 months postplacement, "the birth mother and birth father are involved. So if they were to split up we would have visits with both of them, so two visits once a year." In some cases, the birth parents' intimate relationship did ultimately dissolve, but families were able to maintain contact with both birth parents. Benji, a white gay dermatologist in a large West Coast city, shared that they had maintained a very positive relationship with his 5-year-old Latina daughter Ryanne's birth parents, Emmy and Luis, even though they were no longer together. Benji shared:

> It's not a taboo topic for us. We talk about her birth parents all the time. She'll put something on and I'll be like, "Is that the dress that Luis gave you?" ... It's so open and not taboo. We just treat it all so matter of fact, and I think that's how Ryanne internalizes it. And ... we correspond and send pictures ... two, three times a year. And we have a visit with them once a year. That is going to change going forward, because Emmy has moved to [city] and Luis is still in [city]. So, going forward, we'll probably have a West Coast visit with him and an East Coast visit with her.

Sometimes, birth mothers were relied upon as the conduit to birth fathers—even when they were no longer in a relationship. Daniela and Heather, a white lesbian couple employed as a store owner and bookkeeper, respectively, were living in a midsized Southern city when they established a "very open adoption" with Joy, the birth mother of her daughter Stella, who was white. Throughout Stella's childhood, Daniela, Heather, and Stella traveled at least once a year to visit Joy and her extended family in another state. They also maintained regular email and Facebook contact with Joy as well as Joy's mother. The family did not have much contact with Stella's birth father, Danny, visiting with him only once or twice when Stella was very young. Indeed, Danny was not in regular touch with either Joy or the family—and he had not expressed the same level of interest in or commitment to ongoing contact as Joy had. When Stella began to ask more questions about her birth father at around age 7 or 8, "suddenly there were pictures of Stella's birth father in my email—because Joy happened to see him and thought that Stella and us would like to have it someday so she asked him if she could take the picture" (Heather). As Stella's questions intensified—and she began to imagine reasons why Danny had not been in touch, and also made connections between her own interests (art) and talents and his professional background (designer)—Daniela and Heather reached out to him, through Joy:

> We just had to have a conversation [to] set her mind at ease. So I said, "You want to—you want to *talk* to him?" "Yes." And so we reached out to Danny through Joy, and Danny actually—he made himself very available, which was nice, and quite a gift. So he was able to [have] that conversation with her.

This story serves as an example of how a strong and flexible relationship between adoptive families and birth families can serve the child as their information needs and interests evolve over time. Heather and Daniela actively pursued contact with Danny when Stella requested it. Joy facilitated this request, and Danny agreed to it. All parties, then, were active players in supporting and honoring Stella's desire for contact with and information about her birth father.

It is notable that in a number of cases, parents expected or hoped for birth father contact in the future, even if it had not been part of their original arrangements. Erin, a white lesbian librarian in a large West Coast city, shared her hopefulness that her son's birth father—whom she sent yearly letters and photos via the adoption agency—would be open to contact in the future. According to Erin:

> he had said that when Jeremy is a teenager if he wanted to contact him it's fine. So that's an option in the future. We would encourage that if that's what Jeremy wanted.... I think the birth father was thinking that, like, when he gets into that rebellious phase and is pissed off and wants, you know, answers—he's like, "I'll talk to him."

Often, the possibility of contact with birth fathers was tied to the willingness and efforts of birth mothers to facilitate such contact. One heterosexual mother who maintained contact with her son's birth mother shared that the birth mother had recently "friended the birth father on Facebook because she wanted to kind of keep that contact in case our child wanted it, in the future." In other cases, birth fathers actually reached out to birth mothers with an interest in pursuing contact. One gay father shared how his 5-year-old daughter's birth father, who had not been involved in the beginning, had recently "contacted [birth mother] who then contacted me" about potentially establishing contact—but so far it was unclear as to whether such contact would come to pass:

> There's been some ... sort of preliminary, very tentative outreach from her birth father. But he's not followed up, on sort of what he needs to do in order for us to have contact. We want him to contact the adoption agency, and, and talk—we want him to have the same sort of orientation and understanding of what our relationship means, and what an open adoption relationship looks like, what are his legal rights, what are not his legal rights, some of those kinds of things. Because he was not part of the adoption. So we don't want to start this relationship without a sort of, the established support structure in place and some kind of information for him before we start meeting.

Gendered Dynamics in Relation to Birth Fathers

As noted, certain gendered dynamics arose in regard to how adoptive parents related to birth fathers. Among heterosexual parent couples especially, children's questions about birth fathers sometimes seemed to evoke surprise—the underlying, not always acknowledged sentiment being, "you already have a father; why would you wonder about him?" In a few cases, the possibility of jealousy by heterosexual fathers specifically was raised. One heterosexual mother shared these thoughts about her 8-year-old son's birth father, and how her husband might feel if the birth father were to become involved in the future:

> Over the weekend I said, "Oh, [birth mother], have you talked to [birth father]?" We've never met; he just signed off all rights and didn't want any visitation. And she said, "Yeah, I actually talked to [birth father] this weekend, and he always asks about [child]." She always says he's going to write us a letter. He's . . . not mature himself even though he's [in his 30s]. It's funny because every time she says he's going to do something—and he never has—I always wonder how my husband's going to feel, because you know what, he only has one dad. I have to deal with the birth mother and grandmother. I'm like, how would my husband feel if he met his birth father? I always wonder.
>
> [*Interviewer: Have you ever asked him?*]
>
> No—I don't know, I should. It never really came up because we never thought it would ever be an option, but I'm like, if he ever did meet him, I wonder if my husband would be threatened. [Birth father] and [son] would never have a close relationship so I don't think my husband would be threatened.

Another gendered dynamic that arose concerned children's interest in and curiosity about birth fathers, wherein boys were often described as displaying greater curiosity about birth fathers than girls. This tendency was especially likely to be noted by parents who adopted two children, a boy and a girl, who were therefore able to comment on differences they observed between their two children in this regard. One lesbian mother mused:

> We haven't been talking about "daddy." We've been talking to her about [birth mother], her birth mom. Because she knows [birth mother] is her birth mom, and she was born to her, and she couldn't take care of any babies at that time so we got to have her in our family. . . . She knows these things. The truth [is] we, we almost never talk about her birth father. . . . She doesn't have the same questions—[son] was very interested in birth daddy. But [daughter] doesn't seem to be.

Like gay fathers who spoke easily about birth moms as "moms," several lesbian mothers used the word "daddy" or "dad" in loose reference to the birth father, reflecting the lack of personal relevance of such a term when it came to their own parental roles. Lesbian mothers were also the most likely to state an explicit desire to ensure birth father involvement, given the absence of men within the parental unit ("she's got enough moms; she doesn't have, you know, a dad"). One lesbian mother spoke about her ongoing hope for contact with the birth father "someday"—even though he had not yet been involved in her 5-year-old son's life to date. This mother explained that the birth father's circumstances at the time of the placement (i.e., he was in prison) precluded his involvement; yet she had consistently sent him letters and photos via the agency, hopeful that he might someday make contact, especially given evidence that he had turned a corner in his personal life and was making "better decisions." She said: "He has moved on and gotten married. . . . So, he's trying to make something, trying to do something." In turn, this mother saw the possibility for a "positive relationship that [child] could grow and nurture." In the meantime, she made an effort to acknowledge the existence of the birth father and speak positively about him: "We're never negative about him; whenever we talk about him we talk about how nice-looking he was and how sweet he was and what a great smile he had."

Talking About Birth Fathers: Navigating Conversations Over Time

As children developed more sophisticated ideas about family, reproduction, genetics, and race, they also, in some cases, became more aware of and curious about the existence of birth fathers. In turn, as they increasingly grasped the notion of "birth father," they sometimes asked questions that took their parents by surprise. For example, one gay father explained how his 8-year-old son surprised him by suddenly asking, in the middle of a conversation and amid the presence of extended family, "Daddy, who is my birth father?" With a laugh, this father recalled that there was a "pregnant pause . . . because we didn't know what to say. [The whole family] had no idea what was going on." Then, this father "explained to him that we know don't know who his birth father is and we had made efforts to search but we weren't able to find out more."

Birth fathers were sometimes invoked, either explicitly or implicitly, when discussing heritage, culture, race, ethnicity, and skin tone. Benji, a white gay dermatologist in a large West Coast city, noted that amid his Latina daughter Ryanne's growing curiosity surrounding genealogy and ancestry, her birth father Luis's Mexican origin "frequently came up." Notably, it was much more difficult to avoid the subject of birth parents, and birth fathers specifically, when their children were a different race than their adoptive parents. One lesbian mother, Lindsey, a white physician assistant with an African American daughter named Ava, for example, stated that the multiracial nature of their family meant that people in her community—a large metropolitan area of the Northeast— frequently queried her; her partner, Miri; or Ava about the details of their family-building route and/or Ava's background. Lindsey stated that she typically responded to outsiders' questions about their family structure by saying, "in a positive way . . . 'Yes, I'm her mom.' Or, 'Yes, she has two moms.' Or, 'Yes, her birth father is black.'"

In contrast, another lesbian mother tended to hesitate about sharing her 5-year-old daughter's mixed-race origins:

> We say she's Latina, just to other people, because mentioning the other half . . . begs people to ask about her birth father, and we don't have a lot of information about her birth father. I mean, that just gets into her whole story, and it's not for public consumption, until she knows the full story. . . . It's a very slippery slope once we start saying, "Well, she's half [something else]."

This mother acknowledged the complexity of the issue, further noting: "Once you start down that road, it gets into a whole area that we don't want to keep secret but that's private . . . [and it] brings up all their questions about her heritage and history that she doesn't know the answer to yet."

Their children's growing awareness of skin tone prompted some families to engage more directly in discussions about birth fathers. Hannah, a white lesbian administrative assistant in a large East Coast city, shared that her 5-year-old son Luke, who was biracial (white and African American), was increasingly asking about his birth father, which they attributed to his growing awareness of race and skin tone. Although he had contact with his birth mother, who was white, he did not have contact with his birth father, who was black. "I think it's just on his mind more—where is this person who looks like him?" (Hannah). In this family and others, children's growing awareness that "most families have a mom and a dad" was also seen as prompting their curiosity about birth fathers—particularly in lesbian mother families. By the time that Luke was 8, for example, he was increasingly saying things like "I don't have a daddy" and asserting that he "missed that." Similarly, Charlene, a white lesbian teacher in a midsized city in the Northeast, shared how her daughter Sofia suddenly seemed to "wake up" to the meaning of birth fathers. Although they talked about adoption "all the time," it was only recently that Sofia seemed to grasp the meaning and implications of this previously abstract concept for herself ("she was like, 'Wow, I—I have a birth dad'").

Indeed, as children grew older, they suddenly grasped information about their origins and birth family that they had been told throughout their lives but which took on new meaning as their capacity for complex thought became more refined. Kelly, a white heterosexual environmental planner in a large West Coast city, and mother of a multiracial (African American, Latina, and white) daughter, noted that she had "no confirmation about who Rosa's actual birth father is." In turn, Kelly shared, "We're kind of flummoxed about that because it's unclear what her culture is." After beginning an ancestry unit at school, her 8-year-old daughter Rosa suddenly understood the reality of her unknown birth father, and this missing part of her identity, in a different way: "It landed her with her finally, like, 'Oh my God, I know who my birth mom is but I don't know who my birth father is.'"

Birth Fathers in Child Welfare Adoptions: "He Had His Parental Rights Terminated; He Didn't Give Them Up"

Just as many of the parents who navigated private domestic open adoptions spoke of concerning or difficult birth father circumstances (e.g., substance abuse, criminal involvement, imprisonment), virtually all of the parents who adopted via foster care described such issues—among those who had any knowledge of their children's birth fathers. Such circumstances were, of course, often at least in part responsible for why these men were not in a position to parent: That is, they were in prison, battling drug and alcohol addiction, or struggling with severe mental health issues. By extension, many of these parents were not open to the possibility of birth father involvement postplacement (see also Chapter 5). For example, one lesbian mother shared that after her son's birth father's parental rights were terminated, she was initially fearful that he might come after their family:

> His birth father was involved in a gang and a lot of people were afraid of him, and so we were afraid too when we first got [him], and . . . he had just gotten out of jail. [It was] frightening [initially], but it's not something I worry about now.

At the same time, this mother was not open to future contact, amid her concerns that it would not be "healthy" for her son—or her.

Likewise, one gay father said that he was not open to his son establishing contact with his birth father in light of the circumstances in which he was originally removed from his father's care: "The birth father was violent against [the birth mother]. There's no indication that [child] was hurt, but obviously he would've seen it." In turn, this father did not feel that seeing his birth father would do "any good" for his son. Similarly, another gay father stated simply: "I just think that he's not a very good role model for parenting." Noting that his partner "had much more compassion for the biological dad than I did," this father acknowledged, "I'm choosing to be hard on him."

There were a few exceptions to this trend. For example, one gay father expressed an openness to having his son eventually search for and meet his biological father—something that his son had already expressed an interest in. This father said:

> He really wants to, at some point, get to meet his biological dad. And we've told him, when he gets older he'll have access to more information that will allow him hopefully to find out more about his bio dad, and perhaps locate him. And if that's the case we will certainly support him and help him try and [find] this person. It's perfectly natural to wonder about things like that. His mother was a teenager and she wasn't able to care for him.... He was neglected and taken out of the household. His birth father ... wasn't around.

* * *

As this chapter reveals, birth fathers were often absent from parents' narratives—or, when discussed, regarded as less important than birth mothers. Parents were sometimes surprised when their children asked questions about and wanted to make contact with birth fathers—and some struggled with how and when to share the information that they did know, information that was sometimes sensitive and potentially upsetting. Some parents maintained contact with birth fathers—and in some cases this contact was regarded as quite valuable as it facilitated answers to their children's questions as they grew older and more curious about their birth fathers.

This chapter focused on adoptive parents' feelings about and experiences with birth fathers and, in a few cases, children's growing interest in their birth fathers. Yet we do not know how these children and parents continue to construct the meaning of birth fathers beyond middle childhood. Relevant here is a study of adoptive families with open adoptions, in which the 23 adopted individuals were interviewed in young adulthood (ages 18 to 23) about trajectories of and feelings about birth family contact over time.[24] Few youth had regular contact with birth fathers. More often, they had had ongoing or previous contact with birth mothers and their families (e.g., birth grandparents). Those participants who had not had contact with their birth fathers generally asserted little to no desire to have a relationship with them, feeling as though the birth family relationships they did have "satisfied any need they might otherwise have felt to have contact with the birth father."[25] Most of those who did not want contact explained that they "didn't want to pursue a connection with someone who had been unkind to the birth mother by leaving her during her pregnancy."[26]

This echoes other research showing that the quality of adopted child–birth father relationships may be undermined when the child is aware that their birth father did not take responsibility for or mistreated the mother or child during the period of pregnancy and relinquishment.[27] Such findings highlight how the stories that adoption agencies, adoptive parents, and birth mothers tell about birth fathers are deeply internalized by adopted people. These stories inform children's ideas about their birth fathers and their beliefs about the significance, meaning, and potential consequences of contact.

Also relevant is some research showing that contact between adoptive parents and birth parents serves to facilitate empathy for the birth parents,[28] suggesting that even amid difficult circumstances (e.g., birth fathers' drug use or criminal involvement), adoptive parents may cultivate a more compassionate stance amid some degree of contact. Such compassion, in turn, has the potential to inform how parents talk about birth fathers to their children. Yet even in the absence of genuine compassion, and even in the presence of undeniable "bad behavior" by birth fathers, it is indeed possible to communicate about and with birth fathers in a way that is not entirely hostile or explicitly positive. In a study of 11 adoptive families in open adoptions, two of whom had ongoing contact with birth fathers, the researchers describe how one set of adoptive parents "did not express either positive or negative feelings about the birth father, who had abused their children."[29] Specifically, they did not want to "convey the message that they liked him or were his friends, fearing that this would condone what he had done to the children," but nevertheless tried to make "visits pleasant for everyone" and to "be outwardly accepting towards him."[30] These parents were managing contact well, and their efforts were received gratefully by the birth father, who was also interviewed, and who called them "two nice people in my life."[31]

Ultimately, "children are 50% of their birth fathers. Without knowledge or contact with them, they are missing so much important information."[32] In turn, the onus is on adoptive parents to do the best they can to talk kindly about, solicit information about, and arrange contact with—when appropriate and possible—birth fathers. As Chapter 10 details, adoptive parents should seek to resist the temptation to imagine birth fathers as uninvolved, distant, promiscuous, or cruel—and rather engage the possibility that birth fathers may represent an important source of current and/or future information for their families and their children, even amid challenging circumstances (e.g., drug or alcohol dependence, incarceration, or homelessness). Also, families should not give up on the possibility of establishing birth father contact even many years later. Indeed, birth mothers may soften in their approach to birth fathers over time, ultimately developing a more compassionate stance (e.g., viewing them as scared and immature as opposed to the perpetrators of abandonment), and may therefore be open to providing information to adoptive families that they were not open to sharing at earlier time points.[33]

Notes

1. Goldberg, 2009; Sykes, 2001.
2. Freeark et al., 2005, p. 86.
3. Coles, 2011; Hartmann, 2016; Hughes, 2017.
4. Hartmann, 2016.
5. Ibid.
6. U.S. Department of Health & Human Services, Administration for Children & Families, 2018.
7. Carney, 2014.
8. Ibid.
9. Mann, 2015.
10. Freeark et al., 2005.
11. Franck, 2001; Freeark et al., 2005; French, Henney, Ayers-Lopez, McRoy, & Grotevant, 2013; Miall & March, 2005.
12. Carney, 2014; Mann, 2015; French et al., 2013.
13. Deykin, Campbell, & Patti, 1984; Ettner, 1993; Wrobel, Ayers-Lopez, Grotevant, McRoy, & Friedrick, 1996.
14. Logan; 2010; Siegel, 2012a.
15. Miall & March, 2005.
16. Wrobel et al., 1996, p. 2361.
17. Ge et al., 2008.
18. Farr, Grant-Marsney, & Grotevant, 2014.
19. Farr, Ravvina, & Grotevant, 2018.
20. Ge et al., 2008; Siegel, 2012a.
21. Freeark et al., 2005.
22. Logan & Smith, 1999; Wolfgram, 2008.
23. Freeark et al., 2005.
24. Siegel, 2012a.
25. Ibid., p. 136.
26. Ibid.
27. Passmore & Feeney, 2009.
28. Sykes, 2001; Wolfgram, 2008.
29. Logan & Smith, 2005, p. 19.
30. Ibid.
31. Ibid.
32. Sharon Roszia, adoption consultant, personal communication, November 21, 2017.
33. French et al., 2013.

10
Summing Up
Practical Strategies and Applications for Families

This book has addressed the experiences of contemporary U.S. families who adopted domestically. These families are navigating structural and communicative openness in a context where both adoption agency practices and the rise of the Internet have transformed families' expectations for and reality of ongoing or eventual contact with the birth family. Furthermore, as we have seen, even among families who do not have contact (i.e., they lack structural openness), there is no way to escape the topic of adoption—and nor should there be. This chapter deviates from the format of prior chapters in that it aims to offer parents some guideposts for effectively managing potential challenges and questions across the family life cycle—especially those addressed in this book, and those related to openness in particular.

I offer these suggestions and considerations out of an awareness that many adoptive families do not know about or are unable to access effective postadoption services and supports or adoption-competent therapists, and/or have little contact with other adoptive families. In the absence of adoption-knowledgeable supports and services, families can often feel like they are navigating big issues, challenges, and questions related to adoption on their own. Toward this end, I also provide some resources and guidelines for finding an adoption-competent therapist at the conclusion of this chapter. I also incorporate insights from an interview I conducted with Dr. David Brodzinsky, adoption expert and clinical psychologist, who is well positioned to provide a unique perspective on this topic.

One important caveat: This book, and my recommendations and guideposts, are intended to reflect those issues that are considered "normative" adoption issues—those that are common to most adoptions, and which are not in and of themselves "problems." For some families, the inability to manage common adoption issues can lead to more serious clinical problems; these are not the focus of this book, or this chapter specifically. Furthermore, the strategies and guidance that I offer in this chapter are not directed toward some of the more serious problems that are found in some adopted children and families, which have more to do with preplacement adversity and trauma (e.g., complex developmental trauma), and which may warrant unique parenting and therapeutic interventions.[1] For support and guidance in navigating these types of issues, parents should seek counseling from adoption-competent professionals (see the end of this chapter).

Before moving into a review of the key points raised in the book, and some suggestions and considerations for families—which may also be of interest to practitioners—I provide a brief family vignette to anchor the discussion in this chapter.

Angela and Gordon

Angela and Gordon, a white heterosexual couple employed as an environmental planner and property manager, respectively, lived in a large metropolitan area of the East Coast. The couple encountered infertility, which, although painful and difficult, was viewed by Angela as actually bringing them closer and helping them to function more effectively as a team:

> It's been surprising to me because . . . I have been doing a lot of reading about infertility and how couples stopped having sex or stopped talking to each other. And you know, we were so honest and open with each other that I feel like the whole process has actually strengthened our relationship. Frankly, I got a crash course in trusting him and I don't think I would trust him as much as I do now if we hadn't had to go through all those surgeries and treatments. I had to rely on him. I'm a pretty independent person but he had to take the leadership role [at times].

Angela and Gordon eventually came to the decision to adopt, after several years of failed infertility treatments and several miscarriages. This decision was a relief to both of them. Both Angela and Gordon described feeling hopeful about the future, and connected to one another. Angela, for example, shared that waiting to adopt felt like a "shared pregnancy—and I like that. . . . Plus, I can drink wine! [*laugh*]." Gordon agreed, saying: "We've both been there for each other. We take turns being freaked out or nervous or whatever."

Angela and Gordon attended a great deal of adoption programming, which helped to alleviate their fears and worries about openness. In addition to completing the required classes for their agency, the couple sought out opportunities to learn about adoption, including a conference, online webinars, and a support group for preadoptive and adoptive parents. Both Angela and Gordon came to embrace openness, even considering whether they would decline a placement where the birth parents did not want contact. They were somewhat less open with regard to race. Despite noting that they were open to almost anything, emphasizing several family members' adoption of mixed-race children, they voiced concerns about raising an African American boy specifically. Highlighting the current sociopolitical climate, they expressed a lack of confidence in having the knowledge, skills, or awareness to competently support an African American son to prepare for, respond to, and remain resilient in the face of societal racism, which they viewed as particularly devastating in relation to black boys and men.

The couple ended up matching with a birth mother, Nessa, who gave birth to a biracial (African American and white) girl, whom they named Violet. Although the two parties only knew each other for a short time before Nessa gave birth, both Angela and Gordon had a "great connection" with and respect for Nessa, commenting on her "very mature decision to place [her child]—see, she had no job, no car, nothing. She wanted her daughter to have better. She wanted more for her" (Gordon). The birth father was "not in the picture" (Gordon). The couple maintained contact with Nessa and Nessa's mom—Violet's birth grandma—across Violet's childhood. However, early on, contact was difficult for Nessa, who was "very open with us about having postpartum depression, and it was hard for her to be around people, including us" (Gordon).

Face-to-face contact fluctuated over time, but Facebook contact remained relatively stable and constant throughout Violet's childhood. When Violet was 5, Angela explained their contact with Nessa and Nessa's mom like this: "We text, email, and Facebook a couple times a month. We maintain Facebook contact." According to Angela, Nessa usually "posts something kind of personal on Facebook on Violet's adoption day, just that adoption is hard and also important. . . . And yes; it's hard and it sucks but open adoption is the only way to go." Reflecting on the tricky dance of openness and birth family–adoptive family relationships when Violet was 8, Angela said:

> I think between all of us, there's a high degree of respect and regard. We say "I love you." We enjoy each other's company. I think what's changed is that we're getting better at that. I think there is sort of this blind spot where I wish we could say what we really mean more—I mean I wish I could say what I really want sometimes, like . . ., "Oh, don't send Violet flowers on her birthday. . . . Would you please just send her $30 so she can go buy Legos?" And I need to tell her that. Nessa values truth but sometimes it's like—trying to find the right time for those conversations can be hard. And we've had a little more distance this past year. . . . Nessa just seems to be—she said she wanted to try to have a better relationship with Violet, but yet isn't able to make it happen.

Indeed, when Violet was 8, Angela shared some mild frustration with Nessa, who was not always reliable or dependable when it came to making arrangements for get-togethers and following through on these plans. In turn, contact had faltered over time—particularly over the past few years, alongside instability in Nessa's living, relationship, and employment situations: She had moved and changed jobs several times, and endured several relationship break-ups. About Angela, Gordon said, "She can get frustrated; she will text or send a message to Nessa on Facebook, 'Can we get together?' and then hear nothing back." The inability to get in touch with Nessa reliably or consistently was difficult for Angela, who wanted to protect Violet's feelings: Indeed, when Nessa missed visits, this was a significant trigger for Violet. Most recently, Violet had been profoundly disappointed by Nessa's absence from her birthday gathering. She had developed a deeper understanding of her adoption story over the past few years, which involved a more intense sense of loss and sadness surrounding her birth mom. Gordon said:

> We talk with Violet about it—and you know, with kids, as they grow up, they process it differently. Younger kids just understand the facts and as they get older there's more time for that to sit and ruminate with them and it starts to grow some emotional legs. So I think that's what we're starting to see. When I've heard Violet talk with her friends about it, she's kind of matter of fact—like, "That's my story, I don't feel like talking about it." She's claiming that as part of her story. But whether and how she shares it or doesn't is also something she's developing.

Significantly, part of Angela's and Gordon's discussions with Violet about her story involved helping her to understand how and why her birth mother placed her for adoption—and how the challenges that prevented Nessa from parenting were in some ways the same challenges that prevented her from showing up regularly to visits. As Angela noted, they gradually shared more details with Violet about her story, "from 'she loved you but was not able to care from you' to 'she really struggles to really stick to a job, and has a hard time with taking responsibility, and, you know, some of that probably has to do with how she was raised and the problems she's faced.'" In this way, Angela and Gordon tried to contextualize Nessa's behavior in terms of her own ongoing difficulties—which they expected would continue to become more apparent as Violet grew older.

Both Angela and Gordon were open to Violet developing a more independent relationship with her birth mother as she grew older. Angela said, "I think we're getting into a stage where maybe they can spend an afternoon or something together.... Nessa is looking to get her own place and has said that maybe Violet can spend the night or something. We'll see." As she grew older, Violet seemed to increasingly crave time alone with Nessa. Gordon said:

There have been times she has come to visit us and Violet has asked, "Hey, can you guys go on a walk? I want to spend a little time with Nessa." Like, okay, that's cool.... So I think she enjoys the time alone but also gives her the ability to feel a little more mature. She is starting to develop her own kind of relationship there. I don't know where it's going to go but I think it's great.

Indeed, despite the fact that "it's always been a bit of a struggle to connect—to find opportunities for us or for Violet to spend some time with her birth mother," Angela nevertheless remained committed to openness: "We went into this with what's best for the child. . . . I don't know if we always feel [that our efforts are] reciprocated, but we are committed."

When Violet was 8, Angela and Gordon voiced that they had become increasingly curious about her birth father, amid the reality that Violet's personality was very different from Nessa's, causing Angela to wonder whether "knowing the birth father would help to fill in some of those gaps." Although Violet did not ask questions about her birth father with any regularity, Angela and Gordon were increasingly uneasy about the lack of information they had received from Nessa about him—"we were told that he never responded to her reaching out about the pregnancy" (Angela). They wanted to probe Nessa with additional questions, but hesitated: Nervous about her response, they did not want to do anything to alienate her or jeopardize their relationship. They expressed that they hoped to ask her questions about the birth father "in the future," but noted that they were not exactly sure when that day would come.

Thus, despite their commitment to open adoption, Angela and Gordon, like most couples navigating open adoption, experienced various challenges, at different points in time, in their efforts to support their daughter's relationship with her birth family.

Navigating Infertility and Deciding to Adopt—or Not

As we saw in Chapter 1, same-sex couples, and particularly gay male couples, generally had an easier time arriving at adoption as a route to parenthood than heterosexual couples. Yet couples of all types may experience loss, anger, and/or grief surrounding their inability to have a biological child. Ideally, couples who encounter infertility or barriers to biological parenthood will work with a therapist who is competent in this area—and, in a best-case scenario, one who also possesses basic knowledge about third-party conception routes (e.g., the use of donor eggs and donor sperm), adoption options, and, for same-sex couples, the overall LGBQ family-building experience. (Therapists who are educated about and skilled in working with infertility issues can be identified through the

American Society of Reproductive Medicine's Mental Health Professionals database. Alternatively, both RESOLVE: The National Infertility Association and the American Fertility Association may be able to make referrals to appropriate local therapists.)

Infertility-focused couples counseling will likely address issues of loss, grief, and communication (e.g., within the couple). Individuals, especially women, sometimes use avoidance strategies to cope with infertility stress (e.g., avoiding women with young children)—yet paradoxically, this approach may result in increased distress. Other individuals try to distance themselves from the pain of infertility and may use problem-solving strategies as a means to "fix" the problem (e.g., of infertility, of childlessness, of despair related to infertility). Sometimes, partners within couples differ dramatically from one another in their approach to infertility stress, with one partner using avoidance strategies to cope and the other relying on distancing and/or problem solving. Because each partner's strategy of coping affects the other, couples therapy may be especially useful in treating infertility-related distress and communication breakdowns (as opposed to individual therapy). A counselor, for example, can assist couples by enabling the "problem-solving" partner to let go of the need to "fix" problems and to focus on validating the other partner's distress instead, thus enabling that partner to feel supported and understood.[2] Couples who adopt a "team" approach—seeing infertility as something to be faced and processed together—may fare better. When partners' approach to managing infertility are compatible (i.e., they appraise and cope with the situation similarly), this promotes communication, thereby strengthening a relationship[3]—echoing Angela's perspective that being honest and trusting each other during the process had brought her and Gordon closer during what was otherwise a very stressful time.

Regardless of whether couples choose to work with a therapist, it is important that both partners have sufficient time to process difficult and complex feelings related to not having a biological child. As we saw in Chapter 1, some participants needed more time than others before considering or taking steps toward adoption—and sometimes, partners within couples needed different amounts of time to process and grieve before proceeding to adoption. It is essential that individuals who have experienced infertility fully process, grieve, and, to the extent possible, resolve their infertility prior to moving on to considering adoption. They need to make emotional peace with, and mourn, the loss of the life—and child(ren)—they had envisioned. If infertility is not adequately resolved, individuals who end up adopting can encounter great difficulty in acknowledging and truly "showing up" for their child's own sense of loss surrounding adoption. In turn, this may ultimately lead parents to avoid discussions about adoption or to fail to validate and normalize their child's sense of loss, resulting in a more communicatively closed family system, and possibly contributing to more serious clinical problems for their children down the road.[4]

It is essential that all couples who are considering adoption as a potential path to parenthood receive accurate and comprehensive information about the nature and characteristics of children available for adoption, the adoption process (including wait times and cost), and guidelines surrounding openness and contact. Without this information, prospective adopters are unable to make an informed decision about whether adoption is a good option for them, potentially resulting in poor outcomes for all involved: child, adoptive parents, and the birth family. Significantly, in addition to adoption preparation, certain personal qualities may enhance positive outcomes for families, including flexibility (as opposed to rigidity), a sense of humor, and an openness to seeking out and receiving support.[5] (See the end of this chapter for more detailed discussion of the qualities of successful adoptive parents.) Angela and Gordon demonstrate some of these qualities—for example, laughing about their shared pregnancy (wherein Angela was able to drink alcohol) and seeking education and support opportunities as they pursued adoption.

Meeting and connecting with other adoptive families is one good way to help prospective adopters determine if and what type of adoption is right for them. In addition, seeking out resources—including seminars, webinars, and online resources—to learn more about adoption is essential. For example, the Child Welfare Information Gateway has many excellent resources for individuals and couples considering adoption, such as https://www.childwelfare.gov/topics/adoption/adoptive/before-adoption/.[*]

Navigating Initial Preferences Surrounding Child Characteristics and Openness

Chapter 2 explored couples' preadoptive preferences and decision making related to openness. Participants' narratives revealed that many had experienced shifts in their knowledge of open adoption and their openness to it. Yet as with deciding to adopt, partners within couples were not always immediately on the same page with respect to the amount of openness (and, specifically, structural

---

[*] This chapter—and this book—did not address the experiences of couples who considered adoption and decided not to pursue it. Yet some people do consider adoption and decide that it is not a good choice for them, for a variety of reasons, including a strong prioritization of a biological/genetic tie, concerns about how doing so might impact the couple's relationship, financial concerns, worries about the complex and daunting nature of the adoption process, and concerns about the likelihood and nature of problems (e.g., psychological, developmental, physical) in adopted children (Goldberg & Scheib, 2015; Slauson-Blevins & Park, 2016).

openness, or contact) that they envisioned. Sometimes, agency preparation was important in moving the partner who expressed greater hesitation surrounding contact to a place of greater comfort with it. In other cases, partners continued to have divergent perspectives surrounding contact and had not yet reached a shared agreement about what level and type of contact they would consider.

Maintaining some level of control over the parameters of contact was clearly important to many participants, whereby they were quick to note that they would not hand over the reins to just "any birth parent"—rather, they wanted to be the ultimate arbiter of how much contact would take place, where, and when. This is an important point, and highlights how adoptive parents need to be empowered by the professionals they work with to figure out the type, nature, and frequency of openness that will work for them—rather than feeling compelled to adopt a stance or commitment regarding openness that is not authentic.[6] These participants seemed to be planning for what they imagined as a worst-case scenario—for example, a birth mother with emotional, substance abuse, and criminal problems, who had very poor boundaries, and/or who was demanding constant visits—to which they would have to say no out of concern for their own and their child's safety. Other participants were more focused on the possible benefits of openness than the potential downsides and were careful to center the child's, and in some cases the birth parents', experiences and needs in discussing various contact and openness scenarios. A minority of couples, such as Angela and Gordon, were ultimately so convinced about the importance of openness that they were unsure of whether they would accept a placement with someone who was not also on board with an open adoption and/or who was not also committed to contact.

It is important for couples considering open adoption to actively unearth and explore their fears surrounding contact in a space that is nonjudgmental and also educational—such as in preadoption training sessions and possibly therapy with an adoption-competent therapist. In such a space, they will have a chance to explore the origins and nature of their fears, but also to consider possible scenarios in which those fears come true and how to handle such situations. Fortunately, there are lots of resources for couples in open adoption that are aimed at supporting them in navigating challenging issues, such as when birth parents ask for more visits than the adoptive parents initially agreed to—or, perhaps more often, when the birth parents drop out of sight.[7]

It is clear that participants pursuing child welfare adoption were, in some cases, more likely to assume that a "clean break" was inevitable and optimal in situations where children were adopted via foster care. Few child welfare adopters had thought about, or discussed with their social workers or other adoption professionals, the possibility of ongoing contact with birth family members—such as specific aunts or uncles, grandparents, birth siblings, or even birth parents. This is notable given the very good possibility that in the future, their child and/or their child's birth relatives would be able to find each other online. Amid new technologies, children and their extended birth family, including siblings placed in other homes, can use Google or social media sites to find each other. Couples pursuing child welfare adoption should actively engage with the possibility that contact with some birth family members might benefit their child: For example, such contact may help to guard against the child's idealization of the birth family and/or anger that their parents have separated them from their birth family. And, amid ongoing contact with the birth family, children who receive "out of the blue" contact from the birth family may be less unnerved by, and also more likely to talk to their parents about, such contact.[8]

Regarding race, prospective adopters need to be honest with themselves and adoption professionals about their own racial attitudes, perceptions of competence related to racial socialization, and willingness to inhabit communities—including neighborhoods, churches, and schools—that might be uncomfortable for them (e.g., because they are the racial minority) but will benefit their child's racial identity development.[9] Notably, amid a general attitude of openness surrounding race, Angela and Gordon voiced anxiety about adopting an African American boy specifically, which they had communicated to their adoption agency. Although their honesty suggests that they had seriously considered and deliberated the reality of adopting a black boy, and reflected on their own limitations, their preferences also reveal perhaps overly simplified categorizations of race (and gender), whereby the line is drawn between one group (African American, boy), which is marked as unacceptable, and all others, which are deemed acceptable. This distinction reflects societal constructions of race wherein biracial and multiracial individuals are both designated as "of color" and yet seen as distinct from monoracial black individuals[10]—and therefore presumed to require a different caliber of racial socialization experiences that are perhaps not so "difficult" or unimaginable to engineer.† Yet all white individuals

---

† Some adoption agencies recognize this issue and have now changed their practices regarding how they assess prospective adopters' preferences and openness surrounding race. As opposed to listing every possible combination and permutation of racial/ethnic combinations and allowing prospective adopters to indicate which they are/are not open to, some agencies require that adopters who are open to adopting a biracial or multiracial child also be open to adopting a child who is monoracial and of color. Prospective adopters, then, can no longer indicate an openness to a biracial (African American/white) child, for example, but not a full African American child. The perspective here is that prospective adopters should not go into parenting a child of color thinking that they can "relate to the white part"; they must understand that they are raising a child of color and receive appropriate training and preparation for this reality (Roberta Evantash, Adoptions from the Heart, personal communication, August 30, 2017). The reality is that many adoptive parents view multiracial children as distinct from black children, for example—and, correspondingly, may have incomplete knowledge of or inaccurate beliefs regarding the types of racialized experiences, including discrimination, that a multiracial child will and will not encounter (Khanna & Killian, 2015; Sweeney, 2013). Adoption practitioners should be sensitive to the complex, ambiguous, and sometimes contradictory

who indicate an openness to adopting a child of color, regardless of specific racial makeup, should engage fully with what this means and immerse themselves in readings, webinars, and trainings on transracial adoption—and those on racial justice and racial equity more broadly. Individuals and couples who feel that they have received inadequate information from agencies or adoption professionals related to race should seek out additional resources. Indeed, parents' racial socialization of their children is made innumerably more complex and difficult in the context of transracial adoption.[11] If white prospective adopters are not committed to deeply interrogating their own racial privilege and to seeking immersive and holistic engagement with communities of color, they should not adopt a child of color.

Finally, as we saw in Chapter 2, prospective adoptive parents often possess limited understanding of the nature and effects of prenatal drug/alcohol exposure. Prospective adopters should reach out for additional support and education if they feel inadequately prepared by their agencies or adoption professionals to make informed choices about real or hypothetical placements involving drug and alcohol exposure. The American Academy of Pediatrics (AAP) and the Administration for Children and Families (ACF) are two organizations with many online resources related to prenatal substance abuse and its effects on children at various life stages. Knowledge and understanding of the risks associated with prenatal drug/alcohol exposure can help prospective adopters make informed choices—which in turn are associated with greater satisfaction with and adjustment to an adoptive placement.[12] Ideally, preadoption programming will support prospective adopters in (a) developing empathy for substance-abusing parents, (b) understanding the research on children with prenatal substance exposure as well as learning about relevant caregiving strategies, (c) understanding children's risk for substance abuse and developing a substance abuse prevention plan, and (d) understanding how to communicate with children about birth parents' substance abuse.[13] Shari Levine, executive director of Open Adoption and Family Services, an adoption agency in Oregon, emphasized the significance of empathy for birth parents who are substance abusers—and how to communicate that to children:

> Adoptive parents should be aware of the challenges that the birth parents may have faced. For instance, maybe the birth parent has inherited a family history of addiction and struggles with substance abuse. Maybe that was part of her adoption decision: so, she found herself in a place where she couldn't break that cycle. Given her addiction, she may continue to use during her pregnancy.

beliefs and preferences that prospective adopters may possess regarding race—and seek to address these through comprehensive preadoption training and education.

Addiction is a monster. In an open adoption, the adoptive parents can ideally help the child feel compassion for their birth parent's challenges.[14]

Navigating the Initial Post-Placement Period

Chapter 3 illustrated how the reality of parents' placement situation often differed from what they had imagined. Sometimes parents anticipated more contact than ultimately unfolded; indeed, it was rare that initial contact was more than what they had hoped for or expected. Heterosexual women were the most likely to emphasize the desire or need for boundary management, wherein they felt somewhat threatened by birth mothers' requests for visits and experienced such overtures as undermining their precarious, still developing, sense of parental entitlement. Significantly, couples who are embarking on open adoption should be aware that the initial phase—really the first year or more—is a period of adjustment for everyone, as each member of the adoption system (birth parents, adoptive parents, extended family members on both sides) figures out their role in relation to each other and tries to imagine what their relationships will look like going forward.[15] As Dawn Smith-Pliner, founder and director of Friends in Adoption, an agency in Vermont, said to me:

> The first year is a dance of openness. Everyone is figuring out their relationships to one another; it is new territory for everyone. By the second year, the birth parents and adoptive parents are often more adjusted, but there is still a little bit of a dance. By the third year, patterns are often established.[16]

During the early stages of this "dance," adoptive parents may find it tempting to react quickly to perceived violations or boundary infractions, yet it is sometimes best to override the initial impulse to react and take some time to determine how best to respond—that is, what response will support the relationship going forward. Stacey Stark, an adoptive mother, offers this example of something she often sees in Facebook groups of adoptive parents:[17]

> An adoptive parent sees that their child's birth mother posted a photo of the baby on social media. More often than not, it seems, the adoptive parents feel threatened and bothered. The question comes up, *What should we do?* Do they fire off an emotional email asking that the photo be taken down? Every family's situation is unique, but this is simply an example of how reacting quickly from emotion has potential to inflict hurt or harm to a new open adoption relationship. Take the time to consider what healthy boundaries really entail, and be willing to check your own fear and insecurity beforehand.

In such a situation, checking in with the birth parent to find out what her intention was might be the best option. Indeed, the birth parent in this situation may have seen her actions as a gesture of sharing pride in her child. In doing so, adoptive parents can perhaps affirm the birth parent's pride but also raise concerns about making information about the child public. Additionally, talking to professionals and other experienced adoptive parents in open adoptions may be useful. Speaking to knowledgeable others can help to normalize, validate, and ease the difficult emotions that may come up in this type of scenario, while also providing strategies and practical advice for managing these emotions—and responding in a way that is reflective of one's best self and intentions.

Some parents may find that birth families do not seem to want contact immediately postplacement. Even amid surprise or disappointment, parents should try to maintain a stance that is sensitive to and respectful of the unique vantage point of the birth parents, recognizing that they may be grieving in ways that prevent them from reaching out or being as engaged as they had planned or anticipated. During the initial weeks and months postplacement, adoptive parents can let the birth parents know that they are thinking of them by periodically sending an email, note, and/or photos. These types of actions communicate to the birth parents that they are not forgotten, they are important, and they are welcome to be in touch when they are ready. Angela and Gordon, for example, were aware that their daughter's birth mom, Nessa, was experiencing severe postpartum depression soon after placement. The couple was disappointed in the lack of contact but regularly communicated to Nessa that she was on their minds. They also maintained contact with Nessa's mother during this period to ensure that Nessa had access to mental health professionals.

As Chapter 3 highlights, prospective adoptive parents should be aware that their expectations and hopes surrounding openness and contact may indeed be violated. Even when both parties communicate about and agree to a detailed agreement regarding structural and communicative openness, life circumstances may ultimately disrupt these plans. For example, birth parents may face an unanticipated level of grief, relapse on drugs, move, or face resistance to their adoption plan from their own immediate or extended family (including current partners and parents). Likewise, adoptive parents may move, face unanticipated challenges with regard to their child's health or needs, experience illness or job loss, or endure some other major life change or event. Both parties may experience changes in their feelings about and motivation for contact. Adoptive parents can and should be prepared for a variety of possible scenarios and should balance a commitment to openness and contact with qualities of flexibility and patience, such that they can accept and work with the full range of potential situations that may come to pass. The recognition that open adoption is a lifelong process that will likely undergo changes over time can help parents to anticipate and cope with changes that may occur—and reach out for support from professionals as needed.

Ultimately, it is helpful for adoptive parents to realize and remember that they have a great deal of power. According to Shari Levine, executive director of Open Adoption and Family Services:

> A lot of the quality of the relationship lies with the adoptive parents. When adoptive parents are welcoming and empathic, birth parents are typically very appreciative of that door opening, and can then step through it. When birth parents are not in a position where they can engage, other birth family members might be able to be engaged. It's up to adoptive parents to honor the birth family in the process, and to create a culture of openness which they then communicate to the child.[18]

Navigating the Unexpected in Open Adoption Arrangements

As some of the participants in Chapter 4 emphasized, facing a lack of contact—when parents have bought into open adoption and believe in its importance—can be profoundly disappointing, especially as children grow older and begin to ask questions about why they do not see or hear from their birth parents. Again, parents who find themselves in this situation should understand that birth parents may be experiencing a complex range of emotions for months and years after the placement, including relief, sadness, loss, pride in having made an adoption placement, shame about having placed a child for adoption, grief, hope, and so on. Birth parents may also be experiencing life circumstances that inhibit their being in touch, including ongoing housing issues, employment issues, chaotic family or relationship issues, and substance abuse or mental health challenges.

Postplacement support for birth parents—a place to talk about and process their feelings openly—is so important but might not be sought or obtained, for a number of reasons, including secrecy surrounding the placement, financial constraints, a desire to "move on," and fear that talking about their feelings will be too overwhelming. Specialized and comprehensive postplacement support services for birth parents are also fairly rare overall—with important and notable exceptions.[‡] If faced with a lack of or limited response from birth parents, adoptive parents should, ideally, continue to reach out in a way that is appropriate and

---

[‡] See On Your Feet Foundation for one notable exception (http://www.oyff.org/).

abides by their agreement—for example, sending photos, letters, texts, or emails that communicate that they are thinking of the birth parents and care for them. Such communication may be especially meaningful to birth parents around certain times of year and on certain dates, such as Mother's Day and Father's Day, and the child's birthday.

In talking to children about why there is limited or no contact, it is important not to appear frustrated with the birth parents or blame them for the lack of contact. Parents can acknowledge, in an age-appropriate way, the different circumstances that might be inhibiting the birth parents' ability to be in touch, while also emphasizing the birth parents' strengths and positive qualities. And, of course, parents should listen to and validate their child's desire to see and interact with their birth parents as normal, natural, and expected. Angela and Gordon, for example, found that it was increasingly important to contextualize for their daughter Violet that her birth mother had certain ongoing difficulties—for example, with responsibility and dependability—that were interfering with her ability to show up for important events and scheduled visits. They told Violet that even though Nessa "really and truly wants to be there," her personal challenges sometimes kept her from meeting her expectations for herself and her commitments to others.

Other parents, including those who were very excited about and interested in openness, encountered challenges related to what they perceived as boundary infractions and violations. What should adoptive parents do when faced with what they perceive as inappropriate or disruptive behaviors on the part of birth parents? Ideally, the relationship is solid enough to have a direct conversation that is respectful on both sides, wherein the adoptive parents can communicate how they are feeling and assert their wishes for future interactions, while remaining open to hear what the birth parents are feeling and experiencing. If adoptive parents feel that birth parents are having difficulty respecting the boundary lines that have already been established, it can be useful to talk to an adoption professional. Getting an adoption-competent outsider's perspective on how to respond without fueling further hurt or causing unnecessary disruption to the relationship can be helpful—as can maintaining relationships with other adoptive parents who may have experienced similar issues and can provide a supportive ear.

However, there are inevitably circumstances where adoptive parents need to firmly (re)assert and (re)instate the boundaries in relation to birth family members to protect their child and family from inappropriate, disruptive, or harmful behavior. Birth parents' personal difficulties (e.g., substance use, mental health issues) may become disruptive to the family system, requiring that adoptive parents pull back on contact and/or make changes to the terms, frequency, or type of contact—at least for a period of time. In doing so, the message to birth parents or birth family can be compassionate and empathic, but also firm and clear.[19] For example, adoptive parents can say something along the lines of, "Although we agreed to communicate in certain ways, there have been situations such as _____ that are not good for our child and family. In order to continue with contact, we need _____ to happen. We care about you and we want you in our lives, but we can't continue to uphold our current arrangement." In this way, parents can send a message to birth family members that communicates their care and concern but also firmly upholds their commitment to their child's and family's safety and well-being.

Adoptive parents should ideally receive not only preparatory training from agencies surrounding openness and contact but also ongoing support from adoption professionals. During the preadoptive stage, open adoption is theoretical, and therefore understood at an abstract level more so than a lived experience. In adopting a child and navigating openness across that child's life, the complexity of open adoption becomes real. As Janette Logan, a social work scholar, notes:

> Professionals must . . . help adopters to understand that contact is a complex and dynamic practice in which the needs of children and birth relatives will change over time. Adopters need to be encouraged to anticipate feelings and management issues that will inevitably arise throughout their child's life, and to think about how they can maintain positive communication with all members of the adoptive kinship—even in situations of adversity. Wherever possible, all participants in contact arrangements should be included in discussing and agreeing to detailed plans, and perhaps most importantly, agencies should anticipate that contact arrangements may run into difficulties and preadoption contact planning is only the beginning of a lifelong process for adoptive parents, their children and the birth relatives with whom they are in contact.[20]

Adoption practitioners who are strong advocates for openness in adoption should themselves be prepared to invest a fair amount of time, effort, patience, and emotional energy to facilitate the ongoing process of open adoption. They should aim to provide ongoing, committed support to the adoption triad, particularly at difficult or critical periods during the family life cycle.[21] And, regardless of whether adoptive parents have contact with the birth family, practitioners can support parents in finding ways to celebrate and honor birth families. For example, parents can honor their children's birth families in the form of a meal, special holiday, or celebration, possibly around the holidays or children's birthday. These "life-giver days" can serve as an important means of honoring birth families' importance in the lives of adopted children.[22]

It is important to note that sometimes maintaining contact with the birth family is difficult not because of boundary infractions, personal problems, or lack of communication on the part of birth parents but because of difficulties within the adoptive family. For example, adoptive parents within a couple may have differing feelings about continuing contact or intimate relationship or marital problems that make coping with the complexities of contact too overwhelming or difficult. Or the child may express resistance to or lack of desire for contact. It is essential to emphasize that challenges in open adoption do not just come from birth family members—rather, they can arise because of difficulties within the adoptive families or problems between and across members of the two constellations.

Navigating the Possibility of Contact in Child Welfare Adoptions

Most birth parents involved with the child welfare system do not relinquish their parental rights voluntarily—and when they do, it is often because they are told that unless they do, child welfare professionals will seek involuntarily termination of parental rights. Those who voluntarily relinquish their parental rights are often in a position to develop a relationship with adoptive parents in which there is less mutual suspicion, distrust, and resentment. Further, if both parties are educated about the range of possibilities for contact, voluntary relinquishment by birth parents may facilitate postadoption contract agreements that are mutually agreeable and beneficial—assuming that both parties reside in jurisdictions where child welfare professionals provide education about and support contact with birth family and facilitate such agreements.

As we saw in Chapter 5, parents who adopt via child welfare vary significantly in terms of whether and how much they have been prepared for the possibility of openness, or ongoing contact, with members of their children's birth family. In some cases, it may not be advisable for adoptive parents to maintain communication or contact with birth parents for their children's safety; likewise, in some cases birth parents will not be in a position to maintain contact (e.g., due to serious drug or mental health issues), at least not at the time of placement. It is important for parents who adopt via child welfare to understand and gain information about the range of birth relatives (e.g., siblings, aunts, uncles, siblings) with whom the child may have a relationship, as well as details about the nature of these relationships. When possible, parents should seek to preserve meaningful and important birth family relationships for their child, or any other individuals with whom their child has a strong attachment. As we saw, these relationships could sometimes be sustained—and were quite powerful for children, serving as sources of ongoing connection and support. Likewise, relationships with prior foster parents may also be a source of strength and connection[23]—and maintaining these relationships can benefit children.

At the same time, as we saw in Chapter 5, there are circumstances in which parents may need to establish firm boundaries around contact with birth relatives whom the child wishes to see and/or who reach out to the adoptive parents or child directly. It is often inappropriate to facilitate contact with birth family members who have previously perpetrated abuse against the child, at least until there is clear evidence that such contact would not pose harm for the child. When in doubt, parents should consult with child welfare professionals and adoption experts, particularly those who are savvy about contemporary guidelines surrounding openness in child welfare adoptions.

Talking About Adoption

Parents don't always know how and when to talk about adoption with their child. In turn, as we saw in Chapter 6, parents, armed with this awareness, often started practicing adoption talk before their child was able to understand what they were saying. Parents also sought out guidance from professionals regarding how to talk about adoption and how to respond to their children's questions, especially when birth parents were not readily available to answer their own or their children's questions, and when the details surrounding their birth family or placement were sensitive. A recurring thread throughout parents' narratives was the approach of only answering the question that children asked. This approach—taking the lead from one's child—is developmentally responsive and child centered but, as adoption expert and clinical psychologist David Brodzinsky warns, a bit too simplistic, as it could ultimately have the effect of leaving unanswered the unasked questions. In turn, a better approach is

> to first affirm the importance of what is asked, answer the question, and then ask if the child has other questions he/she would like to ask. If the child says no, then the next message is to say something along the lines of "Okay, but I want you to know that you can always ask me whatever you want, about your adoption or anything else. It's perfectly normal to be curious about this part of your life.... [I]f I were you, I certainly would.... I promise to always try to answer your questions as best as I can." The parent who says, "I will answer exactly the question that is asked and nothing beyond that" may be inadvertently giving the child the impression they actually don't like to talk about adoption.[24]

Parents should not assume that their child's silence on the topic of adoption means that it is not on their minds. Some parents were attuned to this potential error in interpretation, stating that their child did not talk or ask questions about their adoption, but also noting that this did not mean that adoption lacked salience or meaning for their child. Importantly, parents sometimes worried that talking about adoption, especially if their child was not regularly bringing it up, would cause their child to feel "different" or "singled out"—and they did not want to impose an importance on their child that was not there. A very similar rationale was invoked by some parents for not talking about race. But parents *can* cultivate an environment of openness, including an openness to the difficult emotions surrounding adoption, that simultaneously emphasizes a child's sense of belonging to and integration within the adoptive family, and also their origins (e.g., they were born to a set of birth parents that may or may not be involved in their life). If children see that their parents are resistant to or uncomfortable with talking about adoption or race, they are less likely to discuss difficult feelings (e.g., loss surrounding birth family) or events (e.g., racist incidents).[25]

Some parents hinted at anxiety and uncertainty surrounding their children's expressions of loss and grieving related to the birth family. When a child expresses sadness regarding birth parents (e.g., not seeing them, feeling abandoned by them), parents sometimes responded by emphasizing their own joy or luck at being their child's parent—possibly prompted by their own anxiety at their children's expressions of loss.[26] This type of response, though well intentioned, may have the effect of discouraging future expressions of painful emotions: Rather than opening up conversation about loss, a focus on one's own emotions—of joy, no less—suggests that their child's painful feelings are not acceptable or welcomed. Parents should aim to fully acknowledge and "show up" for their child's loss and grief—which is extremely common in adopted individuals[27]—and seek to create and hold space for both positive and negative emotions around adoption and the birth family. By bearing witness to their child's adoption loss, which can be complex and multifaceted, parents affirm the reality and normalcy of what the child is experiencing. As children grow, parents can provide more information, in a developmentally appropriate manner, about the circumstances, if known, that contributed to the birth parents' inability to parent, lack of contact, or upsetting behavior. Sharing such knowledge and engaging in discussion about it can help the adopted child to manage and indeed mitigate their sense of uncertainty related to their origins and adoptive identity.[28]

Some adoptive parents struggled with whether, when, and how to talk about the more difficult aspects of their children's story, such as birth parents' drug use, criminal behavior, violence, and neglect. In some cases, they were cognizant of the need to avoid demonizing birth parents—especially when they themselves were angry or frustrated with the birth parents about birth parents' past (or current) behaviors—and specifically tried to disentangle the birth parents' character from their behavior. That is, parents found ways to discuss the birth parents' behavior and decision making while not communicating the idea that the birth parents were bad people—in fact, in some cases, birth parents' poor decision making was contextualized in terms of their personal circumstances (e.g., poverty, personal difficulties). This, as well as differentiating between action and intent, can help to mitigate against the child's internalization of their birth parents—or themselves—as "bad." As David Brodzinsky states:

> I often suggest using an illness model as part of the explanation. "Your birth mom wanted to be a good mom to you, but she had a problem that made it impossible for her to care for you the way you needed her to. She had an illness; she was addicted to drugs (or she had emotional problems) and when she used drugs she couldn't be the kind of mother she wanted to be and knew that you needed. And you couldn't wait for her to get better, to get off of drugs; you needed someone to feed you, bathe you, consistently—all the time." The idea is to reframe the birth parent's problem into a context that doesn't demonize the parent, or communicate to the child that they came from something "bad." To feel worthy as a human being, you must believe that you came from people who are worthwhile. When birth parents are demeaned or demonized, children's self-image will suffer.[29]

In some cases, parents were not just searching for if, when, and how to talk about issues of parental psychopathology or drug abuse. A key question that lingered in the minds of several parents was whether and how to talk to their child about their conception story if parents believed (or had been told) that it involved rape or incest. Parents may find it helpful to consult with adoption practitioners at different points in their children's life to discuss developmentally appropriate strategies for engaging in these conversations. Many adoption practitioners believe that children should learn their full story—in all its complexity—by the age of 10 or 12.

There are many online resources devoted to providing the rationale for, and guidance surrounding, disclosures of conception via rape or incest—and other "difficult" background information. See, for example, Dawn Davenport's radio show-turned-podcast "Creating a Family" (https://creatingafamily.org), which, since 2007, has explored this and other topics related to adoption. Relevant episodes include, "Should You Tell Your Adopted Child He Was Conceived by Rape, His Mother Is an Addict, etc.?" and "Talking With Tweens and Teens About Adoption."

A general rule for discussing adoption with children is that it is a process, not a one-time event. At the same time, parents should take into account children's emotional, social, and cognitive readiness in deciding when and how to share adoption-related information. In addition to being a process, adoption revelation is also a dialogue, a "give and take": That is, it involves sharing information, asking questions, and listening to children. Through an ongoing dialogue, parents can encourage questions, normalize curiosity, and assess children's understanding of adoption-related issues—and, in turn, address gaps in comprehension. It is important that parents be as equally focused on listening to their children as they are on imparting information. Listening may be especially difficult—but important—when children are distressed or anxious, possibly unsettled by some piece of adoption information that they recently understood in a new way or some adoption-related event that occurred.[30]

As Children Grow: Making Sense of Nature and Nurture

Parents, in general, were prepared for the reality that their children would be different from them. At the same time, as we saw in Chapter 7, many emphasized their intention, and then their efforts, to create social, emotional, and academic scaffolding that would support their children in flourishing to the extent that was possible. Ultimately, what appeared to be most adaptive for parents was being open to a diverse range of possibilities with regard to their children's strengths and challenges, and modifying their expectations—and behaviors (e.g., with respect to the schools that they chose, the academic and social enrichment opportunities they provided)—as their children developed. Furthermore, for the most part, parents demonstrated notable thoughtfulness about how they invoked the birth family with respect to their children's characteristics—and this is important, given that, especially as children grow older, the nature, tone, and messaging of such attributions or wonderings on their parents' part will deepen in meaning and salience. Indeed, as important as it is to not explicitly "blame" children's less-than-desirable qualities on their birth family, it is also necessary to acknowledge and celebrate children's positive qualities (e.g., musical, artistic, or athletic skills) and, at times, to connect these to the birth family.

Some parents, as we saw, had to dramatically alter their expectations for their children. They were faced with evidence of cognitive deficits as well as emotional and behavioral challenges that were more severe than what they had been prepared for. Likewise, some parents were met with attachment-related difficulties, which were especially surprising to them when they had adopted their children at birth. These parents may have benefited from preadoption training specifically aimed at normalizing, and also presenting strategies for addressing, attachment-related difficulties. Curiously, few parents mentioned seeking postadoption support services to navigate unexpected challenges—although some did pursue assessment services, traditional therapies, and school-based interventions. Meeting and talking with adoption-competent professionals—ideally those who are knowledgeable about both trauma and adoption—may be very helpful to parents who are facing unanticipated and/or severe emotional, behavioral, social, neurological, medical, and intellectual challenges in their children. Parents and children need to work with practitioners who can conceptualize children's challenges in ways that reflect and integrate their preadoptive history and provide adoption-informed guidance for parents that enables them to effectively understand and respond to their children's needs. It is essential that therapists and medical professionals understand a child's adoption context, including what is known and not known about the child's prenatal history, genetic risks, and early environment, to ensure appropriate assessment and intervention. Adopted children who do not receive comprehensive, adoption-informed evaluation and assessment are vulnerable to having their difficulties go undiagnosed (e.g., fetal alcohol spectrum disorders, or FASD) or misdiagnosed (e.g., attachment disorders), as well as mistreated (e.g., prescribed medication that may exacerbate or aggravate their symptoms).[31]

Of note is that some parents may consider genetic testing as a means of filling in the gaps in their children's genetic and medical profile. Access to genetic-relative family health history may provide important information to the families of adopted individuals, who often suffer from incomplete or inaccurate medical records, and who may possess unique risks for certain conditions (e.g., due to genetics, poor prenatal environmental conditions, and adverse early circumstances). Genetic testing can help to provide genetic and ancestry information and enhance the ability of adopted individuals to identify hidden or unknown medical risks and/or receive recommended screenings for certain conditions. Yet ethical and practical challenges may accompany the pursuit of genetic testing, warranting careful and thoughtful dialogue with adoption-competent medical practitioners and counselors before (and, if relevant, after) such testing.[32]

Engaging With Social Media in Open Adoption

As we saw in Chapter 8, parents were diverse with respect to their approach to and feelings about the use of social media as a means of accessing information about the birth family and/or connecting with the birth family directly. Some parents saw it as a useful tool—especially when in-person contact was unpredictable or irregular, as in the case of Angela and Gordon. Such parents appreciated the easy, casual, and spontaneous nature of communication via social media—while also sometimes noting its downsides, such as learning unwanted details about birth families' lives and behavior. Others voiced hesitation, even fear, regarding its potential for destabilizing carefully erected boundaries between themselves and the birth family. Rarely, though, did families talk about being fearful of birth family members finding their children and reaching out to them directly—likely because, in most cases, children were not yet at the age when they had an independent social media presence. Among those parents who had begun to guide their children around social media use, concerns were typically mitigated by the fact that they had open adoptions and had shared relevant information with their child, or they had limited identifying information about the birth family and had reason to believe that the birth family also possessed limited information about them.

As noted in Chapter 8, the rise in genetic ancestry testing, alongside the power of the Internet and the pervasiveness of social media, means that many children will have the ability to search for and quite possibly find information about their birth family (and, likewise, the birth family may also use these tools to search for the children they placed). In turn, parents should increasingly share with their children—in an age-graded and developmentally appropriate manner—their reasons for seeking or not seeking out contact with their birth family via social media. They should also support their children in developing an understanding of social media etiquette and online privacy issues—while also ensuring that they themselves are social media savvy.

Parents should seek to support their children's curiosity about their birth family, including online searching, regardless of the level of actual contact the birth family has with the child. Indeed, even if parents have contact with their child's birth mother, that child may ultimately wish to seek out other birth family members. Parents may wish to offer their children additional support options, such as counseling focused on supporting them during the searching process and helping them work through their fantasies and fears surrounding making contact. Youth may also need help—from parents, therapists, and so on—in determining the healthiest and most considerate approach to reaching out to birth family members. And youth may also need practical guidance (e.g., from parents or adoption professionals) in determining the most reliable and ethical web sources and support organizations to facilitate their search (e.g., if they have limited current birth family information and are searching for details such as last names or current city). Parents should recognize that their children will eventually search, if they want to—and therefore it is not in their child's or family's best interest to actively block their child's acquisition of information about the birth family. Parents who experience paralyzing fears about what they or their children might discover in a thorough search, or who feel intensely threatened by the possibility of their child making contact with the birth family online, should get support themselves—so they can be available, emotionally and physically, to their children.

Ultimately, however, some professionals warn that children who contact birth family members via Facebook or other social networking sites may do so spontaneously and independently, and thus without supervision, making it "nearly impossible for the children to have a surrounding support system, third-party social workers, or the guidance necessary to mediate them through an extremely vulnerable time."[33] Lacking the maturity to realize the implications of independent, unguided contact with their birth family on Facebook, children may navigate this relationship online for a period of time before disclosing it to their parents—possibly only if and when the communication fades away, becomes concerning, or seems to move too quickly.[34] It is important for adoptive parents to realize that the best defense against this scenario is, again, keeping communication open and educating their children about social media etiquette and appropriate boundaries. When parents encourage flexible, ongoing communication about adoption within the family, youth are more likely to feel that their parents accept, understand, and will support searching and information seeking—and in turn, youth will likely feel more comfortable engaging in these behaviors and will be less likely to hide them from their parents.[35]

The Missing Birth Fathers

As is evident throughout the book, and as discussed in Chapter 9, birth fathers were often absent from parents' narratives—and when they were discussed, they were frequently invoked as less important or salient in their children's consciousness or identities as compared to birth mothers, reflecting broader narratives about the role of fathers and birth fathers specifically. Yet as children grew, they often asked questions about their birth fathers—a reality that surprised some parents, who had been prepared for questions about birth mothers but downplayed the significance of birth fathers. Some parents struggled with the lack of information they possessed, in some cases doubting the stories that birth mothers told about not knowing the birth fathers. Among those parents who did possess information about birth fathers, some wrestled with when and how to share this information with children, such as the reality that birth fathers were in prison or the possibility that children were conceived through rape. Although some parents said that they would never tell their children certain details about birth fathers, it is important to emphasize that many adoption practitioners, advocates, and scholars strongly recommend that all adopted youth be told their entire stories eventually, albeit in a developmentally graded and sensitive manner.[36] Parents should seek support and guidance for how to talk to their children about the missing or upsetting details of their story, especially regarding birth fathers, with the goal of ensuring that their child is given age-appropriate but also matter-of-fact information about their birth fathers, and thus their full story.

Ideally, prospective adoptive parents can fight against societal stereotypes and misconceptions about birth fathers to imagine and facilitate birth father engagement and involvement. Recognizing that birth fathers do care about their children can go far in terms of developing a sense of compassion for these men, even amid sadness or frustration regarding the circumstances that may surround them (e.g., drug/alcohol dependence, criminal activity, or simply lack of preparedness to be a father). Parents can let birth fathers know how important they are by exerting the same level of effort in making contact (e.g., via letters and visits) as they do with birth mothers. They can accept that birth fathers, like birth mothers, may have life circumstances or personal challenges that interfere with their ability to be present and responsive to such contact, while also affirming birth fathers' symbolic significance and being open to a shift toward more reciprocal contact in the future. If contact with birth fathers was never established early on, parents should not give up on the possibility that it can occur in the future: Indeed, birth mothers who were unwilling to share information about birth fathers early on may ultimately be willing to provide details later on.

But in fact, shifts are needed in the ways that birth fathers are treated beginning in the preadoptive stage. As adoption expert Sharon Roszia observes, often, "birth fathers are still treated as a nuisance by both agencies and families, the idea being, 'Let's get them to sign off.'"[37] Birth (or expectant) fathers need high-quality and comprehensive counseling, preadoption education, and support that is geared toward facilitating their self-determination and ensuring their informed consent, as well as preparing them for the lifelong process of adoption, if this is the path that is ultimately chosen. And birth fathers also need postadoption support and counseling. Birth fathers, from the outset, should be prepared for the possibility that even if they are not interested in ongoing reciprocal contact with adoptive families, there is a good possibility that children may eventually find them using the Internet and social media.

When parents do not possess information about birth fathers—or birth mothers, for that matter—they may feel as though the absence of information means the absence of conversation. That is, they may end up foreclosing on important and helpful conversations simply because they do not have many actual details about birth family. Parents may say to their child, "We just don't know who your birth father was. I'm sorry," thereby ending the conversation there. Yet as David Brodzinsky notes, the absence of information should never be a reason for ending a conversation; indeed, birth family members are psychologically present even if physically absent.[38] Dr. Brodzinsky suggests the following approach as one possibility:

> Parents might say, for example, "We don't have any info about your birth father. . . . We wish we did. . . . How do you feel about not knowing about him? . . . I'm sure you have had many thoughts about who he might be, what he might look like, what he knows about you. . . . I would too. Let's talk about what you've thought about and I'll also share what I've thought about." Or some variation of this exchange. The point is to get the child to engage in a conversation about what he/she believes, hopes, desires, fears, etc., about the missing info. Parents need to affirm the child's curiosity, normalize their thoughts and feelings, and by doing so increase the chances that the child will continue in the "normative" process of searching for self.[39]

Looking to the Future

Most of the parents in this study had children who were school aged—between 8 and 10 years old—the last time that we spoke to each other. What happens next? Parents often looked to the future, anticipating if, when, and how children would take on more of an active and agentic role in their relationship with (or search for) birth family, as in the case of Angela and Gordon, who were increasingly navigating their daughter's desire for time alone with her birth mom. Significantly, some parents noted that they did have concerns about this independent relationship, recognizing their diminished ability to protect or shield their children from potential disappointments or upsetting realities surrounding birth family if and when they were not present, online or in person, to witness the two parties' interactions. Yet assuming that parents are having open and increasingly sophisticated conversations with their children about their birth family, a birth mother's drug addiction, for example, should not come as any surprise—rather, children will just need a new set of tools for navigating this issue if they are faced with any issues related to said addiction on their own. Parents can work with their children to come up with strategies for ensuring safety, such as structuring the time and place of visits or teaching the child or teen to recognize danger signs and/or to know when to leave the situation.[40] In this way, children and teens can hopefully continue to benefit from contact while minimizing negative interactions.

As children grow older, they will be better able to understand the nature of their birth family's challenges, if relevant. That is, a more sophisticated understanding of drug abuse and depression will enable them to better grasp the "how" and "why" of a birth parent's absence or intermittent contact, for example.[41] Yet understanding does not necessarily lessen the pain of not having contact. In turn, it is important for adoptive parents to continue to support their children as they enter adolescence and emerging adulthood, creating space for a variety of emotions toward and surrounding birth family, and a range of preferences for contact (e.g., from none to a great deal).

It is notable that, when interviewed, adopted youth in open adoptions emphasize that they strongly value openness and honesty.[42] They want their adoptive parents and birth parents to be honest with them and to share information with them, recognizing that "facing facts and dealing with pain are preferable to keeping secrets," with one research participant stating that the "truth may be disconcerting and painful, but it's also empowering. The truth can be processed." These youth also understand that caution and discretion are important, and that there is no "one size fits all" approach to open adoption. Finally, they stress the importance of empowering adopted children to form their own relationships with birth family.

Final Thoughts: Guidance for Adoptive Parents

There is no secret formula for a successful open adoption—or a successful adoption for that matter. Nor is there a "best" level of openness; indeed, satisfaction with openness is more predictive of positive individual and family outcomes than the actual extent or level of openness.[43]

However, research and practice tell us that adoptive parents with certain characteristics tend to be more successful in parenting. Namely, characteristics of successful adoptive parents include (a) the ability to find happiness with small steps toward improvement; (b) refusal to be rejected by the child and the ability to delay gratification of parental needs; (c) tolerance of their own ambivalence and/or negative feelings; (d) flexibility with regard to one's parental role (e.g., moving into the caregiving role when one senses overwhelming frustration or burnout in the other parent); (e) having a systems view of the family (i.e., looking at how each member affects the other, not viewing any one member as the villain or the savior); (f) taking charge of one's parental role (i.e., a sense of comfort and entitlement with regard to the parental role); (g) insisting on building an immediate relationship with the child (e.g., not holding back); (h) practicing self-care and self-compassion, and using humor; (i) operating in an open versus a closed family system—that is, being open to accepting help from others, including other parents, therapists, adoption professionals, and so on; (j) realistic expectations and cognitive flexibility—that is, the ability to alter one's expectations in the face of new information and experiences; (k) a strong support system; and (l) viewing help seeking (e.g., individual, couples, and family therapy; assessment services; support groups; consultation with adoption agencies and adoption professionals) as a strength, and not a weakness or failure.[44]

Related to this last point, adoptive parents should, whenever possible, seek out adoption-competent helping professionals. What makes a therapist or clinician adoption competent? Competency is far more than just having experience treating adopted individuals in the past or having personal experiences with adoption (e.g., being an adoptive parent or having friends or family members who have adopted). Ideally, a therapist has completed accredited training in trauma-based adoption issues and, reflecting this training, will be attuned to issues of loss, neglect, and trauma and the effect of these issues on children's behavior (and family dynamics) at various developmental stages. Adoption-competent therapists should, in turn, ask parents for a detailed history of their children's life before adoption, including prenatal history and genetic risk(s), and should account for such early life experiences (including prenatal substance exposure and early neglect/abuse) in their case conceptualization, diagnosis, and treatment. At the same time, they will understand that, as Sharon Roszia notes, "Regardless of adoption type, and even in the most open of open adoptions, there are still losses. The lived experience of adoption for all triad members will not be pain free."[45] Sensitivity to the inevitability of loss in adoption is a key component of adoption-competent practice.

Adoption-competent therapists possess knowledge of how the adoption system works, the diverse routes to adoption, and what both parents and children go through prior to, during, and after family formation. In turn, they should be able to tailor their approach and interventions to diverse adoptive families—including those who are multiracial, those with children with special needs, those with two moms or two dads, and those with extensive, or minimal, birth family contact. They should be flexible, realistic, and growth oriented.

Sometimes, therapists may express a willingness or openness to working with adopted children or families, or even bill themselves as adoption competent—but they are not. Parents should know the "warning signs" of a therapist who does not possess the skills, training, or experience to help them. These include therapists who fail to validate or believe parents' or children's experiences, blame parents for their children's problems, pathologize adoption, question parents' motives for adoption, advise parents not to talk about adoption with children as a means of avoiding conflict, and fail to gather information about children's histories or to address the impact of early life experiences.[46] If parents experience any of these dynamics with a therapist, they should seriously consider terminating treatment and pursuing other options.

There are a number of resources available to support and guide parents in identifying adoption-competent therapists and other professionals. The Center for Adoption Support and Education (CASE), a leader in mental health services for the adoption and foster care community, created the Training for Adoption Competency (TAC) program, which has established sites across 16 states that have trained more than 900 mental health professionals to be "adoption competent" (see http://adoptionsupport.org/about-us/). Parents can search by state for adoption-competent therapists and counselors who have graduated from the TAC program; see http://adoptionsupport.org/member-types/adoption-competent-professionals/. *Psychology Today* also allows consumers to search for adoption therapists—although there is no guarantee they have received training via the TAC model, or any other adoption-specific training program: https://www.psychologytoday.com/us/therapists/adoption. Other guides, such as the Child Welfare Information Gateway's "Selecting and Working With a Therapist Skilled in Adoption," may also be useful to parents (see http://www.childwelfare.gov/pubPDFs/f_therapist.pdf).

Parents who face a paucity of adoption-savvy therapists in their geographic area should look to their adoption agencies for appropriate referrals. They may also find it helpful to (a) travel to a region with adoption-competent professionals to at least gain comprehensive evaluation and assessment; (b) consult by phone or Skype with an adoption-competent professional; (c) attend conferences, webinars, and other programs that allow them to interface with adoption professionals and other adoptive parents virtually or in real time; or (d) find support online, via formal support groups or listservs run for and/or by adoptive parents. There are many, many online resources for adoptive parents; however, they inevitably range in quality, and, in turn, it is best to consult with one's adoption agency or an experienced adoption professional for guidance and suggestions about the most informative and credible online resources. Asking for support and advice from a skilled adoption professional can save parents time and energy as they seek to support themselves and their families in the best way possible.

Notes

1. Kenrick, Lindsey, & Tollemache, 2006.
2. Peterson et al., 2012.
3. Pasch & Sullivan, 2017.
4. Brodzinsky, 1997; David Brodzinsky, personal communication, August 19, 2018.
5. North American Council on Adoptable Children, 2018.
6. David Brodzinsky, personal communication, October 8, 2018.
7. Carney, 2018; Family Education, 2018.
8. Greenhow, Hackett, Jones, & Meins, 2016.
9. Goldberg, Sweeney, Black, & Moyer, 2016.

10. Perry, 2014; Raleigh, 2016.
11. Hughes et al., 2006.
12. Edelstein et al., 2017.
13. Ibid.
14. Shari Levine, personal communication, November 20, 2017.
15. Stark, 2017.
16. Dawn Smith-Pliner, personal communication, August 21, 2017.
17. Ibid.
18. Shari Levine, personal communication, November 20, 2017.
19. David Brodzinsky, personal communication, August 19, 2018.
20. Logan, 2010, p. 322.
21. Towsend, 2003.
22. Sharon Roszia, personal communication, November 21, 2017.
23. Roszia & Silverstein, 1999; Wood, 2018.
24. Brodzinsky, 2011; David Brodzinsky, personal communication, August 19, 2018.
25. Docan-Morgan, 2010.
26. Brodzinsky, 2011.
27. Brodzinsky, 2011; Keefer & Schooler, 2000.
28. Colaner & Kranstuber, 2010.
29. David Brodzinsky, personal communication, August 19, 2018.
30. Brodzinsky, 2011.
31. Chasnoff, Wells, & King, 2015; Woolgar & Scott, 2014.
32. Baptista et al., 2016; May, 2015.
33. Kearney & Millstein, 2013, p. 261.
34. Kearney & Millstein, 2013.
35. Skinner-Drawz, Wrobel, Grotevant, & Von Korff, 2011.
36. Davenport, 2018; Palmer, 2012.
37. Sharon Roszia, personal communication, November 21, 2017.
38. Fravel, McRoy, & Grotevant, 2000; Freeark et al., 2005.
39. David Brodzinsky, personal communication, August 19, 2018.
40. Wright, Flynn, & Welch, 2007.
41. Siegel, 2012b.
42. Ibid.
43. Brodzinsky, 2006, 2011; Siegel & Smith, 2012.
44. David Brodzinsky, personal communication, August 19, 2018; Grotevant, 2009; Katz, 1986; North American Council on Adoptable Children, 2018; Roszia & Silverstein, 1999.
45. Sharon Roszia, personal communication, November 21, 2017.
46. Brodzinsky and the Donaldson Adoption Institute, 2013.

APPENDIX A

Demographic Information for Participants

	Parents' Names, Race	Birth Parents' & Siblings' Names	Region	Parent Profession	Child Name	Child Race	Child Gender	Child Age at Adoption	Adoption Type	Siblings Adopted Later (Number + Gender)
	\multicolumn{10}{l}{LESBIAN COUPLES, PRIVATE DOMESTIC ADOPTION}	
1.	Tammy (White)		Midwest; LARGE CITY[a]	Graphic designer	Madden	White	Boy	Newborn	Open Private Domestic	
	Holly (White)			Civil engineer						
2.	Mariette (White)	BM: Didi BF: Jim	Midwest; SUBURB of large city	Physical therapist	Jacob	Biracial (AA, White)	Boy	Newborn	Private Domestic	
	Jenny (White)			Manager of a medical supply company						
3.	Rachel (White)	BM: Jade	South; LARGE CITY	Computer applications training manager	Moriah	Biracial (AA, White)	Girl	Newborn	Private Domestic	

	Nancy (White)		Manager of a pet store					
4.	Tiffany (White)		South; LARGE CITY	Accounts manager	Patrice	Biracial (AA, White)	Boy	Newborn	Private Domestic
	Karen (White)		Custom framing specialist					
5.	Charlene (White)	BM: Jasmine	Northeast; MEDIUM CITY	Teacher	Sofia	Biracial (Latina, White)	Girl	Newborn	Private Domestic
	Leila (White)		Physical therapist					
6.	Daniela (White)	BM: Joy BF: Danny	South; MEDIUM CITY	Owner of a small bookstore	Stella	White	Girl	Newborn	Private Domestic
	Heather (White)		Bookkeeper					
7.	Stacy (White)	BM: Krista BF: Jay	Northeast; MEDIUM CITY	School administrator	Marlo	Biracial (Latina, White)	Girl	Newborn	Private Domestic
	Deb (White)		Chiropractor					

8.	Miranda (White)	BM: Emily	Northwest; LARGE CITY	Director of career services at university	Eloise	White	Girl	Newborn	Private Domestic	
	Shannon (White)			School psychologist						
9.	Andrea (White)	BM: Luciana	South; MEDIUM CITY	Prison guard	Jessie	Latina	Girl	Newborn	Private Domestic	
	Mary (White)			Manager at a TV production studio						
10.	Molly (White)	BM: Sharla	Northeast; SUBURB of large city	Environmental engineer	Quinn	White	Girl	Newborn	Private Domestic	1 boy, Dillon
	Taryn (White)			Radio personality						
11.	Erin (White)		West; LARGE CITY	Librarian	Jeremy	White	Boy	Newborn	Private Domestic	
	Meredith (White)			Office manager						
12.	Christy (White)	BM: Ann	Northeast; MEDIUM CITY	Director of nonprofit	Arielle	White	Girl	Newborn	Private Domestic	
	Sonja (Native American, White)			Data analyst						

	Parents' Names, Race	Birth Parents' & Siblings' Names	Region	Parent Profession	Child Name	Child Race	Child Gender	Child Age at Adoption	Adoption Type	Siblings Adopted Later (Number + Gender)
13.	Eliza (White)	BM: Amy BS: Reese	Northeast; LARGE CITY	Junior accountant for small county hospital	Luke	Biracial (AA, White)	Boy	Newborn	Private Domestic	1 boy, Stewart
	Hannah (White)			Administrative assistant						
14.	Peggy (White)		Northeast; LARGE CITY	Occupational therapist	Kacie	Biracial (AA, White)	Girl	Newborn	Private Domestic	
	Elana (White)			Web editor						
15.	Miri (White)		Northeast; LARGE CITY	Artist	Ava	AA	Girl	Newborn	Private Domestic	

LESBIAN COUPLES, PUBLIC DOMESTIC ADOPTION

	Parents' Names, Race	Birth Parents' & Siblings' Names	Region	Parent Profession	Child Name	Child Race	Child Gender	Child Age at Adoption	Adoption Type	Siblings Adopted Later (Number + Gender)
1.	Kathleen (White)		West; MEDIUM CITY	Manager of a nonprofit	Ana	Biracial (Latina, White)	Girl	Newborn	Public Domestic	
	Becki (White)			Group home supervisor						

2.	Kate (White)	BM: Camila BF: Rafael	West; LARGE CITY	Director of a women's survival center	Daniel	Latino	Boy	3 months	Public Domestic	2 girls: Gabriela and Adriana
	Cara (White)			Landscape design artist						
3.	Aisha (AA)		Northeast; LARGE CITY	Human resources manager	Elise	Biracial (AA, White)	Girl	5 years	Public Domestic	
	Larissa (White)			Bookstore manager						
4.	Greta (White)	BF: Esteban BB: Mateo	Northeast; SUBURB of large city	Small business owner	Shawn	Latino	Boy	3 years	Public Domestic	
	Robin (White)			Freelance writer						
5.	Eva (Latina)	BB: Rick	Northeast; SUBURB of large city	Communications professor	Devon	Latino	Boy	4 years	Public Domestic	
	Tina (AA, Asian, White)			Engineer						
6.	Lauren (White)	BS: Abigail	Northeast; MEDIUM CITY	Social worker	Kiley	Latina	Girl	6 years	Public Domestic	
	Victoria (White)			Medical assistant						

	Parents' Names, Race	Region	Parent Profession							
7.	Kerry (White)	Northeast; SMALL CITY	Housepainter	Cameron Cole	Biracial (Latino, White)	2 Boys	10 and 6	Public Domestic		
	Shelby (White)		Postal clerk							

GAY COUPLES, PRIVATE DOMESTIC ADOPTION

	Parents' Names, Race	Birth Parents' & Siblings' Names	Region	Parent Profession	Child Name	Child Race	Child Gender	Child Age at Adoption	Adoption Type	Siblings Adopted Later (Number + Gender)
1.	Jamie (White)		South; MEDIUM CITY	Communications manager	Timothy	Biracial (AA, White)	Boy	Newborn	Private Domestic	1 girl, Daria
	Evan (White)			Office manager at a hospital						
2.	Paul (White)	BM: Nina BB: Sebastian	South; SMALL CITY	School principal	Louisa	Biracial (AA, White)	Girl	Newborn	Private Domestic	1 girl, Magdalen
	Greg (White)			Software consultant						
3.	Brent (White)	BM: Adalia	West; LARGE CITY	Brand manager at a small skincare company	Samuel	Latino	Boy	Newborn	Private Domestic	
	Travis (White)			Technical writer						

4.	Leo (Latino)	BM: Leandra	East; SUBURB of large city	Speech therapist	Elizabeth	Biracial (AA, White)	Girl	Newborn	Private Domestic	
	Javier (Latino)			Gastroenterologist						
5.	Roy (White)	BM: Liza	West; LARGE CITY	Sales manager	Ethan	AA	Boy	Newborn	Private Domestic	
	Dante (AA)			Vice president of operations						
6.	Rick (White)	BM: Sara BS: Caitlin BB: Jayden	West; LARGE CITY	Director of a nonprofit	Jack	White	Boy	Newborn	Private Domestic	
	Marcus (White)			Graduate student						
7.	Roger (White)	BM: Beth	East; SUBURB of large city	Director of marketing at a small company	Xavier	Biracial (AA, White)	Boy	Newborn	Private Domestic	1 boy, Corey
8.	Doug (White)	BM: Lara	West; LARGE CITY	Psychologist	Catie	White	Girl	Newborn	Private Domestic	
	Sam (Asian, White)			Human resources director						

#	Parents	Location	Occupation	Child name	Race	Sex	Age	Adoption type	Other children
9.	Phil (White) BM: Elle	South; MEDIUM CITY	Graduate student in physics	Anastasia	Multiracial (AA, Asian, White)	Girl	Newborn	Private Domestic	
	Eddie (White)		Physical therapist						
10.	Adam (AA, White) BM: Julie	West; MEDIUM CITY	Director of marketing	Isaac	Biracial (Latino, White)	Boy	Newborn	Private Domestic	1 girl, Clementine
	Will (White)		Accountant						
11.	Benji (White) BM: Emmy BF: Luis	West; LARGE CITY	Dermatologist	Ryanne	Latina	Girl	Newborn	Private Domestic	
	Darren (White)		Computer programmer						
12.	Dave (White) BM: Keira	Midwest; LARGE CITY	Radiologist	Aidan	Latino	Boy	Newborn	Private Domestic	
	Byron (White)		Graduate student in linguistics						
13.	Rob (Latino) BM: Alena	West; SUBURB of large city	Administrative assistant	David	Biracial (Latino, White)	Boy	Newborn	Private Domestic	1 boy, Nolan
	Terrence (White)		Anesthesiologist						
14.	Seth (White)	South; LARGE CITY	Director of an after-school program	Bobby	White	Boy	Newborn	Private Domestic	1 girl, Samantha

		Dean (White)			Software developer							
15.		Eric (White)		East; LARGE CITY	Editor		Glenn	White	Boy	Newborn	Private Domestic	
		Russell (White)			Policy analyst							

	Parents' Names, Race	Birth Parents' & Siblings' Names	Region	Parent Profession	Child Name	Child Race	Child Gender	Child Age at Adoption	Adoption Type	Siblings Adopted Later (Number + Gender)
	\multicolumn{10}{c}{GAY COUPLES, PUBLIC DOMESTIC ADOPTION}									
1.	Joe (White)	BM: Alison BB: Perry BB: Jax	Northwest; LARGE CITY	Operations manager	Chase	White	Boy	1 year	Public Domestic	
	Jared (White)			Sales associate						
2.	Jake (White)		West; SMALL CITY	Hotel manager	Sharice	AA	Girl	3 years	Public Domestic	1 girl, Sheree 1 boy, Amos
	Carl (AA)			Day care supervisor						
3.	Al (White)	BM: Nina BF: Steve	East; MEDIUM CITY	Insurance sales manager	Nick	White	Boy	10 years	Public Domestic	2 boys, Mitchell and Brad

	Geoff (White)			Waiter					
4.	Nate (White)		South; LARGE CITY	Medical assistant		Biracial (Latino, White)	Boy	5 years	Public Domestic
	Dwight (White)			Health program administrator					
5.	Randy (White)		West; LARGE CITY	Operations manager for a retail chain	Lars	White	Boy	6 years	Public Domestic
	Brendan (White)			Auditor					
6.	Simon (White)	BB: Gamba	Midwest; LARGE CITY	Social worker	Ayo	AA	Boy	1 year	Public Domestic
	Vincent (White)			Director of telecommunications at a small company					
7.	Noah (White)	BB: Robert BB: Mason BS: Bonnie	West; LARGE CITY	School psychologist	Shayne	Biracial (Latino, Native American)	Boy	5 years	Public Domestic
	Reed (White)			Director of alumni relations at a university					

	Parents' Names, Race	Birth Parents' & Siblings' Names	Region	Parent Profession	Child Name	Child Race	Child Gender	Child Age at Adoption	Adoption Type	Siblings Adopted Later (Number + Gender)
	\multicolumn{10}{l}{HETEROSEXUAL COUPLES, PRIVATE DOMESTIC ADOPTION}									
1.	Elora (White)	BM: Shari	West; LARGE CITY	Homemaker	Maeve	Biracial (Latina, White)	Girl	Newborn	Private Domestic	1 girl, Opal
	Dominick (Native American, Asian, White)			Small business owner						
2.	Ellen (White)	BM: Dania BB: Finn	West; LARGE CITY	Travel writer	Anthony	Biracial (Latino, White)	Boy	Newborn	Private Domestic	1 boy, Benny
	Matt (White)			Realtor						
3.	Seana (White)	BM: Dana BF: Brad	Midwest; LARGE CITY	Sales associate at a jewelry store	Joseph	White	Boy	Newborn	Private Domestic	
	Ron (White)			Supervisor at a retail chain						
4.	Laura (White)		Midwest; MEDIUM CITY	Web designer	Dennis	Latino	Boy	Newborn	Private Domestic	1 boy, Tate
	Lou (White)			Cartoonist						
5.	Donna (White)	BM: Gloria	Northeast; LARGE CITY	Manager at a nonprofit	Ace	Biracial (AA, White)	Boy	Newborn	Private Domestic	

6.	Max (White)	BM: Coco						
	Therese (White)		South; SUBURB of large city	Teacher	Josh	Latino	Boy	Newborn	Private Domestic
	Lucas (Latino)			Lawyer					
7.	Lena (White)	BM: Mandy	Northeast; MEDIUM CITY	Operations manager	Joey	White	Boy	Newborn	Private Domestic
	Thomas (White)			Financial planner					
8.	Jackie (White)	BM: Thea BS: Debbie BB: John BB: Jake	Northeast; SUBURB of large city	Pediatric nurse	Serena	White	Girl	Newborn	Private Domestic
	Bob (White)			Financial manager					
9.	Shoshanna (White)	BM: Leanne BF: Tucker	Northeast; SMALL CITY	Project manager	Morgan	White	Girl	Newborn	Private Domestic
	Cal (White)			IT manager					
10.	Georgia (White)		West; LARGE CITY	Realtor	Henry	Biracial (Latino, White)	Boy	Newborn	Private Domestic

	Stan (White)		Program evaluation manager					
11.	Jessica (White)	BM: Carolyn	Midwest; MEDIUM CITY	Homemaker	Jerome	AA	Boy	4 months	Private Domestic
	Ned (White)			Engineer					
12.	Kelly (White)	BM: Zoe	West; LARGE CITY	Environmental planner	Rosa	Multiracial (AA, Latina, White)	Girl	Newborn	Private Domestic
	Gil (White)			Property manager					
13.	Monica (White)	BM: Tracy	West; MEDIUM CITY	Graphic design artist	Olivia	Latina	Girl	Newborn	Private Domestic
	Damian (White)			Software engineer					
14.	Angela (White)	BM: Nessa	West; LARGE CITY	Environmental planner	Violet	Biracial (AA, White)	Girl	Newborn	Private Domestic
	Gordon (White)			Property manager					
15.	Carly (White)		Northeast; LARGE CITY	History professor	Eve	AA	Girl	Newborn	Private Domestic
	Brian (White)			Dentist					

	Parents' Names, Race	Birth Parents' & Siblings' Names	Region	Parent Profession	Child Name	Child Race	Child Gender	Child Age at Adoption	Adoption Type	Siblings Adopted Later (Number + Gender)
	\multicolumn{10}{c}{HETEROSEXUAL COUPLES, PUBLIC DOMESTIC ADOPTION}	
1.	Annie (White)	BB: Christian	Northeast; SUBURB of large city	School administrator	Grayson	White	Boy	3 years	Public Domestic	
	Chuck (White)			IT director						
2.	Sandy (White)		Northeast; SMALL CITY	Health care advocate	Todd	White	Boy	2 years	Public Domestic	
	Lewis (White)			Teacher						
3.	Rosie (White)		Northeast; SUBURB of large city	Magazine editor	Lila	White	Girl	1.5 years	Public Domestic	
	Tony (White)			Small business owner						
4.	Leigh (White)		East; SMALL CITY	Assistant museum director	Kevin	White	Boy	15 months	Public Domestic	
	Billy (White)			Assistant principal						
5.	Mindy (White)	BM: Barbie	East; SUBURB of large city	Career services manager	Brett	Biracial (AA, White)	Boy	4 years	Public Domestic	

		Earl (White)						
6.		Meg (White)	BM: Penny	East; MEDIUM CITY	Therapist	Graduate student	Shaylene	Biracial (AA, Latina)	Girl	1.5 years	
		Michael (White)				Philosophy professor				
7.		Marianna (White)		East; SUBURB of large city		Homemaker	Lola	Biracial (AA, Latina)	Girl	10 years	Public Domestic
		Jerry (White)				Appliance installer				

Note. AA = African American; BB = birth brother; BF = birth father; BM = birth mother; BS = birth sister.

[a] Geographic determinations (large city, medium city, small city, suburb of large city) are based on the CDC Urban-Rural Classification Schemes for Counties.[1] This classification system specifies metropolitan categories (large cities, suburbs of large cities, medium cities, and small metro cities) and nonmetropolitan categories (micropolitan and noncore). A key feature of the NCHS urban–rural scheme is that it separates counties within large metropolitan areas (1 million or more population) into two categories: large "central" metro (akin to inner cities) and large "fringe" metro (akin to suburbs).

Large cities—counties in metropolitan statistical areas (MSAs) of 1 million or more population that (a) contain the entire population of the largest principal city of the MSA, or (b) have their entire population contained in the largest principal city of the MSA, or (c) contain at least 250,000 inhabitants of any principal city of the MSA.

Suburb of large cities—counties in MSAs of 1 million or more population that did not qualify as large central metro counties.

Medium cities—counties in MSAs of populations of 250,000 to 999,999.

Small cities—counties in MSAs of populations less than 250,000.

Micropolitan—counties in micropolitan statistical areas (N/A in this sample).

Noncore—nonmetropolitan counties that did not qualify as micropolitan (N/A in this sample).

Note

1. Centers for Disease Control and Prevention, 2018.

APPENDIX B

Data Analysis Process

Data analysis is a crucial part of any book that relies predominantly on participant interviews and attempts to tell a coherent story based on interview data. In turn, with so many participants (132) and time points (4), it is worth sharing a little bit about the steps and stages of my data analysis process.[1]

I engaged in a multistep approach to data analysis. Initially I wrote short memos on each family that incorporated key information about their family structure (e.g., adoption type, parent and child race, geographic location, if and when parents adopted subsequent children) as well as key details of their adoption (e.g., level/type of openness, changes in openness over time, contact types, specific birth family members with whom the family maintained contact). I also incorporated key phrases or quotes that illustrated, for example, how families talked about adoption, and changes in how they talked or approached adoption over time. Then, I began coding data by time point. For example, I read all of the preadoption interviews carefully, identifying key common themes, as well as differences and similarities across participants. Then, I read all of the 3-month postadoption participant interviews carefully and developed a list of key themes. I then examined these codes across time point and across families. At this point, I moved on to consider the 5-year postadoption interviews, using a similar approach. Then, I carefully read and developed themes for the 8-year postadoption interviews. Comparing and contrasting themes across time points and families was overwhelming and time-consuming, and I enlisted the use of NVivo, a qualitative data analysis software program, to help me to organize key themes and quotes.

After taking a time-centric approach, I moved to a family-centric approach. I read each family's data from each time point, characterizing their journey with a variety of themes and quotes. Of particular interest to me at this stage was gaining an understanding of how families' experiences with and approach to openness had shifted or evolved over time—that is, the trajectories and dynamics associated with openness.

After developing a long list of themes for each family, for each time point, and for each family across time points, it was necessary to distill these into a less lengthy and more digestible "storyline"—which took the form of mapping out, very roughly, the key chapter titles, in order. For example, I knew I wanted to start with a chapter on preadoptive experiences that would address parents' ideas about adoption and openness prior to the adoption, as well as experiences of infertility, if relevant. I also wanted a chapter that captured the immediate transitional phase, as families made contact with birth families for the first time. I wanted a chapter that explored changes in contact and the complex and varied trajectories that took hold in many families. I also wanted a chapter on how parents talk about adoption at different stages. Thus, I began to map themes onto chapter topics. I was at this point able to distill a document that was hundreds of pages long into one that was under 100 pages.

At this stage, after mapping out the primary themes in each chapter, I went back to the data, grouping participants according to subthemes, or subcodes (e.g., those who struggled with infertility, how they moved from infertility to adoption), attending to what distinguished these individuals from each other and from individuals not in that subcode (e.g., those who did not encounter infertility). During this process, I also continued to carefully consider how key participant characteristics—such as adoption type, parent gender, parent and child race—helped to differentiate or make sense of the emergent themes. Effort was also made to search for "negative cases"—that is, those where participants' experiences or perspectives differ from the main body of evidence. The ability to account for or explain a negative case (e.g., how and why did a heterosexual woman not attempt to conceive prior to pursuing adoption?) serves to strengthen the general explanation for the "typical" case (e.g., how and why most heterosexual women do attempt to conceive prior to pursuing adoption).

During the years I spent writing this book, I shared some of my findings—and in some cases, full chapters—with key "players" in the adoption world. Specifically, I shared my work with several executive directors and/or founders of adoption agencies, adoption social workers, adoptive parents who did not participate in my research, and several internationally recognized adoption scholars. My conversations with these individuals, as well as their written feedback, in some cases caused me to return to the data to further refine my coding scheme and data analysis, either to achieve greater clarity or to better explain, account for, or expand upon certain themes. Thus, the coding, analysis, and editing process was iterative in nature, whereby I drew on my colleagues' insights and observations to refine, improve upon, and deepen my analysis.

In sharing details about each family, I made an effort to preserve the integrity of each family's story—namely, to capture the key dynamics and issues for each family, and in doing so, to meaningfully and authentically capture parents' feelings about, changes in, and challenges regarding openness. Yet I was also mindful of the fact that certain family circumstances were fairly unusual or unique, and that providing families' demographic details in addition to their particular birth family dynamics could potentially identify some families. In turn, I made the decision to obscure or subtly change certain demographic details, in order to preserve confidentiality. In doing so, however, I made every effort to ensure that these changes did not meaningfully alter the storyline of that family or the types of conclusions that could be drawn about their experiences. In some cases, such as when discussing participant quotes that discuss highly sensitive information or details that have not been shared among family members, I have chosen not to provide the participants' pseudonyms or demographic details that could identify them. I take seriously my commitment to my participants—but also wish to provide readers with meaningful accounts of real people and their experiences. I juggled this balance throughout the writing of this book and tried to come up with reasonable solutions that would allow me to do both.

Note

1. Bogdan & Biklen, 2007; Dickie, 2003; Goldberg & Allen, 2015.

References

American Academy of Pediatrics, Committee on Early Childhood, Adoption, & Dependent Care. (2000). Developmental issues for young children in foster care. *Pediatrics, 106*, 1145–1150.

Baptista, N., Christensen, K., Carere, D., Broadley, S., Roberts, J., & Green, R. (2016). Adopting genetics: Motivations and outcomes of personal genomic testing in adult adoptees. *Genetics in Medicine, 18*, 924–932.

Barth, R. P., & Berry, M. (1988). *Adoption and disruption: Rates, risks, and responses.* Hawthorne, NY: Aldine de Gruyter.

Baxter, L. A., Norwood, K. M., Asbury, B., & Scharp, K. M. (2014). Narrating adoption: Resisting adoption as "second best" in online stories of domestic adoption. *Journal of Family Communication, 14*, 253–269.

Belbas, N. (1986). Staying in touch: Empathy in open adoptions. *Smith College Studies in Social Work, 57*, 37–55.

Berge, J. M., Mendenhall, T. J., Wrobel, G. M., Grotevant, H. D., & McRoy, R. G. (2006). Adolescents' feelings about openness in adoption: Implications for adoption agencies. *Child Welfare, 85*, 1011–1039.

Black, K., Moyer, A. M., & Goldberg, A. E. (2016). From face-to-face to Facebook: The role of technology and social media in adoptive family relationships with birth family. *Adoption Quarterly, 19*, 306–332.

Bogdan, R. C., & Biklen, S. K. (2007). *Qualitative research for education: An introduction to theory and methods* (5th ed.). Boston, MA: Pearson.

Bouchard, T. (1994). Genes, environment, and personality. *Science, 264*(5166), 1700–1701.

Boyle, C. (2017). What is the impact of birth family contact on children in adoption and long term foster care? A systematic review. *Child & Family Social Work, 22*, 22–33.

Broderick, C. B. (1993). *Understanding family process: Basics of family systems theory.* Thousand Oaks, CA: Sage.

Brodzinsky, D. M. (1987). Adjustment to adoption: A psychosocial perspective. *Clinical Psychology Review, 7*, 25–47.

Brodzinsky, D. (1997). Infertility and adoption adjustment: Considerations and clinical issues. In S. R. Leiblum (Ed.), *Wiley series in couples and family dynamics and treatment. Infertility: Psychological issues and counseling strategies* (pp. 246–262). Oxford, England: Wiley.

Brodzinsky, D. M. (2006). Family structural openness and communication openness as predictors in the adjustment of adopted children. *Adoption Quarterly, 9*, 1–18.

Brodzinsky, D. M. (2011). Children's understanding of adoption: Developmental and clinical implications. *Professional Psychology: Research and Practice, 42*, 200–207.

Brodzinsky, D. (2014). Adoptive identity and children's understanding of adoption: Implications for pediatric practice. In P. Mason, D. Johnson, & L. Albers Prock (Eds.), *Adoption medicine: Caring for children and families* (pp. 367–394). Elk Grove Village, IL: American Academy of Pediatrics.

Brodzinsky, D. M., & the Donaldson Adoption Institute. (2013). *A need to know: Enhancing adoption competence among mental health professionals.* Retrieved from https://www.adoptioninstitute.org/wp-content/uploads/2017/03/2013_08_ANeedToKnow.pdf

Brodzinsky, D. M., & Goldberg, A. E. (2016). Contact with birth family in adoptive families headed by lesbian, gay male, and heterosexual parents. *Children & Youth Services Review, 62,* 9–17.

Brodzinsky, D. M., Schechter, M. D., & Henig, R. M. (1992). *Being adopted: The lifelong search for self.* New York, NY: Anchor Press.

Brodzinsky, D. M., Singer, L. M., & Braff, A. M. (1984). Children's understanding of adoption. *Child Development, 55,* 869–878.

Campbell, L. H., Silverman, P. R., & Patti, P. B. (1991). Reunions between adoptees and birth parents: The adoptees' experience. *Social Work, 36,* 329–335.

Carney, E. N. (2014, June 6). Birth fathers: The forgotten half of the story. *Adoptive Families.* Retrieved from www.adoptivefamilies.com/openness/birth-fathers-and-adoption/

Carney, E. N. (2018). Understanding open adoption. *Adoptive Families.* Retrieved from https://www.adoptivefamilies.com/openness/understanding-open-adoption/

Carter, B., & McGoldrick, M. (Eds.). (2005). *The expanded family life cycle: Individual, family, and social perspectives.* London, UK: Pearson.

Centers for Disease Control and Prevention. (2018). *NCHS urban-rural classification scheme for counties.* Retrieved from https://www.cdc.gov/nchs/data_access/urban_rural.htm

Chasnoff, I. J., Wells, A. M., & King, L. (2015). Misdiagnosis and missed diagnoses in foster and adopted children with prenatal alcohol exposure. *Pediatrics, 135,* 264–270.

Chateaneuf, D., & Ouellette, F. R. (2017). Kinship within the context of new genetics: The experience of infertility from medical assistance to adoption. *Journal of Family Issues, 38*(2), 177–203.

Chaulk, K., & Jones, T. (2011). Online obsessive relational intrusion: Further concerns about Facebook. *Journal of Family Violence, 26,* 245–254.

Child, J. T., & Petronio, S. (2011). Unpacking the paradoxes of privacy in CMC relationships: The challenges of blogging and relational communication on the internet. In K. B. Wright & L. M. Webb (Eds.), *Computer-mediated communication in personal relationships* (pp. 21–40). New York, NY: Peter Lang.

Child, J. T., & Starcher, S. C. (2016). Fuzzy Facebook privacy boundaries: Exploring mediated lurking, vague-booking, and Facebook privacy management. *Computers in Human Behavior, 54,* 1–8.

Child Welfare Information Gateway. (2012). *Sibling issues in foster care and adoption.* Washington, DC: U.S. Department of Health and Human Services, Children's Bureau. Retrieved from https://www.childwelfare.gov/pubpdfs/siblingissues.pdf

Child Welfare Information Gateway. (2013). *Openness in adoption: Building relationships between adoptive and birth families.* Washington, DC: U.S. Department of Health and Human Services, Children's Bureau. Retrieved from https://www.childwelfare.gov/pubs/f-openadopt/

Child Welfare Information Gateway. (2014). *Post adoption contract agreements between birth and adoptive families.* Washington, DC: U.S. Department of Health and Human Services, Children's Bureau. Retrieved from https://www.childwelfare.gov/pubpdfs/cooperative.pdf

Clapton, G. (2003). *Birth fathers and their adoption experiences*. London, UK: Jessica Kingsley Publishers.

Clutter, L. (2017). Open adoption placement by birth mothers in their twenties. *Journal of Maternal/Child Nursing, 42*, 345–351.

Colaner, C. W., & Kranstuber, H. (2010). Forever kind of wondering: Communicatively managing uncertainty in adoptive families. *Journal of Family Communication, 10*, 236–255.

Coles, G. (2011). *The invisible men of adoption*. Melbourne, Australia: Mermerus Books.

Cowan, C. P., & Cowan, P. A. (2000). *When partners become parents: The big life change for couples*. Mahwah, NJ: Lawrence Erlbaum Associates.

Crea, T. M., & Barth, R. P. (2009). Patterns and predictors of adoption openness and contact: 14 years postadoption. *Family Relations, 58*, 607–620.

Cushman, L. F., Kalmuss, D., & Namerow, P. B. (1997). Openness in adoption. *Marriage & Family Review, 25*, 7–18.

Daly, K. (1992). Toward a formal theory of interactive resocialization: The case of adoptive parenthood. *Qualitative Sociology, 15*, 395–417.

Davenport, D. (2018). Should you tell your adopted child he was conceived by rape, his mother is an addict, etc.? *Creating a Family*. Retrieved from https://creatingafamily.org/adoption-category/adopted-child-conceived-rape/

De Wolf, R., Willaert, K., & Pierson, J. (2014). Managing privacy boundaries together: Exploring individual and group privacy management strategies in Facebook. *Computers in Human Behavior, 35*, 444–454.

Deykin, E. Y., Campbell, L., & Patti, P. (1984). The postadoption experience of surrendering parents. *American Journal of Orthopsychiatry, 54*, 271–280.

Dickie, V. A. (2003). Data analysis in qualitative research: A plea for sharing the magic and the effort. *American Journal of Occupational Therapy, 57*, 49–56.

Docan-Morgan, S. (2010). "They don't know what it's like to be in my shoes": Topic avoidance about race in transracially adoptive families. *Journal of Social and Personal Relationships, 27*, 336–355.

Donovan, S. (2013). *No matter what: An adoptive family's story of hope, love and healing*. London, UK: Jessica Kingsley Publishers.

Dunbar, N., Manfred, H., van Dulmen, M., Ayers-Lopez, S., Berge, J., Christian, C., . . . McRoy, R. (2006). Processes linked to contact changes in adoptive kinship networks. *Family Process, 45*, 449–465.

Dusky, L. (2015). *Hole in my heart: Memoir and report from the fault lines of adoption*. Leto Media.

Edelstein, S. B., Gonzalez, A., Langley, A., Waterman, J., Paasivirta, M., & Paczkowski, E. (2017). Preparing and partnering with families to support the adoption of children from foster care. *Adoption Quarterly, 20*, 119–133.

Elder, G. H., Jr. (1994). Time, human agency, and social change: Perspectives on the life course. *Social Psychology Quarterly, 57*, 4–15.

Elder, G. H., Jr. (1998). The life course as developmental theory. *Child Development, 69*, 1–12.

Elkins, R. (2011). *Open adoption, open heart: An adoptive father's inspiring journey*. Aloha Publishing.

Ettner, J. (1993). Levels of cooperation and satisfaction in 56 open adoptions. *Child Welfare, 62*, 257–267.

Family Education. (2018). *Adoption: When problems occur with birth parents*. Retrieved from https://www.familyeducation.com/life/birthparent-adoptive-parent-relations/adoption-when-problems-occur-birthparents

Farr, R. H., Grant-Marsney, H. A., & Grotevant, H. D. (2014). Adoptees' contact with birth parents in emerging adulthood: The role of adoption communication and attachment to adoptive parents. *Family Process*, 53, 656–671.

Farr, R., Ravvina, Y., & Grotevant, H. (2018). Birth family contact experiences among lesbian, gay, and heterosexual adoptive parents with school-aged children. *Family Relations*, 67, 132–146.

Faulkner, M., & Madden, E. (2012). Openness and post adoption birth family contact: A comparison of non-relative foster and private adoptions. *Adoption Quarterly*, 15(1), 35–56.

Felitti, V., Anda, R., Nordenberg, D., Williamson, D., Spitz, A., Edwards, V., . . . Marks, J. (1998). Relationship of childhood abuse and household dysfunction to many of the leading causes of death in adults. *American Journal of Preventative Medicine*, 14, 245–258.

Franck, E. J. (2001). Outreach to birthfathers of children in out-of-home care. *Child Welfare*, 80, 381–399.

Fravel, D. L., McRoy, R. G., & Grotevant, H. D. (2000). Birthmother perceptions of the psychologically present adopted child: Adoption openness and boundary ambiguity. *Family Relations*, 49(4), 425–433.

Freeark, K., Rosenberg, E. B., Bornstein, J., Jozefowicz-Simbeni, D., Linkevich, M., & Lohnes, K. (2005). Gender differences and dynamics shaping the adoption life cycle: Review of the literature and recommendations. *American Journal of Orthopsychiatry*, 75, 86–101.

French, C. A., Henney, S. M., Ayers-Lopez, S., McRoy, R. G., & Grotevant, H. D. (2014). Birth mothers' perspectives on their relationship with the birth father 12 to 20 years after adoption. *Journal of Family Issues*, 35, 579–600.

Fursland, E. (2010a). *Facing up to Facebook*. London, England: British Association for Adoption and Fostering.

Fursland, E. (2010b, June 19). Facebook has changed adoption forever. *The Guardian*. Retrieved from https://www.theguardian.com/lifeandstyle/2010/jun/19/facebook-adoption-tracing-birth-mother

Fursland, E. (2013). *Facing up to Facebook: A survival guide for adoptive families*. London, UK: British Association for Adoption and Fostering.

Ge, X., Natsuaki, M., Martin, D., Leve, L., Neiderhiser, J., Shaw, D. S., & Reiss D. (2008). Bridging the divide: Openness in adoption and postadoption psychosocial adjustment among birth and adoptive parents. *Journal of Family Psychology*, 22, 529–540.

Goldberg, A. E. (2009). Lesbian and heterosexual preadoptive couples' openness to transracial adoption. *American Journal of Orthopsychiatry*, 79, 103–117.

Goldberg, A. E. (2010). The transition to adoptive parenthood. In T. W. Miller (Ed.), *Handbook of stressful transitions across the lifespan* (pp. 165–184). New York, NY: Springer.

Goldberg, A. E. (2012). *Gay dads: Transitions to adoptive fatherhood*. New York, NY: NYU Press.

Goldberg, A. E., & Allen, K. R. (2015). Communicating qualitative research: Some practical guideposts for scholars. *Journal of Marriage and Family*, 77, 3–22.

Goldberg, A. E., Downing, J. B., & Richardson, H. B. (2009). The transition from infertility to adoption: Perceptions of lesbian and heterosexual preadoptive couples. *Journal of Social and Personal Relationships, 26,* 938–963.

Goldberg, A. E., Kinkler, L. A., Richardson, H. B., & Downing, J. B. (2011). Lesbian, gay, and heterosexual couples in open adoption arrangements: A qualitative study. *Journal of Marriage and Family, 73,* 502–518.

Goldberg, A. E., Moyer, A., Kinkler, L. A., & Richardson, H. B. (2012). "When you're sitting on the fence, hope's the hardest part": Challenges and experiences of heterosexual and same-sex couples adopting through the child welfare system. *Adoption Quarterly, 15,* 288–315.

Goldberg, A. E., & Scheib, J. (2015). Why donor insemination and not adoption? Narratives of female-partnered and single mothers. *Family Relations, 64,* 726–742

Goldberg, A. E., & Smith, J. Z. (2009). Predicting non-African American lesbian and heterosexual preadoptive couples' openness to adopting an African American child. *Family Relations, 58,* 346–360.

Goldberg, A. E., & Smith, J. Z. (2013). Predictors of psychological adjustment among early-placed adopted children with lesbian, gay, and heterosexual parents. *Journal of Family Psychology, 27,* 431–442.

Goldberg, A. E., & Smith, J. Z. (2016). Predictors of race, adoption, and sexual orientation related socialization of adoptive parents of young children. *Journal of Family Psychology, 30*(3), 397–408.

Goldberg, A. E., Sweeney, K., Black, K., & Moyer, A. (2016). Lesbian, gay, and heterosexual adoptive parents' socialization approaches to children's minority statuses. *Counseling Psychologist, 44*(2), 267–299.

Greenhow, S., Hackett, S., Jones, C., & Meins, E. (2016). The maintenance of traditional and technological forms of post-adoption contact. *Child Abuse Review, 25,* 373–385.

Gregorian, D. (2015, August 26). Rosie O'Donnell's daughter leaves home to move in with birth mother in Wisconsin after turning 18. *Daily News.* Retrieved from http://www.nydailynews.com/entertainment/gossip/rosie-o-donnell-daughter-moves-birth-mom-wisc-article-1.2338449

Greil, A. L., Leitko, T. A., & Porter, K. L. (1988). Infertility: His and hers. *Gender & Society, 2,* 172–199.

Greil, A. L., Slauson-Blevins, K., & McQuillan, J. (2009). The experience of infertility: A review of recent literature. *Sociology of Health & Illness, 32,* 140–162.

Gritter, J. L. (2000). *Lifegivers: Framing the birthparent experience in open adoption.* Arlington, VA: CWLA Press.

Grotevant, H. D. (2009). Emotional distance regulation over the life course in adoptive kinship networks. In G. Wrobel & E. Neil (Eds.), *International advances in adoption research for practice* (pp. 295–316). Chichester, England: Wiley.

Grotevant, H. D., & McRoy, R. G. (1998). *Openness in adoption: Exploring family connections.* Thousand Oaks, CA: Sage.

Grotevant, H. D., McRoy, R. G., Elde, C. L., & Fravel, D. L. (1994). Adoptive family system dynamics: Variations by level of openness in the adoption. *Family Process, 33,* 125–146.

Grotevant, H. D., McRoy, R. G., Wrobel, G. M., & Ayers-Lopez, S. (2013). Contact between adoptive and birth families: Perspectives from the Minnesota Texas Adoption Research Project. *Child Development Perspectives, 7,* 193–198.

Grotevant, H. D., Wrobel, G. M., Von Korff, L., Skinner, B., Newell, J., Friese, S., & McRoy, R. G. (2007). Many faces of openness in adoption: Perspectives of adopted adolescents and their parents. *Adoption Quarterly, 10*, 79–101.

Hamilton, L., Cheng, S., & Powell, B. (2007). Adoptive parents, adaptive parents: Evaluating the importance of biological ties for parental involvement. *American Sociological Review, 72*, 95–116.

Hampton, K. N., Goulet, L. S., Rainie, L., & Purcell, K. (2011). Social networking sites and our lives. *Pew Research Center's Internet & American Life Project*. Retrieved from http://pewinternet.org/Reports/2011/Technology-and-social-networks.aspx

Hartmann, N. (2016, June 28). Father unknown: How birth fathers became invisible in early adoptions. *SBS*. Retrieved from www.sbs.com.au/news/insight/article/2016/06/27/father-unknown-how-birth-fathers-became-invisible-early-adoptions

Hawkins, A., Beckett, C., Rutter, M., Castle, J., Colvert, E., Kreppner, J., . . . Sonuga-Barke, E. (2007). Communicative openness about adoption and interest in contact in a sample of domestic and intercountry adolescent adoptees. *Adoption Quarterly, 10*, 131–156.

Hays, A. H., Horstman, H. K., Colaner, C. W., & Nelson, L. R. (2016). "She chose us to be your parents": Exploring the content and process of adoption entrance narratives told in families formed through open adoption. *Journal of Social & Personal Relationships, 33*, 917–937.

Heffron, A. (2016). *You don't look adopted: A memoir*. Running Water Press.

Henney, S. M., Ayers-Lopez, S., McRoy, R. G., & Grotevant, H. D. (2007). Evolution and resolution: Birth mothers' experience of grief and loss at different levels of adoption openness. *Journal of Personal and Social Relationships, 24*, 875–889.

Henney, S., McRoy, R. G., Ayers-Lopez, S., & Grotevant, H. D. (2003). The impact of openness on adoption agency practices: A longitudinal perspective. *Adoption Quarterly, 6*, 31–51.

Henry, M. J., & Pollack, D. (2009). *Adoption in the United States: A reference for families, professionals, and students*. New York, NY: Oxford University Press.

Herman, E. (2008). *Kinship by design: A history of adoption in the modern United States*. Chicago, IL: University of Chicago Press.

Hertlein, K. M. (2012). Digital dwelling: Technology in couple and family relationships. *Family Relations, 61*, 374–387.

Holden, L. (2013). *The open-hearted way to open adoption: Helping your child grow up whole*. Lanham, MD: Rowman & Littlefield.

Howard, J. A. (2012). *Untangling the web: The internet's transformative impact on adoption*. The Evan B. Donaldson Institute. Retrieved from http://adoptioninstitute.org/old/publications/2012_12_UntanglingtheWeb.pdf

Howard, J. A., Smith, S. L., & Ryan, S. D. (2004). A comparative study of child welfare adoptions with other types of adopted children and birth children. *Adoption Quarterly, 7*, 1–30.

Hughes, D., Rodriguez, J., Smith, E. P., Johnson, D. J., Stevenson, H. C., & Spicer, P. (2006). Parents' ethnic–racial socialization practices: A review of research and directions for future study. *Developmental Psychology, 42*, 747–770.

Hughes, E. (2017). *Adopted women and biological fathers: Reimagining stories of origin and trauma*. London, UK: Routledge.

Jones, C., & Hackett, S. (2007). Communicative openness within adoptive families: Adoptive parents' narrative accounts of the challenges of adoption talk and the approaches used to manage these challenges. *Adoption Quarterly, 10*, 157–178.

Katz, L. (1986). Parental stress and factors for success in older-child adoption. *Child Welfare, 65,* 569–578.

Kearney, M. K., & Millstein, A. (2013). Meeting the challenges of adoption in an internet age. *Capital University Law Review, 41,* 237–278.

Keefer, B., & Schooler, J. (2000). *Telling the truth to your adopted or foster child: Making sense of the past.* Westport, CT: Bergin & Garvey.

Kenrick, J., Lindsey, C., & Tollemache, L. (Eds.). (2006). *Creating new families: Therapeutic approaches to fostering, adoption, and kinship care.* London, England: Karnac.

Khanna, N., & Killian, C. (2015). "We didn't even think about adopting domestically": The role of race and other factors in shaping parents' decisions to adopt abroad. *Sociological Perspectives, 58,* 570–594

Kirk, D. (1964). *Shared fate: A theory of adoption and mental health.* New York, NY: Free Press.

Kohler, J. K., Grotevant, H. D., & McRoy, R. G. (2002). Adopted adolescents' preoccupation with adoption: Impact of adoptive family dynamics. *Journal of Marriage and Family, 64,* 93–104.

Kranstuber, H., & Koenig Kellas, J. (2011). Instead of growing under her heart I grew in it: The relationship between adoption entrance narratives and adoptees' self-concept. *Communication Quarterly, 59,* 79–99.

Krueger, C. (2014). Should I friend our child's birthmother? *Adoptive Families.* Retrieved from http://www.adoptivefamilies.com/articles/2146/should-i-friend-our-birthmother

Lavner, J., Waterman, J., & Peplau, A. (2012). Can gay and lesbian parents promote healthy development in high-risk children adopted from foster care? *American Journal of Orthopsychiatry, 82,* 465–472.

Leathers, S. J. (2003). Parental visiting, conflicting allegiances, and emotional and behavioral problems among foster children. *Family Relations, 52,* 53–63.

Levine, S. (2017). *A proposal for change from OAFS.* Prepared by Open Adoption & Family Services & Shari Levine, Executive Director.

Levitt, M. (2013). Perceptions of nature, nurture and behavior. *Life Sciences, Society, & Policy, 9,* 13.

Logan, J. (2010). Preparation and planning for face-to-face contact after adoption: The experience of adoptive parents in a UK study. *Child & Family Social Work, 15,* 315–324.

Logan, J., & Smith, C. (1999). Adoption and direct postadoption contact. *Adoption & Fostering, 23*(4), 58–59.

Logan, J., & Smith, C. (2005). Face-to-face contact post adoption: Views from the triangles. *British Journal of Social Work, 35,* 3–35.

Mann, L. (2015, December 5). Birth dads still fighting for bigger role in adoption process. *Chicago Tribune.* Retrieved from www.chicagotribune.com/lifestyles/sc-birth-fathers-family-0105-20151207-story.html

May, T. (2015). An adoptive parental perspective on personal genomic screening. *Pediatrics, 135,* e811–e814.

McNamara, T. (2014, December 31). The top 15 family films about adoption. *Huffington Post.* Retrieved from https://www.huffingtonpost.com/tara-mcnamara/the-top-15-family-films-a_b_6331544.html

Melina, L. R., & Roszia, S. K. (1993). *The open adoption experience: A complete guide for adoptive and birth families.* HarperCollins.

Miall, C. E. (1987). The stigma of adoptive parent status: Perceptions of community attitudes toward adoption and the experience of informal social sanctioning. *Family Relations, 36*, 34–39.

Miall, C. E., & March, K. (2005). Community attitudes toward birth fathers' motives for adoption placement and single parenting, *Family Relations, 54*, 535–546.

National Scientific Council on the Developing Child. (2010). *Early experiences can alter gene expression and affect long-term development* (Working Paper No. 10). Retrieved from http://www.developingchild.net

Neil, E. (2006). Coming to terms with the loss of a child: The feelings of birth parents and grandparents about adoption and post-adoption contact. *Adoption Quarterly, 10*, 1–23.

Neil, E. (2009). The corresponding experiences of adoptive parents and birth relatives in open adoptions. In G. Wrobel & E. Neil (Eds.), *International advances in adoption research for practice* (pp. 269–294). Chichester, England: Wiley.

Neil, E. (2012). Making sense of adoption: Integration and differentiation from the perspective of adopted children in middle childhood. *Children and Youth Services Review, 34*, 409–416.

North American Council on Adoptable Children. (2018). *Nine qualities of successful adoptive and foster parents.* Retrieved from https://www.nacac.org/resource/nine-qualities/

Orenstein, P. (2007). *Waiting for Daisy: A tale of two continents, three religions, five fertility doctors, an Oscar, an atomic bond, a romantic night, and one woman's quest to become a mother.* London, UK: Bloomsbury.

Palmer, B. (2012, August 22). Should a mother tell her child he was conceived in a rape? What psychologists recommend. *Slate.* Retrieved from http://www.slate.com/articles/news_and_politics/explainer/2012/08/rape_and_pregnancy_is_it_best_to_tell_a_child_he_was_conceived_in_a_rape_.html

Pasch, L., & Sullivan, K. (2017). Stress and coping in couples facing infertility. *Current Opinion in Psychology, 13*, 131–135.

Passmore, N., & Feeney, J. (2009). Reunions of adoptees who have met both birth parents: Post-reunion relationships and factors that facilitate and hinder the reunion process. *Adoption Quarterly, 12*, 100–119.

Perry, T. (2014). Race, color, and the adoption of biracial children. *Journal of Gender, Race and Justice, 17*, 73–104.

Pertman, A. (2012). *Adoption nation: How the adoption revolution is transforming our families—and America.* Boston, MA: Harvard Common Press.

Peterson, B., Boivin, J., Norre, J., Smith, C., Thorn, P., & Wischmann, T. (2012). An introduction to infertility counseling: A guide for mental health and medical professionals. *Journal of Assisted Reproduction & Genetics, 29*, 243–248.

Petronio, S. (2002). *Boundary of privacy: Dialectics of disclosure.* New York, NY: State University of New York Press.

Pew Research Center. (2016, November 11). *Social media update 2016.* Retrieved from http://www.pewinternet.org/2016/11/11/social-media-update-2016/

Pew Research Center. (2018, February 5). *Social media fact sheet.* Retrieved from http://www.pewinternet.org/fact-sheet/social-media/

Plomin, R., & Deary, I. J. (2015). Genetics and intelligence differences: Five special findings. *Molecular Psychiatry, 20*, 98–108.

Powell, K., & Afifi, T. (2005). Uncertainty management and adoptees' ambiguous loss of their birth parents. *Journal of Social & Personal Relationships, 22*, 129–151.

Raleigh, E. (2016). The color line exception: The transracial adoption of foreign-born and biracial Black children. *Women, Gender, & Families of Color, 4*(1), 86–107.

Reiss, D., Leve, L., & Whitesel, A. (2009). Understanding links between birth parents and the child they have placed for adoption: Clues for assisting adoptive families and for reducing genetic risk. In G. Wrobel & E. Neil (Eds.), *International advances in adoption research for practice* (pp. 119–146). Chichester, England: Wiley.

Reitz, M., & Watson, K. W. (1992). *Adoption and the family system: Strategies for treatment*. New York, NY: Guilford.

Riggs, D. (2007, February 8). Facilitated openness can benefit children adopted from care. *North American Council on Adoptable Children*. Retrieved from https://www.nacac.org/resource/facilitated-openness-can-benefit-children-adopted-from-care/

Robbins, J. (2016, February 26). *The one adoption question no mom (or kid) should have to hear*. Retrieved from http://www.sheknows.com/parenting/articles/1113593/adoptive-real-mom

Roszia, S. K., & Silverstein, D. N. (1999). Openness: A critical component of special needs adoption. *Child Welfare, 78*, 637–651.

Seek, A. (2016). *God and jetfire: Confessions of a birth mother*. New York, NY: Farrar, Straus and Giroux.

Sharajevska, I., & Stodolska, M. (2015). Redefining boundaries in families through social networking leisure. *Leisure Sciences, 37*, 431–446.

Siegel, D. H. (2012a). Social media and the post-adoption experience. *Social Work Today, 12*, 22. Retrieved from www.socialworktoday.com/archive/091712p22.shtml

Siegel, D. H. (2012b). Growing up in open adoption: Young adults' perspectives. *Families in Society, 93*, 133–139.

Siegel, D., & Smith, S. (2012, March). *Openness in adoption: From secrecy and stigma to knowledge and connections*. The Evan B. Donaldson Institute. Retrieved from https://www.adoptioninstitute.org/publications/openness-in-adoption-from-secrecy-and-stigma-to-knowledge-and-connections/

Silber, K., & Speedlin, P. (1982). *Dear birthmother: Thank you for our baby*. San Antonio, TX: Corona Publishers.

Simmel, S., Barth, R. P., & Brooks, D. (2007). Adopted foster youths' psychosocial functioning: A longitudinal perspective. *Child & Family Social Work, 12*, 336–348.

Simms, M. D., Dubowitz, H., & Szilagyi, M. A. (2000). Health care needs of children in the foster care system. *Pediatrics, 106*(4), 909–918.

Simon, R. J., & Roorda, R. M. (Eds.). (2000). *In their own voices: Transracial adoptees tell their stories*. New York, NY: Columbia University Press.

Skinner-Drawz, B., Wrobel, G. M., Grotevant, H. D., & Von Korff, L. (2011). The role of adoption communicative openness in information seeking among adoptees from adolescence to emerging adulthood. *Journal of Family Communication, 11*, 181–197.

Slauson-Blevins, K., & Park, N. K. (2016). Deciding not to adopt: The role of normative family ideologies in adoption consideration. *Adoption Quarterly, 19*, 237–260.

Smith, D. E. (1993). The standard North American family: SNAF as an ideological code. *Journal of Family Issues, 14*, 50–65.

Sorich, C., & Siebert, R. (1982). Toward humanizing adoption. *Child Welfare, 61*, 207–216.

Stark, S. (2017, October 6). What you should know about the first year of open adoption. *Adoption.com*. Retrieved from https://adoption.com/what-you-should-know-about-the-first-year-of-open-adoption

The Surrogacy Experience. (2018). *U.S. surrogacy law by state*. Retrieved from http://www.thesurrogacyexperience.com/surrogate-mothers/the-law/u-s-surrogacy-law-by-state/

Sweeney, K. (2013). Race-conscious adoption choices, multiraciality, and color-blind racial ideology. *Family Relations, 62*, 42–57.

Sykes, M. (2001). Adoption with contact: A study of adoptive parents and the impact of continuing contact with families of origin. *Journal of Family Therapy, 23*, 296–316.

Towsend, L. (2003). Open adoption: A review of the literature with recommendations to adoption practitioners. *Journal of Child & Adolescent Mental Health, 15*, 1–11.

Turkington, S., & Taylor, B. (2009). Post-adoption face-to-face contact with birth parents: Prospective adopters' views. *Child Care in Practice, 15*, 21–38.

U.S. Department of Health & Human Services, Administration for Children & Families. (2018). *The rights of unmarried fathers*. Retrieved from www.childwelfare.gov/pubPDFs/putative.pdf

U.S. Department of Health & Human Services, Administration for Children and Families, Children's Bureau. (2017). *The AFCARS report #24*. Retrieved from https://www.acf.hhs.gov/sites/default/files/cb/afcarsreport24.pdf

van IJzendoorn, M. H., Juffer, F., & Poelhuis, C. W. K. (2005). Adoption and cognitive development: A meta-analytic comparison of adopted and nonadopted children's IQ and school performance. *Psychological Bulletin, 131*, 301–316.

Vandivere, S., Malm, K., & Radel, L. (2009). *Adoption USA: A chartbook based on the 2007 National Survey of Adoptive Parents*. U.S. Department of Health and Human Services. Retrieved from http://aspe.hhs.gov/hsp/09/NSAP/chartbook/index.pdf

Von Korff, L., & Grotevant, H. D. (2011). Contact in adoption and adoptive identity formation: The mediating role of family conversation. *Journal of Family Psychology, 25*, 393–401.

Von Korff, L., Grotevant, H. D., & McRoy, R. G. (2006). Openness arrangements and psychological adjustment in adolescent adoptees. *Journal of Family Psychology, 20*, 531–534.

Walsh, F. (2015). *Normal family processes: Growing diversity and complexity* (4th ed.). New York, NY: Guilford.

Webb, L., Ledbetter, A., & Norwood, K. (2015). Families and technologically assisted communication. In L. Turner and R. West (Eds.), *The SAGE handbook of family communication* (pp. 354–369). Thousand Oaks, CA: Sage.

Wegar, K. (2000). Adoption, family ideology, and social stigma: Bias in community attitudes, adoption research, and practice. *Family Relations, 49*, 363–369.

Werum, R., Davis, T., Cheng, S., & Browne, I. (2018). Adoption context, parental investment, and children's educational outcomes. *Journal of Family Issues, 39*, 720–746.

Wolfgram, S. M. (2008). Openness in adoption: What we know so far—a critical review of the literature. *Social Work, 53*, 133–142.

Wood, K. (2018). Families beyond boundaries: Conceptualising kinship in gay and lesbian adoption and fostering. *Child & Family Social Work, 23*(2), 155–162.

Woolgar, M., & Scott, S. (2014). The negative consequences of over-diagnosing attachment disorders in adopted children: The importance of comprehensive formulations. *Clinical Child Psychology & Psychiatry, 19*, 355–366.

Wright, L., Flynn, C., & Welch, W. (2007). Adolescent adoption and the birth family. *Journal of Public Child Welfare, 1*(1), 35–63.

Wrobel, G. M., Ayers-Lopez, S., Grotevant, H. D., McRoy, R. G., & Friedrick, M. (1996). Openness in adoption and the level of child participation. *Child Development, 67*, 2358–2374.

Wrobel, G. M., Kohler, J. K., Grotevant, H. D., & McRoy, R. G. (2003). The family adoption communication (FAC) model: Identifying pathways of adoption-related communication. *Adoption Quarterly, 7*, 53–84.

Index

For the benefit of digital users, indexed terms that span two pages (e.g., 52–53) may, on occasion, appear on only one of those pages.

AAP (American Academy of Pediatrics), 286, 374
abandonment, feelings of
    dealing with adopted children's, 239–40
    sensitivity to birth mother's, 114–15
ability to have biological children, 97–98
absent birth fathers, 192–93, 342–43, 350–53
ACEs (adverse childhood experiences), 275, 306–8
ACF (Administration for Children and Families), 374
Adam and Will (research participants)
    birth family contact with, 114–15, 171–73
    on child's medical history, 287
    communicative openness for, 243
    conversations about race for, 264–65
    demographic information on, 395
    and drug/alcohol exposure, 86–87
    lack of desire for biological children of, 37
    and limiting birth family contact, 69–70
    matching process for, 98
    on nature vs. nurture, 282
    on racial preferences, 80–81
    surrogacy for, 43
    timing and nature of match for, 101–2
additional adopted children, 254–55
ADHD. *See* attention deficit/hyperactivity disorder
Administration for Children and Families (ACF), 374
adopted children
    additional, 254–55
    and birth father curiosity, 351–52, 357, 358, 361–62, 387–88
    communication about adoption with, 217–19, 381
    communication about contact with, 378
    components forming identity of, 285–309
    curiosity of, 135, 146, 149–50
    development of, 275–76, 384–85, 389–90
    emphasizing nurture in, 298–301 (*see also* nature vs. nurture)
    family narrative perspectives of (*see* family narratives)
    intellectual ability of, 292–94
    lack of contact desire in, 379–80
    medical and mental health issues in, 286–92
    psychological development of, 15–16
    questions from (*see* questions from adopted child)
    social media use by, 386–87
    talents, personality, and physical features of, 294–98
    understanding of adoption by, 158–59
    views on openness, 390
adoption
    agencies for (*see* adoption agencies)
    choosing against, 371n.*
    history of, 2–3
    narratives of (*see* adoption narrative [adoption story])
    normalization of, 231–32, 251
    "put up for," 233–34n.*
    societal shifts in, 7–10
    timing of, 93–94, 100, 102
    tips for navigating (*see* adoptions, tips for navigating)
    use of word "adoption," 241–42

adoption agencies, 52
  and birth father involvement, 349–50
  and child welfare adoptions, 188
  crafting adoption narrative with, 229
  and drug/alcohol exposure, 88
  financial support from, 109–10
  and "hospital calls", 102–4
  matching process at, 93–94, 97
  and racial preferences, 74n.‡, 78, 373–74n.†
  therapy referrals by, 392
adoption day, celebrating, 14
adoption narrative (adoption story), 217–42
  in Angela and Gordon's family, 366–69
  child's ownership of, 248–50
  delaying/experiencing difficulty with, 230–31
  in Kathleen and Becki's family, 219–22
  loss and sensitive circumstances in, 226–30
  over course of childhood, 217–19
  practicing, in infancy, 222–26
  for school-aged children, 231–42
adoption programming, 366–67, 379
adoptions, tips for navigating
  absent birth fathers, 387–89
  for adoptive parents, 390–92
  birth father absence, 260–61
  child development, 384–85
  contact in child welfare, 380–81
  conversations about, 381–84
  drug/alcohol exposure, 374–75
  future of adopted child, 389–90
  infertility, 369–71
  postplacement period, 375–77
  preferences, 371–75
  social media, 385–87
  unexpected events in, 377–80
adoptive–birth family relationship
  and contact arrangements, 126–27
  matching as start of, 91
  rapport building in, 100–2
adoptive families
  preadoptive preferences of, 371–75
adoptive fathers, 357
  gay, 7–8, 119, 155
adoptive identity development
  and communication about adoption, 218
  components of, 285–309
  structural and communicative openness in, 126–27
adoptive kinship network, 12–13
adoptive mothers
  language used to refer to birth mothers by, 155
  responses to boundary challenges of, 121
adoptive parents
  at birth of child, 104–6
  choosing of, by birth parents, 93–99
  with difficulty communicating about adoption, 230–31
  emotions of, after birth, 106–7
  in family narratives, 285
  Internet facilitating contact with, 8–9 (see also Facebook)
  knowledge of placement circumstances for, 107–13
  preparing for nature vs. nature, 310 (see also nature vs. nurture)
  profession of, contributing to nurture, 281
  with strong engagement in communicative openness, 243
  and structural/communicative openness, 4–5
  successful, 390–91
  tips for, 390–92
adverse childhood experiences (ACEs), 275, 306–8
African American children
  and genetics, 297
  openness to, 77–79, 80, 81, 84–85, 366–67, 373–74
  See also children of color; race
age, 24, 41
agencies, adoption. See adoption agencies
Aisha and Larissa (research participants)
  addressing of racial differences by, 266–68
  communication about adoption for, 231, 239
  communicative openness of, 245
  demographic information on, 395

lack of desire for biological children for, 38, 41
on nature vs. nurture, 300–1
Al and Geoff (research participants)
on birth family contact, 209–10
demographic information on, 395
on nature vs. nurture, 281
on racial preferences, 82
alcohol exposed children. *See* drug or alcohol exposed children
altruism, as factor in matching process, 97
American Academy of Pediatrics (AAP), 286, 374
ancestry.com, 339
Andrea and Mary (research participants)
ceasing of fertility treatments for, 34
demographic information on, 395
on drug/alcohol exposed child, 88
enthusiasm for contact with, 148–50
matching process for, 97, 98–99
on navigating child's challenging questions, 259–60
placement circumstances for, 108
structural openness for, 59–60
Angela and Gordon (research participants)
adoption story of, 366–69
ceasing of fertility treatments for, 28–29, 371
and communication about contact, 378
demographic information on, 395
future planning of, 389
on genetics, 298
on racial preferences, 373–74
social media use by, 385–86
structural openness for, 53, 372
on unreciprocated contact, 376
Annie and Chuck (research participants)
and adverse childhood experiences, 306–7
on child's medical history, 290
communicative openness for, 258
demographic information on, 395
Facebook use by, 327–28
lack of desire for biological children of, 41
placement circumstances for, 112–13
on racial preferences, 86

anonymity, detrimental effects of, 3
anxiety
about contact, 70, 130, 133, 349
about openness, 133, 141–42
about parent–child differences, 276
in adoptive child, 220–21
of adoptive parents after birth, 106–7
and communication about adoption, 243–44, 258
and genetics, 287–88, 296
and infertility, 25, 27, 29
over child sense of loss, 382
over racial differences, 373–74
application process, 23
appreciation, from birth family, 105–6
attention deficit/hyperactivity disorder (ADHD), 277–78, 289, 294, 307
avoidance strategies, and infertility issues, 370
awkwardness
at birth of child, 104–5
at initial meeting with birth parent, 103, 107

behavioral changes and challenges, for school-age children, 15–16
Benji and Darren (research participants)
boundary challenges for, 119–20
on child's medical history, 286–87
communicative openness for, 251
demographic information on, 395
lack of desire for biological children of, 38
on nature vs. nurture, 284–85
structural openness for, 63–64
timing and nature of match for, 102
biological children
ability to have, 97–225
lack of desire for, 37–42
prioritizing adoptive children over, 298
struggles with conceiving (*see* infertility)
biracial children, 77, 98–99. *See also* racial preferences
birth, 104–7
adoptive parents' attendance at, 104–6
communication with expectant mother prior to, 91–92, 102

birth (*cont.*)
   emotions of adoptive parents after, 106–7
   emotions of birth family at, 104–6
   lack of desire to experience, 38–39
   matching process after, 100, 102–4
birth book, 250–51
birth families
   adopted children's questions about, 234
   in adoption narrative, 227–28
   attributing talents to, 294–95
   and child welfare adoptions, 5–6
   choosing of adoptive parents by, 94–99
   contact level determination by, 66–67
   emotions of, at birth, 104–6
   as extended family, 155–56, 224–25
   in family narrative, 285
   fantasies about going to/searching for, 237–39
   initial meetings with, 99–104
   loss of, 234–35
   placement circumstances for, 107–13
   postplacement support for, 377–78
   returning to, 190, 208–10
   view of, 67
   See also adoptive–birth family relationship; *specific family members*
birth family contact, 49–50
   adoption agency-mediated, 127
   arrangements for, 3–4, 65–71
   benefits of, 4–5, 136, 197
   and birth father involvement, 354–55
   boundaries on (*see* boundaries on contact)
   and children's feelings of loss, 238–39
   and child's identity, 285, 296
   and child's medical history, 286–89
   in child welfare adoptions, 6–7, 71–73
   and communicative openness, 224, 247
   concerns/considerations with, 208–9, 215
   demand for, 52–53
   under difficult circumstances, 167–84
   empathy associated with, 362
   flexibility regarding, 65–66, 67
   and genetics, 295
   hesitation about, 63
   importance of, 53–54
   initial, 113–22
   Internet-facilitated, 11–12
   as nonbiological kinship, 56–57
   overcoming barriers to, 139
   and race, 263, 268
   in same-sex couple adoptions, 7–8
   via social media, 8–9, 157, 315–16, 317–31 (*see also* Facebook)
   See also level of contact; structural openness
birth father contact
   in child welfare adoptions, 360–61
   families with, 354–56
   families without, 192–93, 260–61, 342–43, 350–53, 387–89
   hesitation with, 349
   lack of, 192–93, 260–61, 342–43, 350–53, 387–89
   placement circumstances discouraging, 345–50
   research on, 342–43
birth fathers, 341–63
   absent, 192–93, 260–61, 342–43, 350–53, 387–89
   child's challenging questions about, 260–61
   communication about, 247, 358–60
   family vignette on, 344
   gendered dynamics in relation to, 357–58
   marginalization of, 341–42
   mother's declining to acknowledge, 345–46
   parental role tension with, 121
   present, 354–56
   prioritization of mothers over, 350, 361
birth grandparents, 66, 153, 156–57, 177–78, 179–80
birth mother contact
   level of, 92–93
   throughout development, 367–69
birth mothers
   boundary challenges by, 118–22
   child's questions about, 233, 235, 238–39, 260
   considering perspectives of, 52
   counseling for, 52
   "Dear Birth Mother" letters to, 93–94n.*

INDEX   429

disclosing sexual orientation to, 55
parental orientation of gay male couples toward, 91–92
prioritization of, over fathers, 350, 361
protective feelings toward, 105
responding to needs/boundaries of, 92–93
selection of same-sex couples by, 96–97
birth sibling contact, 205
and birth father contact, 344
for children adopted by different families, 145
and child's medical history, 289–90
in child welfare adoptions, 73, 112–13, 190–91, 195–97, 207, 208
in Eliza and Hannah's family, 141
maintaining, 180
unreciprocated, 210–11
via Facebook, 327–28
birth siblings
challenging questions about, 261
communication about, 248
feelings of loss for children with, 113–240
book, birth, 250–51
books about adoption, 223, 224
boundaries on contact
challenges to, 118–22, 173–74, 185, 378
in early postplacement period, 375
fear of overstepping, 116
negotiating, 200, 201, 331–34
and non-communicative birth parents, 137
reasserting/reinstating, 378–79
renegotiating, 168–69
in Rob and Terrence's family, 92–93
setting of, 143, 160–61
social media-related, 166–67
boundaries on information sharing, 248–50
Brent and Travis (research participants)
demographic information on, 395
enthusiasm for contact with, 136–39
Facebook use by, 329
matching process for, 96
placement circumstances for, 111
structural openness for, 55, 60–61
Bright Futures Adoption Center, 47

Broderick, Carlfred, 13–14
Brodzinsky, David, 12–13n.‡, 15, 16, 158–59, 217–18, 242–43, 381, 382–83, 388–89

Carly and Brian (research participants)
boundary challenges for, 121
communicative openness of, 230–31
demographic information on, 395
Facebook contact with, 337–38
fertility issues of, 25
matching process for, 94–95
on nature vs. nurture, 280
placement circumstances for, 107–8
on racial preferences, 84
structural openness for, 62
timing and nature of match for, 103–4
CASE (Center for Adoption Support and Education), 391–92
cautiousness
about communicative openness, 255–59
in birth–adoptive parents' relationship, 101–2
in reaching out to birth mother, 116
celebrations, of birth families, 379
Center for Adoption Support and Education (CASE), 391–92
Charlene and Leila (research participants)
addressing of racial differences by, 266
adoption story by, 248–49
birth father involvement with, 359
communication about adoption for, 237, 247–48
communicative openness of, 253–54
demographic information on, 395
enthusiasm for contact with, 164–67
Facebook use by, 319–20
fertility issues for, 25, 27
matching process for, 94
structural openness for, 52–53, 55
Chaulk, K., 315–16n.‡
Child Protective Services (CPS), 112n.§
children of color, 12
addressing racial differences with, 262–70
biracial children, 98–99
challenges with, 85–86
LGBQ parent adoption of, 7–8

children of color (*cont.*)
  matching process for, 98–99
  muted approach to communicative openness with, 259
  openness to, 83, 373–74
child welfare adoptions, 187–215
  birth fathers in, 360–61
  contact in, 71–73, 189–97, 372–73, 380–81
  disclosing sexuality within, 55–56
  lack of desire for, 61–62n.*
  and nature vs. nurture, 279–82, 303–4
  openness in, 5–7, 197–210
  unreciprocated contact in, 210–15
  See also domestic public adoptions
Child Welfare Information Gateway, 371, 391–92
chosen family, 234–35
Christy and Sonja (research participants)
  communication about adoption for, 231
  demographic information on, 395
  Facebook use by, 329–30
  navigating of child's challenging questions by, 261–62
  timing and nature of match for, 102–3
Clomid, 21–22, 28–29
color-blind philosophy, 86
communication
  about contact, 116
  with expectant mother, 91–92, 102
communication about adoption, 217–73, 381–84
  addressing loss and sensitive circumstances in, 226–30
  addressing racial differences in, 262–70
  answering challenging questions from children, 259–62
  and birth fathers, 352–53, 358–60
  delaying/experiencing difficulty with, 230–31
  failure of children to initiate, 258–59
  and genetic vulnerabilities, 291–92, 294
  with infant children, 222–26
  in Kathleen and Becki's family, 219–22
  minimizing/not emphasizing race in, 270–72
  openness in (*see* communicative openness)
  over course of adoptee's childhood, 217–19
  with school-aged children, 231–42
communication privacy management (CPM) theory, 317
communicative openness, 10–11, 242–59
  and addressing racial differences, 272–73
  benefits of, 4–5
  breaks in, 376–77
  in child welfare adoptions, 201, 203
  defined, 218
  developmentally responsive, 243–50
  facilitating, 250–55
  with high enthusiasm for contact, 145, 146–47, 157–58
  increasing enthusiasm for contact and, 137–38
  with low enthusiasm for contact, 128, 130–31, 134–35
  muted approach to, 255–59
  navigating, 365
  preadoption expectations for, 125–26
  with reduced contact, 170–71
  strong engagement in, 243
  structural openness vs., 218, 242–43
  struggles with, 5
  when birth parents reject contact, 161–62, 163–64, 165, 184–85
community resources, racial preference and, 79
complex feelings, addressing child's, 237–39
conception, struggles with. *See* infertility
confusion, of child about adoption, 245
contact. *See* birth family contact
contact agreements, 113–14n.**, 176, 183–84
counseling, for birth mothers, 52
courageousness, of birth parents, 108–9
CPM (communication privacy management) theory, 317
CPS (Child Protective Services), 112n.§
culture, 264, 358–59

Daniela and Heather (research participants)
  birth father involvement with, 355–56

ceasing of fertility treatments for, 34–35
on child's intelligence, 292–93
on child's talents, 295
communicative openness for, 224–25, 246–47
demographic information on, 395
on flexibility with birth family contact, 66–67
initial contact with birth family for, 115
navigating of child's challenging questions by, 260–61
placement circumstances for, 111
timing and nature of match for, 102
data analysis process, 411–12
Dave and Byron (research participants)
communicative openness for, 256–57
demographic information on, 395
enthusiasm for openness and contact with, 133–35
Facebook contact by, 338
on genetics, 299–300
on limiting birth family contact, 70–71
on nature vs. nurture, 282
placement circumstances for, 108, 111
on racial preferences, 79–80
surrogacy for, 44
DCF (Department of Children and Families), 112n.§
DCYS (Department of Child and Youth Services), 112n.§
"Dear Birth Mother" letters ("Dear Expectant Parent" letters), 93–94n.*
delaying communication about adoption, 230–31
Department of Child and Youth Services (DCYS), 112n.§
Department of Children and Families (DCF), 112n.§
Department of Social Services (DSS), 112–13
depression, 25, 32
developmentally responsive communicative openness, 217, 222–23, 243–50
developmental psychology frameworks, 15–16, 211–12

developmental stages
children's understanding of adoption in, 158–59
and muted approach to communicative openness, 256–57
developmental tasks, for adopted child, 15
DHS (Oregon Department of Human Services), 6–7, 188
"different," feeling and being, 218–19, 245, 257
discomfort, with communication about adoption, 222
discrimination, 55–56, 96
disinterest of child, in adoption communication, 244–45, 256
domestic public adoptions, 5–7, 48–49
Donna and Max (research participants)
addressing of racial differences by, 266, 267–68
boundary challenges for, 121–22
ceasing of fertility treatments for, 33
communication about adoption by, 232
demographic information on, 395
on drug/alcohol exposed child, 88–89
Facebook use by, 332–33
initial contact with birth family for, 116
on limiting birth family contact, 70, 336
matching process for, 96
placement circumstances for, 108
structural openness for, 64
Doug and Sam (research participants)
communication about adoption by, 239–40
communicative openness for, 253
demographic information on, 395
enthusiasm for contact with, 181–84
initial contact with birth family for, 117–18
on intellectual ability, 305–6
matching process for, 96–97
structural openness for, 53, 56–57
surrogacy for, 44
"dream situation" circumstances of placement, 110–12
drug abuse, birth parent 6
drug or alcohol exposed children, 86–89
birth family contact with, 175–76
and genetics, 289, 291, 304

drug or alcohol exposed children (*cont.*)
  reasons for placing, 113
  tips to navigating, 374–75
DSS (Department of Social
    Services), 112–13

early childhood, adoption communication
    in, 217
early life experience, gene expression
    and, 275
early puberty, 288
education, 107–8, 299, 371
Eliza and Hannah (research participants)
  addressing of racial differences by, 272
  ceasing of fertility treatments for, 35
  communicative openness for, 227
  on conversations about race, 263
  demographic information on, 395
  on drug/alcohol exposed child, 88
  enthusiasm for contact with, 139–41
  Facebook use by, 320–21
  matching process for, 97
  openness for, 63
  on racial preferences, 84–85
Ellen and Matt (research participants)
  addressing of racial differences
    by, 270–71
  demographic information on, 395
  enthusiasm for contact with, 144–48
  fertility issues of, 25–26
  openness for, 61
  on racial preferences, 79–80
Elora and Dominick (research
    participants)
  ceasing of fertility treatments by, 31–32
  on child's medical history, 288, 291
  communicative openness for, 244–45
  demographic information on, 395
  enthusiasm for contact with, 155–59
  on flexibility with birth family
    contact, 66
  on racial preferences, 77
emotional distance regulation, 126, 317
emotional issues, contact limitations due
    to, 168–70, 172–73
emotional preparation, for
    parenting, 110–12
emotional resources, of birth parents, 108

emotions
  about infertility, 22–23, 25–33, 370–71
  about racial differences, 266
  of adopted child, 381–82
  of adoptive parents after birth, 106–7
  at birth of child, 104–6
  at fertility treatment cessation, 28–37
  in postplacement period, 122–23
  with unreciprocated contact, 210–15
  See also specific emotions
engagement, in communicative
    openness, 243
enthusiasm for openness (of adoptive
    families)
  high, 150–67
  increasing, 136–50
  low, 127–35
entitlement, maternal, 96–97
Eric and Russell (research participants)
  demographic information on, 395
  matching process for, 96, 99
  on racial preferences, 82
  surrogacy for, 44–45
Erin and Meredith (research participants)
  birth father involvement with, 356
  ceasing of fertility treatments
    for, 35–36
  communication about adoption
    by, 232
  demographic information on, 395
  on limiting birth family contact, 69
  on nature vs. nurture, 283–84
  on racial preferences, 78–79
ethnicity, 264, 358–59. *See also* race
Eva and Tina (research participants)
  on child's medical history, 289–90
  demographic information on, 395
  on nature vs. nurture, 303–4
  placement circumstances for, 112
  on unreciprocated contact, 210–11
Evantash, Roberta, 12–13n.‡
expectant parents
  "Dear Expectant Parent" letters,
    93–94n.*
  defined, 7–8n.*
  matching process for, 93–99
  openness with, 64
  See also birth mothers

expectations, about level of contact, 92–93, 117–18
expected transitions, 14–15
extended family, birth family as, 155–56, 224–25

Facebook, 8–9, 313–39, 367–68
　avoiding contact through, 331–34, 339
　birth father contact via, 356
　birth sibling contact via, 327–28
　boundaries on contact via, 375
　easing communication with, 313–14
　functions of, 315–17, 338–39
　initial contact through, 116
　lack of supervision with, 334–35, 387
　maintaining contact with, 141, 152, 153–54, 157, 166, 178
　passive contact through, 328–31
　reducing contact through, 335–38
　in Rick and Marcus's family, 314–15
failed matches, anxiety about, 106–7
family life cycle, contact during, 125–26
family narratives, 275–310
　adoption story in, 217–18
　birth and adoptive families in, 285
　intellectual ability in, 292–94
　medical and mental health issues in, 286–92
　minimizing differences in biological and adopted children in, 282–85
　nature vs. nurture in (see nature vs. nurture)
　reflecting on origins, 279–80
　talents, personality, and physical features in, 294–98
　in Therese and Lucas's family, 276–79
family obligations, of birth parents, 108–9
family rituals, 14
family systems theory, 4, 13–14, 126
family trees, 230
fantasies, about going to/searching for birth parents, 237–39
fathers
　adoptive, 7–8, 119, 155, 357
　birth (see birth father contact; birth fathers)
　See also two-mom and two-dad families

fear
　of closed adoptions, 53–54
　of overstepping boundaries, 116
female role models, 56
fertility treatments, 21–23
　ceasing, 28–37, 369–71
　emotional toll of, 25–33
fetal alcohol syndrome, 290
financial barriers to surrogacy, 42–43
financial resources, of birth parents, 108–10
financial stability, 94
flexibility, in birth family contact, 65–66, 67
forced adoption, 341
foster care adoptions
　adoption narrative for children in, 228–29
　and child medical history, 290
　contact with, 71–73, 187–88
　medical and mental health issues in, 286
　placement circumstances in, 112–13
　See also child welfare adoptions
Friends in Adoption, 47, 375
Friendster, 313
frustration, about boundary challenges, 120–21
Fursland, Ellen, 9–10

Gates, Gary, 7
gay adoptive fathers
　and birth mothers, 7–8, 155
　boundary challenges for, 119
　See also two-mom and two-dad families
gay male couples
　birth father contact with, 343, 351
　communicative openness in, 98
　drug/alcohol exposed children for, 87
　narratives about selection for, 96–97
　parental orientation toward birth mothers of, 91–92
　as preferential adopters, 37–38
　racial preferences in, 74, 81–82, 85
　surrogacy for, 42–45
　See also same-sex couples
gay men
　birth parents' relationships with, 98
　sensitivity to abandonment feelings of, 114

gender
  and birth fathers, 341, 357–58
  and birth mothers, 92
  as factor in matching process, 96–97
gene expression, 275
genetic ancestry testing, 339, 386
genetics
  and human development, 275
  and nature vs. nurture (*see* nature vs. nurture)
  unknown, 286–88
genetic testing, 288, 339, 385, 386
Georgia and Stan (research participants)
  on child's medical history, 290
  demographic information on, 395
grandparents, birth, 66, 156–57, 177–78, 179–80
Greta and Robin (research participants)
  birth family contact with, 201–4
  communicative openness for, 234
  demographic information on, 395
  on genetics, 296
  lack of desire for biological children of, 37, 38–39
  placement circumstances for, 112–13
grieving
  by adopted child, 239–40, 241–42, 272–73, 382
  of biological parenthood, 30–31, 32, 370–71
  by birth parents, 93, 115, 376–77
  of loss of surrogacy option, 44
Gritter, James, 70
Grotevant, Harold, 3

happiness, family, 94
height, genetics and, 297
heterosexual adoptive mothers
  language used to refer to birth mothers by, 155
  responses to boundary challenges of, 121
heterosexual couples
  adoption narratives for, 98–226
  birth father contact with, 343, 351, 357
  communication about adoption in, 230–31
  emotional toll of infertility on, 25–33
  fertility treatment cessation for, 29–31, 36–37, 369–70
  fertility treatments for, 24
  infertility in, 21–24
  openness to birth family contact with, 215
  postplacement period with, 375
  racial preferences in, 74
high enthusiasm for openness, adoptive families with
  and no level of contact, 159–67
  and some level of contact, 150–59
higher educational goals, of birth mother, 107–8
Hispanic children, 80. *See also* children of color; Latino children; race
hobbies, matching based on, 95
Holden, Lori, 70
holidays, for birth families, 379
homophobia, 34
honesty
  in communication, 217, 243
  in process, 51
"hospital calls," 102–4
hostility, from birth family, 105
Howard, Jeanne, 5–6

idiosyncratic details, matching based on, 95
incest, 229–30, 383
increasing enthusiasm for openness, adoptive families with
  and low level of contact, 144–50
  and some level of contact, 136–44
infancy
  addressing loss and sensitive circumstances in, 226–30
  communication about adoption in, 217, 222–26
  delaying/avoiding communication about adoption in, 230–31
  developmental tasks in, 15
infertility, 21–24
  decision to adopt after, 369–71
  enthusiasm for openness of families with, 128–29, 132, 141–42
  in Jackie and Bob's family, 21–23
  loss associated with, 25–33

infertility-focused couples counseling, 370–71
insemination, 21–22. *See also* fertility treatments
insurance coverage, for fertility treatments, 22–23, 28–29
intellectual ability
 and genetics, 292–94, 302–3, 304–5
 in Therese and Lucas's family, 278–79
interests, matching based on, 95
international adoptions, 48–49
 with heterosexual couples, 62
 with same sex couples, 54, 55–56, 61–62
Internet, accessibility/pervasiveness with, 7–10, 11–12
interpersonal violence, 168
intrauterine insemination (IUI), 21–22
intuition, in matching process, 95
"invisible" birth fathers, 345–50
in vitro fertilization (IVF), 21–22, 24–25
involuntary termination of parental rights. *See* termination of parental rights (TPR)
IUI (intrauterine insemination), 21–22
IVF. *See* in vitro fertilization

Jackie and Bob (research participants)
 communication about adoption by, 227, 240
 demographic information on, 395
 fertility issues for, 21–23
 initial contact with birth family for, 116–17
 openness for, 58–59, 65
 placement circumstances for, 110
Jake and Carl (research participants)
 addressing of racial differences by, 269–70
 on child's medical history, 286–87
 contact concerns of, 190–92
 demographic information on, 395
 on nature vs. nurture, 299–300
Jamie and Evan (research participants)
 communicative openness of, 254
 demographic information on, 395
 on drug/alcohol exposed child, 87–88
 enthusiasm for contact with, 159–62
 matching process for, 97–99

 on nature vs. nurture, 299
 surrogacy for, 45
Jessica and Ned (research participants)
 on adverse childhood experiences, 307–8
 communicative openness for, 235, 245
 demographic information on, 395
 Facebook use by, 326–27
Joe and Jared (research participants)
 on contact in child welfare adoptions, 206–8
 demographic information on, 395
 placement circumstances for, 112
 surrogacy for, 43
Jones, T., 315–16n.[‡]
Juno (film), 10

Kate and Cara (research participants)
 adoption story by, 248
 communicative openness for, 223, 251, 253
 on contact in child welfare adoptions, 71–72, 197–201
 on conversations about race, 264
 demographic information on, 395
 lack of desire for biological children of, 39–41
 on racial preferences, 83–84
Kathleen and Becki (research participants)
 ceasing of fertility treatments for, 33
 communication about adoption by, 219–22, 228, 237
 communicative openness for, 243–44, 249
 contact concerns of, 194–95
 demographic information on, 395
Kelly and Gil (research participants)
 birth father involvement with, 359–60
 communication about adoption by, 241–42
 demographic information on, 395
 enthusiasm for contact with, 173–74
Kerry and Shelby (research participants)
 communicative openness for, 223
 contact concerns of, 189–90
 demographic information on, 395
 lack of desire for biological children for, 38

kinship, 12–13, 56–57
Kirk, David, 14–15, 16, 258–59

language spoken, 95, 264, 266
Latino children, 83–84. *See also* children of color; Hispanic children; race
Laura and Lou (research participants)
    addressing of racial differences by, 271–72
    ceasing of fertility treatments for, 30, 32
    communicative openness for, 255–56
    demographic information on, 395
    openness for, 51–52
Lauren and Victoria (research participants)
    on adverse childhood experiences, 307
    on birth sibling contact, 196–97
    on child's medical history, 286–87
    demographic information on, 395
    on nature vs. nurture, 281–82
    on racial preferences, 81–82
legal interactions, with birth fathers, 348–49
Leigh and Billy (research participants)
    ceasing of fertility treatments for, 36–37
    on child's medical history, 289
    communication about adoption by, 236
    demographic information on, 395
    Facebook use by, 324–25, 334–35
    on nature vs. nurture, 284, 302–3
    placement circumstances for, 113
    on racial preferences, 79
Lena and Thomas (research participants)
    boundary challenges for, 120–21
    ceasing of fertility treatments for, 30
    communicative openness for, 226, 252–53
    demographic information on, 395
    enthusiasm for contact with, 141–44
    Facebook use by, 334
    on flexibility with birth family contact, 67
    on genetics, 297–98
    on nature vs. nurture, 299
    openness for, 61–62, 63–64
    on racial preferences, 76
    timing and nature of match for, 101

Leo and Javier (research participants)
    on birth of child, 105
    boundary challenges for, 119–20
    communicative openness for, 223–24
    on conversations about race, 263
    demographic information on, 395
    on limiting birth family contact, 68–69
    matching process for, 97
    openness for, 59
    on racial preferences, 78, 80–81
lesbian, gay, bisexual, and queer (LGBQ) parents
    gay adoptive fathers, 7–8, 119, 155
    increase in adoption by, 7–8
    lesbian adoptive mothers, 155
    See also same-sex couples; two-mom and two-dad families
lesbian couples
    adoption narratives of, 98, 226
    birth father contact with, 343, 358
    drug/alcohol exposed children for, 87
    emotional toll of infertility on, 25–33
    fertility treatment cessation for, 31, 33–36
    narratives about selection for, 97
    parenthood route of, 24–25
    as preferential adopters, 37, 38–42
    racial preferences for, 81–82, 85
    See also same-sex couples
level of contact, 125–85
    with birth mothers, 92–93
    ceasing, 12–13
    controlling, 372
    determination of, by birth family, 66–67
    differing, families with multiple children and, 254–55
    under difficult circumstances, 167–75
    evolution of, 114–18
    expectations about vs. reality of, 92–93, 117–18
    fluctuation in, 367
    with high enthusiasm for openness, 150–67
    increasing enthusiasm for openness and, 136–50
    limiting, 68–71, 335–38, 339
    low, 125, 127–35, 144–50

with low enthusiasm for
openness, 127–35
maintaining, 175–84, 185
no, 159–67
reduced, 167–75
some, 136–44, 150–59
Levine, Shari, 12–13n.‡, 188, 374
LGBQ parents. *See* lesbian, gay, bisexual, and queer parents
life course theory, 14–15
Life book, for children, 145, 165, 197
Logan, Janette, 379
loss
addressing, in communication about adoption, 226–30, 234–35, 236–42
birth mothers' feelings of, 92–93, 115
and infertility, 25–33
school-age children's feelings of, 234–35, 236–42
love, in communication about adoption, 227, 231, 232
low enthusiasm for openness, adoptive families with, 127–35
low level of contact, families with
and increasing enthusiasm for openness, 144–50
and low enthusiasm for openness, 127–35
regarded as meaningful, 125

marginalization, 98, 341–42
Marianna and Jerry (research participants)
demographic information on, 395
on racial preferences, 79–80
on unreciprocated contact, 214–15
Mariette and Jenny (research participants)
addressing of racial differences by, 265–66
birth father involvement with, 354, 359
on birth of child, 104–5
ceasing of fertility treatments for, 34
on child's intelligence, 292–93
on child's physical features, 297
on child's talents, 295
communicative openness for, 250–51
demographic information on, 395
enthusiasm for contact with, 150–54

Facebook use by, 327
fertility process for, 24
initial contact with birth family for, 117
matching process for, 94, 98–99
on nature vs. nurture, 280, 300
openness for, 55, 56
placement circumstances for, 108–9
Mason, Mary Martin, 343
matching process
and birth–adoptive parents relationship, 91
for expectant parents, 93–99
level of contact informed by, 125
matches that fall through, 91
nature and timing of, 99–104
in Rob and Terrence's family, 91–93, 97
maternal entitlement, 96–97
McRoy, Ruth, 3
media, portrayals of openness in, 10
medical issues
in family narratives, 286–92
and infertility, 24, 28–29
Meg and Michael (research participants)
demographic information on, 395
fertility issues for, 26
placement circumstances for, 112
on unreciprocated contact, 213–14
"memories" of birth mother, child's, 238
men
gay, 98, 114
history with, as factor in matching process, 97
muted approach to communicative openness for, 255–56
See also fathers; gay male couples
mental health issues
child welfare adoptions due to, 188
contact limitations due to, 173–75
Facebook contact for family members with, 332
in family narratives, 286–92
middle childhood
communication about adoption in, 217–18
conversations about race in, 265
Midwestern U.S., children of color in, 98–99

Mindy and Earl (research participants)
  communicative openness for, 234–35
  demographic information on, 395
  on nature vs. nurture, 304
  on unreciprocated contact, 211–13
Miranda and Shannon (research participants)
  communication about adoption by, 249
  demographic information on, 395
  Facebook use by, 321–22, 325, 334
  matching process for, 95
  on navigating child's challenging questions, 261
Miri and Lindsey (research participants)
  addressing of racial differences by, 267–68
  on birth family contributions to identity, 296
  birth father involvement with, 358–59
  on child's medical history, 287–88
  demographic information on, 395
  Facebook contact by, 337
  lack of desire for biological children for, 40–41
  openness for, 53–54, 55
miscarriages, 25–27, 34
Molly and Taryn (research participants)
  ceasing of fertility treatments by, 31
  communicative openness for, 252
  demographic information on, 395
  on drug/alcohol exposed child, 87
  fertility issues for, 27–28
  on genetics, 295–96
  on nature vs. nurture, 283
Monica and Damian (research participants)
  ceasing of fertility treatments for, 30–31, 32
  demographic information on, 395
  emotional aftermath of birth for, 107
  fertility issues for, 26
  initial contact with birth family for, 116
  openness for, 48–51
  on racial preferences, 76–77
mother figures, 56
"mother" role, 96–97, 119, 121
mothers
  adoptive, 121, 155
  birth (see birth mother contact; birth mothers)
  "real mom," 128n.[†]
  See also two-mom and two-dad families
Mother's Day, 338
multiracial children, 77, 98–99. See also racial preferences
multiracial families, communicative openness in, 253–54
muted approach to communicative openness, 255–59
MySpace, 313

name of child, 120, 261–62
Nate and Dwight (research participants)
  contact concerns of, 192–94
  demographic information on, 395
  on nature vs. nurture, 282–83
  on racial preferences, 80–81
  on surrogacy, 44
nature vs. nurture
  accepting nature in, 302–6
  acknowledgment of both factors in, 280–82
  and adverse childhood experiences, 306–8
  and child identity, 285–309
  emphasizing nurture in, 298–301
  minimizing, 282–85
  nurture appreciation in, 308–9
  separating, 309–10
negative early life experiences, 306
"negative space," birth fathers in, 343
neglect, 6
Neil, Elsbeth, 242–43
Noah and Reed (research participants)
  on birth sibling contact, 195–96
  communicative openness for, 259
  demographic information on, 395
  on nature vs. nurture, 281, 304–5
  on racial preferences, 81–82
nonbiological kinship, 56–57
nonnormative transitions, 14–15
nontraditional family, as factor in matching process, 97–98
nontrying partners, emotional toll of infertility on, 28
normative family transitions, 14–15
nurturing, influence of. See nature vs. nurture

OAFS. *See* Open Adoption and Family Services
older children
    addressing racial differences with, 266
    birth family contact with, 71, 190
    birth father curiosity of, 361–62
    medical and mental health issues in, 286
    nature vs. nurture for, 282
online profiles, of prospective adoptive parents, 93–94
Open Adoption and Family Services (OAFS), 6–7, 188, 374
open adoptions
    misconceptions about, 1
    in TAPP, 11
open/fully disclosed adoption, 3–4
openness, 2–7
    adoption programming supporting, 366–67
    benefits of, 3–4, 53
    with birth fathers, 361 (*see also* present birth fathers)
    in child welfare adoptions, 188
    considering, in preadoption stage, 47–51
    contact and, 125
    by default, 61–64
    different desires for, within couples, 59–61, 371–72, 379–80
    in domestic adoptions, 2–5
    hesitation about, 57–59, 63–64
    media portrayal of, 10
    in Monica and Damian's family, 48–51
    negative effects of, 3
    See also communicative openness; enthusiasm for openness (of adoptive families); structural openness
openness, initial desire for, 51–61
    and disclosing sexuality, 54–56
    for female role models, 56
    and nonbiological kinship, 56–57
Oregon Department of Human Services (DHS), 6–7, 188
ownership, of adoption narrative, 248–50

parental drug abuse, 6
parental rights
    relinquishment of, 103–4n.[†], 199, 380
    termination of, 71, 104n.[†], 202, 204–5, 228–29, 360–61
parental role tension, 96–97, 121
parent–child differences
    acknowledging, 5
    minimizing, 282–85
    in race, 223–24, 253–54, 262–70 (*see also* transracial adoption)
    talking about, 276
parents. *See* adoptive parents; birth families
passive contact via Facebook, 328–31
past history, in adoption narrative, 234–35
Paul and Greg (research participants)
    on birth of child, 104
    on conversations about race, 263
    demographic information on, 395
    enthusiasm for contact with, 154–55
    matching process for, 96–97
    openness for, 50–51
Peggy and Elena (research participants)
    demographic information on, 395
    enthusiasm for contact with, 162–64
    lack of desire for biological children of, 39
personality, 95, 294–98
Pew Research Center, 313
Phil and Eddie (research participants)
    demographic information on, 395
    on emotional aftermath of birth, 106
    Facebook use by, 331–32
    initial contact with birth family for, 115
    on navigating child's challenging questions, 260
    openness for, 64
    on parent–child differences, 262–63
    placement circumstances for, 108–9
    on racial preferences, 85
    on surrogacy, 42–43
photos
    as aids in communication about adoption, 223, 224, 246, 250–51
    of birth mother, 237–38
physical features, 224, 297–98
placement circumstances
    addressing, with child, 226–30, 232, 233–35
    child's questions about, 260

placement circumstances (*cont.*)
    "dream situation," 110–12
    in muted approach to communicative openness, 257–59
    reasons for placement, 107–13
placement process
    birth and immediate aftermath in, 104–7
    and circumstances of placement, 107–13
    timing of matching in, 99–104
political beliefs, matching based on, 96
postadoption contact. *See* birth family contact
postplacement period
    adjustment in, 122–23
    communication about adoption in, 222–31
    evolution of contact in, 113–22
    social distance regulation in, 93
    support for birth parents in, 377–78
    tips for navigating, 375–77
preadoption programming, 374–75
preadoption stage, 47–89
    and birth fathers, 388
    nature vs. nurture in, 279–85, 299
    preferences in, 89
    See also matching process
preferential adopters, 37–42
pregnancy
    contact with birth mothers during, 99–102
    lack of desire to experience, 38–39
    matching process during, 100–2
prejudice, 55–56, 96
Prenatal substance use/exposure, 86–89, 284–285, 289, 303–304
preschool-age children, 217
present birth fathers, 354–56
pride, racial, 266–68
privacy, 250, 322–23
private domestic adoptions
    communicative openness in, 227
    openness in, 2–3, 61
    in TAPP, 11
private international adoptions, 61–62
prospective adoptive parents
    connecting, with other adoptive families, 371
    defined, 7–8n.*
    education for, 371
    on unknowns of child, 284–85
protective feelings, toward birth mothers, 105
Psychology Today, 391–92
puberty, early, 288
public adoptions, 11

questions from adopted child
    answering, for school-aged children, 232–33, 235, 238–39
    challenging, 259–62
    and communicative openness of parents, 246, 247–48, 251–52, 258
    lack of, 258

race
    birth fathers as topic in discussions about, 358–59
    as factor in communicative openness, 259
    as factor in matching process, 95
    and genetics, 297
    minimizing/not emphasizing, 270–72
    parent–child similarities in, 269–70
    and privilege, 265
    same race adoptions, 50, 74
    social constructions of, 262
Rachel and Nancy (research participants)
    addressing of racial differences by, 267–68
    communicative openness for, 257–58
    demographic information on, 395
    enthusiasm for contact with, 167–71
    fertility issues for, 26–27
    matching process for, 98
    openness for, 58
racial differences
    as factor in communicative openness, 253–54
    talking about, 223–24, 262–70
    See also transracial adoptions
racial preferences, 73–86
    and adoption agencies, 78, 373–74n.†
    limited openness with, 77–82
    strict, 75–77
    tips for navigating, 373–74
    very open adoptions with, 82–86

racial pride, 266–68
racism, 80–81
Randy and Brendan (research
    participants)
  demographic information on, 395
  on nature vs. nurture, 280
rape, 346–48, 383
rapport building, 100–2
"real mom," 128n.[†]
relational barriers to surrogacy, 43
religion and religious beliefs
  in adoption narrative, 235
  as factor in matching process, 95, 96
relinquishment of parental rights, 103–4n.[†], 199, 380
respect
  for birth mother's space, 115
  for birth parents' decision, 109
returning to birth family, 190, 208–10
Rick and Marcus (research participants)
  boundary challenges for, 118–19
  communicative openness for, 232–33
  demographic information on, 395
  enthusiasm for contact with, 178–81
  Facebook use by, 314–15, 321–22
  lack of desire for biological children
    for, 301
  matching process for, 95
"right choice," adoption as, 108–9
rituals, family, 14
Rob and Terrence (research participants)
  on child's medical history, 288–89, 291
  communication about adoption by,
    225, 238–39
  communicative openness of, 222–23,
    243, 253
  demographic information on, 395
  on emotional aftermath of
    birth, 106–7
  matching process for, 91–93, 97
  openness for, 57–58
  placement circumstances for, 108–9
  on surrogacy, 43
  timing and nature of match for, 102
Roger and Barry (research participants)
  on birth of child, 105–6
  communicative openness for, 256
  demographic information on, 395

initial contact with birth family
    for, 113–14
  matching process for, 96–97
  openness for, 63–64
  placement circumstances for, 108
  on racial preferences, 85–86
  on surrogacy, 42–43
Rosie and Tony (research participants)
  on adverse childhood experiences, 306
  on child's intelligence, 293
  communicative openness for, 223
  demographic information on, 395
Roszia, Sharon, 12–13n.[‡], 388, 391
Roy and Dante (research participants)
  addressing of racial differences
    by, 268–69
  communicative openness for,
    233, 245–46
  demographic information on, 395
  Facebook use by, 322–24
  on flexibility with birth family
    contact, 65–66
  matching process for, 95
  openness for, 54
  timing and nature of match for, 100–1

safety, child, 68, 187, 360–61
same race adoptions, 50, 74
same-sex couples
  adoption narratives of, 226
  adoption rates for, 7–8
  contact in child welfare adoptions
    for, 206–7
  disclosure of sexuality by, 54–56
  international adoptions by, 54,
    55–56, 61–62
  matching process for, 96–99
  preferences of, 85, 89
  as preferential adopters, 37–42
  See also gay male couples; lesbian
    couples
Sandy and Lewis (research
    participants), 78
  on adverse childhood experiences, 307
  birth family contact with, 188–89
  communication about adoption by, 229,
    230–31, 232, 236
  demographic information on, 395

Sandy and Lewis (research participants) (*cont.*)
   on flexibility with birth family contact, 68
   infertility issues for, 41–42
   matching process for, 95
school-aged children
   answering questions of, 232–33, 235, 238–39
   communication about adoption with, 231–42
   communicative openness with, 257
   developmental tasks of, 15–16
Seana and Ron (research participants)
   communicative openness for, 226
   demographic information on, 395
   enthusiasm for openness and contact with, 128–32
   fertility treatment cessation for, 28–29
   on racial preferences, 75–76
second trimester of pregnancy, matching during, 100–2
secrecy
   adoptive parents' feelings about, 253
   avoiding, 54–56
   detrimental effects of, 3, 217
self-concept, 218–19, 231
semiopen/mediated adoptions, 3–4, 127, 329–30
sensory integration issues, 275–76
separate realities, in family systems theory, 14
Seth and Dean (research participants)
   on child's intelligence, 293–94
   communicative openness for, 254–55
   demographic information on, 395
   openness for, 57–58
   on racial preferences, 82–83, 85
   on surrogacy, 42–43
sexual assault, 229
Shared Fate (Kirk), 14–15
shared realities, in family systems theory, 14
Shoshanna and Cal (research participants)
   birth father involvement with, 354–55
   ceasing of fertility treatments for, 29–30, 36
   communicative openness for, 223, 227–28, 251–52
   demographic information on, 395
   Facebook use by, 333–34
   on flexibility with birth family contact, 68
   on nature vs. nurture, 308–9
   openness for, 51–52
   placement circumstances for, 109
   on racial preferences, 77
   timing and nature of match for, 103
siblings. *See* birth sibling contact; birth siblings
Simon and Vincent (research participants)
   addressing of racial differences by, 269
   communication about adoption by, 228–29, 237–38
   communicative openness for, 253–54
   on contact in child welfare adoptions, 72–73, 204–6
   on conversations about race, 265
   demographic information on, 395
   Facebook use by, 327
   on racial preferences, 83
single individuals, adoption by, 7–8
Skype, with birth parents, 114, 115, 155, 161, 168, 171, 333
Substance use of birth parents
   See also: Prenatal substance use/exposure
Smith-Pliner, Dawn, 12–13n.[‡], 294, 375
SNAF (standard nuclear American family), 75
social distance regulation, 13–14, 93
social justice, as factor in matching process, 97
social media, 313–39
   accessibility/pervasiveness of, 7–10, 372–73
   maintaining contact with, 166–67
   rates of use for, 313–14
   tips for navigating, 385–87
   See also Facebook
Social Services, 112n.[§]
society, views of adoption in, 7–10
socioeconomic status, of birth vs. adoptive families, 109–10
some level of contact, families with and high enthusiasm for openness, 150–59

and increasing enthusiasm for
    openness, 136–44
Southern U.S., children of color in, 98–99
sperm banks, 39–40
spiritual element, in matching process, 96
Stacy and Deb (research participants)
    birth father involvement with, 354
    on child's medical history, 292
    communicative openness for,
        233–34, 249–50
    on conversations about race, 263–64
    demographic information on, 395
    enthusiasm for contact with, 175–78
    Facebook use by, 318–19
    on nature vs. nurture, 284
stalking, on Facebook, 325, 331
standard nuclear American family
    (SNAF), 75
Stark, Stacey, 375
stigma, with LGBQ parent adoption, 7–8
storybooks about adoption, 223, 224
strangers, sharing adoption-related
    information with, 248–50
structural openness, 10–11
    benefits of, 4–5
    boundary challenges with, 121–22
    breaks in, 376–77
    in child welfare adoptions, 201, 203
    and communicative openness, 218,
        242–43, 250–53
    navigating, 365
    negative effects of, 3
    preadoption expectations for, 125–26
    struggles with, 5
    See also birth family contact
substance abuse, 179–80, 188, 201
support
    from adoption agencies, 109–10
    for adoptive parents, 391–92
    for birth families, 377–78
    from birth family, 105–6
surrogacy, 21, 42–45
    adoption conceptualized as, 101
    financial barriers to, 42–43
    lack of desire for, 44–45
    relational barriers to, 43
surrogacy laws, 42

TAC (Training for Adoption Competency)
    program, 391–92
talents of child, 285, 294–98
Tammy and Holly (research participants)
    demographic information on, 395
    enthusiasm for openness and contact
        with, 127–28
    fertility issues for, 25–26
    placement circumstances for, 110–11
    timing and nature of match for, 102
TAPP (Transition to Adoptive Parenthood
    Project), 11
technology, for contact, 139, 155
termination of parental rights (TPR)
    for birth fathers, 202, 360–61
    communicative openness about, 228–29
    contact after, 71, 202
    in foster care adoptions, 204–5
    relinquishment vs., 104n.[†]
texting, with birth parents/family or
    text messaging, 137, 138, 141, 321,
        332, 336
therapy
    for adoptive parents, 391–92
    and birth family contact, 372
    and genetics, 310
    for infertility issues, 369–71
Therese and Lucas (research participants)
    on birth of child, 105
    communication about adoption by, 236
    communicative openness for, 259
    demographic information on, 395
    enthusiasm for openness and contact
        with, 132–33
    family narrative by, 276–79
    fertility issues for, 28
    on nature vs. nurture, 283
    openness for, 59
third trimester of pregnancy, matching
    during, 102
Tiffany and Karen (research participants)
    demographic information on, 395
    matching process for, 98–99
    structural openness for, 55–56
timing, of match, 99–104
toddlerhood, 15, 217
TPR. See termination of parental rights

Training for Adoption Competency (TAC) program, 391–92
trajectories, in life course theory, 14–15
transitions, in life course theory, 14–15
Transition to Adoptive Parenthood Project (TAPP), 11
transparency, about process, 51
transracial adoptions, 84, 193, 195. *See also* racial differences; racial preferences
23andme.com, 339
two-mom and two-dad families
   communication about adoption in, 224–25
   communicative openness in, 253
   navigating child's challenging questions in, 260–61

uncertainty, about level of contact, 117, 231
unreciprocated contact, 210–15
   in early postplacement period, 376
   through Facebook, 324–25, 337

values, matching based on, 94–95
violence, interpersonal, 168
voluntary relinquishment of parental rights, 103–4n.[†], 199, 380

wait, length of, in matching process, 94
warning signs with therapists, 391
Wrobel, Gretchen, 218